LEADERSHIP
DEVELOPMENT STUDIES
A Humanities Approach

Fifth Edition

 PHI THETA KAPPA
HONOR SOCIETY

Monika Byrd and Susan Edwards, Editors

HAYDEN McNEIL

For supplemental student and instructor resources
please visit the Book Companion Site at
http://bcs.haydenmcneil.com/phithetakappa

Hayden-McNeil Sustainability

Hayden-McNeil's standard paper stock uses a minimum of 30% post-consumer waste. We offer higher % options by request, including a 100% recycled stock. Additionally, Hayden-McNeil Custom Digital provides authors with the opportunity to convert print products to a digital format. Hayden-McNeil is part of a larger sustainability initiative through Macmillan Higher Ed. Visit http://sustainability.macmillan.com to learn more.

Printed in the United States of America

10 9 8 7 6 5 4 3 2 1

ISBN 978-0-7380-6604-2

Hayden-McNeil Publishing
14903 Pilot Drive
Plymouth, MI 48170
www.hmpublishing.com

ByrdM 6604-2 S14

TABLE OF CONTENTS

HISTORY

The presidents of the Missouri junior colleges for women established Phi Theta Kappa in 1918. The purpose of the Society has remained consistent since then: to recognize and encourage scholarship among associate degree-seeking students. To achieve this purpose, Phi Theta Kappa provides opportunities for the development of leadership and service, for an intellectual climate to exchange ideas and ideals, for lively fellowship for scholars, and for stimulation of interest in continuing academic excellence. Providing leadership development opportunities to those served by community colleges is thus central to the mission of Phi Theta Kappa, and its leaders set forth in 1990 to design a leadership program to inspire and grow the unlimited leadership potential in our communities. More than twenty years later, the program continues to develop the knowledge, skills, and abilities for the effective exercise of leadership. Its growth throughout the world where Phi Theta Kappa facilitates student success helps to meet global leadership development needs. Phi Theta Kappa serves more than 1,280 two-year colleges around the world. The Society's operations are international in scope, with chapters located in all 50 United States, Canada, Germany, Republic of Palau, Republic of the Marshall Islands, Federated States of Micronesia, British Virgin Islands, Peru, the United Arab Emirates, and U.S. Territories. Over two million students have earned membership in Phi Theta Kappa since its founding, with approximately 135,000 students inducted each year. In 1929, the American Association of Community Colleges recognized Phi Theta Kappa as the official honor society for two-year colleges. Today, Phi Theta Kappa is the largest honor society in American Higher Education.

IN MEMORY OF

Phi Theta Kappa Leadership Development Studies: A Humanities Approach is a tribute to the leadership of Margaret James Mosal and Shirley B. Gordon.

Margaret James Mosal (1911–1987)

Phi Theta Kappa alumna Margaret Mosal became Phi Theta Kappa's National Secretary in 1935. For the next 50 years, Dr. Mosal led the organization through periods of explosive growth. By 1967, the Society had grown sufficiently to name a Board of Directors, and Dr. Mosal's title became Executive Director.

Shirley B. Gordon (1922–2008)

Dr. Shirley Gordon was the longest-serving Chairman of Phi Theta Kappa's Board of Directors, a position she filled from 1988 until 2008. She was a founding member of the Phi Theta Kappa Foundation, and one of the first and most acclaimed female community college presidents in the country. Dr. Gordon was one of 18 educators, and the only community college representative, selected to serve on President Ronald Reagan's National Commission on Excellence in Education, which led to the first significant attempts to revitalize the nation's public education system.

FOREWORD

In 1990, Phi Theta Kappa set forth to address a leadership crisis in our country and world by designing a leadership program to build and equip the next generation of leadership at the grass-roots level. Today the need for this innovative leadership program persists, as the critical need to create strong, informed and ethical leaders on a global scale continues to grow. The world as a whole increasingly faces complicated challenges and opportunities, and it is this call to action that Phi Theta Kappa's leadership program continues to answer.

Phi Theta Kappa's leadership course, with its universal relevancy, cultural appreciation, hands-on process, community audiences, worldwide dissemination, and proven outcomes continues to provide unprecedented success in developing well-prepared leaders who effect change and enhance the quality of life in the thousands of communities served around the world. Leaders such as these are a necessity in the new global economy, in which a college credential is more important than ever for citizens of *all* nations. Phi Theta Kappa is committed to leading the charge to increase the number of well-prepared college graduates entering the workforce, and our leadership program is just one of many ways we are answering this demand.

In this program, Phi Theta Kappa makes three important assumptions regarding leadership. First, within every individual there exists leadership potential. Second, leadership can be taught and learned. Third, developing a personal leadership philosophy is a prerequisite to learning and applying leadership skills. After 22 years, the leadership performances of students who have completed the course suggest our initial assumptions were accurate and that the program works.

Since the launch of Phi Theta Kappa's Leadership Development Program in 1991, more than 2,700 college presidents, college administrators, faculty and trainers have become Certified Instructors in the program. More than 700 institutions around the world have Certified Instructors. Student graduates of the Program have gone on to become Rhodes Scholars, Phi Theta Kappa International Officers, All-USA Academic Team winners, legislators and outstanding community leaders, and college presidents and trustees. We are proud that this program was recognized by the W.K. Kellogg Foundation as one of only eight exemplary higher education leadership programs funded by the foundation between 1990 and 1998.

We at Phi Theta Kappa believe that *everyone* has in them an inherent ability to learn and exercise leadership, even those not currently in leadership positions or holding leadership titles. Therefore, it is our charge with this fifth edition to help *everyone* realize this ability, put this ability into practice, and intentionally develop ethical leadership knowledge, skills, and attitudes. It is the objective of this program to unleash the leadership potential of *all* individuals so they might emerge as tomorrow's community leaders.

For Phi Theta Kappa members specifically, this Leadership Development Studies curriculum holds a deeper meaning. The exercise of leadership is a must for success in the Society's key program, Honors in Action, and the leadership program serves as an intentional leadership development tool.

It is said that leadership is an art that demands constant practice. Thus, our leadership course will continue to change in order to remain a state-of-the-art program to meet the needs of a rapidly changing society. What has not changed is the Program's emphasis on the value of humanities-based learning, a prerequisite for becoming an effective and ethical leader. This revised edition includes new Classic Cases, Leadership Profiles, Exercises and Film Studies, which reflect the diverse audience interested in leadership development.

Providing leadership development opportunities is central to the mission of Phi Theta Kappa. We are committed to imbuing in those within our communities the desire to become servant leaders. Phi Theta Kappa is proud to present this proven, state-of-the-art leadership program to emerging and existing leaders with the hope that we are contributing to the solution of our world's leadership crisis.

December 2013

Dr. Rod A. Risley
Executive Director & CEO
Phi Theta Kappa

ACKNOWLEDGEMENTS

Over twenty years ago, the vision and leadership of Phi Theta Kappa Executive Director and CEO Dr. Rod Risley brought together a team of dedicated people who created *Phi Theta Kappa Leadership Development Studies: A Humanities Approach*. This Fifth Edition of the publication is likewise a collaborative effort of many. It continues to reflect the success of the original team's efforts and builds on the foundations established with the first edition. We again acknowledge and express special appreciation to those who worked in the early 1990s to make the curriculum a reality:

- Carlene Feldman, the first department leader of Phi Theta Kappa Leadership Development Programs, for her commitment to launching a leadership development program of the highest order.

- John Clemens, Professor at Hartwick College and Executive Director of the Hartwick Leadership Institute, for his invaluable assistance in developing the framework of the initial manuscript.

- The W.K. Kellogg Foundation for its generous monetary support and confidence in our vision. This support and confidence afforded one hundred community colleges the opportunity to provide the course to thousands of students across the nation, Canada and the British Virgin Islands from 1992–1995. The Foundation also provided Phi Theta Kappa the means to enhance and refine the curriculum during 1995.

- The Phil Hardin Foundation, the Mississippi Humanities Council, and the National Endowment for the Humanities for their generous support that enabled community colleges in Mississippi to be the first to offer the course statewide.

- Community college presidents, administrators and faculty for their initial encouragement to pursue the development of a leadership studies course. They continue to contribute their time, knowledge and expertise in the delivery and continuous improvement of this course.

- The 1995 Course Refinement Task Force: Dr. Jo Marshall, Dr. Lillie McCain, Dr. Kevin Rafferty, Dr. Janice Roberts and Hyla Winters for their knowledgeable, indispensable and tireless efforts.

- Diane Eisenberg and associates for providing the expertise essential for the evaluation and refinement of the text and for providing assistance above and beyond responsibility during the Kellogg grant period between 1992 and 1995.

- Dr. Shirley B. Gordon, Chair of the Phi Theta Kappa Board of Directors, for her dedication to the founding of Phi Theta Kappa Leadership Development Programs and her constant willingness to assist with the development.

In 2000, Phi Theta Kappa organized a Revision Task Force. On behalf of Phi Theta Kappa, we wish to express sincere thanks to the following people who contributed to the significant enhancements of the Third Edition:

- The National Facilitators: Dr. Jo Marshall, Dr. Lillie McCain, Dr. Michael Engs, Dr. Mark McCabe, David Berry and Carlene Feldman, whose experiences with and commitment to the Phi Theta Kappa Leadership Development Program enabled them to create a dedicated team of experts who evaluated the curriculum in its entirety. The team then developed the outline for the revisions and participated in the content review and decision-making process. They contributed as well to several of the background and instructor support sections of the curriculum.

- Participants in the 2000 Leading Edge Conference, the first conference of Phi Theta Kappa Certified Leadership Instructors, who "field tested" several of the Classic Cases, Leadership Profiles and Film Studies for the first major revision of the curriculum.

- John Clemens of the Hartwick Leadership Institute for his continued interest and assistance with the curriculum. His depth of knowledge, reach of innovation and enthusiasm for leadership development is inspirational.

The Fourth Edition of *Phi Theta Kappa Leadership Development Studies: A Humanities Approach* reflected further work and passion to ensure that the curriculum remained accessible and relevant. We have great admiration and respect for our team who worked tirelessly to recommend enhancements for the edition. Our heartfelt thanks to:

- Our National Facilitators, who again formed the core team of content reviewers in 2005: Dr. Jo Marshall, Dr. Lillie McCain, Dr. Michael Engs, Dr. Mark McCabe, David Berry, Judy Gordon, Kevin Brame and Dr. Louis Fetheroff.

- Certified Instructor Mario Ramos-Reyes for many conversations about Latin American leaders and for his contributions to the Fourth Edition's Leadership Profile of Simón Bolivar.

- We are deeply grateful to Tammy Harvey, Michelle Slay, Nell Ewing, Renee Culpepper, Mollie Baker and Jason Quick for their personal and professional contributions to the Fourth Edition of the text. The enhancements of the curriculum would not have been possible without their assistance, creativity and devotion.

The Fifth Edition of *Phi Theta Kappa Leadership Development Studies: A Humanities Approach* includes new material that continues to expand the diversity of perspectives represented. Again, there are many contributors! Many thanks to:

- Members of the Honors Program Council for their recommendations about ways to enhance the Fifth Edition and encourage students to consider the insights on leadership at multiple levels, concerning self-leadership, interpersonal leadership, organizational leadership, and community/global leadership: Dr. Joan Fedor, Jeff Edwards, Josephine Fritts, Dr. Erica Hastert, Dan Rooney, Steve Schroeder, Dr. Sauda Smith, Jennifer Stanford, Dr. Patricia West and Lisa York.

- Certified Leadership Faculty who participated in round table dialogues in 2011 and who sent material and ideas.

- An additional, extremely dedicated group of International Facilitators and Certified Leadership Faculty who presented new material at the 2013 Leading Edge Institute held at the Community College Humanities Association National Conference in Louisville, Kentucky: David Berry, Cindy Carbone, Janis Hatfield, Grace Megnet, Dr. Jo Marshall, Dr. Lillie McCain, Steve Schroeder and Dr. Patricia West.

- Dan Rooney, who devoted a portion of his sabbatical to focus on the revisions for several units.

- The Marketing and Communications Department, especially Clay Meyer, Tracy Kleven and Blair Gillespie for their creative enthusiasm and perseverance through the work for the Fifth Edition.

- The entire staff of Phi Theta Kappa for their support throughout this effort, many of whom participated in trial film studies and dialogue.

May 2014

Monika S. Byrd

Monika S. Byrd
Editor
Dean of Leadership Development and Service Learning
Honors Program Department

Susan F. Edwards

Susan F. Edwards
Editor
Dean of Academic Affairs and Honors Programs
Honors Program Department

INTRODUCTION

Phi Theta Kappa Honor Society's mission is about the pursuit of excellence in three areas: academic and intellectual growth, leadership, and service. We emphasize each of these in *Phi Theta Kappa Leadership Development Studies: A Humanities Approach*. The contents are intellectually stimulating, academically challenging, and values-based with positive examples of the exercise of leadership in service to the common good and in progress for humankind. We value learning, diversity of perspective, critical thought, innovation, and above all, human dignity, and we are intentional about integrating the concept of citizenship into this course of study.

Citizenship requires both an individual identity and a communal identity. It necessitates a sense of self as both unique and part of local, regional, and global communities. As a result, the course will focus on enhancing self-awareness and the exercise of self-leadership as well as developing understanding of the possibilities for the exercise of leadership in groups, organizations and communities, regardless of position, title, or authority. Citizenship on many levels requires knowledge of the world, so the course includes readings from around the world and from many time periods to provide some historical context of the global forces affecting our lives today. World issues are complex and cut across disciplinary boundaries, so the course includes readings from many disciplines in order to hone our intellectual abilities for creating deeper understanding. Diverse knowledge, from many times and places and disciplines, is necessary to move into the arena of constructing truly new ideas and concepts for progress. The course will create new insights into one's own and others' cultural leadership traditions, and thus contribute to an understanding of what is universal about the human experience and leadership.

Grounding the course with values makes the kind of leadership we seek to develop among students transformational leadership, as suggested by James MacGregor Burns in his book *Leadership* (1978). Transformational leadership helps each individual reach his/her fullest potential and in so doing creates the leadership potential for positive change and progress—transformation—for others and for society. Other recent texts of leadership reinforce this outward focus on the needs of others or the group or society, rather than the needs of the individual leader. In his book, *Leadership: Theory and Practice* (2013), Peter G. Northouse defines leadership as "a process whereby an individual influences a group of individuals to achieve a common goal." Northouse clearly indicates that leadership in the modern world focuses on others and on goals—some kind of change or progress—unlike the more self-centered focus of definitions of leadership such as this one, "leadership is the exercise of power," one of thousands of earlier definitions that leadership scholar Ralph Stogdill identified in his encyclopedic study of leadership (*Handbook of Leadership: A Survey of Theory and Research*. New York: Free Press, 1974).

The transformational purpose of this curriculum contains three distinct and constant assumptions about leadership:

* within every individual there exists leadership potential,

* leadership can be taught and learned, and

* developing a personal leadership identity and philosophy is a prerequisite to deeper learning about leadership and to practicing leadership skills authentically in order to create progress.

This course therefore begins with a deep exploration of different perspectives on leadership. The curriculum affords participants an opportunity early in the course to assess their own leadership potential and identify their underlying assumptions about leadership, beginning the process of developing a personal leadership philosophy. The course then continues to examine specific leadership topics and skills through the literature and philosophy of great students of humanity and effective leaders in history who provide prime, real examples of leadership practices and skills. Much can be gleaned to enhance a personal understanding of leadership and to develop or improve essential skills required of effective leaders from the observation and study of these historical, philosophical, and fictional readings. This integration of readings from the humanities is a unique feature of *Phi Theta Kappa Leadership Development Studies*. Traditional leadership development curricula often overlook the leadership wisdom contained in the writings from ancient Greece and China, Renaissance Europe, early America, and twentieth-century Europe, America, Africa, and Asia we include, and therefore miss the opportunity to connect leadership development to global citizenship as this course does.

Around the world, thoughtful people perceive a crisis of leadership as well-established institutions and processes for dealing with social, economic, environmental, and political problems seem incapable of developing solutions or creating progress. Where are the thoughtful, effective leaders who consider innovative global, national, local, and personal solutions to pressing issues such as nuclear proliferation, wars, genocide, terrorist attacks, natural disasters, financial melt-down, community disputes, corporate scandals, failing school systems, pollution, and human rights violations? There is no shortage in sight of opportunities for the exercise of leadership at many levels to make a difference. To help respond to this challenge, and because recognizing and assisting human potential is central to the mission of Phi Theta Kappa Honor Society, we have developed this course of study.

A Note on Abbreviations in This Text

The abbreviation "B.C.E." represents the phrase "Before Common Era," in which "common" refers to the most common calendar in use in the world, the Gregorian calendar. It is a notation replacing "B.C."—"Before Christ"—and, as expected, the notation "C.E."—"Common Era"—replaces "A.D." which is the abbreviation for "Anno Domini," meaning "year of our lord Jesus Christ" in Latin. The new notations of B.C.E. and C.E. can be viewed as inclusive of the diverse people around the globe who use the Gregorian calendar besides Christians.

UNIT 1

DEVELOPING A PERSONAL LEADERSHIP PHILOSOPHY

INTRODUCTION

Developing a personal philosophy of leadership means, first and foremost, thinking deeply about the subject. The Classic Case, Leadership Profile, Readings, Film Studies, as well as the assessment exercises in this unit will focus on the many different facets of leadership, styles of leadership, and tasks of leadership. To develop a personal philosophy of leadership, you must also probe your own assumptions about leadership. Self-awareness is essential for effective interaction with others and it will ultimately enhance your flexibility to make contributions in a variety of situations. Awareness of your personal philosophy (and then through your work in subsequent units, your personal vision and values) will give you confidence in your future by helping you to determine the leadership approaches to take to achieve your goals, work collaboratively and effectively in groups, and apply your philosophy to engage in organizations and communities.

The Unit's Classic Case comes from an ancient source and one of the earliest authors to write extensively about leadership. In "The Philosopher King," excerpted from Plato's *Republic*, Plato's dialogue deals with the important question of selecting those persons who will lead the state or organization. As you will discover, Plato believed strongly that only a few people in a society or organization are meant to lead. The Leadership Profile is of Paulo Freire, an influential Brazilian educator. Freire gave great physical energy and deep thinking to the establishment of effective education in South America and beyond.

Each of the additional readings underscores how deeply individual and unique philosophies of leadership can be, with different assumptions about leaders and followers, different skills emphasized, and different understandings of what is most important to the effective exercise of leadership. The exercises in this Unit are a series of self-assessments chosen to help you discover your priorities and ways of thinking and how these apply to your personal philosophy of leadership. Your ability to understand your priorities, as well as those of others with whom you work or live, and articulating your personal philosophy of leadership can substantially enhance your exercise of leadership in your personal life, in your work with others, and to the benefit of your community. Margaret Wheatley (2006) explains the importance of self-reference:

> We see the world through who we are. All living beings create themselves and then use that "self" to filter new information and co-create their worlds. We refer to this self to determine what's important for us to notice. Through the self, we bring form and meaning to the infinite cacophony of data that always surrounds us...; "Self" includes awareness of those others it must relate to as part of its system...In a living system, self-reference is the source of growth, of increasing vitality. *(Leadership and the New Science: Discovering Order in a Chaotic World)*

As demonstrated throughout this text, films can be useful in the study of leadership. That is certainly true of the films *Twelve O'Clock High* and *Iron Lady*. The contrasting leadership styles between the two military leaders in *Twelve O'Clock High* and with the political leader in *Iron Lady* will provide excellent opportunities for dialogue about their values, perceptions of people, and assumptions regarding leadership.

Learning Objectives

- Recognize leadership and develop a personal understanding of what constitutes the effective exercise of leadership

- Define leadership in terms of the knowledge, skills, and abilities necessary for effective leadership

- Identify the assumptions underlying the leadership philosophies revealed in the Readings and the Film Studies

- Establish a foundation for a personal leadership philosophy based on an enhanced understanding of self

- Appreciate the contributions of the Classic Case and Leadership Profile for assisting with the development of a personal philosophy of leadership

UNIT

1

CLASSIC CASE

"The Philosopher King"

By Plato (428–347 B.C.E.)
Greek Philosopher

Introduction and Historical Background

Plato, along with Socrates, his teacher, and Aristotle, his student, laid the philosophical foundations of Western culture. In fact, Alfred North Whitehead once described the history of philosophy as merely "a series of footnotes to Plato."

Plato wrote in dialogue form. Philosophical ideas were advanced, discussed, and criticized in the context of conversations or debates. By the time of his death in 347 B.C.E., Plato had completed thirty-five dialogues. Today, after 2,400 years, these dialogues are still incomparable studies of the basic issues that confront human beings.

In addition to his writings, Plato, in 387 B.C.E., established the Academy in Athens as an institute for the systematic pursuit of philosophical and scientific research. It was a true educational innovation because he did not allow tedious lecturing. Instead, students, encouraged by their teachers, discussed, argued, and analyzed problems.

The Republic, Plato's most noted dialogue, was a response to the catastrophic leadership failure that led to the defeat of Athens in the Peloponnesian War. American essayist Ralph Waldo Emerson, referring to *The Republic*, once declared, "Burn all the libraries, for their value is in this one book." It is superb reading for philosophers and also those seeking to influence and exercise leadership.

As Plato looked back on the history of Athens, reflecting on its greatness during the Golden Age under Pericles, he could not help but wonder how such a great organization could be brought to its knees. Thus, in *The Republic*, Plato argues against the leadership style of Periclean Athens and offers his ideas for a new kind of leadership for his city-state, a style of leadership that he believed would return Athens to her greatness.

Plato believed strongly that only a few people in an organization are capable of leading the organization. They are, not surprisingly, the organizational philosophers, those who care deeply about truth and are imbued with great integrity and an overriding concern about the welfare of the organization.

The following excerpt from *The Republic* addresses the important question of identifying and selecting capable leaders. You will be introduced to Plato's famous "Philosopher King." Whereas many leadership scholars believe that leadership should be adaptive and responsive to different situations and to the needs of the followers, for Plato there was one style of leadership, and that was the kind of leadership that his "Philosopher King" would provide.

UNIT
1

Points to Consider

1. What qualities did Plato believe those who would be most effective at the exercise of leadership should have that are similar to the qualities of a philosopher? A king? How can an individual develop these talents and qualities?

2. Why does Plato consider the "Philosopher King" concept as important in groups? What might he argue against alternative styles?

3. What does Plato think about the capabilities of large groups (like the people of a city-state, or a large corporation, or a large community) to work together to make wise decisions? Do you agree?

4. To Plato, what is the *purpose* of leadership?

"The Philosopher King"

(Excerpts from *The Republic*, Book 6)
Translated by C.D.C. Reeve

Socrates: Who the philosophers are, then, Glaucon, and who they aren't has, through a somewhat lengthy argument and with much effort, somehow been made clear.

Glaucon: That's probably because it could not easily have been done through a shorter one.

Socrates: I suppose not. Yet, I, at least, think that the matter would have been made even clearer if we had had only that topic to discuss, and not the many others that remain for us to explore if we are to discover the difference between the just life and the unjust one.

Glaucon: What comes after this one, then?

Socrates: What else but the one that comes next? Since the philosophers are the ones who are able to grasp what is always the same in all respects, while those who cannot—those who wander among the many things that vary in every sort of way—are not philosophers, which of the two should be the leaders of a city?

Glaucon: What would be a reasonable answer for us to give?

Socrates: Whichever of them seems capable of guarding a city's laws and practices should be established as guardians.

Glaucon: That's right.

Socrates: So, is the answer to the following question clear: should a guardian who is going to keep watch over something be blind or keen-sighted?

Glaucon: Of course it is.

Socrates: Well, do you think there is any difference, then, between the blind and those who are really deprived of the knowledge of each thing that is, and have no clear model of it in their souls—those who cannot look away, like painters, to what is most true, and cannot, by making constant reference to it and by studying it as exactly as possible, establish here on earth conventional views about beautiful, just, or good things when they need to be established, or guard and preserve those that have been established?

Glaucon: No, by Zeus, there is not much difference between them.

Socrates: Shall we appoint these blind people as our guardians, then, or those who know each thing that is, have no less experience than the others, and are not inferior to them in any other part of virtue?

Glaucon: It would be absurd to choose anyone but philosophers, if indeed they are not inferior in these other things. For the very area in which they are superior is just about the most important one.

Socrates: Shouldn't we explain, then, how the same men can have both sets of qualities?

Glaucon: Certainly.

Socrates: Then, as we were saying at the beginning of this discussion, it is first necessary to understand the nature of philosophers. And I think that if we can agree sufficiently about that, we will also agree that the same people can have both qualities, and that they alone should be leaders in cities.

Glaucon: How so?

Socrates: Let's agree that philosophic natures always love the sort of learning that makes it clear to them some feature of the being that always is and does not wander around between coming-to-be and decaying.

Glaucon: Yes, let's.

Socrates: And further, let's agree that they love all of it and are not willing to give up any part, whether large or small, significant or insignificant, just like the honor-lovers and passionate men we described before.

Glaucon: That's right.

Socrates: Consider next whether there is a further feature they must have in their nature if they are going to be the way we described.

Glaucon: What?

Socrates: Truthfulness; that is to say they must never willingly tolerate falsehood in any form. On the contrary, they must hate it and have a natural affection for the truth.

Glaucon: They probably should have that feature.

Socrates: But it is not only *probable*, my friend; it is entirely necessary for a naturally passionate man to love everything akin to or related to the boys he loves.

Glaucon: That's right.

Socrates: Well, could you find anything that is more intimately related to wisdom than truth?

Glaucon: Of course not.

Socrates: Then is it possible for the same nature to be a philosopher (lover of wisdom) and a lover of falsehood?

Glaucon: Certainly not.

Socrates: So, right from childhood, a genuine lover of learning must strive above all for truth of every kind.

Glaucon: Absolutely.

Socrates: But in addition, when someone's appetites are strongly inclined in one direction, we surely know that they become more weakly inclined in the others, just like a stream that has been partly diverted into another channel.

Glaucon: Of course.

Socrates: Then when a person's desires flow toward learning and everything of that sort, they will be concerned, I imagine, with the pleasures that the soul experiences just by itself, and will be indifferent to those that come through the body—if indeed the person is not a counterfeit, but rather a true philosopher.

Glaucon: That's entirely inevitable.

Socrates: A person like that will be temperate, then, and in no way a lover of money. After all, money and the big expenditures that go along with it are sought for the sake of things that other people may take seriously, but that he does not.

Glaucon: That's right.

Socrates: And of course, there is also this to consider when you are going to judge whether a nature is philosophic or not.

Glaucon: What?

[handwritten margin note: intolerant, narrowminded]

Socrates: You should not overlook its sharing in <u>illiberality</u>; for surely petty-mindedness is altogether incompatible with that quality in a soul that is always reaching out to grasp all things as a whole, whether divine or human.

Glaucon: That's absolutely true.

Socrates: And do you imagine that a thinker who is high-minded enough to look at all time and all being will consider human life to be a very important thing?

Glaucon: He couldn't possibly.

Socrates: Then he won't consider death to be a terrible thing either, will he?

Glaucon: Not in the least.

[handwritten margin note: new opinions]

Socrates: Then a cowardly and <u>liberal</u> nature could not partake, apparently, in true philosophy.

Glaucon: Not in my opinion.

Socrates: Well, then, is there any way that an orderly person, who is not money-loving, illiberal, a lying imposter, or a coward, could come to drive a hard bargain or be unjust?

Glaucon: There is not.

Socrates: Moreover, when you are considering whether someone has a philosophic soul or not, you will consider whether he is just and gentle, right from the time he is young, or unsociable and savage.

Glaucon: Of course.

Socrates: And you won't ignore this either, I imagine.

Glaucon: What?

Socrates: Whether he is a slow learner or a fast one. Or do you expect someone to love something sufficiently well when it pains him to do it and a lot of effort brings only a small return?

Glaucon: No, it could not happen.

Socrates: What if he could retain nothing of what he learned, because he was completely forgetful? Could he fail to be empty of knowledge?

Glaucon: Of course not.

Socrates: Then if he is laboring in vain, don't you think that in the end he is bound to hate himself and what he is doing?

Glaucon: Of course.

Socrates: So let's never include a person with a forgetful soul among those who are sufficiently philosophical; the one we look for should be good at remembering.

Glaucon: Absolutely.

Socrates: Moreover, we would deny that an unmusical and graceless nature is drawn to anything besides what is disproportionate.

Glaucon: Of course.

Socrates: And do you think that is akin to what is disproportionate or to what is proportionate?

Glaucon: To what is proportionate.

Socrates: Then, in addition to those other things, let's look for a mind that has a natural sense of proportion and grace, one whose innate disposition makes it easy to lead to the form of each thing which is.

Glaucon: Indeed.

Socrates: Well, then, do you think the properties we have gone through aren't interconnected, or that any of them is in any way unnecessary to a soul that is going to have a sufficiently complete grasp of what is?

Glaucon: No, they are all absolutely necessary.

Socrates: Is there any criticism you can find, then, of a pursuit that a person cannot practice adequately unless he is naturally good at remembering, quick to learn, high-minded, graceful, and a friend and relative of truth, justice, courage, and temperance?

Glaucon: Not even Momus could criticize a pursuit like that.

Socrates: Well, then, when people of this sort are in perfect condition because of their education and their stage of life, wouldn't you entrust the city to them alone?

And Adeimantus replied: No one, Socrates, would be able to contradict these claims of yours. But all the same, here is pretty much the experience people have on any occasion on which they hear the sorts of things you are now saying: they think that because they are inexperienced in asking and answering questions, they are led astray a little bit by the argument at every question, and that when these little bits are added together at the end of the discussion, a big false step appears that is the opposite of what they said at the outset. Like the unskilled, who are trapped by the clever checkers players in the end and cannot make a move, they too are trapped in the end, and have nothing to say in this different kind of checkers, which is played not with pieces, but with words. Yet they are not a bit more inclined to think that what you claim is true. I say this in relation to the present case. You see, someone might well say now that he is unable to find the words to oppose you as you ask each of your questions. Yet, when it comes to facts rather than words, he sees that of all those who take up philosophy—not those who merely dabble in it while still young in order to complete their upbringing, and then drop it, but those who continue in it for a longer time—the majority become cranks, not to say completely bad, while the ones who seem best are rendered useless to the city because of the pursuit you recommend.

Socrates: When I heard him out, I said: Do you think that what these people say is false?

Adeimantus: I do not know. But I would be glad to hear what you think.

Socrates: You would hear that they seem to me to be telling the truth.

Adeimantus: How, then, can it be right to say that there will be no end to evils in our cities until philosophers—people we agree to be useless to cities—rule in them?

Socrates: The question you ask needs to be answered by means of an image.

Adeimantus: And you, of course, are not used to speaking in images!

Socrates: So! After landing me with a claim that is so difficult to establish, are you mocking me, too? Anyway, listen to my image, and you will appreciate all the more how I have to strain to make up images. What the best philosophers experience in relation to cities is so difficult to bear that there is no other single experience like it. On the contrary, one must construct one's image and one's defense of these philosophers from many sources, just as painters paint goat-stags by combining the features of different things.

Imagine, then, that the following sort of thing happens either on one ship or on many. The shipowner is taller and stronger than everyone else on board. But he is hard of hearing, he is a bit shortsighted, and his knowledge of seafaring is correspondingly deficient. The sailors are quarreling with one another about captaincy. Each of them thinks that he should captain the ship, even though he has not yet learned the craft and cannot name his teacher or a time when he was learning it. Indeed, they go further and claim that it cannot be taught at all, and are even ready to cut to pieces anyone who says it can. They are always crowding around the shipowner himself, pleading with him, and doing everything possible to get him to turn the rudder over to them. And sometimes, if they fail to persuade him and others succeed, they execute those others or throw them overboard. Then, having disabled their noble shipowner with mandragora or drink or in some other way, they rule the ship, use up its cargo drinking and feasting, and make the sort of voyage you would expect of such people. In addition, they praise anyone who is clever at persuading or forcing the shipowner to let them rule, calling him a "sailor," a "skilled captain," and "an expert about ships" while dismissing anyone else as a good-for-nothing. They do not understand that a true captain must pay attention to the seasons of the year, the sky, the stars, the winds, and all that pertains to

his craft if he is really going to be expert at ruling a ship. As for *how* he is going to become captain of the ship, whether people want him to or not, they do not think it possible to acquire the craft or practice of doing this at the same time as the craft of captaincy. When that is what is happening onboard ships, don't you think that a true captain would be sure to be called a "stargazer," a "useless babbler," and a "good-for-nothing" by those who sail in ships so governed?

Adeimantus: I certainly do.

Socrates: I do not think you need to examine the image to see the resemblance to cities and how they're disposed toward true philosophers, but you already understand what I mean.

Adeimantus: Indeed, I do.

Socrates: First teach this image, then, to the person who is surprised that philosophers are not honored in cities, and try to persuade him that it would be far more surprising if they were honored.

Adeimantus: I will.

Socrates: Furthermore, try to persuade him that you are speaking the truth when you say that the best among the philosophers are useless to the masses. But tell him to blame their uselessness on those who do not make use of them, not on those good philosophers. You see, it is not natural for the captain to beg the sailors to be ruled by him, nor for the wise to knock at the doors of the rich. The man who came up with that bit of sophistry was lying. What is truly natural is for the sick person, rich or poor, to go to doctor's doors, and for anyone who needs to be ruled to go to the doors of the one who can rule him. It is not for the ruler—if he is truly any use—to beg the subjects to accept his rule. Tell him he will make no mistake if he likens our present political rulers to the sailors we mentioned a moment ago, and those who are called useless stargazers by them to the true ship's captains.

Adeimantus: That's absolutely right.

Socrates: For those reasons, then, and in these circumstances, it is not easy for the best pursuit to be highly honored by those whose pursuits are its very opposites. But by far the greatest and most serious slander is brought on philosophy by those who claim to practice it—the ones about whom the prosecutor of philosophy declares, as you put it, that the majority of those who take it up are completely bad, while the best ones are useless. And I admitted that what you said was true, didn't I?

Adeimantus: Yes.

Socrates: Haven't we now explained why the good ones are useless?

Adeimantus: We certainly have.

Socrates: Do you next want us to discuss why it is inevitable that the greater number are bad, and try to show, if we can, that philosophy is not responsible for this either?

Adeimantus: Certainly.

Socrates: Then let's begin our dialogue by recalling the starting point of our description of the nature that someone must have if he is to become a fine and good person. First of all, if you remember, he was led by truth, and he had to follow it wholeheartedly and unequivocally, on pain of being a lying imposter with no share at all in true philosophy.

Adeimantus: That's what we said.

Socrates: Well, isn't that fact alone completely contrary to the belief currently held about him?

Adeimantus: It certainly is.

Socrates: So, won't it be reasonable, then, for us to plead in his defense that a real lover of learning naturally strives for what is? He does not linger over each of the many things that are believed to be, but keeps on going, without losing or lessening his passion, until he grasps what the nature of each thing itself is with the part of his soul that is fitted to grasp a thing of that sort because of its kinship with it. Once he has drawn near to it, has intercourse with what really is, and has begotten understanding and truth, he knows, truly lives, is nourished, and—at that point, but not before—is relieved from his labor pains.

Adeimantus: Nothing could be more reasonable.

Socrates: Well, then, will a person of that sort love falsehood or, in completely opposite fashion, will he hate it?

Adeimantus: He will hate it.

Socrates: And if truth led the way, we would never say, I imagine, that a chorus of evils could follow it.

Adeimantus: Of course not.

Socrates: On the contrary, it is followed by a healthy and just character, and the temperance that accompanies it.

Adeimantus: That's right.

Socrates: What need is there, then, to go back to the beginning and compel the rest of the philosophic nature's chorus to line up all over again? You surely remember that courage, high-mindedness, ease in learning, and a good memory all belong to philosophers. Then you objected that anyone would be compelled to agree with what we are saying, but that if he left the arguments aside and looked at the very people the argument is about, he would say that some of those he saw were useless, while the majority of them were thoroughly bad. Trying to discover the reason for this slander, we have arrived now at this question: why are the majority of them bad? And *that* is why we have again taken up the nature of the true philosophers and defined what it necessarily has to be.

Adeimantus: That's right.

Socrates: What we now have to do is look at the ways this nature gets corrupted; how it gets completely destroyed in the majority of cases, while a small number escape—the very ones that are called useless, rather than bad. After that, we must next look at those who imitate this nature and adopt its pursuit. We must see

what natures the souls have that enter into a pursuit that is too valuable and too high for them—souls that, by often striking false notes, give philosophy the reputation that you said it has with everyone everywhere.

Adeimantus: What sorts of corruption do you mean?

Socrates: I will try to explain them to you if I can. I imagine that everyone would agree with us about this: the sort of nature that possesses all the qualities we prescribed just now for the person who is going to be a complete philosopher, is seldom found among human beings, and there will be few who possess it. Or don't you think so?

Adeimantus: I most certainly do.

Socrates: Consider, then, how many great sources of destruction there are for these few.

Adeimantus: What are they?

Socrates: The most surprising thing of all to hear is that each one of the things we praised in that nature tends to corrupt the soul that has it and drag it away from philosophy. I mean courage, temperance, and the other things we mentioned.

Adeimantus: That does sound strange.

Socrates: Furthermore, in addition to those, all so-called good things also corrupt it and drag it away—beauty, wealth, physical strength, powerful family connections in the city, and all that goes along with these. You understand the general pattern of thing I mean?

Adeimantus: I do, and I would be glad to acquire a more precise understanding of it.

Socrates: Grasp the general principle correctly and the matter will become clear to you, and what I said about it before won't seem so strange.

Adeimantus: What are you telling me to grasp?

Socrates: In the case of every seed or growing thing, whether plant or animal, we know that if it fails to get the food, climate, or location suitable for it, then the more vigorous it is, the more it is deficient in the qualities proper to it. For surely bad is more opposed to good than to not-good.

Adeimantus: Of course.

Socrates: So, I suppose it is reasonable that the best nature comes off worse than an inferior one from unsuitable nurture.

Adeimantus: It is.

Socrates: Well, then, Adeimantus, won't we also say that if *souls* with the best natures get a bad education, they become exceptionally bad? Or do you think that great injustices and unalloyed evil originate in an inferior nature, rather than in a vigorous one that has been corrupted by its upbringing? Or that a weak nature is ever responsible for great good things or great bad ones?

Adeimantus: No, you are right.

Socrates: Well, then, if the nature we proposed for the philosopher happens to receive the proper instruction, I imagine it will inevitably grow to attain every virtue. But if it is not sown, planted, and grown in a suitable environment, it will develop in entirely the opposite way, unless some god comes to its aid. Or do you too believe, as the masses do, that some young people are corrupted by sophists—that there are sophists, private individuals, who corrupt them to a significant extent? Isn't it, rather, the very people who say this who are the greatest sophists of all, who educate most effectively and produce young and old men and women of just the sort they want?

Adeimantus: When do they do that?

Socrates: When many of them sit together in assemblies, courts, theaters, army camps, or any other gathering of a majority in public and, with a loud uproar, object excessively to some of the things that are said or done, then approve excessively of others, shouting and clapping; and when, in addition to these people themselves, the rocks and the surrounding space itself echo and redouble the uproar of their praise or blame. In a situation like that, how do you think—as the saying goes—a

young man's heart is affected? How will whatever sort of private education he received hold up for him, and not get swept away by such praise and blame, and go on carried off by the flood wherever it goes, so that he will call the same things beautiful or ugly as these people, practice what they practice, and become like them?

Adeimantus: The compulsion to do so will be enormous, Socrates.

Socrates: And yet we have not mentioned the greatest compulsion of all.

Adeimantus: What is that?

Socrates: It is what these educators and sophists impose by their actions if their words fail to persuade. Or don't you know that they punish anyone who is not persuaded, with disenfranchisement, fines, or death?

Adeimantus: They most certainly do.

Socrates: What other sophist, then, or what sort of private conversations do you think will oppose these and prove stronger?

Adeimantus: None, I imagine.

Socrates: No, indeed, even to try would be very foolish. You see, there is not now, never has been, nor ever will be, a character whose view of virtue goes contrary to the education these provide. I mean a human character, comrade—the divine, as the saying goes, in an exception to the rule. You may be sure that if anything is saved and turns out well in the political systems that exist now, you won't be mistaken in saying that divine providence saved it.

Adeimantus: That is what I think, too.

Socrates: Well, then, you should also agree to this.

Adeimantus: What?

Socrates: Each of those private wage-earners—the ones these people call sophists and consider to be their rivals in craft—teaches anything other than the convictions the masses hold when they are assembled together, and this he calls wisdom. It is just as if someone were

Clever but fallacious (Mistaken)

learning the passions and appetites of a huge, strong beast that he is rearing—how to approach and handle it, when it is most difficult to deal with or most docile and what makes it so, what sounds it utters in either condition, and what tones of voice soothe or anger it. Having learned all this through associating and spending time with the beast, he calls this wisdom, gathers his information together as if it were a craft, and starts to teach it. Knowing nothing in reality about which of these convictions or appetites is fine or shameful, good or bad, just or unjust, he uses all these terms in conformity with the great beast's beliefs—calling the things it enjoys good and the things that angers it bad. He has no other account to give of them, but calls everything he is compelled to do just fine, never having seen how much the natures of necessity and goodness really differ, and being unable to explain it to anyone. Don't you think, by Zeus, that someone like that would make a strange educator?

Adeimantus: I do, indeed.

Socrates: Then does this person seem any different from the one who believes that wisdom is understanding the passions and pleasures of the masses—multifarious people—assembled together, whether in regard to painting, music, or politics for that matter? For if a person associates with the masses and exhibits his poetry or some other piece of craftsmanship to them or his service to the city, and gives them mastery over him to any degree beyond what is unavoidable, he will be under Diomedean compulsion, as it is called, to produce the things of which they approve. But that such things are truly good and beautiful—have you ever heard anyone presenting an argument for that conclusion that was not absolutely ridiculous?

Adeimantus: No, and I do not suppose I ever will.

Socrates: So then, bearing all that in mind, recall our earlier question: can the majority in any way tolerate or accept that the beautiful itself (as opposed to the many beautiful things), or each thing itself (as opposed to the corresponding many), exists?

Diverse

God-like cunning

Adeimantus: Not in the least.

Socrates: It is impossible, then, for the majority to be philosophic.

Adeimantus: It is impossible.

Socrates: And so, those who practice philosophy are inevitably disparaged by them?

Adeimantus: Inevitably.

Socrates: And also by those private individuals who associate with the majority and want to please them.

Adeimantus: Clearly.

Socrates: On the basis of these facts, then, do you see any way to preserve a philosophic nature and ensure that it will continue to practice philosophy and reach the end? Consider the question in light of what we said before. We agreed that ease in learning, a good memory, courage, and high-mindedness belong to the philosophic nature. ✓

Adeimantus: Yes.

Socrates: Right from the start, then, won't someone like that be first among the children in everything, especially if his body's nature matches that of his soul?

Adeimantus: Of course he will.

Socrates: So as he gets older, I imagine his family and fellow citizens will want to make use of him in connection with their own affairs.

Adeimantus: Certainly.

Socrates: They will get down on their knees, begging favors from him and honoring him, flattering ahead of time the power that is going to be his, so as to secure it for themselves.

Adeimantus: That's usually what happens, at least.

Socrates: What do you think someone like that will do in such circumstances—especially if he happens to be from a great city where he is rich and noble, and if he is good-looking and tall as well? Won't he be filled with an impractical expectation and think himself capable of managing the affairs, not only of the Greeks, but of the barbarians, too? And won't he exalt himself to great heights, as a result, and be brimming with pretension and empty, senseless pride?

Adeimantus: He certainly will.

Socrates: Now, suppose someone gently approaches a young man in that state of mind and tells him the truth: that he has no sense, although he needs it, and that it cannot be acquired unless he works like a slave to attain it. Do you think it will be easy for him to hear that message through the evils that surround him?

Adeimantus: Far from it.

Socrates: And suppose that, because of his noble nature and his natural affinity for such arguments, he somehow sees the point and is turned around and drawn toward philosophy. What do we suppose those people will do if they believe that they are losing his services and companionship? Is there anything they won't do or say in his regard to prevent him from being persuaded? Or anything they won't do or say in regard to his persuader to prevent him from succeeding, whether it is in private plots or public court cases?

Adeimantus: There certainly is not.

Socrates: Then is there any chance that such a person will practice philosophy?

Adeimantus: None at all.

Socrates: Do you see, then, that we weren't wrong to say that when a philosophic nature is badly brought up, its very components—together with the other so-called goods, such as wealth and every provision of that sort—are somehow the cause of its falling away from the pursuit?

Adeimantus: No, we were not. What we said was right.

Socrates: There you are, you amazing fellow! That is the extent of the sort of destruction and corruption that the nature best suited for the noblest pursuit undergoes. And such a nature is a rare occurrence anyway, we claim. Moreover, men who possess it are the ones that do the worst things to cities and individuals, and also—if they happen to be swept that way by the current—the greatest good. For a petty nature does anything great, either to a private individual or a city.

Adeimantus: That's very true.

Socrates: So when these men, for whom philosophy is most appropriate, fall away from her, they leave her desolate and unwed, and themselves lead a life that is inappropriate and untrue. Then others, who are unworthy of her, come to her as to an orphan bereft of kinsmen, and shame her. They are the ones responsible for the reproaches that you say are cast upon philosophy by her detractors—that some of her consorts are useless, while the majority deserve many evils.

Adeimantus: Yes, that is what they say.

Socrates: And it is a reasonable thing to say. For other worthless little men see that this position has become vacant, even though it is brimming with fine accolades and pretensions, and—like prisoners escaping from jail who take refuge in a temple—leap gladly from their crafts to philosophy. These are the ones who are most sophisticated at their own petty craft. You see, at least in comparison to other crafts, and even in its present state, philosophy still has a grander reputation. And that is what many people are aiming at, people with defective natures, whose souls are as cramped and spoiled by their menial tasks as their bodies are warped by their crafts and occupations. Isn't that inevitably what happens?

Adeimantus: It certainly is.

Socrates: Do you think that they look any different than a little, bald-headed blacksmith who has come into some money and, newly released from debtor's prison, has taken a bath, put on a new cloak, got himself up as a bride groom, and is about to marry the master's daughter because she is poor and abandoned?

Adeimantus: They are no different at all.

Socrates: What sort of offspring are they likely to beget, then? Won't their children be wretched illegitimates?

Adeimantus: Inevitably.

Socrates: What about when men who are unworthy of education approach philosophy and associate with her in a way unworthy of her? What kinds of thought and beliefs are we to say they beget? Won't they be what are truly and appropriately called sophisms, since they have nothing genuine or truly wise about them?

Adeimantus: Absolutely.

Socrates: Then there remains, Adeimantus, only a very small group who associate with philosophy in a way that is worthy of her: a noble and well brought-up character, perhaps, kept down by exile, who stays true to his nature and remains with philosophy because there is no one to corrupt him; or a great soul living in a small city, who disdains the city's affairs and looks beyond them. A very few might perhaps come to philosophy from other crafts that they rightly despise because they have good natures. And some might be held back by the bridle that restrains our friend Theages—you see, he meets all the other conditions needed to make him fall away from philosophy, but his physical illness keeps him out of politics and prevents it. Finally, my own case is hardly worth mentioning—my diamonic sign—since I don't suppose it has happened to anyone else or to only a few before. Now, those who have become members of this little group have tasted how sweet and blessed a possession philosophy is. At the same time, they have also seen the insanity of the masses and realized that there is nothing healthy, so to speak, in public affairs, and that there is no ally with whose aid the champion of justice can survive; that instead he would perish before he could profit either their city or his friends, and be useless both to himself and to others—like a man who has fallen among wild animals and is neither willing to join them in doing injustice nor sufficiently strong to oppose the general savagery alone. Taking all this into his calculations, he keeps quiet and does his own work,

like someone who takes refuge under a little wall from a storm of dust or hail driven by the wind. Seeing others filled with lawlessness, the philosopher is satisfied if he can somehow lead his present life pure of injustice and impious acts, and depart from it with good hope, blameless and content.

Adeimantus: Well, that is no small thing for him to have accomplished before departing.

Socrates: But no very great one either, since he did not chance upon a suitable constitution. In a suitable one, his own growth will be fuller and he will save the community, as well as himself. Anyway, it seems to me that we have now said enough about the slander brought against philosophy and why it is unjust—unless, of course, you have got something to add.

Adeimantus: I have nothing further to add on that issue. But which of our present constitutions do you think is suitable for philosophy?

Socrates: None of them. But that is exactly my complaint. There is not one city today with a constitution worthy of philosophic nature. That is precisely why it is perverted and altered. It is like foreign seed sown in alien ground: it tends to be overpowered and to fade away into the native species. Similarly, the philosophic species does not maintain its own power at present, but declines into a different character. But if it were to find the best constitution, as it is itself the best, it would be clear that it is really divine and that other natures and pursuits are merely human. Obviously, you are going to ask next what that constitution is.

Adeimantus: You are wrong there. You see, I was not going to ask that, but whether it was the constitution we described when we were founding our city or a different one.

Socrates: In all other respects, it is that one. But we said even then that there must always be some people in the city who have a rational account of the constitution, the same one that guided you, the lawgiver, when you made the laws.

Adeimantus: Yes, we did say that.

Socrates: But we did not explain it clearly enough, for fear of what our own objections have made clear: namely, that the demonstration of it would be long and difficult. Indeed, even what remains is not the easiest of all things to discuss.

Adeimantus: What is that?

Socrates: How a city can engage in philosophy without being destroyed. You see, all great things are prone to fall and, as the saying goes, beautiful things are really difficult.

Adeimantus: All the same, the demonstration won't be complete until this has been cleared up.

Socrates: If anything prevents that, it won't be lack of willingness, but lack of ability. At any rate, you will see how passionate *I* am. Look now, in fact, at how passionately and recklessly I am going to argue that a city should practice philosophy in the opposite way to the present one.

Adeimantus: How?

Socrates: At present, those who take it up at all do so as young men, just out of childhood, who have yet to take up household management and moneymaking. Then, just when they reach the most difficult part they abandon it and are regarded as the most fully trained philosophers. By the most difficult part, I mean the one concerned with arguments. In later life, if others are engaged in it and they are invited and deign to listen to them, they think they have done a lot, since they think this should only be a sideline. And, with a few exceptions, by the time they reach old age they are more thoroughly extinguished than the sun of Heraclitus, since they are never rekindled.

Adeimantus: What should they do instead?

Socrates: Entirely the opposite. As young men and children, they should occupy themselves with an education and philosophy suitable to the young. Their bodies are blooming and growing into manhood at this time, and they should take very good care of them, so as to acquire a helper for philosophy. But as they grow older and their soul begins to reach maturity, they should make its exercises more rigorous. Then, when their strength begins to fail and they have retired from politics and military service, they should graze freely in the pastures of philosophy and do nothing else, except as a sideline—I mean those who are going to live happily and, when the end comes, crown the life they have lived with a fitting providence in that other place.

Adeimantus: You seem to be arguing with real passion, Socrates. But I am sure that most of your hearers will oppose you with even greater passion and won't be convinced in the least—beginning with Thrasymachus.

Socrates: Please do not try to raise a quarrel between me and Thrasymachus just as we have become friends—not that we were enemies before. You see, we won't relax our efforts until we convince him and the others—or at least do something that may benefit them in a later incarnation when, reborn, they happen upon these arguments again.

Adeimantus: You are talking about the short term, I see!

Socrates: It is certainly nothing compared to the whole of time! However, it is no wonder that the masses are not convinced by our arguments. I mean, they have never seen a *man* that matched our *plan*—though they have more often seen words purposely chosen to rhyme with one another than just happening to do so as in the present case. But a man who, as far as possible, matched and rhymed with virtue in word and deed, and wielded dynastic power in a city of the same type—that is something they have never seen even once. Or do you think they have?

Adeimantus: No, definitely not.

Socrates: Nor, bless you, have they spent enough time listening to fine and free arguments that vigorously seek the truth in every way, so as to acquire knowledge and keep their distance from all the sophistries and eristic quibbles that—whether in public trials or private gatherings—strive for nothing except reputation and disputation.

Adeimantus: No, they have not.

Socrates: It was for these reasons, and because we foresaw these difficulties, that we were afraid. All the same, we were compelled by the truth to say that no city, no constitution, and no individual man will ever become perfect until some chance event compels those few philosophers who are not vicious (the ones who are now called useless) to take care of a city, whether they are willing to or not, and compels the city to obey them—or until a true passion for true philosophy flows by some divine inspiration into the sons of the men now wielding dynastic power or sovereignty, or into the men themselves. Now it cannot be reasonably maintained, in my view, that either or both of these things is impossible. But if they were, we would be justly ridiculed for indulging in wishful thinking. Isn't that so?

Adeimantus: It is.

Socrates: Then if, in the limitless past, some necessity forced those who were foremost in philosophy to take charge of a city, or is doing so now in some barbaric place far beyond our ken, or will do so in the future, this is something we are prepared to fight about—our argument that the constitution we have described has existed, does exist, and will exist, at any rate, whenever it is that the muse of philosophy gains mastery of a city. It is not impossible for this to happen, so we are not speaking of impossibilities—that it is *difficult*, we agree ourselves.

Adeimantus: *I* certainly think so.

Socrates: But the masses do not—is that what you are going to say?

Adeimantus: They probably don't.

Socrates: Bless you, you should not make such a wholesale charge against the masses! They will surely come to hold a different belief if, instead of wanting to win a victory at their expense, you soothe them and try to remove their slanderous prejudice against the love of learning.

You must show them what you mean by philosophers and define their nature and pursuit the way we did just now. Then they will realize you do not mean the same people they do. And if they once see it that way, even you will say that they will have a different opinion from the one you just attributed to them and will answer differently. Or do you think that anyone who is gentle and without malice is harsh to one who is not harsh, or malicious to one who is not malicious? I will anticipate you and say that I think a few people may have such a harsh character, but not the majority.

Adeimantus: And I agree, of course.

Socrates: Then don't you also agree that the harshness of the masses toward philosophy is caused by those outsiders who do not belong and who have burst in like a band of revelers, abusing one another, indulging their love of quarreling, and always arguing about human beings—something that is least appropriate in philosophy?

Adeimantus: I do, indeed.

Socrates: For surely, Adeimantus, someone whose mind is truly directed toward the things that are has not the leisure to look down at human affairs and be filled with malice and hatred as a result of entering into their disputes. Instead, as he looks at and contemplates things that are orderly and always the same, that neither do injustice to one another nor suffer it, being all in a rational order, he imitates them and tries to become as like them as he can. Or do you think there is any way to prevent someone from associating with something he admires without imitating it?

Adeimantus: He can't possibly.

Socrates: Then the philosopher, by associating with what is orderly and divine, becomes as divine and orderly as a human being can. Though, mind you, there are always plenty of slanders around.

Adeimantus: Absolutely.

Socrates: And if he should come to be compelled to make a practice—in private and in public—of stamping what he sees there into the people's characters, instead of shaping only his own, do you think he will be a poor craftsman of temperance, justice, and the whole of popular virtue?

Adeimantus: Not at all.

Socrates: And when the masses realize that what we are saying about him is true, will they be harsh with philosophers or mistrust us when we say that there is no way a city can ever find happiness unless its plan is drawn by painters who use the divine model?

Adeimantus: They won't be harsh, if they do realize this. But what sort of drawing do you mean?

Socrates: They would take the city and people's characters as their sketching slate, but first they would wipe it clean—which is not at all an easy thing to do. And you should be aware that this is an immediate difference between them and others—that they refuse to take either a private individual or a city in hand, or to write laws, unless they receive a clean slate or are allowed to clean it themselves.

Adeimantus: And rightly so.

Socrates: And after that, don't you think they would draw the plan of the constitution?

Adeimantus: Of course.

Socrates: And I suppose that, as they work, they would look often in each direction: on the one hand, toward what is in its nature just, beautiful, temperate, and all the rest; and, on the other, toward what they are trying to put into human beings, mixing and blending pursuits to produce a human likeness, based on the one that Homer too called divine and godly when it appeared among human beings.

Adeimantus: Right.

Socrates: They would erase one thing, I suppose, and draw in another, until they had made people's characters as dear to the gods as possible.

Adeimantus: At any rate, the drawing would be most beautiful that way.

Socrates: Are we at all persuading the people you said were rushing to attack us, then, that the philosopher we were praising to them is really this sort of painter of constitutions? They were angry because we were entrusting cities to him; are they any calmer at hearing it now?

Adeimantus: They will be much calmer, if they have any sense.

Socrates: After all, how could they possibly dispute it? Will they deny that philosophers are lovers both of what is and of the truth?

Adeimantus: That would be silly.

Socrates: Or that their nature, as we have described it, is akin to the best?

Adeimantus: They cannot deny that either.

Socrates: Or that such a nature, when it happens to find appropriate pursuits, will not be as completely good and philosophic as any other? Or are they going to claim that the people we excluded are more so?

Adeimantus: Certainly not.

Socrates: Will they still be angry, then, when we say that until the philosopher class gains mastery of a city, there will be no respite from evils for either city or citizens, and the constitution we have been describing in our discussion will never be completed in practice?

Adeimantus: They will probably be less so.

Socrates: If it is all right with you, then, let's not say that they will simply be less angry, but that they will become altogether gentle and persuaded; so that out of shame, if nothing else, they will agree.

Adeimantus: All right.

Socrates: So let's assume that they have been convinced of this. Will anyone contend, then, that there is no chance that the offspring of kings or men in power could be natural-born philosophers?

Adeimantus: No one could.

Socrates: Could anyone claim that if such offspring are born, they must inevitably be corrupted? We agree ourselves that it is difficult for them to be saved. But that in the whole of time not one of them could be saved—could anyone contend that?

Adeimantus: Of course not.

Socrates: But surely the occurrence of one such individual is enough, provided his city obeys him, to bring to completion all the things that now seem so incredible.

Adeimantus: Yes, one is enough.

Socrates: For I suppose that if a ruler established the laws and practices we have described, it is hardly impossible that the citizens would be willing to carry them out.

Adeimantus: Not at all.

Socrates: Would it be either surprising or impossible, then, that others should think as we do?

Adeimantus: I don't suppose so.

Socrates: But I think our earlier discussion was sufficient to show that these arrangements are best, provided they are possible.

Adeimantus: Indeed, it was.

Socrates: It seems, then, that the conclusion we have now reached about legislation is that the one we are describing is best, provided it is possible; and that while it is difficult for it to come about, it certainly is not impossible.

Adeimantus: Yes, that is the conclusion we have reached.

Socrates: Now that this conclusion has, with much effort, been reached, we must next deal with the remaining issues—in what way, by means of what subjects and pursuits, the saviors of our constitution will come to exist, and at what ages they will take up each of them.

Adeimantus: Yes, we must deal with that.

Socrates: I gained nothing by my cleverness, then, in omitting from our earlier discussion the troublesome topic of acquiring women, begetting children, and establishing rulers, because I knew the whole truth would provoke resentment and would be difficult to bring about. As it turned out, the need to discuss them arose anyway. Now, the subject of women and children has already been discussed. But that of the rulers has to be taken up again from the beginning. We said, if you remember, that they must show themselves to be lovers of the city, when tested by pleasures and pains, by not abandoning this conviction through labors, fears, and all other adversities. Anyone who was incapable of doing so was to be rejected, while anyone who always came through pure—like gold tested in a fire—was to be made ruler and receive gifts and prizes, both while he lived and after his death. These were the sorts of things we were saying while our argument veiled its face and slipped by, for fear of stirring up the very problems that now confront us.

Adeimantus: That's absolutely true. I do remember.

Socrates: I was reluctant, my friend, to say the things we have now dared to say anyway. But now, let's also dare to say that we must establish philosophers as guardians in the most exact sense.

Adeimantus: Let's do so.

Socrates: Bear in mind, then, that there will probably be only a few of them. You see, they have to have the nature we described, and its parts rarely consent to grow together in one person; rather, its many parts grow split off from one another.

Adeimantus: How do you mean?

Socrates: Ease of learning, good memory, astuteness, and smartness, as you know, and all the other things that go along with them, such as youthful passion and high-mindedness, are rarely willing to grow together simultaneously with a disposition to live an orderly, quiet, and completely stable life. On the contrary, those who possess the former traits are carried by their quick wits wherever chance leads them, and have no stability at all.

Adeimantus: That's true.

Socrates: Those with stable characters, on the other hand, who do not change easily, whom one would employ because of their greater reliability, and who in battle are not easily moved by fears, act in the same way when it comes to their studies. They are hard to get moving and learn with difficulty, as if they are anesthetized, and are constantly falling asleep and yawning whenever they have to work hard at such things.

Adeimantus: They are.

Socrates: Yet we say that someone must have a good and fine share of both characters, or he won't receive the truest education or honor, or be allowed to rule.

Adeimantus: That's right.

Socrates: Then don't you think this will rarely occur?

Adeimantus: Of course.

Socrates: He must be tested, then, in the labors, fears, and pleasures we mentioned before. He must also be exercised in many other subjects, however, which we did not mention but are adding now, to see whether his nature can endure the most important subjects or will shrink from them like the cowards who shrink from the other tests.

Adeimantus: It is certainly important to find that out. But what do you mean by the most important subjects?

Socrates: Do you remember when we distinguished three kinds of things in the soul in order to help bring out what justice, temperance, courage, and wisdom each is?

Adeimantus: If I didn't, I would not deserve to hear the rest.

Socrates: Do you also remember what preceded it?

Adeimantus: No, what?

Socrates: We said, I believe, that in order to get the finest view of these matters, we would need to take a longer road, which would make them plain to anyone who took it, but that it was possible to give demonstrations that would be up to the standard of the previous discussion. All of you said that was enough. The result was that our subsequent discussion, as it seemed to me, was less than exact. But whether or not it satisfied all of you is for you to say.

Adeimantus: I, at any rate, thought you gave us good measure. And so, apparently, did the others.

Socrates: No, my friend, any measure of such things that falls short in any way of what is, is not good measure at all, since nothing incomplete is a measure of anything. Some people, however, are occasionally of the opinion that an incomplete treatment is already adequate and that there is no need for further inquiry.

Adeimantus: Yes, a lot of people feel like that. Laziness is the cause.

Socrates: Well, that is a feeling that is least appropriate in a guardian of a city and its laws.

Adeimantus: No doubt.

Socrates: He will have to take the longer road then, comrade, and put no less effort into learning than into physical training. For otherwise, as we were just saying, he will never pursue the most important and most appropriate subject to the end.

Adeimantus: Why, aren't these virtues the most important things? Is there something yet more important than justice and the other virtues we discussed?

Socrates: Not only is it more important, but, even in the case of the virtues themselves, it is not enough to look at a mere sketch as we are doing now, while neglecting the most finished portrait. I mean, it is ridiculous, isn't it, to strain every nerve to attain the utmost exactness and clarity about other things of little value, while not treating the most important things as meriting the most exactness?

Adeimantus: It certainly is. But do you think that anyone is going to let you off without asking you what you mean by this most important subject, and what it is concerned with?

Socrates: No, I do not. And you may ask it, too. You have certainly heard the answer often, but now either you are not thinking or you intend to make trouble for me again by interrupting. And I suspect it is more the latter. You see, you have often heard it said that the form of the good is the most important thing to learn about, and that it is by their relation to it that just things and the others become useful and beneficial. And now you must be pretty certain that that is what I am going to say, and, in addition, that we have no adequate knowledge of other things is of no benefit to us, any more than if we acquire any possession without the good. Or do you think there is any benefit in possessing everything but the good? Or to know everything without knowing the good, thereby knowing nothing fine or good?

Adeimantus: No, by Zeus, I do not.

Socrates: Furthermore, you also know that the masses believe pleasure to be the good, while the more refined believe it to be knowledge.

Adeimantus: Of course.

Socrates: And, my friend, that those who believe this cannot show us what sort of knowledge it is, but in the end are forced to say that it is knowledge of the good.

Adeimantus: Which is completely ridiculous.

Socrates: How could it not be, when they blame us for not knowing the good and then turn around and talk to us as if we did know it? I mean, they say it is knowledge of the good—as if we understood what they mean when they utter the word "good."

Adeimantus: That's absolutely true.

Socrates: What about those who define the good as pleasure? Are they any less full of confusion than the others? Or aren't even they forced to admit that there are bad pleasures?

Adeimantus: Most definitely.

Socrates: I suppose it follows, doesn't it, that they have to admit that the same things are both good and bad?

Adeimantus: It certainly does.

Socrates: Isn't it clear, then, that there are lots of serious disagreements about the good?

Adeimantus: Of course.

Socrates: Well, isn't it also clear that many people would choose things that are believed to be just or beautiful, even if they are not, and would act, acquire things, and form beliefs accordingly? Yet no one is satisfied to acquire things that are *believed* to be good. On the contrary, everyone seeks the things that *are* good. In this area, everyone disdains mere reputation.

Adeimantus: Right.

Socrates: That, then, is what every soul pursues, and for its sake does everything. The soul has a hunch that the good is something, but it is puzzled and cannot adequately grasp just what it is or acquire the sort of stable belief about it that it has about other things, and so it misses the benefit, if any, that even those other things may give. Are we to accept that even the best people in the city, to whom we entrust everything, must remain thus in the dark about something of this kind and importance?

Adeimantus: That's the last thing we would do.

[handwritten margin note: the things that are good not just believed to be good]

Reeve, C. D. C. (2004). *Plato: Republic.* Translated From The New Standard Greek Text. Indianapolis, IN: Hackett.

LEADERSHIP PROFILE

Paulo Freire (1921–1997)

Brazilian Educator and Philosopher
"The Fourth Letter: On the Indispensable Qualities of Progressive Teachers
for Their Better Performance"

Introduction and Historical Background

Decades of thoughtful experience clearly go into Paulo Freire's "Fourth Letter." Like handing us carbon beaten over time into diamonds, he shares his life of teaching and writing in gems of concentrated wisdom.

Friere describes the "indispensable"—that is, the absolutely necessary—qualities of a "progressive teacher," but, as he hints, these are the qualities necessary to a progressive mother or father, doctor, farmer, citizen, human being. And while the virtues he describes come from years of experience, knowing of them before we have our own experiences can be both helpful and inspirational.

Globo via Getty Images

Mortimer J. Adler, philosopher, professor, creator of the Great Books program, in 1984 published *Paidea: An Educational Syllabus*, a statement of what every student, K–12, should know, developed with a national committee. "The three great cooperative arts," he says at one point, "are Agriculture, Medicine, and Teaching," to which we can add parenting, ministry, counseling. These "arts," Adler explains, work not with lifeless, controlled oil paint or marble or even mental notes and harmonies, but with living things—plants, soil, people. Without the willing cooperation of the recipient of the artistry, the work is in vain. What Paulo Freire gives us in his "Fourth Letter" can be seen as a list of the virtues of the experienced Cooperative Artist.

Freire's early life in Brazil, particularly through the Great Depression of the 1930s, when his father died, was riddled with hunger and poverty which put him behind four grades in school. "I wasn't dumb. It wasn't lack of interest," but "I didn't understand anything because of my hunger," he said later. As his family and he emerged from these difficulties, Freire became one of those people who are moved to turn back and attempt to help others walking with ragged shoes in his footsteps, a clear motivation for his life's work as an educator and philosopher, particularly of critical pedagogy.

Of Freire's many books, best known is his earliest, *Pedagogy of the Oppressed*, first published in English in 1970 and often used in teacher-training programs. Freire objects strongly to what he calls the "banking" concept of education—the placing of valuable learning into inert brains where it accumulates. Rather, Freire believed education should make it possible for those who are oppressed to work toward a sense of humanity. Liberation is not a gift or a self-achievement, but a "mutual process"; "the oppressed must be their own example in the struggle for their redemption" (p. 54).

Freire's work and writing have been highly influential in North American education circles. The Paulo Freire Institute, established in Brazil in 1991, operates in many other countries as well, with its headquarters now at the UCLA Graduate School of Education and Information Studies, which also holds the Friere archives. At McGill University in Montreal, Canada, is "The Paulo and Nita Freire Project for International Critical Pedagogy," a center for research and dialogue. For nearly twenty years, Omaha, Nebraska has been the site of an annual "Pedagogy and Theatre of the Oppressed Conference."

The "Fourth Letter" is taken from a book published by Westview Press of Boulder, Colorado in 2005: *Teachers as Cultural Workers: Letters to Those Who Dare Teach*. From the beginning, Freire makes it clear that the qualities he describes are "acquired gradually through practice," and become part of the person who sees education as crucial in the world, which of course can be many more than those who teach. He considers teaching an important way to exercise leadership, and the "Fourth Letter" can be seen as an expression of his personal philosophy of leadership.

Points to Consider

1. What might be the problems that could result from "being entrenched in the circuit of [one's] own truth"?

2. How can leaders help others limit and control fear in order to develop courage?

3. To create a climate in which people can practice tolerance, what limits may be important to establish and what principles need to be respected?

4. Why does Freire write that learners (followers) perceive indecision as moral weakness?

"The Fourth Letter: On the Indispensable Qualities of Progressive Teachers for Their Better Performance"

I would like to make it clear that the attributes I am going to speak about, which seem to me to be indispensable to the progressive teacher, are qualities acquired gradually through practice. Furthermore, they are developed through practice in concurrence with a political decision that the educator's role is crucial. Thus the attributes I am going to speak about are not attributes that we can be born with or that can be bestowed upon us by decree or as a gift. In addition, the order in which I list them here is not intended to rank their value. They are all necessary for a progressive educational practice.

I shall start with *humility*, which here by no means carries the connotation of a lack of self-respect, of resignation, or of cowardice. On the contrary, humility requires courage, self-confidence, self-respect, and respect for others.

Humility helps us to understand this obvious truth: No one knows it all; no one is ignorant of everything. We all know something; we are all ignorant of something. Without humility, one can hardly listen with respect to those one judges to be too far below one's own level of competence. But the humility that enables one to listen even to those considered less competent should not be an act of condescension or resemble the behavior of those fulfilling a vow: "I promise the Virgin Mary that, if the problem with my eyes turns out not to be serious, I will listen to the rude and ignorant parents of my students with attention." No. None of that. Listening to all that come to us, regardless of their intellectual level, is a human duty and reveals an identification with democracy and not with elitism.

In fact, I cannot see how one could reconcile adherence to an ideal of democracy and of overcoming prejudice with a proud or arrogant posture in which one feels full of oneself. How can I listen to the other, how can I hold a dialogue, if I can only listen to myself, if I can only see myself, if nothing or no one other than myself can touch me or move me? If while humble, one does undermine oneself or accepts humiliation, one is also always ready to teach and to learn. Humility helps me avoid being entrenched in the circuit of my own truth. One of the fundamental auxiliaries of humility is *common sense*, which serves to remind us that certain attitudes may lead us too close to becoming lost.

The arrogance of "You don't know who you are dealing with…," the *conceit* of the know-it-all with an unrestrained desire to make his or her knowledge known and recognized—none of this has anything to do with the *tameness* (which is not apathy) of the humble. Humility does not flourish in people's insecurities but in the insecure security of the more aware, and thus this insecure security is one of the expressions of humility, as is uncertain certainty, unlike certainty, which is excessively sure of itself. The authoritarians' stance, in contrast, is sectarian. Theirs is the only truth, and it must be imposed on others. It is in their truth that others' salvation resides. Their knowledge "illuminates" the obscurity or the ignorance of others, who then must be subjected to the knowledge and arrogance of the authoritarian.

I will return to my analysis of authoritarianism, whether that of parents or teachers. As one might expect, authoritarianism will at times cause children and students to adopt rebellious positions, defiant of any limit, discipline, or authority. But it will also lead to apathy, excessive obedience, uncritical conformity, lack of resistance against authoritarian discourse, self-abnegation, and fear of freedom.

In saying that authoritarianism may generate various types of reactions, I understand that on a human level things do not happen so mechanically and happily. Thus it is possible that certain children will go through the rigors of arbitrariness unscathed, which does not give us the license to gamble on that possibility and fail to make an effort to become less authoritarian. And if we can't make that effort for our dream for democracy, we should make it out of respect for beings in development, our children and our students.

But to the humility with which teachers perform and relate to their students, another quality needs to be added: lovingness, without which their work would lose its meaning. And here I mean lovingness not only toward the students but also toward the very process of teaching. I must confess, not meaning to cavil, that I do not believe educators can survive the negativities of their trade without some sort of "armed love," as the poet Tiago de Melo would say. Without it they could not survive all the injustice or the government's contempt, which is expressed in the shameful wages and the arbitrary treatment of teachers, not coddling mothers, who take a stand, who participate in protest activities through their union, who are punished, and who yet remain devoted to their work with students.

It is indeed necessary, however, that this love be an "armed love," the fighting love of those convinced of the right and the duty to fight, to denounce, and to announce. It is this form of love that is indispensable to the progressive educator and that we must all learn.

It so happens, however, that this lovingness I speak about, the dream for which I fight and for whose realization I constantly prepare myself, demands that I invent in myself, in my social experience, another quality: *courage*, to fight and to love.

Courage, as a virtue, is not something I can find outside myself. Because it comprises the conquering of my fears, it implies fear.

First of all, in speaking about fear we must make sure that we are speaking of something very concrete. In other words, fear is not an abstraction. Second, we must make sure that we understand that we are speaking of something very normal. And, when we speak about fear, we are faced with the need to be very clear of our choices, and that requires certain concrete procedures and practices, which are the very experiences that cause fear.

To the extent that I become clearer about my choices and my dreams, which are substantively political and attributively pedagogical, and to the extent that I recognize that though an educator I am also a political agent, I can better understand why I fear and realize how far we still have to go to improve our democracy. I also understand that as we put into practice an education that critically provokes the learner's consciousness, we are necessarily working against myths that deform us. As we confront such myths, we also face the dominant power because those myths are nothing but the expression of this power, of its ideology.

When we are faced with concrete fears, such as that of losing our jobs or of not being promoted, we feel the need to set certain limits to our fear. Before anything else, we begin to recognize that fear is a manifestation of our being alive. I do not need to hide my fears. But I must not allow my fears to immobilize me. If I am secure in my political dream, having tactics that may lessen my risk, I must go on with the fight. Hence the need to be in control of my fear, to *educate* my fear, from which is finally born my courage.[1] Thus I must neither, on the one hand, deny my fears nor, on the other, surrender myself to them. Instead, I must control them, for it is in the very exercise of this control that my necessary courage is shared.

That is why though there may be fear without courage, the fear that devastates and paralyzes us, there may never be courage without fear, that which "speaks" of our humanness as we manage to limit, subject, and control it.

Tolerance is another virtue. Without it no serious pedagogical work is possible; without it no authentic democratic experience is viable; without it all progressive educational practice denies itself. Tolerance is not, however, the irresponsible position of those who play the game of make-believe.

Being tolerant does not mean acquiescing to the intolerable; it does not mean covering up disrespect; it does not mean coddling the aggressor or disguising aggression. Tolerance is the virtue that teaches us to live with the different. It teaches us to learn from and respect the different.

On an initial level, tolerance may almost seem to be a favor, as if being tolerant were a courteous, thoughtful way of accepting, of *tolerating*, the not-quite-desired presence of one's opposite, a civilized way of permitting a coexistence that might seem repugnant. That, however, is hypocrisy, not tolerance. Hypocrisy is a defect; it is degradation. Tolerance is a virtue. Thus if I live tolerance, I should embrace it. I must experience it as something that makes me coherent first with my historical being, inconclusive as that may sound, and second with my democratic political choice. I cannot see how one might be democratic without experiencing tolerance, coexistence with the different, as a fundamental principle.

No one can learn tolerance in a climate of irresponsibility, which does not produce democracy. The act of tolerating requires a climate in which limits may be established, in which there are principles to be respected. That is why tolerance in not coexistence with the intolerable. Under an authoritarian regime, in which authority is abused, or a permissive one, in which freedom is not limited, one can hardly learn tolerance. Tolerance requires respect, discipline, and ethics. The authoritarian, filled with sexual, racial, and class prejudices, can never become tolerant without first overcoming his or her prejudices. That is why a bigot's *progressive* discourse, which contrasts

with his or her practice, is a false discourse. That is also why those who embrace scientism are equally intolerant, because they take science for the ultimate truth, outside of which nothing counts, believing that only science can provide certainty. Those immersed in scientism cannot be tolerant, though that fact should not discredit science.

I would also like to add *decisiveness*, *security*, the tension between *patience and impatience*, and *joy of living* to the group of qualities to be nourished in ourselves if we are to be progressive educators. An educator's ability to make decisions is absolutely necessary to his or her educational work. It is by demonstrating an ability to make decisions that an educator teaches the difficult virtue of decisiveness. Making decisions is difficult to the extent that it signifies breaking free to choose. No one ever decides anything without making a trade-off, weighing one thing against another, one point against another, one person against another. Thus every choice that follows a particular decision calls for careful evaluation in comparing and opting for one of the possible sides, persons, or positions. It is evaluation, with all its implications, that helps us to finally make choices.

Decision making is rupture and is not always an easy experience. But it is not possible to exist without rupturing, no matter how hard it may be.

One of the deficiencies that an educator may possess is an inability to make decisions. Such indecision is perceived by learners as either moral weakness or professional incompetence. Democratic educators must not nullify themselves in the name of being democratic. On the contrary, although they cannot take sole responsibility for the lives of their students, they must not, in the name of democracy, evade the responsibility of making decisions. At the same time, they must not be arbitrary in their decisions. Setting an example, as an authority figure, of not taking responsibility for one's duties, of allowing oneself to fall into permissiveness is even more somber a fate for a teacher than abusing authority.

There are plenty of occasions when a good democracy-oriented pedagogical example is to make the decision in question with the students, after analyzing the problem. Other times, when the decision to be made is within the scope of the educator's expertise, there is no reason not to take action, to be negligent.

Indecision reveals a lack of confidence; but confidence is indispensable for anyone with responsibilities in government, whether of a class, a family, an institution, a company, or the state.

Security, confidence, on the other hand, requires scientific competence, political clarity, and ethical integrity.

One cannot be secure in one's actions without knowing how to support those actions scientifically, without at least some idea of what one does, why, and to what end. The same is true of allegiance: One must know whom or what one is for or against. Nor can one be secure in one's actions without being moved by them, or if one hurts the dignity of others, exposing them to embarrassing situations. Such ethical irresponsibility and cynicism show an inability to live up to the educator's task, which demands critically disciplined performance with which to challenge learners. On the one hand, such discipline reflects the educator's competence, as it is gradually revealed to the learners, discreetly and humbly, without arrogant outbursts; on the other, it affects the balance with which the educator exercises authority—secure, lucid, and determined.

None of this, however, can be realized if an educator lacks a taste for permanently seeking justice. No one can prevent a teacher from liking one student more than another, for any number of reasons. That is a teacher's right. What a teacher must not do is disregard the rights of the other students in favoring one student.

UNIT
1

There is another fundamental quality that the progressive educator must not lack: He or she must exercise wisdom in experiencing the tension between *patience* and *impatience.* Neither *patience* nor *impatience* alone is what is called for. Patience alone may bring the educator to a position of resignation, of permissiveness, that denies the educator's democratic dream. Unaccompanied patience may lead to immobility, to inactivity. Conversely, impatience alone may lead the educator to blind activism, to action for its own sake, to a practice that does not respect the necessary relationship between tactics and strategy. Isolated patience tends to hinder the attainment of objectives central to the educator's practice, making it soft and ineffectual. Untempered impatience threatens the success of one's practice, which becomes lost in the arrogance of judging oneself the owner of history. Patience alone consumes itself in mere prattle; impatience alone consumes itself in irresponsible activism.

Virtue, then, does not lie in experiencing either without the other but, rather, in living the permanent tension between the two. The educator must live and work impatiently patiently, never surrendering entirely to either.

Balanced

Alongside this harmonious, balanced way of being and working there must figure another quality, which I have been calling *verbal parsimony.* Verbal parsimony is implied in the assumption of patience-impatience. Those who live impatient patience will rarely lose control over their words; they will rarely exceed the limits of considered yet energetic discourse. Those who predominantly live patience alone stifle their legitimate anger, which then is expressed through weak and resigned discourse. Those, on the other hand, who are all uncontrolled impatience tend toward a lack of restraint in discourse. The patient person's discourse is always well-behaved, whereas that of the impatient person generally goes beyond what reality itself could withstand.

Both of these kinds of discourse, the overly controlled as well as the undisciplined, contribute to the preservation of the status quo. The first falls short of the demands of the status quo; the second surpasses its limits.

The benevolent classroom discourse and practice of those who are only patient suggest to learners that anything, or almost anything, goes. There is in the air a sense of a nearly infinite patience. Nervous, arrogant, uncontrolled, unrealistic, unrestrained discourse will find itself immersed in inconsequence and irresponsibility.

In no way do these discourses contribute to the learners' education.

There are also those who are excessively restrained in their discourse but who once in a while lose control. From absolute patience, they leap unexpectedly into uncontainable impatience, creating a climate of insecurity for everyone around them, always with terrible effects.

Countless mothers and fathers behave so. Today their words and their actions are permissive, but they transform tomorrow into the opposite, a universe of authoritarian discourse and orders, which not only leaves their sons and daughters appalled but, above all, makes them insecure. Such immoderate parental behavior limits children's emotional balance, which they need to grow up. Loving is not enough; one must know how to love.

Though I recognize that these reflections on qualities are incomplete, I would also like to briefly discuss *joy of living* as a fundamental virtue for democratic educational practice.

By completely giving myself to life rather than to death—without meaning either to deny death or to mythicize life—I can free myself to surrender to the joy of living, without having to hide the reasons for sadness in life, which prepares me to stimulate and champion joy in the school.

UNIT
1

Whether or not we are willing to overcome slips or inconsistencies, by living humility, loving-ness, courage, tolerance, competence, decisiveness, patience-impatience, and verbal parsimony, we contribute to creating a happy, joyful school. We forge a school-adventure, a school that marches on, that is not afraid of the risks, and that rejects immobility. It is a school that thinks, that participates, that creates, that speaks, that loves, that guesses, that passionately embraces and says *yes* to life. It is not a school that quiets down and quits.

Indeed the easy way out in dealing with the obstacles posed by governmental contempt and the arbitrariness of antidemocratic authorities is the fatalist resignation in which many of us find ourselves.

"What can I do? Whether they call me teacher or coddling mother, I am still underpaid, disregarded, and uncared for. Well, so be it." In reality, this is the most convenient position, but it is also the position of someone who quits the struggle, who quits history. It is the position of those who renounce conflict, the lack of which undermines the dignity of life. There may not be life or human existence without struggle and conflict. Conflict[2] shares in our conscience. Denying conflict, we ignore even the most mundane aspects of our vital and social experience. Trying to escape conflict, we preserve the status quo.

Thus I can see no alternative for educators to unity within the diversity of their interests in defending their rights. Such rights include the right to freedom in teaching, the right to speak, the right to better conditions for pedagogical work, the right to paid sabbaticals for continuing education, the right to be coherent, the right to criticize the authorities without fear of retaliation (which entails the duty to criticize truthfully), the right to the duty to be serious and coherent and to not have to lie to survive.

We must fight so that these rights are not just recognized but respected and implemented. At times we may need to fight side by side with the unions; at other times we may need to fight against them, if their leadership is sectarian, whether right or left. At other times we also need to fight as a progressive administration against the devilish anger of the obsolete; of the traditional-ists, some of whom judge themselves progressive; and of the neoliberal, who see themselves as the culmination of history.

NOTES

1. See Paulo Freire and Ira Shor, *Medo e Ousadia, o Cotidiano do Professor* (Rio de Janeiro: Paz e Terra, 1987).

2. See Moacir Gadotti, Paulo Freire, and Sergio Guimaraes, *Pedagogy: Dialogue and Conflict* (Rio de Janeiro: Cortez, 1989).

"We do not think of the ordinary person as preoccupied with such difficult and profound questions as: What is truth? What is authority? To whom do I listen? What counts for me as evidence? How do I know what I know? Yet to ask ourselves these questions and to reflect on our answers is more than an intellectual exercise, for our basic assumptions about the nature of truth and reality and the origins of knowledge shape the way we see the world and ourselves as participants in it. They affect our definitions of ourselves, the way we interact with others, our public and private personae, our sense of control over life events, our views of teaching and learning, and our conceptions of morality."

—Mary Field Belenky, Blyth McVicker Clinchy, Nancy Rule Goldberger, and Jill Mattuck Tarule, Professors and Researchers in Human Development and Psychology

REFLECT & FOCUS

READINGS

Leadership Matters:
Unleashing the Power of Paradox

By Thomas Cronin and Michael Genovese

Points to Consider

1. What are some of the things the authors might be referring to when they write that, "Change and success have many parents and multiple causes"? What are or can be the "parents and causes" of *your* personal success?

2. When collaborating with others, how do you think "leadership matters"—in what ways do you agree that leadership is different from management, command, and office holding?

3. Why do Cronin and Genovese contend that humans in a community need hierarchy?

4. What makes the difference between the exercise of leadership in service to good and the exercise of leadership that results in harm?

Humility

Not thinking less of self But... Thinking about yourself less

Leadership Matters:
Unleashing the Power of Paradox

(Excerpts from Chapter Two, "Defining Leadership")

The Greek playwright Euripedes once wrote that ten soldiers wisely led will best one hundred without a head. And this may also have helped the English at Agincourt, for the French national leaders were overconfident and perhaps in disarray. Leo Tolstoy would suggest that ambiguities and events may well have been beyond the control of the leaders that day. But, in the event, new technology, more than rhetorical leadership, carried the day for the English.

What does this teach us about leadership? Leadership matters. But in this case what proved consequential was the leadership and innovation of developing new weaponry as much as, if not more than, battlefield pep talk or the heroics of the twenty-nine-year-old King Henry V.

Great leaders sometimes do make history; yet so do new inventions, social movements, organizational breakthroughs, and timely innovations of all kinds. Change and success have many parents and multiple causes. It is often easy to highlight a single persona and exclaim, "See, he (or she) did it!"; yet what is easy can often be wrong.

This book defines and analyzes leadership, yet we do not contend leaders alone make history, win battles, or cause change. Nor do we contend leaders are inconsequential. Leaders and leadership matter. Not all leaders matter all of the time. Of course leadership matters, yet it is not the only thing that matters. As agents of change or achievers of group goals, social movements or concerted efforts may be important, coalitions of various groups and interests may make a difference, the exercise of force or raw power may be important, technological innovations might cause great changes, the power of an idea may be vital. Leadership matters, yet it is not the be-all and end-all. It is only a part of the puzzle.

On the other hand, what about Winston Churchill's dogged leadership that propelled England to stand up to the Nazis during the darkest days of World War II? Did his grit, drive, and un-relenting determination turn the tide, or might the British on their own have risen to the chal-lenge? We can never definitively know the answer, yet one cannot help but think that Churchill mattered, and mattered greatly.[3]

Another case for the "leadership matters" argument is Mikhail Gorbachev.[4] Who would deny that Gorbachev opened doors in the former Soviet Union that led to dramatic changes, liberating Eastern Europe, breaking up the moribund Soviet dynasty, ending the Cold War, and helping bring about the downfall of communism?[5]

What of Florence Nightingale? After her service as a nurse during the Crimean War, she returned to England where she revolutionized the field of nursing by making it more professional and bet-ter grounded in medical science. Her book, *Notes on Nursing*, plus her extraordinary leadership, had a profound impact on public health.

Or Nelson Mandela? If charisma is in part defined as creating a presence, Mandela's absence, in prison, paradoxically created for his colleagues an indelible presence. After spending twenty-seven years in prison, Mandela emerged as the leader of his cause and people. His strength, moral courage, example, and personal narrative inspired a peaceful transition that toppled apartheid in South Africa and led to his becoming South Africa's president.[6]

Absent Mandela, would the apartheid government of South Africa have fallen? Yes, but later rather than sooner. Would a bloody revolution have ensued? One is hard-pressed to imagine a positive outcome absent the moral and political leadership of Mandela. Yes, at times, leadership *can* matter. Surely the *roles* required to achieve group ends have to be performed by an individual or individuals.

When, why, and how much is leadership likely to matter? Consider a baseball analogy. In base-ball, some managers matter greatly. Good and bad managers can have a significant impact. When Joe Torre left the New York Yankees (where his teams won four World Series championships) to manage the Los Angeles Dodgers in 2008, he took a mediocre team and made them into win-ners. A good manager can do that.

What was Torre's "magic"? He knew the game (he was an all-star) and had experience managing several teams before the Dodgers. As a successful quietly confident coach, he supported his play-ers and earned their trust. As a strategist, he knew just which players to use and when. He helped hire talented players and skilled coaches and built his team around the dimensions of the home field. When his high-maintenance superstar Manny Ramirez was suspended for fifty games for violating the Major League's performance-enhancing drug policy during the 2009 season, Torre's team continued to win (in fact, during Ramirez's absence the Dodgers had the best record in baseball).

Joe Torre was a great player and a great manager. Contrast Torre to Ted Williams. Williams was one of the greatest hitters in the history of the game. He is the last player to hit over .400 in a season, and was a two-time winner of the American League Most Valuable Player award, led the league in hitting six times, and won the Triple Crown. The Hall of Famer had a career batting average of .349.

Williams managed the Washington Senators for three seasons and the Texas Rangers for one (the Senators moved to Texas in 1972). In his four years as a manager, he won 273 games and lost 364, a dismal .429 winning percentage. His only winning season was his first, with an 86–76 record. His teams got worse each year he managed. In his fourth season, his team finished with a 54–100 record.

UNIT
1

Why was so great a player so poor a manager? Williams was a hitter's manager. He knew hitting. Yet, hitting is only part of the game. Williams was notorious for being short with pitchers and he often openly displayed contempt for his pitchers. He was less savvy about overall strategy and could be short-tempered when his team failed. Some players say they felt uncomfortable and anxious playing for Williams, who expected, even demanded, that his team play up to *his* skill level. It was a formula for failure.

If good managers matter a great deal in bringing about positive results and bad managers have a decidedly negative impact, what can be said about "most" managers who are mediocre or merely capable? Thus, a few good managers matter, a few bad managers matter, but most managers have little impact and matter little.

The same is true of leaders in general. Leaders *can* matter, for better or worse. Yet most "leaders" (office holders) matter little.

This is a book about leaders and leadership. This is not a "how-to" book, although we offer classical as well as contemporary insights for leaders. We don't promote a specific theory of leadership although we discuss and analyze many theories and put them to the test. This is not a book that glorifies the cult of leadership, although there are leaders we admire. It looks at how leaders lead, why and when followers follow, what leadership is and how it works, what the limits and possibilities of leadership are, what happens when leaders "go bad," and how leadership can be valued, empowered, *and* constrained in a democratic culture.

We employ a distinct thematic approach to leadership. As discussed, we believe leadership can best be understood by using the conceptual framework of paradoxes. It requires the balancing of competing demands, contradictory lessons, and clashing expectations. Leaders learn to live with, navigate through and master paradoxes. Thus, there are few absolute rules for leadership. What works for one leader, at one time, under one set of circumstances, may not work for another leader. What leads to success today may condemn a leader to failure tomorrow. For leaders to succeed they must learn to lead, adapt, and improvise within the harsh confines of paradox, reality, context, and culture.

The Need for Leadership

Leadership is universal and inescapable—unless, of course, one chooses to live alone in a cave. Sociologist Robert Michaels's "iron law of oligarchy"[7] holds that in all forms of organization, whether democratic or autocratic, leaders emerge, or oligarchies form. Leadership is indispensable and thus ubiquitous.

Humans need organization as well as some form of hierarchy. As soon as our ancestors started living in groups, government became necessary. And as soon as government became necessary, leaders became necessary. Collective work requires coordination, thus government and leadership.

Living systems seek equilibrium or balance. And when knocked out of equilibrium, "living systems summon a set of restorative responses" designed to adapt to the new challenges that jolted us out of balance.[8] Leadership helps identify threats to equilibrium and proposes constructive measures to adapt to threats to social balance.

Real leadership is not afraid to confront the threats of disequilibrium. As Ronald Heifetz points out, "In times of distress, we turn to authority."[9] False leaders lie or give us sugar pills; true leaders give us the truth, as hard as that may be to swallow. It is the difference between maladaptive and adaptive leadership.[10]

Defining Leadership

Despite the impressive writings of Plato, Plutarch, Machiavelli, Shakespeare, Sigmund Freud, Thomas Carlyle, Tolstoy, Max Weber, James MacGregor Burns, and others no grand, unifying theory of leadership exists.[11] One may ever exist. Yet we now know a lot about leadership and leaders, and it is these ideas that are discussed throughout this book. We'll set the stage.

People regularly yearn for transcending leadership for their communities, companies, unions, universities, political parties, and nations. Yet we have ambivalence about power wielders and those who exercise great influence. As noted, we dislike anyone who tries to boss us around. We admire leaders like Washington and Churchill, but Richard Nixon and Hitler and Saddam Hussein were leaders, too—and this highlights a central problem: leadership can be exercised in service of noble, liberating, life-enriching ends; yet it can also be used to manipulate, mislead, and repress.

"One of the most universal cravings of our time," writes James MacGregor Burns, "is a hunger for compelling and creative leadership."[12] But exactly what is creative leadership? Leadership defies simple definition, but it is ultimately a relationship or chemistry between leaders and associates. We understand much of what is involved in leadership—shared values, community goals, vision, collaboration, strategy, cooperation, trust, adaptation, synthesizing, motivation, mobilization, decision making, judgment, and productivity—yet leadership for many people is often a hazy and confusing abstraction. One of the puzzling paradoxes about a leader is that invariably a leader is a follower who emerges as a leader and remains a leader only so long as the followers are willing to follow. Yet exactly when these transitions occur is typically unclear to everyone, including the leader.

Leadership is about making things happen, both good and bad, that might not otherwise happen and preventing things from happening that ordinarily would. It is the process of getting people to work together. Leadership transforms intentions into actions, visions into realities. It turns a group of people into a community with a purpose. It involves the infusion of vision into an enterprise. It entails mobilizing people and resources to undertake desired patterns of cooperation. It often involves directing followers where only their better selves are willing to go.

Leadership is a process of persuasion and example, whereby leaders or a leadership team motivate colleagues to take an action and achieve shared goals.[13] Leadership in common with coaching and conducting is a process where leaders empower the rest of us to rise to our potential, to become engaged and excel. Leadership is about getting people in an organization to discover their comparative advantages and getting them to concentrate their resources on those advantages. It involves conflict, challenge, learning, collaboration, adaptation, renewal, and disciplined, tenacious action in pursuit of desired results.

Bernard Bass, in his *Handbook of Leadership*, suggests leadership should be defined broadly, arguing that "leadership occurs when one group member modifies the motivation or competencies of others in the group."[14]

Other definitions emphasize similar themes:

- Leadership is the process of capturing people's attention and getting people to think about what is important and how this can be achieved.

- Leadership refers to someone of a team who helps a larger group create and achieve mutual goals.

- Leadership involves diagnosing the collective situation, designing ways of dealing with it, and mobilizing support for both a diagnosis and proposed adaptive responses.

UNIT

1

- Leadership is the capacity to shape organizations and mobilize and inspire members to achieve results; the cooperation must be purposeful and the executive exercise of authority involves management as well as vision and imagination.

- Leadership involves intentional action that allocates resources to achieve desired shared aspirations.

What Leaders Do

Any effort to define leadership necessarily involves an analysis of what leaders do. A leader guides the group and, as noted, is at the same time paradoxically guided by the group. No one can lead except from within. Not only must leaders be part of the group, they also must acknowledge their common bonds with the group. Leaders are defined by what they do for others rather than by who they are. The wise leader is dedicated not only to his or her own career but the careers of colleagues and associates. One of the first maxims of leadership is to take care of those one works with and a lot of good things will happen.

Leaders interpret our experiences to us. They are often able to see the different points of view that underlie our activities. Leaders are often better than the rest of us in seeing beyond the horizon, in comprehending the bigger picture, and in sharing storytelling narratives that help us make sense of our story, our situation, and our possibilities and where we should be going. This is sometimes called the "helicopter" factor—the ability to rise above ongoing operations and take a more encompassing view of one's self and one's organization in a societal or global context.

Leaders empower us less by dominating than by expressing our hopes and values and unlocking our collective energies in pursuit of those goals. Leaders inspire us to believe in ourselves and in our power and responsibility to improve our situation, and leaders help convince us of our strengths and help us focus on what we want to achieve. An effective college president, for example, gets the important constituencies to believe their school could and should be an outstanding institution. An effective corporate executive sets goals, articulates vision, and aligns the organization's personnel, resources, and structure to execute its plans. "He is a leader who gives form to the inchoate energy in everyman," wrote Mary Parker Follett in the 1920s. "The person who influences me most is not the person who does great deeds but he who makes me feel I can do great deeds."[15]

The effective leader is variously a listener, learner, teacher, mentor, negotiator, pragmatist, coach, and politician. But too much focus on the function of *the leader* can undermine the effort to understand *leadership*. Leadership needs in contemporary organizations—public and private—are necessarily understood as an *engagement* between partners and collaborators.

To study leaders separate from the loyalties and complex interactions they have with followers, constituents, and team members is to miss the essence of leadership. It is always a two-way loyalty, a two-way communication, and the mutual engagement of leaders and the "led" that are crucial. Leadership scholars rightly insist on putting the "ship," or the followers, back in the leadership equation. Leadership is a collective enterprise, the ongoing, if subtle, interplay between common desires and a leader's capacity to understand and respond to these shared aspirations. The success of effective leadership becomes apparent primarily among the so-called followers. Are they learning? Are they succeeding? Are they productive, efficient, effective? Are they achieving their common goals?

Leadership may be a mutual process of influence among a group's members. Yet normally, we single out one or a few members who exert the most influence and we designate those people as leaders—especially when their exercise of influence has an impact on the group's attainment of a specified set of goals. Still, followers can have considerable influence over their so-called leaders. Influence between leaders and followers is seldom unidirectional.[16] Indeed, as Keith Grant perceptively notes, "What distinguishes a successful from a failed leader is whether the subordinates can and will save the organization from mistakes of its leader."[17]

The mind's eye often sees leaders as larger-than-life figures who act boldly, often alone, make things happen, have and use power. Yet this is seldom the case. Most of the time, leaders stand on the shoulders of others, derive their strength and authority from others, benefit from being a member of an effective team and build on the previous work of others.

Let us clarify some of the definitional ambiguities. Leadership is not *management*; it is not *command* and it is not *office holding*. Management is the practice of directing and coordinating organized activity within a group or organization. It is process oriented, a technical skill, designed to do things right.

Command, as in the military command model, grants someone authority to decide and dictate. In command, an authoritative person has a recognized right to issue orders that are expected to be followed.

Office holding is not leadership. Merely holding office may grant a modicum of authority, an opportunity to lead, and resources to command; yet, mere office holding falls far short of leadership.

Leadership is about mobilizing and inspiring others to get something done for the benefit of the group or the common good. It is interactive and requires leaders to lead and followers to become activated.

In the simplest form, leaders find ways to get things done. There is a telling aphorism that holds: one doesn't need a title or a special position to lead. Leaders may or may not occupy an institutional position or office, yet they see a need and fill it, see a problem and get it solved, see an opportunity and make the most of it. They do not do this alone, but in concert with others. They work with others to get things done, to fill needs, to solve problems.

- Leadership is a *process*, not a single act by a lone individual.
- Leadership involves a leader *and* followers—it is a *group* process.
- Leadership is *influence*, much more than the exercise of raw power.
- Leaders ignite a spark in others.
- Followers *willingly* follow a legitimate leader, just as followers generally validate a leader's legitimacy.
- Leadership is about attaining *mutually desired goals* for the group.
- A key to effective leadership is good judgment.
- Good judgment requires rationality *and* empathy, passion and a sense of proportion.

The U.S. Army, which for obvious reasons has one of the world's most sophisticated leadership training models, strives to create what it calls "pentathlete" leaders. These are the ideal leaders, and are defined as officers "who are not only competent in their core warrior skills, but who are also scholars; men and women who are creative, innovative, strategically minded, culturally competent, and skilled in all aspects of peace, war, politics, and civil administration."[18] That's asking a lot. And it set the bar high.

With some tweaking, that is a definition of an effective leader in most contexts. It is a lot to ask of anyone. But leaders aren't just "anyone." And although everyone can become a better leader, not everyone can become a pentathlete leader.

In the United States, the words "leader" and "leadership" generally have similar associations with the public. Not so in some other cultures. In German, "leader" is translated as *Führer*, a red flag warning if ever there was one. And in some Asian societies, anyone who stands out as above or apart from "the group" risks being resented and resisted.

All leaders have some power, but not all office holders (who have positions of power) are leaders. Leadership is the ability to mobilize a group to achieve a common purpose. Power is the capacity to control decisions and actions via the authoritative use of force or sanctions. Leadership is about working with and for others. Power is the ability of an individual to get his or her way. Leadership is about persuasion, influence, and agreement building. Power is about having your desires implemented. In leadership, followers *agree* to follow. In power, "followers" have little choice.

Effective leadership remains in many ways the most baffling of the performing arts. There is an element of mystery about it. Intuition, passion, flare, and even ability come into play. Individuals with ample leadership qualities do not necessarily become effective leaders, often because of cultural or situational factors. Sometimes, it is because they are insufficiently optimistic or insufficiently tenacious or unwilling to dramatize their values, vision, and ideas. The genius of leadership sometimes comes too early or too late; an effective person in one thing can be a failure in another.

Leaders often emerge as products of newly coalescing interest groups or accidents rather than sole instigators or initiators of such movements. Thus, Lincoln was an emerging star within the recently formed Republican Party in 1860. Not to belittle or slight their courage, contributions, or talents, leaders are often unduly singled out as founders and catalysts of parties and movements that hoisted them to prominence. Textbook writers too often, for example, name eras or movements by the actions of famous individuals—almost as if they acted alone. In Lincoln's case, for example, his role was crucial but so was the rise of the Republican Party, the agitational might of the Abolitionists, and the increasing rebellion and yearnings of African Americans led by Frederick Douglass and others.

In idolizing Mount Rushmore leaders, we underestimate everyone's ability to lead. At the end of his prizewinning biography of Martin Luther King, Jr., David J. Garrow approvingly quotes a friendly observer of King and the civil rights movement, "If people think, that it was Martin Luther King's movement then today they—young people—are more likely to say, 'Gosh, I wish we had Martin Luther King here today to lead us…' If people knew how the movement started, the question they would ask themselves is, 'What can I do?'"[19]

If a group or community wishes to have leaders to follow, they often must first show the way. Citizens, groups, and movements often get the leadership they nurture, encourage, inspire, and ultimately deserve. Here again, leadership is more a bottom-up than a top-down proposition.

There are a number of generic tasks leaders typically perform. Leaders direct and coordinate the effort of a group toward goals. "The leader generally plans, organizes, directs, and supervises the activities of group members and develops and maintains sufficient cohesiveness and motivation among group members to keep them together as a functioning unit."[20]

Leaders get organizations interested in what they are going to become as well as remind them of what they have been. They show the direction and help people get there.

Leaders help groups to plan, gather data, develop action strategies, understand their challenges and competition, understand both the positive and negative technological developments of the day, and then make decisions and assess outcomes. Leaders also motivate and rally people to make commitments that permit the group to achieve much more than they thought possible.

Leaders have ideas. Yet leaders seldom come up with all or even most of the ideas as much as they are users and integrators of available new ideas. Still leaders must contribute to the substantive thinking necessary to move an organization beyond problems and toward achievements. A leader helps to define reality, to clarify options and opportunities, and to remove the obstacles that make it difficult for the members of an organization to succeed in their work. A leader helps to set the agenda, spelling out strategies, timetables, and objectives for achieving an organization's mission. Leaders are listeners, yet they also raise group consciousness and unlock the energies and talents of fellow associates.

Leaders define, defend, and promote values. They also help redefine values and understand, in Abraham Lincoln's phrase, when the dogmas of the past are inadequate for the stormy present, when new circumstances call for new vision. "Good business leaders create a vision, articulate the vision, passionately own the vision, and relentlessly drive it to completion," wrote former General Electric chairman Jack Welch.[21] Leaders carefully appreciate their colleagues' values, beliefs, and passions.

Leaders merge hopes and needs with organizational purposes and shared aspirations. The task of leadership is one of closing the gap between an individual's needs and abilities and the organization's goals. In this sense, leaders mediate, direct, negotiate, motivate, and in general, "mesh things up."

Leaders capitalize on the strengths of their talented members while simultaneously upgrading the competencies and the morale of their less prepared members. Although everyone needs motivation or training, some people need more of one than the other. Some top performers are can-do, will-do contributors. But certain laggards need more specialized skills training. Still others need additional motivation and clarification about the central purpose and meaning of a venture. Yet others need better skills and inspiration. The leader's job never ends.

Leaders recruit new blood and, preferably, the right kind of blood. They are responsible for identifying, developing, and nurturing future leaders. A primary job of a leader is helping talented people blossom. Equally important, they fire people who need to be let go. As management consultant Jim Collins famously wrote, leaders get the right people in the right seats on the bus and the wrong people off the bus as well as making sure the bus is headed in the proper direction.[22]

According to the mountain climbing classic *Mountaineering: The Freedom of the Hills*, fellow climbers look instinctively to the person who inspires confidence. This may not be the person with the most experience, nor is it always the person who has the most skill. It is, mountaineering experts say, the person who displays the most common sense and sensible judgment. What matters is the climbers' willingness to follow a leader's judgment and decisions. Consideration of both safety and success is important. "Knowledge, experience, and climbing skills help with these responsibilities, but of far greater importance is the ability to deal with others, to be sensitive to their attitudes, physical requirements and limitations, to inspire and encourage them and to guide them in the exercise of their own initiative so that their efforts contribute to the achievement of their goals." It is in this sense that effective leaders give us an idea not only of who they are, but also of who we are, and where we are going.[23]

Of course, leaders do so much more. They delegate. They thank people. They listen. They teach. They motivate. They evaluate. They praise. They get everyone involved and focused. "Leadership is diving for a loose ball, getting the crowd involved, getting other players involved," said basketball legend Larry Bird. "It's being able to take it as well as dish it out. That's the only way you're going to get the respect of the players."

Leaders are expected to see farther and more accurately than others to balance present and future, to think big and take certain risks, and to use their intuition and imagination as well as their analytic reasoning abilities to define meaningful relations with followers, customers, and important external stakeholders. It often falls to presidents and corporate leaders, for example, to be the necessary intermediaries between internal and external forces, between micro and macro, between national and transnational relations.[24]

Hockey great Wayne Gretzky used to credit some of his legendary success to a key point in sports as well as leadership. "I go," he said, "where the puck is going to be, not where it is." In a similar way, effective leaders read the context, diagnose the current situation and see where things are headed before the fact. This is strategic anticipation or contextual intelligence, and it allows a leader to be ahead of the wave rather than swallowed up by it. This was, we are told, the genius Steve Jobs provided for Apple.[25]

Leaders have to prepare, modify, and simplify plans so everyone understands and "owns" a share in the organization's goals. They must have a personal vision of where they want to lead, yet just having a vision isn't enough. Effective leaders get the best people they can find to improve, share, help implement, and achieve their vision. Leaders shape their organization's culture, ideology, and values. And since values can decay over time, leaders are constantly reviewing, renewing and reaffirming the values and integrity of an organization.

Leaders are hope dealers. They activate positive emotions and imaginations. They create, in Ted Turner's phrase, "infectious enthusiasm." Exuberance enlists followers and inspires support.[26]

Humans do not live by reason alone. Dreams and myths are an age-old form of motivation as well as entertainment and escape. People turn to civic and societal leaders just as tribesmen turn to shamans—searching for meaning, healing, improvement, legitimacy, assurance, and a sense of purpose. Leaders lead us in part by tapping into the myths, legends, symbols, and aspirations of our culture. Alexander the Great did this, Henry V did this, Lincoln did this, MLK Jr. did this, Mandela did this.

NOTES

3.   See, among other works, Max Hastings, *Winston's War: Churchill, 1940–1945* (New York: Knopf, 2010).

4.   George W. Breslauer, *Gorbachev and Yeltsin as Leaders* (Cambridge: Cambridge University Press, 2002).

5.   Akan Malici, *When Leaders Learn; and When They Don't* (Albany: SUNY Press, 2008).

6.   Tom Lodge, *Mandela: A Critical Life* (Oxford: Oxford University Press, 2006).

7.   Robert Michaels, *Political Parties: A Sociological Study of the Oligarchical Tendencies of Modern Democracy* (New York: Free Press, 1915).

8.   Ronald A. Heifetz, *Leadership Without Easy Answers* (Cambridge, MA: Belknap Press, 1994), p. 28.

9.   Ibid., p. 69. See also Ronald A. Heifetz and Marty Linsky, *Leadership on the Line: Staying Alive Through the Dangers of Leading* (Boston: Harvard Business Press, 2002).

10. See Joseph S. Nye Jr., *The Powers to Lead* (New York: Oxford University Press, 2008); and John J. Mearsheimer, *Why Leaders Lie* (New York: Oxford University Press, 2011).

11. For a few overviews of the ideas and theories of leadership that do exist, see Bernard Bass, *Bass and Stogdill's Handbook of Leadership*, 3rd ed. (New York: Free Press, 1990); James MacGregor Burns, *Leadership* (New York: Harper & Row, 1978); Kenneth E. and Miriam C. Clark, eds., *Measures of Leadership* (West Orange: Leadership Library of America, 1990); and Nitin Nohria and Rakesh Khurana, eds., *Handbook of Leadership Theory and Practice* (Boston: Harvard Business Press, 2010). See also George R. Goethals and Georgia Sorenson, eds., *The Quest for a General Theory of Leadership* (Cheltenham: Edward Elgar, 2007).

12. James MacGregor Burns, *Leadership* (New York: Harper & Row, 1978), p. 1.

13. John W. Gardner, *On Leadership* (New York: Free Press, 1990).

14. Bernard M. Bass, *Bass and Stogdill's Handbook of Leadership*, 3rd ed. (New York: Free Press, 1990), p. 20.

15. Mary Parker Follett, *The New State* (New York: Longman's, 1923), p. 230.

16. Gary A. Yukl, *Leadership in Organizations* (Englewood Cliffs: Prentice Hall, 1981), p. 10.

17. Keith Grim, *The Arts of Leadership* (Oxford: Oxford University Press, 2000), p. 419.

18. Crispin Burke, "T. E. Lawrence: A Leadership Vignette for the Successful Counter-Insurgent," *Small Wars Journal*, posted by SLOJ Editors, February 19, 2009, www.smallwarsjournal.com.

19. David J. Garrow, *Bearing the Cross: Martin Luther King and the Southern Leadership Conference* (New York: Vintage Books, 1986), p. 625. See also the helpful essay by Clayborne Carson, "Martin Luther King, Jr.: Charismatic Leadership in a Mass Struggle," *Journal of History* 74 (September 1987): 448–454.

20. Fred E. Fiedler and Joseph E. Garcia, *New Approaches to Effective Leadership* (New York: Wiley, 1987), p. 2.

21. Quoted in Noel Tichy and Ram Charan, "Speed, Simplicity, Self-Confidence: An Interview with Jack Welch," *Harvard Business Review*, September–October 1989, 113. See also Jack Welch with Suzy Welch, *Winning* (New York: Harper Business, 2005).

22. Jim Collins, *Good to Great: Why Some Companies Make the Leap and Others Don't* (New York: Harper Business, 2001), Chapter 3.

23. Ed Peters, ed., *Mountaineering: The Freedom of the Hills*, 4th ed. (Seattle: The Mountaineers, 1982), p. 414. But see the vivid case study of a failed Everest expedition in Jon Krakauer, *Into Thin Air* (New York: Anchor Books, 1997).

24. Proctor and Gamble CEO A. G. Lafley reflects on these responsibilities in "What Only the CEO Can Do," *Harvard Business Review*, May 2009, 54–62.

25. Walter Isaacson, *Steve Jobs* (New York: Simon & Schuster, 2011).

26. See, in general, Kay Redfield Jamison, *Exuberance: The Passion for Life* (New York: Knopf, 2004).

Cronin, T. E., and Genovese, M. A. (2012). *Leadership Matters: Unleashing the Power of Paradox*. Used by permission of Paradigm Publishers.

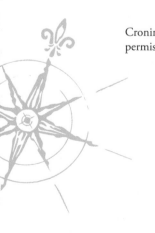

"The Female Advantage"

By Sally Helgesen

Points to Consider

1. Note the two images that Sally Helgesen uses to contrast male and female leadership philosophies. What other images are possible (think about the imagery that might match the philosophies in the other readings of this Unit)? Which coincides most clearly with your own ideas about leadership?

2. What are the advantages of "the web" when exercising leadership in groups?

3. How could the web philosophy of leadership work in large organizations?

"The Female Advantage"

Far into the night, while the other creatures slept, Charlotte worked on her web. First she ripped out a few of the orb lines near the center. She left the radial lines alone, as they were needed for support. As she worked, her eight legs were a great help to her. So were her teeth. She loved to weave, and she was an expert at it.

Charlotte's Web
E. B. White

It is lunchtime in the pink-and-green garden dining room of the Cosmopolitan Club in upper Manhattan, the all-women's club started by Abigail Rockefeller when the Union, her husband's club, refused to serve her. The atmosphere is genteel, with stone planters, trailing petunias, and women mostly over fifty…

It seems an unlikely place in which to be discussing modern leadership and management techniques, but I am with Frances Hesselbein, chief executive of the Girl Scouts, a woman who bridges the paradox with ease…the woman who brought modern management to her organization with such success that Peter Drucker called her "perhaps the best professional manager in America."

I am attempting to interview her, despite the club's rather archaic ban on "visible paper"; apparently ladies are not to engage in business over lunch. So I am balancing my notebook on my knees under a napkin and scribbling without looking while an elderly waitress serves Parker House rolls with silver tongs. Frances Hesselbein is describing the management structure she devised for the Girl Scouts, a replacement for the old hierarchical pyramid.

The new system is circular, she explains; positions are represented as circles, which are then arranged in an expanding series of orbits. "I use circles," she says, "because symbolically they are important. The circle is an organic image. We speak of the family circle. The circle is inclusive, but it allows for flow and movement; the circle doesn't box you in! I've always conceived of management as a circular process. When I was head of my regional organization, I devised a structure similar to the one I'm using now. It wasn't something I'd read I should do, it was just something I felt. These days, there are all these theories about the circular management model, but with me it was intuitive—this attraction I've always had to the circle."

Suddenly, Frances Hesselbein seizes a wooden pepper mill and sets it in the middle of our table. "This is me," she says, "in the center of the organization." She moves a glass of iced tea and several packets of sugar to form a circle around the pepper mill. "And this is my management team, the first circle." Using cups and saucers, Frances Hesselbein constructs a second circle around the first. "These are the people who report to the first team. And beyond this outer circle, there's another, and another beyond that. And they're all interrelated." She picks up knives and forks and begins fashioning radials to link up the orb lines. "As the circles extend outward, there are more and more connections. So the galaxy gets more interwoven as it gets bigger!"

The table at the Cosmopolitan Club is a mess, but I am fascinated. Frances Hesselbein has created the perfect image of a spider's web. And the image of the web has been haunting me lately, for I have been thinking about structure. More specifically, about how women structure things differently from men—companies, office spaces, human relationships, even their own presumed place in the universe.

The Web as Structure

In my studies, women, when describing their roles in their organizations, usually referred to themselves as being in the middle of things. Not at the top, but in the center; not reaching down, but reaching out. The expressions were spontaneous, part of the women's language, indicating unconscious notions about what was desirable and good. Inseparable from their sense of themselves as being in the middle was the women's notion of being connected to those around them, bound as if by invisible strands or threads. This image of an interrelated structure, built around a strong central point and constructed of radials and orbs, quite naturally made me think of a spider's web—that delicate tracery, compounded of the need for survival and the impulse of art, whose purpose is to draw other creatures to it.

The image of the web not only imbued the language of the women in the studies; it was also evident in the management structures they devised, and in the way they structured their meetings. Frances Hesselbein's "circular management chart," drawn with cutlery and sugar packets, was the most obvious example, and perhaps the most fully articulated. Jokingly called the Girl Scouts' "Wheel of Fortune" by Peter Drucker, the wheel actually spins; most management staff jobs are rotated every two or three years. Frances Hesselbein explains that job rotation used in conjunction with the circular chart is ideal for team-building.

A sense of having a larger concern—a concern for the group or whole—is of course implicit in the imagery of the web. The orb and radial lines bind the whole together; every point of contact is also a point of connection. The principle, as Frances Hesselbein observed about the circle, is inclusion. You can't break a web into single lines or individual components without tearing the fabric, injuring the whole.

From Hierarchy to Web

Carol Gilligan, in *A Different Voice*, consistently opposes the image of the hierarchy to that of the "web of connection" in describing the difference between what women and men view as valuable in this world. She writes, "The images of hierarchy and web, drawn from the texts of men's and women's fantasies and thoughts, convey different ways of structuring relationships, and are associated with different views of morality and self." She notes that these images are in their way mirror opposites, because the most desirable place in the one is the most feared spot in the other. "As the top of the hierarchy becomes the edge of the web, and as the center of the network of connection becomes the middle of the hierarchical progression, each image marks as dangerous the place which the other defines as safe." In the hierarchical scheme of things, "reaching the top"—where others cannot get close is the ultimate goal; in the web, the top is too far from the center. The ideal center spot in the web is perceived in the hierarchical view as "being stuck" in the middle going nowhere.

The contrasting models also reveal different notions of what constitutes effective communication. Hierarchy, emphasizing appropriate channels and the chain of command, discourages diffuse or random communication; information is filtered, gathered, and sorted as it makes its way to the top. By contrast, the web facilitates direct communication, free-flowing and loosely structured, by providing points of contact and direct tangents along which to connect.

The Point of Authority in the Web

When organizations are structured in a top-to-bottom chain of command, lines of authority are extremely clear. The old "if it moves, salute it" mentality prevails. But how does authority manifest itself when the head of an organization sees herself as being at its center? How does a manager in her various roles as information gatherer, decision maker, planner, figurehead, and information disseminator exert authority from the fixed point at the center of the web?

First, it must be noted that, although lines of authority in a web structure may appear diffuse, even tangled, the women in the studies are very much the leaders in their organizations, the ones upon whom final responsibility rests. All could be characterized as strong leaders: they have vivid personalities, are direct, and, most important, have specific visions of where they wish to lead and the methods they must use to achieve their goals. Nor are their organizations run as participatory democracies, with everyone contributing in a haphazard way. The women are authorities as much as if they sat at the very top of a hierarchical ladder, but that authority has more subtle ways of manifesting itself.

A prime example is in information-gathering. In a top-down management, information flows upward through channels; authority is established by having access to this progressively filtered information. The chain of command is broken, however, if the authority bypasses established channels in order to ask direct questions down the ladder. By contrast, being at the center, connected to every point in the whole, makes it possible to gather information directly from all sources. Frances Hesselbein made it a practice to receive and answer herself any suggestions made by any member of the 500-person paid staff, whether an accountant or mailroom employee. The most important aspect of this direct contact was that there was no filter, no supervisory layer through whom "lower-downs" were expected to go.

In terms of planning for the future, the process of leading from the center of the web is very subtle, and derives its strength from nourishing and fortifying the bonds between intersecting points. In Frances Hesselbein's management team meeting, when conflict arose over issues relating to future plans, she asked the antagonists to work out a plan between themselves and then bring it to her for discussion—which of course implied that the final judgment would be hers. But handling the conflict in this way assured her that the plan the team members devised would meet the requirements of both their departments, while also helping them forge tighter bonds to strengthen the fabric of the organization as a whole. Further, because her circular management chart eliminates ups and downs as well as layers, Frances Hesselbein was able to invite the antagonists to work things out among themselves without regard to who was above or below whom in rank. As a disseminator of information, the leader who operates from the center of the web has the same advantages as when in an information-gathering role. She has direct access to anyone within the organization without having to resort to channels, and thus avoids the attendant risks of dilution and distortion. Further, because releasing information does not lessen authority in the web (as happens in the top-down structure whenever information flows down), that information can function as a tool to draw people together.

The Strategy of the Web

Books such as *The Managerial Woman* attributed some measure of men's success in the workplace to what the authors saw as the male focus on "winning; on achieving a goal or reaching an objective." These goals or objectives were conceived of in very specific terms: bring in six new customers next month, make vice president within three years. By contrast, women were supposed to be hampered by a more diffuse, less goal-oriented notion of their careers: by tending to see their work "as personal growth, as self-fulfillment, as satisfaction, as making a contribution to others, as doing what one wants to do." The difference, then, came down to a question of strategy: men had a definite, objective plan for getting to where they wanted, while women, as a general rule, lacked such a plan.

And yet, when we consider the contrasting images of hierarchy and web, the question falls into a different focus. For what the authors of *The Managerial Woman* define as strategy is in fact the strategy of the hierarchy. It is preoccupied with targeting position, climbing the ladder, knocking out the competition, playing factions against each other, achieving an objective by manipulating the chain of command. Both its goals and methods assume the existence of a hierarchical structure.

This is surely how strategy is generally perceived, but it need not be the only way. The strategy of the web employs different methods in order to achieve different goals. Since the most desirable spot in the web is the center, the strategy of the web concentrates on drawing closer to that center by drawing others closer, and by strengthening the lines and orbs that knit the fabric together.

The strategy of the web is less direct, less focused on specific goals, and so less driven by pure will than the strategy of the hierarchy. Thus it is appropriate to the diffuse and growth-centered notions of success that women have been criticized for holding. Proceeding by means of strengthening the fabric as well as defining a series of objectives, it works in a less linear fashion than hierarchical strategies.

British Prime Minister Margaret Thatcher, so often thought of as a woman who exemplifies male values, nevertheless gave perfect expression to this female sense of strategy when asked how she had attained her success. She replied that she had never spelled out specific goals for herself or aspired to a particular position, but had rather seized opportunities as they came and made the best of them.

The strategy of the web is guided by opportunity, proceeds by the use of intuition, and is characterized by a patience that comes of waiting to see what comes next. It is the strategy used by the spider Charlotte in E. B. White's *Charlotte's Web*. When Charlotte is confronted by the need to save Wilbur, the barnyard pig facing slaughter, she does not devise a list of objectives in order to decide how to proceed. Instead of being "like men, who rush, rush, rush every minute," she relies on intuition and patience. "Charlotte knew from experience that if she waited long enough, a fly would come into her web; she felt sure if she thought long enough about Wilbur's problem, an idea would come into her mind." And the solution, when it came, required her to weave a web; after all, Charlotte "loved to weave, and she was an expert at it."

The image of weaving is one of the most ancient associated with the female domain; the archaic word for woman, distaff, also refers to a skein of flax, and to the staff on the loom that holds the unspun wool. In mythologies all over the world, female deities are depicted at the loom, knitting together the fabric of human life, spinning out the thread that links the events of the past with the potentialities—the unborn people and events—of the future. Thus the strategy of the web, of weaving, acknowledges the importance of what Frances Hesselbein called "the continuum," that sense that one is a part of what has gone before, and of what will follow.

Helgesen, Sally. *The Female Advantage: Women's Ways of Leadership*. New York: Doubleday, 1990. Used by permission of Doubleday, a Division of Random House, Inc.

"Seek and Speak Your Truth"

By Sheryl Sandberg

Points to Consider

1. What are the personal, individual challenges associated with communicating honestly? How can you overcome these challenges to "speak your truth"?

2. Sandberg makes the case for open, honest communication as a foundation for leadership, and also describes some risks and cautions. What are the risks of open, honest communications in groups, and how can you prevent the potential problems?

3. How can you be sure to solicit input broadly in large organizations?

4. What is the ethical value, personally and in the larger context, of seeking feedback?

"Seek and Speak Your Truth"

My friend Betsy Cohen was pregnant with her second child when her toddler, Sam, became curious about where the baby was in her body. "Mommy," he asked, "are the baby's arms in your arms?" "No, the baby is in my tummy." "Really, the whole baby is in your tummy? Are you sure?" "Yes, the whole baby is in my tummy." "Then, Mommy, what's growing in your butt?"

This kind of honesty is common from children and virtually unheard of from adults. As kids grow up, we teach them to be polite, watch what they say, not hurt others' feelings. This is not a bad thing. As a former pregnant "whale," I'm glad that most people keep some observations to themselves. But as we learn to speak appropriately, we lose something in authenticity.

Authentic communication is not always easy, but it is the basis for successful relationships at home and real effectiveness at work. Yet people constantly back away from honesty to protect themselves and others. This reticence causes and perpetuates all kinds of problems: uncomfortable issues that never get addressed, resentment that builds, unfit managers who get promoted rather than fired, and on and on. Often these things don't improve because no one tells anyone what is really happening. We are so rarely brave enough to tell the truth.

Being honest in the workplace is especially difficult. All organizations have some form of hierarchy, which means that someone's performance is assessed by someone else's perception. This makes people even less likely to tell the truth. Every organization faces this challenge, no matter how flat it tries to be. At Facebook, we work hard to be nonhierarchical. Everyone sits at open desks in big open spaces—no offices, cubes, or partitions for any of us. We hold a company-wide Q & A every Friday where anyone can ask a question or make a comment. When people disagree with decisions, they post to the company-wide Facebook group. Still, I would be an idiot, or not telling myself the truth, if I thought that my coworkers always felt free to criticize me, Mark, or even their peers.

When psychologists study power dynamics, they find that people in low-power positions are more hesitant to share their views and often hedge their statements when they do.[1] This helps explain why for many women, speaking honestly in a professional environment carries an additional set of fears: Fear of not being considered a team player. Fear of seeming negative or nagging. Fear that constructive criticism will come across as just plain old criticism. Fear that by speaking up, we will call attention to ourselves, which might open us up to attack (a fear brought to us by that same voice in the back of our heads that urges us not to sit at the table).

Communication works best when we combine appropriateness with authenticity, finding that sweet spot where opinions are not brutally honest but delicately honest. Speaking truthfully without hurting feelings comes naturally to some and is an acquired skill for others. I definitely needed help in this area. Fortunately, I found it.

When Dave was at Yahoo, he attended a management training program taught by Fred Kofman, a former MIT professor and author of *Conscious Business*. Dave hates training of any kind, and the human resources team at Yahoo had to force him to attend the two-day session. When he came home after the first day, he surprised me by describing the training as "not too bad." By the end of the second day, he started quoting Fred and making observations about our communication. I was in shock; this guy must *good*. So I called Fred, introduced myself, and said, "I don't know what you do, but I want you to do it for my team at Google."

Fred showed up at Google, and his teaching changed my career and my life. He is one of the most extraordinary thinkers on leadership and management I have ever encountered. Many of the concepts discussed in this chapter originated with him and reflect his belief that great leadership is "conscious" leadership.

I learned from Fred that effective communication starts with the understanding that there is my point of view (my truth) and someone else's point of view (his truth). Rarely is there one absolute truth, so people who believe that they speak *the* truth are very silencing of others. When we recognize that we can see things only from our own perspective, we can share our views in a nonthreatening way. Statements of opinion are always more constructive in the first person "I" form. Compare these two statements: "You never take my suggestions seriously" and "I feel frustrated that you have not responded to my last four e-mails, which leads me to believe that my suggestions are not that important to you. Is that so?" The former can elicit a quick and defensive "That's not true!" The latter is much harder to deny. One triggers a disagreement; the other sparks a discussion. I wish I could always maintain this perspective in all my communication. I don't—but I continue to try.

Truth is also better served by using simple language. Office-speak often contains nuances and parentheticals that can bury not just the lead but the entire point. Comedies like *Office Space* ring true for a reason. People fear insulting others, especially the boss, so they hedge. Rather than stating, "I disagree with our expansion strategy," they say, "While I think there are many good reasons why we are opening this new line of business and I feel confident that the management team has done a thorough ROI analysis, I am not sure we have completely thought through all of the downstream effects of taking this step forward at this time." Huh? With all of these caveats, it's hard to decipher what the speaker actually thinks.

When communicating hard truths, less is often more. A few years ago, Mark Zuckerberg decided to learn Chinese. To practice, he spent time with a group of Facebook employees who were native speakers. One might think that Mark's limited language skills would have kept these conversations from being substantively useful. Instead, they gave him greater insight into what was going on in the company. For example, one of the women was trying to tell Mark something about her manager. Mark didn't understand so he said, "Simpler, please." Then she spoke again, but he still didn't understand, so he had to ask her to simplify further. This happened a few more times. Eventually, she got frustrated and just blurted out, "My manager is bad!" She was still speaking Chinese, but simply enough that Mark understood. If more people were this clear, the performance of many organizations would improve dramatically.

The ability to listen is as important as the ability to speak. From the time my siblings and I were very young, whenever we had arguments, our mother taught us—or more like forced us—to

mirror each other, which means restating the other person's point before responding to it. For example, one day my sister and I were fighting over a lollipop. "Sheryl ate the last lollipop!" Michelle screamed. "But she had a lollipop yesterday and I didn't!" I screamed back, making an excellent point. My mother sat us down facing each other. I was not allowed to explain how gravely inequitable the lollipop allocation was until I acknowledged my sister's feelings. "Michelle, I understand that you are upset because I ate the last lollipop and you wanted it." As painful as this was at the time, reflecting someone's viewpoint clarifies the disagreement and becomes a starting point for resolution. We all want to be heard, and when we focus on showing others that we are listening, we actually become better listeners. I now do this with my children. And while they probably dislike the process as much as I did when I was their age, I love hearing my son explain to my daughter, "I'm sorry you're upset because you lost at Monopoly, but I'm older than you so I should win." Not bad for a seven-year-old. (Although Fred would caution my son to take out the "but" and everything after, since it tends to deny the preceding statement. Imagine someone saying, "I really like you, but . . .")

Being aware of a problem is the first step to correcting it. It is nearly impossible to know how our actions are perceived by others. We can try to guess what they're thinking, but asking directly is far more effective. With real knowledge, we can adjust our actions and avoid getting tripped up. Still, people rarely seek enough input. A few years ago, Tom Brokaw interviewed me for a piece on Facebook. Tom is a magnificent interviewer, and I felt that I stumbled through some of my answers. After we wrapped, I asked him how I could have done better. He seemed surprised by my question, so I asked him again. He then told me that in his entire career, I was only the second person to ask him for feedback.

The strategy of soliciting input broadly was first demonstrated for me by Robert Rubin, secretary of the Treasury when I joined the department in 1996. During my first week there, I was invited to a meeting on structuring the IRS. About ten senior staffers were sitting at the table when we entered. Since I knew nothing about the topic, I took a seat in the back corner of the room (yup, not even close to the table). Toward the end of the meeting, Secretary Rubin suddenly turned and asked, "Sheryl, what do you think?" I was stunned silent—my mouth opened but nothing came out. When he saw how shocked I was, Secretary Rubin explained why he had put me on the spot: "Because you're new and not fully up to speed on how we do things, I thought you might see something we were missing." Apparently not in my case. But Secretary Rubin sent a powerful message to all of us about the value of soliciting ideas from every corner (literally).

Secretary Rubin was also aware of the dangers of blindly following leaders, or in his case, being blindly followed. Before becoming Treasury secretary, Rubin served as co-chairman of the board of Goldman Sachs. At the end of his first week as co-chairman, he noticed that Goldman was heavily invested in gold. He asked someone why the firm had taken such a big position. The startled employee answered, "That was you, sir." "Me?" Rubin replied. Apparently, the day before he had been taking his initial tour of the trading floor and commented, "Gold looks interesting." This got repeated as "Rubin likes gold," and someone spent millions of dollars to please the new boss.

More than a decade later, I experienced my own "Rubin likes gold" moment. When I joined Facebook, I faced a dilemma: I needed to bolster the business side of the company while respecting its unconventional culture. Most corporations love PowerPoint presentations, so I encouraged people *not* to prepare them for meetings with me, but instead to come with a simple list of topics. I repeated this frequently, but every meeting seemed to include a detailed PowerPoint presentation anyway. After more than two years of frustration, I announced that although I hated making rules, I was making one: no more PowerPoint in my meetings.

A few weeks later, as I was getting ready to speak to our global sales team, Kirsten Nevill-Manning, a skilled human resources leader at Facebook, came to find me. Kirsten thought I should know that everyone in Europe was upset with me. *Really? I angered an entire continent?* She explained that client meetings were very difficult without PowerPoint and asked why I would make such a stupid rule. I explained that I intended the rule to apply only to presentations to *me*. But just as the Goldman team heard "Gold=good," the Facebook team heard "PowerPoint=bad." I got onstage in front of our entire sales team and apologized for the misunderstanding. I also let them know that if they hear a bad idea, even one they believe is coming from me or Mark, they should either fight it or ignore it.

As hard as it is to have an honest dialogue about business decisions, it is even harder to give individuals honest feedback. This is true for entry-level employees, senior leaders, and everyone in between. One thing that helps is to remember that feedback, like truth, is not absolute. Feedback is an opinion, grounded in observations and experiences, which allows us to know what impression we make on others. The information is revealing and potentially uncomfortable, which is why all of us would rather offer feedback to those who welcome it. If I make an observation or recommendation and someone reacts badly—or even just visibly tenses up—I quickly learn to save my comments for things that really matter. This is why I so admire Molly Graham's approach. Molly joined Facebook in 2008 and held a number of jobs throughout the company in communications, human resources, and mobile products. She performed extraordinarily well in all of these very different roles, not just because she is uniquely talented but because she is always learning. One day, she and I hosted a tricky client meeting. She navigated the discussion effectively, and after the clients left, I praised her effort. She paused and said, "Thanks, but you must have ideas for me on what more I could have done."

"How can I do better?" "What am I doing that I don't know?" "What am I *not* doing that I don't see?" These questions can lead to many benefits. And believe me, the truth hurts. Even when I have solicited feedback, any judgment can feel harsh. But the upside of painful knowledge is so much greater than the downside of blissful ignorance.

Requesting advice can also help build relationships. At Facebook, I knew that the most important determinant of my success would be my relationship with Mark. When I joined, I asked Mark for a commitment that he would give me feedback every week so that anything that bothered him would be aired and discussed quickly. Mark not only said yes but immediately added that he wanted it to be reciprocal. For the first few years, we stuck to this routine and voiced concerns big and small every Friday afternoon. As the years went by, sharing honest reactions became part of our ongoing relationship. Now we do so in real time rather than waiting for the end of the week. I wouldn't suggest that all relationships need this much feedback—there is such a thing as asking for too much—but for us, it has been critically important.

I have also learned the hard way that being open to hearing the truth means taking responsibility for mistakes. In my first week as chief of staff at Treasury, I had the chance to work directly with the heads of the department bureaus. There is a right and a wrong way to start a working relationship. I chose the wrong way. My first call was to Ray Kelly, who was then commissioner of the U.S. Customs Service and now serves as New York City's police commissioner. Instead of reaching out to offer assistance, I called Commissioner Kelly with a request from the secretary. The impression I made was that my job was to demand and his job was to listen. It was a mistake. Ray's response was quick and clear. "[Expletive], Sheryl," he explained. "Just because I'm not in Larry Summers's [expletive] thirty-year-old brain trust doesn't mean that I don't know what I'm doing! If Secretary Summers wants something from me, tell him to [expletive] call me himself!" Then he hung up the phone. I thought, *This is not going well.* My first week on the job and I'd angered a man who knows a thing or two about firearms.

After I stopped shaking, I realized that Commissioner Kelly had done me a huge favor. His "feedback" was extremely helpful and delivered in a way that I would never forget. I reassessed my outreach strategy. With the other bureau chiefs, I initiated conversation by asking what I could do to help them achieve *their* goals. It's no surprise that they reacted more positively and with far fewer expletives. And after I employed my "What have I done for you lately?" approach, they were far more eager to return the favor.

As often as I try to persuade people to share their honest views, it is still a challenge to elicit them. When I started building my team at Google, I interviewed every candidate before we made an offer. Even when the team had grown to about one hundred people, I still spoke with each finalist. One day at a meeting of my direct reports, I offered to stop interviewing, fully expecting everyone to insist that my input was an essential part of the process. Instead, they applauded. They all jumped in to explain—*in unison*—that my insistence on speaking personally to every candidate had become a huge bottleneck. I had no idea that I had been holding the team back and was upset that no one had told me. I spent a few hours quietly fuming, which, given that I have no poker face, was probably obvious to everyone. Then I realized that if my colleagues had kept this to themselves, I was clearly not communicating that I was open to their input. Miscommunication is always a two-way street. If I wanted more suggestions, I would have to take responsibility for making that clear. So I went back to my team and agreed that I would not interview anymore. And more important, I told them that I want their input early and often.

Another way I try to foster authentic communication is to speak openly about my own weaknesses. To highlight just one, I have a tendency to get impatient about unresolved situations. My reaction is to push for people to resolve them quickly, in some cases before they realistically can. David Fischer and I have worked closely together for fifteen years at Treasury, Google, and Facebook. He jokes that he can tell from my tone of voice whether he should bother to complete a task or if I'm about to just do it myself. I acknowledge my impatience openly and ask my colleagues to let me know when I need to chill out. By mentioning this myself, I give others permission to bring up my impatience—and joke about it too. My colleagues will say to me, "Sheryl, you asked us to tell you when you get nervous and push the teams too hard. I think you're doing that now." But if I never said anything, would anyone at Facebook walk up to me and announce, "Hey, Sheryl, calm down! You're driving everyone nuts!" Somehow I doubt it. They would think it. They might even say it to one another. But they wouldn't say it to me.

When people are open and honest, thanking them publicly encourages them to continue while sending a powerful signal to others. At a meeting with about sixty Facebook engineers, I mentioned that I was interested in opening more Facebook offices around the world, especially in one particular region. Since the group included members of the security team, I asked what they were most worried about. Without being called on, Chad Greene blurted out, "Opening a Facebook office in that region." He explained why it wouldn't work and why I was dead wrong in front of the entire group. I loved it. We had never met before, and I will never forget that strong introduction. I ended the meeting by thanking Chad for his candor and then posted the story on Facebook to encourage the rest of the company to follow his example. Mark feels the same way. At a summer barbecue four years ago, an intern told Mark that he should work on his public speaking skills. Mark thanked him in front of everyone and then encouraged us to extend him a full-time job offer.

Humor can be an amazing tool for delivering an honest message in a good-natured way. A recent study even found that "sense of humor" was the phrase most frequently used to describe the most effective leaders.[2] I have seen humor get results so many times. After working in the Obama White House, Marne Levine joined Facebook to run global public policy. Marne is polished, professional, and highly competent. During her first week at her job, she needed a colleague from another team to finish drafting a few paragraphs for an upcoming congressional testimony. The colleague was dragging his heels. He kept coming to Marne to ask questions, which she would duly answer, then she would wait, but still no paragraphs. When he came to her again with yet another question, she turned to him with a huge smile and said, "I am going to answer all of your questions. I really am. But right now, the only thing that is going to keep me from falling down on the floor and having a heart attack right in front of you is for you to get out of your chair, go back to your desk, and write the paragraphs we need for Congress." It worked beautifully.

A colleague at Google, Adam Freed, and I were frustrated by someone at work who was making our jobs very difficult. I met with her several times and earnestly explained that I felt that she was second-guessing our every move and preventing progress. During each heartfelt discussion, she would listen and nod and thank me for raising the matter. I would leave feeling better. Then the situation would get worse. Adam took a totally different approach. He invited her to lunch. They met at the Google café, chatted a bit, and then he looked at her and jokingly asked, "Why do you hate me?" Where I had failed repeatedly, Adam broke through. She asked why he would make that joke, which gave him a chance to explain in a way she was able to hear.

Unfortunately, our sense of humor sometimes fails us when we need it most. When I get emotional, it's very hard for me to treat a problem lightly. I had been at Google about three months when an uncomfortable situation erupted. I had started at the company reporting to Eric Schmidt but was transitioning to work for Omid Kordestani. During that process, Omid and I had a major misunderstanding. I went to discuss it with him, intending to explain calmly why I was upset, but as soon as I started talking, I burst into tears. I was horrified to be crying in front of my new boss whom I barely knew—which just made more tears flow. But I got lucky. Omid was patient and reassuring, insisting, "Everyone gets upset at work. It's okay."

Most women believe—and research suggests—that it is not a good idea to cry at work.[3] It is never something that I plan to do and is hardly recommended in *The Seven Habits of Highly Effective People*, but on those rare occasions when I have felt really frustrated, or worse, betrayed, tears have filled my eyes. Even as I have gotten older and more experienced, it still happens every so often.

I had been working at Facebook for almost a year when I learned that someone had said something about me that was not just false, but cruel. I started telling Mark about it and, despite my best efforts, started to cry. He assured me that the accusation was so untrue that no one could possibly believe it. And then he asked, "Do you want a hug?" I did. It was a breakthrough moment for us. I felt closer to him than ever before. I then recounted this story publicly, figuring that it might make it easier for others who have faced unwanted tears. The press reported the incident as "Sheryl Sandberg cried on Mark Zuckerberg's shoulder," which is not exactly what happened. What happened was that I expressed my feelings and Mark responded with compassion.

Sharing emotions builds deeper relationships. Motivation comes from working on things we care about. It also comes from working with people we care about. To really care about others, we have to understand them—what they like and dislike, what they feel as well as think. Emotion drives both men and women and influences every decision we make. Recognizing the role emotions play and being willing to discuss them makes better managers, partners, and peers.

I did not always understand this. I used to think that being professional meant being organized and focused and keeping my personal life separate. Early on at Google, Omid and I would have a one on one meeting each week. I would enter his office with a typed agenda and get right to it. I thought I was being so efficient, but my colleague Tim Armstrong (who later become CEO of AOL) kindly pulled me aside one day to give me some advice. He told me that I should take a moment to connect with Omid before diving in. Since Omid and I were the only people in those meetings, it was clear who had mentioned this to Tim. I made the adjustment and started asking Omid how he was before leaping into my to-do list. It was a good lesson. An all-business approach is not always good business.

It has been an evolution, but I am now a true believer in bringing our whole selves to work. I no longer think people have a professional self for Mondays through Fridays and a real self for the rest of the time. That type of separation probably never existed, and in today's era of individual expression, where people constantly update their Facebook status and tweet their every move, it makes even less sense. Instead of putting on some kind of fake "all-work persona," I think we benefit from expressing our truth, talking about personal situations, and acknowledging that professional decisions are emotionally driven. I should have learned this lesson years earlier. When I was graduating from business school in 1995, Larry Summers offered me a job at Treasury. I wanted the job desperately, but there was an issue: I did not want to move back to D.C., where my soon-to-be ex-husband lived. One of the hardest calls I've ever had to make was to tell Larry that I could not accept the job. Larry pressed me on why, and I thought about telling him that I really wanted to try consulting in Los Angeles. Instead, I opened up. I explained that I was getting divorced and wanted to move far away from D.C., which held too many painful memories. Larry argued that it was a big city, but it didn't seem big enough for me. A year later, when enough time had passed and I felt ready to return to D.C., I called Larry and asked if the opportunity was still available. It was one of the easiest calls I have ever made, in part because I had been honest the year before. If I had told Larry that I was passing on the job for professional reasons, I would have appeared impulsive when I reversed that decision. Since the real reason was personal, sharing it honestly was the best thing to do.

People often pretend that professional decisions are not affected by their personal lives. They are afraid to talk about their home situations at work as if one should never interfere with the other, when of course they can and do. I know many women who won't discuss their children at work out of fear that their priorities will be questioned. I hope this won't always be the case.

My sister-in-law, Amy Schefler, had a college roommate, Abby Hemani, who is a partner in one of Boston's most prestigious law firms. The line between personal and professional was erased for Abby when her seven-month-old daughter was diagnosed with Dravet syndrome, a rare and severe form of epilepsy. Abby explained that her mostly male partners got used to seeing her cry at the office and their response was heartwarming. "It was as if they envisioned me as one of their own daughters and wanted to comfort me," she said. Abby insists that her public emotion improved her work situation both by turning her colleagues into a source of support and by leading to more flexible hours. "I know several men at my firm who have had similar experiences with sick children, but they didn't feel they could be as forthcoming as I was," she said. "So, in the end, I think my female manner of relating served me well."

Not every workplace and every colleague will be as generous and caring. But I do think we are moving toward at least blurring the line between personal and professional. Increasingly, prominent thinkers in the field of leadership studies like Marcus Buckingham are challenging traditional notions of leadership. Their research suggests that presenting leadership as a list of carefully defined qualities (like strategic, analytical, and performance oriented) no longer holds. Instead, true leadership stems from individuality that is honestly and sometimes imperfectly expressed.[4] They believe leaders should strive for authenticity over perfection. This shift is good news for women, who often feel obliged to suppress their emotions in the workplace in an attempt to come across as more stereotypically male. And it's also good news for men, who may be doing the exact same thing.

I had the opportunity to see the power of authentic communication in a leader firsthand when I served on the board of Starbucks. Howard Schultz was CEO of Starbucks from 1987 through 2000, and during his tenure, the company grew from just a few stores into a global retail powerhouse. Howard stepped down as CEO in 2000, and over the next eight years Starbucks' performance faltered. When Howard returned as CEO in 2008, he held a meeting with all of the company's global managers in New Orleans. He openly admitted that the company was in serious trouble. Then he allowed his emotions to show, tearing up as he confessed that he felt that he had let down his employees and their families. The entire company rose to the challenge. Starbucks turned around and delivered it highest revenue and earnings a few years later.

Maybe someday shedding tears in the workplace will no longer be viewed as embarrassing or weak, but as a simple display of authentic emotion. And maybe the compassion and sensitivity that have historically held some women back will make them more natural leaders in the future. In the meantime, we can all hasten this change by committing ourselves to both seek—and speak—our truth.

NOTES

1. Denise L. Loyd et al., "Expertise in Your Midst: How Congruence Between Status and Speech Style Affects Reactions to Unique Knowledge," *Group Processes & Intergroup Relations* 13, no. 3 (2010): 379–95; and Lawrence A. Hosman, "The Evaluative Consequences of Hedges, Hesitations, and Intensifiers: Powerful and Powerless Speech Styles," *Human Communication Research* 15, no. 3 (1989): 383–406. For a review of how power shapes behavior, see Dacher Keltner, Deborah H. Gruenfeld, and Cameron Anderson, "Power, Approach, Inhibition," *Psychological Review* 110, no. 2 (2003): 265–84. For a review of gender and speech, see Cecilia L. Ridgeway and Lynn Smith-Lovin, "The Gender System and Interaction," *Annual Review of Sociology* 25, no. 1 (1999): 202–3.

2. Bell Leadership Institute, *Humor Gives Leaders the Edge* (2012), http://www.bellleaderhip.com/pressreleases/press_template.php?id=15.

3. Research by Kimberly D. Elsbach, professor of management at the University of California at Davis, and her colleagues found that most of the time when women cry at work, they receive negative reactions from colleagues and coworkers, unless the crying is related to a serious personal issue such as a death in the family or a divorce. Crying during a meeting or because of professional pressures or a disagreement is viewed as "unprofessional," "disruptive," "weak," and even "manipulative." For further description of Professor Elsbach's findings, see Jenna Goudreau, "Crying at Work, a Woman's Burden," *Forbes*, January 11, 2011, http://www.forbes.com/sites/jennagoudreau/2011/01/11/crying-at-work-a-womans-burden-study-men-sex-testosterone-tears-arousal/.

4. Marcus Buckingham, "Leadership Development in the Age of the Algorithm," *Harvard Business Review* 90, no. 6 (2012): 86–94; and Bill George et al., "Discovering Your Authentic Leadership," *Harvard Business Review* 85, no. 2 (2007): 129–38.

"The Mindsets"

By Carol Dweck

Points to Consider

1. Consider examples of leaders in your own life; what evidence is there that they had either fixed mindsets or growth mindsets?

2. In groups or teams, how would the fixed mindset manifest? The growth mindset?

3. How can the exercise of leadership affect the mindset of individuals in organizations or communities?

4. What are some of the ethical issues related to the different mindsets?

"The Mindsets"

When I was a young researcher, just starting out, something happened that changed my life. I was obsessed with understanding how people cope with failures, and I decided to study it by watching how students grapple with hard problems. So I brought children one at a time to a room in their school, made them comfortable, and then gave them a series of puzzles to solve. The first ones were fairly easy, but the next ones were hard. As the students grunted, perspired, and toiled, I watched their strategies and probed what they were thinking and feeling. I expected differences among children in how they coped with the difficulty, but I saw something I never expected.

Confronted with the hard puzzles, one ten-year-old boy pulled up his chair, rubbed his hands together, smacked his lips, and cried out, "I love a challenge!" Another, sweating away on these puzzles, looked up with a pleased expression and said with authority, "You know, I was *hoping* this would be informative!"

What's wrong with them? I wondered. I always thought you coped with failure or you didn't cope with failure. I never thought anyone *loved* failure. Were these alien children or were they on to something?

Everyone has a role model, someone who pointed the way at a critical moment in their lives. These children were my role models. They obviously knew something I didn't and I was determined to figure it out—to understand the kind of mindset that could turn a failure into gift.

What did they know? They knew that human qualities, such as intellectual skills, could be cultivated through effort. And that's what they were doing—getting smarter. Not only weren't they discouraged by failure, they didn't even think they were failing. They thought they were learning.

Whether human qualities are things that can be cultivated or that are carved in stone is an old issue. What these beliefs mean for you is a new one: What are the consequences of thinking that your intelligence or personality is something you can develop, as opposed to something that is a fixed, deep-seated trait? Let's first look in on the age-old, fiercely waged debate about human nature and then return to the question of what these beliefs mean for you.

Why Do People Differ?

Since the dawn of time, people have thought differently, acted differently, and fared differently from each other. It was guaranteed that someone would ask the question of why people differed—why some people are smarter or more moral—and whether there was something that made them permanently different. Experts lined up on both sides. Some claimed that there was a strong, physical basis for these differences, making them unavoidable and unalterable. Through the ages, these alleged physical differences have included bumps on the skull (phrenology), the size and shape of the skull (craniology), and, today, genes.

Others pointed to the strong differences in people's backgrounds, experiences, training, or ways of learning. It may surprise you to know that a big champion of this view was Alfred Binet, the inventor of the IQ test. Wasn't the IQ test meant to summarize children's unchangeable intelligence? In fact, no. Binet, a Frenchman working in Paris in the early twentieth century, designed this test to identify children who were not profiting from the Paris public schools, *so that new educational programs could be designed to get them back on track*. Without denying individual differences in children's intellects, he believed that education and practice could bring about fundamental changes in intelligence. Here is a quote from one of his major books, *Modern Ideas About Children*, in which he summarizes his work with hundreds of children with learning difficulties:

> A few modern philosophers…assert that an individual's intelligence is a fixed quantity, a quantity which cannot be increase. We must protest and react against this brutal pessimism … With practice, training, and above all, method, we manage to increase our attention, our memory, our judgment and literally to become more intelligent than we were before.

Who's right? Today most experts agree that it's not either-or. It's not nature or nurture, genes or environment. From conception on, there's a constant give and take between the two. In fact, as Gilbert Gottlieb, an eminent neuroscientist, put it, not only do genes and environment cooperate as we develop, but genes *require* input from the environment to work properly.

At the same time, scientists are learning that people have more capacity for lifelong learning and brain development than they ever thought. Of course, each person has a unique genetic endowment. People may start with different temperaments and different aptitudes, but it is clear that experience, training, and personal effort take them the rest of the way. Robert Sternberg, the present-day guru of intelligence, writes that the major factor in whether people achieve expertise "is not some fixed prior ability, but purposeful engagement." Or, as his forerunner Binet recognized, it's not always the people who start out the smartest who end up the smartest.

What Does All This Mean for You? The Two Mindsets

It's one thing to have pundits spouting their opinions about scientific issues. It's another thing to understand how these views apply to you. For twenty years, my research has shown that *the view you adopt for yourself* profoundly affects the way you lead your life. It can determine whether you become the person you want to be and whether you accomplish the things you value. How does this happen? How can a simple belief have the power to transform your psychology and, as a result, your life?

Believing that your qualities are carved in stone—the *fixed mindset*—creates an urgency to prove yourself over and over. If you have only a certain amount of intelligence, a certain personality, and a certain moral character—well, then you'd better prove that you have a healthy dose of them. It simply wouldn't do to look or feel deficient in these most basic characteristics.

Some of us are trained in this mindset from an early age. Even as a child, I was focused on being smart, but the fixed mindset was really stamped in by Mrs. Wilson, my sixth-grade teacher. Unlike Alfred Binet, she believed that people's IQ scores told the whole story of who they were. We were seated around the room in IQ order, and only the highest-IQ students could be trusted to carry the flag, clap the erasers, or take a note to the principal. Aside from the daily stomachaches she provoked with her judgmental stance, she was creating a mindset in which everyone in the class had one consuming goal—look smart, don't look dumb. Who cared about or enjoyed learning when our whole being was at stake every time she gave us a test or called on us in class?

I've seen so many people with this one consuming goal of proving themselves—in the classroom, in their careers, and in their relationships. Every situation calls for a confirmation of their intelligence, personality, or character. Every situation is evaluated: *Will I succeed or fail? Will I look smart or dumb? Will I be accepted or rejected? Will I feel like a winner or a loser?*

But doesn't our society value intelligence, personality, and character? Isn't it normal to want these traits? Yes, but…

There's another mindset in which these traits are not simply a hand you're dealt and have to live with, always trying to convince yourself and others that you have a royal flush when you're secretly worried it's a pair of tens. In this mindset, the hand you're dealt is just the starting point for development. The *growth mindset* is based on the belief that your basic qualities are things you can cultivate through your efforts. Although people may differ in every which way—in their initial talents and aptitudes, interests, or temperaments—everyone can change and grow through application and experience.

Do people with this mindset believe that anyone can be anything, that anyone with proper motivation or education can become Einstein or Beethoven? No, but they believe that a person's true potential is unknown (and unknowable); that it's impossible to foresee what can be accomplished with years of passion, toil, and training.

Did you know that Darwin and Tolstoy were considered ordinary children? That Ben Hogan, one of the greatest golfers of all time, was completely uncoordinated and graceless as a child? That the photographer Cindy Sherman, who has been on virtually every list of the most important artists of the twentieth century, *failed* her first photography course? That Geraldine Page, one of our greatest actresses, was advised to give it up for lack of talent?

You can see how the belief that cherished qualities can be developed creates a passion for learning. Why waste time proving over and over how great you are, when you could be getting better? Why hide deficiencies instead of overcoming them? Why look for friends or partners who will just shore up your self-esteem instead of ones who will also challenge you to grow? And why seek out the tried and true, instead of experiences that will stretch you? The passion for stretching yourself and sticking to it, even (or especially) when it's not going well, is the hallmark of the growth mindset. This is the mindset that allows people to thrive during some of the most challenging times in their lives.

A View from the Two Mindsets

To give you a better sense of how the two mindsets work, imagine—as vividly as you can—that you are a young adult having a really bad day:

> One day, you go to a class that is really important to you and that you like a lot. The professor returns the midterm papers to the class. You got a C+. You're very disappointed. That evening on the way back to your home, you find that you've gotten a parking ticket. Being really frustrated, you call your best friend to share your experience but are sort of brushed off.

What would you think? What would you feel? What would you do?

When I asked people with the fixed mindset, this is what they said: "I'd feel like a reject." "I'm a total failure." "I'm an idiot." "I'm a loser." "I'd feel worthless and dumb—everyone's better than me." "I'm slime." In other words, they'd see what happened as a direct measure of their competence and worth.

This is what they'd think about their lives: "My life is pitiful." "I have no life." "Somebody upstairs doesn't like me." "The world is out to get me." "Someone is out to destroy me." "Nobody loves me, everybody hates me." "Life is unfair and all efforts are useless." "Life stinks. I'm stupid. Nothing good ever happens to me." "I'm the most unlucky person on this earth."

Excuse me, was there death and destruction, or just a grade, a ticket, and a bad phone call?

Are these just people with low self-esteem? Or card-carrying pessimists? No. When they aren't coping with failure, they feel just as worthy and optimistic—and bright and attractive—as people with the growth mindset.

So how would they cope? "I wouldn't bother to put so much time and effort into doing well in anything." (In other words, don't let anyone measure you again.) "Do nothing." "Stay in bed." "Get drunk." "Eat." "Yell at someone if I get a chance to." "Eat chocolate." "Listen to music and pout." "Go into my closet and sit there." "Pick a fight with somebody." "Cry." "Break something." "What is there to do?"

What is there to do! You know, when I wrote the vignette, I intentionally made the grade a C+, not an F. It was a midterm rather than a final. It was a parking ticket, not a car wreck. They were "sort of brushed off," not rejected outright. Nothing catastrophic or irreversible happened. Yet from this raw material the fixed mindset created the feeling of utter failure and paralysis.

When I gave people with the growth mindset the same vignette, here's what they said. They'd think:

"I need to try harder in class, be more careful when parking the car, and wonder if my friend had a bad day."

"The C+ would tell me that I'd have to work a lot harder in the class, but I have the rest of the semester to pull up my grade."

There were many, many more like this, but I think you get the idea. Now, how would they cope? Directly.

"I'd start thinking about studying harder (or studying in a different way) for my next test in that class, I'd pay the ticket, and I'd work things out with my best friend the next time we speak."

"I'd look at what was wrong on my exam, resolve to do better, pay my parking ticket, and call my friend to tell her I was upset the day before."

"Work hard on my next paper, speak to the teacher, be more careful where I park or contest the ticket, and find out what's wrong with my friend."

You don't have to have one mindset or the other to be upset. Who wouldn't be? Things like a poor grade or a rebuff from a friend or loved one—these are not fun events. No one was smacking their lips with relish. Yet those people with the growth mindset were not labeling themselves and throwing up their hands. Even though they felt distressed, they were ready to take the risks, confront the challenges, and keep working at them.

So, What's New?

Is this such a novel idea? We have lots of sayings that stress the importance of risk and the power of persistence, such as "Nothing ventured, nothing gained" and "If at first you don't succeed, try, try again" or "Rome wasn't built in a day." (By the way, I was delighted to learn that the Italians have the same expression.) What is truly amazing is that people with the fixed mindset would not agree. For them, it's "Nothing ventured, nothing lost." "If at first you don't succeed, you probably don't have the ability." "If Rome wasn't built in a day, maybe it wasn't meant to be." In other words, risk and effort are two things that might reveal your inadequacies and show that you were not up to the task. In fact, it's startling to see the degree to which people with the fixed mindset do not believe in effort.

What's also new is that people's ideas about risk and effort grow out of their more basic mindset. It's not just that some people happen to recognize the value of challenging themselves and the importance of effort. Our research has shown that this *comes directly* from the growth mindset. When we teach people the growth mindset, with its focus on development, these ideas about challenge and effort follow. Similarly, it's not just that some people happen to dislike challenge and effort. When we (temporarily) put people in a fixed mindset, with its focus on permanent traits, they quickly fear challenge and devalue effort.

We often see books with titles like *The Ten Secrets of the World's Most Successful People* crowding the shelves of bookstores, and these books may give many useful tips. But they're usually a list of unconnected pointers, like "Take more risks!" or "Believe in yourself!" While you're left admiring people who can do that, it's never clear how these things fit together or how you could ever become that way. So you're inspired for a few days, but basically the world's most successful people still have their secrets.

Instead, as you begin to understand the fixed and growth mindsets, you will see exactly how one thing leads to another—how a belief that your qualities are carved in stone leads to a host of thoughts and actions, and how a belief that your qualities can be cultivated leads to a host of different thoughts and actions, taking you down an entirely different road. It's what we psychologists call an *Aha!* experience. Not only have I seen this in my research when we teach people a new mindset, but I get letters all the time from people who have read my work.

They recognize themselves: "As I read your article I literally found myself saying over and over again, 'This is me, this is me!'" They see the connections: "Your article completely blew me away. I felt I had discovered the secret of the universe!" They feel their mindsets reorienting: "I can certainly report a kind of personal revolution happening in my own thinking, and this is an exciting feeling." And they can put this new thinking into practice for themselves *and* others: "Your work has allowed me to transform my work with children and see education through a different lens," or "I just wanted to let you know what an impact—on a personal and practical level—your outstanding research has had for hundreds of students."

Self-Insight: Who Has Accurate Views of Their Assets and Limitations?

Well, maybe the people with the growth mindset don't think they're Einstein or Beethoven, but aren't they more likely to have inflated views of their abilities and try for things they're not capable of? In fact, studies show that people are terrible at estimating their abilities. Recently, we set out to see who is most likely to do this. Sure, we found that people greatly misestimated their performance and their ability. *But it was those with the fixed mindset who accounted for almost all the inaccuracy.* The people with the growth mindset were amazingly accurate.

When you think about it, this makes sense. If, like those with the growth mindset, you believe you can develop yourself, then you're open to accurate information about your current abilities, even if it's unflattering. What's more, if you're oriented toward learning, as they are, you need accurate information about your current abilities in order to learn effectively. However, if everything is either good news or bad news about your precious traits—as it is with fixed-mindset people—distortion almost inevitably enters the picture. Some outcomes are magnified, others are explained away, and before you know it you don't know yourself at all.

Howard Gardner, in his book *Extraordinary Minds*, concluded that exceptional individuals have "a special talent for identifying their own strengths and weaknesses." It's interesting that those with the growth mindset seem to have that talent.

What's in Store

The other thing exceptional people seem to have is a special talent for converting life's setbacks into future successes. Creativity researchers concur. In a poll of 143 creativity researchers, there was wide agreement about the number one ingredient in creative achievement. And it was exactly the kind of perseverance and resilience produced by the growth mindset.

You may be asking again, *How can one belief lead to all this—the love of challenge, belief in effort, resilience in the face of setbacks, and greater (more creative!) success?* In the chapters that follow, you'll see exactly how this happens: how the mindsets change what people strive for and what they see as success. How they change the definition, significance, and impact of failure. And how they change the deepest meaning of effort. You'll see how these mindsets play out in school, in sports, in the workplace, and in relationships. You'll see where they come from and how they can be changed.

Grow Your Mindset

Which mindset do you have? Answer these questions about intelligence. Reach each statement and decide whether you mostly agree with it or disagree with it.

1. Your intelligence is something very basic about you that you can't change very much.

2. You can learn new things, but you can't really change how intelligent you are.

3. No matter how much intelligence you have, you can always change it quite a bit.

4. You can always substantially change how intelligent you are.

Questions 1 and 2 are the fixed-mindset questions. Questions 3 and 4 reflect the growth mindset. Which mindset did you agree with more? You can be a mixture, but most people lean toward one or the other.

You also have beliefs about other abilities. You could substitute "artistic talent," sports ability," or "business skill" for "intelligence." Try it.

It's not only your abilities; it's your personal qualities too. Look at these statements about personality and character and decide whether you mostly agree or mostly disagree with each one.

1. You are a certain kind of person, and there is not much that can be done to really change that.

2. No matter what kind of person you are, you can always change substantially.

3. You can do things differently, but the important parts of who you are can't really be changed.

4. You can always change basic things about the kind of person you are.

Here, questions 1 and 3 are the fixed-mindset questions and questions 2 and 4 reflect the growth mindset. Which did you agree with more?

Did it differ from your intelligence mindset? It can. Your "intelligence mindset" comes into play when situations involve mental ability.

Your "personality mindset" comes into play in situations that involve your personal qualities—for example, how dependable, cooperative, caring, or socially skilled you are. The fixed mindset makes you concerned with how you'll be judged; the growth mindset makes you concerned with improving.

Here are some more ways to think about mindsets:

*   Think about someone you know who is steeped in the fixed mindset. Think about how they're always trying to prove themselves and how they're supersensitive about being wrong or making mistakes. Did you ever wonder why they were this way? (Are you this way?) Now you can begin to understand why.

*   Think about someone you know who is skilled in the growth mindset—someone who understands that important qualities can be cultivated. Think about the ways they confront obstacles. Think about the things they do to stretch themselves. What are some ways you might like to change or stretch yourself?

Okay, now imagine you've decided to learn a new language and you've signed up for a class. A few sessions into the course, the instructor calls you to the front of the room and starts throwing questions at you one after another.

Put yourself in a fixed mindset. Your ability is on the line. Can you feel everyone's eyes on you? Can you see the instructor's face evaluating you? Feel the tension, feel your ego bristle and waver. What else are you thinking and feeling?

Now put yourself in a growth mindset. You're a novice—that's why you're here. You're here to learn. The teacher is a resource for learning. Feel the tension leave you, feel your mind open up.

The message is: You can change your mindset.

FILM STUDIES

Twelve O'Clock High (1949)

Screenplay by Sy Bartlett and Beirne Lay, Jr.
Directed by Henry King

Character Guide

Colonel Davenport
(Original Commanding Officer) . . . . . . Gary Merrill

General Savage (Commanding Officer
who replaces Davenport) . . . . Gregory Peck

General Pritchard
(Savage's superior officer) . . . . Millard Mitchell

Major Stoval (Adjutant trained as a lawyer and
serving as Ground Executive Officer) . . . . Dean Jagger

Col. Gately (Executive demoted to airplane
commander of "Leper Colony") . . . . . . Hugh Marlowe

Major Cobb (Appointed to replace Gately
as Air Executive Officer) . . . . John Kellogg

Introduction

The film *Twelve O'Clock High* illustrates contrasting philosophies of leadership. Sy Bartlett and Beirne Lay, Jr. wrote the screenplay for this 1949 film based on their novel about the heavy bomber group in the U.S. Army's Eighth Air Force in which they served during World War II.

The film examines the human crisis which results when the army, early in the air war, demands "maximum effort" from its bomber pilots and crews. It depicts the story of an unyielding general and his mission: rebuilding a bomber group whose shattered morale threatens to discredit precision bombing and undermine the whole aerial offensive against German-held Europe.

Brigadier General Frank Savage, a character largely inspired by much-decorated Major General Frank A. Armstrong, Jr., who led the first Flying Fortress daylight assault across the continent, approaches the task with the cold passion of a martinet and the inner torment of a man of good will.

Savage's leadership philosophy and style greatly contrasts with that of Colonel Keith Davenport, the bomber squadron's original Commanding Officer. Both leaders, Savage and Davenport, work with the same group and hope to achieve the same goal; however, the results are very different.

Dialogue Questions

1. What is the Bomber Group's mission?

2. What problems keep the group from achieving its mission?

3. What is Davenport's leadership style?

4. Why does Davenport fail as a leader?

5. Why does General Pritchard ask Savage to replace Davenport?

6. What major problems does Savage face as he assumes the role of leader?

7. When does Savage recognize that Stoval can play a major role in helping him succeed? What is Stoval's role?

8. Why does Savage succeed as a leader?

9. Why do the pilots withdraw their applications to transfer?

10. What is Savage's leadership style?

11. Where along the Theory X–Y continuum would you place the behaviors displayed by Davenport and Savage? Cite examples. (You explore Theory X and Theory Y with your instructor following the exercise Assumptions About People, page 61–62.)

Iron Lady (2011)

Screenplay by Abi Morgan
Directed by Phyllida Lloyd

Character Guide

Margaret Thatcher. . . . .   Meryl Streep

Denis Thatcher . . . .   Jim Broadbent

Carol Thatcher . . . .   Olivia Colman

Introduction

The film covers aspects of Prime Minister of the United Kingdom's Margaret Thatcher's early life, first election to Parliament, and difficulties during her eleven year term of office from 1979–90 (Irish Republican Army bombings, labor strikes, Falkland War) by taking her memories looking back on her life from an increasingly frail and demented old age.

Dialogue Questions

1. What is Thatcher's philosophy of leadership and governing?

2. Why does she resist accepting the suggestion of what attention to appearances it takes to get elected?

3. How can these two matters (philosophy and appearances) be reconciled? When she says, finally, that she will surrender her hats but not her pearls, since they were given her by her husband at the birth of their twins, how does this represent a reconciliation, especially for a woman?

4. Throughout the film, Thatcher is frequently seen as a swatch of pastel in a gray and black crowd of men. How can this uniqueness, this stark difference, be made into a positive part of leadership rather than a negative one?

EXERCISES

Values Sort

Introduction

This activity allows you to reflect on your core beliefs and values and identify those of highest priority.

Instructions

Your Instructor will provide you with the instructions and handouts for this exercise.

Adapted from the California Public Safety Leadership and Ethics Institute Course—Developing a Personal Philosophy of Leadership Facilitator Guide—Section V, January 2005. Adapted with permission from the International Public Safety Leadership and Ethics Institute.

Assumptions About People

Introduction

According to Douglas McGregor, the assumptions you make about people affect your leadership style. The purpose of this exercise is to help you better understand the assumptions you make about people and to recognize more fully your perceptions about human nature. McGregor named the two extremes possible Theory X and Theory Y. Your instructor will provide scoring instructions and further explore Theory X and Theory Y.

Instructions

- Assign a weight from 0 to 10 to EACH STATEMENT IN EACH PAIR to show the relative strength of your belief in the statement compared to the other in the pair.

- The points assigned for each pair must total 10.

- Be as honest with yourself as you can and resist the natural tendency to respond as you would "like to think things are."

- This instrument is not a "test." There are no right or wrong answers. It is designed to be a stimulus for personal reflection and dialogue.

1. __2__ a. It's only human nature for people to do as little work as they can get away with.

   __8__ b. When people avoid work, it's usually because their work has been deprived of its meaning.

2. __5__ c. If employees have access to any information they want, they tend to have better attitudes and behave more responsibly.

   __5__ d. If employees have access to more information than they need to do their immediate tasks, they will usually misuse it.

3. ___0___ e. One problem in asking for the ideas of employees is that their perspective is too limited for their suggestions to be of much practical value.

    ___10___ f. Asking employees for their ideas broadens their perspective and results in the development of useful suggestions.

4. ___2___ g. If people don't use much imagination and ingenuity on the job, it's probably because relatively few people have much of either.

    ___8___ h. Most people are imaginative and creative but may not show it because of limitations imposed by supervision and the job.

5. ___1___ i. People tend to raise their standards if they are accountable for their own behavior and for correcting their own mistakes.

    ___3___ j. People tend to lower their standards if they are not punished for their misbehaviors and mistakes.

6. ___8___ k. It's better to give people both good and bad news because most employees want the whole story, no matter how painful.

    ___3___ l. It's better to withhold unfavorable news about business because most employees really want to hear only the good news.

7. ___0___ m. Because a supervisor is entitled to more respect than those below him in the organization, it weakens his prestige to admit that a subordinate was right and he was wrong.

    ___10___ n. Because people at all levels are entitled to equal respect, a supervisor's prestige is increased when he supports this principle by admitting a subordinate was right and he was wrong.

8. ___0___ o. If you give people enough money, they are less likely to be concerned with such intangibles as responsibility and recognition.

    ___10___ p. If you give people interesting and challenging work, they are less likely to complain about such things as pay and benefits.

9. ___8___ q. If people are allowed to set their own goals and standards of performance, they tend to set them higher than the boss would.

    ___2___ r. If people are allowed to set their own goals and standards of performance, they tend to set them lower than the boss would.

10. ___2___ s. The more knowledge and freedom a person has regarding his job, the more controls are needed to keep him in line.

    ___8___ t. The more knowledge and freedom a person has regarding his job, the fewer controls are needed to ensure satisfactory job performance.

SUGGESTED READING

This selected bibliography is intended to supplement the excerpts and articles of authors included in this Unit. There is an emphasis on books that are pivotal and recent publications. Numerous journals regularly offer articles related to these topics, but are not included in this selected bibliography. For further research, you may wish to include searches of the following journals: (alphabetically) *Academy of Management Executive, Academy of Management Journal, Harvard Business Review, Journal of Leadership Studies, Leadership in Action, Leadership Quarterly,* and *Leader To Leader.*

This list is organized by author's last name using Modern Language Association-style citations.

Avolio, Bruce J., and Francis J. Yammarino, eds. *Transformational and Charismatic Leadership: The Road Ahead.* Emerald Group Publishing, 2013.
This is an updated compendium of theoretical, empirical, and practical writing on transformational and charismatic leadership.

Ashby, Ruth, and Deborah D. G. Ohrn, eds. *Herstory: Women Who Changed the World.* New York: Viking, 1995.
A history of women's leadership detailing the historical and social significance of over 100 women from all areas of the world and in various areas of influence, including politics, religion, society, and the arts.

Burns, James MacGregor. *Leadership.* New York: Harper and Row Publishers, 1978.
A seminal, intellectual analysis of leadership provided by James MacGregor Burns, a political scientist and historian. This work is separated into five parts: Leadership: Power and Purpose; Origins of Leadership; Transforming Leadership; Transactional Leadership; and Implications: Theory and Practice.

Clemens, John K., and Douglas F. Mayer. *The Classic Touch: Lessons in Leadership from Homer to Hemingway.* Homewood, IL: Dow-Jones-Irwin, 1987.
This book taps the collective wisdom found in the classic works of Western philosophy, history, biography, and drama and applies it to the problems of modern leaders. It addresses such issues as how to build a team and keep it together, how to manage an acquisition once it is in place, how to eliminate daily distractions and how better to trust intuition.

Covey, Stephen R., A. Roger Merrill, and DeWitt Jones. *The Nature of Leadership.* Salt Lake City: Franklin Covey, 1998.
A unique integration of the humanities into the study of leadership, this book is a celebration of nature through stunning photographs that illustrate leadership principles such as interdependence, change, growth, diversity, and inspiration.

Gardner, Howard, and Emma Laskin. *Leading Minds: An Anatomy of Leadership.* New York: Basic Books, 1995.
This book raises the question of which type of leadership has greater influence: the direct leadership of a president or prime minister, or the indirect leadership of a creative mind. For example, during World War II, which was more influential—the allied force that Franklin D. Roosevelt and Winston Churchill forged or Albert Einstein's theory of nuclear reaction?

Heifetz, Ronald A. *Leadership Without Easy Answers.* **Cambridge: Belknap Press, 1994.**
Heifetz reflects on years of teaching leadership at Harvard to varied groups from undergraduates to executives and draws conclusions about the role of leadership in a complex society. He suggests that leadership is a social responsibility and that everyone, with and without authority, should take leadership roles to strengthen our democratic society.

James, Joy. *Transcending the Talented Tenth: Black Leaders and American Intellectuals.* **New York: Routledge, 1997.**
A densely researched book on how historically "leadership has been articulated in and for black communities."

Komives, Susan R., Nance Lucas, and Timothy R. McMahon. *Exploring Leadership: For College Students Who Want to Make a Difference.* **San Francisco: Jossey-Bass, 2013.**
This text explains a "Relational Leadership Model," and then offers an in-depth focus on self-exploration and relationships with others, followed by a section focusing on collaborative processes, and concluding with an examination of the importance of group and individual renewal.

Kouzes, James M., and Barry Z. Posner. *The Leadership Challenge: How to Make Extraordinary Things Happen in Organizations.* **San Francisco: Jossey-Bass, 2012.**
Kouzes' and Posner's research proposes five exemplary leadership practices: challenging the process, inspiring a shared vision, enabling others to act, modeling the way, and encouraging the heart.

Pearson, Carol S. *The Hero Within: Six Archetypes We Live By.* **San Francisco: Harper Collins, 1998.**
A self-development book based on the six Jungian archetypes and beginning a "heroic journey." It includes a self-test for readers to determine the archetype in their own personalities.

Wheatley, Margaret. *Leadership and the New Science: Discovering Order in a Chaotic World.* **San Francisco: Berrett-Koehler, 2010.**
Wheatley contrasts scientific management theory, which she sees as based upon Newtonian physics and the thinking which developed in the Age of Reason, with a new understanding of leading and managing based upon recent scientific discoveries and quantum physics.

UNIT2

LEADING BY SERVING

INTRODUCTION

The concept of servant leadership examines the exercise of leadership from an unexpected perspective. According to this view, the key to resolving at least part of society's leadership crisis is for those who exercise leadership to understand that they are, in fact, servants, and to recognize that the function of leadership is not merely to influence or change just for the sake of influence or change, but to serve by seeking to uplift and create a better society.

For many people, serving others in this way has always been a top priority. For example, a quick look at the resumés of many people identified as effective leaders will reveal that they are actively involved in challenging injustices and other complex problems in the world. Effective leaders understand that engaging society—in both its successes, to increase them, and in its challenges, to correct them—is the cornerstone of excellent leadership.

"The Servant as Leader" is a powerful article by Robert K. Greenleaf about the growing body of wisdom on leadership which urges leaders to serve society and their followers. Greenleaf was inspired to develop his philosophy of leadership by Hermann Hesse in his novel, *Journey to the East*, excerpts from which make the Classic Case for this Unit. To Greenleaf, and to the fictional character of the servant, Leo, in *Journey to the East*, leadership goes beyond organizational boundaries and must also seek to create a better society through service to those within and outside the organization. "Becoming a Servant-Leader: The Personal Development Path," by Isabel Lopez, builds on Greenleaf's ideas and provides additional descriptions of the concept of servant leadership and examples of implementing them. Paul Woodruff complements the concepts presented by Greenleaf and Lopez through his writing, *Reverence*.

The Leadership Profile for this Unit is of Harriet Tubman, providing an excellent example of servant leadership with a touch of "tough love." In leading people out of the bondage of slavery, she provided the ultimate service to others and inspired others to accomplish similar goals toward a new vision of freedom for all. Similarly, David Bornstein provides a description of how Florence Nightingale, through discipline and determination, transformed the field of nursing.

The Film Studies for this Unit are *Born Free*, a story about preparing an orphaned lion cub to successfully return to its intended life in the wild, and *Hotel Rwanda*, a dramatic account of the transformation of a hotel assistant manager into a servant leader during the horrendous African genocide of the 1990s.

The Unit concludes with an exercise designed to allow students to better appreciate the concept of servant leadership.

Learning Objectives

- Understand the paradoxes inherent in the concept of servant leadership

- Recognize the need for servant leadership and its benefits in organizations or society

- Identify the qualities and values important to the exercise of servant leadership

- Examine the role of individual initiative for combating evil and spreading good in the world

- Discover the impact of the exercise of servant leadership in many settings

- Recognize the benefits for organizations of serving others and serving society

- Appreciate the contributions made by the humanities selections in the Unit toward understanding the concept and importance of servant leadership

UNIT
2

CLASSIC CASE

Journey to the East

By Hermann Hesse (1877–1962)
German Novelist and Poet

Introduction and Historical Background

Hermann Hesse's writing is rich in human sympathy, imagination, and ironic humor. His writing was influenced by the Romantic tradition, and he was skilled at combining the ideas of widely varying times and cultures into a single whole as he does in *Journey to the East*. His writing is characterized by an individualized style and an original view of humanity that combines, among other things, ideas from psychoanalysis and Eastern religion. Hesse won the Nobel Prize for Literature in 1946.

Journey to the East, a fictional story written as though autobiographical, is an account of Hesse joining a mystical organization called "The League." A variety of members are described, among them artists, musicians, and poets; the narrator himself serves as the group's chorister and storyteller. One of the lesser-noticed members is a man known only as Leo, one of the servants. Each member of the group has his own personal goal in relation to the journey. The narrator's personal goal is to find the beautiful princess of Arabia. Leo's personal goal is to search for Solomon's wisdom.

Once, in a conversation with Leo, reference is made to a "law," the law of service. Leo explains to the narrator that the person "who wishes to live long must serve, but he who wishes to rule does not live long." Shortly after the conversation, while the group moves through a gorge called Morbio Inferiore, Leo suddenly disappears. No one knows why; a search party is organized, but Leo is not found, and no one understands why he might have left. For the narrator, and for the entire group for that matter, the departure of the servant Leo has dire results. Faith begins to diminish; dissension destroys the peaceful unity the group had enjoyed from the beginning. It seems that when Leo left, with him went the prosperity of the League and the cohesion of the entire group of travelers. The narrator himself becomes depressed and distrustful of the others, begins to neglect his duties and becomes very nervous and quarrelsome. It isn't long before the narrator, too, deserts the journey.

Points to Consider

1. Do you agree or disagree with Leo's "law of service"? Why or why not?

2. What are the implications for servant leaders if they, like mothers, become "invisible," as attention is diverted to those whom they lead? What strategies might such leaders take to remain relevant, while, at the same time, allowing others to step up as leaders?

3. The narrator states that Leo was never seen, other than when he was needed, "in fact, an ideal servant." Is this also a description of an ideal servant leader of a project team? Of a large organization? Explain your response.

4. Why are the motives of the servant leader often seen as suspect in our society?

Journey to the East

(Excerpts)

Chapter I

I was very fond of many of my comrades and leaders, but not one of them subsequently occupied my thoughts as much as Leo, while at that time he was apparently hardly noticed. Leo was one of our servants (who were naturally volunteers, as we were). He helped to carry the luggage and was often assigned to the personal service of the Speaker. This unaffected man had something so pleasing, so unobtrusively winning about him that everyone loved him. He did his work gaily, usually sang or whistled as he went along, was never seen except when needed—in fact, an ideal servant. Furthermore, all animals were attached to him. We nearly always had some dog or other with us which joined us on account of Leo; he could tame birds and attract butterflies to him. It was his desire for Solomon's key which would enable him to understand the language of the birds that had drawn him to the East. This servant Leo worked in a very simple and natural manner, friendly in an unassuming way, alongside the many forms of our League, which, without doing harm to the value and sincerity of the League, had within them something exalting, something singular, solemn, or fantastic. What makes my account particularly difficult is the great disparity in my individual recollections. I have already said that sometimes we marched along only as a small group; sometimes we formed a troop or even an army, but sometimes I remained in a district with only a few friends, or even quite alone, without tents, without leaders and without a Speaker. My tale becomes even more difficult because we not only wandered through Space, but also through Time. We moved towards the East, but we also traveled into the Middle Ages and the Golden Age; we roamed through Italy or Switzerland, but at times we also spent the night in the 10th century and dwelt with the patriarchs or the fairies. During the times I remained alone, I often found again places and people of my own past. I wandered with my former betrothed along the edges of the forest of the Upper Rhine, caroused with friends of my youth in Tübingen, in Basle or in Florence, or I was a boy and went with my school-friends to catch butterflies or to watch an otter, or my company consisted of the beloved characters of my books; Almansor and Parsifal, Witiko or Goldmund rode by my side, or Sancho Panza, or we were guests at the Barmekides. When I found my way back to our group in some valley or another, heard the League's songs and camped by the leaders' tents, it was immediately clear to me that my excursion into my childhood and my ride with Sancho belonged essentially to this journey. For our goal was not only the East, or rather the East was not only a country and something geographical, but it was the home and youth of the soul, it was everywhere and nowhere, it was the union of all times. Yet I was only aware of this for a moment, and therein lay the reason for my great happiness at that time. Later, when I had lost this happiness again, I clearly understood these connections without deriving the slightest benefit or comfort from them. When something precious and irretrievable is lost, we have the feeling of having awakened from a dream. In my case this feeling is strangely correct, for my happiness did indeed arise from the same secret as the happiness in dreams, it arose from the freedom to experience everything imaginable simultaneously, to exchange outward and inward easily, to move Time and Space about like scenes in a theatre. And as we League brothers traveled throughout the world without motor-cars or ships, as we conquered the war-shattered world by our faith and transformed it into Paradise, we creatively brought the past, the future and the fictitious into the present moment.

And again and again, in Swabia, at Bodensee, in Switzerland, everywhere, we met people who understood us, or were in some way thankful that we and our League and our Journey to the East existed. Amid the tramways and banks of Zurich we came across Noah's Ark guarded by several old dogs which all had the same name, and which were bravely guided across the shallow waters of a calm period by Hans C. to Noah's descendant, to the friend of the arts. We went to Winterthur, down into Stocklin's Magic Closet; we were guests in the Chinese Temple where the incense holders gleamed beneath the bronze Maja and the black king played the flute sweetly to the vibrating tone of the temple gong. And at the foot of the Sun Mountains we came across Suon Mali, a colony of the King of Siam, where, amongst the stone and brazen Buddhas, we offered up our libations and incense as grateful guests.

One of the most beautiful experiences was the League's celebration in Bremgarten; the magic circle surrounded us closely there. Received by Max and Tilli, the lords of the castle, we heard Othmar play Mozart on the grand piano in the lofty hall. We found the grounds occupied by parrots and other talking birds. We heard the fairy Armida sing at the fountain. With blown locks the heavy head of the astrologer Longus nodded by the side of the beloved countenance of Henry of Ofterdingen. In the garden, the peacocks screeched, and Louis conversed in Spanish with Puss in Boots, while Hans Resom, shaken after his peeps into the masked game of life, vowed he would go on a pilgrimage to the grave of Charles the Great. It was one of the triumphant periods of our journey; we had brought the magic wave with us; it cleansed everything. The native paid homage on his knees to beauty, the lord of the castle produced a poem which dealt with our evening activities. The animals from the forest lurked close to the castle walls, and in the river the gleaming fishes moved in lively swarms and were fed with cakes and wine.

The best of these experiences really worth relating are those which reflect the spirit of it. My description of them seems poor and perhaps, foolish, but everyone who participated in and celebrated the days at Bremgarten would confirm every single detail and supplement them with hundreds which are more beautiful. I shall always remember how the peacocks' tails shimmered when the moon rose amongst the tall trees, and on the shady bank the emerging mermaids gleamed fresh and silvery amongst the rocks; how Don Quixote stood alone under the chestnut-tree by the fountain and held his first night-watch while the last Roman candles of the firework display fell so softly over the castle's turrets in the moonlight, and my colleague Pablo, adorned with roses, played the Persian reed-pipe to the girls. Oh, which of us ever thought that the magic circle would break up so soon! That almost all of us—and also I, even I—should again lose myself in the soundless deserts of mapped out reality, just like officials and shop-assistants who, after a party or a Sunday outing, adapt themselves again to everyday business life!

In those days none of us was capable of such thoughts. From the castle's turrets of Bremgarten, the fragrance of lilac entered my bedroom. I heard the river flowing beyond the trees. I climbed out of the window in the depth of the night, intoxicated with happiness and yearning. I stole past the knight on guard and the sleeping banqueters down to the riverbank, to the flowing waters, to the white, gleaming mermaids. They took me down with them into the cool, moonlit crystal world of their home, where they played dreamily with the crowns and golden chains from their treasure-chambers. It seemed to me that I spent months in the sparkling depths and when I emerged and swam ashore, thoroughly chilled, Pablo's reed-pipe was still to be heard from the garden far away, and the moon was still high in the sky. I saw Leo playing with two white poodles, his clever, boyish face radiating happiness. I found Longus sitting in the wood. On his knees was a book of parchment in which he was writing Greek and Hebrew characters; dragons flew out of the letters, and colored snakes reared themselves. He did not look at me; he went on painting, absorbed in his colored snake-writing. For a long time I looked over his bent shoulders into the book. I saw the snakes and dragons emerge from his writing, whirl about and silently disappear into the dark wood. "Longus," I said to him softly, "dear friend!" He did not hear me, my world was far from his; and quite apart, under the moonlit trees, Anselm wandered about with an iris in his hand; lost in thought, he stared and smiled at the flower's purple calyx.

Something that I had observed several times during our journey, without having fully considered it, impressed me again during the days at Bremgarten, strangely and rather painfully. There were amongst us many artists, painters, musicians and poets. Ardent Klingsor was there and restless Hugo Wolf, taciturn Lauscher and vivacious Brentano—but however animated and lovable the personalites [sic] of these artists were, yet without exception their imaginary characters were more animated, more beautiful, happier and certainly finer and more real than the poets and creators themselves. Pablo sat there with his flute in enchanting innocence and joy, but his poet slipped away like a shadow to the river-bank, half transparent in the moonlight, seeking solitude. Stumbling and rather drunk, Hoffman ran here and there amongst the guests talking a great deal, small and elfish, and he also, like all of them, was only half-real, only half there, not quite solid, not quite real. At the same time, the archivist Lindhorst, playing at dragons for a joke, continually breathed fire and discharged energy like an automobile. I asked the servant Leo why it was that artists sometimes appear to be only half-alive, while their creations seemed so irrefutably alive. Leo looked at me, surprised at my question. Then he released the poodle he was holding in his arms and said,

"It is just the same with mothers. When they have borne their children and given them their milk and beauty and strength, they themselves become invisible, and no one asks about them any more."

"But that is sad," I said, without really thinking very much about it.

"I do not think it is sadder than all other things," said Leo. "Perhaps it is sad and yet also beautiful. The law ordains that it shall be so."

"The law?" I asked curiously. "What law is that, Leo?"

"The law of service. He who wishes to live long must serve, but he who wishes to rule does not live long."

"Then why do so many strive to rule?"

"Because they do not understand. There are few who are born to be masters; they remain happy and healthy. But all the others who have only become masters through endeavor, end in nothing."

"In what nothing, Leo?"

"For example, in the sanitoria."

I understood little about it and yet the words remained in my memory and left me with a feeling that this Leo knew all kinds of things, that he perhaps knew more than us, who were ostensibly his masters.

Chapter II

Each participant in this unforgettable journey had his own ideas as to what made our faithful Leo suddenly decide to leave us in the middle of the dangerous gorge of Morbio Inferiore. It was only very much later that I began in some measure to suspect and review the circumstances and deeper significance of this occurrence. It also seemed that this apparently incidental but in reality extremely important event, the disappearance of Leo, was in no way an accident, but a link in that chain of events through which the eternal enemy sought to bring disaster to our undertaking. On that cool autumn morning when it was discovered that our servant Leo was missing and that all search for him remained fruitless, I was certainly not the only one who, for the first time, had a feeling of impending disaster and menacing destiny.

However, for the moment, this was the position. After we had boldly crossed half Europe and a portion of the Middle Ages, we camped in a very narrow rocky valley, a wild mountain gorge on the Italian border, and looked for the inexplicably missing Leo. The longer we looked and the more our hopes of finding him again dwindled during the course of the day, the more we were oppressed by the thought that it was not only the question of a popular, pleasant man amongst our servants who had either met with an accident or run away or had been captured by an enemy, but that this was the beginning of trouble, the first indication of a storm which would break over us. We spent the whole day, far into the twilight, searching for Leo. The whole of the gorge was explored, and while these exertions made us weary, and a feeling of hopelessness and futility grew amongst us all, it was very strange and uncanny how from hour to hour the missing servant seemed to increase in importance and our loss created difficulties. It was not only that each pilgrim, and without doubt the whole of the staff, were worried about the handsome, pleasant and willing youth, but it seemed that the more certain his loss became, the more indispensable he seemed; without Leo, his handsome face, his good humor and his songs, without his enthusiasm for our great undertaking, the undertaking itself seemed in some mysterious way to lose meaning. At least, that is how it affected me. Despite all the strain and many minor disillusionments during the previous months of the journey, I had never had a moment of inner weakness. Of serious doubt; no successful general, no bird in the swallows' flight to Egypt, could be more sure of his goal, of his mission, of the rightness of his actions and aspirations than I was on this journey. But now, in this fateful place, while I continually heard the calls and signals of our sentinels during the whole of the blue and golden October day, and awaited again and again with growing excitement the arrival of a report, only to suffer disappointment and to gaze at perplexed faces, I had feelings of sadness and doubt for the first time. The stronger these feelings became, the clearer it seemed to me that it was not only that I had lost faith in finding Leo again, but everything now seemed to become unreliable and doubtful; the value and meaning of everything was threatened: our comradeship, our faith, our vow, our Journey to the East, our whole life.

Even if I was mistaken in presuming that we all had these feelings, indeed even if I was subsequently mistaken about my own feelings and inner experiences and many things which were in reality experienced much later and erroneously attributed to that day, there still remains, despite everything, the strange fact about Leo's luggage. Quite apart from all personal moods, this was, in fact, rather strange, fantastic, and an increasing source of worry. Even during this day in the Morbio gorge, even during our eager search for the missing man, first one man, then another missed something important, something indispensable from the luggage which could not be found anywhere. It appeared that every missing article must have been in Leo's luggage, and although Leo, like all the rest of us, had only carried the usual linen haversack on his back, just one bag amongst about thirty others, it seemed that in this one lost bag there were all the really important things which we carried with us on our journey. And although it is a well-known human weakness that a thing at the time we miss it has an exaggerated value and seems less dispensable than the things we have, and although the loss of many of the articles which troubled us so much in the Morbio gorge did, in fact, turn up again later, or finally did not prove so indispensable—yet, despite all this, it is unfortunately true that we did at that time, with quite justifiable alarm, confirm the loss of a whole series of extremely important things.

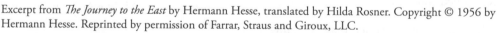

Excerpt from *The Journey to the East* by Hermann Hesse, translated by Hilda Rosner. Copyright © 1956 by Hermann Hesse. Reprinted by permission of Farrar, Straus and Giroux, LLC.

LEADERSHIP PROFILE

Harriet Tubman (1821?–1913)

Escaped Slave and Underground Railroad Leader
Excerpts from
The Underground Railroad: First-Person Narratives of Escape to Freedom in the North
By Charles L. Blockson

UNIT
2

Introduction and Historical Background

Harriet Tubman (1821?–1913), a truly outstanding American abolitionist leader, was born a slave. As a young girl she worked as a field hand and house servant on a Maryland plantation. After marrying John Tubman, a free black, she escaped to the North.

Tubman was the most famous "conductor" or guide on the Underground Railroad, an escape route to assist slaves fleeing the South. The Underground was established before the Civil War by Northern abolitionists, free blacks in the North, and escaped slaves. Traveling by night to avoid detection, escapees used the North Star for guidance. This was a very dangerous enterprise for both the fleeing slaves and the conductors. The conductors faced imprisonment if caught. Escaped slaves acting as conductors could be returned to slavery, or worse, if recaptured. Professional slave catchers and vigilant officials were paid rewards for seizing runaway slaves. In fact, the federal Fugitive Slave Act

Library of Congress, Prints and
Photographs Division,
LC-USZ62-7816

of 1850 allowed bounty hunters to pursue escaped slaves across state lines into free states and use force, if necessary, to secure the return of the slave owners' property. The law further stated that all citizens were required to return fugitive slaves to the proper authorities. Violation of the law was punishable by imprisonment. Defiance of existing slavery laws by the North outraged Southerners, and certainly the Underground Railroad played a major role in fanning the flames of the pending Civil War.

Tubman, making approximately nineteen return trips to the South, personally assisted an estimated three hundred slaves in their escape to the free states and Canada. Her home was an important station on the escape route. Among the slaves, she became universally known as Moses the Deliverer. She was lionized by Northern writers. She was vilified by Southerners, however, who offered a price for her capture or death. During the Civil War, Tubman served in the Union Army as a cook, nurse, spy, and scout. In later years, she maintained a home for aged blacks in Auburn, New York.

Harriet Tubman is considered one of the greatest heroines of African-American history. To honor this remarkable woman who helped free others through the Underground Railroad and for her activities as a Union spy, the anniversary of her death, March 10th, is observed as Harriet Tubman Day.

The following Leadership Profile is based on interviews appearing in the *Commonwealth* on July 17, 1863, and in the first volume of the *Freeman's Record* dated March 1865.

Points to Consider

1. What are some ways that Harriet Tubman practiced self-leadership, ensuring that she would be able to do the most good for the most people?

2. To protect the group, Harriet Tubman would not tolerate any man acting out. As a leader, how might you deal with a team member whose behavior is detrimental to the goals of the group?

3. To what extent is it important to sacrifice personal aims in order to focus on a broader mission?

4. What are the potential benefits/detriments to bringing a "Can't die but once" attitude into a leadership situation in an organization?

Narrative of Harriet Tubman

By Charles L. Blockson
(Excerpt from *The Underground Railroad*)

One of the teachers lately commissioned by the New England Freedmen's Aid Society is probably the most remarkable woman of this age. That is to say, she has performed more wonderful deeds by the native power of her own spirit against adverse circumstances than any other. She is well known to many by the various names which her eventful life has given her; Harriet Garrison, Gen. Tubman, etc.; but among the slaves she is universally known by her well earned title of Moses,—Moses the Deliverer. She is a rare instance, in the midst of high civilization and intellectual culture, of a being of great native powers, working powerfully, and to beneficent ends, entirely untaught by schools or books.

Her maiden name was Araminta Ross. She is the granddaughter of a native African, and has not a drop of white blood in her veins. She was born in 1820 or 1821, on the Eastern Shore of Maryland. Her parents were slaves, but married and faithful to each other, and the family affection is very strong. She claims that she was legally freed by a will of her first master, but his wishes were not carried into effect.

She seldom lived with her owner, but was usually "hired out" to difficult persons. She once "hired her time," and employed it in rudest farming labors, ploughing, carting, driving the oxen, etc., to so good advantage that she was able in one year to buy a pair of steers worth forty dollars.

When quite young she lived with a very pious mistress; but the slaveholder's religion did not prevent her from whipping the young girl for every slight or fancied fault. Araminta found that this was usually a morning exercise; so she prepared for it by putting on all the thick clothes she could procure to protect her skin. She made sufficient outcry, however, to convince her mistress that her blows had full effect; and in the afternoon she would take off her wrappings, and dress as well as she could. When invited into family prayers, she preferred to stay on the landing, and pray for herself; "and I prayed to God," she says "to make me strong and able to fight and that's what I've allers prayed for ever since." It is in vain to try to persuade her that her prayer was a wrong one. She always maintains it to be sincere and right, and it has certainly been fully answered.

In her youth she received a severe blow on her head from a heavy weight thrown by her master at another slave, but which accidentally hit her. The blow produced a disease of the brain which was severe for a long time, and still makes her very lethargic. She cannot remain quiet fifteen minutes without appearing to fall asleep. It is not refreshing slumber; but a heavy, weary condition which

exhausts her. She therefore loves great physical activity, and direct heat of the sun, which keeps her blood actively circulating. She was married about 1844 to a free colored man named John Tubman, but never had any children. Owing to changes in her owner's family, it was determined to sell her and some other slaves; but her health was so much injured, that a purchaser was not easily found. At length she became convinced that she would soon be carried away and she decided to escape. Her brothers did not agree with her plans; and she walked off alone, following the guidance of the brooks, which she had observed to run North. The evening before she left, she wished very much to bid her companions farewell, but was afraid of being betrayed, if any one knew of her intentions; so she passed through the street singing "good bye, I'm going to leave you, Good bye, I'll meet you in the kingdom," and similar snatches of Methodist songs. As she passed on singing, she saw her master, Dr. Thompson, standing at his gate, and her native humor breaking out, she sung yet louder, bowing down to him, "Good bye, I'm going for to leave you." He stopped and looked after her as she passed on; and he afterwards said, that, as her voice came floating back in the evening air it seemed as if "A wave of trouble never rolled across her peaceful breast."

Wise judges are we of each other!—She was only quitting home, husband, father, mother, friends, to go out alone, friendless and penniless into the world.

She remained two years in Philadelphia working hard and carefully hoarding her money. Then she hired a room, furnished it as well as she could, bought a nice suit of men's clothes, and went back to Maryland for her husband. But the faithless man had taken to himself another wife. Harriet did not dare venture into her presence, but sent word to her husband where she was. He declined joining her. At first her grief and anger were excessive. She said, "she did not care what massa did to her, she thought she would go right in and make all the trouble she could, she was determined to see her old man once more;" but finally she thought "how foolish it was just for temper to make mischief;" and that, "if he could do without her, she could without him," and so "he dropped out of her heart," and she determined to give her life to brave deeds. Thus all personal aims died out of her heart; and with her simple brave motto, "I can't die but once," she began the work which has made her Moses,—the deliverer of her people. Seven or eight times she has returned to the neighborhood of her former home, always at the risk of death in the most terrible forms, and each time has brought away a company of fugitive slaves, and led them safely to the free States, or to Canada. Every time she went, the dangers increased. In 1857 she brought away her old parents, and, as they were too feeble to walk, she was obliged to hire a wagon, which added greatly to the perils of the journey. In 1860 she went for the last time, and among her troop was an infant whom they were obliged to keep stupefied with laudanum to prevent its outcries. This was at a period of great excitement, and Moses was not safe even in New York State; but her anxious friends insisted upon her taking refuge in Canada. So various and interesting are the incidents of the journeys, that we know not how to select from them. She has shown in them all the characteristics of a great leader: courage, foresight, prudence, self-control, ingenuity, subtle perception, command over others' minds. Her nature is at once profoundly practical and highly imaginative. She is as economical as Dr. Franklin, and as firm in the conviction of supernatural help as Mahomet. A clergyman once said, that her stories convinced you of their truth by their simplicity as do the gospel narratives.

She never went to the South to bring away fugitives without being provided with money; money for the most part earned by drudgery in the kitchen, until within the last few years, when friends have aided her. She had to leave her sister's two orphan children in slavery the last time, for the want of thirty dollars. Thirty pieces of silver; an embroidered handkerchief or a silk dress to one, or the price of freedom to two orphan children to another! She would never allow more to join her than she could properly care for, though she often gave others directions by which they succeeded in escaping. She always came in the winter when the nights are long and dark, and people who have homes stay in them. She was never seen on the plantation herself; but appointed a rendezvous for her company eight or ten miles distant, so that if they were discovered at the first start she was not compromised. She started on Saturday night; the slaves at that time being allowed to go away from home to visit their friends—so that they would not be missed until Monday morning. Even then they were supposed to have loitered on the way, and it would often be late on Monday afternoon before the flight would be certainly known. If by any further delay the advertisement was not sent out before Tuesday morning, she felt secure of keeping ahead of it; but if it were, it required all her ingenuity to escape. She resorted to various devices, she had confidential friends all along the road. She would hire a man to follow the one who put up the notices, and take them down as soon as his back was turned. She crossed creeks on railroad bridges by night, she hid her company in the woods while she herself not being advertised went into the towns in search of information. If met on the road, her face was always to the south, and she was always a very respectable looking darkey, not at all a poor fugitive. She would get into the cars near her pursuers and manage to hear their plans.

The expedition was governed by the strictest rules. If any man gave out, he must be shot. "Would you really do that?" she was asked. "Yes," she replied, "if he was weak enough to give out, he'd be weak enough to betray us all, and all who had helped us; and do you think I'd let so many die just for one coward man." "Did you ever have to shoot any one?" she was asked. "One time," she said, "a man gave out the second night; his feet were sore and swollen, he couldn't go any further; he'd rather go back and die, if he must." They tried all arguments in vain, bathed his feet, tried to strengthen him, but it was of no use, he would go back. Then she said, "I told the boys to get their guns ready, and shoot him. They'd have done it in a minute; but when he heard that, he jumped right up and went on as well as any body." She can tell the time by the stars, and find her way by natural signs as well as any hunter; and yet she scarcely knows of the existence of England or any other foreign country.

When going on these journeys she often lay alone in the forests all night. Her whole soul was filled with awe of the mysterious Unseen Presence, which thrilled her with such depths of emotion, that all other care and fear vanished. Then she seemed to speak with her Maker "as a man talketh with his friend;" her child-like petitions had direct answers, and beautiful visions lifted her up above all doubt and anxiety into serene trust and faith. No man can be a hero without this faith in some form; the sense that he walks not in his own strength, but leaning on an almighty arm. Call it fate, destiny, what you will, Moses of old, Moses of to-day, believed it to be Almighty God.

She loves to describe her visions, which are very real to her; but she must tell them word for word as they lie in her untutored mind, with endless repetitions and details; she cannot shorten or condense them, whatever be your haste. She has great dramatic power; the scene rises before you as she saw it, and her voice and language change with her different actors. Often these visions came to her in the midst of her work. She once said, "We'd been carting manure all day, and t'other girl and I were gwine home on the sides of the cart, and another boy was driving, when suddenly I heard such music as filled all the air;" and, she saw a vision which she described in language which sounded like the old prophets in its grand flow; interrupted now and then by what t'other girl said, by Massa's coming and calling her to wake up, and her protests that she wasn't asleep.

One of her most characteristic prayers was when on board a steamboat with a party of fugitives. The clerk of the boat declined to give her tickets, and told her to wait. She thought he suspected her, and was at a loss how to save herself and her charge, if he did; so she went alone into the bow of the boat, and she says, "I drew in my breath and I sent it out to the Lord, but that was all I could say; and then again the third time, and just then I felt a touch on my shoulder, and looked round, and the clerk said, 'Here's your tickets.'"

Her efforts were not confined to the escape of slaves. She conducted them to Canada, watched over their welfare, collected clothing, organized them into societies, and was always occupied with plans for their benefit. She first came to Boston in the spring of 1859, to ask aid of the friends of her race to build a house for her aged father and mother. She brought recommendations from Gerrit Smith, and at once won many friends who aided her to accomplish her purpose. Her parents are now settled in Auburn, and all that Harriet seems to desire in reward for her labors is the privilege of making their old age comfortable. She has a very affectionate nature, and forms the strongest personal attachments. She has great simplicity of character; she states her wants very freely, and believes you are ready to help her; but if you have nothing to give, or have given to another, she is content. She is not sensitive to indignities to her color in her own person; but knows and claims her rights. She will eat at your table if she sees you really desire it; but she goes as willingly to the kitchen. She is very abstemious in her diet, fruit being the only luxury she cares for. Her personal appearance is very peculiar. She is thoroughly negro, and very plain. She has needed disguise so often, that she seems to have command over her face, and can banish all expression from her features, and look so stupid that nobody would suspect her of knowing enough to be dangerous; but her eye flashes with intelligence and power when she is roused.

Blockson, Charles L. *The Underground Railroad: First-Person Narratives of Escape to Freedom in the North*. New York: Simon & Schuster, 1987. Reprinted by permission of Simon & Schuster, Inc.

UNIT
2

REFLECT & FOCUS

"To know is to comprehend. Do you know, do you comprehend, in this moment, who or what you serve? We must all be serving someone or something. Whom or what are you choosing to serve right now? It takes courage to ask this question of yourself. But without courage, you can't practice any other value consistently."

— Maya Angelou, American Poet, Educator, Historian, Civil Rights Activist

READINGS

"The Servant as Leader"

By Robert K. Greenleaf

Points to Consider

1. According to Greenleaf, withdrawal is a key self-management technique for a servant leader. Where do you fit in terms of his description of two extreme types of leaders? How would you evaluate your own ability to withdraw?

2. Greenleaf states, "The servant always accepts and empathizes, never rejects." Have you been in environments (e.g., work, school) where you have seen this type of leadership? Conversely, have you been in situations where a leader rejected the person? What has been the impact?

3. Greenleaf states, "A new moral principle is emerging which holds that the only authority deserving one's allegiance is that which is freely and knowingly granted by the led to the leader…To the extent that this principle prevails in the future, the only truly viable institutions will be those that are predominantly servant-led." To what extent do you feel this principle holds true today?

4. Is the present-day world too jaded for the notion of servant leadership?

"The Servant as Leader"

Servant and leader—can these two roles be fused in one real person, in all levels of status or calling? If so, can that person live and be productive in the real world of the present? My sense of the present leads me to say yes to both questions. This chapter is an attempt to explain why and to suggest how.

The idea of The Servant as Leader came out of reading Hermann Hesse's *Journey to the East*. In this story we see a band of men on a mythical journey, probably also Hesse's own journey. The central figure of the story is Leo who accompanies the party as the servant who does their menial chores, but who also sustains them with his spirit and his song. He is a person of extraordinary presence. All goes well until Leo disappears. Then the group falls into disarray and the journey is abandoned. They cannot make it without the servant Leo. The narrator, one of the party, after some years of wandering—finds Leo and is taken into the Order that had sponsored the journey. There he discovers that Leo, whom he had known first as servant, was in fact the titular head of the Order, its guiding spirit, a great and noble leader.

One can muse on what Hesse was trying to say when he wrote this story. We know that most of his fiction was autobiographical, that he led a tortured life, and that *Journey to the East* suggests a turn toward the serenity he achieved in his old age. There has been much speculation by critics on Hesse's life and work, some of it centering on this story which they find the most puzzling. But to me, this story clearly says that the great leader is seen as servant first, and that simple fact is the key to his greatness. Leo was actually the leader all the time, but he was servant first because that was what he was, deep down inside. Leadership was bestowed upon a man who was by nature a servant. It was something given, or assumed, that could be taken away. His servant nature was the real man, not bestowed, not assumed, and not to be taken away. He was servant first.

I mention Hesse and *Journey to the East* for two reasons. First, I want to acknowledge the source of the idea of The Servant as Leader. Secondly, I want to use this reference as an introduction to a brief discussion of prophecy.

Fifteen years ago when I first read about Leo, if I had been listening to contemporary prophecy as intently as I do now, the first draft of this piece might have been written then. As it was, the idea lay dormant for eleven years until, four years ago, I concluded that we in this country were in a leadership crisis and that I should do what I could about it. I became painfully aware of how dull my sense of contemporary prophecy had been. And I have reflected much on why we do not hear and heed the prophetic voices in our midst (not a new question in our times, nor more critical than heretofore).

I now embrace the theory of prophecy which holds that prophetic voices of great clarity, and with a quality of insight equal to that of any age, are speaking cogently all of the time. Men and women of a stature equal to the greatest of the past are with us now addressing the problems of the day and pointing to a better way and to a personality better able to live fully and serenely in these times.

The variable that marks some periods as barren and some as rich in prophetic vision is in the interest, the level of seeking, the responsiveness of the hearers. The variable is not in the presence or absence or the relative quality and force of the prophetic voices. Prophets grow in stature as people respond to their message. If their early attempts are ignored or spurned, their talent may wither away.

It is seekers, then, who make prophets, and the initiative of any one of us in searching for and responding to the voice of contemporary prophets may mark the turning point in their growth and service. But since we are the product of our own history, we see current prophecy within the context of past wisdom. We listen to as wide a range of contemporary thought as we can attend to. Then we choose those we elect to heed as prophets—both old and new—and meld their advice with our own leadings. This we test in real-life experiences to establish our own position.

Some who have difficulty with this theory assert that their faith rests on one or more of the prophets of old having given the "word" for all time and that the contemporary ones do not speak to their condition as the older ones do. But if one really believes that the "word" has been given for all time, how can one be a seeker? How can one hear the contemporary voice when one has decided not to live in the present and has turned that voice off?

Neither this hypothesis nor its opposite can be proved. But I submit that the one given here is the more hopeful choice, one that offers a significant role in prophecy to every individual. One cannot interact with and build strength in a dead prophet, but one can do it with a living one. "Faith," Dean Inge has said, "is the choice of the nobler hypothesis."

One does not, of course, ignore the great voices of the past. One does not awaken each morning with the compulsion to reinvent the wheel. But if one is servant, either leader or follower, one is always searching, listening, expecting that a better wheel for these times is in the making. It may emerge any day. Any one of us may find it out from personal experience. I am hopeful.

I am hopeful for these times, despite the tension and conflict, because more natural servants are trying to see clearly the world as it is and are listening carefully to prophetic voices that are speaking now. They are challenging the pervasive injustice with greater force, and they are taking sharper issue with the wide disparity between the quality of society they know is reasonable and possible with available resources, and, on the other hand, the actual performance of the whole range of institutions that exist to serve society.

A fresh critical look is being taken at the issues of power and authority, and people are beginning to learn, however haltingly, to relate to one another in less coercive and more creatively supporting ways. A new moral principle is emerging which holds that the only authority deserving one's allegiance is that which is freely and knowingly granted by the led to the leader in response to, and in proportion to, the clearly evident servant stature of the leader. Those who choose to follow this principle will not casually accept the authority of existing institutions. Rather, they will freely respond only to individuals who are chosen as leaders because they are proven and trusted as servants. To the extent that this principle prevails in the future, the only truly viable institutions will be those that are predominantly servant-led.

I am mindful of the long road ahead before these trends, which I see so clearly, become a major society-shaping force. We are not there yet. But I see encouraging movement on the horizon.

What direction will the movement take? Much depends on whether those who stir the ferment will come to grips with the age-old problem of how to live in a human society. I say this because so many, having made their awesome decision for autonomy and independence from tradition, and having taken their firm stand against injustice and hypocrisy, find it hard to convert themselves into affirmative builders of a better society. How many of them will seek their personal fulfillment by making the hard choices, and by undertaking the rigorous preparation that building a better society requires? It all depends on what kind of leaders emerge and how they—we—respond to them.

My thesis, that more servants should emerge as leaders, or should follow only servant-leaders, is not a popular one. It is much more comfortable to go with a less demanding point of view about what is expected of one now. There are several undemanding, plausibly-argued alternatives to choose. One, since society seems corrupt, is to seek to avoid the center of it by retreating to an idyllic existence that minimizes involvement with the "system" (with the "system" that makes such withdrawal possible). Then there is the assumption that since the effort to reform existing institutions has not brought instant perfection, the remedy is to destroy them completely so that fresh, new perfect ones can grow. Not much thought seems to be given to the problem of where the new seed will come from or who the gardener to tend them will be. The concept of the servant-leader stands in sharp contrast to this kind of thinking.

Yet it is understandable that the easier alternatives would be chosen, especially by young people. By extending education for so many so far into the adult years, the normal participation in society is effectively denied when young people are ready for it. With education that is preponderantly abstract and analytical it is no wonder that there is a preoccupation with criticism and that not much thought is given to "What can I do about it?"

Criticism has its place, but as a total preoccupation it is sterile. In a time of crisis, like the leadership crisis we are now in, if too many potential builders are taken in by a complete absorption with dissecting the wrong and by a zeal for instant perfection, then the movement so many of us want to see will be set back. The danger, perhaps, is to hear the analyst too much and the artist too little.

Albert Camus stands apart from other great artists of his time, in my view, and deserves the title of prophet, because of his unrelenting demand that each of us confront the exacting terms of our own existence, and like Sisyphus, accept our rock and find our happiness in dealing with it. Camus sums up the relevance of his position to our concern for the servant as leader in the last paragraph of his last published lecture, entitled: Create Dangerously:

One may long, as I do, for a gentler flame, a respite, a pause for musing. But perhaps there is no other peace for the artist than what he finds in the heat of combat. "Every wall is a door," Emerson correctly said. Let us not look for the door, and the way out, anywhere but in the wall against which we are living. Instead, let us seek the respite where it is—in the very thick of battle. For in my opinion, and this is where I shall close, it is there. Great ideas, it has been said, come into the world as gently as doves. Perhaps, then, if we listen attentively, we shall hear, amid the uproar of empires and nations, a faint flutter of wings, the gentle stirring of life and hope. Some will say that this hope lies in a nation, others, in a man. I believe rather that it is awakened, revived, nourished by millions of solitary individuals whose deeds and works every day negate frontiers and the crudest implications of history. As a result, there shines forth fleetingly the ever-threatened truth that each and every man, on the foundations of his own sufferings and joys, builds for them all.

One is asked, then, to accept the human condition, its sufferings and its joys, and to work with its imperfections as the foundation upon which the individual will build wholeness through adventurous creative achievement. For the person with creative potential there is no wholeness except in using it. And, as Camus explained, the going is rough and the respite is brief. It is significant that he would title his last university lecture Create Dangerously. And, as I ponder the fusing of servant and leader, it seems a dangerous creation: dangerous for the natural servant to become a leader, dangerous for the leader to be servant first, and dangerous for a follower to insist on being led by a servant. There are safer and easier alternatives available to all three. But why take them?

As I respond to the challenge of dealing with this question in the ensuing discourse, I am faced with two problems.

First, I did not get the notion of the servant as leader from conscious logic. Rather it came to me as an intuitive insight as I contemplated Leo. And I do not see what is relevant from my own searching and experience in terms of a logical progression from premise to conclusion. Rather I see it as fragments of data to be fed into my internal computer from which intuitive insights come. Serving and leading are still mostly intuition-based concepts in my thinking.

The second problem, and related to the first, is that, just as there may be a real contradiction in the servant as leader, so my perceptual world is full of contradictions. Some examples: I believe in order, and I want creation out of chaos. My good society will have strong individualism amidst community. It will have elitism along with populism. I listen to the old and to the young and find myself baffled and heartened by both. Reason and intuition, each in its own way, both comfort and dismay me. There are many more. Yet, with all of this, I believe that I live with as much serenity as do my contemporaries who venture into controversy as freely as I do but whose natural bent is to tie up the essentials of life in neat bundles of logic and consistency. But I am deeply grateful to the people who are logical and consistent because some of them, out of their natures, render invaluable services for which I am not capable.

My resolution of these two problems is to offer the relevant gleanings of my experience in the form of a series of unconnected little essays, some developed more fully than others, with the suggestion that they be read and pondered on separately within the context of this opening section.

Who Is the Servant-Leader?

The servant-leader is servant first—as Leo was portrayed. It begins with the natural feeling that one wants to serve, to serve first. Then conscious choice brings one to aspire to lead. That person is sharply different from one who is leader first, perhaps because of the need to assuage an unusual power drive or to acquire material possessions. For such it will be a later choice to serve—after leadership is established. The leader-first and the servant-first are two extreme types. Between them there are shadings and blends that are part of the infinite variety of human nature.

The difference manifests itself in the care taken by the servant-first to make sure that other people's highest priority needs are being served. The best test, and difficult to administer, is: Do those served grow as persons? Do they, while being served, become healthier, wiser, freer, more autonomous, more likely themselves to become servants? And, what is the effect on the least privileged in society; will they benefit, or, at least, not be further deprived?

As one sets out to serve, how can one know that this will be the result? This is part of the human dilemma; one cannot know for sure. One must, after some study and experience, hypothesize—but leave the hypothesis under a shadow of doubt. Then one acts on the hypothesis and examines the result. One continues to study and learn and periodically one reexamines the hypothesis itself.

Finally, one chooses again. Perhaps one chooses the same hypothesis again and again. But it is always a fresh open choice. And it is always a hypothesis under a shadow of doubt. "Faith is the choice of the nobler hypothesis." Not the noblest; one never knows what that is. But the nobler, the best one can see when the choice is made. Since the test of results of one's actions is usually long delayed, the faith that sustains the choice of the nobler hypothesis is psychological self-insight. This is the most dependable part of the true servant.

The natural servant, the person who is servant first, is more likely to persevere and refine a particular hypothesis on what serves another's highest priority needs than is the person who is leader first and who later serves out of promptings of conscience or in conformity with normative expectations.

My hope for the future rests in part on my belief that among the legions of deprived and unsophisticated people are many true servants who will lead, and that most of them can learn to discriminate among those who presume to serve them and identify the true servants whom they will follow.

Everything Begins with the Initiative of an Individual

The forces for good and evil in the world are propelled by the thoughts, attitudes, and actions of individual beings. What happens to our values, and therefore to the quality of our civilization in the future, will be shaped by the conceptions of individuals that are born of inspiration. Perhaps only a few will receive this inspiration (insight) and the rest will learn from them. The very essence of leadership, going out ahead to show the way, derives from more than usual openness to inspiration. Why would anybody accept the leadership of another except that the other sees more clearly where it is best to go? Perhaps this is the current problem: too many who presume to lead do not see more clearly and, in defense of their inadequacy, they all the more strongly argue that the "system" must be preserved—a fatal error in this day of candor.

But the leader needs more than inspiration. A leader ventures to say: "I will go; come with me!" A leader initiates, provides the ideas and the structure, and takes the risk of failure along with the chance of success. A leader says: "I will go; follow me!" while knowing that the path is uncertain, even dangerous. One then trusts those who go with one's leadership.

Paul Goodman, speaking through a character in *Making Do*, has said, "If there is no community for you, young man; young man, make it yourself."

UNIT
2

What Are You Trying to Do?

"What are you trying to do?" is one of the easiest to ask and most difficult to answer of questions.

A mark of leaders, an attribute that puts them in a position to show the way for others, is that they are better than most at pointing the direction. As long as one is leading, one always has a goal. It may be a goal arrived at by group consensus, or the leader, acting on inspiration, may simply have said, "Let's go this way." But the leader always knows what it is and can articulate it for any who are unsure. By clearly stating and restating the goal the leader gives certainty and purpose to others who may have difficulty in achieving it for themselves.

The word goal is used here in the special sense of the overarching purpose, the big dream, the visionary concept, the ultimate consummation which one approaches but never really achieves. It is something presently out of reach; it is something to strive for, to move toward, or become. It is so stated that it excites the imagination and challenges people to work for something they do not yet know how to do, something they can be proud of as they move toward it.

Every achievement starts with a goal—but not just any goal and not just anybody stating it. The one who states the goal must elicit trust, especially if it is a high risk or visionary goal, because those who follow are asked to accept the risk along with the leaders. Leaders do not elicit trust unless one has confidence in their values and competence (including judgment) and unless they have a sustaining spirit (entheos) that will support the tenacious pursuit of a goal.

Not much happens without a dream. And for something great to happen, there must be a great dream. Behind every great achievement is a dreamer of great dreams. Much more than a dreamer is required to bring it to reality; but the dream must be there first.

Listening and Understanding

One of our very able leaders recently was made the head of a large, important, and difficult-to-administer public institution. After a short time he realized that he was not happy with the way things were going. His approach to the problem was a bit unusual. For three months he stopped reading newspapers and listening to news broadcasts; and for this period he relied wholly upon those he met in the course of his work to tell him what was going on. In three months his administrative problems were resolved. No miracles were wrought; but out of a sustained intentness of listening that was produced by this unusual decision, this able man learned and received the insights needed to set the right course. And he strengthened his team by so doing.

Why is there so little listening? What makes this example so exceptional? Part of it, I believe, with those who lead, is that the usual leader in the face of difficulty tends to react by trying to find someone else on whom to pin the problem, rather than by automatically responding: "I have a problem. What is it? What can I do about my problem?" The sensible person who takes the latter course will probably react by listening, and somebody in the situation is likely to say what the problem is and what should be done about it. Or enough will be heard that there will be an intuitive insight that resolves it.

I have a bias about this which suggests that only a true natural servant automatically responds to any problem by listening first. When one is a leader, this disposition causes one to be seen as servant *first*. This suggests that a non-servant who wants to be a servant might become a *natural* servant through a long arduous discipline of learning to listen, a discipline sufficiently sustained that the automatic response to any problem is to listen first. I have seen enough remarkable transformations in people who have been trained to listen to have some confidence in this approach. It is because true listening builds strength in other people.

Most of us at one time or another, some of us a good deal of the time, would really like to communicate, really get through to a significant level of meaning in the hearer's experience. It can be terribly important. The best test of whether we are communicating at this depth is to ask ourselves first: Are we really listening? Are we listening to the one we want to communicate to? Is our basic attitude, as we approach the confrontation, one of wanting to understand? Remember that great line from the prayer of St. Francis, "Lord, grant that I may not seek so much to be understood as to understand."

One must not be afraid of a little silence. Some find silence awkward or oppressive, but a relaxed approach to dialogue will include the welcoming of some silence. It is often a devastating question to ask oneself—but it is sometimes important to ask it—"In saying what I have in mind will I really improve on the silence?"

UNIT
2

Language and Imagination

Alfred North Whitehead once said, "No language can be anything but elliptical, requiring a leap of imagination to understand its meaning in its relevance to immediate experience." Nothing is meaningful until it is related to the hearer's own experience. One may hear the words, one may even remember them and repeat them, as a computer does in the retrieval process. But *meaning*, a growth in experience as a result of receiving the communication, requires that the hearer supply the imaginative link from the hearer's fund of experience to the abstract language symbols the speaker has used. As a leader (including teacher, coach, administrator) one must have facility in tempting the hearer into that leap of imagination that connects the verbal concept to the hearer's own experience. The limitation on language, to the communicator, is that the hearer must make that leap of imagination. One of the arts of communicating is to say just enough to facilitate that leap. Many attempts to communicate are nullified by saying too much.

The physicist and philosopher Percy Bridgman takes another view of it when he says, "No linguistic structure is capable of reproducing the full complexity of experience… The only feasible way of dealing with this is to push a particular verbal line of attack as far as it can go, and then switch to another verbal level which we might abandon when we have to… Many people…insist on a single self-consistent verbal scheme into which they try to force all experience. In doing this they create a purely verbal world in which they can live a pretty autonomous existence, fortified by the ability of many of their fellows to live in the same verbal world." This, of course, is what makes a cult—a group of people who thus isolate themselves from the evolving mainstream. By staying within their own closed verbal world they forfeit the opportunity to lead others. One of the great tragedies is when a proven able leader becomes trapped in one of these closed verbal worlds and loses the ability to lead.

A commentator once observed: "If you have something important to communicate, if you can possibly manage it—put your hand over your mouth and point." Someday we will learn what a great handicap language is.

Withdrawal—Finding One's Optimum

People who go for leadership (whether they are servants or non-servants) may be viewed as one of two extreme types. There are those who are so constituted physically and emotionally that they like pressure—seek it out—and they perform best when they are totally intense. And there are those who do not like pressure, do not thrive under it, but who want to lead and are willing to endure the pressure in order to have the opportunity. The former welcome a happy exhaustion and the latter are constantly in defense against that state. For both the art of withdrawal is useful. To the former it is a change of pace; to the latter it is a defense against an unpleasant state. The former may be more the natural leader; the latter needs a tactic to survive. The art of withdrawal serves them both.

The ability to withdraw and reorient oneself, if only for a moment, presumes that one has learned the art of systematic neglect, to sort out the more important from the less important—and the important from the urgent—and attend to the more important, even though there may be penalties and censure for the neglect of something else. One may govern one's life by the law of the optimum (optimum being that pace and set of choices that give one the best performance over a lifespan)—bearing in mind that there are always emergencies and the optimum includes carrying an unused reserve of energy in all periods of normal demand so that one has the resilience to cope with the emergency.

Pacing oneself by appropriate withdrawal is one of the best approaches to making optimal use of one's resources. The servant-as-leader must constantly ask: How can I use myself to serve best?

Acceptance and Empathy

These are two interesting words, acceptance and empathy. If we can take one dictionary's definition, acceptance is receiving what is offered, with approbation, satisfaction, or acquiescence, and empathy is the imaginative projection of one's own consciousness into another being. The opposite of both, the word reject, is to refuse to hear or receive—to throw.

The servant always accepts and empathizes, never rejects. The servant as leader always empathizes, always accepts the person but sometimes refuses to accept some of the person's effort or performance as good enough.

A college president once said, "An educator may be rejected by students and must not object to this. But one may never, under any circumstances, regardless of what they do, reject a single student."

We have known this a long time in the family. For a family to be a family, no one can ever be rejected. Robert Frost in his poem "The Death of the Hired Man" states the problem in a conversation on the farmhouse porch between the farmer and his wife about the shiftless hired man, Silas, who has come back to their place to die. The farmer is irritated about this because Silas was lured away from his farm in the middle of the last haying season. The wife says that theirs is the only home he has. They are then drawn into a discussion of what a home is. The husband gives his view:

> "Home is the place where, when you have to go there, they have to take you in." [The wife sees it differently. What is a home? She says,] "I should have called it Something you somehow haven't to deserve."

Because of the vagaries of human nature, the halt, the lame, half-made creatures that we all are, the great leader (whether it is the mother in her home or the head of a vast organization) would say what the wife said about home in Robert Frost's poem. The interest in and affection for one's followers which a leader has—and it is a mark of true greatness when it is genuine—is clearly something the followers "haven't to deserve." Great leaders, including "little" people, may have gruff, demanding, uncompromising exteriors. But deep down inside the great ones have empathy and an unqualified acceptance of the persons of those who go with their leadership.

Acceptance of the person, though, requires a tolerance of imperfection. Anybody could lead perfect people—if there were any. But there aren't any perfect people. And the parents who try to raise perfect children are certain to raise neurotics.

It is a part of the enigma of human nature that the "typical" person—immature, stumbling, inept, lazy—is capable of great dedication and heroism if wisely led. Many otherwise able people are disqualified to lead because they cannot work with and through the half-people who are all there are. The secret of institution building is to be able to weld a team of such people by lifting them up to grow taller than they would otherwise be.

People grow taller when those who lead them empathize and when they are accepted for what they are, even though their performance may be judged critically in terms of what they are capable of doing. Leaders who empathize and who fully accept those who go with them on this basis are more likely to be trusted.

Community—The Lost Knowledge of These Times

Men and women once lived in communities, and, in the developing world, many still do. Human society can be much better than it is (or was) in primitive communities. But if community itself is lost in the process of development, will what is put in its place survive? At the moment there seems to be some question. What is our experience?

Within my memory, we once cared for orphaned children in institutions. We have largely abandoned these institutions as not good for children. Children need the love of a real home—in a family, a community.

Now we realize that penal institutions, other than focusing the retributive vengeance of society and restraining anti-social actions for a period, do very little to rehabilitate. In fact they dehabilitate and return more difficult offenders to society. What should we do with these people? It is now suggested that most of them should be kept in homes, in community.

There is now the beginning of questioning of the extensive building of hospitals. We need some hospitals for extreme cases. But much of the recent expansion has been done for the convenience of doctors and families, not for the good of patients—or even for the good of families. Only community can give the healing love that is essential for health. Besides, the skyrocketing cost of such extensive hospital care is putting an intolerable burden on health-care systems.

The school, on which we pinned so much of our hopes for a better society, has become too much a social-upgrading mechanism that destroys community. Now we have the beginnings of questioning of the school as we know it, as a specialized, separate-from-community institution. And much of the alienation and purposelessness of our times is laid at the door, not of education, but of the school.

We are in the process of moving away from institutional care for the mentally retarded and toward small community-like homes. Recent experience suggests that, whereas the former provides mostly custodial care, the small community can actually lift them up, help them grow. Now the care of old people is a special concern, because there are so many more of them and they live so much longer. But the current trend is to put them in retirement homes that segregate the old from the normal community. Already there is the suggestion that these are not the happy places that were hoped for. Will retirement homes shortly be abandoned as orphan homes were?

As a generalization, I suggest that human service that requires love cannot be satisfactorily dispensed by specialized institutions that exist apart from community, that take the problem out of sight of the community. Both those being cared for and the community suffer.

Love is an undefinable term, and its manifestations are both subtle and infinite. But it begins, I believe, with one absolute condition: unlimited liability! As soon as one's liability for another is qualified to any degree, love is diminished by that much.

UNIT
2

Institutions, as we know them, are designed to limit liability for those who serve through them. In the British tradition, corporations are not "INC" as we know them, but "LTD"—Limited. Most of the goods and services we now depend on will probably continue to be furnished by such limited liability institutions. But any human service where the one who is served should be loved in the process requires community, a face-to-face group in which the liability of each for the other and all for one is unlimited, or as close to it as it is possible to get. Trust and respect are highest in this circumstance and an accepted ethic that gives strength to all is reinforced. Where there is not community; trust, respect, and ethical behavior are difficult for the young to learn and for the old to maintain. Living in community as one's basic involvement will generate an exportable surplus of love which the individual may carry into his many involvements with institutions which are usually not communities: businesses, churches, governments, schools.

Out of the distress of our seeming community-less society, hopeful new forms of community are emerging: young people's communes, Israeli kibbutzes, and therapeutic communities like Synanon. Seen through the bias of conventional morality, the communes are sometimes disturbing to the older generation. But among them is a genuine striving for community, and they represent a significant new social movement which may foretell the future.

The opportunities are tremendous for rediscovering vital lost knowledge about how to live in community while retaining as much as we can of the value in our present urban, institution-bound society.

All that is needed to rebuild community as a viable life form for large numbers of people is for enough servant-leaders to show the way, not by mass movements, but by each servant-leader demonstrating his own unlimited liability for a quite specific community-related group.

From Servant Leadership: A Journey into the Nature of Legitimate Power & Greatness by Robert K. Greenleaf. Copyright © 2002. Used by permission of Paulist Press.

Reverence

By Paul Woodruff

Points to Consider

1. How can a deep understanding of your human limitations enhance your leadership skills?

2. Woodruff states that reverence is compatible "with almost every form of mockery. Reverence and a keen eye for the ridiculous are allies: both keep people from being pompous or stuck up." How can both reverence and mockery be qualities of an effective group leader?

3. Can an organization demonstrate reverence? What examples can you think of that show an organization demonstrating reverence or irreverence?

4. Is it irreverent to seek to achieve peace through war? Is it always irreverent to believe that the end justifies the means? Explain.

Reverence

Reverence is an ancient virtue that survives among us in half forgotten patterns of civility, in moments of inarticulate awe, and in nostalgia for the lost ways of traditional cultures. We have the word "reverence" in our language, but we scarcely know how to use it. Right now it has no place in secular discussions of ethics or political theory. Even more surprisingly, reverence is missing from modern discussions of the ancient cultures that prized it.

Reverence begins in a deep understanding of human limitations; from this grows the capacity to be in awe of whatever we believe lies outside our control—God, truth, justice, nature, even death. The capacity for awe, as it grows, brings with it the capacity for respecting fellow human beings, flaws and all. This in turn fosters the ability to be ashamed when we show moral flaws exceeding the normal human allotment. The Greeks before Plato saw reverence as one of the bulwarks of society, and the immediate followers of Confucius in China thought much the same. Both groups wanted to see reverence in their leaders, because reverence is the virtue that keeps leaders from trying to take tight control of other people's lives. Simply put, reverence is the virtue that keeps human beings from trying to act like gods.

To forget that you are only human, to think you can act like a god—this is the opposite of reverence. Ancient Greeks thought that tyranny was the height of irreverence, and they gave the famous name of *hubris* to the crimes of tyrants. An irreverent soul is arrogant and shameless, unable to feel awe in the face of things higher than itself. As a result, an irreverent soul is unable to feel respect for people it sees as lower than itself—ordinary people, prisoners, children. The two failures go together, in both Greek and Chinese traditions. If an emperor has a sense of awe, this will remind him that Heaven is his superior—that he is, as they said in ancient China, the Son of Heaven. And any of us is better for remembering that there is someone, or Someone, to whom we are children; in this frame of mind we are more likely to treat all children with respect. And vice versa: If you cannot bring yourself to respect children, you are probably deficient in the ability to feel that anyone or anything is higher than you.

Reverence has more to do with politics than with religion. We can easily imagine religion without reverence; we see it, for example, wherever religion leads people into aggressive war or violence. But power without reverence—that is a catastrophe for all concerned. Power without reverence is aflame with arrogance, while service without reverence is smoldering toward rebellion. Politics without reverence is blind to the general good and deaf to advice from people who are powerless. And life without reverence? Entirely without reverence? That would be brutish and selfish, and it had best be lived alone.

It is a natural mistake to think that reverence belongs to religion. It belongs, rather, to community. Wherever people try to act together, they hedge themselves around with some form of ceremony or good manners, and the observance of this can be an act of reverence. Reverence lies behind civility and all of the graces that make life in society bearable and pleasant. But in our time we hear more praise of *ir*reverence than we do of reverence, especially in the media. That is because we naturally delight in mockery and we love making fun of solemn things. It is not because, in our heart of hearts, we despise reverence. In my view, the media are using the word "irreverent" for qualities that are not irreverent at all. A better way to say what they have in mind would be "bold, boisterous, unrefined, unimpressed by pretension"—all good things. Reverence is compatible with these and with almost every form of mockery. The one great western philosopher who praises reverence is Nietzsche, who is also the most given to mockery. Reverence and a keen eye for the ridiculous are allies: both keep people from being pompous or stuck up. So don't think that this book is an attack on laughter. Far from it.

UNIT

2

Another easy mistake to make about reverence is to confuse it with respect. Respect is sometimes good and sometimes bad, sometimes wise and sometimes silly. It is silly to respect the pratings of a pompous fool; it is wise to respect the intelligence of any student. Reverence calls for respect only when respect is really the right attitude. To pay respect to a tyrant would not be reverent; it would be weak and cowardly. The most reverent response to a tyrant is to mock him. All of this is because reverence is a kind of virtue. A virtue is a capacity to do what is right, and what is right in a given case—say, respect or mockery for an authority figure—depends on many things.

Reverence is one of the strengths in any good person's character. Such strengths are called "virtues," and the study of virtues forms an important branch of ethics. Virtue ethics makes a strong assumption: that some people are better than others because they have greater strengths of character—stronger virtues, in other words. Virtues are sources of good behavior. Moral rules and laws set standards for doing right, but there is nothing about a rule that makes you feel like following it. In fact, there is something about many rules that makes most people feel like breaking them. According to virtue ethics, a good person is one who feels like doing what is right. People who do good are aware of moral rules, but so are people who do bad. The difference is virtue. Virtue is the source of the feelings that prompt us to behave well. Virtue ethics takes feelings seriously because feelings affect our lives more deeply than beliefs do.

Virtue ethics holds that you learn a virtue as your capacity for feelings is attuned over years of experience. You may learn rules intellectually, and therefore you may learn or forget them very quickly. But virtues are habits of feeling, and these are much harder to learn or to forget. A fine violin that has not been played for many years will not stay in tune, and when it is first played it will have an ugly sound. A superior instrument must be played well, year after year, for it to sound beautiful. So it is with moral character. You may have as good equipment as anyone, but if your feelings have not been well played upon over the years, you will not stay in tune, and you will not respond well to life's challenges.

Virtues grow in us through being used. And they are used mainly by people living or working together. A family develops common virtues by the way its members live together, a team by the way its members play together, and so on. If you are surrounded by vice, you will find it hard to stay in tune with virtue. By the same token, a team or family will find it hard to cultivate virtues unless every member helps. Virtue ethics, then, deals with strengths that people develop in communities. Communities, in turn, depend on the strengths of their members.

I am interested in the virtues we should be cultivating today, as I write. But I begin my work from two classic models, one ancient Greek, and the other ancient Chinese, because of their clarity, their beauty, and their apparent difference from each other. These two ancient civilizations were set too far apart to have any communication (unlike India, which had early communication with both). If we find a common thread in Greek and Chinese ideals, we should take it seriously. It may well turn out to be a kind of thread that any society needs if it is to sew itself into an enduring shape. If so, reverence is a cardinal virtue, like justice or courage, and not the particular property of this culture or that. I don't think we should imitate ancient Greek or Chinese culture, but I believe we are better off for studying them. Both peoples cared deeply and thought long about the meaning of ceremonies in the texture of their religious and political lives, and in this meaning they saw the deeper value of reverence.

We have ceremonies in our own times too, but we try not to think about what they mean. In fact, I believe reverence gives meaning to much that we do, yet the word has almost passed out of our vocabulary. Because we do not understand reverence, we don't really know what we are doing in much of our lives, and therefore we are in no position to think about how to do it better.

Defining Reverence

Reverence compels me to confess that I do not know exactly what reverence is. I can't do any better for justice or courage or wisdom, though I have a pretty good idea in each case. Take courage. I would say that courage is a well-developed capacity for feeling confidence and fear in the right places, at the right times, and in the right degrees of intensity; that is, courage lies somewhere between fearlessness (which often looks like courage) and timidity (which no one would mistake for courage). This account of courage has a grand history—it comes from Aristotle—but is hardly a complete definition. I would call it a definition-schema—something like a form full of blanks that we need to fill in as best we can, after life experience and critical reflection. The schema for courage tells us that we can't go wrong by being courageous, but it does not tell us how to be courageous. It points to a distinction between courage and fearless, but it does not spell out the difference between them—aside from the obvious point that one is always good while the other can go too far. Before filling in the blanks in the schema we would need to know the difference between right and wrong. That looks easy enough in some cases, but it seems to call for divine wisdom in others.

I cannot claim divine wisdom, and so I cannot offer a full account of any of the virtues, least of all reverence. My schema for reverence looks like this: Reverence is the well-developed capacity to have the feelings of awe, respect, and shame when these are the right feelings to have. This says that reverence is a good thing, but not much more, except by pointing to further questions. Sometimes it is right to be respectful and sometimes wrong; that's obvious. Sometimes our feelings should rise to the level of awe, but not always. So when should we be respectful, and how deep should our respect be in each case? Of what should we be in awe? No capsule definition will tell you. Nor can any human wisdom give you a complete and final answer. The best answer I can give is this book.

Some writers use the words "reverence" and "respect" as synonyms, but these words are not synonyms in this book. I need one word for an ideal, "Reverence," and other words for the feelings—respect, awe, and shame—that may or may not serve that ideal. You can never follow an ideal too closely, but you can have too much—or too little—of the feelings to which it gives rise. You are too lavish with awe, for example, if you are in awe of your own wisdom and treat it as sacred. That's arrogant, and it's not much better if you feel that way about the accumulated wisdom of your own tradition, for both are human products. On the other hand, you are too niggardly with awe if you never feel awe for a great whale, a majestic redwood, or a range of tall mountains. You need not enjoy these things—awe can be frightening, after all—and you need not be moved by them every time you encounter them. But if you do not have the capacity to be awestruck at the sight of the majesties of nature you are missing part of the usual human endowment.

Why This Book

The topic surprised me. I never expected to write a book about reverence, but I came to this as I explored material for a footnote to a chapter I was writing in a still unfinished tome on ancient Greek humanism. But I soon came to think that this abandoned topic deserves to have a new life.

My footnote was on Thucydides, the most thoughtful of the ancient Greek historians. Writing in the fifth and fourth centuries BCE, Thucydides adopted the humanist position that gods do not intervene in human affairs. He believed that purely human currents in history would bring the most of the results that traditional thinkers expected from the gods: If a tyrant rises too far and too fast, or if he exercises his power with too much arrogance, other people will fear him and hate him, and they—not the gods—will unite to bring him down. But if the gods never punish human beings, why bother with reverence? I used to think that it was only fear of the gods that made the ancient Greeks reverent. Thucydides does not seem to fear the gods, but he fears human arrogance, and therefore he cares a great deal about reverence, which he treats as a cardinal virtue. Some scholars argue, in spite of appearances, that he does believe the gods punish human beings when they violate reverence. But then why doesn't he say so? That was the puzzle I took on in my footnote.

The footnote exploded as I went deeper and deeper into the concept of reverence. I had been content in former years to accept Plato's view that reverence is not a primary virtue at all. Plato taught that all you need do for reverence is to practice the other virtues that the gods favor, principally justice. Plato was afraid that the Greeks of his day were trying to use reverence to win over the gods, in the hope that the gods would forgive any kind of wickedness on the part of people who gave abundant sacrifices. That is why Plato treated reverence as a part of justice, so that no one would think you could be reverent without also being just. But if reverence is part of justice, then you will have it all if you cultivate justice as a whole—as you should—and you need not spend another moment's thought on reverence.

After Plato, I turned to the ancient poets and became disenchanted with Plato's simple theory. From Homer through Euripides, the poets treat reverence as a substantial virtue, and I began to see their point. More surprising, I began to suspect that reverence has more to do with power than with religion. I was struck by the fact that Thucydides prizes reverence while condemning credulity in people who persist in seeing a divine plan behind the natural consequences of their own mistakes. If Thucydides believes that reverence is good but that credulity is foolish, he is plainly thinking of reverence as a moral virtue that is detachable from traditional beliefs about the gods. Could this be possible? Could reverence be detached from belief? The answer turned out to be complicated. Reverence depends to some extent on belief, but not at all on formal creeds. And so I realized with shock and delight that reverence could—in theory, at least—be shared across religions. In fact, what religious people today admire in other religions cannot be faith (since they reject most of the content of other faiths), but reverence. So they know about reverence, though they don't know to call it by that name.

I began to feel that something has been lost in modern times. This virtue, so important to the ancients, has fallen beneath the horizon of our intellectual vision. And yet reverence is all around us, even in the most ordinary ceremonies of our lives. It is as if we have forgotten one of the cylinders that has been chugging along in the vehicle of human society since its beginning. And now, because we do not know the cylinder is there, we have no idea how to tune it up, or even how we might gum it up completely by inattention. The more I pondered this, the more I wanted to know what reverence is, not just to the ancient Greeks, but for us, for all of us trying to live good human lives. If reverence is a cardinal virtue, it belongs to the family of justice and courage and wisdom, and those are ideals that bear study in their own right, not merely as they occur within the boundaries of this or that culture.

My quest for universal reverence took me out of ancient Greece and across to ancient China, back to the European tradition and to writers of our own time. I soon found that I had been reading the wrong books. Most modern philosophers have forgotten about reverence. But poets are aware of it, as they have always been. I might have expected that Yeats would turn out to be a poet of reverence. And Tennyson. But Philip Larkin? This has all been a delightful surprise.

In studying reverence I have come to a new view about how ethics should be discussed and about how a book like this should be written. A writer who is serious about virtue can't stay behind the boundaries of a single academic discipline; the subject brings together poetry and philosophy and the history of ideas and puts them all to work on a huge live wire of a question—how should we live our lives. Also, a writer about virtue must not expect to deliver the sharp-edged definitions or the clear criteria that some philosophers crave. Aristotle urges us—with virtue in mind—not to ask the same precision of ethics that we would of mathematics. Poets often understand virtues better than philosophers, so that the wisdom of poets over time is essential to this subject. Also essential to the study of virtue is the experience that you, the reader, bring to the subject. Virtues are about emotions, and you can't learn much about emotions from a book. I could write a volume ten times the length of this one, and it would still leave many questions for you to work out on your own. Reverent students of ethics will understand that this is a project not for a book but a lifetime.

Why Reverence?

Why write about reverence? Because we have forgotten what it means. Because reverence fosters leadership and education. Most important, because reverence kindles warmth in friendship and family life. And because without reverence, things fall apart. People do not know how to respect each other and themselves. An army cannot tell the difference between what it is and a gang of bandits. Without reverence, we cannot explain why we should treat the natural world with respect. Without reverence, a house is not a home, a boss is not a leader, an instructor is not a teacher. Without reverence, we would not even know how to learn reverence. To teach reverence, you must find the seeds of reverence in each person and help them grow.

Religious wars are endemic in our time, which is a time with little care for reverence. Perhaps these wars are cooling down in some places, but they are heating up in others, even as I write this book. If a religious group thinks it speaks and acts as God commands in all things, this is a failure of reverence. A group like that may turn violent and feel they are doing so in good faith. Nothing is more dangerous than that feeling.

War is nothing new, and neither are killer strains of religion, pathogens that take hold of a people and send them into paroxysms of violence. War and religion will always be with us; we can't expect to shake them off. But we can ask what it is in religion that might keep the dogs of war on leash, and what it is that whips them into a frenzy and lets them loose. It is reverence that moderates war in all times and cultures, irreverence that urges it on to brutality. The voices that call in the name of God for aggressive war have lost sight of human limitations. They have lost reverence, even when they serve a religious vision. So it is when a people believe that their god commands them to take land from others, or insists that they force others into their way of thinking. Even when the goal of war is something as noble as freedom or peace, it may be irreverent to think we can impose these goals by violence.

When Agamemnon waited on the beach with his ships and chariots and with the men who hungered to capture Troy, the winds remained hostile, and he asked a diviner what he should do. He had faith in his diviner, and the diviner had faith in his power to speak for the gods. He said he knew what the gods desired—the life of the king's daughter. And so Iphigenia came, summoned to her wedding in all the veiled finery of the bride. At the altar stood her father with the priest. But there was no young husband, only the great sharp knife poised to end her life.

The poet Lucretius tells this take, as I have done, to be the introduction for his work of philosophy. He ends with the strong line, *tantum religio potuit suadere malorum* (1.101)—"so great is the power of religion to lead us to evil." He gives us Iphigenia to stand for all the huge unholy cost of war when it is driven by men who believe they know what the gods want. But he does not mean to condemn everything that falls under religion. Lucretius may be hostile to some kinds of faith, but he begins his work with an invocation to the goddess who stands for Nature. He too is a poet of reverence.

Reverence runs across religions and even outside them through the fabric of community, however secular. We may be divided from one another by our beliefs, but never by reverence. If you desire peace in the world, do not pray that everyone share your beliefs: Pray instead that all may be reverent.

Woodruff, Paul. (2001). Introducing Reverence. In *Reverence: Renewing a Forgotten Virtue*. Oxford University Press. Pp. 1–15.

"The Fixed Determination of an Indomitable Will— Florence Nightingale, England: Nursing"

By David Bornstein

Points to Consider

1. Based on this reading, what are the characteristics that enabled Nightingale to exercise leadership in the nursing field? How do these characteristics compare to those outlined by Greenleaf and Lopez in discussing servant leaders?

2. Nightingale's family discouraged her from pursuing nursing because of the "low moral standards" associated with the profession at the time. How and why did the perception of the nursing profession change? Can you think of professions in today's society that may struggle to attract an adequate workforce due to a low public perception of its importance or potential? What might someone who exercises leadership change in the profession that could lead to changed public perception?

3. Despite her own health conditions, Nightingale still managed to be successful in her quest "to initiate new orders of things." How was she able to effect this change? What are some skills that are necessary to lead an organization through a period of dramatic change?

4. The author states, "The existence of knowledge and the widespread application of knowledge are very different things." Other than in the field of medicine, where can you see this gap in today's society?

5. Define "social entrepreneurism" as it relates to Nightingale's journey in changing the health care system of Victorian England.

"The Fixed Determination of an Indomitable Will— Florence Nightingale, England: Nursing"

When Drayton calls someone a leading social entrepreneur, he is describing a specific and rare personality type. He doesn't mean a businesswoman who gives jobs to homeless people or devotes a percentage of profits to the environmental movement. He doesn't mean someone running a nonprofit organization who has developed a business to generate revenue. He means someone like Florence Nightingale.

Most people know a little about the "lady of the lamp" who tended to British soldiers during the Crimean War. But what did Florence Nightingale really do? Why are nursing students still assigned Nightingale's 1860 book *Notes on Nursing: What It Is and What It is Not?*[1]

In *Eminent Victorians*, biographer Lytton Strachey observes that, as children in the nursery, while Florence Nightingale's sister displayed "a healthy pleasure in tearing her dolls to pieces," young Florence already displayed "an almost morbid one in sewing them up again." As a girl, Nightingale was driven "to minister to the poor in their cottages, to watch by sick-beds, to put her dog's wounded paw into elaborate splints as if it was a human being." She imagined her family's country home turned into a hospital "with herself as matron moving about among the beds."[2]

In 1845, at the age of twenty-five, Nightingale expressed a desire to work as a nurse in Salisbury Hospital. But when her father, William, a wealthy landowner, was informed of the low moral standards then associated with nursing, he forbade his daughter to take the position. For a woman of wealth and social standing in Victorian England, seeking work was odd enough; seeking work as a nurse was almost unimaginable. At the time a "nurse" implied "a coarse old woman, always ignorant, usually dirty, often brutal…in bunched-up sordid garments, tippling at the brandy bottle or indulging in worse irregularities."[3]

Nightingale was devastated by her family's refusal. Still, she found ways to apprentice herself. On family trips to London and European capitals, she toured hospitals, slums, schools, and workhouses. Privately, she studied the history of hospitals and convalescent homes and devoured reports from sanitary authorities and medical commissions. After a friend sent her a copy of the yearbook of the Institution of Protestant Deaconesses at Kaiserswerth, Germany, which trained girls of good character to nurse the sick, Nightingale fought with her parents for four years until she was permitted to take the training course.

When a suitor made an offer of marriage, Nightingale declined. She was torn between her "passional nature" and her "moral" and "active nature." Although she found her suitor attractive and intellectually stimulating, she felt the need to remain independent to pursue her work—even though her family still opposed it. "In my thirty-first year," she wrote, "I see nothing desirable but death."[4]

In 1853, at age thirty-three, Nightingale was finally permitted to accept an unpaid position as superintendent of the Institution for the Care of Sick Gentlewomen in London, where she gained a reputation as an excellent administrator. Then, in the fall of 1854, English soldiers were dispatched to Crimea, on the north coast of the Black Sea, to fight alongside Turkish forces at war with Russia. Through the advent of war journalism, the English public began receiving reports about wounded soldiers in the Crimean campaign being left to die without basic medical attention.

In response to the public outcry, on October 15, 1854, Nightingale's friend, Sidney Herbert, secretary at war, sent her a letter asking if she would take charge of nursing in the military hospitals in Scutari, a district of Istanbul. Herbert's words were prescient: "If this succeeds…a prejudice will have been broken through and a precedent established which will multiply the good to all time."[5]

Nightingale had already sent a letter to Herbert offering her services; within six days she had assembled thirty-eight nurses and departed for Constantinople. When she arrived in Scutari on November 4, Nightingale encountered a catastrophe: total system collapse. The barracks and general hospitals contained almost 2,400 sick and wounded soldiers. They lay in filthy clothes along four miles of cots. Not only were basic surgical and medical supplies unavailable, the hospital barracks were infested with rats and fleas, and the wards stank from underground sewage. Water was tightly rationed. Cholera, typhus, and dysentery were endemic, causing deaths almost at the rate of one in two—deaths that Nightingale found were not even being properly recorded in hospital registers.

The army surgeons thought it preposterous that the War Office had dispatched a boatload of civilian women to the rescue, and promptly informed Nightingale that her nurses would not be permitted to enter the wards. However, within days, the doctors had no choice but to solicit Nightingale's assistance following the Battle of Inkerman, when more than 500 soldiers, suffering from wounds, malnutrition, exposure, dysentery, and scurvy, began lining the hospital corridors on straw litters. "In all our corridor, I think we have not an average of three Limbs per man," wrote Nightingale.[6]

Immediately Nightingale set out to fix the system that was producing such a high death toll. She requisitioned 200 scrubbing brushes and saw to it that the wards were cleaned and the soldiers' clothes were taken outside for washing. She visited the army purveyor to see what could be done about the supply shortages. When he proved uncooperative, Nightingale took over his job, using the £30,000 (raised from private donations) that she had brought with her. When she discovered that supplies were being held up in Turkish customs, she persuaded the War Office to straighten out the problem. She raised additional funds from private sources in England and built a warehouse for supplies. When she received advance word of an impending battle, over the surgeons' objections she authorized the construction of new ward.[7]

With a combination of tact, good sense, political influence, and calm authority, Nightingale reorganized the military hospitals in Scutari. She introduced meticulous record-keeping, built new kitchens and laundry rooms, and made sure that soldiers ate with sterilized cutlery, washed with fresh towels and soap, and wore clothes that had been laundered in boiled water. She made nightly rounds to comfort patients, speaking in a "soft, silvery voice."[8] She established reading rooms, recreation rooms, classes and lectures, and even got soldiers to send remittances home, a feat the army had deemed impossible. Soldiers stopped cursing when Nightingale was in earshot. Their morale soared. They came to adore her. In February 1855 the death rate in the British army hospitals in Scutari was 43 percent; by May it had dropped to 2 percent.[9]

"Certainly she was heroic," Strachey wrote. "Yet her heroism was not of that simple sort so dear to the readers of novels and the compilers of hagiologies—the romantic sentimental heroism with which mankind loves to invest its chosen darlings: it was made of sterner stuff....It was not by gentle sweetness and womanly self-abnegation that she brought order out of chaos in Scutari Hospitals, that, from her own resources, she had clothed the British Army, that she had spread her dominion over the serried and reluctant powers of the official world; it was by strict method, by stern discipline, by rigid attention to detail, by ceaseless labor, by the fixed determination of an indomitable will."[10]

After the war, Nightingale returned to England a national heroine. But she declined all public receptions and accepted only those invitations—such as an interview with Queen Victoria—that could advance her work, which she now determined was to improve the health of the British army.

Because of poor sanitation, ventilation, and food in army barracks, mortality rates among soldiers in England were nearly double those for civilians. "[Allowing such a high mortality rate] is as criminal...as it would be to take 1,100 men per annum out upon Salisbury Plain and shoot them," Nightingale wrote.[11] The weapon she wielded in this battle was not a lamp, but an extensive collection of health statistics.

As a young woman, Nightingale pleaded with her father to teach her mathematics. She was deeply influenced by the development in her day of the theory of probability, particularly the work of the Belgian statistician Adolphe Quételet, who is regarded as one of the founders of modern social statistics. Nightingale believed that statistics were a means of discerning the will of God.

After returning from Turkey, she worked with the leading statistician in England, William Farr, and produced and printed at her own expense an 800-page book entitled *Notes on Matters Affecting the Health, Efficiency and Hospital Administration of the British Army* (1858), which featured an extensive statistical analysis of the causes of sickness and death in the army. Nightingale was a pioneer in the use of graphical tools (such as polar-area or "pie" charts), which she employed to dramatize the need for change. She went so far as to frame her statistical charts and present them to officials in the army medical department and War Office.[12]

Nightingale didn't do these things in person. In fact, she rarely ventured outside her home. Having suffered from a bout of Crimean fever during the war, she suffered thereafter from frequent fainting fits and chronic physical exhaustion, and remained bedridden much of the remainder of her life. Yet from her sofa, she greeted countless visitors, and issued an unending stream of orders, memos, and letters to a group of devotees.

She operated principally through her friend and political ally Sidney Herbert, who pushed for the establishment of a series of Royal Commissions to investigate health in the military and in society. As a woman, Nightingale was not permitted to sit on these commissions, but she guided their recommendations and ensured that they were carried out. Due to her efforts, the army established a medical school and statistical department and remodeled barracks across the country. Among other things, Nightingale taught the British army about the salutary effects of sunlight, pure water, and clean kitchens. In two and a half years, the mortality rate among troops in England was cut in half.[13]

Nightingale later applied the same strategy in India, where the death rate for British troops was *six* times higher than the rate for civilian young men in England. Through sanitary reforms, between 1863 and 1873, the annual mortality rate of soldiers in India was reduced by 75 percent.[14]

In 1859 Nightingale published the first edition of *Notes on Hospitals*, which would go on to revolutionize the theory of hospital construction. In 1860, with the support of contributions from the public, she established the Nightingale Training School for Nurses, based on the principle that nurses should receive instruction in teaching hospitals while residing in homes that formed moral character. In so doing, Nightingale began the process that transformed nursing into a modern, respectable profession. Over the next four decades the number of nurses in Britain increased from 28,000 to 64,000. Perhaps more telling, by the end of the nineteenth century, nursing had been reclassified in the British Census from the list of occupations headed "Domestics" to the list headed "Medicine."[15]

Nightingale never recovered from the Crimean fever she suffered while in her thirties. For five and a half decades after her return to England until her death in 1910, she continued to experience fainting fits and often was too weak to stand. Nevertheless, during her life, she authored an estimated 12,000 letters and 200 books, reports, and monographs.

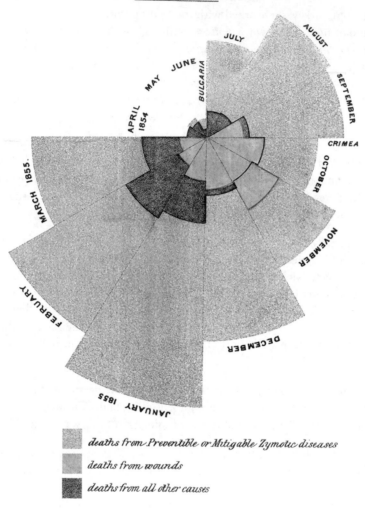

DIAGRAM OF THE CAUSES OF MORTALITY
IN THE ARMY IN THE EAST.

APRIL 1854 TO MARCH 1855.

deaths from Preventible or Mitigable Zymotic diseases

deaths from wounds

deaths from all other causes

In accordance with her wishes, Nightingale did not receive a national funeral and was not buried at Westminster Abbey.

"The first thought I can remember, and the last," she wrote, "was nursing work."[16]

As a child, I imagined Florence Nightingale to be sweet and gentle, which she was not. I certainly never thought of her as an administrator, statistician, or lobbyist. I still can't get used to thinking of her as an "entrepreneur," although she certainly fits the original definition, having increased the "productivity" or "yield" of healthcare resources by many orders of magnitude. In addition to blazing a trail for nurses, Nightingale established standards for sanitation and hospital management that have shaped norms worldwide.

Given the march of medical science over the past 150 years, one might imagine that these changes would have occurred with or without her. That is impossible to say. What we can say is that the existence of knowledge and the widespread application of knowledge are very different things. If knowledge alone were enough, millions of children would not still be dying each year of dehydration due to diarrhea. (Stopping these preventable deaths was the obsession of James P. Grant, whose work is detailed in Chapter 19 [of Bornstein's book, *How to Change the World: Social Entrepreneurs and the Power of New Ideas*].)

Changing a system means changing attitudes, expectations, and behaviors. It means overcoming disbelief, prejudice, and fear. Old systems do not readily embrace new ideas or information; defenders of the status quo can be stubbornly impervious to common sense, as Nightingale's many battles with British army officers can attest. In his classic analysis of politics and power, *The Prince*, Niccolò Machiavelli observed: "[T]here is nothing more difficult to carry out, nor more doubtful of success, nor more dangerous to handle, than to initiate a new order of things. For the reformer has enemies in all those who profit by the old order, and only lukewarm defenders in all those who would profit by the new order."[17]

This may be one reason why society needs ethically driven social entrepreneurs like Florence Nightingale to break out of negative patterns and to initiate new orders of things. It takes concentrated focus, practical creativity, and a long-term source of energy to advance a system change and to ensure that the change becomes well rooted in institutions and cultures. Certain people, because of the quality of their motivation—their inexplicable obsessions, their action and growth orientation, their unwavering belief in the rightness of their ideas—seem particularly well suited to lead this process.

NOTES

1. The Florence Nightingale section is drawn from the following sources: Florence Nightingale, *Notes on Nursing* (New York: Dover Publications, 1969); Lytton Strachey, *Eminent Victorians* (New York: Modern Library, 1999); Cecil Woodham-Smith, *Florence Nightingale* (New York: McGraw-Hill, 1951); Edward Tyas Cook, *The Life of Florence Nightingale*, vols. 1 and 2 (New York: Macmillan, 1913); Michael D. Calabria and Janet A. Macrae, eds., *Suggestions for Thought, by Florence Nightingale, Selections and Commentaries* (Philadelphia: University of Pennsylvania Press, 1994); Martha Vicinus and Bea Nergaard, eds., *Ever yours, Florence Nightingale, Selected Letters* (London: Varago Press, 1989); *Encyclopaedia Brittanica*, 2001 CD-ROM Edition, entry on "Florence Nightingale"; I. Bernard Cohen, "Florence Nightingale," *Scientific American*, 250 (March 1984): 128–37; and Edwin W. Kopf, "Florence Nightingale as Statistician," *Journal of the American Statistical Association*, 15, Issue 116 (December 1916): 388–404.

2. Strachey, *Eminent Victorians*, 102.

3. Ibid., 103.

4. Ibid., 105.

5. Cook, *The Life of Florence Nightingale*, vol. 1, 153.

6. The description of the scene in Scutari is summarized from Cook, *The Life of Florence Nightingale*, vol. 1, 183–84.

7. Nightingale's administrative reforms are detailed in Strachey, *Eminent Victorians*, 108–16.

8. Cook, *The Life of Florence Nightingale*, vol. 1, 186.

9. Cohen, "Florence Nightingale," 131. The exact death rates in February and May 1855 were 42.7 and 2.2 percent respectively.

10. Strachey, *Eminent Victorians*, 116–17.

11. Ibid.

12. See Kopf, "Florence Nightingale as Statistician," 388–404; and Cohen, "Florence Nightingale," 128–37.

13. Cohen, "Florence Nightingale," 136–37.

14. The mortality rate among British troops in India was reduced from 69 to 18 per 1,000 from 1863 to 1873. Kopf, "Florence Nightingale as Statistician," 403.

15. Cohen, "Florence Nightingale," 137.

16. Strachey, *Eminent Victorians*, 105.

17. Niccolò Machiavelli, *The Prince* (New York: New American Library, 1980), 49–50.

Bornstein, David. *How to Change the World: Social Entrepreneurs and the Power of New Ideas*. Updated ed. Oxford: Oxford UP, 2007. Print.

"Becoming a Servant-Leader: The Personal Development Path"

By Isabel O. Lopez

Points to Consider

1. What strategies can/have you used to "know self well" as a leader? What are some ways that this concept is addressed in readings/activities in Unit 1: Developing a Personal Leadership Philosophy?

2. What strategies have you used or seen used to build community in a group? How might this process differ in a large organization, versus a small group?

3. Lopez states, "Builders of community understand the value of each person and how each person contributes to the whole. In workgroups, they insist on teams led by *primus inter pares*, or 'first among equals.'" Describe ways in which you have observed others effectively achieve this in group or organizational settings.

4. At the time of this writing, Lopez identifies a decline in trust and an increase in the fear of the future. How would you evaluate these attitudes today?

"Becoming a Servant-Leader: The Personal Development Path"

Becoming a Servant Leader

My earliest introduction to servant-leadership was my family: My mother, who cared, taught, guided, encouraged, and laughed; my grandmother, who imparted wisdom, joy, teachings, and acceptance of others; and my father, who taught me simplicity, honor and the capacity to love. How wonderful to be served—to have others in both our personal and institutional lives caring for us and being concerned with our growth as persons. I was lucky to have such models and to be on the receiving end of the actions of these simple and powerful servant-leaders.

When I went to school, I met other servant-leaders: Teachers who caused me to stretch, who encouraged, who loved. But, for the first time, I was also exposed to people who were leaders but not servants and to servants who were not leaders. Somewhere in the movement from family to institution, I began to learn about the dark side of life; not everyone was concerned with the other, and some were even invested in the failure, not the growth of others. Servant-leadership—leaders because they serve first. Then they are chosen to lead.

Robert Greenleaf defines the servant-leader as being a servant first. He acknowledges the difficulty of the term servant-leader. In workshops on servant-leadership, participants often struggle with this language. The traditional Western image of a leader is a person who is in charge and in control of others. The image of servant is one who is submissive, takes orders and does as told. How can one possibly be both?

If these are our images, do we even want to be servant-leaders? So we struggle with the correctness of these traditional images, begin to understand the limitations of our understanding, create new images, and still have trouble with being both a servant and a leader in action. This is the beginning of the path to becoming a servant leader—struggling with the paradox. Charles Handy, in *The Age of Paradox*, says, "Paradox...confuses us because it asks us to live with simultaneous opposites."

And besides dealing with the paradox, Greenleaf puts a test of our performance as servant-leaders before us. The test, in Greenleaf's words, is as follows: "The best test, and difficult to administer, is: Do those served grow as persons? Do they, while being served, become healthier, wiser, freer, more autonomous, more likely themselves to become servants? And what is the effect on the least privileged in society, will (s)he benefit, or at least not be further deprived?"

In order to develop our personal path to becoming servant leaders, it might be of help to review the steps that Greenleaf took. In his essay, "Old Age: The Ultimate Test of the Spirit," Greenleaf gives a retrospective. He says:

> So I, in my eighty-third year and with a much larger view of the world than my father had, now lament what seems the small number among those who see themselves as able, conscientious, and dedicated, and who are disposed to respond to a vision of the larger roles they might play and the much greater service to society that the institutions they influence might render. We have plenty of people with the stamina to build and lead a much more serving society and I believe they would lead fuller lives, if they would rise to their opportunities. What they seem to lack is spirit, and I wonder what they will be like when they grow old. Will they find it the 'best' that is yet to be? I said at the outset that I cannot define spirit. But I have tried in what I have said to give human spirit a meaning that is beyond rational definition.

Earlier in his essay, he says that "spirit can be said to be the driving force behind the motive to serve." Perhaps, Greenleaf, in his gentle way, smiles as more and more people are drawn to servant-leadership and toward developing themselves to be servant-leaders.

The steps that Robert Greenleaf took that resulted in his becoming a servant-leader are as follows:

- He took meditative intervals.
- He engaged in conversation with people.
- He analyzed his dreams.

He developed close relationships with several institutions.

  He became interested in the ethics of his company and developed relationships with others that had a similar interest.

Although he did not consider himself a scholar and did not focus on reading as part of his development at this time, he did read deeply into the history of two institutions: AT&T and the Religious Society of Friends.

What strikes me about Greenleaf's development path is that it was a path of self development that led to him becoming a servant-leader. As Director of Management Research at AT&T, he undoubtedly had developed his analytical skills: the skills that allowed him to analyze, see gaps, and refine information. His path to servant-leadership seemed to focus on the developing or deepening of new skills; those developed from other than the rational and that were relational in nature.

In becoming a servant-leader, this essay assumes that one has developed the logical and analytical skills that are taught, rewarded, and reinforced by our teaching institutions. This essay is also built around the premise that the mind is a tool of the heart—a concept that goes back to ancient Greece, or perhaps even further back. The personal development suggestions that will be made in this chapter focus on the characteristics of servant-leaders and how we might develop them in ourselves.

What **are** the characteristics of servant-leaders that we might emulate?

- Servant-leaders express unlimited liability for others.
- Servant-leaders know self well.
- Servant-leaders are holders of liberating vision.
- Servant-leaders are users of persuasion.
- Servant-leaders are builders of community.
- Servant-leaders use power ethically.

These characteristics will be explored one at a time.

Expressing Unlimited Liability for Others

This characteristic, as well as the others, is a difficult one. In our litigious society, we struggle with the implications of the legalistic framework of liability. Greenleaf speaks about liability in the context of "s/he who is served should be loved in the process" and that "living in community as one's basic involvement will generate an exportable surplus of love which the individual may carry into his or her many involvements with institutions…." So, there is a root of unconditional love in servant-leadership. How might we point ourselves in this direction?

First, we accept others as they are. This is a more spiritual than psychological approach. There is beauty in each person, and we focus on that beauty. I am reminded of one of Anthony De Mello's stories. In *The Song of the Bird*, he tells this story.

I was a neurotic for years. I was anxious and depressed and selfish. Everyone kept telling me to change. I resented them, and I agreed with them, and I wanted to change, but simply couldn't, no matter how hard I tried.

What hurt the most was that, like the others, my best friend kept insisting that I change. So I felt powerless and trapped. Then, one day, he said to me, "Don't change. I love you just as you are." These words were music to my ears; "don't change. Don't change. Don't change . . . I love you as you are."

I relaxed. I came alive. And suddenly I changed! Now I know that I couldn't really change until I found someone who would love me whether I changed or not.

Second, we must learn to empathize. This entails learning to walk in someone else's shoes. Being able to empathize is a sign of our maturity. Sympathy, on the other hand, only allows us to feel sorry for someone else. The outcome of acceptance and sympathy is that we will not reject the other and will therefore be practicing "unlimited liability."

To develop this characteristic, try the following exercises. When someone brings you a problem, an issue, or an idea, listen first. Do not assume you know what they want. Just listen. Listening is an intense activity. You may want to ask someone to talk to you for five minutes while you listen. After they have finished, repeat what you heard. Did you hear what they were saying? The more emotional the conversation, the more intense is the listening required. Ask yourself the following questions:

- Was I able to concentrate?
- Did I have other thoughts running through my head while the other person was talking?
- How often was I framing solutions to what I perceived was the "problem" rather than listening?

Although the practice of listening is intense, the opportunities to practice present themselves all the time.

Another activity that will help to develop the characteristic of expressing unlimited liability for others is to view those we serve as the acquirers rather than the recipients of service. In other words, they have a choice and we do not have all the answers for them. Practice asking questions rather than giving answers. Some questions you might ask are:

- How might I be of help?
- What is it that you need from me?
- What resources do I have that would be of use to you in your circumstances?
- How can I help you think through your choices in this matter?
- Would it be helpful for me to share my experiences with you?

Again, the opportunity to practice asking questions will present itself as often as the current opportunity to give answers does. The danger in providing our answers to someone else's issue is that our experience and circumstance may not match theirs.

Know Self Well

The development of this characteristic is critical to the servant-leader. The old Chinese saying, "S/he who feels punctured must have once been a balloon" speaks to this characteristic. Our actions can spring from our own needs for recognition, acknowledgement, and power unless we know ourselves well. The development of this characteristic is a life-long commitment, but is the foundation of becoming the servant-leaders of which Robert Greenleaf speaks.

One step we might take to know ourselves well is to be active learners who are immersed in the world. Greenleaf's learning path included conversing with people, developing institutional relationships, developing deeper relationships with people around a common interest, and doing some in-depth reading. We might engage in some of the same activities. Some guiding questions for us might be:

- Who is missing from my circle of friends and acquaintances? Missing might be people of color, people of other religious beliefs or lifestyles, people from other countries or areas of our country, or even people from professions different from ours.

- Who do I know that has relationships with a variety of people who are not part of my circle?

- What institutions do I know the least about? How might I find out more?

- Who is interested in some of the deeper issues that concern me? ✔

- In what areas do I normally read? How can I expand my learning through reading?

Another step we might take is to start inside ourselves and light our own lamps. Another De ✔ Mello story, *The Truth Shop*, talks to the difficulty of this step.

I could hardly believe my eyes when I saw the name of the shop: The Truth Shop.

The saleswoman was very polite: What type of truth did I wish to purchase, partial or whole? The whole truth, of course. No deceptions for me, no defenses, no rationalizations. I wanted my truth plain and unadulterated. She waved me on to another side of the store.

The salesman there pointed to the price tag. "The price is very high, Sir," he said. "What is it?" I asked, determined to get the whole truth, no matter what it cost. "Your security, Sir," he answered.

I came away with a heavy heart. I still need the safety of my unquestioned beliefs.

Starting inside ourselves requires a great commitment on our part. The value is that we know who we are, our behavior becomes more consistent, and we become worthy of the trust of others. Activities to engage in include the following:

- Analyze your dreams, as Greenleaf did.

- Keep a journal.

- Be aware of feedback that is given to us.

- Meditate.

- Find a teacher.

- Develop your own path.

Another step to take in knowing self is to withdraw, be silent, or reorient. This step is the place from which we gain perspective. With the speed of change in our world today, it is easy to lose perspective. Without perspective, we can too easily lose our way.

Hold a Liberating Vision

This characteristic is key in relationship to being allowed to serve, to helping point the way, and to allowing others to join us. A liberating vision will serve to enlarge and create spaces in which our work can become more focused, more excellent, and more apt to make a difference in both our personal and institutional lives. Elements of this characteristic include being comfortable with the use of intuition. Striving to embody this characteristic helps us to develop our foresight—we learn to see a way and point to it. Suggestions that might help us develop this characteristic are:

- Develop the creative part of you.
- Draw rather than write your ideas.
- Write a poem about your vision.
- Use metaphors to capture your ideas.
- Practice reading between the lines in written items.
- Practice hearing between the words in oral communication on both personal and business matters. (Sometimes what is spoken or written is only the surface.)
- Work at understanding what is really important to you, both personally and professionally.

Use Persuasion

This characteristic assumes that servant-leaders do not control others. Rather than control, they share their wisdom. Their approach is one person at a time while seeking always to develop understanding. Servant-leaders use this characteristic now, but the impact of their persuasion withstands the test of time and affects the future. Look at Greenleaf himself. His major essay was published 25 years ago. Today, his model of servant-leadership informs much of the current leadership literature.

Two basic principles underscore the use of persuasion in this context: one is the reinforcement of hope; the second is that others can do for themselves what they must do.

The use of this characteristic allows the servant-leader to offer hope to the cynical and to those who have forgotten how to hope. This characteristic also allows us to persuade others to see themselves as empowered people—we are not the empowerers. Suggestions in this area are:

- Check your own quotient of hope.
- Point out the possibilities for others.
- Develop a patient attitude.
- Do not expect quick results but notice the beginnings of change, the seedlings that are growing.
- Share your joy.
- Smile often.

Build Community

Builders of community invent the ways that we will live together, either personally or institutionally. Greenleaf quotes Camus when he speaks of builders of community:

> Great ideas, it has been said, come into the world as gently as doves. Perhaps, then, if we listen attentively, we shall hear, amid the uproar of empires and nations, a faint flutter of wings, the gentle stirring of life and hope. Some will say this hope lies in a nation, others, in a man. I believe rather that it is awakened, revived, nourished by millions of solitary individuals whose deeds and works every day negate frontiers and the crudest implications of history. As a result there shines forth fleetingly the ever-threatened truth that each and every person, on the foundations of his or her own suffering and joys, builds for them all. (Camus, "Create Dangerously," 1961)

Wendell Berry in *What are People For?* expands on this thought.

He says:

> …when a community loses its memory, its members no longer know one another. How can they know one another if they have forgotten one another's stories, how can they know whether or not to trust one another? People who do not trust one another do not help one another, and moreover they fear one another. And this is our predicament now. Because of a general distrust and suspicion, we not only lose another's help and companionship, but we are now living in jeopardy of being sued.

Builders of community understand that we each build for all. Builders of community also understand that work is as essential for the worker as what is being produced.

In these times of corporate competition, mergers, and buyouts, I often wonder how many executives cry over the effects of their actions on their workers. And I wonder how many workers resist the temptation to become bitter and powerless in the aftermath of corporate layoffs. I also wonder about the effects on the products being produced. Certainly we see many new programs coming into place to respond to these effects, TQM (Total Quality Management) being just one of the many. Sometimes I wonder if the effects of the current environment drive us to look for solutions that are more meaningful, which might explain the deeper interest in Greenleaf and others who speak a similar language: the language of ethics, of values, of principles, and of love.

Builders of community understand the value of each person and how each person contributes to the whole. In workgroups, they insist on teams led by *primus inter pares*, or "first among equals." The concept of first among equals can be implemented either formally or informally.

Formally, one might ask a team to choose its leader. Informally, a group can develop an attitude of first among equals, rather than power by formal position. The informal way requires much discussion and consensus building so that the philosophy frames the work. Some suggestions to develop this characteristic are:

- Share your story.
- Look for the good in each person.
- Create spaces that allow people to bloom personally and to perform professionally.
- Listen for the "faint fluttering of wings."
- Practice hospitality: the art of letting the stranger in to be who they are; not who we are.

Use Power Ethically

The more we know ourselves, the less apt we will be to abuse power. Servant-leaders have made this connection. They assure that no one is harmed by the actions of the team. They accept authority that is freely and knowingly granted. And they are aware that giving is a potential moral act. In many ways, this characteristic is developed as an outcome of the development of the other characteristics.

The suggestion for our progress on this characteristic is to apply the servant-leader test. Do those served grow as persons? Do they, while being served, become healthier, wiser, freer, more autonomous, more likely themselves to become servants? And, what is the effect on the least privileged in society? Will they benefit or, at least, not be further deprived? The bottom line of this characteristic is to be able to respond with a "yes" to this test.

To develop the characteristics of a servant-leader is not easy—and not fast. For us to be able to express unlimited liability for each other, to know ourselves well, to be holders of liberating vision, to use persuasion wisely, to be builders of community, and to use power ethically sets a high standard for us. We are required to be committed and can only take one step at a time. Another Chinese saying, which tells us that the journey of 10,000 miles begins with a single step, points to the requirement of commitment. And, before we know it, we have gone many miles. Each of us individually must decide on our first steps.

Servant-leadership and servant-leaders fit into a larger context. We begin our development as individuals. We then become healthier, wiser, more autonomous, and more disposed to serve. Because of who we have become, we are then asked to choose to lead. From this dual role we can become the roots of communications and institutions that enlarge and liberate. Our institutions can then become distinctive through raising their level of performance as servants. Institutions play such a critical role in our society. If they become servant-leaders, a society can emerge that is more just and caring where the less able and the more able serve each other. We start with one person, and then with another, and then yet another.

Perhaps this time is ours. In 1992, DDB Needham, a marketing and research firm, released the results of a 16-year survey on lifestyles. I was struck by some of their findings.

Trust continues its steady decline: (in 1992) 66 percent of women and 62 percent of men said, "Most people are honest," down from their peaks of 77 percent and 74 percent respectively in 1976.

…79 percent believe, "Most big companies are just out for themselves," up from about 65 percent in the mid-70s.

The number of people saying, "It is hard to get a good job these days," has climbed sharply since 1989, to 79 percent of women and 75 percent of men, approaching the high of 83 percent for both men and women in 1983.

After dipping in the late 1980's, "dread of the future" has risen since 1989 to 29 percent.

If they could do it all again, 60 percent would "sure do things differently," up from 56.5 percent in 1988. Paradoxically, 79 percent say consistently over the years that they "would be content to live in the same town the rest of my life."

But there's been an increase in people who have trouble getting to sleep, and reach for pain relievers "right away" when they don't feel well.

Perhaps in light of these indicators, servant-leaders will be those who provide a "sense of continuity, a sense of connection and a sense of direction," to use Charles Handy's words from *The Age of Paradox.*

Robert Greenleaf died in 1990, and now our generations are called to become the servant-leaders who will act on the legacies we have been left. Welcome to paradox. Welcome to joy.

Lopez, Isabel O. "Becoming a Servant-Leader: The Personal Development Path." *Reflections on Leadership*. Ed. Larry C. Spears. New York: John Wiley & Sons, 1995. 149–60. Reprinted with permission of John Wiley and Sons, Inc.

FILM STUDIES

Born Free (1966)

Screenplay by Lester Cole
Directed by James Hill

Character Guide

Joy Adamson. . . . .   Virginia McKenna

George Adamson . . . .   Bill Travers

Geoffrey Keen . . . .   John Kendall

Introduction

A naturalist, artist, and author, Joy Adamson wrote *Born Free* to document her efforts to raise Elsa, a lion cub whose mother was shot by Adamson's husband in self-defense. When it became too difficult to keep Elsa, the Adamsons, rather than sending Elsa to a zoo, chose to release her back into the wild. This was a risky venture, as there was no record of anyone having successfully accomplished this task. As the film documents, the couple spent extensive time teaching Elsa to hunt and to interact with other lions. They were, eventually, successful, and Elsa would have cubs of her own and would return to visit the Adamsons. Joy Adamson would later repeat this process with a young cheetah.

Ironically, while Joy Adamson demonstrates characteristics of servant leadership in her work with animals, her interactions with people were, reportedly, different. One associate said that she "was so stubborn and unyielding and people did not live up to her expectations." In 1980, she was murdered by a disgruntled employee, who claimed that she had not paid him and had mistreated him.

Dialogue Questions

1. Joy resists the suggestion of sending the lion to a zoo, stating that Elsa would be miserable there. Instead, Joy wants to teach Elsa how to survive in the wild. How does this situation relate to principles of servant leadership?

2. Part of the teaching of Elsa involved leaving her on her own overnight. What were the risks versus the potential rewards of this strategy? What examples from human culture can you think of that parallel this experience?

3. Why is Elsa tentative about meeting up with the male lion? How can you, in a leadership role, help people to face situations for which they may not feel adequately prepared?

4. Joy's clear affection for Elsa arguably clouded her vision, making her believe that she could accomplish what no one else had ever done before (successfully returning a domesticated lion to the wild). As a servant leader, how can one effectively balance compassion for individuals with the need to make rational decisions that are for the good of the whole?

Hotel Rwanda (2004)

Screenplay by Keir Pearson and Terry George
Directed by Terry George

Character Guide

Paul Rusesabagina	Don Cheadle
Tatiana Rusesabagina	Sophie Okonedo
Dubé	Desmond Dubé
George Rutaganda	Hakeem Kae-Kazin
General Bizimungu	Fana Mokoena
Colonel Oliver (United Nations) . . .	Nick Nolte
Jack Daglish (Camera man)	Joaquin Phoenix
Pat Archer (Red Cross)	Cara Seymour
Mr. Tillens (Sabena President)	Jean Reno

Introduction

Hotel Rwanda portrays the leadership of one man in the face of horrendous circumstances. Paul Rusesabagina does not immediately seek to protect anyone beyond his immediate family from the violence descending upon his city and his country, but as the movie progresses he changes and becomes a servant leader who uses his skills, his position, his influence, and his heart to save over 1,000 lives during the Rwandan Genocide of 1994. Paul Rusesabagina does this with the simple but profound realization that he may not change the world, but he nevertheless has an obligation to get involved and serve those whom he can reach.

Dialogue Questions

1. Who or what does Paul serve at the beginning of the movie? How does this change as the movie progresses?

2. How and why does Paul's rationale for decision making change?

3. What role does Tatiana play in shaping Paul's decisions?

4. What talents and skills did Paul have and how did he use them to respond to the crisis? Are these similar to the skills mentioned in the readings about servant leadership?

5. What resources were at Paul's disposal and how did he use them?

6. What role did the Rwandan media play in the genocide? The international media?

EXERCISE

Service Beyond Self

Introduction

This exercise will demonstrate principles of servant leadership, of supporting those around you to achieve a common goal. Your instructor will provide instructions for this activity.

SUGGESTED READING

This selected bibliography is intended to supplement the excerpts and articles of authors included in this Unit. There is an emphasis on books that are pivotal and recent publications. Numerous journals regularly offer articles related to these topics, but are not included in this selected bibliography. For further research, you may wish to include searches of the following journals: (alphabetically) *Academy of Management Executive, Academy of Management Journal, Harvard Business Review, Journal of Leadership Studies, Leadership in Action, Leadership Quarterly,* and *Leader To Leader.*

This list is organized by author's last name using Modern Language Association-style citations.

Autry, James A. *The Servant Leader: How to Build a Creative Team, Develop Great Morale, and Improve Bottom-Line Performance.* **Crown Business, 2004.**
Autry emphasizes success through love and caring. Part of his creed is, "I choose to believe that most of the market place is driven by people who want to do good work for others and for themselves."

Block, Peter. *Stewardship: Choosing Service Over Self-Interest.* **San Francisco: Berrett-Koehler, 2013.**
Block writes in detail that makes implementation possible for an alternative to traditional patriarchy and hierarchy in organizations.

Erikson, Erik H. *Gandhi's Truth: On the Origins of Militant Nonviolence.* **New York: Norton, 1970.**
Erikson looks closely at what had always been considered a minor episode in Gandhi's life—the Abmedabad Mill Strike of 1918 and Gandhi's first fast.

Nair, Keshavan. *A Higher Standard of Leadership: Lessons from the Life of Gandhi.* **San Francisco: Berrett-Koehler, 1994.**
Nair focuses on Gandhi's bravery and moral purpose.

Preskill, Stephen and Stephen Brookfield. *Learning as a Way of Leading: Lessons from the Struggle for Social Justice.* **San Francisco: Jossey-Bass, 2008.**
The authors consider topics such as "learning to support the growth of others" and "learning to build community."

Trompenaars, Fons and Ed Voerman. *Servant-Leadership Across Cultures: Harnessing the Strengths of the World's Most Powerful Management Philosophy.* **New York: McGraw-Hill, 2009.**
This book includes many corporate examples where management and executive leadership put the philosophy and principles of servant leadership into practice.

van Dierendonck, Dirk, and Kathleen Patterson, eds. *Servant leadership: Developments in theory and research.* **London: Palgrave Macmillan, 2010.**
The editors are noted researchers on servant leadership and have compiled a comprehensive collection of recent writing about the practice of servant leadership and an overview of recent quantitative research using the Servant Leadership Assessment Instrument (SLAI) and qualitative research.

UNIT 3

UNDERSTANDING ETHICAL LEADERSHIP

INTRODUCTION

Ethics, the principles or standards of human conduct, are often defined as simply "actions based on a concept of what is right." However, what may be ethical—the right action—in one situation or culture may be deemed unethical in another. The question of an action's ethical basis is much larger than simply determining if it is legal or not, and this Unit provides you with readings that give examples of such dilemmas and explore the complexity of ethical decision making. Perhaps the most difficult task for any leader is deciding on a course of action when there are many ethical choices. Excerpts from Victor Hugo's novel, *Les Misérables*, provide the Classic Case for this Unit. Hugo presents situations in which two leaders face contradictory choices, which may be ethical from different perspectives of people with different priorities. Jean Valjean and Inspector Javert spend years in both their thoughts and actions espousing divergent views about what constitutes the ethical course of action. The Leadership Profile looks at ethics from the perspective of a very different time and place with excerpts from *The Analects of Confucius*, providing an opportunity to consider how much standards of human conduct change with time and place and whether or not there are any universal ethical principles.

Family, peers, moral values, and life experiences all have an impact on an individual's application of ethics. All these influences add up to the ethical position an individual takes through many acts each day. It is important to keep in mind that ethical standards are determined by individuals, not by organizations. When individuals exercise leadership, therefore, their actions affect the ethical environment. A compelling exploration of the difficult road that individuals must take if they are to maintain high ethical standards for a group or organization is presented in the reading from Mohandas Gandhi. *The Argumentative Indian* explores a key ethical question related to the exercise of leadership. To what extent are we bound by duty to promote a just cause and in the process ignore the potentially negative consequences for others? Another reading describes the conclusions. In "Making Meaning of Being Bad," Barbara Kellerman asks the question, "Should followers follow the leader, or the dictates of their consciences?" The final reading for the Unit offers a framework for ethical decision making. Such a framework can offer guidance for our decisions when we are confronted with difficult ethical dilemmas such as Billy Budd faces in a life-and-death situation in the classic Film Study for the Unit and as Nurse Evers does in the contemporary Film Study for the Unit, *Miss Evers' Boys* (1997). Nurse Evers must decide her course of action in a situation in which none of her options seems truly the right thing to do.

We often make unconscious "value" decisions. However, we need to articulate our ethical priorities and must therefore be aware of the values on which we base our actions. The exercise for this Unit, "Whom to Choose: Values and Group Decision Making," is designed to help us clarify the values and morals on which we base decisions for ethical actions and then learn to work in a group where individuals may have competing ethical priorities. The exercise provides an opportunity to examine the nature of attitude and value acquisition and to assess the degree to which members of a group have common values and the impact this has on the group's action.

Learning Objectives

- Recognize the impact ethical behavior has on effective leadership

- Define the elements of ethical leadership

- Examine the nature of attitude and value acquisition and the influence they have on ethical decisions

- Evaluate personal ethical priorities

- Understand the origin of organizational ethics and the influence they exert upon the lives of people in the organization

- Appreciate the contributions made by the Classic Case and Leadership Profile in this Unit toward understanding ethical leadership

UNIT
3

CLASSIC CASE

Les Misérables

By Victor Hugo (1802–1885)
French Novelist and Poet

Introduction and Historical Background

Victor Hugo was born in Besançon, France to a high-ranking military officer and his Catholic Royalist wife in a time of political upheaval. Educated principally by his mother, but influenced by his early travels with both his parents, by the age of 13 Hugo had begun writing award-winning poems, earning mentions from the *Academie Française* to which he was elected in 1841. He managed both admiration and popularity for his literary efforts. His fame grew, and by the 1820s Hugo was a leader in the French Romantic movement. His interest in politics led Hugo to initially support the French monarchy, but he became disenchanted with political colleagues he realized did not share his values and became a vocal supporter of republicanism. Hugo's opposition to Louis Bonaparte in 1851 led to his exile in the Channel Islands. He was allowed to return to France in 1859, but chose to stay in the Channel Islands until 1870. *Les Misérables* (1862) was one of the works Hugo completed during his nineteen years as an expatriate in Guernsey.

The story was inspired by Hugo's dissatisfaction with the criminal justice system in France and by events he witnessed or read about during his life. The author loosely based Jean Valjean, the novel's protagonist, on the life of an ex-convict whose story of strength lifting a cart off a factory worker made an impression on the author. Hugo based other characters on people he had met, knew well, or simply read about. He first thought about writing a novel highlighting social misery and injustice in the 1830s. From conception to publication, the novel took him seventeen years to write. *Les Misérables* caused a stir when it was first published. Hugo himself thought the book good, and his publisher created a marketing campaign, which was unusual for the time. It launched six months before the serialization of the part of the book focusing on the character Fantine. It sold out its first printing.

In *Les Misérables*, Jean Valjean has served nineteen years in prison, four of them for stealing bread to feed his sister's seven children and the others for repeatedly trying to escape. As he is released in 1815, Inspector Javert reminds him he is a criminal and will wear that mark for the rest of his life. Valjean travels to Digne, but can only find shelter for the night with the town's bishop. Bitter, Valjean steals the bishopric's silver. The police capture him, but the Bishop spares him by telling the police he has given Valjean the silver as a gift. The Bishop then tells Valjean to take this second chance and use the silver to forge an honest life. Valjean once again steals a forty-sous coin from a boy, thinks better of it and tries to return the coin. Unable to do so, he flees and starts a virtuous and prosperous life.

Six years later, Valjean is appointed mayor of a town for which Javert works as an inspector. The two don't recognize each other until Valjean saves a life by lifting a heavy cart from a factory worker. Valjean had hesitated doing so, but thought no one was watching. Javert, in fact, saw the feat and realized he was watching Valjean, the strongest man he had ever met. From that moment, the two men square off, both of them facing ethical dilemmas they must resolve.

Points to Consider

1. What factors shape the ethical frameworks of Jean Valjean and Inspector Javert? How and why are the frameworks different for each individual?

2. When members of small groups passionately disagree about ethical decisions, how can they resolve their issues?

3. In what ways does social structure factor into the choices Valjean and Javert make? What was Victor Hugo's perspective on the ways ethical decisions made by organizational leaders have consequences for an individual's ethical decision making?

4. To what degree could Valjean and Javert have made different ethical choices to resolve their issues and perhaps alter the course of their lives?

Les Misérables

(Excerpts)

How Jean Can Become Champ

One morning M. Madeleine was in his study, occupied in arranging in advance some pressing matters connected with the mayor's office, … when he was informed that Police Inspector Javert was desirous of speaking with him. Madeleine could not refrain from a disagreeable impression on hearing this name. Javert had avoided him more than ever since the affair of the police-station, and M. Madeleine had not seen him.

"Admit him," he said.

Javert entered.

M. Madeleine had retained his seat near the fire, pen in hand, his eyes fixed on the docket which he was turning over and annotating, and which contained the trials of the commission on highways for the infraction of police regulations. He did not disturb himself on Javert's account. … It suited him to be glacial in his manner.

Javert bestowed a respectful salute on the mayor, whose back was turned to him. The mayor did not look at him, but went on annotating this docket.

Javert advanced two or three paces into the study, and halted, without breaking the silence.

If any physiognomist who had been familiar with Javert, and who had made a lengthy study of this savage in the service of civilization, … this spy who was incapable of a lie, this unspotted police agent—if any physiognomist had known his secret and long-cherished aversion for M. Madeleine, … and had examined Javert at that moment, he would have said to himself, "What has taken place?" It was evident to any one acquainted with that clear, upright, sincere, honest, austere, and ferocious conscience, that Javert had but just gone through some great interior struggle. Javert had nothing in his soul which he had not also in his countenance. … On entering he bowed to M. Madeleine with a look in which there was neither rancor, anger, nor distrust; he halted a few paces in the rear of the mayor's arm-chair, and there he stood, perfectly erect, in an attitude almost of discipline, with the cold ingenuous roughness of a man who has never been gentle and who has always been patient; he waited without uttering a word, without making a movement, in genuine humility and tranquil resignation, calm, serious, hat in hand, with eyes cast down, and an expression which was half-way between that of a soldier in the presence of his officer and a criminal in the presence of his judge, until it should please the mayor to turn round. All the sentiments

UNIT
3

as well as all the memories which one might have attributed to him had disappeared. That face, as impenetrable and simple as granite, no longer bore any trace of anything but a melancholy depression. His whole person breathed lowliness and firmness and an indescribable courageous despondency.

At last the mayor laid down his pen and turned half round.

"Well! What is it? What is the matter, Javert?"

Javert remained silent for an instant as though collecting his ideas, then raised his voice with a sort of sad solemnity, which did not, however, preclude simplicity.

"This is the matter, Mr. Mayor; a culpable act has been committed."

"What act?"

"An inferior agent of the authorities has failed in respect, and in the gravest manner, towards a magistrate. I have come to bring the fact to your knowledge, as it is my duty to do."

"Who is the agent?" asked M. Madeleine.

"I," said Javert.

"You?"

"I."

"And who is the magistrate who has reason to complain of the agent?"

"You, Mr. Mayor."

M. Madeleine sat erect in his arm-chair. Javert went on, with a severe air, and his eyes still cast down.

"Mr. Mayor, I have come to request you to instigate the authorities to dismiss me."

M. Madeleine opened his mouth in amazement. Javert interrupted him:—

"You will say that I might have handed in my resignation, but that does not suffice. Handing in one's resignation is honorable. I have failed in my duty; I ought to be punished; I must be turned out."

And after a pause he added:—

"Mr. Mayor, you were severe with me the other day, and unjustly. Be so to-day, with justice."

"Come, now! Why?" exclaimed M. Madeleine. "What nonsense is this? What is the meaning of this? What culpable act have you been guilty of towards me? ... You accuse yourself; you wish to be superseded—"

"Turned out," said Javert.

"Turned out; so it be, then. That is well. I do not understand."

"You shall understand, Mr. Mayor."

Javert sighed from the very bottom of his chest, and resumed, still coldly and sadly:—

"Mr. Mayor, six weeks ago, in consequence of the scene over that woman, I was furious, and I informed against you."

"Informed against me!"

"At the Prefecture of Police in Paris."

M. Madeleine, who was not in the habit of laughing much oftener than Javert himself, burst out laughing now:—

"As a mayor who had encroached on the province of the police?"

"As an ex-convict."

The Mayor turned livid.

Javert, who had not raised his eyes, went on:—

"I thought it was so. I had had an idea for a long time; a resemblance; inquiries which you had caused to be made at Faverolles; ... the adventure with old Fauchelevant; your skill in marksmanship; your leg, which you drag a little;—I hardly know what all,—absurdities! But, at all events, I took you for a certain Jean Valjean."

"A certain—What did you say the name was?"

"Jean Valjean. He was a convict whom I was in the habit of seeing twenty years ago, when I was adjutant-guard of convicts at Toulon. On leaving the galleys, this Jean Valjean, as

it appears, robbed a bishop; then he committed another theft, accompanied with violence, on a public highway on the person of a little Savoyard. He disappeared eight years ago, no one knows how, and he has been sought, I fancied. In short, I did this thing! Wrath impelled me; I denounced you at the Prefecture!"

M. Madeleine, who had taken up the docket again several moments before this, resumed with an air of perfect indifference:—

"And what reply did you receive?"

"That I was mad."

"Well?"

"Well, they were right."

"It is lucky that you recognize the fact."

"I am forced to do so, since the real Jean Valjean has been found."

The sheet of paper which M. Madeleine was holding dropped from his hand; he raised his head, gazed fixedly at Javert, and said with his indescribable accent:—

"Ah!"

Javert continued:—

"This is the way it is, Mr. Mayor. It seems that there was in the neighborhood near Ailly-le-Haut-Clocher an old fellow who was called Father Champmathieu. He was a very wretched creature. No one paid any attention to him. No one knows what such people subsist on. Lately, last autumn, Father Champmathieu was arrested for the theft of some cider apples from—Well, no matter, a theft had been committed, a wall scaled, branches of trees broken. My Champmathieu was arrested. He still had the branch of apple-tree in his hand. The scamp is locked up. Up to this point it was merely an affair of a misdemeanor. But here is where Providence intervened.

"The jail being in a bad condition, the examining magistrate finds it convenient to transfer Champmathieu to Arras, where the departmental prison is situated. In this prison at Arras there is an ex-convict named Brevet, who is detained for I know not what, and who has been appointed turnkey of the house, because of good behavior. Mr. Mayor, no sooner had Champmathieu arrived than Brevet exclaims: 'Eh! Why, I know that man! … Take a good look at me, my good man! You are Jean Valjean!' Champmathieu feigns astonishment. 'Don't play the innocent dodge,' says Brevet. 'You are Jean Valjean! You have been in the galleys of Toulon; it was twenty years ago; we were there together.' Champmathieu denies it. Parbleu! You understand. The case is investigated. The thing was well ventilated for me. This is what they discovered: This Champmathieu had been, thirty years ago, a pruner of trees in various localities, notably at Faverolles. There all trace of him was lost. A long time afterwards he was seen again in Auvergne; then in Paris, … Now, before going to the galleys for theft, what was Jean Valjean? A pruner of trees. Where? At Faverolles. Another fact. This Valjean's Christian name was Jean, and his mother's surname was Mathieu. What more natural to suppose that, on emerging from the galleys, he should have taken his mother's name for the purpose of concealing himself, and called himself Jean Mathieu? He goes to Auvergne. The local pronunciation turns Jean into Chan—he is called Chan Mathieu. Our man offers no opposition, and behold him transformed to Champmathieu. You follow me, do you not? Inquiries were made at Faverolles. The family of Jean Valjean is no longer there. It is not known where they have gone. … And then, as the beginning of the story dates thirty years back, there is no longer any one at Faverolles who knew Jean Valjean. Inquiries were made at Toulon. Besides Brevet, there are only two convicts in existence who have seen Jean Valjean; they are Cochepaille and Chenildieu, and are sentenced for life. They are taken from the galleys and confronted with the pretended Champmathieu. They do not hesitate; he is Jean Valjean for them as well as for Brevet. The same age,—he is fifty-four,—the same height, the same air, the same man; in short, it is he. It was precisely at this moment that I forwarded my denunciation to the Prefecture in Paris. I was told that I had lost my reason, and that Jean Valjean is at Arras, in the power of the authorities. You can imagine whether this surprised me, when I thought that I had that same Jean Valjean here. I write to the examining judge; he sends for me; Champmathieu is conducted to me—"

"Well?" interposed M. Madeleine.

Javert replied, his face incorruptible, and as melancholy as ever:—

"Mr. Mayor, the truth is the truth. I am sorry; but that man is Jean Valjean. I recognized him also."

M. Madeleine resumed in, a very low voice:—

"You are sure?"

Javert began to laugh, with that mournful laugh which comes from profound conviction.

"O! Sure!"

…he added:—

"And even now that I have seen the real Jean Valjean, I do not see how I could have thought otherwise. I beg your pardon, Mr. Mayor."

Javert, as he addressed these grave and supplicating words to the man, who six weeks before had humiliated him in the presence of the whole station-house, and bade him "leave the room,"—Javert, that haughty man, was unconsciously full of simplicity and dignity,—M. Madeleine made no reply to his prayer than the abrupt question:—

"And what does this man say?"

"Ah! Indeed, Mr. Mayor, it's a bad business. If he is Jean Valjean, he has his previous conviction against him. To climb a wall, to break a branch, to purloin apples, is a mischievous trick in a child; for a man it is a misdemeanor; for a convict it is a crime. Robbing and house-breaking—it is all there. It is no longer a question of correctional police; it is a matter for the Court of Assizes. It is no longer a matter of a few days in prison; it is the galleys for life. And then, there is the affair with the little Savoyard, who will return, I hope. The deuce! there is plenty to dispute in the matter, is there not?

Yes, for any one but Jean Valjean. But Jean Valjean is a sly dog. That is the way I recognized him. Any other man would have felt that things were getting hot for him; he would struggle, he would cry out—the kettle sings before the first; he would not be Jean Valjean, et cetera. But he has not the appearance of understanding; he says, 'I am Champmathieu, and I won't depart from that!' He has an astonished air, he pretends to be stupid; it is far better. Oh! the rogue is clever! But it makes no difference. The proofs are there. He has been recognized by four persons; the old scamp will be condemned. The case has been taken to the Assizes at Arras. I shall go there to give my testimony. I have been summoned."

M. Madeleine had turned to his desk again, and taken up his docket, and was turning over the leaves tranquilly, reading and writing by turns, like a busy man. He turned to Javert:—

"That will do, Javert. In truth, all these details interest me but little. We are wasting our time, and we have pressing business on hand. Javert, you will betake yourself at once to the house of the woman Buseaupied, who sells herbs at the corner of the Rue Saint-Saulve…[T]ell her that she must enter complaint against carter Pierre Chesnelong. The man is a brute, who came near crushing this woman and her child. He must be punished…[T]hen go to M. Charcellay, Rue Montre-de-Champigny. He complained that there is a gutter on the adjoining house which discharges rain-water on his premises, undermining the foundations of his house. After that, you will verify the infractions of police regulations which have reported to me in the Rue Guibourg, … and you will prepare documents. But I am giving you a great deal of work. Are you not to be absent? Did you not tell me that you were going to Arras on that matter in a week or ten days?"

"Sooner than that, Mr. Mayor."

"On what day, then?"

"Why, I thought that I had said to Monsieur le Maire that the case was to be tried to-morrow, and that I am to set out by diligence to-night."

M. Madeleine made an imperceptible movement.

"And how long will the case last?"

"One day, at the most. The judgment will be pronounced to-morrow evening at latest. But I shall not wait for the sentence, which is certain; I shall return here as soon as my deposition has been taken."

"That is well," said M. Madeleine.

And he dismissed Javert with a wave of the hand.

Javert did not withdraw.

"Excuse me, Mr. Mayor," said he.

"What is it now?" demanded M. Madeleine.

"Mr. Mayor, there is still something of which I must remind you."

"What is it?"

"That I must be dismissed."

M. Madeleine rose.

"Javert, you are a man of honor, and I esteem you. You exaggerate your fault. Moreover, this is an offence which concerns me. Javert, you deserve promotion instead of degradation. I wish you to retain your post."

Javert gazed at M. Madeleine with his candid eyes, in whose depths his not very enlightened but pure and rigid conscience seemed visible, and said in a tranquil voice:—

"Mr. Mayor, I cannot grant you that."

"I repeat," replied M. Madeleine, "that the matter concerns me."

But Javert, heeding his own thought only, continued:—

"So far as exaggeration is concerned, I am not exaggerating. This is the way I reason: I have suspected you unjustly. That is nothing. It is our right to cherish suspicion, although suspicion directed above ourselves is an abuse. But without proofs, in a fit of rage, with the object of wreaking my vengeance, I have denounced you as a convict, you, a respectable man, a mayor, a magistrate! That is serious, very serious. I have insulted authority in your person, I, an agent of the authorities! If one of my subordinates had done what I have done, I should have declared him unworthy of the service, and have expelled him. ... I have often been severe in the course of my life towards others. That is just. ... Now, if I were not severe towards myself, all the justice that I have done would become injustice. Ought I to spare myself more than others? No! What! I should be good for nothing but to chastise others, and not myself! ... Mr. Mayor, I do not desire that you should treat me kindly; your kindness roused sufficient bad blood in me when it was directed to others. I want none of it for myself. The kindness which consists in upholding a woman of the town against a citizen, the police agent against the mayor, the man who is down against the man who is up in the world, is what I call false kindness. That is the sort of kindness which disorganizes society. Good God! it is very easy to be kind; the difficulty lies in being just. Come! if you had been what I thought you, I should not have been kind to you, not I! You would have seen! Mr. Mayor, I must treat myself as I would treat any other man. When I have subdued malefactors, when I have proceeded with vigor against rascals, I have often said to myself, 'If you flinch, if I ever catch you at fault, you may rest at your ease!' I have flinched, I have caught myself in a fault. So much the worse! Come, discharged, cashiered, expelled! That is well. I have arms. I will till the soil; it makes no difference to me. Mr. Mayor, the good of the service demands an example. I simply require the discharge of Inspector Javert."

All this was uttered in a proud, humble, despairing, yet convinced tone, which lent indescribable grandeur to this singular, honest man.

"We shall see," said M. Madeleine.

And he offered him his hand.

Javert recoiled, and said in a wild voice:—

UNIT
3

"Excuse me, Mr. Mayor, but this must not be. A mayor does not offer his hand to a police spy."

He added between his teeth:—

"A police spy, yes; from the moment when I have misused the police. I am no more than a police spy."

Then he bowed profoundly, and directed his steps towards the door.

There he wheeled round, and with eyes still downcast:—

"Mr. Mayor," he said, "I shall continue to serve until I am superseded."

He withdrew. M. Madeleine remained thoughtfully listening to the firm, sure step, which died away on the pavement of the corridor.

A Tempest in a Skull

...

We have but little to add to what the reader already knows of what had happened to Jean Valjean after the adventure with Little Gervais. From that moment forth he was ... a totally different man. ... It was more than a transformation; it was a transfiguration.

He succeeded in disappearing, sold the Bishop's silver, reserving only the candlesticks as a souvenir, crept from town to town, traversed France, ... accomplished what we have related, succeeded in rendering himself safe from seizure and inaccessible, and, thenceforth, ... he lived in peace, reassured and hopeful, having henceforth only two thoughts,—to conceal his name and to sanctify his life; to escape men and to return to God.

These two thoughts were so closely intertwined in his mind that they formed but a single one there; both were equally absorbing and imperative and ruled his slightest actions. In general, they conspired to regulate the conduct of his life; ... they rendered him kindly and simple; they counselled him to the same things. Sometimes, however, they conflicted. In that case, ... M. Madeleine did not hesitate to sacrifice the first to the second—his security to his virtue. Thus, in spite of all his reserve and all his prudence, he had preserved the Bishop's candlesticks, worn mourning for him, summoned and interrogated all the little Savoyards

who passed that way, collected information regarding the families at Faverolles, and saved old Fauchelevent's life, despite the disquieting insinuations of Javert. It seemed ... as though he thought, following the example of all those who have been wise, holy, and just, that his first duty was not towards himself.

At the same time, it must be confessed, nothing just like this had yet presented itself.

Never had the two ideas which governed the unhappy man whose sufferings we are narrating, engaged in so serious a struggle. He understood this confusedly but profoundly at the very first words pronounced by Javert, when the latter entered his study. At the moment when that name, which he had buried beneath so many layers, was so strangely articulated, he was struck with stupor, and as though intoxicated with the sinister eccentricity of his destiny; and through this stupor he felt that shudder which precedes great shocks. He bent like an oak at the approach of a storm, like a soldier at the approach of an assault. ... As he listened to Javert, the first thought which occurred to him was to go, to run and denounce himself, to take that Champmathieu out of prison and place himself there; this was as painful and as poignant as an incision in the living flesh. Then it passed away, and he said to himself, "We will see! We will see!" He repressed this first, generous instinct, and recoiled before heroism.

It would be beautiful, no doubt, after the Bishop's holy words, after so many years of repentance and abnegation, in the midst of a penitence admirably begun, if this man had not flinched for an instant, even in the presence of so terrible a conjecture, but had continued to walk with the same step towards this yawning precipice, at the bottom of which lay heaven; that would have been beautiful; but it was not thus. … He was carried away, at first, by the instinct of self-preservation; he rallied all his ideas in haste, stifled his emotions, took into consideration Javert's presence, that great danger, postponed all decision with the firmness of terror, shook off thought as to what he had to do, and resumed his calmness as a warrior picks up his buckler.

He remained in this state during the rest of the day, a whirlwind within, a profound tranquility without. He took no "preservative measures," as they may be called. Everything was still confused, and jostling together in his brain. His trouble was so great that he could not perceive the form of a single idea distinctly, and he could have told nothing about himself, except that he had received a great blow.

…

He dined with a good deal of appetite.

On returning to his room, he communed with himself.

He examined the situation, and found it unprecedented; so unprecedented that in the midst of his reverie he rose from his chair, moved by some inexplicable impulse of anxiety, and bolted his door. He feared lest something more should enter. He was barricading himself against possibilities.

A moment later he extinguished his light; it embarrassed him.

It seemed to him as though he might be seen.

By whom?

Alas! That on which he desired to close the door had already entered; that which he desired to blind was staring him in the face,—his conscience.

His conscience; that is to say, God.

Nevertheless, he deluded himself at first; he had a feeling of security and of solitude; the bolt once drawn, he thought himself impregnable; the candle extinguished, he felt himself invisible. Then he took possession of himself: he set his elbows on the table, leaned his head on his hand, and began to meditate in the dark.

"Where do I stand? Am not I dreaming? What have I heard? Is it really true that I have seen that Javert, and that he spoke to me in that manner? Who can that Champmathieu be? So he resembles me! Is it possible? When I reflect that yesterday I was so tranquil, and so far from suspecting anything! What was I doing yesterday at this hour? What is there in this incident? What will the end be? What is to be done?"

This was the torment in which he found himself. His brain had lost its power of retaining ideas; they passed like waves, and he clutched his brow in both hands to arrest them.

Nothing but anguish extricated itself from this tumult which overwhelmed his will and his reason, and from which he sought to draw proof and resolution.

His head was burning. He went to the window and threw it wide open. There were no stars in the sky. He returned and seated himself at the table.

The first hour passed in this manner.

Gradually, however, vague outlines began to take form and to fix themselves in his meditation, and he was able to catch a glimpse with precision of the reality,—not the whole situation, but some of the details. He began by recognizing the fact that, critical and extraordinary as was this situation, he was completely master of it.

This only caused an increase of his stupor.

Independently of the severe and religious aim which he had assigned to his actions, all that he had made up to that day had been nothing but a hole in which to bury his name. That which he had always feared most of all in his hours of self-communion, during his sleepless nights, was to ever hear that name pronounced; he had said to himself, that that would be the end of all things for him; that on the day when that name made its reappearance it would cause his new life to vanish from about him, and—who knows?—perhaps even his new soul within him, also. He shuddered at the very thought that this was possible. Assuredly, if any one had said to him at such moments that the hour would come when that name would ring in his ears, when the hideous words, Jean Valjean, would suddenly emerge from the darkness and rise in front of him, … and that that name would not menace him,… that this earthquake would solidify his edifice, that this prodigious incident would have no other result…than that of rendering his existence at once clearer and more impenetrable, and that, out of his confrontation with the phantom of Jean Valjean, the good and worthy citizen Monsieur Madeleine would emerge more honored, more peaceful, and more respected than ever—if any one had told him that, he would have … regarded the words as those of a madman. Well, all this was precisely what had just come to pass; all that accumulation of impossibilities was a fact, and God had permitted these wild fancies to become real things!

…

It seemed to him that he had but just waked up from some inexplicable dream, and that he found himself slipping down … on the very brink of the abyss. He distinctly perceived in the darkness a stranger, a man unknown to him, whom destiny had mistaken for him, and whom she was thrusting into the gulf in his stead; in order that the gulf might close once more, it was necessary that some one, himself or that other man, should fall into it: he had only let things take their course.

The light became complete, and he acknowledged this to himself: That his place was empty in the galleys; that do what he would, it was still awaiting him; that the theft from little Gervais had led him back to it; that this vacant place would await him, and draw him on until he filled it; that this was inevitable and fatal;

and then he said to himself, "that, at this moment, he had a substitute; that it appeared that a certain Champmathieu had that ill luck, and that, as regards himself, being present in the galleys in the person of that Champmathieu, present in society under the name of M. Madeleine, he had nothing more to fear, provided that he did not prevent men from sealing over the head of that Champmathieu this stone of infamy which, like the stone of the sepulchre, falls once, never to rise again."

All this was so strange and so violent, that there suddenly took place in him that indescribable movement, which no man feels more than two or three times in the course of his life, a sort of convulsion of the conscience which stirs up all that there is doubtful in the heart…

He hastily relighted his candle.

"Well, what then?" he said to himself; "what am I afraid of? What is there in all that for me to think about? I am safe; all is over. I had but one partly open door through which my past might invade my life, and behold that door is walled up forever! That Javert, who has been annoying me so long; that terrible instinct which seemed to have divined me, which had divined me—good God! and which followed me everywhere; that frightful hunting-dog, always making a point at me, is thrown off the scent, engaged elsewhere, absolutely turned from the trail: henceforth he is satisfied; he will leave me in peace; he has his Jean Valjean. Who knows? it is even probable that he will wish to leave town! And all this has been brought about without any aid from me, and I count for nothing in it! Ah! but where is the misfortune in this? Upon my honor, people would think, to see me, that some catastrophe had happened to me! After all, if it does bring harm to some one, that is not my fault in the least: it is Providence which has done it all; it is because it wishes it so to be, evidently. Have I the right to disarrange what it has arranged? What do I ask now? Why should I meddle? It does not concern me; what! I am not satisfied: but what more do I want? The goal to which I have aspired for so many years, the dream of my nights, the object of my prayers to Heaven,—security,—I have now attained;

it is God who wills it; I can do nothing against the will of God, and why does God will it? In order that I may continue what I have begun, that I may do good, that I may one day be a grand and encouraging example, that it may be said at last, that a little happiness has been attached to the penance which I have undergone, and to that virtue to which I have returned….It is settled; let things take their course; let the good God do as he likes!"

Thus did he address himself in the depths of his own conscience, bending over what may be called his own abyss; he rose from his chair, and began to pace the room: "Come," said he, "let us think no more about it; my resolve is taken!" but he felt no joy.

Quite the reverse.

One can no more prevent thought from recurring to an idea than one can the sea from returning to the shore: the sailor calls it the tide; the guilty man calls it remorse; God upheaves the soul as he does the ocean.

After the expiration of a few moments, do what he would, he resumed the gloomy dialogue in which it was he who spoke and he who listened, saying that which he would have preferred to ignore, and listened to that which he would have preferred not to hear….

So he asked himself where he stood. He interrogated himself upon that "settled resolve." He confessed to himself that all that he had just arranged in his mind was monstrous, that "to let things take their course, to let the good God do as he liked," was simply horrible; to allow this error of fate and of men to be carried out, not to hinder it, to lend himself to it through his silence, to do nothing, in short, was to do everything! that this was hypocritical baseness in the last degree! that it was a base, cowardly, sneaking, abject, hideous crime!

For the first time in eight years, the wretched man had just tasted the bitter savor of an evil thought and of an evil action.

He spit it out with disgust.

He continued to question himself. He asked himself severely what he had meant by this, "My object is attained!" He declared to himself that his life really had an object; but what object? To conceal his name? To deceive the police? Was it for so petty a thing that he had done all that he had done? Had he not another and a grand object, which was the true one—to save, not his person, but his soul; to become honest and good once more; to be a just man? Was it not that above all, that alone, which he had always desired, which the Bishop had enjoined upon him—to shut the door on his past? But he was not shutting it! great God! he was re-opening it by committing an infamous action! He was becoming a thief once more, and the most odious of thieves! He was robbing another of his existence, his life, his peace, his place in the sunshine. He was becoming an assassin. He was murdering, morally murdering, a wretched man. He was inflicting on him that frightful living death, that death beneath the open sky, which is called the galleys. On the other hand, to surrender himself to save that man, struck down with so melancholy an error, to resume his own name, to become once more, out of duty, the convict Jean Valjean, that was, in truth, to achieve his resurrection, and to close forever that hell whence he had just emerged; to fall back there in appearance was to escape from it in reality. This must be done! He had done nothing if he did not do all this; his whole life was useless; all his penitence was wasted. There was no longer any need of saying, "What is the use?" He felt that the Bishop was there, that the Bishop was present all the more because he was dead, that the Bishop was gazing fixedly at him, that henceforth Mayor Madeleine, with all his virtues, would be abominable to him, and that the convict Jean Valjean would be pure and admirable in his sight; that men beheld his mask, but that the Bishop saw his face; that men saw his life, but that the Bishop beheld his conscience. So he must go to Arras, deliver the false Jean Valjean, and denounce the real one. Alas! that was the greatest of sacrifices, the most poignant of victories, the last step to take; but it must be done. Sad fate! he would enter into sanctity only in the eyes of God when he returned to infamy in the eyes of men.

"Well," said he, "let us decide upon this; let us do our duty; let us save this man." He uttered these words aloud, without perceiving that he was speaking aloud.

…

"Go! Tell your name! Denounce yourself!"

In the same way he beheld, as though they had passed before him in visible forms, the two ideas which had, up to that time, formed the double rule of his soul,—the concealment of his name, the sanctification of his life. For the first time they appeared to him as absolutely distinct, and he perceived the distance which separated them. He recognized the fact that one of these ideas was, necessarily, good, while the other might become bad; that the first was self-devotion, and that the other was personality; that the one said, my neighbor, and that the other said, myself; that one emanated from the light, and the other from darkness.

They were antagonistic. He saw them in conflict. In proportion as he meditated, they grew before the eyes of his spirit. They had now attained colossal statures, and it seemed to him that he beheld within himself, in that infinity of which we were recently speaking, in the midst of the darkness and the lights, a goddess and a giant contending.

He was filled with terror; but it seemed to him that the good thought was getting the upper hand.

He felt that he was on the brink of the second decisive crisis of his conscience and of his destiny; that the Bishop had marked the first phase of his new life, and that Champmathieu marked the second. After the grand crisis, the grand test.

But the fever, allayed for an instant, gradually resumed possession of him. A thousand thoughts traversed his mind, but they continued to fortify him in his resolution.

One moment he said to himself that he was, perhaps, taking the matter too keenly; that, after all, this Champmathieu was not interesting, and that he had actually been guilty of theft.

He answered himself: "If this man has, indeed, stolen a few apples, that means a month in prison. It is a long way from that to the galleys. And who knows? Did he steal? Has it been proved? The name of Jean Valjean overwhelms him, and seems to dispense with proofs. Do not the attorneys for the Crown always proceed in this manner? He is supposed to be a thief because he is known to be a convict."

In another instant the thought had occurred to him that, when he denounced himself, the heroism of his deed might, perhaps, be taken into consideration, and his honest life for the last seven years, and what he had done for the district, and that they would have mercy on him.

But this supposition vanished very quickly, and he smiled bitterly as he remembered that the theft of the forty sous from little Gervais put him in the position of a man guilty of a second offence after conviction, that this affair would certainly come up, and, according to the precise terms of the law, would render him liable to penal servitude for life.

He turned aside from all illusions, detached himself more and more from earth, and sought strength and consolation elsewhere. He told himself that he must do his duty; that perhaps he should not be more unhappy after doing his duty than after having avoided it; that if he allowed things to take their own course, … his good name, his good works, the deference and veneration paid to him, his charity, his wealth, his popularity, his virtue, would be seasoned with a crime. And what would be the taste of all these holy things when bound up with this hideous thing? while, if he accomplished his sacrifice, a celestial idea would be mingled with the galleys, the post, the iron necklet, the green cap, unceasing toil, and pitiless shame.

At length he told himself that it must be so, that his destiny was thus allotted, that he had not authority to alter the arrangements made on high, that, in any case, he must make his choice: virtue without and abomination within, or holiness within and infamy without.

The stirring up of these lugubrious ideas did not cause his courage to fail, but his brain to grow weary. He began to think of other things, of indifferent matters, in spite of himself.

The veins in his temples throbbed violently; he still paced to and fro; midnight sounded first from the parish church, then from the town-hall; he counted the twelve strokes of the two clocks, and compared the sounds of the two bells....

He was cold; he lighted a small fire; it did not occur to him to close the window.

In the meantime he had relapsed into his stupor; he was obliged to make a tolerably vigorous effort to recall what had been the subject of his thoughts before midnight had struck; he finally succeeded in doing this.

"Ah! yes," he said to himself, "I had resolved to inform against myself."

...

Here a fresh crisis declared itself.

...

"Ah! but I have hitherto considered no one but myself; it is proper for me to hold my tongue or to denounce myself, to conceal my person or to save my soul, to be a despicable and respected magistrate, or an infamous and venerable convict; it is I, it is always I and nothing but I: but, good God! all this is egotism; these are diverse forms of egotism, but it is egotism all the same. What if I were to think a little about others? The highest holiness is to think of others; come, let us examine the matter. The *I* excepted, the *I* effaced, the *I* forgotten, what would be the result of all this? What if I denounce myself? I am arrested; this Champmathieu is released; I am put back in the galleys; that is well—and what then? What is going on here? Ah! here is a country, a town, here are factories, an industry, workers, both men and women, aged grandsires, children, poor people! All this I have created; all these I provide with their living; everywhere where there is a smoking chimney, it is I who have placed the brand on the hearth and meat in the pot; I have created ease, circulation, credit; before me there was nothing; I have elevated, vivified, informed with life, fecundated, stimulated, enriched the whole country-side; lacking me, the soul is lacking; I take myself off, everything dies... If I do not denounce myself? come, let us see how it will be if I do not denounce myself."

After putting this question to himself, he paused; he seemed to undergo a momentary hesitation and trepidation; but it did not last long, and he answered himself calmly:—

"Well, this man is going to the galleys; it is true, but what the deuce! he has stolen! There is no use in my saying that he has not been guilty of theft, for he has! I remain here; I go on: in ten years I shall have made ten millions; I scatter them over the country; I have nothing of my own; what is that to me? It is not for myself that I am doing it; the prosperity of all goes on augmenting; industries are aroused and animated; factories and shops are multiplied; families, a hundred families, a thousand families, are happy; the district becomes populated; villages spring up where there were only farms before; farms rise where there was nothing; wretchedness disappears, and with wretchedness debauchery, prostitution, theft, murder; all vices disappear, all crimes:...and behold a whole country rich and honest! Ah! I was a fool! I was absurd! what was that I was saying about denouncing myself? I really must pay attention and not be precipitate about anything. What! because it would have pleased me to play the grand and generous; this is melodrama, after all; because I should have thought of no one but myself, the idea! for the sake of saving from a punishment, a trifle exaggerated, perhaps, but just at bottom, no one knows whom, a thief, a good-for-nothing, evidently, a whole country-side must perish! ... and all that for the sake of an old wretch of an apple-thief who, most assuredly, has deserved the galleys for something else, if not for that;

UNIT
3

fine scruples, indeed, which save a guilty man and sacrifice the innocent, which save an old vagabond who has only a few years to live at most, and who will not be more unhappy in the galleys than in his hovel, and which sacrifice a whole population, mothers, wives, children. …and I was going to neglect my duty towards all these poor creatures; and I was going off to denounce myself; and I was about to commit that unspeakable folly! Let us put it at the worst: suppose that there is a wrong action on my part in this, and that my conscience will reproach me for it some day, to accept, for the good of others, these reproaches which weigh only on myself; this evil action which compromises my soul alone; in that lies self-sacrifice; in that alone there is virtue."

He rose and resumed his march; this time, he seemed to be content.

Diamonds are found only in the dark places of the earth; truths are found only in the depths of thought. It seemed to him, that, after having descended into these depths, after having long groped among the darkest of these shadows, he had at last found one of these diamonds, one of these truths, and that he now held it in his hand, and he was dazzled as he gazed upon it.

"Yes," he thought, "this is right; I am on the right road; I have the solution; I must end by holding fast to something; my resolve is taken; let things take their course; let us no longer vacillate; let us no longer hang back; this is for the interest of all, not for my own; I am Madeleine, and Madeleine I remain. Woe to the man who is Jean Valjean! I am no longer he; I do not know that man; I no longer know anything; it turns out that some one is Jean Valjean at the present moment; let him look out for himself; that does not concern me; it is a fatal name which was floating abroad in the night; if it halts and descends on a head, so much the worse for that head."

He looked into the little mirror which hung above his chimney-piece, and said:—

"Hold! it has relieved me to come to a decision; I am quite another man now."

He proceeded a few paces further, then he stopped short.

"Come!" he said, "I must not flinch before any of the consequences of the resolution which I have once adopted; there are still threads which attach me to that Jean Valjean; they must be broken; in this very room there are objects which would betray me, dumb things which would bear witness against me; it is settled; all these things must disappear."

He fumbled in his pocket, drew out his purse, opened it, and took out a small key; he inserted the key in a lock whose aperture could hardly be seen, so hidden was it in the most sombre tones of the design which covered the wall-paper; a secret receptacle opened…; in this hiding-place there were some rags—a blue linen blouse, an old pair of trousers, an old knapsack, and a huge thorn cudgel shod with iron at both ends. Those who had seen Jean Valjean at the epoch when he passed through D—in October, 1815, could easily have recognized all the pieces of this miserable outfit.

He had preserved them as he had preserved the silver candlesticks, in order to remind himself continually of his starting-point.…

He cast a furtive glance towards the door, as though he feared that it would open in spite of the bolt which fastened it; then, with a quick and abrupt movement, he took the whole in his arms at once, without bestowing so much as a glance on the things which he had so religiously and so perilously preserved for so many years, and flung them all, rags, cudgel, knapsack, into the fire.

…

He did not look at the fire, but paced back and forth with the same step.

All at once his eye fell on the two silver candlesticks, which shone vaguely on the chimney-piece, through the glow.

"Hold!" he thought; "the whole of Jean Valjean is still in them. They must be destroyed also."

He seized the two candlesticks.

There was still fire enough to allow of their being put out of shape, and converted into a sort of unrecognizable bar of metal.

He bent over the hearth and warmed himself for a moment. He felt a sense of real comfort. "How good warmth is!" said he.

He stirred the live coals with one of the candlesticks.

A minute more, and they were both in the fire.

At that moment it seemed to him that he heard a voice within him shouting: "Jean Valjean! Jean Valjean!"

His hair rose upright: he became like a man who is listening to some terrible thing.

"Yes, that's it! finish!" said the voice. "Complete what you are about! Destroy these candlesticks! Annihilate this souvenir! Forget the Bishop! Forget everything! Destroy this Champmathieu, do! That is right! Applaud yourself! So it is settled, resolved, fixed, agreed: here is an old man who does not know what is wanted of him, who has, perhaps, done nothing, an innocent man, whose whole misfortune lies in your name, upon whom your name weighs like a crime, who is about to be taken for you, who will be condemned, who will finish his days in abjectness and horror. That is good! Be an honest man yourself; … remain honorable and honored; enrich the town; nourish the indigent; rear the orphan; live happy, virtuous, and admired; and, during this time, while you are here in the midst of joy and light, there will be a man who will wear your red blouse, who will bear your name in ignominy, and who will drag your chain in the galleys. Yes, it is well arranged thus. Ah, wretch!"

The perspiration streamed from his brow. He fixed a haggard eye on the candlesticks. But that within him which had spoken had not finished. The voice continued:—

"Jean Valjean, there will be around you many voices, which will make a great noise, which will talk very loud, and which will bless you, and only one which no one will hear, and which will curse you in the dark. Well! listen, infamous man! All those benedictions will fall back before they reach heaven, and only the malediction will ascend to God."

This voice, feeble at first, and which had proceeded from the most obscure depths of his conscience, had gradually become startling and formidable, and he now heard it in his very ear. It seemed to him that it had detached itself from him, and that it was now speaking outside of him. He thought that he heard the last words so distinctly, that he glanced around the room in a sort of terror.

"Is there any one here?" he demanded aloud, in utter bewilderment.

Then he resumed, with a laugh which resembled that of an idiot:—

"How stupid I am! There can be no one!"

There was some one; but the person who was there was of those whom the human eye cannot see.

He placed the candlesticks on the chimney-piece.

…

He now recoiled in equal terror before both the resolutions at which he had arrived in turn. The two ideas which counselled him appeared to him equally fatal. What a fatality! What conjunction that that Champmathieu should have been taken for him; to be overwhelmed by precisely the means which Providence seemed to have employed, at first, to strengthen his position!

There was a moment when he reflected on the future. Denounce himself, great God! Deliver himself up! With immense despair he faced all that he should be obliged to leave, all that he should be obliged to take up once more. He should have to bid farewell to that existence which was so good, so pure, so radiant, to the respect of all, to honor, to liberty. He should never more stroll in the fields; he should never more hear the birds sing in the month of May; he should never more bestow alms on

UNIT
3

the little children; he should never more experience the sweetness of having glances of gratitude and love fixed upon him; he should quit that house which he had built, that little chamber! Everything seemed charming to him at that moment. Never again should he read those books; never more should he write on that little table of white wood; his old portress, the only servant whom he kept, would never more bring him his coffee in the morning. Great God! instead of that, the convict gang, the iron necklet, the red waistcoat, the chain on his ankle, fatigue, the cell, the camp bed, all those horrors which he knew so well! At his age, after having been what he was! If he were only young again! but to be addressed in his old age as "thou" by any one who pleased; to be searched by the convict-guard; to receive the galley-sergeant's cudgellings; to wear iron-bound shoes on his bare feet; to have to stretch out his leg night and morning to the hammer of the roundsman who visits the gang; …and at night, dripping with perspiration, overwhelmed with lassitude, their green caps drawn over their eyes, to remount, two by two, the ladder staircase of the galleys beneath the sergeant's whip. Oh, what misery! Can destiny, then, be as malicious as an intelligent being, and become as monstrous as the human heart?

And do what he would, he always fell back upon the heartrending dilemma which lay at the foundation of his reverie: "Should he remain in paradise and become a demon? Should he return to hell and become an angel?"

What was to be done? Great God! what was to be done?

…

At intervals, as he combated his lassitude, he made an effort to recover the mastery of his mind. He tried to put to himself, for the last time, and definitely, the problem over which he had, in a manner, fallen prostrate with fatigue: Ought he to denounce himself? Ought he to hold his peace? He could not manage to see anything distinctly. The vague aspects of all the courses of reasoning which had been sketched out by his meditations quivered and vanished, one after the other, into smoke. He only felt that, to whatever course of action he made up his mind, something in him must die, and that of necessity, and without his being able to escape the fact; that he was entering a sepulchre on the right hand as much as on the left; that he was passing through a death agony,—the agony of his happiness, or the agony of his virtue.

Alas! all his resolution had again taken possession of him. He was no further advanced than at the beginning.

…

Javert

Javert passed slowly down the Rue de l'Homme Arme.

He walked with drooping head for the first time in his life, and likewise, for the first time in his life, with his hands behind his back.

Up to that day, Javert had borrowed from Napoleon's attitudes, only that which is expressive of resolution, with arms folded across the chest; that which is expressive of uncertainty—with the hands behind the back—had been unknown to him. Now, a change had taken place; his whole person, slow and sombre, was stamped with anxiety.

He plunged into the silent streets.

Nevertheless, he followed one given direction.

He took the shortest cut to the Seine,…and halted at some distance from the post of the Place du Chatelet, at the angle of the Pont Notre-Dame. There…the Seine forms a sort of square lake, traversed by a rapid.

This point of the Seine is dreaded by mariners. Nothing is more dangerous than this rapid, hemmed in, at that epoch, and irritated by the piles of the mill on the bridge, now demolished. The two bridges, situated thus close together, augment the peril; the water hurries in formidable … through the arches. It rolls in vast and terrible waves; it accumulates and piles up there; the flood attacks the piles of the bridges as though in an effort to pluck them up…. Men who fall in there never re-appear; the best of swimmers are drowned there.

Javert leaned both elbows on the parapet, his chin resting in both hands, and, while his nails were mechanically twined in the abundance of his whiskers, he meditated.

A … revolution, a catastrophe had just taken place in the depths of his being; and he had something upon which to examine himself.

Javert was undergoing horrible suffering.

For several hours, Javert had ceased to be simple. He was troubled; that brain, so limpid in its blindness, had lost its transparency; that crystal was clouded. Javert felt duty divided within his conscience, and he could not conceal the fact from himself. When he had so unexpectedly encountered Jean Valjean on the banks of the Seine, there had been in him something of the wolf which regains his grip on his prey, and of the dog who finds his master again.

He beheld before him two paths, both equally straight, but he beheld two; and that terrified him; him, who had never in all his life known more than one straight line. And, the poignant anguish lay in this, that the two paths were contrary to each other. One of these straight lines excluded the other. Which of the two was the true one?

His situation was indescribable.

To owe his life to a malefactor, to accept that debt and to repay it; to be, in spite of himself, on a level with a fugitive from justice, and to repay his service with another service; to allow it to be said to him, "Go," and to say to the latter in his turn: "Be free"; to sacrifice to

personal motives duty, that general obligation, and to be conscious, in those personal motives, of something that was also general, and, perchance, superior, to betray society in order to remain true to his conscience; that all these absurdities should be realized and should accumulate upon him,—this was what overwhelmed him.

One thing had amazed him,—this was that Jean Valjean should have done him a favor, and one thing petrified him,—that he, Javert, should have done Jean Valjean a favor.

Where did he stand? He sought to comprehend his position, and could no longer find his bearings.

What was he to do now? To deliver up Jean Valjean was bad; to leave Jean Valjean at liberty was bad. In the first case, the man of authority fell lower than the man of the galleys, in the second, a convict rose above the law, and set his foot upon it. In both cases, dishonor for him, Javert. There was disgrace in any resolution at which he might arrive. Destiny has some extremities which rise perpendicularly from the impossible, and beyond which life is no longer anything but a precipice. Javert had reached one of those extremities.

One of his anxieties consisted in being constrained to think. The very violence of all these conflicting emotions forced him to it. Thought was something to which he was unused, and which was peculiarly painful.

In thought there always exists a certain amount of internal rebellion; and it irritated him to have that within him.

Thought on any subject whatever, outside of the restricted circle of his functions, would have been for him in any case useless and a fatigue; thought on the day which had just passed was a torture. Nevertheless, it was indispensable that he should take a look into his conscience, after such shocks, and render to himself an account of himself.

What he had just done made him shudder. He, Javert, had seen fit to decide, contrary to all the regulations of the police, contrary to the whole social and judicial organization, contrary to the entire code, upon a release; this had suited him; he had substituted his own affairs for the affairs of the public; was not this unjustifiable? Every time that he brought himself face to face with this deed without a name which he had committed, he trembled from head to foot. Upon what should he decide? One sole resource remained to him; to return in all haste to the Rue de l'Homme Arme, and commit Jean Valjean to prison. It was clear that that was what he ought to do. He could not.

Something barred his way in that direction.

Something? What? Is there in the world, anything outside of the tribunals, executory sentences, the police and the authorities? Javert was overwhelmed.

A galley-slave sacred! A convict who could not be touched by the law! And that the deed of Javert!

Was it not a fearful thing that Javert and Jean Valjean, …these two men who were both the things of the law, should have come to such a pass, that both of them had set themselves above the law? What then! such enormities were to happen and no one was to be punished! Jean Valjean, stronger than the whole social order, was to remain at liberty, and he, Javert, was to go on eating the government's bread!

His reverie gradually became terrible.

…

Jean Valjean was the load which weighed upon his spirit.

Jean Valjean disconcerted him. All the axioms which had served him as points of support all his life long, had crumbled away in the presence of this man. Jean Valjean's generosity towards him, Javert, crushed him. Other facts which he now recalled, and which he had formerly treated as lies and folly, now recurred to him as realities. M. Madeleine re-appeared behind Jean Valjean, and the two figures were superposed in such fashion that they now

formed but one, which was venerable. Javert felt that something terrible was penetrating his soul—admiration for a convict. Respect for a galley-slave—is that a possible thing? He shuddered at it, yet could not escape from it. In vain did he struggle, he was reduced to confess, in his inmost heart, the sublimity of that wretch. This was odious.

A benevolent malefactor, merciful, gentle, helpful,… a convict, returning good for evil, giving back pardon for hatred, preferring pity to vengeance, preferring to ruin himself rather than to ruin his enemy, saving him who had smitten him, kneeling on the heights of virtue, more nearly akin to an angel than to a man. Javert was constrained to admit to himself that this monster existed.

Things could not go on in this manner.

Certainly, and we insist upon this point, he had not yielded without resistance to that monster, to that infamous angel, to that hideous hero, who enraged almost as much as he amazed him. Twenty times, as he sat in that carriage face to face with Jean Valjean, the legal tiger had roared within him. A score of times he had been tempted to fling himself upon Jean Valjean, to seize him and devour him, that is to say, to arrest him. What more simple, in fact? To cry out at the first post that they passed:—"Here is a fugitive from justice, who has broken his ban!" to summon the gendarmes and say to them: "This man is yours!" then to go off, leaving that condemned man there, to ignore the rest and not to meddle further in the matter. This man is forever a prisoner of the law; the law may do with him what it will. What could be more just? Javert had said all this to himself; he had wished to pass beyond, to act, to apprehend the man, and then, as at present, he had not been able to do it; and every time that his arm had been raised convulsively towards Jean Valjean's collar, his hand had fallen back again, as beneath an enormous weight, and in the depths of his thought he had heard a voice, a strange voice crying to him:—"It is well. Deliver up your savior. Then have the basin of Pontius Pilate brought and wash your claws."

Then his reflections reverted to himself and beside Jean Valjean glorified he beheld himself, Javert, degraded.

A convict was his benefactor!

…

His supreme anguish was the loss of certainty. He felt that he had been uprooted. The code was no longer anything more than a stump in his hand. He had to deal with scruples of an unknown species. There had taken place within him a sentimental revelation entirely distinct from legal affirmation, his only standard of measurement hitherto. To remain in his former uprightness did not suffice. A whole order of unexpected facts had cropped up and subjugated him. A whole new world was dawning on his soul: kindness accepted and repaid, devotion, mercy, indulgence, violences committed by pity on austerity, respect for persons, no more definitive condemnation, no more conviction, the possibility of a tear in the eye of the law, no one knows what justice according to God, running in inverse sense to justice according to men. He perceived amid the shadows the terrible rising of an unknown moral sun; it horrified and dazzled him. An owl forced to the gaze of an eagle.

He said to himself that it was true that there were exceptional cases, that authority might be put out of countenance, that the rule might be inadequate in the presence of a fact, that everything could not be framed within the text of the code, that the unforeseen compelled obedience, that the virtue of a convict might set a snare for the virtue of the functionary, that destiny did indulge in such ambushes, and he reflected with despair that he himself had not even been fortified against a surprise.

He was forced to acknowledge that goodness did exist. This convict had been good. And he himself, unprecedented circumstance, had just been good also. So he was becoming depraved.

He found that he was a coward. He conceived a horror of himself.

Javert's ideal was not to be human, to be grand, to be sublime; it was to be irreproachable.

Now, he had just failed in this.

How had he come to such a pass? How had all this happened? He could not have told himself. He clasped his head in both hands, but in spite of all that he could do, he could not contrive to explain it to himself.

…

All sorts of interrogation points flashed before his eyes. He put questions to himself, and made replies to himself, and his replies frightened him. He asked himself: "What has that convict done, that desperate fellow, whom I have pursued even to persecution, and who has had me under his foot, and who could have avenged himself, and who owed it both to his rancor and to his safety, in leaving me my life, in showing mercy upon me? His duty? No. Something more. And I in showing mercy upon him in my turn—what have I done? My duty? No. Something more. So there is something beyond duty?" Here he took fright; his balance became disjointed; one of the scales fell into the abyss, the other rose heavenward, and Javert was no less terrified by the one which was on high than by the one which was below…being…respectful by instinct, towards the established church, he knew it only as an august fragment of the social whole; order was his dogma, and sufficed for him; ever since he had attained to man's estate and the rank of a functionary, he had centered nearly all his religion in the police…. [U]p to that day he had never dreamed of that other superior, God.

This new chief, God, he became unexpectedly conscious of, and he felt embarrassed by him. This unforeseen presence threw him off his bearings; he did not know what to do with this superior, he, who was not ignorant of the fact that the subordinate is bound always to bow, that he must not disobey, nor find fault, nor discuss, and that, in the presence of a superior who amazes him too greatly, the inferior has no other resource than that of handing in his resignation.

But how was he to set about handing in his resignation to God?

UNIT 3

However things might stand,—and it was to this point that he reverted constantly,—one fact dominated everything else for him, and that was, that he had just committed a terrible infraction of the law. He had just shut his eyes on an escaped convict who had broken his ban. He had just set a galley-slave at large. He had just robbed the laws of a man who belonged to them. That was what he had done. He no longer understood himself. The very reasons for his action escaped him; only their vertigo was left with him. Up to that moment he had lived with that blind faith which gloomy probity engenders. This faith had quitted him, this probity had deserted him. All that he had believed in melted away. Truths which he did not wish to recognize were besieging him, inexorably. Henceforth, he must be a different man. He was suffering from the strange pains of a conscience abruptly operated on for the cataract. He saw that which it was repugnant to him to behold. He felt himself emptied, useless, put out of joint with his past life, turned out, dissolved. Authority was dead within him. He had no longer any reason for existing.

A terrible situation! to be touched.

To be granite and to doubt! ... [T]o be the watch-dog, and to lick the intruder's hand! to be ice and melt!... —what a terrible thing!

...

To be obliged to confess this to oneself: infallibility is not infallible, there may exist error in the dogma, all has not been said when a code speaks, society is not perfect, authority is complicated with vacillation, a crack is possible in the immutable, judges are but men, the law may err, tribunals may make a mistake! to behold a rift in the immense blue pane of the firmament!

...

God, always within man, and refractory, He, the true conscience, to the false; a prohibition to the spark to die out; an order to the ray to remember the sun; an injunction to the soul to recognize the veritable absolute when confronted with the fictitious absolute, humanity which cannot be lost; the human heart indestructible; that splendid phenomenon, the finest, perhaps, of all our interior marvels, did Javert understand this? Did Javert penetrate it? Did Javert account for it to himself? Evidently he did not. But beneath the pressure of that incontestable incomprehensibility he felt his brain bursting.

He was less the man transfigured than the victim of this prodigy. In all this he perceived only the tremendous difficulty of existence. It seemed to him that, henceforth, his respiration was repressed forever. He was not accustomed to having something unknown hanging over his head.

Up to this point, everything above him had been, to his gaze, merely a smooth, limpid and simple surface; there was nothing incomprehensible, nothing obscure; nothing that was not defined, regularly disposed, linked, precise, circumscribed, exact, limited, closed, fully provided for; authority was a plane surface; there was no fall in it, no dizziness in its presence. Javert had never beheld the unknown except from below. The irregular, the unforeseen, the disordered opening of chaos, the possible slip over a precipice—this was the work of the lower regions, of rebels, of the wicked, of wretches. Now Javert threw himself back, and he was suddenly terrified by this unprecedented apparition: a gulf on high.

What! one was dismantled from top to bottom! one was disconcerted, absolutely! In what could one trust! That which had been agreed upon was giving way! What! the defect in society's armor could be discovered by a magnanimous wretch! What! an honest servitor of the law could suddenly find himself caught between two crimes—the crime of allowing a man to escape and the crime of arresting him! everything was not settled in the orders given by the State to the functionary! There might be blind alleys in duty! What,—all this was real! was it true that an ex-ruffian, weighed down with convictions, could rise erect and end by being in the right? Was this credible? were there cases in which the law should retire before transfigured crime, and stammer its excuses?—Yes, that was the state of the case! and Javert saw it! and Javert had touched it! and not only could he not deny it, but he had taken part in it. These were realities. It was abominable that actual facts could reach such deformity. If facts did their duty, they would confine themselves to being proofs of the law; facts—it is God who sends them. Was anarchy, then, on the point of now descending from on high?

Thus,—and in the exaggeration of anguish, … society, and the human race, and the universe were, henceforth, summed up in his eyes, in one simple and terrible feature,—thus the penal laws, the thing judged, the force due to legislation, the decrees of the sovereign courts, … the government, … official cruelty, wisdom, legal infallibility, the principle of authority, all the dogmas on which rest political and civil security, sovereignty, justice, public truth, all this was rubbish, a shapeless mass, chaos; he himself, Javert, the spy of order, incorruptibility in the service of the police, the bull-dog providence of society, vanquished and hurled to earth; … this was the fearful vision which he bore within his soul.

Was this to be endured? No.

A violent state, if ever such existed. There were only two ways of escaping from it. One was to go resolutely to Jean Valjean, and restore to his cell the convict from the galleys. The other….

The darkness was complete. It was the sepulchral moment which follows midnight. A ceiling of clouds concealed the stars. Not a single light burned in the houses of the city; no one was passing; all of the streets and quays which could be seen were deserted; Notre-Dame and the towers of the Court-House seemed features of the night. A street lantern reddened the margin of the quay. The outlines of the bridges lay shapeless in the mist one behind the other. Recent rains had swollen the river.

The spot where Javert was leaning was, it will be remembered, situated precisely over the rapids of the Seine, perpendicularly above that formidable spiral of whirlpools which loose and knot themselves again like an endless screw.

Javert bent his head and gazed. All was black. Nothing was to be distinguished. A sound of foam was audible; but the river could not be seen. At moments, in that dizzy depth, a gleam of light appeared, and undulated vaguely, water possessing the power of taking light, no one knows whence, and converting it into a snake. The light vanished, and all became indistinct once more. Immensity seemed thrown open there. What lay below was not water, it was a gulf. The wall of the quay, abrupt, confused, mingled with the vapors, instantly concealed from sight, produced the effect of an escarpment of the infinite. Nothing was to be seen, but the hostile chill of the water and the stale odor of the wet stones could be felt. A fierce breath rose from this abyss. The flood in the river, divined rather than perceived, the tragic whispering of the waves, the melancholy vastness of the arches of the bridge, the imaginable fall into that gloomy void, into all that shadow was full of horror.

Javert remained motionless for several minutes, gazing at this opening of shadow; he considered the invisible with a fixity that resembled attention. The water roared. All at once he took off his hat and placed it on the edge of the quay. A moment later, a tall black figure, which a belated passer-by in the distance might have taken for a phantom, appeared erect upon the parapet of the quay, bent over towards the Seine, then drew itself up again, and fell straight down into the shadows; a dull splash followed; and the shadow alone was in the secret of the convulsions of that obscure form which had disappeared beneath the water.

UNIT
3

Hugo, Victor. *Les Misérables*. (Translator: Isabel F. Hapgood). New York: Thomas Y. Crowell & Co. 1887. eBook Retrieved from www.gutenberg.org.

Abridgment for Phi Theta Kappa by William Albright.

LEADERSHIP PROFILE

K'ung Fu-tzu—"Confucius" (551?–479 B.C.E.)

Chinese Philosopher
Excerpts from *Lún Yû* or *The Analects*

Introduction and Historical Background

K'ung Fu-tzu, or "Master K'ung," known in the West as Confucius, was a Chinese political and ethical philosopher, educator, and reformer. Confucius lived during a time of political disorder when might often made right, and in which dealings and relations were often managed on the basis of personal advantage. In the aristocratic Chinese society of the time, those with influence and power had inherited it. Confucius himself was born into a noble family and served the state in minor official capacities. However, he sought to establish a more equitable hierarchical system that was not based on birth. He wished to end the political infighting and to establish political order, and he advocated transforming the martial society into a more civil one—one in which leadership and government would be based on more than military prowess and strength. *The Analects* purport to be a record of conversations and sayings of Confucius and often focus on issues related to this social and political

Shutterstock

transformation he desired. He raises questions of what constitutes merit, how one recognizes it, and how one develops it. He also often refers to historical and legendary figures, good and bad, to illustrate his points. He says that what he proposes has historical precedent and can thus be accomplished again. In this way, his thinking is practical and he promotes a union of theory and practice. His theories were based on a worldly, rational philosophy emphasizing humanity and goodness (*jen*), propriety (*li*), reverence for the ancient sages, and government by personal virtue.

By the second century B.C.E., Confucianism had become the dominant philosophy in China. Confucius had also identified texts that he thought a person should study, and throughout much of subsequent Chinese history, his program of reading and activities was considered central to a person's education. In fact, for a span of nearly 700 years, from the thirteenth century to the beginning of the twentieth century, *The Analects* was considered essential to the education of those preparing for official careers in the Chinese imperial government—the leaders and managers of Chinese society.

During the Enlightenment period in Europe (eighteenth century), the Chinese governmental system was much admired, and it served as a pattern for civil service systems in England, and indirectly in the United States. Confucian thought fell into disrepute early in the twentieth century, after the Chinese empire crumbled as a result of Western encroachment and a host of economic and political problems. Chinese leaders believed that Confucianism was part of China's backwardness and tried to institute reforms based on different, Western ideas. The influence of Confucianism, however, has proved to be persistent, if the various anti-Confucian campaigns

launched by the Chinese communist party are any indication. Another, perhaps stronger, indicator of the continuing vitality and adaptability of Confucian thought is the economic rise in the late twentieth century of Taiwan, Hong Kong, Singapore, and South Korea. The success of these four economies has been attributed at least in part to Confucianism and has led to renewed interest in this tradition of thought.

The Analects has been one of the most influential texts in East Asian history. The statements of Confucius offer a challenging way to examine and reflect on a number of leadership topics, including ethics, power, motivation, authority, and communication. *The Analects* was compiled some time after Confucius' death, and Confucius is usually referred to as "The Master," a term of veneration. The text is organized into twenty "books," which are themselves divided into brief chapters. Some chapters consist of a single saying by Confucius. More often, chapters consist of a conversation between Confucius and one or more of his disciples. In such chapters, *The Analects* give an idea of how Confucius taught and how he adapted his thinking to the various capacities of his students. Often the chapters seem almost to stand as an independent unit, and there is frequently no narrative or logical connection between the chapters in each book. Sometimes the books do not always seem to have a coherent focus. In this way, the structure of *The Analects* frustrates a linear reading process. The intent seems to be to focus a reader's attention more closely on the content of each chapter, to force a reader to concentrate fully on the thought expressed. On first reading, the application and relevance of many of these sayings may not be immediately apparent. Deeper reflection and discussion, however, should allow Confucius' wisdom to emerge.

UNIT
3

Points to Consider

1. What values does Confucius praise?

2. What do *The Analects* tell us about followership? How can individuals effectively assess when to exercise leadership and when to follow?

3. To what extent do Confucius' beliefs about punishment work in practice with small groups or larger organizations?

4. Is the Confucian leader autocratic or participative? What difference in organizational culture do those styles make in practice?

The Analects of Confucius

(Excerpts from *Lún Yǔ* or *The Analects*)
Translated by Edward Slingerland

Book One

One of the central themes of this Book is that learning (xue) has more to do with actual behavior than academic theory, and that virtuous public behavior as an adult is rooted in such basic familial virtues as filial piety (xiao) and respect for elders (ti).

1.1 The Master said, "To learn and then have occasion to practice what you have learned—is this not satisfying? To have friends arrive from afar—is this not a joy? To be patient even when others do not understand—is this not the mark of the gentleman?"

1.2   Master You said, "A young person who is filial and respectful of his elders rarely becomes the kind of person who is inclined to defy his superiors, and there has never been a case of one who is disinclined to defy his superiors stirring up rebellion.

"The gentleman applies himself to the roots. 'Once the roots are firmly established, the Way will grow.' Might we not say that filial piety and respect for elders constitute the root of Goodness?"

1.3   The Master said, "A clever tongue and fine appearance are rarely signs of Goodness."

1.4   Master Zeng said, "Every day I examine myself on three counts: in my dealings with others, have I in any way failed to be dutiful? In my interactions with friends and associates, have I in any way failed to be trustworthy? Finally, have I in any way failed to repeatedly put into practice what I teach?

1.5   The Master said, "To guide a state of one thousand chariots, be respectful in your handling of affairs and display trustworthiness; be frugal in your expenditures and cherish others; and employ the common people only at the proper times."

1.6   The Master said, "A young person should be filial when at home and respectful of his elders when in public. Conscientious and trustworthy, he should display a general care for the masses but feel a particular affection for those who are Good. If he has any strength left over after manifesting these virtues in practice, let him devote it to learning the cultural arts (*wen*)."

1.7   Zixia said, "Imagine someone who recognizes and admires worthiness and therefore changes his lustful nature, who is able to fully exhaust his strength in serving his parents and extend himself to the utmost in serving his lord, and who is trustworthy in speech when interacting with friends and associates. Even if you said of such a person, 'Oh, but he is not learned (*xue*),' I would still insist that it is precisely such qualities that make one worthy of being called 'learned.'"

1.8   The Master said, "If a gentleman is not serious, he will not inspire awe, and what he learns will be grasped only superficially.

Let your actions be governed by dutifulness and trustworthiness, and do not accept as a friend one who is not your equal. If you have committed a transgression, do not be afraid to change your ways."

1.9   Master Zeng said, "Take great care in seeing off the deceased and sedulously maintain the sacrifices to your distant ancestors, and the common people will sincerely return to Virtue."

1.10   Ziqin and Zigong, "When our Master arrives in a state, he invariably finds out about its government. Does he actively seek out this information? Surely it is not simply offered to him!"

Zigong answered, "Our Master obtains it through being courteous, refined, respectful, restrained, and deferential. The Master's way of seeking it is entirely different from other people's way of seeking it, is it not?"

1.11   The Master said, "When someone's father is still alive, observe his intentions; after his father has passed away, observe his conduct. If for three years he does not alter the ways of his father, he may be called a filial son."

1.12 Master You said, "When it comes to the practice of ritual, it is harmonious ease (*he*) that is to be valued. It is precisely such harmony that makes the Way of the Former Kings so beautiful. If you merely stick rigidly to ritual in all matters, great and small, there will remain that which you cannot accomplish. Yet if you know enough to value harmonious ease but try to attain it without being regulated by the rites, this will not work either."

1.13 Master You said, "Trustworthiness comes close to rightness, in that your word can be counted upon. Reverence comes close to ritual propriety, in that it allows you to keep shame and public disgrace at a distance. Simply following these virtues, never letting them out of your sight—one cannot deny that this is worthy of respect."

1.14 The Master said, "The gentleman is not motivated by the desire for a full belly or a comfortable abode. He is simply scrupulous in behavior and careful in speech, drawing near to those who possess the Way in order to be set straight by them. Surely this and nothing else is what it means to love learning."

1.15 Zigong said, "Poor without being obsequious, rich without being arrogant—what would you say about someone like that?"

The Master answered, "That is acceptable, but it is still not as good as being poor and yet joyful, rich and yet loving ritual."

Zigong said, "An ode says,

'As if cut, as if polished;

As if carved, as if ground.'

Is this not what you have in mind?"

The Master said, "Zigong, you are precisely the kind of person with whom one can begin to discuss the *Odes*. Informed as to what has gone before, you know what is to come."

1.16 The Master said, "Do not be concerned about whether or not others know you; be concerned about whether or not you know others."

UNIT
3

Book Two

In this book, we see elaborations of a theme suggested in 1.2: political order is not obtained by means of force or government regulations, but rather by the non-coercive influence of the morally perfected person. Several descriptions of such wu-wei perfection appear in this book (including Confucius' famous spiritual autobiography in 2.4), and we also find an extended discussion of the "root" virtue of filial piety that emphasizes the importance of having the proper internal dispositions.

2.1 The Master said, "One who rules through the power of Virtue is analogous to the Pole Star: it simply remains in its place and receives the homage of the myriad lesser stars."

2.2 The Master said, "The *Odes* number several hundred, and yet can be judged with a single phrase: 'Oh, they will not lead you astray.'"

2.3 The Master said, "If you try to guide the common people with coercive regulations (*zheng*) and keep them in line with punishments, the common people will become evasive and will have no sense of shame. If, however, you guide them with Virtue, and keep them in line by means of ritual, the people will have a sense of shame and will rectify themselves."

2.4   The Master said, "At fifteen, I set my mind upon learning; at thirty, I took my place in society; at forty, I became free of doubts; at fifty, I understood Heaven's Mandate; at sixty, my ear was attuned; and at seventy, I could follow my heart's desires without overstepping the bounds of propriety."

2.5   Meng Yizi asked about filial piety. The Master replied, "Do not disobey."

Later, Fan Chi was driving the Master's chariot. The Master said to him, "Just now Meng Yizi asked me about filial piety, and I answered, 'Do not disobey.'"

Fan Chi said, "What did you mean by that?"

The Master replied, "When your parents are alive, serve them in accordance with the rites; when they pass away, bury them in accordance with the rites and sacrifice to them in accordance with the rites."

2.6   Meng Wubo asked about filial piety. The Master replied, "Give your parents no cause for anxiety other than the possibility that they might fall ill."

2.7   Ziyou asked about filial piety. The Master said, "Nowadays 'filial' means simply being able to provide one's parents with nourishment. But even dogs and horses are provided with nourishment. If you are not respectful, wherein lies the difference?"

2.8   Zixia asked about filial piety. The Master said, "It is the demeanor that is difficult. If there is work to be done, disciples shoulder the burden, and when wine and food are served, elders are given precedence, but surely filial piety consists of more than this."

2.9   The Master said, "I can talk all day long with Yan Hui without him once disagreeing with me. In this way, he seems a bit stupid. And yet when we retire and I observe his private behavior, I see that it is in fact worthy to serve as an illustration of what I have taught. Hui is not stupid at all."

2.10 The Master said, "Look at the means a man employs, observe the basis from which he acts, and discover where it is that he feels at ease. Where can he hide? Where can he hide?"

2.11 The Master said, "Both keeping past teachings alive and understanding the present—someone able to do this is worthy of being a teacher."

2.12 The Master said, "The gentleman is not a vessel."

2.13 Zigong asked about the gentleman.

The Master said, "He first expresses his views, and then acts in accordance with them."

2.14 The Master said, "The gentleman is broad and not partial; the petty person is partial and not broad."

2.15 The Master said, "If you learn without thinking about what you have learned, you will be lost. If you think without learning, however, you will fall into danger."

2.16 The Master said, "Working from the wrong starting point will lead to nothing but harm."

2.17 The Master said, "Zilu, remark well what I am about to teach you! This is wisdom: to recognize what you know as what you know, and recognize what you do not know as what you do not know."

2.18 Zizhang asked about obtaining official position.

Confucius said, "If you first learn as much as you can, then guard against that which is dubious and speak carefully about the rest, you will seldom speak in error. If you first observe as much as you can, then guard against that which is perilous and carefully put the rest into action, you will seldom have cause for regret. If in your speech you seldom err, and in your behavior you seldom have cause for regret, an official position will follow naturally."

2.19 Duke Ai asked, "What can I do to induce the common people to be obedient?"

Confucius replied, "Raise up the straight and apply them to the crooked, and the people will submit to you. If you raise up the crooked and apply them to the straight, the people will never submit."

2.20 Ji Kangzi asked, "How can I cause the common people to be respectful, dutiful, and industrious?"

The Master said, "Oversee them with dignity, and the people will be respectful; oversee them with filiality and kindness, and the people will be dutiful; oversee them by raising up the accomplished and instructing those who are unable, and the people will be industrious."

2.21 Some people said of Confucius, "Why is it that he is not participating in government?"

[Upon being informed of this,] the Master remarked, "*The Book of Documents* says,

'Filial, oh so filial,

Friendly to one's elders and juniors; [In this way] exerting an influence upon those who govern.'

Thus, in being a filial son and good brother one is already taking part in government. What need is there, then, to speak of 'participating in government'?"

2.22 The Master said, "I cannot see how a person devoid of trustworthiness could possibly get along in the world. Imagine a large ox-drawn cart without a linchpin for its yolk, or a small horse drawn cart without a linchpin for its collar: how could they possibly be driven?"

2.23 Zizhang asked, "Can we know what it will be like ten generations from now?"

The Master responded, "The Yin followed the rituals of the Xia, altering them only in ways that we know. The Zhou followed the rituals of the Yin, altering them only in ways that we know. If some dynasty succeeds the Zhou, we can know what it will be like even a hundred generations from now."

2.24 The Master said, "To sacrifice to spirits that are not one's own is to be presumptuous. To see what is right, but to fail to do it, is to be lacking in courage."

UNIT 3

"Among the tribes of northern Natal in South Africa, the most common greeting—the equivalent of 'hello' in English—is the expression *sawu bona*. Literally it means 'I see you.' If you are a member of the tribe you might reply by saying *sikhona*, which translates into English as 'I am here.' The order of the exchange is significant. It means that until you see me I do not exist; when you do see me, you bring me into existence. The meaning implicit in the perennial wisdom of these tribespeople is part of what is called *ubuntu*, a frame of mind or world-view characteristic of sub-Sahara African peoples. *Ubuntu* is the key word used to shorten a phrase in the Zulu language that translates 'a person is a person because of other people.'"

—Bennett J. Sims

Sims, B. (2005). *Servanthood: Leadership for the third millenium.* Used by permission of Wipf and Stock Publishers. www.wipfandstock.com .

REFLECT & FOCUS

READINGS

"Satyagraha"

By Mohandas K. Gandhi (1869–1948)
Leader of Indian Independence

Mohandas K. Gandhi (1869–1948) pursued an education and career in law but dedicated his life to progress for the disadvantaged, the dispossessed, the oppressed, and the downtrodden, first in South Africa and then in his native India. His causes included Indian independence from Great Britain, Hindu-Muslim unity, and the end of "untouchability"—the discrimination against the lower orders of India's caste system of social hierarchy. His new method of provoking change was ultimately successful and earned him fame, the title "Mahatma"—Great Soul, and great admiration around the world: Gandhi preached and practiced non-violence—"soul force" or *satyagraha*, not physical force—and inspired millions to emulate his example in his country and elsewhere, including Martin Luther King, Jr. and the Civil Rights activists of the United States. In this reading, Gandhi responds as an editor and writer to questions from readers of papers and journal articles.

Points to Consider

1. Why does Gandhi contend that individuals exhibit more courage with passive resistance than aggressive resistance?

2. What leadership characteristics does *Satyagraha* require? To what extent do these characteristics translate to other leadership situations?

3. In what ways is *Satyagraha* an effective organizational strategy? How effective as a long-term strategy is *Satyagraha*?

4. What does Gandhi mean when he says that passive resistance is an "all-sided sword"?

"Satyagraha"

Moral Requirements for Satyagraha
Reader: I deduce that passive resistance is a splendid weapon of the weak, but that when they are strong they may take up arms.

Editor: This is gross ignorance. Passive resistance, that is, soul-force, is matchless. It is superior to the force of arms. How, then, can it be considered only a weapon of the weak? Physical-force men are strangers to the courage that is requisite in a passive resister. Do you believe that a coward can ever disobey a law that he dislikes? Extremists are considered to be advocates of brute force. Why do they, then, talk about obeying laws? I do not blame them. They can say nothing else. When they succeed in driving out the English and they themselves become governors, they will want you and me to obey their laws. And that is a fitting thing for their constitution. But a passive resister will say he will not obey a law that is against his conscience, even though he may be blown to pieces at the mouth of a cannon.

What do you think? Wherein is courage required—in blowing others to pieces from behind a cannon, or with a smiling face to approach a cannon and be blown to pieces? Who is the true warrior—he who keeps death always as a bosom-friend, or he who controls the death of others? Believe me that a man devoid of courage and manhood can never be a passive resister.

This, however, I will admit: that even a man weak in body is capable of offering this resistance. One man can offer it just as well as millions. Both men and women can indulge in it. It does not require the training of an army; it needs no jiu-jitsu. Control over the mind is alone necessary and when that is attained, man is free like the king of the forest and his very glance withers the enemy.

Passive resistance is an all-sided sword, it can be used anyhow; it blesses him who uses it and him against whom it is used. Without drawing a drop of blood it produces far-reaching results. It never rusts and cannot be stolen. Competition between passive resisters does not exhaust. The sword of passive resistance does not require a scabbard. It is strange indeed that you should consider such a weapon to be a weapon merely of the weak.

Reader: You have said that passive resistance is a specialty of India. Have cannons never been used in India?

Editor: Evidently, in your opinion, India means its few princes. To me it means its teeming millions on whom depends the existence of its princes and our own.

Kings will always use their kingly weapons. To use force is bred in them. They want to command, but those who have to obey commands do not want guns: and these are in a majority throughout the world. They have to learn either body-force or soul-force. Where they learn the former, both the rulers and the ruled become like so many mad men; but where they learn soul-force, the commands of the rulers do not go beyond the point of their swords, for true men disregard unjust commands. Peasants have never been subdued by the sword, and never will be. They do not know the use of the sword, and they are not frightened by the use of it by others. That nation is great which rests its head upon death as its pillow. Those who defy death are free from all fear. For those who are labouring under the delusive charms of brute-force, this picture is not overdrawn. The fact is that, in India, the nation at large has generally used passive resistance in all departments of life. We cease to co-operate with our rulers when they displease us. This is passive resistance.

Hind Swaraj or Indian Home Rule, chap. XVII

Conditions for Successful Satyagraha

There can be no Satyagraha in an unjust cause. Satyagraha in a just cause is vain, if the men espousing it are not determined and capable of fighting and suffering to the end; and the slightest use of violence often defeats a just cause. Satyagraha excludes the use of violence in any shape or form, whether in thought, speech, or deed. Given a just cause, capacity for endless suffering and avoidance of violence, victory is a certainty.

Young India, 27-4-'21

Qualifications for Satyagraha

Satyagraha presupposes self-discipline, self-control, self-purification, and a recognized social status in the person offering it. A Satyagrahi must never forget the distinction between evil and the evil-doer. He must not harbour ill-will or bitterness against the latter. He may not even employ needlessly offensive language against the evil person, however unrelieved his evil might be. For it should be an article of faith with every Satyagrahi that there is none so fallen in this world but can be converted by love. A Satyagrahi will always try to overcome evil by good, anger by love, untruth by truth, *himsa* by *ahimsa*. There is no other way of purging the world of evil. Therefore a person who claims to be a Satyagrahi always tries by close and prayerful self-introspection and self-analysis to find out whether he is himself completely free from the taint of anger, ill-will and such other human infirmities, whether he is not himself capable of those very evils against which he is out to lead a crusade. In self-purification and penance lies half the victory of a Satyagrahi. A Satyagrahi has faith that the silent and undemonstrative action of truth and love produces far more permanent and abiding results than speeches or such other showy performances.

But although Satyagraha can operate silently, it requires a certain amount of action on the part of a Satyagrahi. A Satyagrahi, for instance, must first mobilize public opinion against the evil which he is out to eradicate, by means of a wide and intensive agitation. When public opinion is sufficiently roused against a social abuse even the tallest will not dare to practice or openly to lend support to it. An awakened and intelligent public opinion is the most potent weapon of a Satyagrahi.

Young India, 8-8-'29

UNIT
3

For "Followers"

A friend sends me the following:

"It will be very helpful if you will kindly guide your followers about their conduct when they have to engage in a political controversy. Your guidance on the following points is particularly needed: (a) Vilification so as to lower the opponent in public estimation; (b) Kind of criticism of the opponent permissible; (c) Limit to which hostility should be carried; (d) Whether effort should be made to gain office and power."

I have said before in these pages that I claim no followers. It is enough for me to be my own follower. It is by itself a sufficiently taxing performance. But I know that many claim to be my followers. I must therefore answer the questions for their sakes. If they will follow what I endeavour to stand for rather than me they will see that the following answers are derived from truth and *ahimsa.*

(a) Vilification of an opponent there can never be. But this does not exclude a truthful characterization of his acts. An opponent is not always a bad man because he opposes. He may be as honourable as we may claim to be and yet there may be vital differences between him and us.

(b) Our criticism will therefore be if we *believe* him to be guilty of untruth to meet it with truth, of discourtesy with courtesy, of bullying with calm courage, of violence with suffering, of arrogance with humility, of evil with good. "My follower" would seek not to condemn but to convert.

(c) There is no question of any limit to which hostility may be carried. For there should be no hostility to persons. Hostility there must be to acts when they are subversive of morals or the good of society.

(d) Office and power must be avoided. Either may be accepted when it is clearly for greater service.

Young India, 7-5-'31

The Future

A friend writing from America propounds the following two questions:

1. *Granted that Satyagraha is capable of winning India's independence, what are the chances of its being accepted as a principle of State policy in a free India? In other words, would a strong and independent India rely on Satyagraha as a method of self-preservation, or would it lapse back to seeking refuge in the age-old institution of war, however defensive its character? To restate the question on the basis of a purely theoretic problem: Is Satyagraha likely to be accepted only in an up-hill battle, when the phenomenon of martyrdom is fully effective, or is it also to be the instrument of a sovereign authority which has neither the need nor the scope of behaving on the principle of martyrdom?*

2. *Suppose a free India adopts Satyagraha as an instrument of State policy[;] how would she defend herself against probable aggression by another sovereign State? To restate the question on the basis of a purely theoretic problem: What would be the Satyagrahic action-patterns to meet the invading army at the frontier? What kind of resistance can be offered the opponent before a common area of action, such as the one now existing in India between the Indian nationalists and the British Government, is established? Or should the Satyagrahis withhold their action until after the opponent has taken over the country?*

The questions are admittedly theoretical. They are also premature for the reason that I have not mastered the whole technique of non-violence. The experiment is still in the making. It is not even in its advanced stage. The nature of the experiment requires one to be satisfied with one step at a time. The distant scene is not for him to see. Therefore, my answers can only be speculative.

In truth, as I have said before, now we are not having unadulterated non-violence even in our struggle to win independence.

As to the first question, I fear that the chances of non-violence being accepted as a principle of State policy are very slight, so far as I can see at present. If India does not accept non-violence as her policy after winning independence, the second question becomes superfluous.

But I may state my own individual view of the potency of non-violence. I believe that a State can be administered on a non-violent basis if the vast majority of the people are non-violent. So far as I know, India is the only country which has a possibility of being such a State. I am conducting my experiment in that faith. Supposing, therefore, that India attained independence through pure non-violence, India could retain it too by the same means. A non-violent man or society does not anticipate or provide for attacks from without. On the contrary, such a person or society firmly believes that nobody is going to disturb them. If the worst happens, there are two ways open to non-violence. To yield possession but non-co-operate with the aggressor. Thus, supposing that a modern edition of Nero descended upon India, the representatives of the State will let him in but tell him that he will get no assistance from the people. They will prefer death to submission. The second way would be non-violent resistance by the people who have been trained in the non-violent way. They would offer themselves unarmed as fodder for the aggressor's cannon. The underlying belief in either case is that even a Nero is not devoid of a heart. The unexpected spectacle of endless rows upon rows of men and women simply dying rather than surrender to the will of an aggressor must ultimately melt him and his soldiery. Practically speaking there will be probably no greater loss in men than if forcible resistance was offered; there will be no expenditure in armaments and fortifications. The non-violent training received by the people will add inconceivably to their moral height. Such men and women will have shown personal bravery of a type far superior to that shown in armed warfare. In each case the bravery consists in dying, not in killing. Lastly, there is no such thing as defeat in non-violent resistance. That such a thing has not happened before is no answer

to my speculation. I have drawn no possible picture. History is replete with instances of individual non-violence of the type I have mentioned. There is no warrant for saying or thinking that a group of men and women cannot by sufficient training act non-violently as a group or nation. Indeed the sum total of the experience of mankind is that men somehow or other live on. From which fact I infer that it is the law of love that rules mankind. Had violence, i.e. hate, ruled us, we should have become extinct long ago. And yet the tragedy of it is that the so-called civilized men and nations conduct themselves as if the basis of society was violence. It gives me ineffable joy to make experiments proving that love is the supreme and only law of life. Much evidence to the contrary cannot shake my faith. Even the mixed non-violence of India has supported it. But if it is not enough to convince an unbeliever, it is enough to incline a friendly critic to view it with favour.

Harijan, 13-4-'40

Gandhi, M. (1956/2013). *Harijan: A journal of applied Gandhism*. Used by permission of Navajivan Trust.

UNIT 3

The Argumentative Indian

By Amartya Sen

Points to Consider

1. In what situations might an individual feel it necessary to follow duty, rather than conscience? How might an individual follow conscience when charged with a particular duty? What are the potential consequences of doing so?

2. How can a group reach consensus about the ethical path to follow when faced with the choice between duty and conscience?

3. In what ways can traditional societal roles for individuals shape the choices made between duty and conscience?

4. Why does Amartya Sen believe arguments are vital when making ethical decisions?

The Argumentative Indian

(Excerpts)

Editors' Note: These excerpts retain the British spelling
and punctuation conventions of the original.

Prolixity is not alien to us in India. We are able to talk at some length. Krishna Menon's record of the longest speech ever delivered at the United Nations (nine hours non-stop), established half a century ago (when Menon was leading the Indian delegation), has not been equaled by anyone from anywhere. Other peaks of loquaciousness have been scaled by other Indians. We do like to speak.

This is not a new habit. The ancient Sanskrit epics the *Rāmāyana* and the *Mahābhārata*, which are frequently compared with the *Iliad* and the *Odyssey*, are colossally longer than the works that the modest Homer could manage. Indeed, the *Mahābhārata* alone is about seven times as long as the *Iliad* and the *Odyssey* put together. The *Rāmāyana* and the *Mahābhārata* are certainly great epics: I recall with much joy how my own life was vastly enriched when I encountered them first as a restless youngster looking for intellectual stimulation as well as sheer entertainment. But they proceed from stories to stories woven around their principal tales, and are engagingly full of dialogues, dilemmas and alternative perspectives. And we encounter masses of arguments and counterarguments spread over incessant debates and disputations.

Dialogue and Significance

The arguments are also, often enough, quite substantive. For example, the famous *Bhagavad Gītā*, which is one small section of the *Mahābhārata*, presents a tussle between two contrary moral positions—Krishna's emphasis on doing one's duty, on one side, and Arjuna's focus on avoiding bad consequences (and generating good ones), on the other. The debate occurs on the eve of the great war that is a central event in the *Mahābhārata*. Watching the two armies readying for war, profound doubts about the correctness of what they are doing are raised by Arjuna, the peerless and invincible warrior in the army of the just and honourable royal family (the Pāndavas) who are about to fight the unjust usurpers (the Kauravas). Arjuna questions whether it is right to be concerned only with one's duty to promote a just cause and be indifferent to the misery and slaughter—even of one's kin—that the war itself would undoubtedly cause. Krishna, a divine incarnation in the form of a human being (in fact, he is also Arjuna's charioteer), argues against Arjuna. His response takes the form of articulating principles of action—based on the priority of doing one's duty—which have been repeated again and again in Indian philosophy. Krishna insists on Arjuna's duty to fight, irrespective of his evaluation of the consequences. It is a just cause, and, as a warrior and general on whom his side must rely, Arjuna cannot waver from his obligations, no matter what the consequences are.

Krishna's hallowing of the demands of duty wins the argument, at least as seen in the religious perspective.[1] Indeed, Krishna's conversations with Arjuna, the *Bhagavad Gītā*, became a treatise of great theological importance in Hindu philosophy, focusing particularly on the 'removal' of Arjuna's doubts. Krishna's moral position has also been eloquently endorsed by many philosophical and literary commentators across the world, such as Christopher Isherwood and T. S. Eliot. Isherwood in fact translated the *Bhagavad Gītā* into English.[2] This admiration for the *Gītā*, and for Krishna's arguments in particular, has been a lasting phenomenon in parts of European culture. It was spectacularly praised in the early nineteenth century by Wilhelm von Humboldt as 'the most beautiful, perhaps the only true philosophical song existing in any known tongue'.[3] In a poem in *Four Quartets*, Eliot summarizes Krishna's view in the form of an admonishment: 'And do not think of the fruit of action. / Fare forward.' Eliot explains: 'Not fare well, / But fare forward, voyagers.'[4]

And yet, as a debate in which there are two reasonable sides, the epic *Mahābhārata* itself presents, sequentially, each of the two contrary arguments with much care and sympathy.[5] Indeed, the tragic desolation that the post-combat and post-carnage land—largely the Indo-Gangetic plain—seems to face towards the end of the *Mahābhārata* can even be seen as something of a vindication of Arjuna's profound doubts. Arjuna's contrary arguments are not really vanquished, no matter what the 'message' of the *Bhagavad Gītā* is meant to be. There remains a powerful case for 'faring well', and not just forward.[*]

----

* As a high school student, when I asked my Sanskrit teacher whether it would be permissible to say that the divine Krishna got away with an incomplete and unconvincing argument, he replied: 'Maybe you could say that, but you must say it with adequate respect.' I have presented elsewhere a critique—I hope with adequate respect—of Krishna's deontology, along with a defence of Arjuna's consequential perspective, in 'Consequential Evaluation and Practical Reason', *Journal of Philosophy* 97 (Sept. 2000).

J. Robert Oppenheimer, the leader of the American team that developed the ultimate 'weapon of mass destruction' during the Second World War, was moved to quote Krishna's words ('I am become death, the destroyer of worlds') as he watched, on 16 July 1945, the awesome force of the first nuclear explosion devised by man.[6] Like the advice that Arjuna had received about his duty as a warrior fighting for a just cause, Oppenheimer the physicist could well find justification in his technical commitment to develop a bomb for what was clearly the right side. Scrutinizing—indeed criticizing—his own actions, Oppenheimer said later on: 'When you see something that is technically sweet, you go ahead and do it and you argue about what to do about it only after you have had your technical success.'[7] Despite that compulsion to 'fare forward', there was reason also for reflecting on Arjuna's concerns: How can good come from killing so many people? And why should I seek victory, kingdom or happiness for my own side?

These arguments remain thoroughly relevant in the contemporary world. The case for doing what one sees as one's duty must be strong, but how can we be indifferent to the consequences that may follow from our doing what we take to be our just duty? As we reflect on the manifest problems of our global world (from terrorism, wars and violence to epidemics, insecurity and grueling poverty), or on India's special concerns (such as economic development, nuclear confrontation or regional peace), it is important to take on board Arjuna's consequential analysis, in addition to considering Krishna's arguments for doing one's duty. The univocal 'message of the *Gītā*' requires supplementation by the broader argumentative wisdom of the *Mahābhārata*, of which the *Gītā* is only one small part.

There will be an opportunity in this essay, and in the others to follow, to examine the reach and significance of many of the debates and altercations that have figured prominently in the Indian argumentative tradition. We have to take note not only of the opinions that won—or allegedly won—in the debates, but also of the other points of view that were presented and are recorded or remembered. A defeated argument that refuses to be obliterated can remain very alive.

…

The Importance of Arguments

Before closing this essay, I should make clear what is and, no less important, what is not being claimed. There is, in particular, no proposal here to seek a single-factor explanation of India's 'past and present' through an exclusive and separate focus on one particular feature out of a multitude that can be found in India's constantly evolving traditions. To recognize the importance of an argumentative heritage and of the history of heterodoxy does not in any way do away with the need to look at the impact of other influences, nor obviate the necessity of investigating the interactions of different influences.

It also definitely does not encourage us to think of any social feature as an unchanging, perennial characteristic of an 'eternal India'. India has undergone radical developments and changes over its long history which cannot be understood without bringing in a variety of factors, circumstances and causal connections that have had—and are continuing to have—their impact. The particular point of the focus on heterodoxy and loquaciousness is not so much to elevate the role of tradition in the development of India, but to seek a fuller reading of Indian traditions, which have interacted with other factors in the dynamism of Indian society and culture.

Consider the relevance of ongoing traditions for the development of democracy—an issue that was briefly discussed earlier. In his autobiography, *Long Walk to Freedom*, Nelson Mandela notes that as a young boy he learned about the importance of democracy from the practice of the local African meetings that were held in the regent's house in Mqhekezweni:

Everyone who wanted to speak did so. It was democracy in its purest form. There may have been a hierarchy of importance among the speakers, but everyone was heard, chief and subject, warrior and medicine man, shopkeeper and farmer, landowner and laborer.... The foundation of self-government was that all men were free to voice their opinions and equal in their value as citizens.[50]

In arguing that his 'long walk to freedom' began at home, Mandela was not claiming that nothing else mattered in taking him towards the fight for democracy, nor that democracy would have no relevance to South Africa had its social heritage been different. The point is, rather, that the traditions Mandela saw at home were momentous, and they interacted with other significant factors that influenced him—and others—in South Africa. And since the democratic precursors in Africa had been fairly widely neglected in discussions on politics and colonial history, it was particularly important for Mandela to bring out the role of Africa's historical traditions.[51]

It is in this broad context that one can see the importance of the contributions made by India's argumentative tradition to its intellectual and social history, and why they remain relevant today. Despite the complexity of the processes of social change, traditions have their own interactive influence, and it is necessary to avoid being imprisoned in formulaic interpretations that are constantly, but often uncritically, repeated in intellectual as well as political discussions on historical traditions. For example, seeing Indian traditions as overwhelmingly religious, or deeply anti-scientific, or exclusively hierarchical, or fundamentally unsceptical (to consider a set of diagnoses that have received some championing in cultural categorizations) involves significant oversimplification of India's past and present. And in so far as traditions are important, these mischaracterizations tend to have a seriously diverting effect on the analysis of contemporary India as well as of its complex history. It is in that broad context that the corrective on which this essay concentrates comes particularly into its own. The claim is that the chosen focus here is useful and instructive, not that it is uniquely enlightening.

It is in this broad context that it becomes particularly important to note that heterodoxy has been championed in many different ways throughout Indian history, and the argumentative tradition remains very much alive today. This tradition has received understanding and support from many of the modern leaders of India—not only political leaders such as Mohandas Gandhi, but also people in other walks of life, such as Rabindranath Tagore. Tagore, who was proud of the fact that his family background reflected 'a confluence of three cultures, Hindu, Mohammedan and British',[52] emphasized the need to be vigilant in defence of this open-minded tradition and to help it to flower more fully.

Like Akbar's championing of *rahi aql* (the path of reason), Tagore emphasized the role of deliberation and reasoning as the foundation of a good society:

> Where the mind is without fear and the head is held high;
> Where knowledge is free;
> Where the world has not been broken up into fragments by narrow domestic walls; ...
> Where the clear stream of reason has not lost its way into the dreary desert sand of dead habit; ...
> Into that heaven of freedom, my Father, let my country awake. [53]

That task, momentous as it is, is made easier, I have argued, by the long history and consummate strength of our argumentative tradition, which we have reason to celebrate and to defend.

I end on a positive (if somewhat light-hearted) note, by recollecting a nineteenth-century Bengali poem by Ram Mohun Roy which bears on the subject matter of this essay.* Roy explains what is really dreadful about death:

> Just consider how terrible the day of your death will be.
> Others will go on speaking, and you will not be able to argue back.

We are told, in line with our loquacious culture, that the real hardship of death consists of the frustrating—very frustrating—inability to argue. There is, actually, an interesting vision behind this extraordinary diagnosis.

NOTES

1. Arjuna is supposed to have ended with abject surrender: 'I stand firm with my doubts dispelled. I shall act according to Thy word' (Sarvapalli Radhakrishnan, *The Bhagavadgita*, New Delhi: HarperCollins, 1993, p. 381).

2. In collaboration with Swami Prabhavananda (Madras: Sri Ramakrishna Math, 1989).

3. Jawaharlal Nehru, who quotes Humboldt, does however point out that 'every school of thought and philosophy . . . interprets [the Gītā] in its own way' (The Discovery of India, Calcutta: The Signet Press, 1946; repr. Delhi: Oxford University Press, 1981, pp. 108–9).

4. T. S. Eliot, 'The Dry Salvages', in *Four Quartets* (London: Faber & Faber, 1944), pp. 29–31.

5. For a good discussion of some other interesting arguments in the *Mahābhārata*, see Bimal Matilal, *Moral Dilemmas in the Mahābhārata* (Shimla: Indian Institute of Advanced Study, and Delhi: Motilal Banarsidass, 1989). See also his collection of papers, edited by Jonardan Ganeri, *The Collected Essays of Bimal Krishna Matilal*, vol. ii: *Ethics and Epics* (Delhi and Oxford: Oxford University Press, 2002). Shashi Tharoor conveys well the excitements offered by the stories and substories in the *Mahābhārata*, in his adapted tale, *The Great Indian Story* (Harmondsworth: Penguin, 1990).

6. See Len Giovannitti and Fred Freed, *The Decision to Drop the Bomb* (London: Methuen, 1957).

7. See *In the Matter of J. Robert Oppenheimer: USAEC Transcript of the Hearing before Personnel Security Board* (Washington, DC: Government Publishing Office, 1954). See also the play, based on these hearings, by Heinar Kipphardt, *In the matter of J. Robert Oppenheimer*, trans. Ruth Speirs (London: Methuen, 1967).

…

50. Nelson Mandela, *Long Walk to Freedom* (Boston: Little, Brown & Co., 1994), p. 21.

---

* Ram Mohun Roy was one of the pioneering reformers in nineteenth-century India, whose intellectual contributions matched his public work and leadership. In his far-reaching history of the emergence of the modern world, C.A. Bayly illuminatingly discusses the role of Ram Mohun Roy, 'who made in two decades an astonishing leap from the status of a late-Moghul state intellectual to that of the first Indian liberal', and who 'independently broached themes that were being simultaneously developed in Europe by Garibaldi and Saint-Simon' (*The Birth of the Modern World 1780–1914*, Oxford: Blackwell, 2004, p. 293). Ram Mohun Roy's love of reasoned arguments combined well with the independence and reach of his mind.

51. In the presence of multiple and interdependent causation, which actor we decide to emphasize must depend on what features are being highlighted already. Facing a different act of balancing in the context of British history, Eric Hobsbawm discussed, half a century ago, why it was important for Marxist historians (he was writing as one) to bring out the role of 'ideals, passions and movements' (increasingly neglected by orthodox historians), rather than concentrating mainly on material conditions—the traditional focus of Marxist analysis: 'In the pre-Namier days Marxists regarded it as one of the chief historical duties to draw attention to the material bases of politics.... But since bourgeois historians have adopted what is a particular form of vulgar materialism, Marxists have had to remind them that history is the struggle of men for ideas, as well as a reflection of their material environment' ('Where Are British Historians Going?', *Marxist Quarterly*, 2 Jan. 1955, p. 22).

52. Rabindranath Tagore, *The Religion of Man* (London: Unwin, 1931, 2nd, ed., 1961), p. 105.

53. From *Gitanjali*. See also Essay 5.

Excerpts from "Voice and Heterodoxy" from *The Argumentative Indian: Writings on Indian History, Culture and Identity*. Copyright © 2005 by Amartya Sen. Reprinted by permission of Farrar, Straus and Giroux, LLC.

"Universal Human Values: Finding an Ethical Common Ground"

By Rushworth M. Kidder

Points to Consider

1. Note the nations, cultures, and professions represented in the group of people Kidder interviewed for this study. To what extent do you think that the group is diverse enough for him to conclude that their individual opinions on a code of values can develop a universal code of human values?

2. What specific issues trouble you and help prove Kidder's assertion that there is a "pressing need for shared values in our age of global interdependence without consensus"?

3. To what degree is it possible to have universal human values in a diverse, often stratified world?

4. If Kidder interviewed you, how would you answer the question "If you could help create a global code of ethics, what would be in it?"

"Universal Human Values: Finding an Ethical Common Ground"

Universal Human Values

In the remote New Zealand village of Panguru, tucked into the mountains at the end of a winding gravel road, a Maori woman nearly a century old pauses for a moment as she talks about the moral values of her people. "This is God's country!" says Dame Whina Cooper with great feeling, gesturing toward the flowers blooming among the bird songs outside her modest frame house. "Only we the people running it must be doing something wrong."

Halfway around the world, in a United Nations office perched under the eaves of a fifteenth-century building in Florence, a leading journalist from Sri Lanka is asked what will happen if the world enters the twenty-first century with the ethics of the twentieth. "I feel it will be disastrous," Varindra Tarzie Vittachi replies simply.

Midway between, in his well-appointed residence in San José, Costa Rica, former president Oscar Arias explains that our global survival "will become more complicated and precarious than ever before, and the ethics required of us must be correspondingly sophisticated."

Turn where you will in the world and the refrain is the same. The ethical barometer is falling, and the consequences appear to be grave. That, at least, is one of the impressions to be drawn from the two dozen individuals from sixteen nations interviewed over the past few years by the Institute for Global Ethics.

These interviews did not seek to discover the ethical failings of various nations, but rather to find the moral glue that will bind us together in the twenty-first century. These voices speak powerfully of an underlying moral presence shared by all humanity—a set of precepts so fundamental that they dissolve borders, transcend races, and outlast cultural traditions.

There is a pressing need for shared values in our age of global interdependence without consensus. But there is one very real question unanswered: Is there in fact a single set of values that wise, ethical people around the world might agree on? Can there be a global code of ethics? If there is a common core of values "out there" in the world, it ought to be identifiable through examination of contemporary modes of thought in various cultures around the world. Can it be found?

On that topic, the two dozen "men and women of conscience" interviewed had a clear point of view. "Yes," they said, "there is such a code, and it can be clearly articulated." These interviewees were chosen not because they necessarily know more about ethics than their peers—although some do, having made it a lifelong study. Nor were they chosen because they are the single most exemplary person of their nation or community, though some could easily be nominated for that honor. They are, however, ethical thought-leaders within their different cultures, each viewed by his or her peers as a kind of ethical standard-bearer, a keeper of the conscience of the community, a center of moral gravity.

Each of the interviews began with a common question: If you could help create a global code of ethics, what would be in it? What moral values, in other words, would you bring to the table from your own culture and background?

In an ideal world, one would have assembled all the interviewees around a table, had each talk for an hour, had each listen intently to all the others, and finally had them arrive at a consensus. If they could have done so, here's the core of moral values upon which they probably would have agreed:

Love

Despite the concern of foundation executive James A. Joseph in Washington that "the L-word, Love," is falling sadly into disuse, it figured prominently in these interviews. "Love, yes," said children's author Astrid Lindgren in Stockholm. "This is the main word for what we need—love on all stages and with all people."

"The base of moral behavior is first of all solidarity, love, and mutual assistance," said former first lady Graça Machel of Mozambique. Buddhist monk Shojun Bando in Tokyo agreed, detailing three different kinds of love and insisting that "it shouldn't be that *others* should tell you to love others: It should just come of its own will, spontaneously." Or, as author Nien Cheng from China put it, "You cannot guide without love."

For tribal chief Reuben Snake of Nebraska, the central word is *compassion*. "We have to be compassionate with one another and help one another, to hold each other up, support one another down the road of life," he recalled his grandfather telling him. Thinking back on her dealings with a global spectrum of cultures at the United Nations, former ambassador Jeanne Kirkpatrick in Washington noted that, no matter how severe the political differences, "there was a kind of assumption, on the part of almost everyone, that people would help one another at the personal level."

Truthfulness

Of the four theses that form Harvard University ex-president Derek Bok's code of ethics, two center on truth. "You should not obtain your ends through lying and deceitful practices," he said, and you have a "responsibility to keep [your] promises." Astrid Lindgren put it with equal clarity when she spoke of the need to "be honest, not lying, not afraid to say your opinion."

Looking through the lens of science, the late economist Kenneth Boulding of Colorado also put "a very high value on veracity—telling the truth. The thing that gets you run out of the scientific community is being caught out telling a lie." Fortunately, said Bangladeshi banker Muhammad Yunus, the spread of technology makes it increasingly difficult for the truth to be hidden. In the future, "people will be forced to reveal themselves," he said. "Nothing can be kept hidden secret—not in computers, not in the halls of government, nothing. People will feel much more comfortable when they're dealing in truth. You converge around and in truth."

Here, however, as with many of these global values, there was also a residue of concern—a fear that trust, which is central to honesty and truthfulness, seems to be falling into abeyance. "The idea that you ought to be able to trust somebody is out of fashion," worried Katharine Whitehorn, columnist for *The Observer* of London. That's a point seconded by corporate executive James K. Baker of Indiana. "Little by little," he said, "if we let that trust go out of our personal dealings with one another, then I think the system really begins to have trouble."

Fairness

Elevating the concept of justice to the top of his list, philosopher and author John W. Gardner of Stanford University said, "I consider that probably the number-one candidate for your common ground." By justice, he meant "fair play, or some word for even-handedness."

"Here, one could get caught up in the very complicated theories of social justice," warned James A. Joseph. "Or one could simply look at the Golden Rule. I relate fairness to treating other people as I would want to be treated. I think that [rule] serves humanity well. It ought to be part of any ethic for the future."

For many, the concern for fairness goes hand in hand with the concept of equality. "The pursuit of equality is basic," said columnist and editor Sergio Muñoz of Mexico City and Los Angeles. "The people who come from Mexico and El Salvador have the same values, in my point of view, as the person who comes from Minnesota or from Alabama or from California—those basic principles that are common to all civilizations."

For some, like Joseph, the concept of fairness and equality focuses strongly on racial issues. Others, like author Jill Ker Conway from Australia, see the need for "greater equity between the sexes." Still others, like UNESCO Director-General Federico Mayor of Spain, see the problem as one of international relations: Despite the groundswell of interest in democracy arising within the former East Bloc nations, Westerners "have not reacted as humans, but only as economic individuals.... Even equity—the most important value in all the world—has collapsed."

Freedom

Very early in human history, said John Gardner, "the concept of degrees of freedom of my action—as against excessive constraints on my action by a tyrant or by military conquerors—emerged." Even the earliest peoples "knew when they were subjugated"—and didn't like it. That desire for liberty, he said, persists to the present as one of the defining values of humanity.

But liberty requires a sense of individuality and the right of that individual to express ideas freely, many of the interviewees said. "Without the principle of individual conscience, every attempt to institutionalize ethics must necessarily collapse," said Oscar Arias. "The effect of one upright individual is incalculable. World leaders may see their effects in headlines, but the ultimate course of the globe will be determined by the efforts of innumerable individuals acting on their consciences."

Such action, for many of these thinkers, is synonymous with democracy. "I think democracy is a must for all over the world," said Salim El Hoss, former prime minister of Lebanon. He defined the ingredients of democracy as "freedom of expression plus accountability plus equal opportunity." While he worried that the latter two are lacking in many countries, he noted that the first condition, freedom of expression, is increasingly becoming available to "all peoples."

Unity

As a counterbalance to the needs of individual conscience, however, stands the value that embraces the individual's role in a larger collective. Of the multitude of similar terms used for that concept in these interviews (*fraternity, solidarity, cooperation, community, group allegiance, oneness*) *unity* seems the most encompassing and the least open to misconstruction. For some, it is a simple *cri de coeur* in a world that seems close to coming undone. "I want unity," said Dame Whina Cooper of New Zealand, adding that "God wants us to be one people." For Tarzie Vittachi of Sri Lanka, the idea of unity embraces a global vision capable of moving humanity from "unbridled competition" to cooperation. "That is what is demanded of us now: putting our community first, meaning the earth first, and all living things."

The problem arises when the common good is interpreted "by seeing the relation between the individual and the common in individualistic terms," said Father Bernard Przewozny of Rome. Carried to the extreme, individualism is "destructive of social life, destructive of communal sharing, destructive of participation," he said, adding that "the earth and its natural goods are the inheritance of all peoples."

Tolerance

"If you're serious about values," said John Gardner, "then you have to add tolerance very early—*very* early. Because you have to have constraints. The more you say, 'Values are important,' the more you have to say, 'There are limits to which you can impose your values on me.'"

"It is a question of respect for the dignity of each of us," said Graça Machel. "If you have a different idea from mine, it's not because you're worse than me. You have the right to think differently." Agreeing, Derek Bok defined tolerance as "a decent respect for the right of other people to have ideas, an obligation or at least a strong desirability of listening to different points of view and attempting to understand why they are held."

"You have your own job, you eat your own food," said Vietnamese writer and activist Le Ly Hayslip. "How you make that food is up to you, and how I live my life is up to me."

UNIT

3

Reuben Snake traced the idea of tolerance back to a religious basis. "The spirit that makes you stand up and walk and talk and see and hear and think is the same spirit that exists in me—there's no difference," he said. "So when you look at me, you're looking at yourself—and I'm seeing me in you."

Abstracting from the idea of tolerance the core principle of respect for variety, Kenneth Boulding linked it to the environmentalist's urgency over the depletion of species. "If the blue whale is endangered, we feel worried about this, because we love the variety of the world," he explained. "In some sense I feel about the Catholic Church the way I feel about the blue whale: I don't think I'll be one, but I would feel diminished if it became extinct."

Responsibility

Oxford don A. H. Halsey placed the sense of responsibility high on his list of values because of its impact on our common future. "We are responsible for our grandchildren," he explained, "and we will make [the world] easier or more difficult for our grandchildren to be good people by what we do right here and now." This was a point made in a different way by Katharine Whitehorn, who noted that, while as a youth "it's fun to break away," it's very much harder to "grow up and have to put it together again."

For Nien Cheng, the spotlight falls not so much on the actions of the future as on the sense of self-respect in the present. "This is Confucius' teaching," she said. "You must take care of yourself. To rely on others is a great shame."

Responsibility also demands caring for others, Hayslip said. But, under the complex interactions of medicine, insurance, and law that exists [sic] in the West, "If you come into my house and see me lying here very sick, you don't dare move me, because you're not a doctor," she pointed out. "So where is your human obligation? Where is your human instinct to try to save me? You don't have it. You lost it, because there are too many rules."

Yet, paradoxically, "responsibility is not often mentioned in discussions of world politics or ethics," said Oscar Arias. "There, the talk is all of rights, demands, and desires." Human rights are "an unquestionable and critical priority for political societies and an indispensable lever for genuine development," he said. "But the important thing is not just to assert rights, but to ensure that they be protected. Achieving this protection rests wholly on the principle of responsibility."

Chicago attorney Newton Minow agreed. "I believe the basic reason we got off the track was that rights became more important than responsibilities, that individuals became more important than community interests. We've gotten to the point where everybody's got a right and nobody's got a responsibility."

At its ultimate, this sense of responsibility extends to the concept of right use of force. "You shouldn't perpetrate violence," said Derek Bok simply, finding agreement with Jeane Kirkpatrick's insistence that "war is always undesirable" and that "any resort to force should be a very late option, never a first option."

Respect for Life

Growing out of this idea of the responsible use of force, but separate from and extending beyond it, is a value known most widely in the West from the Ten Commandments: Thou shalt not kill. For Shojun Bando, it is an inflexible principle: Even if ordered in wartime to defend his homeland by killing, he said, "I would refuse. I would say, 'I cannot do this.'"

Such an idea, expressed in today's peaceable Japan, may seem almost naïve when examined through the lens of such war-riddled areas as the Middle East. Yet, Salim El Hoss took much the same view. "I was a prime minister [of Lebanon] for seven and a half years. I can't imagine myself signing a death penalty for anybody in the world. I think that is completely illegitimate, and I think that is the kind of thing a code of ethics should deal with."

Reuben Snake, noting that the North American Indians have a war-like reputation, said, "Probably the most serious shortcoming of tribal governments is their inability to effectively resolve conflict within the tribe and externally." He described earlier Indian traditions, however, in which great efforts were made by the tribal elders to prevent killing. That's a point with which Tarzie Vittachi—himself from the much-bloodied nation of Sri Lanka—felt perfectly at home. The first element of the Buddhist "daily prayer" under which he was raised, he recalled, is "I shall not kill." It is also central to the Ten Commandments of the Jewish decalogue under which Newton Minow was raised and which he said he still feels forms the basis for the world's code of ethics.

Other Shared Values

There were, of course, other significant values that surfaced in these interviews. Nien Cheng, for instance, pointed to *courage*. "One should basically know what is right and what is wrong," she said, "and, when you know that, be courageous enough to stand for what is right."

Figuring strongly in Shojun Bando's pantheon was *wisdom*, which he defined as "attaining detachment, getting away from being too attached to things."

Whina Cooper put *hospitality* high on her list, recalling that her father said, "If you see any strangers going past, you call them—*Kia Ora*—that means to call them to come here." Astrid Lindgren put an emphasis on *obedience*—a quality that runs throughout the life of her most famous character, Pippi Longstocking, though usually in reverse.

Kenneth Boulding pointed to *peace*, which he defined simply as "well-managed conflict." Thinking of peace brought Salim El Hoss to the concept of *stability*. "Peace is equivalent to stability," he said, adding that "stability means a long-term perspective of no problems." These and other values, while they don't find broad support, had firm proponents among those we interviewed and deserve serious attention.

Other values mentioned included the burning public concerns for racial harmony, respect for women's place, and the protection of the environment. Many of the interviewees touched on them, and some elevated them to high priority. Speaking of the need for racial harmony, James Joseph put at the top of his list a sense of "respect for the cultures of other communities, respect for the need to begin to integrate into our collective memory appreciation of the contributions and traditions of those who are different." Jill Conway topped her list with a warning about the "increasing exploitation of women" around the world. And of the many human rights identified by Father Bernard Przewozny, the one to which he has dedicated his life is the "right to a healthy environment."

So what good is this code of values? It gives us a foundation for building goals, plans, and tactics, where things really happen and the world really changes. It unifies us, giving us a home territory of consensus and agreement. And it gives us a way—not *the* way, but a way—to reply when we're asked, "Whose values will you teach?" Answering this last question, as we tumble into the twenty-first century with the twentieth's sense of ethics, may be one of the most valuable mental activities of our time.

Kidder, R. (1994). Universal Human Values: Finding an Ethical Common Ground. *The Futurist* (July/August, 1994). Originally published in *The Futurist*. Used with permission from the World Future Society (www.wfs.org).

UNIT
3

"Making Meaning of Being Bad"

By Barbara Kellerman

Points to Consider

1. What, according to Kellerman, is the difference between ineffective leadership and unethical leadership?

2. What are the characteristics of ethical leaders? What are the characteristics of ethical followers? How can individuals cultivate these characteristics in themselves and others in ways that benefit groups?

3. What are the seven types of "bad" leadership? To what extent is it possible for an organizational leader to possess some of these qualities and still be effective? To what degree is it possible for a leader to possess some of these qualities and still be ethical?

4. What are the implications for an individual, a group, or an organization when a "bad" leader holds power?

"Making Meaning of Being Bad"

In a talk I once gave to the New Haven Jewish community, I referred to Hitler as a bad leader. The words were hardly out of my mouth when a member of the audience rose to differ. "Hitler may have been 'bad' as in 'ethically bad,'" he said. "But he was a good leader in that he was very effective."

The man was right. Given the ideology of National Socialism and the particulars of the Nazi agenda from 1933 to 1941 (when Germany made the mistake of invading the Soviet Union), Hitler's political and military strategies were nearly impeccable. Moreover, even between 1941 and 1945—the period leading up to Germany's defeat—at least one of Hitler's most cherished objectives, the annihilation of European Jewry, was realized with astonishing efficiency. Does this make Hitler a "good" leader?

If the lines of demarcation between effective and ethical blur for a leader as obviously evil as Adolph Hitler, it is no wonder that judging other leaders, less extreme, is harder. Was Ronald Reagan a good president? In many ways he was effective, much more effective than his Hollywood career might have predicted. But to liberal Democrats, who even in retrospect detest his domestic agenda in particular, to label Reagan a "good" president seems absurd.

The lack of clarity about what exactly defines a good leader, and how to distinguish a good leader from a bad one, is mirrored in the follower. Consider this question: Should followers follow the leader, or the dictates of their consciences? On the one hand, a strong argument can be made that to maintain order and get work done, followers should go along with their leaders except in dire circumstances. On the other hand, followers are not sheep, nor should they necessarily be part of any herd.

When Argentines took to the streets in early 2002 to protest the parties and politicians who had been discredited by the country's economic collapse, one might say that by noisily insinuating themselves into the political process they were being disruptive. Or one might take the opposite view: that by speaking out for what they believed, they were doing what good followers should do.

In an infamous case, Sherron Watkins, at the time vice president of corporate development at Enron, sent Kenneth Lay, Enron's CEO, a six-page memo in 2001 detailing her fears that the company would implode in a wave of accounting scandals. At first glance Watkins appears to be a good, even a very good, follower. But a closer look suggests that the picture is more complex. After the scandal broke and Watkins testified before Congress, some saw a traitor, a woman who was flagrantly disloyal to former colleagues at every level and indeed to Enron itself.

If we ask whether the end justifies the means, we further complicate the conversation. A letter sent anonymously to the president of a major university complained about the coach of the women's basketball team. The coach, a woman, was described as abusive to the point of creating an "extremely unhealthy and unproductive team environment." Specifically, her "primary leadership tools" were "criticism, public humiliation, demands of compliance, screaming and yelling, pitting players against one another, and other 'old-school' boot camp techniques."[1] Here's the question: Should the coach be judged on the basis of her performance, or that of her team?

The same issue arose with regard to Bobby Knight, once the legendary basketball coach at Indiana University (since 2000 he has been at Texas Tech University). Although as individuals his players were at the mercy of his frequent verbal and infrequent physical abuse, his team as a whole did brilliantly. How should Knight be judged? He got the end part right: His team was a winner. But his means were questionable: He browbeat undergraduates. So, finally, our assessment of a coach or leader, such as Knight, is bound to be subjective, personal, and value-driven. You might not like the idea of anyone ever striking a twenty-year-old. But given Knight's remarkable record as a winning coach, I might not find it so objectionable.

Clearly, means versus ends issues are like good versus bad issues: impossible to sort out with precision. No wonder the leadership industry simplifies things. No wonder it defines leaders simply as "people who do the right thing."[2]

But as we know, sometimes leaders do the *wrong* thing. Even the best and brightest aren't precluded from being seduced by power. Some of the twentieth century's most eminent intellectuals fell for really bad leaders in a really big way. The great German philosopher Martin Heidegger joined the Nazi Party because he longed to "return to some imaginary pre-modern idyll." Other Europeans of high repute, such as the leading French writer and philosopher Jean-Paul Sartre, became enamored of Stalin because there was nothing they hated so much as bourgeois capitalism.[3]

Nor were Americans exempt from such foolish flirtations, especially, again, with Stalin. Out of willful ignorance and misguided optimism, writers such as Lillian Hellman and John Steinbeck spent years making excuses for the Soviet despot, apparently believing that all would be right in the end.

I do not underestimate the challenge of explaining followers like these, nor do I minimize the task of explaining bad leadership more generally. But if we have any hope of moving from bad leadership to better leadership, we must strike a balance between looking at the light and seeing in the dark.

Ineffective Leadership versus Unethical Leadership

Bad leadership falls into two categories: bad as in ineffective and bad as in unethical. This distinction is not a theoretical construct. Rather, it is based on the empirical evidence. Look around and you will see that all bad leadership is bad in one, or sometimes both, of these ways.

The distinction between ineffective and unethical brings us back to the question of means and ends. Let's assume that Bill and Hillary Clinton's ambitious health care proposal was a well-intentioned initiative that, initially at least, had the support of most of their followers. But the

UNIT
3

means used—the ways in which the president and the first lady tried to get the American body politic from point A to point B—were inadequate to the point of being hapless. By the time the proposal was dead, even many of its early supporters had abandoned it. We can say, then, that at least in the area of health care policy, President Clinton was not a good leader. His good intentions notwithstanding, he was ineffective. Even his supporters would have to admit that his strategies and tactics were not up to the task, and so the job never got done.

By the same token, sometimes leaders and followers deploy effective means to unethical ends. It has become clear that for many years Boston's Cardinal Bernard Law (along with others in the Roman Catholic hierarchy) considered it his main mission to protect the good standing of the church. The problem was that this mission took precedence over the more immediate and humane one: to shield parishioners from predatory priests. Finally, the wrongdoing that kept the clergy's misconduct hidden from public view—the transfers, the payments, and the cover-ups—undermined the very church that the Cardinal wanted so badly to secure.[4]

Ineffective Leadership

Ineffective leadership fails to produce the desired change. For reasons that include missing traits, weak skills, strategies badly conceived, and tactics badly employed, ineffective leadership falls short of its intention.

One way to think about an ineffective leader is to reverse the ideal: If the ideal leader has traits such as intelligence, persistence, flexibility, and an even disposition, the leader who lacks many of these will likely run into trouble. The same holds for leadership skills. If the ideal leader is able to communicate, mobilize, collaborate, and make good decisions, leaders who are unwilling or unable to employ such skills are less likely to perform well than their better-disposed and better-endowed counterparts.

The rule for followers is analogous: Ineffective followers lack, or do not demonstrate, the traits and skills necessary for good followership. Robert Kelley found that the best followers were "strong, independent partners with leaders. They think for themselves, self-direct their work, and hold up their end of the bargain. They continuously work at making themselves integral to the enterprise, honing their skills and focusing their contributions, and collaborating with their colleagues."[5] By these measures, ineffective followers are weak and dependent, and they refuse in any significant way to commit or contribute to the group.

A final point: Leaders are generally judged ineffective because of the means they employ (or fail to employ) rather than the ends they pursue. Most leaders set goals that seem reasonable to at least a substantial minority of their constituents. But not many leaders and followers have the capacity to reach these goals. To be sure, the deck is often stacked against them. Context matters a great deal, and the challenges they face are, objectively, difficult. But in many cases leaders and their immediate followers simply lack the traits and skills required to surmount the long odds.

By all accounts Gray Davis, California's erstwhile governor, was in a situation fraught with political peril. The state was faced with formidable challenges, in areas ranging from deficits to demographics, and the citizens were restless. Even though no one complained that Davis was unethical, the impression gradually became widespread that he and his team were ineffective—so ineffective that in a special recall election he was unceremoniously dumped.

Unethical Leadership

Unethical leadership fails to distinguish between right and wrong. Because common codes of decency and good conduct are in some way violated, the leadership process is defiled.

In chapter 1, I take issue with James MacGregor Burns' definition of the word *leadership*, in which leadership is, necessarily, an ethical act. Let me now return to the exact way that Burns uses the word, particularly in the phrase "transforming leadership." For Burns, leadership is implicitly ethical in that it "is done to realize goals mutually held by leaders and followers." In his view, transforming leadership goes a step further; it's even better. "Such leadership occurs when one or more persons engage with others in such a way that leaders and followers raise one another to higher levels of motivation and morality."[6]

In Joanne Ciulla's collection of essays, *Ethics: The Heart of Leadership*, Burns takes yet another cut. Here he distinguishes among three types of leadership values: ethical values, moral values, and end values. Although he does not so group them, Burns is writing, on the one hand, about the leader's private self (the leader is honest, kind, and so on) and, on the other hand, about the leader's public self (the leader furthers the common interest).[7]

UNIT 3

Burns goes on to suggest the following.

- Ethical leaders put their followers' needs before their own.
  Unethical leaders do not.

- Ethical leaders exemplify private virtues such as courage and temperance.
  Unethical leaders do not.

- Ethical leaders exercise leadership in the interest of the common good.
  Unethical leaders do not.

Most contemporary leadership scholars agree that the first principle is critical. Robert Greenleaf's "servant leader" leads because of a desire to serve others.[8] Joseph Rost sees leadership as "non-coercive influence" that leaves followers free to decide for themselves whether to go along.[9] And Edwin Hollander is content to bestow on leaders benefits, such as money and prestige, if in turn the leaders are accountable to followers.[10]

The second principle might seem new, and especially pertinent in a time of relentless media intrusion into the private lives of leaders such as Bill Clinton and Jack Welch. Although in recent years the question of whether a leader's private behavior impinges on public performance has been a hot topic, political philosophers have been interested in the issue for centuries. In general, the tolerance for moral fallibility, even if evident only behind closed doors, has been low. Confucius declared, "He who rules by virtue is like the polestar, which remains unmoving in its mansion while all the other stars revolve respectfully around it." In response to a question from Lord Ji Kang ("What should I do in order to make the people respectful, loyal, and zealous?"), Confucius urged him to be what today we call a role model: "Approach them with dignity and they will be respectful. Be yourself a good son and a kind father, and they will be loyal. Raise the good and train the incompetent, and they will be zealous."[11]

To act in accordance with the third principle is to exercise power, authority, and influence in the interest of the public welfare. To be sure, the contemporary literature on democratic theory argues that each of us, every citizen, bears the individual burden of assessing "the moral authority of political mandates."[12] But a good case can be made for the proposition that political leaders have a special responsibility to support the government and uphold the law only if they can do so in good conscience. If they cannot—if they are expected, for example, to uphold what they consider an unjust law—they are morally obliged to try to change course. One need hardly add that corporate, nonprofit, and military leaders should be held similarly accountable.

Ciulla argues that "leaders who do not look after the interests of their followers are not only unethical but ineffective."[13] At the same time, she takes the position that the standards to which we hold leaders should be the same as those we hold for everyone else—no lower and no higher. How then might this translate? If we accept Aristotle's dictum that virtues such as honesty and justice are acquired by practicing them, then leaders should do as Aristotle instructed: They should practice virtue because they want and intend to be virtuous.[14]

Nor are followers exempt. Like leaders, they are accountable for what they do.

- Ethical followers take the leader into account. Unethical followers do not.

- Ethical followers exemplify private virtues such as courage and temperance. Unethical followers do not.

- Ethical followers engage the leader and also other followers on behalf of the common good. Unethical followers do not.

Kelley found that followers were more troubled by ethical issues than were leaders. It's common for followers to be faced with an ethical dilemma: a situation in which they feel obliged by authorities to behave in ways that make them uncomfortable. Kelley writes that exemplary followers address the problem by demonstrating a "courageous conscience." Such followers have "the ability to judge right from wrong and the fortitude to take alternative steps toward what they believe is right."[15] Followers who lack a courageous conscience, particularly those who do not act even when something is obviously and egregiously wrong, are unethical.

Kelley is not, of course, suggesting that followers take on leaders freely and easily. In fact, his work supports the first principle, which clearly implies that leaders cannot be effective without cooperative followers. But followers are more obligated to the community as a whole than they are to any single individual, including the leader.

Kelley's research was conducted in the corporate sector. In contrast, John Rawls's seminal volume *A Theory of Justice* is about public life. Here too followers—citizens—are obliged to resist if resistance, rather than acquiescence, is in the common interest. Rawls describes civil disobedience as a "public, nonviolent, conscientious yet political act contrary to law usually done with the aim of bringing about a change in the law or policies of the government."[16]

Note that if a protest such as this one is successful, followers become leaders. Consider first the followership and then the leadership of Martin Luther King, Jr.—a subtle transition he described in a letter. "As the weeks and months unfolded," King wrote from his Birmingham, Alabama, jail cell in 1963, "we [Negroes] realized that we were the victims of a broken promise. The signs remained. Like so many experiences of the past we were confronted with blasted hopes, and the dark shadow of a deep disappointment settled upon us. So we had no alternative except that of preparing for direct [nonviolent] action, whereby we would present our very bodies as a means of laying our case before the conscience of the local and national community."[17]

The mixture of the ineffective and the unethical in bad leadership can never be known or measured precisely. This is a truth of the human condition. The important tasks then are to develop a greater awareness of the dynamics of bad leadership, and a better understanding of the different ways that leaders' actions can be both ineffective and unethical. Thus, I propose a typology of bad leadership that will highlight and distinguish the various ways in which we lead badly.

Types of Bad Leadership

After looking at hundreds of contemporary cases involving bad leaders and bad followers in the private, public, and nonprofit sectors, and in domains both domestic and international, I found that bad leadership falls into seven groups, which I have typed as follows:

- Incompetent
- Rigid
- Intemperate
- Callous
- Corrupt
- Insular
- Evil

To posit a typology is to invite argument. No less an expert than Max Weber, the German sociologist whose three types of authority—rational-legal, traditional, and charismatic—continue to influence leadership scholars some eighty years after his death, was wary of his critics. "The fact that none of these three ideal types…is usually to be found in historical cases in 'pure' form, is naturally not a valid objection to attempting their conceptual formulation in the sharpest possible form," Weber wrote. "Analysis in terms of sociological types has, after all…certain advantages which should not be minimized."[18]

Let me echo Weber's defense and provide a few cautionary notes about this typology in particular:

- These types are no "purer" than any other types, including Weber's.

- The range is wide. Some leaders and followers are very bad; others are less bad. Moreover, in some cases the consequences of bad leadership are major, in others minor.

- Opinions change. When Harry Truman left office in 1953, his approval rating was a dismal 32 percent. But in 2000, historians rated him among the greatest of American presidents, just behind Lincoln, Franklin Roosevelt, Washington, and Theodore Roosevelt.[19]

- Views differ. About Thomas Krens, controversial director of New York's Guggenheim Museum, two contrasting questions were asked. Was Krens "an egomaniac who squandered the museum's resources on a quest to expand his empire"? Or was he instead a "brilliant, misunderstood radical who inherited an institution with a relatively small endowment and stagnant program and wanted to try something more daring than mounting the umpteenth Picasso show"?[20]

- As it is used here, the word *type* does not mean personality type, nor do I intend to suggest that to be rigid, for example, is a personal trait in evidence at every turn. Rather, *rigid* refers to a set of behaviors in which leaders and followers mutually engage and that results in bad leadership.

Nevertheless, dividing the universe of bad leadership into seven types gives us, as Weber says, certain advantages. First, the ability to distinguish among the ways of being bad orders an untidy world, where the idea of bad leadership is as confusing as it is ubiquitous. Second, the seven types serve a practical purpose. They make it easier to detect inflection points—points at which an intervention might have stopped bad leadership or at least cut it short. Finally, the types make meaning of being bad. They enable us to know better and more clearly what bad leadership consists of.

UNIT

3

Before I describe the seven types, two additional notes. First, the first three types of bad leadership tend to be bad as in ineffective, and the last four types tend to be bad as in unethical. I set up a continuum in which the first type of bad leadership, incompetence, is far less onerous than the last type of bad leadership, evil. But of course the lines blur: Sometimes leaders and followers are ineffective and unethical. For this reason I simply describe the seven types of bad leadership in sequence. Second, although one of my themes is that bad followers are as integral to bad leadership as are bad leaders, in the following section the brief examples allude only to the leader.

Incompetent

Bernadine Healy served effectively as dean of the Ohio State University Medical School and as the first woman director of the National Institutes of Health. But during her brief tenure (1999–2001) as head of the American Red Cross, Healy lost her touch. She was a driven professional, determined rapidly to change the deeply ingrained Red Cross culture, with which she was unfamiliar. In short order, members of the staff, as well as the fifty-member Red Cross board, decided that Healy was too assertive, too critical, and too pitiless. Once she compounded her errors by presiding over a debacle involving donations accumulated in the wake of the attack on the World Trade Center, she was dismissed. In short, whatever Healy's previous successes, and for whatever reasons, as leader of the Red Cross she was incompetent.[21]

***Incompetent Leadership**—the leader and at least some followers lack the will or skill (or both) to sustain effective action. With regard to at least one important leadership challenge, they do not create positive change.*

Incompetent leaders are not necessarily incompetent in every aspect. Moreover, there are many ways of being incompetent. Some leaders lack practical, academic, or emotional intelligence.[22] Others are careless, dense, distracted, slothful, or sloppy, or they are easily undone by uncertainty and stress, unable effectively to communicate, educate, or delegate, and so on. Note also that the impact of incompetent leadership is highly variable. Sometimes, as in the case of pilot error, it leads to disaster. At other times it amounts to mere bungling.[23]

The case of incompetent leadership on which this book centers is that of Juan Antonio Samaranch, president of the International Olympic Committee from 1981 to 2000. His accomplishments were considerable, but toward the end of his tenure something went badly wrong. During his final years in office, Samaranch and his close followers ignored and thus implicitly sanctioned wide spread corruption in the Olympic movement, thereby disgracing the very games they were supposed to honor as well as sustain.

Rigid

As soon as he took office, Thabo Mbeki, who succeeded Nelson Mandela as president of South Africa in 1999, took issue with the West and its approach to AIDS. Mbeki maintained that HIV did not cause AIDS, that leading AIDS drugs were useless and even toxic, and that poverty and violence were at the root of his country's rapidly growing problem with the lethal disease.

As a result of his hostility to the West and his notoriously unyielding quest for an African remedy, Mbeki continued to withhold from HIV-positive pregnant women the antiretroviral drugs that would have cut in half the transmission of the disease to their babies.[24]

***Rigid Leadership**—the leader and at least some followers are stiff and unyielding. Although they may be competent, they are unable or unwilling to adapt to new ideas, new information, or changing times.*

Mbeki can be described by Barbara Tuchman's phrase "wooden headed"—a leader who consistently refuses to be "deflected by the facts."[25] Rigid leaders can be successful up to a point. But if they refuse to change with the changing wind, the result will be bad leadership.

The case of rigid leadership examined in chapter 5 is that of financial analyst Mary Meeker. During the 1990s, while the prices of technology stocks skyrocketed, Meeker rode high. But when the market changed, she did not. Unable or unwilling to acknowledge that the party was over, Meeker and her like-minded collaborators told her legions of listeners to hold on to their stocks even as the market tanked.

Intemperate

Russian President Boris Yeltsin, an alcoholic, was often intoxicated in private and in public, much to the embarrassment of his government and the Russian people. In 1999, to take only one example, Yeltsin was too drunk to get off a plane to greet the visiting prime minister of Ireland, who was left cooling his heels on the tarmac.[26] Alcoholism is a disease. But Yeltsin's failure to treat his problem affected his capacity to serve as Russia's head of state.

Intemperate Leadership—*the leader lacks self-control and is aided and abetted by followers who are unwilling or unable effectively to intervene.*

In their book *Leadership on the Line*, Ronald Heifetz and Marty Linsky cautioned leaders to control their impulses: "We all have hungers that are expressions of our normal human needs. But sometimes those hungers disrupt our capacity to act wisely or purposefully."[27] Because we live in a time when all top leaders are grist for the media mill, the risk of such disruption is far greater than it was in the past.

The case of intemperate leadership on which this book focuses is that of Marion Barry Jr. Although Barry was elected mayor of Washington, D.C., no fewer than four times, almost throughout his time in office he lived a life of excess. In the end, his own inability to control his various hungers, particularly for crack cocaine, and his followers' inability to get him the proper help, dearly cost him as well as the city he had been elected to govern.

Callous

Most Americans who have any interest in such matters know the story of Martha Stewart. She has become rich and famous by figuring out that homemaking—cooking, gardening, sewing, entertaining, cleaning, indeed every conceivable domestic chore—could reflect artistry as well as drudgery.

But even before her indictment on charges stemming from insider trading, Stewart had acquired a bad reputation. Although she is a brilliantly accomplished and hard-working businesswoman, nearly from the start of her career she has been rumored to be unpleasant and unkind, particularly to employees. How many of these personal attacks are the consequence of Stewart's being a woman in a man's world is difficult to say. Most observers would agree that the rules for women at the top of the corporate hierarchy are different from the rules for men. Most would likely also agree that if Stewart is not exactly a monster or a sociopath, she can be mean. Described variously as a harridan, an uncaring mother, and nasty to those in her employ, Stewart has made bad manners part of her legend: "Neighbors and acquaintances said she was aloof, inconsiderate, and selfish. Employees said she was 'hot-tempered and unreasonable and left them little time to cultivate a garden of their own.' It was as if she created a vision that none around her could live in."[28]

Callous Leadership—*the leader and at least some followers are uncaring or unkind. Ignored or discounted are the needs, wants, and wishes of most members of the group or organization, especially subordinates.*

Al Dunlap, the former CEO of Sunbeam Corporation, is the case of callous leadership described in chapter 7. Brought in in 1996 to turn around the fortunes of the appliance maker, Dunlap, through his abrasiveness, instead depleted morale and impaired the company's ability to function. As Sunbeam continued its downward spiral, Dunlap, with the support of his closest followers, cut himself off from the company and willfully ignored its ignominious descent. By the end of his tenure in 1998, Sunbeam had filed for bankruptcy.

Corrupt

In 1983, Michigan mall developer A. Alfred Taubman bought Sotheby's, the legendary auction house known, along with Christie's, for having cornered the market on the sale of fine art, jewelry, and furniture. Because the auction business had become increasingly competitive, by the mid-1990s Taubman and his Christie's counterpart, Sir Anthony Tennant, were illegally conspiring to raise commission rates.

A few years later the scheme was discovered, and in 2001 Taubman was found guilty of price-fixing, sentenced to a year and a day in prison, and ordered to pay a $7.5 million fine. In addition, Sotheby's and Christie's were ordered to settle class action suits with more than one hundred thousand customers for $512 million.[29]

Taubman did not act alone. For her part in the price-fixing scheme, Sotheby CEO Diana (Dede) Brooks was sentenced to six months of home detention, three years of probation, and one thousand hours of community service. Brooks, a Yale-educated former Citibank executive whose tenure at Sotheby's had been viewed as highly successful, was spared a more severe sentence only because she cooperated with government investigators to provide evidence against Taubman.

Corrupt Leadership—*the leader and at least some followers lie, cheat, or steal. To a degree that exceeds the norm, they put self-interest ahead of the public interest.*

Corrupt leaders are usually motivated by power or greed—the desire, in any case, to acquire more of a scarce resource. For example, to make more money, corrupt leaders take bribes, sell favors, evade taxes, exaggerate corporate earnings, engage in insider trading, cook the books, defraud governments and businesses, and in other ways cut corners, bend rules, and break the law.

Chapter 8 tells the story of William Aramony, once the highly respected head of United Way of America. Aramony's tale is not unfamiliar: It is about the head of a large organization caught lying, cheating, and stealing. But it is at odds with how we think about charitable organizations and those who lead and manage them.

Insular

When the streets of Monrovia began to run with blood, Liberians begged President George W. Bush to intervene, to stop the conflict by sending troops. At first he dithered, siding for a time with those who said, in effect, "Our hands are too full to rescue a distant people determined to murder one another."[30]

Those who chose to differ, Secretary of State Colin Powell among them, argued for intervention on the grounds of national interest and because they considered it the right thing to do. "Liberia is not just another African country," one interventionist argued. "It is an American creation, founded by former slaves 150 years ago, reflecting our image and legacy."[31]

In terms of American foreign policy this might be considered yet another debate between isolationists and interventionists. But as far as the quality of leadership is concerned, the debate over whether or not to intervene in Liberia reflected the tension between those who believe that leaders are responsible only to their own constituencies and those who consider that they have a broader mandate—one that includes trying to stop large numbers of men, women, and children from being hacked to death, even in a distant land.

Insular Leadership—*the leader and at least some followers minimize or disregard the health and welfare of "the other"—that is, those outside the group or organization for which they are directly responsible.*

Bill Clinton is the exemplar of insular leadership, as profiled in chapter 9. Although the president knew of the genocide in Rwanda, he paid it little attention. Having been burned by his experience in Somalia in particular, Clinton, along with the rest of his foreign policy team, made the decision to steer clear of a calamity that was taking place far from home.

Evil

In 1991, Foday Sankoh, an itinerant photographer and army corporal with a primary school education, gathered a group of guerillas and started a civil war in Sierra Leone. Sankoh was known for his extraordinary charisma. But his followers, many of them poor boys from the countryside, were notorious above all for their brutality. They killed, raped, and spread terror across the small West African nation by chopping off the hands, arms, and legs of innocent civilians—men, women, and children alike. Sankoh was unperturbed. In fact, when some of his close associates spoke out against the flagrant abuses and violations of human rights, they were summarily executed.[32] In 2000, Sankoh was captured by British troops operating under the auspices of the United Nations; later he was turned over to the Special Court for Sierra Leone. The seventeen-count indictment charged him with crimes against humanity, including murder, rape, and extermination. Foday Sankoh died in custody in July 2003.

Evil Leadership—*the leader and at least some followers commit atrocities. They use pain as an instrument of power. The harm done to men, women, and children is severe rather than slight. The harm can be physical, psychological, or both.*

Evil leaders are not necessarily sadistic. But some experts argue that our notion of evil should include the intent not only to terrorize but also to prolong suffering. They believe that all evildoers derive some sort of satisfaction from hurting others.[33]

The case of evil leadership described in chapter 10 is that of Radovan Karadzic. As Bosnian Serb president during the early and mid-1990s, Karadzic, along with his followers, was responsible for the rape, murder, and pillaging of thousands of Bosnian Muslims and Croats, and for the infamous massacre in Srebrenica.

The Heart of Darkness

Making meaning of being bad is difficult. Consider this confusion: The *American Heritage Dictionary of the English Language* properly refers to Hitler as an "absolute dictator." But, perhaps because he was a wartime ally, the same dictionary describes Stalin only as a "Soviet politician who was general secretary of the Communist Party and premier of the U.S.S.R." This, even though we now know that Stalin was directly responsible for the deaths of some twenty million people.[34]

Moreover, like all typologies, the one in this book raises questions just as it provides answers. It's fair to ask, for example, whether leaders should be considered incompetent if the demands on their time preclude attention to all matters of importance. Similarly, one might reasonably wonder whether leaders are intemperate if they are not monogamous but still not promiscuous. The questions pertain to followers as well. Are you corrupt if you cheat, ever so slightly, on your taxes, knowing that many others are doing the same thing? Am I evil if my leader compels me to commit evil acts?

To avoid as far as possible the inevitable pitfalls of the inevitable complexities, I use only cases in which the evidence of bad leadership is overwhelming. In other words, because I recognize that even generally competent leaders are sometimes incompetent and that even generally kind leaders are sometimes callous, the examples of bad leadership used in this book are at the extreme—virtually indisputable.

The paradoxes of leadership—leaders who are, for example, corrupt and effective at the same time—further complicate the difficulty of making meaning of being bad. As I describe in more detail later, in 2000 Vincent A. (Buddy) Cianci Jr., the mayor of Providence, Rhode Island, was sentenced to five years and four months in jail after being convicted of soliciting bribes for city contracts. But before being thrown into prison, Cianci had "transformed Providence from a grimy industrial backwater into the liveliest, most appealing city in New England."[35]

New York mayor Rudolph Giuliani presents a different kind of paradox. In the wake of 9/11, Giuliani was hailed as a hero, a leader worthy of comparison to Churchill. But before his appointment with history, Giuliani's approval ratings had been low. The mayor's rigid refusal to reach out to members of New York City's minority communities, particularly to people of color, meant that in at least one important way, he was inadequate, a bad leader.

Finally, problems of objectivity and subjectivity inevitably muddy the water. In all but the most egregious cases, opinions will differ about who deserves to be called a bad leader and why. As far as possible I head off this argument by choosing to focus on cases of bad leadership on which there is broad consensus.

The heavy lifting notwithstanding, we know three important things:

1. Sometimes leaders, and followers, make a difference.

2. Sometimes this difference is significant.

3. Sometimes the outcome is bad.[36]

We turn now to the seven types of bad leadership: incompetent, rigid, intemperate, callous, corrupt, insular, and evil. The chapters that follow are about the dark side—about how we get caught in webs we ourselves spin. It is my hope and intention that by discussing and distinguishing among the primary form of bad leadership, we might ourselves avoid becoming entangled both as bad leaders and as bad followers.

NOTES

1. Letter dated 9 December 2001 to the president of a leading West Coast university.

2. Warren Bennis and Burt Nanus, *Leaders: The Strategies for Taking Charge* (New York: Harper & Row, 1985), 21. Bennis and Nanus were making a distinction between managers "who do things right" and leaders "who do the right thing."

3. Mark Lilla, interviewed by Eric Alterman, "Q&A: Why are Deep Thinkers Shallow About Tyranny," *New York Times* (10 November 2001), A15.

4. For a full accounting of how the investigative staff of the *Boston Globe* uncovered this story, see Investigative Staff of the *Boston Globe, Betrayal: The Crisis in the Catholic Church* (Boston: Little, Brown, 2002).

5. Robert E. Kelley, *The Power of Followership: How to Create Leaders People Want to Follow and Followers Who Lead Themselves* (New York: Doubleday, 1992), 166.

6. James MacGregor Burns, *Leadership* (New York: Harper & Row, 1978), 18, 20.

7. James MacGregor Burns, foreword to Joanne B. Ciulla, *Ethics: The Heart of Leadership* (Westport, CT: Praeger, 1998), x.

8. Robert K. Greenleaf, *Servant Leadership: A Journey into the Nature of Legitimate Power* (New York: Paulist Press, 1977).

9. Joseph C. Rost, *Leadership for the Twenty-First Century* (Westport, CT: Praeger, 1991), 82.

10. Edwin P. Hollander, "Ethical Challenges in the Leader-Follower Relationship," in Ciulla, *Ethics: The Heart of Leadership*, 49–61.

11. Confucius, *Analects of Confucius* (New York: Norton, 1977), 6, 8.

12. Arthur Isak Applebaum, "Democratic Legitimacy and Official Discretion," *Philosophy and Public Affairs* 21, no. 3 (1992): 240. Also see Dennis F. Thompson, "Moral Responsibility of Public Officials: The Problem of Many Hands," *American Political Science Review* 74 (1980): 905–915.

13. Joanne B. Ciulla, "Carving Leaders from the Warped Wood of Humanity," Review Canadienne des Sciences de l'Administration (Montreal) 18, no. 4 (December 2001): 313.

14. Aristotle, *The Ethics* (London: Penguin, 1953), 91.

15. Kelley, *The Power of Followership*, 168.

16. John Rawls, *A Theory of Justice* (Cambridge, MA: Harvard University Press, 1971), 364.

17. Martin Luther King, Jr., "Letter from a Birmingham Jail," in *Blessed Are the Peacemakers*, by S. Jonathan Bass (Baton Rouge: Louisiana State University Press, 2001). The letter is dated 16 April 1963.

18. Max Weber, *The Theory of Social and Economic Organizations* (New York: Free Press, 1947), 329.

19. "Presidential Rankings," 2000 poll from C-Span survey of historians, *CNN*, 21 February 2000.

20. Deborah Solomon, "Is the Go-Go Guggenheim Going, Going." *New York Times Magazine*, 20 June 2002.

21. For an excellent description of Healy's tenure at the Red Cross, see Deborah Sontag, "Who Brought Bernadine Healy Down?" *New York Times Magazine*, 23 December 2001, 32.

22. Daniel Goleman, *Working with Emotional Intelligence* (New York: Bantam, 1999), 317. For an interesting exchange about leadership and practical intelligence, see Robert Sternberg and Victor Vroom, "The Person Versus the Situation in Leadership," *The Leadership Quarterly* 13, no. 3 (June 2002): 301–321.

23. For example, the failure by South Carolina governor Jim Hodges to communicate during Hurricane Floyd resulted in a monumental traffic jam. "Traffic Backs Up for Miles as Coastal Dwellers Flee Island," *St. Louis Post Dispatch*, 16 September 1999, A9. See also Leigh Strope, "Hodges Said He Should Control Emergency Response," *Associated Press State and Local Wire*, 1 October 1999; and David Firestone, "Hurricane Floyd: The Overview," *New York Times*, 16 September 1999, A1.

24. "S. African Leader Claims AIDS Drug Is Unsafe," *St. Louis Post Dispatch*, 3 November 1999, A5; Barton Gelman, "S. African President Escalates AIDS Feud: Mbeki Challenges Western Remedies," *Washington Post*, 19 April 2000, A1; Samson Mulugeta, "S. Africa: A Country in Denial—AIDS Victims Suffer in Silence,

UNIT

3

President Dismisses Problem," *Newsday*, 21 August 2001, A16; Rachel Swarns, "In a Policy Shift, South Africa Will Make AIDS Drugs Available to Pregnant Women," *New York Times*, 20 April 2002, A8. In 2002 Mbeki's position on antiretroviral drugs softened slightly, at least in part because of the intervention of Canadian Prime Minister Jean Chretien. For a fuller description of Mbeki's rigid intransigence, see Samantha Power, "The AIDS Rebel," *New Yorker*, 19 May 2003.

25. Barbara Tuchman, *The March of Folly: Troy to Vietnam* (New York: Ballantine, 1984) 7.

26. Fred Hiatt, "Ex-Aides Raise Questions about Yeltsin's Drinking," *Washington Post*, 8 October 1994, A21.

27. Ronald A. Heifetz and Marty Linsky, *Leadership on the Line: Staying Alive Through the Dangers of Leading* (Boston: Harvard Business School Press, 2002), 164.

28. "Image and Reality for Martha Stewart," *Greenwich Time*, 10 June 2003. See also Jerry Oppenheimer, *Just Desserts: The Unauthorized Biography of Martha Stewart* (New York: William Morrow, 1997), especially 236 ff. and 308 ff; and Christopher M. Byron, *Martha, Inc.: The Incredible Story of Martha Stewart Living Omnimedia* (New York: John Wiley & Sons, 2003).

29. Peter Watson, "Under the Hammer," *The Guardian*, 7 December 2001, 2; Carol Vogei and Ralph Blumenthal, "Ex-Chairman of Sotheby's Gets Jail Time," *New York Times*, 13 April 2002. B1.

30. Nicholas D. Kristof, "Hearing Liberia's Pleas." *New York Times*, 29 July 2003, A13.

31. Chester Crocker, "A War Americans Can Afford to Stop," *New York Times*, 1 August 2003, A21.

32. James Traub, "The Worst Place on Earth," *New York Review of Books*, 29 June 2000, 61–65. The quotation is from Somini Sengupta, "African Held for War Crimes Dies in Custody of Tribunal" *New York Times*, 31 July 2003, A6.

33. Psychiatrist Michael Weiner has this view of evil, as cited by Sharon Begley, "The Roots of Evil," *Newsweek*, 21 May 2002, 32.

34. Sidney Goldberg, "Learning Lexicons: Dictionaries Call Castro a Leader and Stalin a 'Statesman,'" 5 July 2002, Wall Street Journal Online. <www.opinionjournal.com/tasre/?id= 110001946> (accessed 5 July 2002).

35. Alan Ehrenhalt, "The Paradox of Corrupt Yet Effective Leadership," *New York Times*, 30 September 2002, A2S.

36. For example, in a 2002 presentation titled "Crisis in Corporate Governance," Bill George estimated that corrupt leaders at Global Crossing, Enron, Qwest, Tyco and WORLDCOM cost shareholders $460 billion.

Kellerman, Barbara. *Bad leadership: What it is, how it happens, why it matters.* Boston, MA: Harvard Business School Press, 2004, pp. 29–48.

"A Framework for Thinking Ethically"

Developed by Manuel Velasquez, Dennis Moberg, Michael J. Meyer, Thomas Shanks, Margaret R. McLean, David DeCosse, Claire André, and Kirk O. Hanson

Points to Consider

1. When you think of leaders whom you know, can you identify which of the five ethical approaches that each seems to use most often?

2. Which of the five ethical approaches is best suited for small groups?

3. To what extent can individuals take different ethical approaches within a larger organization and still be effective?

4. To what degree are ethics situational?

"A Framework for Thinking Ethically"

This document is designed as an introduction to thinking ethically. We all have an image of our better selves—of how we are when we act ethically or are "at our best." We probably also have an image of what an ethical community, an ethical business, an ethical government, or an ethical society should be. Ethics really has to do with all these levels—acting ethically as individuals, creating ethical organizations and governments, and making our society as a whole ethical in the way it treats everyone.

What Is Ethics?

Simply stated, ethics refers to standards of behavior that tell us how human beings ought to act in the many situations in which they find themselves—as friends, parents, children, citizens, businesspeople, teachers, professionals, and so on.

It is helpful to identify what ethics is NOT:

- Ethics is not the same as feelings. Feelings provide important information for our ethical choices. Some people have highly developed habits that make them feel bad when they do something wrong, but many people feel good even though they are doing something wrong. And often our feelings will tell us it is uncomfortable to do the right thing if it is hard.

- Ethics is not religion. Many people are not religious, but ethics applies to everyone. Most religions do advocate high ethical standards but sometimes do not address all the types of problems we face.

- Ethics is not following the law. A good system of law does incorporate many ethical standards, but law can deviate from what is ethical. Law can become ethically corrupt, as some totalitarian regimes have made it. Law can be a function of power alone and designed to serve the interests of narrow groups. Law may have a difficult time designing or enforcing standards in some important areas, and may be slow to address new problems.

- Ethics is not following culturally accepted norms. Some cultures are quite ethical, but others become corrupt—or blind to certain ethical concerns (as the United States was to slavery before the Civil War). "When in Rome, do as the Romans do" is not a satisfactory ethical standard.

UNIT
3

- Ethics is not science. Social and natural science can provide important data to help us make better ethical choices. But science alone does not tell us what we ought to do. Science may provide an explanation for what humans are like. But ethics provides reasons for how humans ought to act. And just because something is scientifically or technologically possible, it may not be ethical to do it.

Why Identifying Ethical Standards Is Hard

There are two fundamental problems in identifying the ethical standards we are to follow:

1. On what do we base our ethical standard?

2. How do those standards get applied to specific situations we face?

If our ethics are not based on feelings, religion, law, accepted social practice, or science, what are they based on? Many philosophers and ethicists have helped us answer this critical question. They have suggested at least five different sources of ethical standards we should use.

Five Sources of Ethical Standards

The Utilitarian Approach

Some ethicists emphasize that the ethical action is the one that provides the most good or does the least harm, or to put it another way, produces the greatest balance of good over harm. The ethical corporate action, then, is the one that produces the greatest good and does the least harm for all who are affected—customers, employees, shareholders, the community, and the environment. Ethical warfare balances the good achieved in ending terrorism with the harm done to all parties through death, injuries, and destruction. The utilitarian approach deals with consequences; it tries both to increase the good done and to reduce the harm done.

The Rights Approach

Other philosophers and ethicists suggest that the ethical action is the one that best protects and respects the moral rights of those affected. This approach starts from the belief that humans have a dignity based on their human nature per se or on their ability to choose freely what they do with their lives. On the basis of such dignity, they have a right to be treated as ends and not merely as means to other ends. The list of moral rights—including the rights to make one's own choices about what kind of life to lead, to be told the truth, not to be injured, to a degree of privacy, and so on—is widely debated: some now argue that non-humans have rights, too. Also, it is often said that rights imply duties—in particular, the duty to respect others' rights.

The Fairness or Justice Approach

Aristotle and other Greek philosophers have contributed the idea that all equals should be treated equally. Today we use this idea to say that ethical actions treat all human beings equally—or if unequally, then fairly based on some standard that is defensible. We pay people more based on their harder work or the greater amount that they contribute to an organization, and say that is fair. But there is a debate over CEO salaries that are hundreds of times larger than the pay of others; many ask whether the huge disparity is based on a defensible standard or whether it is the result of an imbalance of power and hence is unfair.

The Common Good Approach

The Greek philosophers have also contributed the notion that life in community is a good in itself and our actions should contribute to that life. This approach suggests that the interlocking relationships of society are the basis of ethical reasoning and that respect and compassion for all others—especially the vulnerable—are requirements of such reasoning. This approach also calls attention to the common conditions that are important to the welfare of everyone. This may be a system of laws, effective police and fire departments, health care, a public education system, or even public recreational areas.

The Virtue Approach

A very ancient approach to ethics is that ethical actions ought to be consistent with certain ideal virtues that provide for the full development of our humanity. These virtues are dispositions and habits that enable us to act according to the highest potential of our character and on behalf of values like truth and beauty. Honesty, courage, compassion, generosity, tolerance, love, fidelity, integrity, fairness, self-control, and prudence are all examples of virtues. Virtue ethics asks of any action, "What kind of person will I become if I do this?" or "Is this action consistent with my acting at my best?"

UNIT
3

Putting the Approaches Together

Each of the approaches helps us determine what standards of behavior can be considered ethical. There are still problems to be solved, however.

The first problem is that we may not agree on the content of some of these specific approaches. We may not all agree to the same set of human and civil rights.

We may not agree on what constitutes the common good. We may not even agree on what is a good or what is a harm.

The second problem is that the different approaches may not all answer the question "What is ethical?" in the same way. Nonetheless, each approach gives us important information with which to determine what is ethical in a particular circumstance. And much more often than not, the different approaches do lead to similar answers.

Making Decisions

Making good ethical decisions requires a trained sensitivity to ethical issues and a practiced method for exploring the ethical aspects of a decision and weighing the considerations that should impact our choice of a course of action. Having a method for ethical decision making is absolutely essential. When practiced regularly, the method becomes so familiar that we work through it automatically without consulting the specific steps.

The more novel and difficult the ethical choice we face, the more we need to rely on discussion and dialogue with others about the dilemma. Only by careful exploration of the problem, sided by the insights and different perspectives of others, can we make good ethical choices in such situations.

We have found the following framework for ethical decisions making a useful method for exploring ethical dilemmas and identifying ethical courses of action.

A Framework for Ethical Decision Making

Recognize an Ethical Issue

1. Is there something wrong personally, interpersonally, or socially? Could the conflict, the situation, or the decision be damaging to people or to the community?

2. Does the issue go beyond legal or institutional concerns? What does it do to people, who have dignity, rights, and hopes for a better life together?

Get the Facts

3. What are the relevant facts of the case? What facts are unknown?

4. What individuals and groups have an important stake in the outcome? Do some have a greater stake because they have a special need or because we have special obligations to them?

5. What are the options for acting? Have all the relevant persons and groups been consulted? If you showed your list of options to someone you respect, what would that person say?

Evaluate Alternative Actions from Various Ethical Perspectives

6. Which option will produce the most good and do the least harm?

Utilitarian Approach: The ethical action is the one that will produce the greatest balance of benefits over harms.

7. Even if not everyone gets all they want, will everyone's rights and dignity still be respected?

Rights Approach: The ethical action is the one that most dutifully respects the rights of all affected.

8. Which option is fair to all stakeholders?

Fairness or Justice Approach: The ethical action is the one that treats people equally, or if unequally, that treats people proportionately and fairly.

9. Which option would help all participate more fully in the life we share as a family, community, and society?

Common Good Approach: The ethical action is the one that contributes most to the achievement of a quality common life together.

10. Would you want to become the sort of person who acts this way (e.g., a person of courage or compassion)?

Virtue Approach: The ethical action is the one that embodies the habits and values of humans at their best.

Make a Decision and Test It

11. Considering all these perspectives, which of the options is the right or best thing to do?

12. If you told someone you respect why you chose this option, what would that person say? If you had to explain your decision on television, would you be comfortable doing so?

Act, Then Reflect on the Decision Later

13. Implement your decisions. How did it turn out for all concerned? If you had it to do over again, what would you do differently?

Velasquez, M., Andre, C., Shanks, T., Meyer, S., & Meyer, M. (n.d). Thinking ethically: A framework for moral decision making. Retrieved from http://www.scu.edu/ethics/practicing/decision/thinking.html. Reprinted with permission of The Markkula Center for Applied Ethics at Santa Clara University (www.scu.edu/ethics).

UNIT

3

FILM STUDIES

Billy Budd (1962)

Adapted from the novel by Herman Melville
Screenplay by Peter Ustinov and DeWitt Bodeen
Directed by Peter Ustinov

Character Guide

Billy Budd.	Terrence Stamp
Edwin Fairfax Vere	Peter Ustinov
John Claggart (Master-at-Arms) . . .	Robert Ryan
The Dansker (Sailmaker)	Melvyn Douglas
Philip Seymour (First Lieutenant) . . .	Paul Rogers
Julian Radcliffe (Second Lieutenant) . .	John Neville
Steven Wyatt (Gunnery Officer) . . .	David McCallum

Introduction and Historical Background

In *Billy Budd*, Billy is a supremely good, innocent, kind sailor aboard *Bellipotent*, despite the fact that he had been impressed (removed from a merchant ship and forced into military service) in the British Navy. Claggart, the evil master-at-arms aboard *Bellipotent*, cruelly antagonizes Billy. When Claggart falsely accuses Billy of conspiracy to mutiny, Billy becomes speechless with rage and strikes Claggart, who falls hard enough to produce a fatal head injury. In the Naval Code, striking a superior officer requires the death penalty. The matter is complicated, however, because Captain Vere has great affection for Billy as do all the officers and sailors aboard *Bellipotent*, and it is further complicated by recent mutinies aboard other British war ships (the *Nore* is mentioned in this excerpt) and a new Mutiny Act designed to prevent further mutinies. The following excerpts from *Billy Budd* detail the deliberations of the drumhead court that Captain Vere summons to issue a verdict in the matter.

Dialogue Questions

1. Why does Captain Vere choose the course to uphold justice according to the British Naval Rules rather than choosing the course of mercy for Billy Budd?

2. What is the ethical basis for Captain Vere's decision to execute Billy Budd?

3. Was it ethical for Captain Vere to act as a witness to the drumhead court proceedings and also to intercede and persuade the drumhead court to change its verdict? Why or why not?

4. What would have been the ethical basis for Captain Vere to pardon Billy Budd?

Miss Evers' Boys (1997)

Based on the play by David Feldshuh
Teleplay by Walter Bernstein
Directed by Joseph Sargent

Character Guide

Eunice Evers (Nurse) . . . . Alfre Woodard

Dr. Brodus . . . . Joe Morton

Dr. Douglas . . . . Craig Sheffer

Caleb Humphries (Patient) . . . . Laurence Fishburne

Willie Johnson (Patient) . . . . . Obba Babatunde

UNIT
3

Introduction

Miss Evers' Boys is based on the history of the Tuskegee Experiment, a 40-year, government-backed medical research effort on the effects of syphilis in black men of Alabama. In 1932, an eager and dedicated Nurse Eunice Evers is invited to work with Dr. Brodus and Dr. Douglas on a federally funded program to treat syphilis patients in Alabama. Men who test positive for the disease will receive free treatment, as the doctors determine the effectiveness of various alternatives. The government withdraws the funding for the free treatments, and instead offers money for what will become known as "The Tuskegee Experiment," a study of the effects of syphilis on patients who do not receive any treatments known to be effective. Nurse Evers must decide if she will remain with the project that the doctors tell her still has benefits for medical science. She would have to work to convince the men that they are being cared for, even after an effective cure, penicillin, becomes available. Alternatively, she could leave the project and tell the men that they are no longer receiving effective treatment, knowing that they cannot afford the treatment anyway.

Dialogue Questions

1. Do you arrive at different answers to the question "Was the Tuskegee Experiment ethical?" using the five different approaches to ethical decision making explained in the article "A Framework for Thinking Ethically"?

2. What arguments convince Eunice Evers to continue working with the study?

3. Are lies ever justified? In what circumstances?

4. In what situations or circumstances is it ethical to use people? Explain.

EXERCISE

Whom to Choose:
Values and Group Decision Making

Introduction

It is much more difficult to make ethical choices based on values than on facts. However, we often make unconscious "value" decisions. Part of self-growth can include understanding one's own value system in order to make more intelligent or appropriate ethical choices.

This exercise provides an opportunity to: (1) examine and make choices concerning one's own values, (2) assess the degree to which members of a group have common values and the impact of this on group decision making, and (3) observe problem-solving strategies in groups.

Instructions

Your Instructor will provide you with the Whom to Choose Nominees list and further instructions based on one of the following situations or an alternative scenario.

Whom to Choose Situation Description: Kidney Transplant

Since kidney dialysis has become very rare, people who have nonfunctioning kidneys all want transplants. Those who cannot receive these transplants will probably die in one or two years. Unfortunately, there are many more applicants than there are available kidneys. Scandinavian Medical Center in Houston, Texas, has become renowned for its kidney transplants. A committee of doctors screens all applicants to see who would physically benefit most from a kidney transplant. For instance, a person with chronic emphysema or some other debilitating disease might not recover well from the operation.

You are on the hospital's final screening committee. All the applicants on your list have been determined to benefit equally from the transplant. Assume they will all match the donors. Now it is up to you to make a choice about which six people will receive kidneys this year. Rank the six by importance, because it may be that only four or five kidneys will be available. In addition, rank two alternatives, since there might be as many as eight kidneys available for transplants.

You will then share your choices with your group, and it will make a final decision.

Whom to Choose Situation Description: Lifeboat

The *S.S. Titanic II* has just hit an iceberg and will sink in one hour. All lifeboats are assigned except one. For this last lifeboat you must select six people from the list.

After that is done, your next task is the allocation of resources. The lifeboat contains enough food and water for seven days. Assume rescue will not occur before seven days and may take as many as fourteen. If this is so, food must be severely rationed. You must decide what to do in case a fourteen-day lifeboat stay is required:

1. Reduce everyone's food by one-half.

2. Reduce some of the group (of six) members' food and not others, so that those with full allocations of food have a greater chance to make it through the fourteen days.

You will then share your choices with your group, and it will make a final decision.

Whom to Choose Situation Description: Spaceship

The Spaceship Foundation is preparing to send a craft on a journey through our galaxy. It will contain information on the earth's cultures, history, and notable people.

You must choose six notable people from a list. Their biographies will be included with the Foundation's material. This material is intended to be intercepted by extraterrestrial beings and will serve as the basis for the impressions they form of the United States and of Earth in general.

You will then share your choices with your group, and it will make a final decision.

UNIT 3

SUGGESTED READING

This selected bibliography is intended to supplement the excerpts and articles of authors included in this Unit. There is an emphasis on books that are pivotal and recent publications. Numerous journals regularly offer articles related to these topics, but are not included in this selected bibliography. For further research, you may wish to include searches of the following journals: (alphabetically) *Academy of Management Executive*, *Academy of Management Journal*, *Harvard Business Review*, *Journal of Leadership Studies*, *Leadership in Action*, *Leadership Quarterly*, and *Leader To Leader*.

This list is organized by author's last name using Modern Language Association-style citations.

Covey, Stephen R. *Principle Centered Leadership*. New York: Summit Books, 1991.
Principles are "natural laws and governing values that are universally valid." Leadership is the ability to apply these principles to problems resulting in win-win relationships. Covey has designed models of leadership levels, power processes, and conditions of empowerment.

Cuilla, Joanne B., Ed. *Ethics, The Heart of Leadership*. Westport: Praeger, 1998.
Contributors to this collection of essays were members of a Kellogg Leadership Project focus group on leadership and ethics. There are philosophical, psychological, management, and historical perspectives represented.

Fluker, Walter E. *Ethical Leadership: The Quest for Character, Civility and Community*. Minneapolis: Fortress Press, 2009.
Fluker explains his ethical model of leadership which encompasses the key values of character, civility and community. He stresses the need for lifelong leadership development, the use of civility in dealing with people and the importance of community for leaders who hope to advance social justice and good in the world.

Johnson, Craig E. *Meeting the Ethical Challenges of Leadership: Casting Light or Shadow, 4th Edition*. Los Angeles: SAGE Publications, 2012.
Johnson contends we tend to see leadership in a positive light. We should also pay attention to the shadows of leadership, which can come in many forms and can color a leader's perspective. Leaders can make ethical choices that do good in the world, or they can make toxic choices that harm followers in organizations. The choices aware leaders make can make all the difference.

Price, Terry L. *Understanding Ethical Failures in Leadership*. New York: Cambridge University Press, 2005.
Price argues that many ethical failures in leadership are because of the way leaders often think about leadership itself rather than about choosing self-interest over the interests of others.

Vanourek, Bob and Gregg Vanourek. *Triple Crown Leadership: Building Excellent, Ethical, and Enduring Organizations*. New York: McGraw-Hill, 2012.
Vanourek and Vanourek utilize a horse racing metaphor to offer five strategies for creating outstanding and enduring organizations that feature ethical behavior on the parts of both leaders and followers. They offer interviews with people who have created and developed innovative organizations and those who have turned around failing groups with teamwork, heart, character, ethical clarity, and inspired leadership.

UNIT 4

ARTICULATING A VISION

INTRODUCTION

Vision and visionaries are a common theme in leadership scholarship. However, simply developing a vision is not enough. The exercise of leadership requires that a vision is clearly articulated and communicated. Communicating the vision powerfully and convincingly is the critical link between the vision and others' potential contributions to achieving the vision. It is what inspires others to work toward that vision and stay focused on the vision. Most students of leadership agree that this ability to create and articulate a vision, and thus inspire and focus followers is the *sine qua non* of effective leadership and is a key element that separates leadership from management.

Four well-known speeches appear in this unit. The Classic Case is Henry V's St. Crispin's Day speech, excerpted from Shakespeare's play *The Life of King Henry V*. In *Henry V*, we find the story of Henry's personal growth into leadership. Henry effectively communicates his vision of a victory and greatness for England, and in addition he shows how each individual has a part and a future in his vision; he inspires them to follow him in the pursuit of the vision regardless of the risks. Martin Luther King, Jr. is the subject of the Leadership Profile. Close study of his "I Have a Dream" speech from the March on Washington in 1963 also teaches a great deal about articulating a vision and inspiring others. King's style and passion gave new life to a vision of equality for all. Following the Leadership Profile there are two short speeches: Abraham Lincoln's Gettysburg Address and Sojourner Truth's "Ain't I a Woman?" appear in the Reflect & Focus feature of this Unit. For brevity and impact there are probably no finer examples of articulating a vision. Lincoln's speech offers insights on how to direct attention to organizational goals, how to bring together diverse elements within an organization, and how to propel the organization in the direction of the vision. Sojourner Truth's candid and direct language with common-sense appeal contrasts with Lincoln's eloquence, but it is no less powerful to inspire action for a vision of equal rights regardless of race *or* gender.

In the Readings, the authors provide specific points about what a vision is and about articulating one effectively. Stavros and her co-authors outline a process with the acronym SOAR for developing a vision and using it to guide strategic planning. James Vaughan points out in his article "Vision and Meaning: Two Sides of the Same Coin," that it is not easy to develop a vision, nor to pursue excellence, but it is important, even essential.

The Film Studies for this Unit are the 1941 Oscar winner for Best Original Screenplay, *Citizen Kane*, based in part on the life of newspaper magnate William Randolph Hearst, and the award-winning 2004 teleplay *Iron Jawed Angels*. *Citizen Kane* provides a cautionary tale of a vision that erodes. *Iron Jawed Angels* portrays the women of the National Women's Party whose vision for a constitutional amendment guaranteeing the right to vote for women was controversial in the nation and among older suffragists.

Unit Four concludes with the exercise "Hollow Square—A Communications Experiment." This challenging communication exercise demonstrates the difficulties often encountered when attempting to share a vision.

Learning Objectives

- Recognize specific skills and techniques to affect the quality of the communication process

- Evaluate the effectiveness of personal communication techniques

- Identify the elements of successful intragroup and intergroup communication

- Develop and articulate a personal vision statement

- Consider potential strategies available to enhance communication effectiveness

- Apply the skills and techniques used in effective communication

- Appreciate the contributions made by the humanities selections in the Unit toward understanding the concept and importance of articulating a vision

UNIT

4

CLASSIC CASE

The Life of King Henry V

By William Shakespeare (1564–1616)
English Poet and Dramatist

Character Guide

King Henry V . . . . Protagonist; the person around whom the play revolves

Humphrey, Duke of Gloucester . . . King's brother

John, Duke of Bedford . . . . . . King's brother and primary military advisor

Duke of Exeter . . . . King's uncle and primary military advisor

Duke of York . . . . King's cousin

Introduction and Historical Background

Shakespeare's *The Life of King Henry V* is about conflict, royal succession, and above all, redemption and leadership.

As the play opens, Henry V has become king after a youth of dissolution, heavy drinking, and carousing. As a result, he has little credibility with either his followers or with the French, with whom he is soon to come into serious conflict over the matter of succession to the French throne. Through marriages of his predecessors and historical accident, Henry V is a claimant to the throne of France and intends to press his claim even if it means going to war. The French reject his claim and insult him, leading him to declare war and press his claim militarily.

In France, Henry V's troops meet with success but pay a terrible price in death, hardship, and exposure to the elements. Throughout the campaign, we see Henry V grow in stature and ability, developing skills and credibility in the eyes of his followers. They are willing to follow him anywhere, even into what appears to be a hopeless battle with the French army at Agincourt. The English are outnumbered five-to-one and seemingly doomed to defeat. In the high point of the play, Henry V gives his "Saint Crispin's Day Speech," in which he extols the brotherhood in arms and exhorts the English to feats they had believed impossible.

The English triumph, and Henry V marries the daughter of the King of France to secure his claim to the throne.

The play follows Henry V's development as a leader and how he both creates and articulates his vision and inspires others to follow him regardless of the risks.

Points to Consider

1. What is Henry V's vision? How does he express it clearly and memorably?

2. How does his appeal convince others to face overwhelming odds?

3. Compare Henry V's speech with those of Abraham Lincoln, Sojourner Truth, and Martin Luther King, Jr. How are they similar and how are they different in their form, content, and aims?

The Life of King Henry V

(Excerpts from Act 4, Scene 3, Lines 1–67)

SCENE III. The English camp.
Enter **Gloucester, Bedford, Exeter, Erpingham,** *with all his host*: **Salisbury** *and* **Westmoreland**.

UNIT
4

Glou. Where is the king?
Bed. The king himself is rode to view their battle.
West. Of fighting men they have full three score thousand.
Exe. There's five to one; besides, they all are fresh.
Sal. God's arm strike with us! 'tis a fearful odds.
God be wi' you, princes all; I'll to my charge:
If we no more meet till we meet in heaven,
Then, joyfully, my noble Lord of Bedford,
My dear Lord Gloucester, and my good Lord
    Exeter,
And my kind kinsman, warriors all, adieu!
Bed. Farewell, good Salisbury; and good luck go with thee!
Exe. Farewell, kind lord; fight valiantly to-day:
And yet I do thee wrong to mind thee of it.
For thou art framed of the firm truth of valour.
    [Exit Salisbury]
Bed. He is as full of valour as of kindness;
Princely in both.

Enter the **King**

West. O that we now had here
But one ten thousand of those men in England
That do no work today!
K. Hen. What's he that wishes so?
My cousin Westmoreland? No, my fair cousin:
If we are mark'd to die, we are enow   20
To do our country loss; and if to live,
The fewer men, the greater share of honour.
God's will! I pray thee, wish not one man more.
By Jove, I am not covetous for gold,
Nor care I who doth feed upon my cost;
It yearns me not if men my garments wear;
Such outward things dwell not in my desires:

But if it be a sin to covet honour,
I am the most offending soul alive.
No, faith, my coz, wish not a man from
   England: 30
God's peace! I would not lose so great an honour
As one man more, methinks, would share from me
For the best hope I have. O, do not wish one more!
Rather proclaim it, Westmoreland, through my host,
That he which hath no stomach to this fight,
Let him depart; his passport shall be made
And crowns for convoy put into his purse:
We would not die in that man's company.
That fears his fellowship to die with us.
This day is call'd the feast of Crispian: 40
He that outlives this day, and comes safe home,
Will stand a tip-toe when this day is named,
And rouse him at the name of Crispian.
He that shall live this day, and see old age,
Will yearly on the vigil feast his neighbours,
And say 'To-morrow is Saint Crispian:'
Then will he strip his sleeve and show his scars,
And say 'These wounds I had on Crispin's day.'
Old men forget; yet all shall be forgot,
But he'll remember with advantages 50
What feats he did this day. Then shall our names,
Familiar in his mouth as household words,
Harry the king, Bedford and Exeter,
Warwick and Talbot, Salisbury and Gloucester,
Be in their flowing cups freshly remember'd,
This story shall the good man teach his son;
And Crispin Crispian shall ne'er go by,
From this day to the ending of the world,
But we in it shall be remembered;
We few, we happy few, we band of brothers;
For he today that sheds his blood with me 61
Shall be my brother; be he ne'er so vile,
This day shall gentle his condition:
And gentlemen in England now a-bed
Shall think themselves accursed they were not here,
And hold their manhoods cheap whiles any speaks
That fought with us upon Saint Crispin's Day.

Shakespeare, W. ( ). *The life of King Henry V*, (line reference - 4:3:1–67)

LEADERSHIP PROFILE

Martin Luther King, Jr. (1929–1968)

American Clergyman, Civil Rights Leader,
and Nobel Laureate

Introduction and Historical Background

Martin Luther King, Jr., an ordained Baptist minister at the age of seventeen, was one of the principal leaders of the American civil rights movement and a prominent advocate of nonviolent resistance to racial oppression. King's own philosophy of nonviolent protest was heavily influenced by the work of Indian nationalist Mohandas K. Gandhi. Although King advocated nonviolent resistance, he, like many civil rights activists, was a victim of violence. His home was bombed, repeated threats were made against his life, he was arrested several times, and he lost his life to an assassin in 1968.

National Archives and
Records Administration

In 1955, a group of middle-class black women, the Women's Political Council, was considering a boycott of the segregated public transportation system in Montgomery, Alabama. The arrest of Rosa Parks, a black woman who had refused to give her seat to a white passenger, led them to put their boycott into motion. However, they knew that their own jobs, primarily as teachers within institutions that whites controlled, would be threatened. They needed the boycott to make leadership from black citizens less vulnerable to easy economic retaliation. A larger meeting of Montgomery's black civic leaders met within days, and twenty-six-year-old King was asked to lead the boycott. King had been pastor of the Dexter Avenue Baptist Church for a little more than a year. King had not sought the position, and in the weeks that followed he only reluctantly accepted the stressful and dangerous position he was in. The boycott, which lasted 381 days, ended with a mandate from the United States Supreme Court outlawing all segregated public transportation in Montgomery. King's nonviolent resistance strategy was highly successful in the Montgomery boycott and was employed in numerous campaigns he led during the civil rights movement. In 1964, King was awarded the Nobel Peace Prize. King understood that his talent for articulating the vision and mission was a small contribution to the movement; he owed his celebrity and success to the efforts of many activists. When he accepted the Nobel award, King went out of his way to emphasize that he was accepting the award not as a personal honor, but simply as a trustee on behalf of the entire movement.

On April 4, 1968, an escaped convict, James Earl Ray, assassinated King in Memphis, Tennessee. More than 100,000 people attended King's funeral in Atlanta, Georgia. In honor of King, the third Monday in January is observed as a federal holiday. Both his Atlanta birthplace and gravesite are national historic sites.

King delivered the following words as part of the speech that came to be known by the title "I Have a Dream," on August 28, 1963, on the steps of the Lincoln Memorial before a crowd of 250,000 during the historic March on Washington for Jobs and Freedom.

UNIT
4

Points to Consider

1. Through his speech, how did King inspire others to continue the long and arduous struggle he saw ahead of them?

2. In what ways can King's speech be seen as a continuation of Lincoln's words? (See Reflect & Focus feature in this Unit.)

"I Have a Dream"

By Martin Luther King, Jr.
Washington D.C., August 28, 1963

…So even though we face the difficulties of today and tomorrow, I still have a dream. It is a dream deeply rooted in the American dream.

I have a dream that one day this nation will rise up and live out the true meaning of its creed: "We hold these truths to be self-evident; that all men are created equal."

I have a dream—that one day on the red hills of Georgia the sons of former slaves and the sons of former slaveowners will be able to sit down together at the table of brotherhood.

I have a dream—that one day even the state of Mississippi, a state sweltering with the heat of injustice and sweltering with the heat of oppression, will be transformed into an oasis of freedom and justice.

I have a dream—that my four little children will one day live in a nation where they will not be judged by the color of their skin but by the content of their character.

I have a dream today!

I have a dream—that one day, down in the state of Alabama, with its vicious racists, with its governor having his lips dripping with the words of interposition and nullification, one day right down in Alabama, little black boys and black girls will be able to join hands with little white boys and white girls and walk together as sisters and brothers.

I have a dream today.

I have a dream that one day every valley shall be exalted, every hill and mountain shall be made low, the rough places will be made plain, and the crooked places will be made straight, and the glory of the Lord shall be revealed, and all flesh shall see it together!

This is our hope. This is the faith that I go back to the South with. With this faith we will be able to hue out of the mountain of despair a stone of hope. With this faith we will be able to transform the jangling discords of our nation into a beautiful symphony of brotherhood. With this faith we will be able to work together, to pray together, to struggle together, to go to jail together, to stand up for freedom together, knowing that we will be free one day.

This will be the day when all of God's children will be able to sing with new meaning, "My country 'tis of thee, sweet land of liberty, of thee I sing. Land where my fathers died, land of the pilgrim's pride, from every mountainside, let freedom ring."

And if America is to be a great nation this must become true.

So let freedom ring from the prodigious hilltops of New Hampshire!

Let freedom ring from the mighty mountains of New York!

Let freedom ring from the heightening Alleghenies of Pennsylvania!

Let freedom ring from the snowcapped Rockies of Colorado!

Let freedom ring from the curvaceous slopes of California!

But not only that; let freedom ring from Stone Mountain of Georgia!

Let freedom ring from Lookout Mountain of Tennessee!

Let freedom ring from every hill and molehill of Mississippi!

From every mountainside, let freedom ring!

When we allow freedom to ring; when we let it ring from every village and every hamlet, from every state and every city, we will be able to speed up that day when all of God's children—black men and white men, Jews and Gentiles, Protestants and Catholics—will be able to join hands and sing in the words of the old Negro spiritual, "Free at last! Free at last! Thank God almighty, we are free at last!"

UNIT
4

The Gettysburg Address

"Fourscore and seven years ago our fathers brought forth upon this continent a new nation, conceived in Liberty, and dedicated to the proposition that all men are created equal.

"Now we are engaged in a great civil war, testing whether that nation, or any nation so conceived and so dedicated can long endure. We are met on a great battle-field of that war. We are met to dedicate a portion of it as the final resting place of those who here gave their lives that the nation might live. It is altogether fitting and proper that we should do this.

"But in a larger sense we can not dedicate—we can not consecrate—we can not hallow—this ground. The brave men, living and dead, who struggled here have consecrated it, far above our poor power to add or detract. The world will little note, nor long remember what we say here, but it can never forget what they did here. It is for us the living, rather, to be dedicated here to the unfinished work that they who fought here have thus far so nobly advanced. It is rather for us to be here dedicated to the great task remaining before us—that from these honored dead we take increased devotion to that cause for which they gave the last full measure of devotion—that we here highly resolve that these dead shall not have died in vain—that this nation, under God, shall have a new birth of freedom—and that government of the people, by the people, for the people, shall not perish from the earth."

—Abraham Lincoln (1809–1865), Sixteenth President of the United States (1861–1865)

Delivered at the Dedication of the National Cemetery at Gettysburg, November 19, 1863

REFLECT & FOCUS

Ain't I a Woman?

"Well, children, where there is so much racket there must be something out of kilter. I think that 'twixt the [N]egroes of the South and the women at the North, all talking about rights, the white men will be in a fix pretty soon. But what's all this here talking about?

"That man over there says that women need to be helped into carriages, and lifted over ditches, and to have the best place everywhere. Nobody ever helps me into carriages, or over mud-puddles, or gives me any best place! And ain't I a woman? Look at me! Look at my arm! I have ploughed and planted, and gathered into barns, and no man could head me! And ain't I a woman? I could work as much and eat as much as a man—when I could get it—and bear the lash as well! And ain't I a woman? I have borne thirteen children, and seen most all sold off to slavery, and when I cried out with my mother's grief, none but Jesus heard me! And ain't I a woman?

"Then they talk about this thing in the head; what's this they call it? [member of audience whispers, "intellect"] That's it, honey. What's that got to do with women's rights or [N]egroes' rights? If my cup won't hold but a pint, and yours holds a quart, wouldn't you be mean not to let me have my little half measure full?

"Then that little man in black there, he says women can't have as much rights as men, 'cause Christ wasn't a woman! Where did your Christ come from? Where did your Christ come from? From God and a woman! Man had nothing to do with Him.

"If the first woman God ever made was strong enough to turn the world upside down all alone, these women together ought to be able to turn it back, and get it right side up again! And now they is asking to do it, the men better let them.

"Obliged to you for hearing me, and now old Sojourner ain't got nothing more to say."

—Sojourner Truth (1797–1883)

Delivered at the Women's Convention, Akron, Ohio, 1851

REFLECT & FOCUS

READINGS

"Strategic Inquiry → Appreciative Intent: Inspiration to SOAR—A New Framework for Strategic Planning"

By Jacqueline Stavros, David Cooperrider, and D. Lynn Kelley

Points to Consider

1. How is appreciative thinking different from the traditional approach to strategic planning?

2. What do the authors mean by "enabling objectives"? Enabling what or whom?

3. How would you ensure that all stakeholders genuinely contribute to the SOAR process?

4. The authors replace the process of "assessment, planning, implementation, and control" with "inquire, imagine, innovate, and inspire"—what is the essence of the difference in the two processes to you?

"Strategic Inquiry → Appreciative Intent: Inspiration to SOAR—A New Framework for Strategic Planning"

Overview: The Field of Strategic Planning

The corporate mantra over the last ten years has been change, change, and change. Many of the principles that corporations held as stable and immutable have been turned upside down. Books such as *Reengineering the Corporation*, *The Strategy Focused Organization*, *The Balanced Scorecard*, *Strategic Thinking: An Executive Approach*, *Strategy From the Top* and *Leading Strategic Change* have become bestsellers in the corporate world. Corporations that were traditionally considered dominant within industries have shrunk or disappeared, and the march towards globalization has accelerated. For example, in 1976, the majority of the world's fifty largest companies were U.S. based; by 1995 the number was just 17 (Pattison, 1996).

At the heart of the change one often finds competition. When two similar entities compete for the same scarce resources, often one will win and the other will lose. Competition is not a new phenomenon. The very essence of Darwin's "survival of the fittest" is competition. The difference is that when similar species compete for the same scarce resources, the outcome is based not on a strategic plan that results in a win—but simply that the species that was naturally the "most fit" to its environment wins. Look how far we have evolved! We now have the ability to plan for survival. Now, it is not the company that unwittingly finds itself the "fittest" that survives—but the company that is best able to strategically think, plan, manage its resources, lead its people, and sustain its future that becomes "fit" enough to survive and indeed thrive.

Given the acceleration of change in recent years, how are companies proactively responding? Obviously, some companies are ignoring the change and are being left in the dust. However, the majority of companies that are responding to the change are limiting their responses to operational and tactical areas. Companies are answering the "call of the changing world" with such approaches as new processes, new procedures, downsizing, rightsizing, lean manufacturing, Six Sigma, virtual integration, core versus context exercises, value chain analysis, e-business models and other new ways of running their business. These methods have shown the ability to produce dramatic results. However, the common theme that runs through all of these responses is their focus on new ways of performing the daily operations of the organization. There has been a great void in new methods to be used in the one area specifically designed to prepare for the changing future—an appreciative-based approach to strategic planning. We need to change the way we strategically think, plan and implement strategy.

Think about this:

- Change requires action.
- Action requires a plan.
- A plan requires a strategy.
- A strategy requires goals and enabling objectives.
- Goals and objectives require a mission.
- A mission is defined by a vision.
- A vision is set by one's values.

The Appreciative Inquiry (AI) approach to strategic planning starts by focusing on the strengths of an organization and its stakeholders' values and shared vision.

In spite of the tumultuousness of our competitive environment, with few exceptions, the core of the strategic planning approach used by U.S. corporations has been virtually unchanged over the last fifty years. For instance, almost all strategic planning processes contain the "old standby" of completing a SWOT (strengths, weaknesses, opportunities, threats) analysis, or its counterpart TOWS (threats, opportunities, weaknesses, and strengths) Analysis. The question this raises, is if companies are using the traditional strategic planning approach—and are failing in spite of it, perhaps we need to change or challenge the approach. We want to offer an alternative to the SWOT analysis. Our alternative is to SOAR (strengths, opportunities, aspirations, results). But first let's take a brief look at history of strategic planning.

The first writings on the topic predominantly relate to military strategy. The earliest surviving Western book on the subject, published in the fourth century BC, was written by Aineias the Tactician, an ancient Athenian. Within this book and others that followed the same vein (such as *The Art of War* by Sun Tzu), authors identified "job requirements" for strategists, guidelines for developing strategy, resource and manpower allocation, integration of different branches of the military, and characteristics held by good strategists. It was strategic thinking based on "divide and conquer."

Another serious writer in the Eastern tradition of strategic planning was the Samurai warrior, Miyamoto Mushahi, who wrote his book on strategic thinking in Japan over three hundred years ago. This book, full of ancient wisdom, was published in the United States in 1974 under the title *A Book of Five Rings* (Musashi, 1974). During the early 1980s Japanese literature became required reading for American businesspeople. In particular, *A Book of Five Rings* was touted as being the key to understanding the Japanese mind in business. The author based his writings on the principles of Zen, stressing a victorious, warrior-like strategic attitude toward all aspects of life. The "tag line" on the book states, "The classic text of principles, craft, skill, and Samurai strategy that changed the American way of doing business." The cover drawing shows an archetypal Samurai warrior armed with the weapons of business: a phone and a computer printout. Although this novel approach was fundamentally different from the existing American-based writings on strategic planning, in spite of its self-promotion it really did little to "change the American way of doing business."

Around the same time as this tome was published in the U.S., Americans were just cutting their baby teeth on the formal notion of business strategic planning. Strategic planning was presented as a brand new discipline during the 1960s at Harvard Business School, when several pioneering professors taught and published articles on the holistic notion of business planning from the scope of the entire business, rather than from individual disciplines such as marketing and finance. By the late 1970s, the key elements of strategic planning as we know it today began popping up in many of the publications on the topic. A typical strategic planning flowchart during that time looked like Figure 1.

Figure 1: Strategic Planning Process (1970s–1980s)

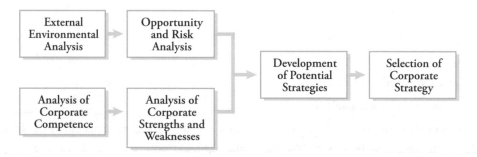

Look familiar? Although this flowchart is fifty years old, it is not radically different from the flowcharts published in today's strategic management textbooks. By the mid-1980s, Strategic Planning had become an official discipline with courses offered at over 2900 business schools, and some improvements to the strategic planning method were added. For instance, Peter Drucker's work in the 1970s urged companies to articulate the business they were in. This led to the development of a mission statement, a subsequent addition to the strategic planning model presented in Figure 1. Other additions to the model occurred when people realized that the best plan is useless unless it is acted upon. Subsequent steps were added at the end of the original strategic planning process to help the organization deploy the plan and evaluate its success. Thus, steps such as: establishing objectives, allocating resources, and monitoring the implementation of the plan appeared as additions to the original model.

Thus, a typical strategic planning flowchart in contemporary business textbooks looks like Figure 2 (below).

Figure 2: Strategic Planning Process (1990s–Present)

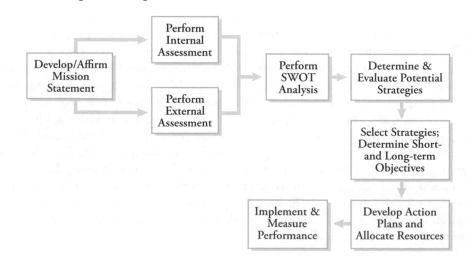

During the 1990s, several publications appeared decrying the existing strategic planning methodology. In 1994, Mintzberg published "The Rise and Fall of Strategic Planning" in the *Harvard Business Review*. The article denounced traditional strategic planning methods as producing rigid documents that are filed away and serve little or no purpose in the day-to-day activities of corporations. In *Beyond Strategic Vision*, Cowley and Domb (1997) noted additional problems with strategic planning:

- Unrealistic forecasts lead to over-optimistic strategic plans.

- Arbitrary goals have no support within the strategic plan.

- Companies fail to focus on a few high-leverage goals.

- Companies select the wrong goals.

- There is no "shared vision."

- The goals have no plans to support them.

- The planned activities are not frequently reviewed and evaluated.

- The review of progress toward strategic goals is punitive, which stifles risk-taking.

- Planning is an event rather than a process.

- A department that is not responsible for implementation develops strategic plans.

Companies began looking for other methods of strategic planning that would address these problems. One of the proposed solutions was the Japanese method called Hoshin Planning. During the 1960s when the U.S. was first developing its form of strategic planning, Japan was independently inventing its own methods of strategic planning. American companies became aware of Hoshin planning in the early 1990s, following the translation into English publications on Hoshin planning. In the late 1980s, two books (Mizuno, 1988; Brassard, 1989) presented some of the tools used in Hoshin planning. However, since these tools were not overtly linked with strategic planning in the early publications, the strategic planning community did not immediately notice them. During the 1990s, additional books presented the Hoshin method as a form of strategic planning (Bechtell, 1995), and major U.S. companies such as Hewlett-Packard, Ford and Xerox began using the method.

The Hoshin approach is based on the premise that organizations should choose just one or two "breakthrough strategy" areas each year. A major emphasis of the Hoshin method is the continuous improvement that occurs within the implementation cycle. Although many models for the Hoshin planning process have been published (including company-specific models, such as those of Xerox and Hewlett-Packard), a typical flowchart for Hoshin strategic planning looks as shown in Figure 3:

UNIT

4

Figure 3: Hoshin Planning Process

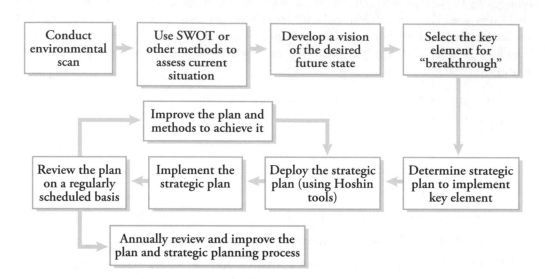

As you can see, Hoshin planning uses some of the same tools as the typical U.S.-based strategic planning methods. However, it should be noted that the specific inclusion of SWOT analysis is an American addition to the traditional Japanese approach—albeit one that is widely included in U.S. utilization of the method. Two of the advantages touted by Hoshin devotees are the associated tools that help gain employee involvement and buy-in during the development and the subsequent deployment of the plan, and the built-in links between the strategic plan and the operations plans. In particular, a deployment matrix is used once the strategy is identified. The matrix is cascaded throughout the organization, creating a vehicle for each successive department to build its objectives in support of the preceding department's objectives—all of which are tied at the top to the strategic plan. The matrix shows the correlations and interrelationships necessary for strategy deployment and identifies corresponding measurements and subsequent impacts as the strategy is rolled out at all levels of the organization.

This brief review of strategic planning history over the last fifty years shows us that the process of planning has undergone some improvements—but very little deviation from its core structure that begins with a SWOT analysis. The biggest departure from the process most U.S. companies use appears in the Japanese Hoshin process. Exposure to the Hoshin process has also led to other approaches such as, A Systems Thinking Approach to Strategic Planning and Management (Haines, 2000), wherein Haines says we should "stamp out the outmoded way of planning, which no longer works in today's dynamic world" (p. i) (referring to traditional U.S. strategic planning).

We agree with Haines. Given the radical changes in the competitive environment, the old model is not up to the task of producing the types of strategy and strategic plans that will propel businesses forward in the rapidly evolving future.

Dozens of models have been available since the 1930s to help organizations do strategic planning. What is needed is not another strategic planning model, but a strategic thinking framework and approach to quickly and smoothly guide an organization through this complex process while engaging the whole system. We will present an emerging framework that involves an appreciative approach of creating an organization's future. This framework allows an organization's stakeholders to see where they are today and establish a vision of where they want to go. The strategic plan will be a co-creation involving various stakeholders at differing levels in the organization. This new approach helps stakeholders to clearly identify, understand and, most importantly, communicate individual and organizational values, direction (vision), purpose (mission), core and unique capabilities (internal analysis), strategic opportunities (external analysis), strategies and tactics, structures and systems to create a positive organizational environment and build upon an organization's positive core to sustain its unique value offering (UVO).

Appreciative Inquiry and Its Integration to Strategic Planning

Appreciative Inquiry (AI) is a vision-based approach of open dialogue that is designed to help organizations and their partners create a shared vision for the future and a mission to operate in the present (Srivastva & Cooperrider, 1990). Today's organizations can benefit from an appreciative approach of inquiry, which invites organizational members to learn and value the history of their organization and its culture. The AI approach allows them to:

- Build on their strengths (the positive core).
- Discover profitable opportunities.
- Visualize goals and strategic alternatives.
- Identify enabling objectives.
- Design strategies and tactics that are integrated with their most successful programs and supply chain partners.
- Implement a strategic plan that is a dynamic, continuous, and living document.

Such a plan will include the best organizational structure and systems to realize its vision. Numerous organizations have used AI, including:

- Private and public nonprofit organizations
- For-profit organizations
- Government and international agencies worldwide.

AI has allowed hundreds of organizations to discover and grow the best practices of capacity building for their organizations as well as their value chain partners' organizations.

The AI approach to strategic planning involves identifying and building on existing strengths and profitable opportunities rather than dwelling on problems, deficiencies, weaknesses, and threats. Think about the traditional strategic planning process—at its very core is the good old standby SWOT analysis—Strengths, Weaknesses, Opportunities, Threats. If we split it 50/50, we would spend about half of our time thinking about our positives (Strengths/Opportunities) and the other half thinking about our negatives (Weaknesses/Threats). But let's be honest. Even though the tool looks 50/50, human nature tends to dwell disproportionately on our weaknesses and threats. Unfortunately, by concentrating on what we do wrong we tend to amplify the negative. Welcome to the world of AI where, instead, we disproportionately focus on our strengths and opportunities, so that we can grow them until they crowd out our weaknesses and threats.

The AI approach also builds capacity by moving stakeholders of an association beyond organizational boundaries to form new relationships and thus expand the organization's potential. What do we mean by this? Many companies are bounded by the limitations of their organizations. Few executives think "outside of the box" of their corporation when they are brainstorming their

UNIT

4

future strategies. AI opens up dialogues with the organization's partners and external stakeholders. These dialogues result in an expansion of the current capacity of the organization, as partners look for ways to create shared directions that benefit both organizations. You can actually think of AI as an approach that expands organizational boundaries, just in the same way the familiar exercise below requires expansion beyond boundaries.

Instructions: Connect all nine dots above using four straight lines without lifting your pencil from the page.

Answer: This can only be accomplished if you allow your pencil to move outside of the box.

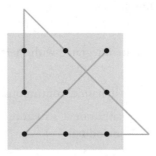

Now, imagine that box is your organization. When creating a strategic plan, most people are bound unconsciously within the rectangle [sic], limiting their organizational capability. The AI approach actually creates opportunities and incentives to move outside the box so the organization's strategic plan may further expand organizational capacity to multi-organizational and global capacity.

One of the pitfalls of the traditional strategic planning process is that it is generally conducted by top management. The process fails to glean wisdom from all levels of the organization. In this failure, it also neglects to obtain stakeholder buy-in from the very people who must ultimately carry out the activities that support the strategic plan. Most of us have had the experience at some point in our careers of being presented with a strategic plan that we were expected to implement, despite our lack of input into the plan. AI allows and in fact encourages all stakeholders to have a voice in the planning dialogue, leading to full participation in an organization's future, resulting in stakeholder ownership of the strategic plan throughout the organization.

The collaborative process of open dialogue helps an organization and its partners understand what happens when their organizations are working at their best. This information is used to create an image of "the best of what can be" for the future. The power of AI is its potential to co-create a visual image of the organization. Stakeholders participate in envisioning a shared set of values, a vision, mission, goals and enabling objectives, strategic alternatives, integrated tactical programs to support the recommended strategies, an actionable implementation plan, and the best structure and systems for a sustainable future.

The advantages of the AI approach to strategic planning are that it:

- Focuses on the positive to crowd out the negative.

- Builds organizational capacity beyond existing boundaries.

- Invites stakeholders into the strategy process.

- Builds relationships with partners.

- Obtains input from all levels of the organization.

- Obtains buy-in from all levels of the organization.

- Allows the planning process to become much more of a process that incorporates and connects values, vision, and mission statement to strategic goals, strategies, plans and a positive and objective review of goals.

- Creates a shared set of organizational values and vision of the future organization.

AI allows for the strategic assessment process to take on a life of its own starting with an inquiry to discover what has made the organization a success in the past and present. The process helps to build a sustainable competitive advantage for the future by identifying the organization's Unique Value Offering (UVO). This phenomenon occurs through an on-going dialogue with the identified stakeholders of the organization. Through this dialogue, appreciative ways of knowing and learning about an organization's history and core capabilities are enriched. Srivastva and Cooperrider (1990) explained it as follows:

> Organizations are, to a much larger extent than normally assumed, *affirmative systems*—they are guided in their actions by anticipatory "forestructures" of positive knowledge that, like a movie projects on a screen, project a horizon of confident expectation which energizes, intensifies, and provokes action in the present. The forestructures or guiding images of the future are not the property of individuals but cohere within patterns of relatedness in the form of dialogue…. In this view Appreciative Inquiry refers to a process of knowing that draws one to inquire beyond superficial appearances to the deeper life-enhancing essentials and potentials of organizational existence. (p.14)

AI is used as a co-inquiry from multiple perspectives to understand organizational efforts to create a vision, serve its mission, obtain desired goals and objectives and design the best strategies.

AI is best known for its 4-D Cycle:

> a cycle of activities that guide members of an organization, group, or community through four stages: *discovery*—finding out about moments of excellence, core values and best practices; *dream*—envisioning positive possibilities; *design*—creating the structure, processes and relationships that will support the dream; and *destiny*—developing an effective inspirational plan for implementation.

These four phases are closely linked to the phases of inquiry necessary in the strategic planning process, as shown at the end of this article.

AI plays a critical role in the strategic planning process. It provides a framework for the organization to complete a strategic assessment and it emphasizes a collaborative process of open dialogue to help the organization's stakeholders understand what they see happening when the organization is working at its best. As the stakeholders identify and describe the "life-giving" forces of their organization, together they can imagine and impart innovation to the future of their organizations with energy, vitality, and commitment. The positive language and affirmation should fit with the value system of the organization. In addition, the process can be a helpful approach in any strategic planning effort because it requires a "strategic vision, collective action, multiple parties and an empowering context for innovation and development" (Liebler, 1997, p. 31).

The final part of this article introduces our relational approach to strategic assessment and planning to assist with co-creation of an organization's future. Our strategic planning framework serves as only a beginning to help organizations dialogue about how best to go about building and delivering their UVO. As demonstrated by case studies in the November 2003 issue of the *AI Practitioner*, when the strategic planning process is being implemented and sustained, the visible outcomes can be:

- Definition and communication of organizational values.

- Clarity of vision, mission, goals, and objectives.

- Openness to new ideas and opportunities from the outside.

- Self-confidence, self-reliance and self-respect at the organizational level.

- Improved organizational capacities and individual and functional capabilities.

- Build multi-organizational and global capacity.

- Stakeholder ownership and responsibility for the organization's existence and future.

- A participatory strategic planning process where everyone is free to voice concerns and opinions.

- Creation of new knowledge that is practical and useful.

- Consideration for important issues and needs of stakeholders.

- Acceptance of new relationships and responsibilities that will build strategic capacity at all levels.

Integrating AI and Strategic Planning is a living concept that has the freedom to grow and change through dialogue. It is much more than a plan. We believe that those organizations with the greatest capacity possess skills and the spirit, enthusiasm, energy, and synergy required for change. If leadership embraces the strategic planning process as an opportunity to work closely with its stakeholders for a profitable sustainable future, they will need the "spirit of cooperation" in which to pursue their organization's vision and mission. To this end, we offer our readers a road map to help organizations get focused and organized for growth.

Strategic Inquiry: Appreciative Intent: Inspiration to SOAR

To illustrate the application of SOAR within the strategic planning process, a corporation (Tendercare) is presented as it first pursued [a] traditional strategic plan, and then how it applied the SOAR principles, to take its strategic plan to a higher level at three levels of strategy: corporate, business, and functional.

Typically, the first step in the traditional strategic planning process is to review the current strategic posture of an organization. It begins with a review of the existing *mission statement*. A mission statement is a statement of purpose or function for the organization. For example, the following is the mission statement of Tendercare, which is a company that operates in the long-term care industry:

The mission of Tendercare (Michigan) Inc. is to be a dynamic, quality-oriented and significant provider of long-term care and diversified health care services.

To emphasize high standards of performance and integrity that will enhance the quality of life of our residents.

To provide our employees opportunities for growth through participation, achievement, recognition, and reward.

To maintain a strong economic base through sound practices in support of these goals.

The mission statement provides the reason for which the organization exists. It describes the products/services to be supplied, the markets served, and operating philosophy. Yet a mission statement should not be developed without a guiding *vision statement*. The vision statement answers the question, *what do we ultimately want to become?* For example:

To be the healthcare provider of choice in our market areas.

The vision statement represents senior management's strategic intent—"a broad (vision) statement that identifies the guiding business concept or driving force that will propel the company forward toward the achievement of that intent," (DeKluyver, 2002, p.9). Then, prior year *goals*, *objectives*, *strategies*, *plans*, and *policies* are reviewed.

Goals are set as a refinement to open-ended statements about such wishes as "being profitable" or "achieving growth in the long-term care market." Then, more specific measurables are defined called *objectives*. For example, Tendercare's objective is to be number one in the long-term care market in Michigan by 2005. It is a quantifiable statement about a desired strategic goal. Next, the effectiveness of *strategies* is evaluated. A *strategy* is simply the "how to" means or guiding actions to achieve the long-term objectives. Strategies are usually viewed at the following levels:

UNIT
4

1. Corporate level: what type of business should we continue to be in? Where should we grow, remain status quo or divest?

2. Business level: How do we compete?

3. Functional level: what should each functional area do to synchronize with the business and corporate level strategies?

After an audit of the current and past situation, a SWOT analysis begins. This analysis is also referred to as environmental scanning. During the environmental scan, data are collected to answer questions about the present and future of the organization and the markets/industry served. The strategic planning team fragments those forces that determine the present and future of the corporation into internal and external variables using the **SWOT** format to analyze **strengths**, **weaknesses**, **opportunities**, and **threats**.

Figure 4: SWOT Model

Internal Assessment	Strengths	Weaknesses
	Where we can outperform others	Where others can outperform us
External Assessment	Opportunities	Threats
	How we might exploit the market	What/who might take our market

Based on the SWOT analysis, a set of recommendations [is] made as to what strategic alternatives would best serve the organization. From there, policies are reviewed or created to link the formulation of strategy with implementation. Policies and guidelines provide clear guidance to employees for implementation often in the form of programs, budgets, and procedures. Then, evaluation and control mechanisms are put into place to measure activities and performance results.

This organization quickly discovered that the AI approach and SOAR framework to strategic planning offers several benefits over the traditional model. The first is that its strategic planning process is both results-oriented and co-constructive at the same time. Whereas the traditional process offers a distinct demarcation between the assessment, planning, implementation, and control stages, the AI framework actually allows participants to co-create their desired future throughout the process by inquiry, imagination, innovation, and inspiration. This starts with a strategic inquiry that values the organizational members' insights. An inquiry is done to best understand organizational members' values and the peak moments/experiences of what has worked well in the past. The inquiry also includes questions about the core factor that gives life to the organization's continued existence and wishes for the future. Its internal focus is on organizational strengths. AI is also used with customers, suppliers and partners to perform external analysis.

In many organizations, strategic planning takes place only at the highest levels of the organization and involves relatively few stakeholders. In contrast this new framework encourages strategic planners and all possible stakeholders to embrace change based on a foundation of executive and organizational integrity. The issue of integrity is important because stakeholders must be aware of the underlying assumptions that drive corporate leaders as questions are developed for the strategic inquiry. The aspiration principle of AI suggests that systems grow toward the collective vision of the future. Through relational discourse, we build our desired image of the most preferred future.

The Appreciative Inquiry (AI) approach transforms the **SWOT** model into **SOAR** (strengths, opportunities, aspirations, results). It can liberate us to focus on what really matters: the future of our people and organization. The AI strategist or strategic planner poses the question of inquiry to shape the direction of the strategic planning process and inform the content based on its strengths and opportunities. This is what we call a strategic inquiry with an appreciative intent.

Figure 5: Strategic Inquiry → Appreciative Intent: Inspiration to SOAR

Strategic Inquiry	Strengths	Opportunities
	What are our greatest assets	What are the best possible market opportunities
Appreciative Intent	Aspirations	Results
	What is our preferred future	What are the measurable results

(Stavros, Cooperrider, and Kelley, 2003)

The **SOAR** approach to strategy starts with a **strategic inquiry**. During this inquiry an organization's greatest **Strengths** and **Opportunities** are discovered and explored among the participants. The participants are invited to share their **Aspirations** and co-construct their most preferred future. Then, recognition and reward programs are designed to inspire employees to achieve measurable **Results**.

Like the original AI 4-D model, the AI approach to strategic planning starts with an **inquiry**—using unconditional positive questions to discover the organization's core values, vision, strengths, and potential opportunities. The inquiry is a time of reflection into the strengths of the past and how these have been constructed with an eye towards creating the change we may desire. Next, the participants enter the **imagination** phase, in which time is spent dreaming and co-constructing the preferred future. At this transformation point, values are affirmed and a vision and mission statement are created or re-created. Long-term objectives and strategic alternatives and recommendations are presented in this phase. The third phase is a time of **innovation** to begin the strategic design of short-term objectives, tactical and functional plans, integrated programs, structures, and systems to best achieve the desired future. To ensure that measurable results are achieved, the AI approach and SOAR framework recognize that employees must be **inspired** through authentic recognition and reward systems. In short, the process of assessment, planning, implementation, and control is replaced with the concepts of "inquire," "imagine," "innovate," and "inspire."

Three Stories of Applying the SOAR Framework

Strategic planning is an opportunity to help organizations soar with their strengths and to elevate an entire system's learning capacity to innovate from initial thought to finish. It can be absolutely thrilling. While we do not often talk about strategic business planning this way it is clear that strategic planning can be one of the most positive occurrences in an organization's life; to which it can be:

- A rarefied time that cultivates the most elevated thought and action.

- A ritual-like time for the public re-creation of high-quality connections across an entire system.

- A precious time for drawing upon the "positive core" of a system in ways that ignite upward spirals in purposeful vision and dynamic action.

When we reflect back over the past several years of our organization development work across many types of corporations, we were surprised: every single one of the high point moments were linked with times of strategic planning.

- It is crucial to cultivate a context that inspires natural curiosity; that is, the thrill of something historians of business innovation have surprisingly called "esthetic appreciation" in contrast to the more limited attitude of calculation or practical utility.

- The second perspective is something that magnifies the first—and it does so more consistently and effortlessly than anything else we have ever experienced. It is the leap from talking about systems thinking to doing systems thinking. It is the enactment of the power of wholeness, which means, quite simply, bringing the whole system into the room together to do the inquiry and strategizing.

Esthetic appreciation and systems thinking are what the first two stories below help illustrate. Each story is briefly described, and then expanded upon in detail in the next section.

The first story involves the strength-based SOAR framework used at Roadway Express, one of the largest trucking companies in America. Terminals from Chicago Heights to Winston-Salem have used this methodology to perform strategic business planning at their decentralized locations. To date Roadway has held over twenty strategic planning summits using the appreciative approach, and now have twelve more summits planned for the upcoming year.

The second story illustrates the use of strategic planning at one of the top management schools in the world. It was a full engagement process guided by a combination of Ernst and Young's strategic planning framework and Appreciative Inquiry (AI). For years Ernst and Young has been a leader in strategic planning as well as AI in their change-management offerings. But this was the first time the two were brought together. The result helps us understand the vast potential of the SOAR sequence.

The third story is a story of a different kind. It is not one of great growth or amazing returns, but one of appreciative divestiture. For years Tendercare, a regional long-term care provider, had been operating an assisted living center in an eroding market. The company, hesitant to continue to invest more resources in a center that was failing, used the SOAR model. They had come to the conclusion that the building did not fit into their aspirations and as a result needed to be closed.

In a previous issue of this journal we spoke about the Roadway case, so let's start with a brief overview of Roadway and explore their special techniques related to the mapping strengths, opportunities, aspirations, and results (or measures of success).

Roadway Express: An Amazing Story of Business Planning

A recent videotape captures it all: the energy, the positive connections between all levels, the enthusiasm of the SOAR model in action as Roadway Express, a Fortune 500 trucking company based in Akron, Ohio holds a strategic planning summit (you can see a web-video of the whole thing at http://ai.cwru.edu). Nearly 300 dockworkers and truck drivers gather with management and customers to discuss Roadway's strategy for becoming the leading "LTL carrier" in a fiercely competitive industry. The mix included dockworkers, sales reps, CEO, drivers, administration, mechanics, customers, and more—literally "the whole system."

At a more recent strategic planning session at their Winston-Salem facility, Joanne Gordon, a *Forbes* Magazine business writer, surprised Roadway by asking if she could participate in the three-day event. The "AI Summit" would engage and involve every kind of stakeholder at the Winston-Salem North Carolina terminal and Joanne Gordon had never seen anything like it. We explained to her how Roadway was doing something nobody else in the industry was doing. Furthermore, Roadway had already successfully piloted this appreciative SOAR framework at five of their 300 terminals around the country.

Prior to the summit the *Forbes* journalist was quite convinced that the session was going to be some kind of large-group "cheerleading" or "therapy" session—not the real thing of joint business planning. She even talked about it that way. So she arrived at the summit asking tough, skeptical questions. Here are the opening lines in the feature story she later wrote: "Teamsters and managers writing business plans together?...It was a scene not often seen in the history of labor-management relations."

As the article unfolded, the reporter's skepticism began to soften. She even sounded shocked at the level of business capability and passion demonstrated, for example, by the dockworkers and drivers. It was clearly hard for this writer to let go of preconceptions such as, how can a large group of hundreds come together to do the real business planning? Fortunately, she was involved first-hand. The Roadway team went through the powerful sequence:

- Day 1: they mind-mapped all the distinctive strengths of Roadway in relationship to the marketplace.

- Day 2: they identified new business opportunities followed by a more selective articulation of aspirations—clear articulations of strategic intent for the future.

- Day 3: The aspirations were themselves made more concrete and specific and were then translated into anticipated results including careful selection of business measures.

The skeptical *Forbes* journalist then wrote descriptively about what she saw:

> A team of short-haul drivers came up with 12 cost-cutting and revenue-generating ideas. One of the most ambitious: Have each of the 32 drivers in Winston-Salem deliver just one more customer order each hour. Using management data, the drivers calculated the 288 additional daily shipments, at average revenue of $212 each and with a 6% margin, would generate just about $1 million a year of operating profit.

Still cautious however, the *Forbes* reporter offered her view that the visions in the business plan were too much of a stretch and results would be "unlikely." But the gloomy prediction was soon shattered. At its analyst meeting several months later on January 22, 2003, Roadway Corporation reported revenues for the sixteen weeks constituting the Company's fourth quarter were $1,074,110,000, up 25.7% over revenues of $854,640,000 for the same period the last year. For the fourth quarter of 2002, the Company reported income from continuing operations of $25,923,000, or $1.37 per share (diluted), compared to income from continuing operations of $13,477,000, or $0.72 per share (diluted), for the fourth quarter of 2001. Operating ratios improved significantly and, according to later analysis, the employee driven "W&I" improvements translated into an additional $17 million dollars in additional revenue for the year and $7 million annual profit. This exciting breakthrough was a result of the combined efforts across all 300 terminals of the 27,000 employee system. But here is the telling fact: of the five terminals leading the company in the gains, *all* were sites that had worked as organizational effectiveness sites using AI in one way or another, and three of the top five sites leading the company in gains had in fact held large-scale Summits using the SOAR sequence for business planning.

So what would be Roadway's approach in 2004? Twelve more locations have already been selected as sites for introducing this kind of strength-based and opportunity-focused strategic planning. For Roadway the more business-focused the better. Here the goal is not only better strategies but also human development. Roadway wants leadership at every level and realizes that strategy is not simply a one moment special event. Roadway wants to embed a strategic thought process that can be used every day to seize new opportunities and to make strategizing an ongoing occurrence. After the Akron terminal summit, for example, a team of switchers and mechanics created a vision that has the potential to save the company millions every year. At Winston-Salem the

UNIT

4

drivers have voluntarily become some of the organization's best sales people. Within months of their summit the drivers secured over a million dollars of new business. One driver used his "off-time" to take a potential customer trout fishing. The result was a major new account. Strategic thinking is becoming part of the culture. Jim Staley, Roadway's CEO, spoke in another magazine article about strategy as a way to build leadership at every level: "The AI approach unleashes tremendous power, tremendous enthusiasm, and gets people engaged in the right way in what we're trying to accomplish."

Formulating sound strategy requires both analysis and synthesis; it is and is as much a rational act as it is a creative and emergent one. But this case emphasizes the later. The strength-based framework we call SOAR creates an energy that lasts. It fuels creative emergence. It supports a view of strategy where every success and strength is noticed, not just in the planning session itself, but all the time. And this is how it works: big things always emerge from little things with one condition as key—that they are noticed and appreciated.

Esthetic Appreciation as the Root of Good Strategy:

Cyril Stanley Smith, an MIT professor emeritus, spent a lifetime studying how humanity's most strategically useful inventions came to be created. He discovered that the creativity and risk-taking required for major innovation came from unexpected expression of personal curiosity, not the result of detailed, long-range planning. Metallurgy, for example, began with curiosity about making jewelry, not from a program plan to develop new tools. Railroad technology started as a London amusement park ride.

 "All big things grow from little things" Smith wrote in a 1975 article in the *New York Times*. "But new little things are destroyed by their environment unless they are cherished for reasons more like esthetic appreciation than practical utility."

Jane Jacobs in her work looking more broadly at emergent strategies made a similar point: "successful economic development has to be open-ended rather than goal-oriented" she said, "and has to make itself up expediently and empirically as it goes along". For example, in the 1890s, the bicycle was, in Smith's terms, a "little thing" that was cherished only by bicycle enthusiasts for reasons of "esthetic appreciation." No one saw the bicycle as a key invention of practical utility or strategic worth as a core industry. Bicycle entrepreneurs were left to make things up as they went along. They soon had a dazzling array of small inventions: ball bearings, pneumatic tires, chain-and-sprocket drives, tubular metal frames, and caliper brakes. This revolutionary new technology passed through the Dayton bicycle shop of Wilbur and Orville Wright. The brothers used these little innovations of the unimportant bicycle. They created the transforming invention of the airplane. The Wrights were strategic not in the typical sense but could see an omnipresence of capacities others could not. They knew how to notice and use existing little things to make up totally new things as they went along. Open-ended curiosity and appreciation was more important than detailed plans or big threats.

This was the approach the Weatherhead School of Management at Case Western Reserve University took when Dean Mohsen Anvari arrived in August of 2001. With the help of Ernst and Young and faculty from the school that knew the strength-based approach of AI, a transformational process of strategic planning was enacted rapidly (for a University) over a six-month period of time. The outcomes were: a whole new elevated mission; a clear articulation of values and core beliefs; strategies in each of the areas of research, education, and service; aspirational images of success in relation to each of the school's stakeholder groups; and finally an agreement on results—key measures of success.

The first meeting set the tone. For the first time in the school's history the "whole system" of faculty, students, alumni, administrators, and community leaders were brought together to formulate strategy. Within fifteen minutes of the opening, people were involved in appreciative interviews mapping the distinctive strengths of the school and "collecting" insights from every innovation, small and large, over a fifty-year period of time. The analysis was astonishing. In one accelerated day every step in the SOAR framework—strengths, opportunities, aspirations, and results—was covered and a foundation was built. Task forces were then formed and given the mandate from the whole to move the analysis and planning to a new depth. Ernst and Young consultants worked with the task forces over the next several months, enacting an iterative process moving deeper and deeper. Finally the whole thing was capped off with another whole system one-day retreat, with hundreds of people participating interactively.

Today the school has a powerful five-year strategy that will propel it into the top tier academically and financially in terms of endowment. The content of the plan was so strong it has been published as a special book. A summary of the strategy is available on http://weatherhead.edu.

Without going into too many details we must point out how unusual this positive, strength-based framework was for a business school. Academia, for example, is known for its problem-based skills in critique and analytic focus on weaknesses. Too often strategic planning creates precisely the deficit-based environment that destroys the "little things" because of a theory that says the threats must by ramped up before really bold thinking will ensue. Most management schools teach it. In fact John Kotter (2002), in the Harvard Business School book on strategy, argues that it is essential, right at the outset, to make the status quo look dangerous and that, if in fact it is not, then it is important to even manufacture crises. Kotter writes: "In a few of the most successful cases, a group has manufactured a crisis. One CEO deliberately engineered the largest accounting loss in the company's history, creating huge pressure from Wall Street in the process. One division president commissioned first-ever customer satisfaction surveys knowing full well that the results would be terrible. He then made these findings public…. When the urgency rate is not pumped up enough, the transformation process cannot succeed and the long-term future of the organization is put in jeopardy."

Clearly this was not the approach the Weatherhead School of Management took. The appreciative approach, right from the beginning when it ignited a day of whole system strength-based analysis, created a DNA for the entire process to follow. Currently, for example, the school is announcing a whole new branding strategy. Every aspect of it can be traced directly to the notes taken when the school used the SOAR framework and AI that very first day of the process. The power of "esthetic appreciation" needs, we believe, to be better studied by the field of strategic planning, just as Cyril Stanley Smith did in his lifetime of study on how humanity's most useful inventions came to be created. The impact of esthetic appreciation can perhaps be felt in this press release, recently out, that reads:

> Weatherhead School of Management Launches New Brand Positioning
>
> CLEVELAND, August 29, 2003—Continuing to build upon its success as a premier business school, the Weatherhead School of Management at Case Western Reserve University today announced its new brand positioning. Intended to formalize how the School is described and better articulate its unique attributes, the School's complete brand position statement reads, "Among the world's best business schools, Weatherhead is a leading catalyst for advancing bold ideas that have a lasting impact on business and society." The most visible expression of the new brand will be the tagline "*Bold Ideas. Lasting Impact.*"

"Our new positioning is the culmination of over a year of work and part of a larger process implemented to ensure our continued success that includes the formation of an aggressive five-year strategic plan and a structured program for promoting Weatherhead at the regional, national and international levels," said Michael Devlin, Executive Director of Relationship Management at Weatherhead. "Through comprehensive research on our competitors as well as in-depth interviews and focus groups with our faculty, students, staff, the business community, corporate recruiters and others, the common theme that emerged was that Weatherhead has a strong legacy for generating new and exciting ideas."

Devlin added that another important realization during the research process was that the ideas generated at Weatherhead drive everything the School does. "Although new ideas happen at every educational institution, at Weatherhead new thinking is developed for real-world applications and implemented by companies around the world every day."

"'Bold Ideas. Lasting Impact.' is a simple phrase, but a very important one that encapsulates our focus on research, teaching and practical application of ideas, as well as the amazing people—students, faculty and staff—that makes [sic] Weatherhead what it is," said Mohsen Anvari, Dean of Weatherhead. "The new positioning not only describes what we are today but also expresses who we aspire to be."

The brand was officially unveiled to the students, faculty and staff at a ceremony and reception on August 28th in the Peter B. Lewis Building, that among other things, highlighted past examples of Weatherhead's bold thinking including the launch of the first MBA specialization for bioscience entrepreneurship, the first PhD in Organizational Behavior, and the introduction of the first competency-based MBA program in the U.S., to name a few.

According to Weatherhead, the new brand is already being put into action with initiatives like the Bold Thinkers Series, which brings to Weatherhead speakers who are challenging convention and creating new standards, as well as the upcoming Bold Ideas in Leadership Conference, a half-day program showcasing Weatherhead's latest research on leadership in the 21st century.

Cultivating a Positive Core at Tendercare

Strategic planning is not always about finding new ways to grow a company. The other two alternatives can be to remain status quo or divest of assets. Tendercare is a regional long-term care provider that operates a chain of skilled nursing homes, assisted living residences and various other long-term care services in the state of Michigan. Tendercare's vision is to be the provider of choice in each of the markets in which it operates, and while most of its centers live up to this vision a few do not. In 2002, the company embarked on a carefully thought out strategic plan which included a thorough review of its properties and their contribution to the company's vision and mission. For years the company had taken a defensive posture in their markets[,] working hard to maintain a solid footing in the communities in which they operated. This meant that even when a center did not meet its vision of being the provider of choice the company maintained the center for fear that it might cause more problems than to seek alternatives. While senior management recognized that a couple of buildings regularly lost money, no action was taken for fear of losing market share, stirring up regulatory issues, attracting negative press, angering families and residents, and damaging the reputation of the company.

In early 2002 the company brought in a team of consultants to one such center that had been losing money for over three years. This assisted living center had a unionized staff and currently operated at 75% of capacity. The initial goal of using Appreciative Inquiry (AI) was to bring the

staff, management, residents, and family members together as a unified team to create a positive working culture, and then to get them to work together towards a final attempt to improve the center's census and reputation.

Using the SOAR-based framework the core care team worked with the center and its stakeholders over a six-week period. During this time, a strategic inquiry with a purposeful appreciative intent was carried out using the new five "I" model (inquiry, imagine, innovation, and inspiration built on a foundation of integrity). Integrity was maintained in that employees were told the facility may be closed or sold. With a focus on the center's strengths, opportunities, aspirations, and results (SOAR) it became clear that the best option for the company might be to discontinue operation of the center. While measurable results included an 8% increase in census and a successful deunionization vote, the center simply was not able to effectively compete within its market. As a result, 18 months later, the company made the decision to, for the first time in their history, take the bold step of closing one of its centers due to a significant change in the uncontrollable environment.

Closing an assisted living center which residents consider their home for many years is not a simple task in the best of circumstances. Because the staff, residents, families, and management had the opportunity to work together openly and honestly in sharing information, ideas, stories, and plans, the transition went very smoothly. From the date the closure was announced, until the last resident moved out, the timeframe involved was less than thirty days. Several noteworthy points include the fact that during the entire transition every staff member showed up for work; no one left his or her position prematurely; the company worked to find employment opportunities for every employee that desired it; and every resident was placed without incident.

Because of this successful divestiture the company is planning to use the strategic inquiry with appreciative intent approach and the SOAR model to review several additional centers that do not meet its vision and mission. In the words of Tendercare's Vice President of Market Development, "We have seen a dramatic shift from a defensive posture of fear to a new level of excitement about our ability to truly make the company into what we want it to be while considering each and every stakeholder. By taking a positive and proactive approach we are able to invest in our good centers instead of spending enormous amounts of time, energy and resources in the couple of centers that seem to drain energy and resources." The corporate Tendercare marketing and business development team is also planning to use the SOAR framework to take one of its strongest regions to the next level of growth in 2004.

Summary

We started this article by stating that the corporate mantra over the past couple of decades has been: change, change, and change. While change is inevitable no one has ever advocated change for the sake of change. So don't. Instead, change with purpose. Decide what you are going to be—the best, the most customer service oriented, the friendliest, the most profitable—whatever it might be and then don't begrudge your weaknesses but celebrate what you do well. The unconditional strategic inquiry into strengths and opportunities is the quest. The SOAR framework is an exciting breakthrough and a new way of thinking about strategic planning. Just as AI has brought a bold new approach to the field of organizational development and change, SOAR offers a break from the tradition deficit based planning process. It is, quite literally, the inspiration to SOAR.

UNIT

4

References

Bechtel, M., (1995). "The Management Compass", AMA Management Briefing, New York, NY.

Brassard, M., (1989). *The Memory Jogger Plus+*, Goal/QPC, Meuthuen, MA.

Cowley, M. & Domb, E., (1997). *Beyond Strategic Vision*, Butterworth-Heinemann, Boston, MA.

Cooperrider, Whitney, and Stavros (2003). *Appreciative Inquiry Handbook: The First in a Series of AI Workbooks for Leaders of Change*, Lakeshore Communications, Cleveland, OH.

DeKluyver, C. (2000). *Strategic Thinking: An Executive Perspective*, Prentice Hall, Upper Saddle River, New Jersey.

Haines, S. G., (2000). *The Systems Thinking Approach to Strategic Planning and Management*, St. Lucie Press, New York, NY.

Kotter, J., (2002). *Heart of Change*, Harvard Business Review. [sic]

Mintzberg, H., (January/February 1994). "The Fall and Rise of Strategic Planning, *Harvard Business Review*, 107–114.

Mizuno, S., (1988). *Management for Quality Improvement: The Seven New QC Tools*. Productivity Press, Cambridge, MA.

Musashi, M., (1974). *A Book of Five Rings*. The Overlook Press, Woodstock, NY.

Pattison, J. E., (1996). *Breaking Boundaries*. Pattersons/Pacesetter Books, Princeton, NJ.

Sun Tzu, (1971). *The Art of War*. Oxford University Press.

Srivastva & Cooperrider (1990). *Appreciative Management and Leadership: The Power of Positive Thought and Action in Organizations*, Lakeshore Communications, Cleveland, OH.

Stavros, J., Cooperrider, D., & Kelley, D. L. (2003). Strategic inquiry—appreciative intent: Inspiration to SOAR, a new framework for strategic planning. *AI Practitioner* (November 2003). Special acknowledgement to *AI Practitioner: International Journal of Appreciative Inquiry*, to review more SOAR related articles, please visit www.aipractitioner.com *AI Practitioner* is the international journal focusing on positive relational approaches to change. The original article first appeared in this journal.

"Vision and Meaning: Two Sides of the Same Coin"

By James A. Vaughan

Points to Consider

1. Do you agree with Vaughan that "you never achieve your vision"?

2. Why is a shared vision so important according to Vaughan?

3. How can you keep others in a group motivated to work toward a vision that is lofty?

4. How can you encourage reflection on the relationship between corporate vision and individual purpose? Why is it important to do so?

"Vision and Meaning: Two Sides of the Same Coin"

Vision and Meaning

Vision and meaning are inextricably intertwined. We create meaning in our lives by pursuing worthy visions, and we refine our visions based on the meaning we are discovering. Let's examine the relationship between corporate vision, individual purpose, and meaning.

The first, and most important, continuing task of leadership is to define and nurture a shared vision that energizes and brings out the best in people. This is not to imply that vision creation is the sole province of the CEO or even a small group of senior managers. Many executives mistakenly think they must come up with a vision that others will sign on to. In fact, the broader the participation in creating a vision, the greater the commitment people will have to it.

A compelling vision paints in broad strokes how the organization intends to grow and serve its customers through individual, team, and organizational excellence. It's the loftiest future you can imagine. You never achieve your vision. You work toward it. Your vision may or may not include a direct expression of your core values, but certainly it emerges from your core values and is an indirect expression of them. It tells others who you are and who you want to become—not what you have achieved.

The centerpiece of a corporate vision is a clear image of how you will satisfy some important customer need(s). It is crucial that this image be developed from what customers perceive to satisfy their needs—not what you think ought to satisfy them. This is widely accepted as the key to excellent customer service, but it is not widely practiced—primarily because it takes such discipline to truly listen to customers.

The pursuit of excellence in any form is a serious and often challenging undertaking. It implies the ability to perform at a consistently high level, which in turn depends on the mastery of the fundamentals in whatever you are doing. Even a golfing duffer hits an excellent drive every once in a while, but an excellent golfer hits outstanding drives consistently. The difference is mastery of the fundamentals. There is no end point in the pursuit of excellence. There is always another increment of improvement.

Three Interrelated Forms of Excellence

Organizational Excellence is the most challenging of the three forms of excellence because of the persistent commitment, cooperation, and alignment required of so many people. A shared vision provides the focal point and the broad guidelines that make it all possible. As an organization grows, it is inevitable that members must often work in isolation from one another. A rapidly changing business environment also means individuals must often deal with new situations without the opportunity to consult others. Without a strong commitment to a shared vision, there is little hope of sustaining alignment and acting as one under these conditions. The core values that are part of a corporate vision should be immutable, but some elements of the vision should change to reflect the changing business environment. Everyone needs to share in the task of keeping the vision fresh and current. It may involve no more than changing the way the vision is expressed to reflect current word usage, but this too is important.

Team Excellence is an absolute prerequisite to organizational excellence, since most work is accomplished by teams. Each team needs to have its own vision that reflects its particular mission and its unique character. Of course, it's important that the team vision also support the organizational vision and aligns with other related teams. Informed Cooperation should be the goal within teams and between teams throughout the organization. Almost all large organizations

UNIT

4

have at least one and perhaps several excellent teams. The difficult part is making excellence the norm within and between all teams.

Individual Excellence in support of team and organizational goals should be encouraged and rewarded. At the same time, the pursuit of individual excellence without regard for its impact on team performance and other parts of the system should be discouraged. This is one of the tradeoffs we make when we join an organization. We give up some of our freedom to do exactly what we wish, and we agree to cooperate with others in the pursuit of shared goals. This does not rule out the pursuit of individual excellence—it does mean we must define individual excellence in the context of team and organizational performance.

Most people want to excel as individuals and as members of a team. When desired outcomes are clearly defined under the umbrella of an organizational vision, it's possible to achieve a synergistic effect from the pursuit of all three forms of excellence. It will not happen automatically, however. It's easy to lose sight of the larger picture when you're engaged in something that is deeply satisfying or exciting to you personally.

The really good news is that people want to be part of something significant. They want to do important work. They want to grow. They want to experience new things. They want to relate to other people whom they trust and respect. And perhaps most of all, they want to make a difference. In short, they want to create meaning in their own lives, and joining others in the pursuit of a shared vision is one way they can do it.

Since the beginning of recorded history, people have sought to understand the world around them—to figure out what life itself is all about—what it all means. I believe every person has a hunger for meaning—a need to know. In the early childhood years our need to know takes the form of an insatiable curiosity about how things work. We need to understand how things work in order to gain some degree of control over our immediate experience. The more we learn about how things work, the more we want to understand why things work the way they do. Ultimately, we come face to face with the deeper questions about existence itself. Who am I? Why am I here? What difference do I make?

A few people discover or develop a sense of purpose or vision early in their lives. They know who they are and what they want to become at a deep level—and they organize their lives around that purpose. In contrast, most people go through life wishing they had the passion and the energy evidenced by people with a purpose.

I don't believe anyone is born with a specific purpose, but I believe strongly that we can all discover a purpose that provides meaning and direction for our lives. It involves a careful examination of our values and priorities—an honest look at how we spend our time—at what energizes us and what drains us of energy. Finally, it entails listening to our innermost hopes and fears—and a willingness to knock down some boundaries that we may have come to accept about who we are and what we can do. A compelling organizational vision often attracts people to its pursuit because it's challenging and it's important. It touches the hunger for meaning that resides in all of us. It energizes and motivates those who choose it at a deep level. It serves as a guide for decisions and actions in the face of an unknowable future. It also provides the glue that holds people together when the going gets tough, as it inevitably does in significant undertakings.

Four forces of change are heightening the importance of vision today:

1. Downsizing and the demise of the unwritten employment contract in which employers promised lifetime employment in exchange for loyalty have created a degree of cynicism and distrust in the workplace that makes wholehearted cooperation and participation

extremely unlikely. A compelling corporate vision that treats employees as partners instead of hired hands and that adds meaning to their lives is a far more promising way to develop a psychological contract that serves individual and corporate needs. It is probably wise to treat all your employees like volunteer partners, but certainly this is true of your most talented ones. They always have other choices.

2. The information age is challenging people's ability to sort through the mass of data that comes their way every day. Everyone uses mental models to figure out what to pay attention to and what to ignore. A shared vision serves a useful purpose in organizing this filtering/screening process. To meet the competition in the information age, you will need more focus—more alignment—and more learning. A shared vision is your best path to all of these.

3. The global marketplace has changed the nature of competition. To a large degree, time and space have been taken out of the equation. You cannot choose your competitors by the geographic place where you locate your business. No matter what business you're in, you must be prepared to take on all comers—and you cannot assume they will be playing by the same rules you've grown accustomed to. The surest prediction is that if you have valuable customers, the competition for those customers will intensify. If you know who you are and what you're about, you'll have a better chance to stay on course or change course as needed.

4. Continuous, rapid change is creating a level of uncertainty that many people find distracting and uncomfortable. Engage your people in defining and pursuing a compelling vision that deals head-on with the same realities of our times. Give them real responsibility and hold them accountable for results—not just managers—everyone. People will give their best when you give them a chance to make a difference and pay them fairly for their contributions. This is the ultimate answer to how you motivate people.

Apparently creating a compelling vision is a lot easier said than done. There is general agreement that a vision is important, yet few corporations can legitimately claim to have a vision that is meaningful to their employees. I believe this is so because too many CEOs take vision too lightly. They underestimate the power of a shared vision and they don't appreciate the time and effort that go into creating one. They also get distracted with some of the details of the final vision. It's important to express the vision in plain talk that everyone can readily understand, but it isn't essential that it all fit on a business card. It would be nice if the language were always as elegant as Martin Luther King, Jr.'s "I Have A Dream" speech, but what's really crucial is that it communicate clearly to all your key stakeholders in language they're comfortable with.

There are no shortcuts to developing a vision, just as there are no shortcuts to excellence. The serious pursuit of excellence requires leaders who can sustain a pointed focus on an important purpose, who value teamwork above individual achievement, and who are constantly working for the best fit between all parts of the organizational system.

Pursuing a vision of excellence is synonymous with continuous improvement. It means learning every day. It means trying new things and failing, but not becoming a failure. It means listening to customers in a way very few companies have done in the past. It means developing partnerships with customers, suppliers, and associates in such a way that everyone benefits and everyone is empowered. It means setting high performance standards today and raising them tomorrow. It means a commitment to the development of people that never wavers—and it means you can finally stop asking the question, how do you motivate people?

Vaughan, J. (n.d.). Vision and meaning: Two sides of the same coin. Used by permission of James Vaughan, PhD. www.life-planning101.com

UNIT
4

FILM STUDIES

Citizen Kane (1941)

Screenplay by Herman Mankiewicz and Orson Welles
Directed by Orson Welles

Character Guide

Jedediah Leland.	Joseph Cotton
Susan Alexander Kane	Dorothy Comingore
Mary Kane	Agnes Moorehead
Emily Monroe Norton Kane.	Ruth Warrick
James W. Gettys	Ray Collins
Herbert Carter	Erskine Sanford
Mr. Bernstein	Everett Sloane
Jerry Thompson	William Alland
Mr. Kane	Orson Welles

Introduction

This Academy-Award-winning film (Best Original Screenplay) is based in part on the life of newspaper magnate William Randolph Hearst. The movie is organized around a newspaper reporter's search for the meaning of the character Charles Foster Kane's dying word: "Rosebud." Jerry Thompson's vision of completing the story of Kane's life by solving the riddle of "Rosebud" takes him to interview many of those whose lives intersected with Kane's. Professionally, Kane envisioned the power of newspapers to shape public opinion and to protect the interests of ordinary people. As successful as Kane was as a newspaper magnate, Kane's story is nonetheless a cautionary one about the importance of vision that inspires both professional and personal achievement, and communicating the vision with clarity and integrity for others to work toward it. Interviewing people from Kane's early, impoverished but mostly happy boyhood, his early newspaper founding, his first and second wives, Thompson the newsman finally concludes that all Kane "wanted out of life was love," that he "was not ever brutal, just did brutal things," and that he had a "generous mind, but never believed in anything but Charlie Kane."

Dialogue Questions

1. The opening and closing frames of the movie show a chain-linked fence with a "No Trespassing" sign. Why does looking into the internal life and the early life of someone who exercised leadership on the world stage seem to be one of the unwritten "No-Nos"

that the media increasingly violate? What are the pros and cons of examining a leader's early life and personal life?

2. What can be learned from asking the question "who was he?", not just "what did he do?" Do the two questions divide into the public self ("What did he do?") and the private one ("Who was he?")?

3. Do ideals of the young expressed in a lofty vision often die off in old age? If so, why? Is there any way the early ideals can be maintained? What can corrupt, dilute, or dissipate ideals, and how can one prevent it?

4. Kane's career is an example of a creation built on the vision of one man. Do such creations inevitably die with the person who starts and grows them? What is necessary for a sustainable vision that others take up beyond the person who created and articulated the vision?

5. When he begins his newspaper career, Kane writes a "Declaration of Principles," including a determination to give "all of the news honestly" and to be a champion of the readers' rights "as citizens and as human beings." Later, when Kane is rich and famous and has fired his most trusted colleague, the man gives the statement back to Kane and Kane tears it up. Why? How does this scene illustrate an ethical dilemma of sustaining a vision that is about others rather than related to oneself?

Iron Jawed Angels (2004)

Story by Jennifer Friedes
Directed by Katja von Garnier

UNIT

4

Character Guide

Alice Paul	Hilary Swank
Lucy Burns	Frances O'Connor
Inez Mulholland	Julia Ormond
Carrie Chapman Catt	Anjelica Huston
Anna Howard Shaw	Lois Smith
Mabel Vernon	Brooke Smith
Doris Stevens	Laura Fraser
Emily Leighton	Molly Parker
Senator Thomas Leighton	Joseph Adams
Ruza Wenclawska	Vera Famiga
Ben Weisman	Patrick Dempsey
President Woodrow Wilson	Bob Gunton

Introduction

This Golden Globe-winning teleplay (Anjelica Huston, Best Supporting Actress, 2005) recounts the story of Alice Paul, Lucy Burns, Inez Mulholland and other young women who propelled a constitutional amendment for women's right to vote to ratification in the early 1900s. At the time, the primary organization seeking the right to vote for women was the National American Woman Suffrage Association (NAWSA) founded in 1890 by Elizabeth Cady Stanton and Susan B. Anthony (see the Leadership Profile in Unit Nine for more on the work of these women in initiating change regarding voting rights in the United States). In 1912, when the film opens, the vision of the older NAWSA suffragists like Carrie Chapman Catt and Anna Howard Shaw was not a constitutional amendment; they favored a state-by-state approach. The film illustrates multiple methods the younger women employ to communicate their vision and gain increasing support despite resistance from many quarters including within NAWSA. As criticism and suspicion of them mounts in NAWSA, they break away and form the National Women's Party in an effort to more effectively continue the work toward attaining their vision. Their picket line and banners at the White House are extremely controversial, inviting intense public criticism that dramatically increases when the United States enters World War I. When the women are arrested and charged with "obstructing traffic," they refuse to pay any fines for a crime they did not commit and must go to prison. There they face harsh and cruel treatment when they demand their rights as political prisoners, not criminals. Their strength, determination, and solidarity through a hunger strike, solitary confinement or straitjackets for some, and force-feeding is a true story of courage. These women demonstrate the power of effectively and creatively communicating a vision to motivate others into action and sacrifice.

Dialogue Questions

1. What evidence is there that Alice Paul very carefully and thoughtfully developed the message for particular groups of stakeholders?

2. How does Alice Paul communicate her vision in a way that eventually overcomes others' doubts or resistance to it?

3. Why do you think she is so effective at convincing others to make sacrifices in order to make progress toward the vision?

4. What keeps the suffragists so focused on the vision?

5. How do these women create opportunities to repeatedly, and in a variety of ways, articulate their vision? Why is this important?

EXERCISE

Hollow Square—A Communications Experiment

Introduction

Communication skills may seem to be a fairly straightforward part of the leadership process. But when you actually try to build a cohesive group, things get a bit more difficult. This is especially true when planning and executing are divided between two groups.

This exercise is designed to help you understand more about communication skills. You may be involved in planning a task that is to be carried out by others, or you may be asked to accomplish a task that has been planned by others. In addition, you will explore both helpful and hindering communication behaviors that can occur when a leader either assigns a task to others or is asked to complete a task for others.

Instructions

Your Instructor will provide you with all materials and specific instructions for this exercise.

UNIT

4

"Hollow Square: A Communications Experiment," from: *A Handbook of Structured Experiences for Human Relations Training, Volume II*, J. William Pfeiffer and John E. Jones (Eds.). Copyright © 1974 by Pfeiffer and Company. Reprinted by permission of Jossey-Bass, Inc., a subsidiary of John Wiley & Sons, Inc.

SUGGESTED READING

This selected bibliography is intended to supplement the excerpts and articles of authors included in this Unit. There is an emphasis on books that are pivotal and recent publications. Numerous journals regularly offer articles related to these topics, but are not included in this selected bibliography. For further research, you may wish to include searches of the following journals: (alphabetically) *Academy of Management Executive*, *Academy of Management Journal*, *Harvard Business Review*, *Journal of Leadership Studies*, *Leadership in Action*, *Leadership Quarterly*, and *Leader To Leader*.

This list is organized by author's last name using Modern Language Association-style citations.

Astin, Helen S., and Carole Leland. *Women of Influence, Women of Vision: A Cross-Generational Study of Leaders and Social Change.* **San Francisco: Jossey-Bass, 1991.**
The authors present an inspiring look at the achievements of women leaders in America from the 1960s to the 1980s and they offer provocative insights into what these leaders have in common and how individuals can improve their own leadership skills. Drawing on an in-depth study of seventy-seven women leaders, Astin and Leland demonstrate how personal commitment, a passion for justice, and a willingness to take risks can prompt remarkable achievements.

Bolman, Lee G., and Terrence E. Deal. *Leading with Soul: An Uncommon Journey of Spirit.* **San Francisco: Jossey-Bass, 2011.**
The authors link leadership with spirituality, and using the ancient literary style of conversations the book reveals the process of finding, believing, sharing, and leading with soul.

Conger, Jay A. *Winning 'em Over: A New Model for Managing in the Age of Persuasion.* **New York: Simon & Schuster, 2001.**
Conger describes four components of effective management by persuasion: building credibility, finding common ground, finding compelling positions and evidence, and connecting emotionally with co-workers.

DePree, Max. *Leadership Jazz—Revised Edition: The Essential Elements of a Great Leader.* **New York: Currency/Doubleday, 2008.**
DePree identifies two things that successful leaders must perfect: voice and touch. Voice is the ability to express one's beliefs, and touch is the ability to demonstrate competence and resolve. Jazz musicians have mastered these concepts. DePree compares leadership to an inspired jazz performance.

Dyson, Michael Eric. *I May Not Get There With You: The True Martin Luther King, Jr.* **New York: Touchstone, 2001.**
Dyson thoroughly studies King's words and the interpretive literature about him, concentrating on King's legacy rather than on his part in events from 1955 to 1968.

Felton, Keith S. *Warriors' Words: A Consideration of Language and Leadership.* **Westport: Praeger, 1995.**
Felton features the public speeches of history's great communicators and examines the rhetoric, impact on listeners, and influence on society of the words.

Oates, Stephen B. *Let The Trumpet Sound: The Life of Martin Luther King, Jr.* **New York: New American Library, 1994.**
A magnificent recreation of King's life. Oates portrays the forces that shaped "a very human man"—parental, cultural, spiritual, and intellectual—and depicts the force he became at a crucial moment in American history.

Wills, Garry. *Lincoln at Gettysburg: The Words that Remade America.* **New York: Simon & Schuster, 2006.**
Wills closely examines Lincoln's personal history and his Gettysburg address itself to understand the power of communication.

UNIT

4

UNIT5

BUILDING A TEAM

INTRODUCTION

An effective leader engages in team-building activities to increase the satisfaction of individuals who work in groups or teams and to promote synergy among them so that the group is more effective as well. Most team-building experts believe that the exercise of leadership is necessary to transform a gathering of individuals into a team, the whole of which is greater than the sum of the parts.

Loren Gary of Harvard Business School Publications summarized scholarship on teamwork. There are three areas in which a team must excel in order to perform successfully: the team members must have a highly developed, shared understanding of goals and values; the team members must have practiced interaction skills that create a synergy and allow the team to solve complex problems beyond the capabilities of individuals' expertise, developing solutions that can withstand the scrutiny of the rest of the organization; and the team members must be able to renew and expand their capabilities in response to change. These dimensions of effective team-work have interwoven, mutually beneficial interactions—improved performance in any one of the three areas creates improvements in the others. Enhanced performance in any of the areas also leads to genuine personal development for the individuals, which builds skills for success for the individual as well as for the team (*Harvard Management Update*, v.6, n.9, September 2001).

The Classic Case for Building a Team is an excerpt from *The Grapes of Wrath* by John Steinbeck. The portion excerpted is Steinbeck's exposition on the formation of "worlds"—groups of people who cooperate to accomplish their goals that are both individual and collective. The world of the migrant workers is an idealized society that forms spontaneously during the migration of thousands of families from the dust bowl to California. Their idealized society is, essentially, a team. Steinbeck shows how teams develop around common, shared purposes and goals, and how they are strengthened through common values and agreed-upon rules and regulations. The Leadership Profile of Cesar Chavez looks at a more formally organized team and the requirements of mobilizing it, specifically the United Farm Workers of America Union.

The Readings for this Unit look at the specific team-building skills and tasks of group leaders. Warren Bennis offers a unique description of effective group leaders as "catalytic completers." Patrick Lencioni provides further explanation about how teams fail to reach their potential in *The Five Dysfunctions of a Team*. A team assessment instrument is included that will help you develop a plan to apply Lencioni's recommendations.

In an inspiring look at real team building, one Film Study for this Unit, *Remember the Titans*, portrays the team-building efforts of now-legendary Coach Herman Boone of T.C. Williams High School in Alexandria, Virginia. The classic Film Study, *The Wizard of Oz*, takes a look at how teamwork enables an unlikely quartet to achieve their goals.

Unit Five concludes with an exercise providing an opportunity to build a team and compete to meet a challenging objective. It is also an excellent opportunity to experience and reflect on team dynamics.

Learning Objectives

- Identify the foundations of effective teamwork
- Recognize the significance of team building as a leadership skill
- Recognize the role of teams within organizations
- Describe ways to augment team-building efforts and improve teamwork
- Appreciate the contributions made by the Classic Case and Leadership Profile in this Unit toward understanding effective team building

UNIT

5

CLASSIC CASE

The Grapes of Wrath

By John Steinbeck (1902–1968)
American Novelist

Introduction and Historical Background

The Grapes of Wrath, by John Steinbeck, is a moving and highly successful proletarian novel that tells of the hardships of the Joad family, forced out of their home in the Oklahoma dust-bowl region, and their migration to California in search of work. Throughout the novel, Steinbeck has a distinctly collectivist stance. The portion excerpted here is Steinbeck's exposition on the formation of "worlds"—groups of people who cooperate to accomplish their goals that are both individual and collective. The world of the migrant workers is an idealized society that forms spontaneously during the migration of thousands of families from the dust bowl to California. Their idealized society is, essentially, a team. Steinbeck shows how teams of people develop around common, shared purposes and goals, and how these common values and agreed-upon rules and regulations strengthen the group. Socializing and sharing joys, sorrows, or small triumphs are important to the effectiveness of the teams. The selection also shows that a common vulnerability (facing adversity together), as well as a shared future orientation are key elements in team building. In the utopian "worlds" of the migrant camps, equality reigns and no real ruler or ruling class emerges. This is one way in which *The Grapes of Wrath* is a powerful statement for the American egalitarian dream, showing that the poor, have-nots, and vulnerable still have strengths, talents, and vital contributions to make to society.

John Steinbeck was born in Salinas, California in 1902. Salinas is in a fertile agricultural valley about twenty-five miles from the Pacific Coast, and both valley and coast would serve as settings for some of his best fiction. In 1919, he went to Stanford University, where he intermittently enrolled in literature and writing courses until he left in 1925, without taking a degree. During the next five years, he supported himself as a laborer and journalist in New York City and then as a caretaker for a Lake Tahoe estate, all the time working on his first novel, *Cup of Gold* (1929). Much of Steinbeck's literary success comes from his realistic studies of life among the depressed economic classes of the U.S., especially the itinerant farm laborers of California. Popular success and financial security came only with *Tortilla Flat* (1935), stories about Monterey's paisanos. Three powerful novels of the late 1930s focused on the California laboring class: *In Dubious Battle* (1936), *Of Mice and Men* (1937), and the book considered by many his finest, *The Grapes of Wrath* (1939). He was a ceaseless experimenter throughout his career, testing filmmaking and writing dramas as well. Steinbeck received the Pulitzer Prize in 1940 and the Nobel Prize in Literature in 1962. He died in 1968.

Points to Consider

1. What roles does Steinbeck identify for effective team building in the camps? What roles do you naturally play in a group setting?

2. How does Steinbeck suggest that groups should incorporate newcomers effectively?

3. How can one effectively critique or challenge norms that are well established within a group?

4. In what ways are Steinbeck's team-building principles relevant to modern organizations?

5. How does an individual make choices related to individual rights or privileges to support effectiveness and goals of a team or organization?

The Grapes of Wrath

(Excerpt)

The cars of the migrant people crawled out of the side roads onto the great cross-country highway, and they took the migrant way to the West. In the daylight they scuttled like bugs to the westward; and as the dark caught them, they clustered like bugs near to shelter and to water. And because they were lonely and perplexed, because they had all come from a place of sadness and worry and defeat, and because they were all going to a new mysterious place, they huddled together; they talked together; they shared their lives, their food, and the things they hoped for in the new country. Thus it might be that one family camped near a spring, and another camped for the spring and for company, and a third because two families had pioneered the place and found it good. And when the sun went down, perhaps twenty families and twenty cars were there.

In the evening a strange thing happened: the twenty families became one family, the children were the children of all. The loss of home became one loss, and the golden time in the West was one dream. And it might be that a sick child threw despair into the hearts of twenty families, of a hundred people; that a birth there in a tent kept a hundred people quiet and awestruck through the night and filled a hundred people with the birth-joy in the morning. A family which the night before had been lost and fearful might search its goods to find a present for a new baby. In the evening, sitting about the fires, the twenty were one. They grew to be units of the camps, units of the evenings and the nights. A guitar unwrapped from a blanket and tuned—and the songs, which were all of the people, were sung in the nights. Men sang the words, and women hummed the tunes.

Every night a world created, complete with furniture—friends made and enemies established; a world complete with braggarts and with cowards, with quiet men, with humble men, with kindly men. Every night relationships that make a world, established; and every morning the world torn down like a circus.

At first the families were timid in the building and tumbling worlds, but gradually the technique of building worlds became their technique. Then leaders emerged, then laws were made, then codes came into being. And as the worlds moved westward they were more complete and better furnished, for their builders were more experienced in building them.

The families learned what rights must be observed—the right of privacy in the tent; the right to keep the black past hidden in the heart; the right to talk and to listen; the right to refuse help or to accept, to offer help or to decline it; the right of son to court and daughter to be courted; the right of the hungry to be fed; the rights of the pregnant and the sick to transcend all other rights.

UNIT
5

And the families learned, although no one told them, what rights are monstrous and must be destroyed: the right to intrude upon privacy, the right to be noisy while the camp slept, the right of seduction or rape, the right of adultery and theft and murder. These rights were crushed, because the little worlds could not exist for even a night with such rights alive.

And as the worlds moved westward, rules became laws, although no one told the families. It is unlawful to foul near the camp; it is unlawful in any way to foul the drinking water; it is unlawful to eat good rich food near one who is hungry, unless he is asked to share.

And with the laws, the punishments—and there were only two—a quick and murderous fight or ostracism; and ostracism was the worst. For if one broke the laws his name and face went with him, and he had no place in any world, no matter where created.

In other worlds, social conduct became fixed and rigid, so that a man must say "Good morning" when asked for it, so that a man might have a willing girl if he stayed with her, if he fathered her children and protected them. But a man might not have one girl one night and another the next, for this would endanger the worlds.

The families moved westward, and the technique of building the worlds improved so that the people could be safe in their worlds; and the form was so fixed that a family acting in the rules knew it was safe in the rules.

There grew up government in the worlds, with leaders, with elders. A man who was wise found that his wisdom was needed in every camp; a man who was a fool could not change his folly with his world. And a kind of insurance developed in these nights. A man with food fed a hungry man, and thus insured himself against hunger. And when a baby died a pile of silver coins grew at the door flap, for a baby must be well buried, since it has had nothing else of life. An old man may be left in a potter's field, but not a baby.

A certain physical pattern is needed for the building of a world—water, a riverbank, a

stream, a spring, or even a faucet unguarded. And there is needed enough flat land to pitch the tents, a little brush or wood to build the fires. If there is a garbage dump not too far off, all the better; for there can be found equipment—stove tops, a curved fender to shelter the fire, and cans to cook in and eat from.

And the worlds were built in the evening. The people, moving in from the highways, made them with their tents and their hearts and their brains.

In the morning the tents came down, the canvas was folded, the tent poles tied along the running board, the beds put in place on the cars, the posts in their places. And as the families moved westward, the technique of building up a home in the evening and tearing it down with the morning light became fixed; so that the folded tent was packed in one place, the cooking pots counted in their box. And as the cars moved westward, each member of the family grew into his proper place, grew into his duties; so that each member, old and young, had his place in the car; so that in the weary, hot evening, when the cars pulled into the camping places, each member had his duty and went to it without instruction: children to gather wood, to carry water; men to pitch the tents and bring down the beds; women to cook the supper and to watch while the family fed. And this was done without command. The families, which had been units of which the boundaries were a house at night, a farm by day, changed their boundaries. In the long hot light, they were silent in the cars moving slowly westward; but at night they integrated with any group they found.

Thus they changed their social life—changed as in the whole universe only man can change. They were not farm men any more, but migrant men. And the thought, the planning, the long staring silence that had gone out to the fields, went now to the roads, to the distance, to the West. That man whose mind had been bound with acres lived with narrow concrete miles. And his thought and his worry were not any more with rainfall, with wind and dust, with the thrust of the crops. Eyes watched the tires, ears listened to the clattering motors, and minds struggled with oil, with gasoline, with the thinning rubber between air and road. Then a broken gear was a tragedy. Then water in the evening was the yearning, and food over the fire. Then health to go on was the need and strength to go on, and spirit to go on. The wills thrust westward ahead of them, and fears that had once apprehended drought or flood now lingered with anything that might stop the westward crawling.

The camps became fixed—each a short day's journey from the last.

And on the road the panic overcame some of the families, so that they drove night and day, stopped to sleep in the cars, and drove on to the West, flying from the road, flying from movement. And these lusted so greatly to be settled that they set their faces into the West and drove toward it, forcing the clashing engines over the roads.

But most of the families changed and grew quickly into the new life. And when the sun went down—

Time to look out for a place to stop.

And—there's some tents ahead.

The car pulled off the road and stopped, and because others were there first, certain courtesies were necessary. And the man, the leader of the family, leaned from the car.

Can we pull up here an' sleep?

Why, sure, be proud to have you. What State you from?

Come all the way from Arkansas.

They's Arkansas people down that fourth tent.

That so?

And the great question, How's the water?

Well, she don't taste so good, but they's plenty.

Well, thank ya.

No thanks to me.

But the courtesies had to be. The car lumbered over the ground to the end tent, and stopped. Then down from the car the weary people climbed, and stretched stiff bodies. Then the new tent sprang up; the children went for water and the older boys cut brush or wood. The fires started and supper was put on to boil or to fry. Early comers moved over, and States were exchanged, and friends and sometimes relatives discovered.

Oklahoma, huh? What county?

Cherokee.

Why, I got folks there. Know the Allens? They's Allens all over Cherokee. Know the Willises?

Why, sure.

And a new unit was formed. The dusk came, but before the dark was down the new family was of the camp. A word had been passed with every family. There were known people—good people.

I knowed the Allens all my life. Simon Allen, ol' Simon, had trouble with his first wife. She was part Cherokee, purty as—as a black colt.

Sure, an' young Simon, he married a Rudolph, didn' he? That's what I thought. They went to live in Enid an' done well—real well.

Only Allen that ever done well. Got a garage.

When the water was carried and the wood cut, the children walked shyly, cautiously among the tents. And they made elaborate acquaintanceship gestures. A boy stopped near another boy and studied a stone, picked it up, examined it closely, spat on it, and rubbed it clean and inspected it until he forced the other to demand, What you got there?

And casually, Nothin'. Jus' a rock.

Well, what you lookin' at it like that for?

Thought I seen gold in it.

How'd you know? Gold ain't gold, it's black in a rock.

UNIT
5

Sure, every'body knows that.

I bet it's fool's gold, an' you figgered it was gold.

That ain't so, 'cause Pa, he's foun' lots a gold an' he tol' me how to look.

How'd you like to pick up a big ol' piece a gold?

Sa-a-ay! I'd git the bigges' old son-a-bitchin' piece a candy you ever seen.

I ain't let to swear, but I do, anyways.

Me too. Le's go to the spring.

And young girls found each other and boasted shyly of their popularity and their prospects. The women worked over the fire, hurrying to get food to the stomachs of the family—pork if there was money in plenty, pork and potatoes, and onions. Dutch-oven biscuits or cornbread, and plenty of gravy to go over it. Side-meat or chops and a can of boiled tea, black and bitter. Fried dough in drippings if money was slim, dough fried crisp and brown and the drippings poured over it.

Those families which were very rich or very foolish with their money ate canned beans and canned peaches and packaged bread and bakery cake; but they ate secretly, in their tents, for it would not have been good to eat such fine things openly. Even so, children eating their fried dough smelled the warming beans and were unhappy about it.

When supper was over and the dishes dipped and wiped, the dark had come, and then the men squatted down to talk.

And they talked of the land behind them. I don' know what it's coming to, they said, The country's spoilt.

It'll come back though, on'y we won't be there.

Maybe, they thought, maybe we sinned some way we didn't know about.

Fella says to me, gov'ment fella, an' he says, she's gullied up on ya. Gov'ment fella. He says, if ya plowed 'cross the contour, she won't gully.

Never did have no chance to try her. An' the new super' ain't plowin' 'cross the contour. Runnin' a furrow four miles long that ain't stoppin' or goin' aroun' Jesus Christ Hisself.

And they spoke softly of their homes: They was a little cool-house under the win'mill. Use' ta keep milk in there to cream up, an' watermelons. Go in there midday when she was hottern' a heifer, an' she'd be jus'as cool, as cool as you'd want. Cut open a melon in there an' she'd hurt your mouth, she was so cool. Water drippin' down from the tank.

They spoke of their tragedies: Had a brother Charley, hair as yella as corn, an' him a growed man. Played the 'cordeen nice too. He was harrowin' one day an' he went up to clear his lines. Well, a rattlesnake buzzed an' them horses bolted an' the harrow went over Charley, an' the points dug into his guts an' his stomach, an' they pulled his face off an'—God Almighty!

They spoke of the future: Wonder what it's like out there?

Well, the pitchers sure do look nice. I seen one where it's hot an' fine, an' walnut trees an' berries; an' right behind, close as a mule's as to his withers, they's a tall up mountain covered with snow. That was a pretty thing to see.

If we can get work it'll be fine. Won't have no cold in the winter. Kids won't freeze on the way to school. I'm gonna take care my kids don't miss no more school. I can read good, but it ain't no pleasure to me like with a fella that's used to it.

And perhaps a man brought out his guitar to the front of his tent. And he sat on a box to play, and everyone in the camp moved slowly in toward him, drawn in toward him. Many men can chord a guitar, but perhaps this man was a picker. There you have something—the deep chords beating, beating, while the melody runs on the strings like little footsteps. Heavy hard fingers marching on the frets. The man played and the people moved slowly in on him until the circle was closed and tight, and then he sang, "Ten-Cent Cotton and Forty-Cent Meat." And the circle sang softly with him. And he sang "Why Do You Cut Your Hair, Girls?" And the circle sang. He wailed the song, "I'm Leaving Old Texas," that eerie song that was sung before the Spaniards came, only the words were Indian then.

And now the group was welded to one thing, one unit, so that in the dark the eyes of the people were inward, and their minds played in other times, and their sadness was like rest, like sleep. He sang the "McAlester Blues" and then, to make up for it to the older people, he sang "Jesus Calls Me to His Side." The children drowsed with the music and went into the tents to sleep, and the singing came into their dreams.

And after a while the man with the guitar stood up and yawned. Good night, folks, he said.

And they murmured, Good night to you.

And each wished he could pick a guitar, because it is a gracious thing. Then the people went to their beds, and the camp was quiet. And the owls coasted overhead, and the coyotes gabbled in the distance, and into the camp skunks walked, looking for bits of food—waddling, arrogant skunks, afraid of nothing.

The night passed, and with the first streak of dawn the women came out of the tents, built up the fires, and put the coffee to boil. And the men came out and talked softly in the dawn.

When you cross the Colorado River, there's the desert, they say. Look out for the desert. See you don't get hung up. Take plenty water, case you get hung up.

I'm gonna take her at night.

Me too. She'll cut the living Jesus outa you.

The families ate quickly, and the dishes were dipped and wiped. The tents came down. There was a rush to go. And when the sun arose, the camping place was vacant, only a little litter left by the people. And the camping place was ready for a new world in a new night.

But along the highway the cars of the migrant people crawled out like bugs, and the narrow concrete miles stretched ahead.

UNIT
5

LEADERSHIP PROFILE

Cesar E. Chavez (1927–1993)

President of the United Farm Workers of America
"Address to the Commonwealth Club of California," November 9, 1984

Introduction and Historical Background

Cesar Estrada Chavez was born on a small farm near Yuma, Arizona. At age ten, during the Great Depression, his family lost the farm, and his life became that of a migrant farm worker. The Chavez family migrated throughout the Southwest, laboring in fields and vineyards. Young Cesar's schooling was sporadic, and he left school for good following the eighth grade to support his family full-time. He served in the U.S. Navy at the end of World War II and married following the war. He continued to work as a farm laborer after beginning his own family. In his spare time, he taught Mexican farm workers to read and write so that they could take the United States citizenship test.

© Najlah Feanny/Corbis

In 1952, Chavez met Fred Ross, an organizer for the Community Service Organization (CSO), a barrio-based, self-help group sponsored by Chicago-based Saul Alinsky's Industrial Areas Foundation. Within several months, Chavez began organizing full-time with CSO. He coordinated voter registration drives and fought against racial and economic discrimination toward Hispanic residents of California and Arizona. By the late 1950s, Chavez was the national CSO director. He had hoped that the CSO would commit to organizing farm workers, but he could not convince the leadership to begin. In 1962, he resigned as national director and founded the National Farm Workers Association (NFWA). Recalling such a risky move—leaving the first regularly paying job he ever had—Chavez said, "If you're outraged at conditions, then you can't possibly be free or happy until you devote all your time to changing them and do nothing but that. But you can't change anything if you want to hold onto a good job, a good way of life and avoid sacrifice."

Within three years, the NFWA had 1,200 member families. This is particularly significant since repeated attempts to unionize California's 400,000 farm workers had failed between 1900 and 1962, despite the major efforts of four different unions. Chavez led his union in joining an AFL-CIO strike already in progress against California grape growers. The strikers took a pledge of non-violence. The strike-boycott lasted five years and rallied millions of supporters for the efforts of the AFL-CIO-sponsored union and the NFWA. The support coalition included unions, church groups, students, minority groups, and consumers. The two unions merged in 1966, forming the United Farm Workers, and affiliated with the AFL-CIO. In 1968, Chavez conducted a 25-day fast to reaffirm the union's commitment to non-violence. By 1970, the grape growers signed contracts with the UFW. In 1973, when the contracts came up for renegotiation, growers signed "sweeter" contracts for themselves with the Teamsters Union, prompting 10,000 farm workers in California to walk out of the fields in protest. Chavez called for a new, worldwide grape boycott. Growers then agreed to support a collective bargaining law for farm workers, the 1975 Agricultural Labor Relations Act. By the 1980s, UFW-negotiated contracts provided tens of thousands of farm workers with higher pay, family health coverage, and pension benefits. Throughout the 1980s, the UFW continued to work for the protection of farm workers as the California Farm Labor Board ceased to enforce the 1975 law. In 1988, Chavez again undertook a fast—this time lasting 36 days—to protest the pesticide poisoning of grape workers and their children.

Cesar Chavez died in 1993. More than 40,000 people attended his funeral at Delano, California. He received the Presidential Medal of Freedom, the highest civilian honor in the United States, posthumously, in 1994.

Points to Consider

1. What kind of persuasive appeals work best in motivating you to take action for a group?

2. How does Chavez's speech seek to unify his group's members and supporters? How does it seek to motivate them?

3. What strategies do you think work best in encouraging team members to sacrifice for the organization's mission/vision?

4. Why do you think Chavez succeeded in organizing farm workers into a group or team that could successfully negotiate labor contracts with growers, when other organizers had failed?

5. To what extent should oppositional arguments be given some credence when attempting to galvanize an organization?

"Address to the Commonwealth Club of California"

By Cesar E. Chavez
San Francisco, November 9, 1984

UNIT
5

Twenty-one years ago last September, on a lonely stretch of railroad track paralleling U.S. Highway 101 near Salinas, 32 Bracero farm workers lost their lives in a tragic accident.

The Braceros had been imported from Mexico to work on California farms. They died when their bus, which was converted from a flatbed truck, drove in front of a freight train.

Conversion of the bus had not been approved by any government agency. The driver had "tunnel" vision.

Most of the bodies lay unidentified for days. No one, including the grower who employed the workers, even knew their names.

Today, thousands of farm workers live under savage conditions—beneath trees and amid garbage and human excrement—near tomato fields in San Diego County, tomato fields which use the most modern farm technology.

Vicious rats gnaw on them as they sleep. They walk miles to buy food at inflated prices. And they carry in water from irrigation pumps.

Child labor is still common in many farm areas.

As much as 30 percent of Northern California's garlic harvesters are under-aged children. Kids as young as six years old have voted in state-conducted union elections since they qualified as workers.

Some 800,000 underaged children work with their families harvesting crops across America. Babies born to migrant workers suffer 25 percent higher infant mortality than the rest of the population.

Malnutrition among migrant worker children is 10 times higher than the national rate.

Farm workers' average life expectancy is still 49 years—compared to 73 years for the average American.

All my life, I have been driven by one dream, one goal, one vision: To overthrow a farm labor system in this nation which treats farm workers as if they were not important human beings.

Farm workers are not agricultural implements. They are not beasts of burden—to be used and discarded.

That dream was born in my youth. It was nurtured in my early days of organizing. It has flourished. It has been attacked.

I'm not very different from anyone else who has ever tried to accomplish something with his life. My motivation comes from my personal life—from watching what my mother and father went through when I was growing up; from what we experienced as migrant farm workers in California.

That dream, that vision, grew from my own experience with racism, with hope, with the desire to be treated fairly and to see my people treated as human beings and not as chattel.

It grew from anger and rage—emotions I felt 40 years ago when people of my color were denied the right to see a movie or eat at a restaurant in many parts of California.

It grew from the frustration and humiliation I felt as a boy who couldn't understand how the growers could abuse and exploit farm workers when there were so many of us and so few of them.

Later, in the '50s, I experienced a different kind of exploitation. In San Jose, in Los Angeles and in other urban communities, we—the Mexican American people—were dominated by a majority that was Anglo.

I began to realize what other minority people had discovered: That the only answer—the only hope—was in organizing. More of us had to become citizens. We had to register to vote. And people like me had to develop the skills it would take to organize, to educate, to help empower the Chicano people.

I spent many years—before we founded the union—learning how to work with people.

We experienced some successes in voter registration, in politics, in battling racial discrimination—successes in an era when Black Americans were just beginning to assert their civil rights and when political awareness among Hispanics was almost non-existent.

But deep in my heart, I knew I could never be happy unless I tried organizing the farm workers. I didn't know if I would succeed. But I had to try.

All Hispanics—urban and rural, young and old—are connected to the farm workers' experience. We had all lived through the fields—or our parents had. We shared that common humiliation.

How could we progress as a people, even if we lived in the cities, while the farm workers—men and women of our color—were condemned to a life without pride?

How could we progress as a people while the farm workers—who symbolized our history in this land—were denied self-respect?

How could our people believe that their children could become lawyers and doctors and judges and business people while this shame, this injustice was permitted to continue?

Those who attack our union often say, 'It's not really a union. It's something else: A social movement. A civil rights movement. It's something dangerous.'

They're half right. The United Farm Workers is first and foremost a union. A union like any other. A union that either produces for its members on the bread and butter issues or doesn't survive.

But the UFW has always been something more than a union—although it's never been dangerous if you believe in the Bill of Rights.

The UFW was the beginning! We attacked that historical source of shame and infamy that our people in this country lived with. We attacked that injustice, not by complaining; not by seeking hand-outs; not by becoming soldiers in the War on Poverty.

We organized!

Farm workers acknowledged we had allowed ourselves to become victims in a democratic society—a society where majority rule and collective bargaining are supposed to be more than academic theories or political rhetoric. And by addressing this historical problem, we created confidence and pride and hope in an entire people's ability to create the future.

UNIT

5

The UFW's survival—its existence—was not in doubt in my mind when the time began to come—after the union became visible—when Chicanos started entering college in greater numbers, when Hispanics began running for public office in greater numbers—when our people started asserting their rights on a broad range of issues and in many communities across the country.

The union's survival—its very existence—sent out a signal to all Hispanics that we were fighting for our dignity, that we were challenging and overcoming injustice, that we were empowering the least educated among us—the poorest among us.

The message was clear: If it could happen in the fields, it could happen anywhere—in the cities, in the courts, in the city councils, in the state legislatures.

I didn't really appreciate it at the time, but the coming of our union signaled the start of great changes among Hispanics that are only now beginning to be seen.

I've traveled to every part of this nation. I have met and spoken with thousands of Hispanics from every walk of life—from every social and economic class.

One thing I hear most often from Hispanics, regardless of age or position—and from many non-Hispanics as well—is that the farm workers gave them hope that they could succeed and the inspiration to work for change.

From time to time you will hear our opponents declare that the union is weak, that the union has no support, that the union has not grown fast enough. Our obituary has been written many times.

How ironic it is that the same forces which argue so passionately that the union is not influential are the same forces that continue to fight us so hard.

The union's power in agriculture has nothing to do with the number of farm workers under union contract. It has nothing to do with the farm worker's ability to contribute to Democratic politicians. It doesn't even have much to do with our ability to conduct successful boycotts.

The very fact of our existence forces an entire industry—unionized and non-unionized—to spend millions of dollars year after year on improved wages, on improved working conditions, on benefits for workers.

If we're so weak and unsuccessful, why do the growers continue to fight us with such passion?

Because so long as we continue to exist, farm workers will benefit from our existence—even if they don't work under union contract.

It doesn't really matter whether we have 100,000 members or 500,000 members. In truth, hundreds of thousands of farm workers in California—and in other states—are better off today because of our work.

And Hispanics across California and the nation who don't work in agriculture are better off today because of what the farm workers taught people about organization, about pride and strength, about seizing control over their own lives.

Tens of thousands of the children and grandchildren of farm workers and the children and grandchildren of poor Hispanics are moving out of the fields and out of the barrios—and into the professions and into business and into politics. And that movement cannot be reversed!

Our union will forever exist as an empowering force among Chicanos in the Southwest. And that means our power and our influence will grow and not diminish.

Two major trends give us hope and encouragement.

First, our union has returned to a tried and tested weapon in the farm worker's non-violent arsenal—the boycott!

After the Agricultural Labor Relations Act became law in California in 1975, we dismantled our boycott to work with the law.

During the early- and mid-'70s, millions of Americans supported our boycotts. After 1975, we redirected our efforts from the boycott to organizing and winning elections under the law.

The law helped farm workers make progress in overcoming poverty and injustice. At companies where farm workers are protected by union contracts, we have made progress in overcoming child labor, in overcoming miserable wages and working conditions, in overcoming sexual harassment of women workers, in overcoming dangerous pesticides which poison our people and poison the food we all eat.

Where we have organized, these injustices soon pass into history.

But under Republican Governor George Deukmejian, the law that guarantees our right to organize no longer protects farm workers. It doesn't work anymore.

In 1982, corporate growers gave Deukmejian one million dollars to run for governor of California. Since he took office, Deukmejian has paid back his debt to the growers with the blood and sweat of California farm workers.

Instead of enforcing the law as it was written against those who break it, Deukmejian invites growers who break the law to seek relief from the governor's appointees.

What does all this mean for farm workers?

It means that the right to vote in free elections is a sham. It means that the right to talk freely about the union among your fellow workers on the job is a cruel hoax. It means the right to be free from threats and intimidation by growers is an empty promise.

It means the right to sit down and negotiate with your employer as equals across the bargaining table—and not as peons in the field—is a fraud.

It means that thousands of farm workers—who are owed millions of dollars in back pay because their employers broke the law—are still waiting for their checks.

It means that 36,000 farm workers—who voted to be represented by the United Farm Workers in free elections—are still waiting for contracts from growers who refuse to bargain in good faith.

It means that, for farm workers, child labor will continue. It means that infant mortality will continue. It means malnutrition among our children will continue. It means the short life expectancy and the inhumane living and working conditions will continue.

Are these make-believe threats? Are they exaggerations?

Ask the farm workers who are still waiting for growers to bargain in good faith and sign contracts. Ask the farm workers who've been fired from their jobs because they spoke out for the union. Ask the farm workers who've been threatened with physical violence because they support the UFW.

Ask the family of Rene Lopez, the young farm worker from Fresno who was shot to death last year because he supported the union.

These tragic events forced farm workers to declare a new international boycott of California table grapes. That's why we are asking Americans once again to join the farm workers by boycotting California grapes.

The Louis Harris poll revealed that 17 million American adults boycotted grapes. We are convinced that those people and that good will have not disappeared.

That segment of the population which makes our boycotts work are the Hispanics, the Blacks, the other minorities and our allies in labor and the church. But it is also an entire generation of young Americans who matured politically and socially in the 1960s and '70s—millions of people for whom boycotting grapes and other products became a socially accepted pattern of behavior.

If you were young, Anglo and on or near campus during the late '60s and early '70s, chances are you supported farm workers.

Fifteen years later, the men and women of that generation are alive and well. They are in their mid-30s and '40s. They are pursuing professional careers. Their disposable income is relatively high. But they are still inclined to respond to an appeal from farm workers. The union's mission still has meaning for them.

UNIT 5

Only today we must translate the importance of a union for farm workers into the language of the 1980s. Instead of talking about the right to organize, we must talk about protection against sexual harassment in the fields. We must speak about the right to quality food—and food that is safe to eat.

I can tell you that the new language is working; the 17 million are still there. They are responding—not to picket lines and leafleting alone, but to the high-tech boycott of today—a boycott that uses computers and direct mail and advertising techniques which have revolutionized business and politics in recent years.

We have achieved more success with the boycott in the first 11 months of 1984 than we achieved in the 14 years since 1970.

The other trend that gives us hope is the monumental growth of Hispanic influence in this country and what that means in increased population, increased social and economic clout, and increased political influence.

South of the Sacramento River in California, Hispanics now make up more than 25 percent of the population. That figure will top 30 percent by the year 2000.

There are 1.1 million Spanish-surnamed registered voters in California; 85 percent are Democrats; only 13 percent are Republicans.

In 1975, there were 200 Hispanic elected officials at all levels of government. In 1984, there are over 400 elected judges, city council members, mayors and legislators.

In light of these trends, it is absurd to believe or suggest that we are going to go back in time—as a union or as a people!

The growers often try to blame the union for their problems—to lay their sins off on us—sins for which they only have themselves to blame.

The growers only have themselves to blame as they begin to reap the harvest from decades of environmental damage they have brought upon the land—the pesticides, the herbicides, the soil fumigants, the fertilizers, the salt deposits from thoughtless irrigation—the ravages from years of unrestrained poisoning of our soil and water.

Thousands of acres of land in California have already been irrevocably damaged by this wanton abuse of nature. Thousands more will be lost unless growers understand that dumping more poisons on the soil won't solve their problems—on the short term or the long term.

Health authorities in many San Joaquin Valley towns already warn young children and pregnant women not to drink the water because of nitrates from fertilizers which have contaminated the groundwater.

The growers only have themselves to blame for an increasing demand by consumers for higher quality food—food that isn't tainted by toxics; food that doesn't result from plant mutations or chemicals which produce red, luscious-looking tomatoes—that taste like alfalfa.

The growers are making the same mistake American automakers made in the '60s and '70s when they refused to produce small economical cars—and opened the door to increased foreign competition.

Growers only have themselves to blame for increasing attacks on their publicly-financed handouts and government welfare: Water subsidies; mechanization research; huge subsidies for not growing crops.

These special privileges came into being before the Supreme Court's one-person, one-vote decision—at a time when rural lawmakers dominated the Legislature and the Congress. Soon, those hand-outs could be in jeopardy as government searches for more revenue and as urban taxpayers take a closer look at farm programs—and who they really benefit.

The growers only have themselves to blame for the humiliation they have brought upon succeeding waves of immigrant groups which have sweated and sacrificed for 100 years to make this industry rich. For generations, they have subjugated entire races of dark-skinned farm workers.

These are the sins of the growers, not the farm workers. We didn't poison the land. We didn't open the door to imported produce. We didn't covet billions of dollars in government hand-outs. We didn't abuse and exploit the people who work the land.

Today, the growers are like a punch-drunk old boxer who doesn't know he's past his prime. The times are changing. The political and social environment has changed. The chickens are coming home to roost—and the time to account for past sins is approaching.

I am told, these days, why farm workers should be discouraged and pessimistic: The Republicans control the governor's office and the White House. They say there is a conservative trend in the nation.

Yet we are filled with hope and encouragement. We have looked into the future and the future is ours!

History and inevitability are on our side. The farm workers and their children—and the Hispanics and their children—are the future of California. And corporate growers are the past!

Those politicians who ally themselves with the corporate growers and against the farm workers and the Hispanics are in for a big surprise. They want to make their careers in politics. They want to hold power 20 and 30 years from now.

UNIT

5

But 20 and 30 years from now—in Modesto, in Salinas, in Fresno, in Bakersfield, in the Imperial Valley, and in many of the great cities of California—those communities will be dominated by farm workers and not by growers, by the children and grandchildren of farm workers and not by the children and grandchildren of growers.

These trends are part of the forces of history that cannot be stopped. No person and no organization can resist them for very long. They are inevitable.

Once social change begins, it cannot be reversed.

You cannot uneducate the person who has learned to read. You cannot humiliate the person who feels pride. You cannot oppress the people who are not afraid anymore.

Our opponents must understand that it's not just a union we have built. Unions, like other institutions, can come and go.

But we're more than an institution. For nearly 20 years, our union has been on the cutting edge of a people's cause—and you cannot do away with an entire people; you cannot stamp out a people's cause.

Regardless of what the future holds for the union, regardless of what the future holds for farm workers, our accomplishments cannot be undone. "La Causa"—our cause—doesn't have to be experienced twice.

The consciousness and pride that were raised by our union are alive and thriving inside millions of young Hispanics who will never work on a farm!

Like the other immigrant groups, the day will come when we win the economic and political rewards which are in keeping with our numbers in society. The day will come when the politicians do the right thing by our people out of political necessity and not out of charity or idealism.

That day may not come this year. That day may not come during this decade. But it will come, someday!

And when that day comes, we shall see the fulfillment of that passage from the Book of Matthew in the New Testament, "That the last shall be first and the first shall be last."

And on that day, our nation shall fulfill its creed—and that fulfillment shall enrich us all.

Thank you very much.

REFLECT & FOCUS

"Individual commitment to a group effort—that is what makes a team work, a company work, a society work, a civilization work."

"People who work together will win, whether it be against complex football defenses, or the problems of modern society."

—Vince Lombardi (1913–1970), National Football League
Green Bay Packers Head Coach, 1959–1967

READINGS

"The Secrets of Great Groups"

By Warren Bennis

Points to Consider

1. In considering Bennis' notion of catalytic completers, what leadership roles do you see as challenging to fulfill? How will you overcome those challenges?

2. If indeed Bennis is correct in asserting that great groups are usually young, in what ways can older, more established groups regain their youth?

3. Reflecting back to Unit 4 on Articulating a Vision, how can leaders effectively get their organization to adopt a "shared dream"?

4. For a group to be a "Great Group," why does Bennis assert that there must always be a price to pay on the part of the individual members?

5. What are the difficulties of abandoning individual egos in pursuit of a group's dream?

"The Secrets of Great Groups"

Personal leadership is one of the most studied topics in American life. Indeed, I have devoted a big chunk of my professional life to better understanding its workings. Far less studied—and perhaps more important—is *group* leadership. The disparity of interest in those two realms of leadership is logical, given the strong individualist bent of American culture. But the more I look at the history of business, government, the arts, and the sciences, the clearer it is that few great accomplishments are ever the work of a single individual.

Our mythology refuses to catch up with our reality. So we cling to the myth of the Lone Ranger, the romantic idea that great things are usually accomplished by a larger-than-life individual working alone. Despite the evidence to the contrary—including the fact that Michelangelo worked with a group of sixteen to paint the ceiling of the Sistine Chapel—we still tend to think of achievement in terms of the Great Man or the Great Woman, instead of the Great Group.

As they say, "None of us is as smart as all of us." That's good, because the problems we face are too complex to be solved by any one person or any one discipline. Our only chance is to bring people together from a variety of backgrounds and disciplines who can refract a problem through the prism of complementary minds allied in common purpose. I call such collections of talent *Great Groups*. The genius of Great Groups is that they get remarkable people—strong individual achievers—to work together to get results. But these groups serve a second and equally important function: they provide psychic support and personal fellowship. They help generate courage. Without a sounding board for outrageous ideas, without personal encouragement and perspective when we hit a roadblock, we'd all lose our way.

The Myths of Leadership

Great Groups teach us something about effective leadership, meaningful missions, and inspired recruiting. They challenge not only the myth of the Great Man but also the 1950s myth of the Organization Man—the sallow figure in the gray flannel suit, giving his life to the job and conforming to its mindless dictates.

Neither myth is a productive model for behavior, and neither holds up to current reality. In fact, I believe that behind every Great Man is a Great Group, an effective partnership. And making up every Great Group is a unique construct of strong, often eccentric individuals. So the question for organizations is, How do you get talented, self-absorbed, often arrogant, incredibly bright people to work together?

The impetus for my current work in groups was a meeting more than forty years ago with anthropologist Margaret Mead. I had heard her speak at Harvard, and afterward I asked her whether anyone had ever studied groups whose ideas were powerful enough to change the world. She looked at me and said, "Young man, you should write a book on that topic and call it *Sapiential Circles*." I gasped, and she went on to explain that *sapiential circles* meant knowledge-generating groups. Like a lot of good ideas, it took a while to gestate, but over the years the power of groups became a recurrent theme for me. Recently, work by leading thinkers such as Michael Shrage in the nature of technology and collaboration, Hal Leavitt and Jean Lipman-Blumen in *Hot Groups*, and Richard Hackman in his writing on the remarkable Orpheus Chamber Orchestra highlights the significance of this inquiry.

To see what makes Great Groups tick, I studied some of the most noteworthy groups of our time, including the Manhattan Project, the paradigmatic Great Group that invented the atomic bomb; the computer revolutionaries at Xerox's Palo Alto Research Center (PARC) and at Apple Computer, whose work led to the Macintosh and other technical breakthroughs; the Lockheed Skunk Works, which pioneered the fast, efficient development of top-secret aircraft; and the Walt Disney Studio animators. Every Great Group is extraordinary in its own way, but my study suggests ten principles common to all—and that apply as well to their larger organizations.

UNIT
5

- *At the heart of every Great Group is a shared dream.* All Great Groups believe that they are on a mission from God, that they could change the world, make a dent in the universe. They are obsessed with their work. It becomes not a job but a fervent quest. That belief is what brings the necessary cohesion and energy to their work.

- *They manage conflict by abandoning individual egos to the pursuit of the dream.* At a critical point in the Manhattan Project, George Kistiakowsky, a great chemist who later served as Dwight Eisenhower's chief scientific advisor, threatened to quit because he couldn't get along with a colleague. Project leader Robert Oppenheimer simply said, "George, how can you leave this project? The free world hangs in the balance." So conflict, even with these diverse people, is resolved by reminding people of the mission.

- *They are protected from the "suits."* All Great Groups seem to have disdain for their corporate overseers and all are protected from them by a leader—not necessarily the leader who defines the dream. In the Manhattan Project, for instance, General Leslie Grove kept the Pentagon brass happy and away, while Oppenheimer kept the group focused on its mission. At Xerox PARC, Bob Taylor kept the honchos in Connecticut (referred to by the group as "toner heads") at bay and kept the group focused. Kelly Johnson got himself appointed to the board of Lockheed to help protect his Skunk Works. In all cases, physical distance from headquarters helped.

- *They have a real or invented enemy.* Even the most noble mission can be helped by an onerous opponent. That was literally true with the Manhattan Project, which had real enemies—the Japanese and the Nazis. Yet most organizations have an implicit mission to destroy an adversary, and that is often more motivating than their explicit mission. During their greatest years, for instance, Apple Computer's implicit mission was, Bury IBM. (The famous 1984 Macintosh TV commercial included the line, "Don't buy a computer you can't lift.") The decline of Apple follows the subsequent softening of their mission.

- *They view themselves as winning underdogs.* World-changing groups are usually populated by mavericks, people at the periphery of their disciplines. These groups do not regard the mainstream as the sacred Ganges. The sense of operating on the fringes gives them a don't-count-me-out scrappiness that feeds their obsession.

- *Members pay a personal price.* Membership in a Great Group isn't a day job; it is a night and day job. Divorces, affairs, and other severe emotional fallout are typical, especially when a project ends. At the Skunk Works, for example, people couldn't even tell their families what they were working on. They were located in a cheerless, rundown building in Burbank, of all places, far from Lockheed's corporate headquarters and main plants. So groups strike a Faustian bargain for the intensity and energy that they generate.

- *Great Groups make strong leaders.* On the one hand, they're all nonhierarchical, open, and very egalitarian. Yet on the other hand, they all have strong leaders. That's the paradox of group leadership. You cannot have a great leader with out a Great Group—and vice versa. In an important way, these groups made the leader great. The leaders I studied were seldom the brightest or best in the group, but neither were they passive players. They were connoisseurs of talent, more like curators than creators.

- *Great Groups are the product of meticulous recruiting.* It took Oppenheimer to get a Kistiakowsky and a Niels Bohr to come to his godforsaken outpost in the desert. Cherry-picking the right talent for a group means knowing what you need and being able to spot it in others. It also means understanding the chemistry of a group. Candidates are often grilled, almost hazed, by other members of the group and its leader. You see the same thing in great coaches. They can place the right people in the right role—and get the right constellations and configurations within the group.

- *Great Groups are usually young.* The average age of the physicists at Los Alamos was about twenty-five. Oppenheimer—"the old man"—was in his thirties. Youth provides the physical stamina demanded by these groups. But Great Groups are also young in their spirit, ethos, and culture. Most important, because they're young and naïve, group members don't know what's supposed to be impossible, which gives them the ability to do the impossible. As Berlioz said about Saint-Saens, "He knows everything; all he lacks is inexperience." Great Groups don't lack the experience of possibilities.

- *Real artists ship.* Steve Jobs constantly reminded his band of Apple renegades that their work meant nothing unless they brought a great product to market. In the end, Great Groups have to produce a tangible outcome external to themselves. Most dissolve after the product is delivered; but without something to show for their efforts, the most talented assemblage becomes little more than a social club or a therapy group.

New Rules for Leaders

These principles not only define the nature of Great Groups, they also redefine the roles and responsibilities of leaders. Group leaders vary widely in style and personality. Some are facilitators, some are doers, some are contrarians. Leadership is inevitably dispersed, however, sometimes in formal rotation, more often with people playing ad hoc leadership roles at different points.

Furthermore, the formal leaders, even when delegating authority, are catalytic *completers*; they take on roles that nobody else plays—cajoler, taskmaster, protector, or doer—and that are needed for the group to achieve its goal. They intuitively understand the chemistry of the group and the dynamics of the work process. They encourage dissent and diversity in the pursuit of a shared vision, and they understand the difference between healthy, creative dissent and self-serving obstructionism. They are able to discern what different people need at different times.

In short, despite their differences in style, the leaders of Great Groups share four behavioral traits. Without exception, the leaders of Great Groups:

- *Provide direction and meaning.* They remind people of what's important and why their work makes a difference.

- *Generate and sustain trust.* The group's trust in itself—and its leadership—allows members to accept dissent and ride through the turbulence of the group process.

- *Display a bias toward action, risk taking, and curiosity.* A sense of urgency—and a willingness to risk failure to achieve results—is at the heart of every Great Group.

- *Are purveyors of hope.* Effective team leaders find both tangible and symbolic ways to demonstrate that the group can overcome the odds.

There's no simple recipe for developing these skills; group leadership is far more an art than a science. But we can start by rethinking our notion of what collaboration means and how it is achieved. Our management training and educational institutions need to focus on group development as well as individual development. Universities, for instance, rarely allow group Ph.D. theses or rewards for joint authorship. Corporations usually reward individual rather than group achievement, even as leaders call for greater teamwork and partnership.

Power of the Mission

It's no accident that topping both lists—the principles of Great Groups and the traits of group leaders—is the power of the mission. All great teams—and all great organizations—are built around a shared dream or motivating purpose. Yet organizations' mission statements often lack real meaning and resonance. Realistically, your team need not believe that it is literally saving the world, as the Manhattan Project did; it is enough to feel that it is helping people in need or battling a tough competitor. Simply punching a time clock doesn't do it.

UNIT
5

Articulating a meaningful mission is the job of leaders at every level—and it's not an easy task. In Shakespeare's *Henry IV, Part 1*, Glendower, the Welsh seer, boasts to Hotspur that he can "call spirits from the vasty deep," and Hotspur retorts, so can I, so can anybody—"but will they come when you do call for them?" That is the test of inspiring leadership.

I learned firsthand how critical a sense of mission—or its absence—can be to an employer. Several years ago, I had an assistant who handled the arrangements for my speeches and travel; at night she did volunteer work for a nonprofit, self-help organization. Her work for me was acceptable but perfunctory. It was clear that she was much more involved and committed to her unpaid work. Frankly, I was jealous. I came to resent the fact that I was not getting her best efforts; after all, I was paying her and they weren't. We talked about it, and she was very honest about the fact that it was her volunteer work that had real meaning for her; there she felt she was making a difference. So you can't expect every employee to be zealously committed to your cause. But you can accept the fact that part of the responsibility for uninspired work lies with the leader.

Great Groups remind us how much we can really accomplish by working toward a shared purpose. To be sure, Great Groups rely on many long-established practices of good management—effective communication, exceptional recruitment, genuine empowerment, personal commitment. But they also remind us of author Luciano de Crescanzo's observation that "we are all angels with only one wing; we can only fly while embracing one another." In the end, these groups cannot be managed; they can only be led in flight.

Bennis, Warren. "The Secrets of Great Groups." *Leader to Leader: Enduring Insights on Leadership from the Drucker Foundation's Award Winning Journal.* San Francisco: Jossey-Bass, 1999. Reprinted by Permission of Jossey-Bass, Inc., a subsidiary of John Wiley & Sons, Inc.

The Five Dysfunctions of a Team

By Patrick Lencioni

Points to Consider

1. What factors impact your comfort level in being able to show vulnerability within a group?
2. What are some strategies for encouraging ideological conflict, while discouraging personality-based conflict in a group?
3. What are some strategies for encouraging buy-in, when a consensus decision isn't possible?
4. Lencioni refers to peer pressure as "the most effective and efficient means of maintaining high standards of performance on a team." Do you agree? Is there a point at which peer pressure crosses an ethical boundary? Explain.

The Five Dysfunctions of a Team

An Overview of the Model

In the course of my experience working with CEOs and their teams, two critical truths have become clear to me. First, genuine teamwork in most organizations remains as elusive as it has ever been. Second, organizations fail to achieve teamwork because they unknowingly fall prey to five natural but dangerous pitfalls, which I call the five dysfunctions of a team.

These dysfunctions can be mistakenly interpreted as five distinct issues that can be addressed in isolation of the others. But in reality they form an interrelated model, making susceptibility to even one of them potentially lethal for the success of a team. A cursory overview of each dysfunction, and the model they comprise, should make this clearer.

Inattention to RESULTS
Avoidance of ACCOUNTABILITY
Lack of COMMITMENT
Fear of CONFLICT
Absence of TRUST

1. The first dysfunction is an **absence of trust** among team members. Essentially, this stems from their unwillingness to be vulnerable within the group. Team members who are not genuinely open with one another about their mistakes and weaknesses make it impossible to build a foundation for trust.

2. This failure to build trust is damaging because it sets the tone for the second dysfunction: **fear of conflict**. Teams that lack trust are incapable of engaging in unfiltered and passionate debate of ideas. Instead, they resort to veiled discussions and guarded comments.

3. A lack of healthy conflict is a problem because it ensures the third dysfunction of a team: **lack of commitment**. Without having aired their opinions in the course of passionate and open debate, team members rarely, if ever, buy in and commit to decisions, though they may feign agreement during meetings.

4. Because of this lack of real commitment and buy-in, team members develop an **avoidance of accountability**, the fourth dysfunction. Without committing to a clear plan of action, even the most focused and driven people often hesitate to call their peers on actions and behaviors that seem counterproductive to the good of the team.

5. Failure to hold one another accountable creates an environment where the fifth dysfunction can thrive. **Inattention to results** occurs when team members put their individual needs (such as ego, career development, or recognition) or even the needs of their divisions above the collective goals of a team.

And so, like a chain with just one link broken, teamwork deteriorates if even a single dysfunction is allowed to flourish.

Another way to understand this model is to take the opposite approach—a positive one—and imagine how members of truly cohesive teams behave:

UNIT
5

1. They trust one another.

2. They engage in unfiltered conflict around ideas.

3. They commit to decisions and plans of action.

4. They hold one another accountable for delivering against those plans.

5. They focus on the achievement of collective results.

If this sounds simple, it's because it is simple, at least in theory. In practice, however, it is extremely difficult because it requires levels of discipline and persistence that few teams can muster.

Before diving into each of the dysfunctions and exploring ways to overcome them, it might be helpful to assess your team and identify where the opportunities for improvement lie in your organization.

Team Assessment

The questionnaire on the following pages is a straightforward diagnostic tool for helping you evaluate your team's susceptibility to the five dysfunctions. At the end of the questionnaire, there is a simple explanation of how to tabulate the results and interpret the possible conclusions. If possible, have all members of your team complete the diagnostic and review the results, discussing discrepancies in the responses and identifying any clear implications for the team.

Instructions: Use the scale below to indicate how each statement applies to your team. It is important to evaluate the statements honestly and without over-thinking your answers.

3 = Usually   2 = Sometimes   1 = Rarely

_____ 1. Team members are passionate and unguarded in their discussion of issues.

_____ 2. Team members call out one another's deficiencies or unproductive behaviors.

_____ 3. Team members know what their peers are working on and how they contribute to the collective good of the team.

_____ 4. Team members quickly and genuinely apologize to one another when they say or do something inappropriate or possibly damaging to the team.

_____ 5. Team members willingly make sacrifices (such as budget, turf, head count) in their departments or areas of expertise for the good of the team.

_____ 6. Team members openly admit their weaknesses and mistakes.

_____ 7. Team meetings are compelling, and not boring.

_____ 8. Team members leave meetings confident that their peers are completely committed to the decisions that were agreed on, even if there was initial disagreement.

_____ 9. Morale is significantly affected by the failure to achieve team goals.

_____ 10. During team meetings, the most important—and difficult—issues are put on the table to be resolved.

_____ 11. Team members are deeply concerned about the prospect of letting down their peers.

_____ 12. Team members know about one another's personal lives and are comfortable discussing them.

_____ 13. Team members end discussions with clear and specific resolutions and calls to action.

_____ 14. Team members challenge one another about their plans and approaches.

_____ 15. Team members are slow to seek credit for their own contributions, but quick to point out those to others.

Scoring

Combine your scores for the preceding statements as indicated below.

Dysfunction 1: Absence of Trust		Dysfunction 2: Fear of Conflict		Dysfunction 3: Lack of Commitment		Dysfunction 4: Avoiding Accountability		Dysfunction 5: Inattention to Results	
Statement 4:		Statement 1:		Statement 3:		Statement 2:		Statement 5:	
Statement 6:		Statement 7:		Statement 8:		Statement 11:		Statement 9:	
Statement 12:		Statement 10:		Statement 13:		Statement 14:		Statement 15:	
Total:		Total:		Total:		Total:		Total:	

A score of 8 or 9 is a probable indication that the dysfunction is not a problem for your team.

A score of 6 or 7 indicates that the dysfunction could be a problem.

A score of 3 to 5 is probably an indication that the dysfunction needs to be addressed.

Regardless of your scores, it is important to keep in mind that every team needs constant work, because without it, even the best ones deviate toward dysfunction.

Understanding and Overcoming the Five Dysfunctions

Dysfunction 1: Absence of Trust

Trust lies at the heart of a functioning, cohesive team. Without it, teamwork is all but impossible.

Unfortunately, the word *trust* is used—and misused—so often that it has lost some of its impact and begins to sound like motherhood and apple pie. That is why it is important to be very specific about what is meant by trust.

In the context of building a team, trust is the confidence among team members that their peers' intentions are good, and that there is no reason to be protective or careful around the group. In essence, teammates must get comfortable being vulnerable with one another.

This description stands in contrast to a more standard definition of trust, one that centers around the ability to predict a person's behavior based on past experience. For instance, one might "trust" that a given teammate will produce high-quality work because he has always done so in the past.

As desirable as this may be, it is not enough to represent the kind of trust that is characteristic of a great team. It requires team members to make themselves vulnerable to one another, and be confident that their respective vulnerabilities will not be used against them. The vulnerabilities I'm referring to include weaknesses, skill deficiencies, interpersonal shortcomings, mistakes, and requests for help.

As "soft" as all of this might sound, it is only when team members are truly comfortable being exposed to one another that they begin to act without concern for protecting themselves. As a result, they can focus their energy and attention completely on the job at hand, rather than on being strategically disingenuous or political with one another.

UNIT
5

Achieving vulnerability-based trust is difficult because in the course of career advancement and education, most successful people learn to be competitive with their peers, and protective of their reputations. It is a challenge for them to turn those instincts off for the good of a team, but that is exactly what is required.

The cost of failing to do this are great. Teams that lack trust waste inordinate amounts of time and energy management their behaviors and interactions within the group. They tend to dread team meetings, and are reluctant to take risks in asking for or offering assistance to others. As a result, morale on distrusting teams is usually quite low, and unwanted turnover is high.

Members of teams with an absence of trust...

- Conceal their weaknesses and mistakes from one another
- Hesitate to ask for help or provide constructive feedback
- Hesitate to offer help outside their own areas of responsibility
- Jump to conclusions about the intentions and aptitudes of others without attempting to clarify them
- Fail to recognize and tap into one another's skills and experiences
- Waste time and energy managing their behaviors for effect
- Hold grudges
- Dread meetings and find reasons to avoid spending time together

Members of trusting teams...

- Admit weaknesses and mistakes
- Ask for help
- Accept questions and input about their areas of responsibility
- Give one another the benefit of the doubt before arriving at a negative conclusion
- Take risks in offering feedback and assistance
- Appreciate and tap into one another's skills and experiences
- Focus time and energy on important issues, not policies
- Offer and accept apologies without hesitation
- Look forward to meetings and other opportunities to work as a group

Suggestions for Overcoming Dysfunction 1

How does a team go about building trust? Unfortunately, vulnerability-based trust cannot be achieved overnight. It requires shared experiences over time, multiple instances of follow-through and credibility, and in-depth understanding of the unique attributes of team members. However, by taking a focused approach, a team can dramatically accelerate the process and achieve trust in relatively short order. Here are a few tools that can bring this about.

Personal Histories Exercise

In less than an hour, a team can take the first steps toward developing trust. This low-risk exercise requires nothing more than going around the table during a meeting and having team members answer a short list of questions about themselves. Questions need not be overly sensitive in nature and might include the following: number of siblings, hometown, unique challenges of childhood, favorite hobbies, first job, and worst job. Simply by describing these relatively innocuous attributes or experiences, team members begin to relate to one another on a more personal basis, and see one another as human beings with life stories and interesting backgrounds. This encourages greater empathy and understanding, and discourages unfair and inaccurate behavioral attributions. It is amazing how little some team members know about one another, and how just a small amount of information begins to break down barriers. (Minimum time required: 30 minutes.)

Team Effectiveness Exercise

This exercise is more rigorous and relevant than the previous one, but may involve more risk. It requires team members to identify the single most important contribution that each of the peers makes to the team, as well as the one area that they must either improve upon or eliminate for the good of the team. All members then report their responses, focusing on one person at a time, usually beginning with the team leader.

While this exercise may seem somewhat intrusive and dangerous at first glance, it is remarkable how manageable it can be and how much useful information, both constructive and positive, can be extracted in about an hour. And though the Team Effectiveness Exercise certainly requires some degree of trust in order to be useful, even a relatively dysfunctional team can often make it work with surprisingly little tension. (Minimum time required: 60 minutes.)

Personality and Behavioral Preference Profiles

Some of the most effective and lasting tools for building trust on a team are profiles of team members' behavioral preferences and personality styles. These help break down barriers by allowing people to better understand and empathize with one another.

UNIT

5

The best profiling tool, in my opinion, is the Myers-Briggs Type Indicator (MBTI). However, a number of others are popular among different audiences. The purpose of most of these tools is to provide practical and scientifically valid behavioral descriptions of various team members according to the diverse ways that they think, speak, and act. Some of the best characteristics of tools like the MBTI are their nonjudgmental nature (no type is better than another, although they differ substantially), their basis in research (they are not founded upon astrology or new age science), and the extent to which participants take an active role in identifying their own types (they don't simply receive a computer printout or test score that alone dictates their type). Many of these tools do require the participation of a licensed consultant, which is important to avoid the misuse of their powerful implications and applications. (Minimum time required: 4 hours.)

360-Degree Feedback

These tools have become popular over the past twenty years and can produce powerful results for a team. They are riskier than any of the tools or exercises described so far because they call for peers to make specific judgments and provide one another with constructive criticism. The key to making a 360-degree program work, in my opinion, is divorcing it entirely from compensation and formal performance evaluation. Rather, it should be used as a developmental tool, one that allows employees to identify strengths and weaknesses without any repercussions. By being even slightly connected to formal performance evaluation or compensation, 360-degree programs can take on dangerous political undertones.

Experiential Team Exercises

Ropes courses and other experiential team activities seem to have lost some of their luster over the course of the past ten years, and deservedly so. Still, many teams do them with the hope of building trust. And while there are certainly some benefits derived from rigorous and creative outdoor activities involving collective support and cooperation, those benefits derived from rigorous and creative outdoor activities involving collective support and cooperation, those benefits do not always translate directly to the working world. That being said, experiential teams exercises can be valuable tools for enhancing teamwork as long as they are layered upon more fundamental and relevant processes.

While each of these tools and exercises can have a significant short-term impact on a team's ability to build trust, they must be accompanied by regular follow-up in the course of daily work. Individual developmental areas must be revisited to ensure that progress does not lose momentum. Even on a strong team—and perhaps especially so—atrophy can lead to the erosion of trust.

The Role of a Leader

The most important action that a leader must take to encourage the building of trust on a team is to demonstrate vulnerability first. This requires that a leader risk losing face in front of the team, so that subordinates will take the same risk themselves. What is more, team leaders must create an environment that does not punish vulnerability. Even well-intentioned teams can subtly discourage trust by chastising one another for admissions of weakness or failure. Finally, displays of vulnerability on the part of a team leader must be genuine; they cannot be staged. One of the best ways to lose the trust of a team is to feign vulnerability in order to manipulate the emotions of others.

Connection to Dysfunction 2

How does all of this relate to the next dysfunction, the fear of conflict? By building trust, a team makes conflict possible because team members do not hesitate to engage in passionate and sometimes emotional debate, knowing that they will not be punished for saying something that might otherwise be interpreted as destructive or critical.

Dysfunction 2: Fear of Conflict

All great relationships, the ones that last over time, require productive conflict in order to grow. This is true in marriage, parenthood, friendship, and certainly business.

Unfortunately, conflict is considered taboo in many situations, especially at work. And the higher you go up the management chain, the more you find people spending inordinate amounts of time and energy trying to avoid the kind of passionate debates that are essential to any great team.

It is important to distinguish productive ideological conflict from destructive fighting and interpersonal politics. Ideological conflict is limited to concepts and ideas, and avoids personality-focused, mean-spirited attacks. However, it can have many of the same external qualities of interpersonal conflict—passion, emotion, and frustration—so much that an outside observer might easily mistake it for unproductive discord.

But teams that engage in productive conflict know that the only purpose is to produce the best possible solution in the shortest period of time. They discuss and resolve issues more quickly and completely than others, and they emerge from heated debates with no residual feelings or collateral damage, but with an eagerness and readiness to take on the next important issue.

Ironically, teams that avoid ideological conflict often do so in order to avoid hurting team members' feelings, and then end up encouraging dangerous tension. When team members do not openly debate and disagree about important ideas, they often turn to back-channel personal attacks, which are far nastier and more harmful than any heated argument over issues.

It is also ironic that so many people avoid conflict in the name of efficiency, because healthy conflict is actually a time saver. Contrary to the notion that teams waste time and energy arguing, those that avoid conflict actually doom themselves to revisiting issues again and again without resolution. They often ask team members to take their issues "off-line," which seems to be a euphemism for avoiding dealing with an important topic, only to have it raised again at the next meeting.

Teams that fear conflict...

- Have boring meetings
- Create environments where back-channel politics and personal attacks thrive
- Ignore controversial topics that are critical to team success
- Fail to tap into all the opinions and perspectives of team members
- Waste time and energy with posturing and interpersonal risk management

Teams that engage in conflict...

- Have lively, interesting meetings
- Extract and exploit the ideas of all team members
- Solve real problems quickly
- Minimize politics
- Put critical topics on the table for discussion

UNIT

5

Suggestions for Overcoming Dysfunction 2

How does a team go about developing the ability and willingness to engage in healthy conflict? The first step is acknowledging that conflict is productive, and that many teams have a tendency to avoid it. As long as some team members believe that conflict is unnecessary, there is little chance that it will occur. But beyond mere recognition, there are a few simple methods for making conflict more common and productive.

Mining

Members of team that tend to avoid conflict must occasionally assume the role of a "miner of conflict"—someone who extracts buried disagreements within the team and sheds the light of day on them. They must have the courage and confidence to call out sensitive issues and force team members to work through them. This requires a degree of objectivity during meetings and a commitment to staying with the conflict until it is resolved. Some teams may want to assign a member of the team to take on this responsibility during a given meeting or discussion.

Real-Time Permission

In the process of mining for conflict, team members need to coach one another not to retreat from healthy debate. One simple but effective way to do this is to recognize when the people engaged in conflict are becoming uncomfortable with the level of discord, and then interrupt to remind them that what they are doing is necessary. As simple and paternal as this may sound, it is a remarkably effective tool for draining tension from a productive but difficult interchange, giving the participants the confidence to continue. And once the discussion or meeting has ended, it is helpful to remind participants that the conflict they just engaged in is good for the team and not something to avoid in the future.

Other Tools

As mentioned earlier in this section, there are a variety of personality style and behavioral preference tools that allow team members to better understand one another. Because most of these include descriptions of how different types deal with conflict, they can be useful for helping people anticipate their approach or resistance to it. Another tool that specifically relates to conflict is the Thomas-Kilmann Conflict Mode Instrument, commonly referred to as the TKI.

It allows team members to understand natural inclinations around conflict so they can make more strategic choices about which approaches are most appropriate in different situations.

The Role of a Leader

One of the most difficult challenges that a leader faces in promoting healthy conflict is the desire to protect members from harm. This leads to premature interruption of disagreements, and prevents team members from developing coping skills for dealing with conflict themselves. This is not unlike parents who overprotect their children from quarrels or altercations with siblings. In many cases, it serves only to strain the relationships by depriving the participants of an opportunity to develop conflict management skills. It also leaves them hungry for resolution that never occurs.

Therefore, it is key that leaders demonstrate restraint when their people engage in conflict, and allow resolution to occur naturally, as messy as it can sometimes be. This can be a challenge because many leaders feel that they are somehow failing in their jobs by losing control of their teams during conflict.

Finally, as trite as it may sound, a leader's ability to personally model appropriate conflict behavior is essential. By avoiding conflict when it is necessary and productive—something many executives do—a team leader will encourage this dysfunction to thrive.

Connection to Dysfunction 3

How does all this relate to the next dysfunction, the lack of commitment? By engaging in productive conflict and tapping into team members' perspectives and opinions, a team can confidently commit and buy in to a decision knowing that they have benefited from everyone's ideas.

Dysfunction 3: Lack of Commitment

In the context of a team, commitment is a function of two things: clarity and buy-in. Great teams make clear and timely decisions and move forward with complete buy-in from every member of the team, even those who voted against the decision. They leave meetings confident that no one on the team is quietly harboring doubts whether to support the actions agreed on.

The two greatest causes of the lack of commitment are the desire for consensus and the need for certainty:

Consensus

Great teams understand the danger of seeking consensus, and find ways to achieve buy-in even when complete agreement is impossible. They understand that reasonable human beings do not need to get their way in order to support a decision, buy only need to know that their opinions have been heard and considered. Great teams ensure that everyone's ideas are genuinely considered, which then creates a willingness to rally around whatever decision is ultimately made by the group. And when that is not possible due to impasse, the leader of the team is allowed to make the call.

Certainty

Great teams also pride themselves on being able to unite behind decisions and commit to clear courses of action even when there is little assurance about whether the decision is correct. That's because they understand the old military axiom that *a* decision is better than *no* decision. They also realize that it is better to make a decision boldly and be wrong—and then change direction with equal boldness—than it is to waffle.

Contrast this with the behavior of dysfunctional teams that try to hedge their bets and delay important decisions until they have enough data to feel certain that they are making the right decision. As prudent as this might seem, it is dangerous because of the paralysis and lack of confidence it breeds within a team.

It is important to remember that conflict underlies the willingness to commit without perfect information. In many cases, teams have all the information they need, but it resides within the hearts and minds of the team itself and must be extracted through unfiltered debate. Only when everyone has put their opinions and perspectives on the table can the team confidently commit a decision knowing that it has tapped into the collective wisdom of the entire group.

Regardless of whether it is caused by the need for consensus or certainty, it is important that one of the greatest consequences for an *executive* team that does not commit to clear decisions is unresolvable discord deeper in the organization. More than any of the dysfunctions, this one creates dangerous ripple effects for subordinates. When an executive team fails to achieve buy-in from all team members, even if the disparities that exist seem relatively small, employees who report to those executives will inevitably clash when they try to interpret marching orders that are not clearly aligned with those of colleagues in other departments. Like a vortex, small gaps between executives high up in an organization become discrepancies by the time they reach employees below.

UNIT

5

A team that fails to commit…

- Creates ambiguity among the team about direction and priorities
- Watches windows of opportunity close due to excessive analysis and unnecessary delay
- Breeds lack of confidence and fear of failure
- Revisits discussions and decisions again and again
- Encourages second-guessing among team members

A team that commits...

- Creates clarity around direction and priorities
- Aligns the entire team around common objectives
- Develops an ability to learn from mistakes
- Takes advantage of opportunities before competitors do
- Moves forward without hesitation
- Changes direction without hesitation or guilt

Suggestions for Overcoming Dysfunction 3

How does a team go about ensuring commitment? By taking specific steps to maximize clarity and achieve buy-in, and resisting the lure of consensus or certainty. Here are a few simple but effective tools and principles.

Cascading Messaging

One of the most valuable disciplines that any team can adopt takes just a few minutes and is absolutely free. At the end of a staff meeting or off-site, a team should explicitly review the key decisions made during the meeting, and agree on what needs to be communicated to employees or other constituencies about those decisions. What often happens during this exercise is that members of the team learn that they are not all on the same page about what has been agreed upon and that they need to clarify specific outcomes before putting them into action. Moreover, they become clear on which of the decisions should remain confidential, and which must be communicated quickly and comprehensively. Finally, by leaving meetings clearly aligned with one another, leaders send a powerful and welcomed message to employees who have grown accustomed to receiving inconsistent and even contradictory statements from managers who attended the same meeting. (Minimum time required: 10 minutes.)

Deadlines

As simple as it seems, one of the best tools for ensuring commitment is the use of clear deadlines for when decisions will be made, and honoring those dates with discipline and rigidity. The worst enemy of a team that is susceptible to this dysfunction is ambiguity, and timing is one of the most critical factors that must be made clear. What is more, committing to deadlines for intermediate decisions and milestones is just as important as final deadlines, because it ensures that misalignment among team members is identified and addressed before the costs are too great.

Contingency and Worst-Case Scenario Analysis

A team that struggles with commitment can begin overcoming this tendency by briefly discussing contingency plans up front or, better yet, clarifying the worst-case scenario for a decision they are struggling to make. This usually allows them to reduce their fears by helping them realize that the costs of an incorrect decision are survivable, and far less damaging than they had imagined.

Low-Risk Exposure Therapy

Another relevant exercise for a commitment-phobic team is the demonstration of decisiveness in relatively low-risk situations. When teams force themselves to make decisions after substantial discussion but little analysis or research, they usually come to realize that the quality of the decision they made was better than they had expected. What is more, they learn that the decision would have been much different had the team engaged in lengthy, time-consuming study. This is not to say that research and analysis are not necessary or important, but rather that teams with this dysfunction tend to overvalue them.

The Role of a Leader

More than any other member of the team, the leader must be comfortable with the prospect of making a decision that ultimately turns out to be wrong. And the leader must be constantly pushing the group for closure around issues, as well as adherence to schedules that the team has set. What the leader cannot do is place too high a premium on certainty or consensus.

Connection to Dysfunction 4

How does all of this relate to the next dysfunction, the avoidance of accountability? In order for teammates to call each other on their behaviors and actions, they must have a clear sense of what is expected. Even the most ardent believers in accountability usually balk at having to hold someone accountable for something that was never bought in to or made clear in the first place.

Dysfunction 4: Avoidance of Accountability

Accountability is a buzzword that has lost much of its meaning as it has become as overused as terms like *empowerment* and *quality*. In the context of teamwork, however, it refers specifically to the willingness of team members to call their peers on performance or behaviors that might hurt the team.

The essence of this dysfunction is the unwillingness of team members to tolerate the interpersonal discomfort that accompanies calling a peer on his or her behavior and the more general tendency to avoid difficult conversations. Members of great teams overcome these natural inclinations, opting instead to "enter the danger" with one another.

UNIT
5

Of course, this is easier said than done, even among cohesive teams with strong personal relationships. In fact, team members who are particularly close to one another sometimes hesitate to hold one another accountable precisely because they fear jeopardizing a valuable personal relationship. Ironically, this only causes the relationship to deteriorate as team members begin to resent one another for not living up to expectations and for allowing the standards of the group to erode. Members of great teams improve their relationships by holding one another accountable, thus demonstrating that they respect each other and have high expectations for one another's performance.

As politically incorrect as it sounds, the most effective and efficient means of maintaining high standards of performance on a team is peer pressure. One of the benefits is the reduction of the need for excessive bureaucracy around performance management and corrective action. More than any policy or system, there is nothing like the fear of letting down respected teammates that motivates people to improve their performance.

A team that avoids accountability…

- Creates resentment among team members who have different standards of performance
- Encourages mediocrity
- Misses deadlines and key deliverables
- Places an undue burden on the team leader as the sole source of discipline

A team that holds one another accountable….

- Ensures that poor performers feel pressure to improve
- Indentifies potential problems quickly by questioning one another's approaches without hesitation
- Establishes respect among team members who are held to the same high standards
- Avoids excessive bureaucracy around performance management and corrective action

Suggestions for Overcoming Dysfunction 4

How does a team go about ensuring accountability? The key to overcoming this dysfunction is adhering to a few classic management tools that are as effective as they are simple.

Publication of Goals and Standards

A good way to make it easier for team members to hold one another accountable is to clarify publicly exactly what the team needs to achieve, who needs to deliver what, and how everyone must behave in order to succeed. The enemy of accountability is ambiguity, and even when a team has initially committed to a plan or a set of behavioral standards, it is important to keep those agreements in the open so that no one can easily ignore them.

Simple and Regular Progress Reviews

A little structure goes a long way toward helping people take action that they might not otherwise be inclined to do. This is especially true when it comes to giving people feedback on their behavior or performance. Team members should regularly communicate with one another, either verbally or in written form, about how they feel their teammates are doing against stated objectives and standards. Relying on them to do so on their own, with no clear expectations or structure, is inviting the potential for the avoidance of accountability.

Team Rewards

By shifting rewards away from individual performance to team achievement, the teams can create a culture of accountability. This occurs because a team is unlikely to stand by quietly and fail because a peer is not pulling his or her weight.

The Role of the Leader

One of the most difficult challenges for a leader who wants to instill accountability on a team is to encourage and allow the team to serve as the first and primary accountability mechanism. Sometimes strong leaders naturally create an accountability vacuum within the team, leaving themselves as the only source of discipline. This creates an environment where team members assume that the leader is holding others accountable, and so they hold back even when they see something that isn't right.

Once a leader has created a culture of accountability on a team, however, he or she must be willing to serve as the ultimate arbiter of discipline when the team itself fails. This should be a rare occurrence. Nevertheless, it must be clear to all team members that accountability has not been relegated to a consensus approach, but merely to a shared team responsibility, and that the leader of the team will not hesitate to step in when it is necessary.

Connection to Dysfunction 5

How does all of this relate to the next dysfunction, the inattention to results? If teammates are not being held accountable for their contributions, they will be more likely to turn their attention to their own needs, and to the advancement of themselves or their departments. An absence of accountability is an invitation to team members to shift their attention to areas other than collective results.

Dysfunction 5: Inattention to Results

The ultimate dysfunction of a team is the tendency of members to care about something other than the collective goals of the group. An unrelenting focus on specific objectives and clearly defined outcomes is a requirement for any team that judges itself on performance.

It should be noted here that results are not limited to financial measures like profit, revenue, or shareholder returns. Though it is true that many organizations in a capitalist economic environment ultimately measure their success in these terms, this dysfunction refers to a far broader definition of results, one that is related to outcome-based performance.

UNIT 5

Every good organization specifies what it plans to achieve in a given period, and these goals, more than the financial metrics that they drive, make up the majority of near-term, controllable results. So, while profit may be the ultimate measure of results for a corporation, the goals and objectives that executives set for themselves along the way constitute a more representative example of the results it strives for as a team. Ultimately, these goals drive profit.

But what would a team be focused on other than results? Team status and individual status are the prime candidates:

Team Status

For members of some teams, merely being part of the group is enough to keep them satisfied. For them, the achievement of specific results might be desirable, but not necessarily worthy of great sacrifice or inconvenience. As ridiculous and dangerous as this might seem, plenty of teams fall prey to the lure of status. These often include altruistic nonprofit organizations that come to believe that the nobility of their mission is enough to justify their satisfaction. Political groups, academic departments, and prestigious companies are also susceptible to this dysfunction, as they often see success in merely being associated with their special organizations.

Individual Status

This refers to the familiar tendency of people to focus on enhancing their own positions or career prospects at the expense of their team. Though all human beings have an innate tendency toward self-preservation, a functional team must make the collective results of the group more important to each individual than individual members' goals.

As obvious as this dysfunction might seem at first glance, and as clear as it is that it must be avoided, it is important to note that many teams are simply not results focused. They do not live and breathe in order to achieve meaningful objectives, but rather merely to exist or survive. Unfortunately for these groups, no amount of trust, conflict, commitment, or accountability can compensate for a lack of desire to win.

> A team that is not focused on results...
>
> - Stagnates/fails to grow
> - Rarely defeats competitors
> - Loses achievement-oriented employees
> - Encourages team members to focus on their own careers and individual goals
> - Is easily distracted

> A team that focuses on collective results...
>
> - Retains achievement-oriented employees
> - Minimizes individualistic behavior
> - Enjoys success and suffers failure acutely
> - Benefits from individuals who subjugate their own goals/interests for the good of the team
> - Avoids distractions

Suggestions for Overcoming Dysfunction 5

How does a team go about ensuring that its attention is focused on results? By making results clear, and rewarding only those behaviors and actions that contribute to those results.

Public Declaration of Results

In the mind of a football or basketball coach, one of the worst things a team member can do is publicly guarantee that his or her team will win an upcoming game. In the case of an athletic team, this is a problem because it can unnecessarily provoke an opponent. For most teams, however, it can be helpful to make public proclamations about intended success.

Teams that are willing to commit publicly to specific results are more likely to work with a passionate, even desperate desire to achieve those results. Teams that say, "We'll do our best," are subtly, if not purposefully, preparing themselves for failure.

Results-Based Rewards

An effective way to ensure that team members focus their attention on results is to tie their rewards, especially compensation, to the achievement of specific outcomes. Relying on this alone can be problematic because it assumes that financial motivation is the sole driver of behavior. Still, letting someone take home a bonus merely for "trying hard," even in the absence of results, sends a message that achieving the outcome may not be terribly important after all.

The Role of the Leader

Perhaps more than with any of the other dysfunctions, the leader must set the tone for a focus on results. If team members sense that the leader values anything other than results, they will take that as permission to do the same for themselves. Team leaders must be selfless and objective, and reserve rewards and recognition for those who make real contributions to the achievement of group goals.

Summary

As much information as is contained here, the reality remains that teamwork ultimately comes down to practicing a small set of principles over a long period of time. Success is not a matter of mastering subtle, sophisticated theory, but rather of embracing common sense with uncommon levels of discipline and persistence.

Ironically, teams succeed because they are exceedingly human. By acknowledging the imperfections of their humanity, members of functional teams overcome the natural tendencies that make trust, conflict, commitment, accountability, and a focus on results so elusive.

Lencioni, Patrick. *The Five Dysfunctions of a Team: A Leadership Fable.* San Francisco: Jossey-Bass, 2002.

UNIT
5

FILM STUDIES

The Wizard of Oz (1939)

Screenplay by Noel Langley, Florence Ryerson, and Edgar Allan Woolf
Directed by Victor Fleming

Character Guide

Dorothy . . . . Judy Garland

Scarecrow . . . . Ray Bolger

Cowardly Lion . . . . Bert Lahr

Tin Man . . . . Jack Haley

Wizard of Oz . . . . Frank Morgan

Introduction

There is certainly no question that a lost girl, a brainless scarecrow, a heartless tin man, and a cowardly lion make an unusual team. Nevertheless, the four of them, despite their individual limitations, share a common goal—to find the man who, they believe, can solve their problems for them. Working together, the four embark on a danger-filled journey that none of them would likely have been able to complete alone. Working together with, admittedly, a little help from Glinda the good witch, the team is able to conquer all challenges and reach their collective goal. While the focus of this Unit is on building teams, *The Wizard of Oz* says as much about servant leadership as it does about building a team. In order to successfully make their way to the Emerald City and negotiate a meeting with the wizard, the four must build one another up so that they can persevere in the face of their limitations. Even the wizard, with significant limitations of his own, ultimately demonstrates qualities of servant leadership in helping the four with their respective desires.

Dialogue Questions

1. Cite examples of how each member of the team (Dorothy, the scarecrow, the tin man, and the lion) contribute to the team's successful accomplishment of their shared goal.

2. In what ways does one member of the team seem to assume the role of leader? In what ways is there shared leadership? How do teams operate effectively in the absence of a clear leader? Are there specific criteria/situations that define when a team may or may not need a specific leader?

3. The four members of the team highlighted in *The Wizard of Oz* certainly have individual limitations, yet they successfully achieve their goal. What are some strategies for ensuring that "the whole is greater than the sum of the parts"?

4. The Wizard presents some ethical issues; how are these resolved? In what ways is the Wizard exercising leadership?

5. Identify and support the type of leadership you think the characters in the movie exercise. In what ways is their exercise of leadership effective for team building?

Remember the Titans (2000)

Written by Gregory Allen Howard
Directed by Boaz Yakin

Character Guide

Coach Herman Boone . . . . Denzel Washington

Coach Bill Yoast . . . . Will Patton

Student Gerry Bertier . . . . Ryan Hurst

Student Julius Campbell . . . . . . Wood Harris

UNIT
5

Introduction

Remember the Titans follows the true story of the T.C. Williams High School football team during the forced integration combining an all-white school and an all-black school in Alexandria, Virginia during 1971. Racial strife envelopes the community, and tempers flair when a black football coach, Herman Boone (Denzel Washington), replaces the white coach, Bill Yoast (Will Patton). Yoast stays on as assistant coach. Boone is a charismatic leader with a brutal, military-style of coaching. Yoast is more laid-back and feels Boone is pushing the players too hard. This difference in coaching styles leads to several confrontations between the two coaches and among the players.

Dialogue Questions

1. Will Coach Boone's tough approach always work? Explain.

2. Is Coach Boone a Theory X leader or a Theory Y leader (Unit One, Assumptions About People Exercise)?

3. Coach Boone demands nothing less than perfection. In what ways is he realistic or unrealistic?

4. How is Coach Boone a "catalytic completer"—a phrase of Warren Bennis', meaning he knows what is required for the team to reach its goal?

EXERCISE

Team Work!

Introduction

In this exercise you will be part of a group that will have a complicated task to complete. The exercise is designed for you to learn about team-building dynamics, especially how individual roles develop and how alternative approaches to the task develop.

Instructions

Your Instructor will divide the class into teams and provide instructions for your task.

Observers will monitor team member behavior during the process of planning and completing the tasks. The observers will give their individual teams feedback on how members used resources, how they worked together on an interpersonal basis, what leadership behaviors were present, and what roles developed within the team.

UNIT

5

SUGGESTED READING

This selected bibliography is intended to supplement the excerpts and articles of authors included in this Unit. There is an emphasis on books that are pivotal and recent publications. Numerous journals regularly offer articles related to these topics, but are not included in this selected bibliography. For further research, you may wish to include searches of the following journals: (alphabetically) *Academy of Management Executive, Academy of Management Journal, Harvard Business Review, Journal of Leadership Studies, Leadership in Action, Leadership Quarterly,* and *Leader To Leader.*

This list is organized by author's last name using Modern Language Association-style citations.

Bennis, Warren, and Patricia Ward Biederman. *Organizing Genius: The Secrets of Creative Collaboration.* Reading, MA: Addison Wesley, 1998.
Bennis and Bierderman explain the importance of assembling effective teams and the "collaborative advantage."

Fisher, Robert, and Bo Thomas. *Real Dream Teams: Seven Practices Used by World Class Leaders to Achieve Extraordinary Results.* Delray Beach: St. Lucie Press, 1996.
Fisher and Thomas identified 12 world-class team leaders—coaches, business leaders, academics, artists, and military leaders—and interviewed them. Based on the interviews, the authors define seven practices essential to effective teams.

Kearns Goodwin, Doris. *Team of Rivals: The Political Genius of Abraham Lincoln.* New York: Simon & Schuster, 2005.
Kearns Goodwin describes Lincoln's masterful understanding of human motivation and behavior to accomplish collective goals and preserve a nation.

McClure, Bud A. *Putting a New Spin on Groups: The Science of Chaos.* Mahwah: Lawrence Erlbaum, 1998.
McClure integrates small-group dynamic theory with chaos theory to explore the importance of conflict in group development and growth, how groups change, evolve, and mature. It also discusses the specific leadership skills required in group activities.

Riggio, Ronald, Ira Chaleff, and Jean Lipman-Blumen, eds. *The Art of Followership: How Great Followers Create Great Leaders and Organizations.* San Francisco: Jossey-Bass, 2008.
This collection provides interdisciplinary perspectives on the complexity of relationships in groups and organizations.

Torres, Cresencio. *The Tao of Teams: A Guide to Team Success.* San Diego: Pfeiffer, 1994.
Eighty-one passages reinforce lessons on trust, flexibility, diversity, intuition, power, and conflict resolution.

Van Nostrand, Catharine Herr. *Gender-Responsible Leadership: Detecting Bias, Implementing Interventions.* Newbury Park, CA: Sage Publishers, Inc., 1993.
In an easy-to-read and practical style—with checklists and case studies—Van Nostrand shows how gender affects group process, how leaders "buy into" these power dynamics, and what can be done about it.

UNIT 6

LEADING WITH GOALS

INTRODUCTION

Over 50 years of studies related to goal setting largely support how critical goals are to successful leadership. A close look at the anatomy of successful leadership often reveals a leader intent on a very specific goal. Goals are the bedrock of a leader's ambition, aspiration, design, intent, and purpose. They can be motivational to individuals, a group, or an organization. It's almost as if there is magic in goals, something inexplicable, but highly powerful. Psychologists understand how this leadership dynamic works, because they understand just how goal-oriented human beings are. Goals that have some degree of difficulty, are specific rather than general, and result in concrete rewards that motivate people can be powerful motivators for excellence. In recent years, however, researchers are also considering the pitfalls and detrimental effects of intent focus on goal setting and goals. This Unit includes readings that present both of these perspectives.

There are three different examples of leaders working toward goals. The Classic Case from George Bernard Shaw's *Pygmalion* focuses on the dynamics between Professor Higgins and Eliza Doolittle regarding an important goal they share, but for different reasons. The Leadership Profile of Frederick Douglass illustrates the motivating power when one sets personal goals that have deeper or broader significance in the world. Douglass' goal of successful escape from slavery was important to him personally, but in the excerpts from *Narrative of the Life of Frederick Douglass* it becomes apparent that in achieving his goal, Douglass understood that it was an important step in achieving the greater good for all.

It is fairly easy to talk about the importance of setting goals for a person or in an organization, but making it happen is something else entirely. Although nearly everyone agrees that goals are vital, we as individuals often find it difficult to set and stick to goals, and, likewise, leaders often find it difficult to instill a goal-oriented attitude in their organizations. Imagine the added difficulty if conditions are harsh or the odds of success are overwhelming. Viktor Frankl, a Holocaust survivor, demonstrates the importance of goals and provides an example of goal setting in horrendous conditions in the excerpts from *Man's Search for Meaning*. There are some powerful hints about how to be a better goal achiever contained in the article "The Power of Goals," by Stephen R. Covey, A. Roger Merrill, and Rebecca R. Merrill. In "Seven Reasons Why Carrots and Sticks (Often) Don't Work," Daniel H. Pink reminds us that goals are not inherently good; they must be well-conceived and appropriate.

The Film Studies for this Unit include *Mr. Smith Goes to Washington*, the story of a naïve man who is appointed to fill a vacancy in the U.S. Senate. There, he must navigate through corruption and scandal to achieve his goal. *Argo*, the other film for this unit, chronicles the efforts to achieve the goal of rescuing hostages during the 1980 U.S. hostage crisis in Iran.

The Exercise for this Unit provides an experience working with others to arrive at a consensus about community priorities and setting community goals that follow the criteria for effective goal setting established in the Unit.

Learning Objectives

- Recognize the importance of clearly defined goals for effective leadership

- Recognize the criteria for effective goal setting in various settings—personal life, group, and organizations

- Formulate personal goals that translate into specific and concrete actions

- Apply concepts of effective goal setting to personal, interpersonal, and career development

- Appreciate the contributions made by the humanities readings in this Unit toward learning about leading with goals

CLASSIC CASE

Pygmalion

By George Bernard Shaw (1856–1950)
Irish Dramatist

Introduction and Historical Background

George Bernard Shaw based his play *Pygmalion* on the classical Greek legend of Pygmalion, a sculptor and king of Cyprus. Though he hates women, Pygmalion falls in love with a statue he created of Aphrodite. He prays earnestly to the goddess Aphrodite and she gives life to the statue. Pygmalion ends up marrying the living statue. In Shaw's *Pygmalion*, Professor Henry Higgins represents Pygmalion, a phonetics expert, researcher, and teacher. He begins teaching Eliza Doolittle, a Cockney flower girl from the streets of Covent Garden, as a challenge to his skills and his notion that speech is the ultimate definer of class. Eliza transforms from a "guttersnipe" into an elegant woman, and in the process, she develops feelings for the professor that he only slowly and slightly realizes are mutual. He admires, even loves, his "creation" (a lady with perfect speech) as the sculptor Pygmalion loved his living statue, but in true life, the creation is more complicated and problematic than simply "a lady with perfect speech," and Higgins' callous personality cannot grow to accept the complexity of the relationship.

The play is about more than the relationship between Higgins and his "creation," Eliza, however. It is also a commentary on the artificiality of class distinctions. It is an example of how Shaw never wrote his essays and plays solely to entertain; the witty, humorous or satirical stories were vehicles for his theories. He is known as a dramatist, but also as a critic and social reformer. He wrote a great deal on socialism, politics, and economics, and also counted spelling reform and vegetarianism among his causes. He began writing purposeful, theoretical drama in the 1880s in the style of Henrik Ibsen (Norwegian, 1828–1906; known for bringing contemporary ideas and issues to the stage), as well as musical and literary criticism in London at the suggestion of a friend who thought his wit would work better in these forms than it had in the five failed socialist novels he wrote before 1884. His early plays were either censored or refused production until 1900 when U.S. and German theaters produced a few of his plays. Success came in England when renowned actor and dramatist H. Granville-Barker promoted Shaw's plays. Shaw wrote his best plays, including *Pygmalion*, just before, during, and after World War I. He was outspoken against British policy during the war, but his world-wide fame by that time allowed him to speak and write as he pleased. Shaw received the Nobel Prize in literature in 1925.

Pygmalion contains insights about the transformational power of goals. Higgins is a transformational leader by the power of his commitment and drive to achieve a goal in which he believes and for which he believes he has the skill to lead.

The fictional Professor Higgins is a phonetician—a linguist who deals with the sounds of speech and their production, combination, description, and representation by written symbols. For Eliza, goal setting is powerfully transformational because the goal sets her on a path to achieve a dream. The goal is related to Higgins' higher purpose, which mirrors Shaw's in real life. Shaw had a lifelong interest in phonetics, shorthand, and reformed spelling and was convinced that the English alphabet could not represent accurately all the sounds of the language. Readers will notice Shaw's phonetic spelling and unique, personal "rules" in this excerpt. He actually developed a new alphabet in which each letter stood for one sound and one sound only. In addition, Shaw, again somewhat like his character Higgins, was intensely interested in debating about the relations between the social classes.

For Higgins, dialect is the greatest barrier that keeps the classes separate. He believes completely that if people erase traces of their class dialects, then no one can ever question their background or discriminate in employment or social matters. For Higgins, equal speech creates equal opportunity. This is his vision, and as the story unfolds, he sets out to create this vision with the goal of erasing Eliza's dialect. As are many visionaries, Higgins is quirky, confident, and passionate, even forceful or obstinate about his goal. On this matter there are additional insights on goal setting and on leadership in general—for those times when a leader has difficulty connecting with people. Such a quirky visionary as Higgins needs talented managers and followers to help communicate and work toward the goal, especially since he is often exceptionally insulting and rude. The connection between Higgins and Eliza is tenuous, and neither can achieve the goal without the other. Other characters in the play aid Higgins to hold the relationship, and thus the goal, together.

Points to Consider

1. Why does Eliza seek out Professor Higgins in spite of her first, rude encounter with him? How do you handle situations where you must interact with someone who has not made a good initial impression on you?

2. How do Higgins' housekeeper, Mrs. Pearce, and Colonel Pickering both help Professor Higgins with the goal even though they do not have the phonetics expertise?

3. Psychologists say that the most motivational goals have some level of difficulty, are very specific, and have concrete rewards. Does the goal described in *Pygmalion* meet these standards?

4. What are some ways in which organizations form their own, internal "class distinctions"? Are such distinctions ever justifiable?

5. Is there merit in judging people based on things like appearance and speech or is it invariably unethical to do so?

Pygmalion

(Excerpts)

Note to readers: As mentioned in the Introduction and Historical Background, Shaw uses phonetic spelling and unique, personal "rules" in this excerpt; they are not errors.

ACT I

London at 11:15 p.m. Torrents of heavy summer rain. Cab whistles blowing frantically in all directions. Pedestrians running for shelter into the portico of St. Paul's church (not Wren's cathedral but Inigo Jones's church in Covent Garden vegetable market), among them a lady and her daughter in evening dress. All are peering out gloomily at the rain, except one man with his back turned to the rest, wholly preoccupied with a notebook in which he is writing.

The church clock strikes the first quarter.

The Daughter: *[in the space between the central pillars, close to the one on her left]* I'm getting chilled to the bone. What can Freddy be doing all this time? He's been gone twenty minutes.

The Mother: *[on her daughter's right]* Not so long. But he ought to have got us a cab by this.

A Bystander: *[on the lady's right]* He wont get no cab not until half-past eleven, missus, when they come back after dropping their theatre fares.

The Mother: But we must have a cab. We cant stand here until half-past eleven. It's too bad.

A Bystander: Well, it aint my fault, missus.

The Daughter: If Freddy had a bit of gumption, he would have got one at the theatre door.

The Mother: What could he have done, poor boy?

The Daughter: Other people got cabs. Why couldn't he?

Freddy rushes in out of the rain from the Southampton Street side, and comes between them closing a dripping umbrella. He is a young man of twenty, in evening dress, very wet round the ankles.

The Daughter: Well, havnt you got a cab?

Freddy: Theres not one to be had for love or money.

The Mother: Oh, Freddy, there must be one. You cant have tried.

The Daughter: It's too tiresome. Do you expect us to go and get one ourselves?

Freddy: I tell you theyre all engaged. The rain was so sudden: nobody was prepared; and everybody had to take a cab. Ive been to Charing Cross one way and nearly to Ludgate Circus the other; and they were all engaged.

The Mother: Did you try Trafalgar Square?

Freddy: There wasnt one at Trafalgar Square.

The Daughter: Did you try?

Freddy: I tried as far as Charing Cross Station. Did you expect me to walk to Hammersmith?

The Daughter: You havent tried at all.

The Mother: You really are very helpless, Freddy. Go again; and dont come back until you have found a cab.

Freddy: I shall simply get soaked for nothing.

The Daughter: And what about us? Are we to stay here all night in the draught, with next to nothing on? You selfish pig—

Freddy: Oh, very well: I'll go, I'll go. *[He opens his umbrella and dashes off Strandwards, but comes into collision with a flower girl, who is hurrying in for shelter, knocking her basket out of her hands. A blinding flash of lightning, followed instantly by a rattling peal of thunder, orchestrates the incident].*

The Flower Girl: Nah then, Freddy: look wh' y' gowin, deah.

Freddy: Sorry *[he rushes off].*

The Flower Girl: *[picking up her scattered flowers and replacing them in the basket]* Theres menners f' yer! Te-oo banches o voylets trod into the mad. *[She sits down on the plinth of the column, sorting her flowers, on the lady's right. She is not at all an attractive person. She is perhaps eighteen, perhaps twenty, hardly older. She wears a little sailor hat of black straw that has long been exposed to the dust and soot of London and has seldom if ever been brushed. Her hair needs washing rather badly: its mousy color can hardly be natural. She wears a shoddy black coat that reaches nearly to her knees and is shaped to her waist. She has a brown skirt with a coarse apron. Her boots are much the worse for wear. She is no doubt as clean as she can afford to be; but compared to the ladies she is very dirty. Her features are no worse than theirs; but their condition leaves something to be desired; and she needs the services of a dentist].*

The Mother: How do you know that my son's name is Freddy, pray?

The Flower Girl: Ow, eez ye-ooa san, is e? Wal, fewd dan y' de-ooty bawmz a mather should, eed now bettern to spawl a pore gel's flahrzn than ran awy athaht pyin. Will ye-oo py me f'them? *[Here, with apologies, this desperate attempt to represent her dialect without a phonetic alphabet must be abandoned as unintelligible outside London].*

The Daughter: Do nothing of the sort, mother. The idea!

The Mother: Please allow me, Clara. Have you any pennies?

The Daughter: No. I've nothing smaller than sixpence.

The Flower Girl: *[hopefully]* I can give you change for a tanner, kind lady.

The Mother: *[to Clara]* Give it to me. *[Clara parts reluctantly].* Now *[to the girl]* This is for your flowers.

The Flower Girl: Thank you kindly, lady.

The Daughter: Make her give you the change. These things are only a penny a bunch.

The Mother: Do hold your tongue, Clara. *[To the girl]* You can keep the change.

The Flower Girl: Oh, thank you, lady.

The Mother: Now tell me how you know that young gentleman's name.

The Flower Girl: I didnt.

The Mother: I heard you call him by it. Dont try to deceive me.

The Flower Girl: *[protesting]* Who's trying to deceive you? I called him Freddy or Charlie same as you might yourself if you was talking to a stranger and wished to be pleasant.

The Daughter: Sixpence thrown away! Really, mamma, you might have spared Freddy that. *[She retreats in disgust behind the pillar].*

An elderly gentleman of the amiable military type rushes into shelter, and closes a dripping umbrella. He is in the same plight as Freddy, very wet about the ankles. He is in evening dress, with a light overcoat. He takes the place left vacant by the daughter.

The Gentleman: Phew!

The Mother: *[to the gentleman]* Oh, sir, is there any sign of its stopping?

The Gentleman: I'm afraid not. It started worse than ever about two minutes ago *[he goes to the plinth beside the flower girl; puts up his foot on it; and stoops to turn down his trouser ends].*

The Mother: Oh, dear! *[She retires sadly and joins her daughter].*

The Flower Girl: *[taking advantage of the military gentleman's proximity to establish friendly relations with him]* If it's worse it's a sign it's nearly over. So cheer up, Captain; and buy a flower off a poor girl.

The Gentleman: I'm sorry, I havnt any change.

The Flower Girl: I can give you change, Captain.

The Gentleman: For a sovereign? Ive nothing less.

The Flower Girl: Garn! Oh do buy a flower off me, Captain. I can change half-a-crown. Take this for tuppence.

The Gentleman: Now dont be troublesome: theres a good girl. *[Trying his pockets]* I really havnt any change—Stop: heres three hapence, if thats any use to you *[he retreats to the other pillar].*

The Flower Girl: *[disappointed, but thinking three halfpence better than nothing]* Thank you, sir.

The Bystander: *[to the girl]* You be careful: give him a flower for it. Theres a bloke here behind taking down every blessed word youre saying. *[All turn to the man who is taking notes].*

The Flower Girl: *[springing up terrified]* I aint done nothing wrong by speaking to the gentleman. Ive a right to sell flowers if I keep off the kerb. *[Hysterically]* I'm a respectable girl: so help me, I never spoke to him except to ask him to buy a flower off me.

General hubbub, mostly sympathetic to the flower girl, but deprecating her excessive sensibility. Cries of Dont start hollerin. Whos hurting you? Nobody's going to touch you. Whats the good of fussing? Steady on. Easy, easy, etc., *come from the elderly staid spectators, who pat her comfortingly. Less patient ones bid her shut her head, or ask her roughly what is wrong with her. A remoter group, not knowing what the matter is, crowd in and increase the noise with question and answer:* Whats the row? What-she do? Where is he? A tec taking her down. What! him? Yes: him over there: Took money off the gentleman, etc.

The Flower Girl: *[breaking through them to the gentleman, crying wildly]* Oh, sir, dont let him charge me. You dunno what it means to me. Theyll take away my character and drive me on the streets for speaking to gentlemen. They —

The Note Taker: *[coming forward on her right, the rest crowding after him]* There! there! there! there! whos hurting you, you silly girl? What do you take me for?

The Bystander: It's aw rawt: he's a gentleman: look at his bə-oots. *[Explaining to the note taker]* She thought you was a copper's nark, sir.

The Note Taker: *[with quick interest]* Whats a copper's nark?

The Bystander: *[inapt at definition]* It's a— well, it's a copper's nark, as you might say. What else would you call it? A sort of informer.

The Flower Girl: *[still hysterical]* I take my Bible oath I never said a word —

The Note Taker: *[overbearing but good-humored]* Oh, shut up, shut up. Do I look like a policeman?

The Flower Girl: *[far from reassured]* Then what did you take down my words for? How do I know whether you took me down right? You just shew me what youve wrote about me. *[The note taker opens his book and holds it steadily under her nose, though the pressure of the mob trying to read it over his shoulders would upset a weaker man]*. Whats that? That aint proper writing. I cant read that.

The Note Taker: I can. *[Reads, reproducing her pronunciation exactly]* "Cheer ap, Keptin; n' baw ya flahr orf a pore gel."

The Flower Girl: *[much distressed]* It's because I called him Captain. I meant no harm. *[To the gentleman]* Oh, sir, dont let him lay a charge agen me for a word like that. You —

The Gentleman: Charge! I make no charge. *[To the note taker]* Really, sir, if you are a detective, you need not begin protecting me against molestation by young women until I ask you. Anybody could see that the girl meant no harm.

The Bystanders Generally: *[demonstrating against police espionage]* Course they could. What business is it of yours? You mind your own affairs. He wants promotion, he does. Taking down people's words! Girl never said a word to him. What harm if she did? Nice thing a girl cant shelter from the rain without being insulted, etc., etc., etc. *[She is conducted by the more sympathetic demonstrators back to her plinth, where she resumes her seat and struggles with her emotion]*.

The Bystander: He aint a tec. Hes a blooming busybody: thats what he is. I tell you, look at his bə-oots.

The Note Taker: *[turning on him genially]* And how are all your people down at Selsey?

The Bystander: *[suspiciously]* Who told you my people come from Selsey?

The Note Taker: Never you mind. They did. *[To the girl]* How do you come to be up so far east? You were born in Lisson Grove.

The Flower Girl: *[appalled]* Oh, what harm is there in my leaving Lisson Grove? It wasnt fit for a pig to live in; and I had to pay four-and-six a week. *[In tears]* Oh, boo—hoo—oo—

The Note Taker: Live where you like; but stop that noise.

The Gentleman: *[to the girl]* Come, come! he cant touch you: you have a right to live where you please.

A Sarcastic Bystander: *[thrusting himself between the note taker and the gentleman]* Park Lane, for instance. I'd like to go into the Housing Question with you, I would.

The Flower Girl: *[subsiding into a brooding melancholy over her basket, and talking very low-spiritedly to herself]* I'm a good girl, I am.

The Sarcastic Bystander: *[not attending to her]* Do you know where I come from?

The Note Taker: *[promptly]* Hoxton.

Titterings. Popular interest in the note taker's performance increases.

The Sarcastic One: *[amazed]* Well, who said I didnt? Bly me! You know everything, you do.

The Flower Girl: *[still nursing her sense of injury]* Aint no call to meddle with me, he aint.

The Bystander: *[to her]* Of course he aint. Dont you stand it from him. *[To the note taker]* See here: what call have you to know about people what never offered to meddle with you?

The Flower Girl: Let him say what he likes. I dont want to have no truck with him.

The Bystander: You take us for dirt under your feet, dont you? Catch you taking liberties with a gentleman!

The Sarcastic Bystander: Yes: tell him where he come from if you want to go fortune-telling.

The Note Taker: Cheltenham, Harrow, Cambridge, and India.

The Gentleman: Quite right.

Great laughter. Reaction in the note taker's favor. Exclamations of He knows all about it. Told him proper. Hear him tell the toff where he come from? *etc.*

The Gentleman: May I ask, sir, do you do this for your living at a music hall?

The Note Taker: I've thought of that. Perhaps I shall some day.

The rain has stopped; and the persons on the outside of the crowd begin to drop off.

The Flower Girl: *[resenting the reaction]* He's no gentleman, he aint, to interfere with a poor girl.

The Daughter: *[out of patience, pushing her way rudely to the front and displacing the gentleman, who politely retires to the other side of the pillar]* What on earth is Freddy doing? I shall get pneumonia if I stay in this draught any longer.

The Note Taker: *[to himself, hastily making a note of her pronunciation of "monia"]* Earlscourt.

The Daughter: *[violently]* Will you please keep your impertinent remarks to yourself?

The Note Taker: Did I say that out loud? I didnt mean to. I beg your pardon. Your mother's Epsom, unmistakeably.

The Mother: *[advancing between her daughter and the note taker]* How very curious! I was brought up in Largelady Park, near Epsom.

The Note Taker: *[uproariously amused]* Ha! ha! What a devil of a name! Excuse me. *[To the daughter]* You want a cab, do you?

The Daughter: Don't dare speak to me.

The Mother: Oh, please, please Clara. *[Her daughter repudiates her with an angry shrug and retires haughtily]* We should be so grateful to you, sir, if you found us a cab. *[The note taker produces a whistle]* Oh, thank you. *[She joins her daughter]*.

The note taker blows a piercing blast.

The Sarcastic Bystander: There! I knowed he was a plain-clothes copper.

The Bystander: That aint a police whistle: thats a sporting whistle.

The Flower Girl: *[still preoccupied with her wounded feelings]* He's no right to take away my character. My character is the same to me as any lady's.

The Note Taker: I dont know whether youve noticed it; but the rain stopped about two minutes ago.

The Bystander: So it has. Why didnt you say so before? and us losing our time listening to your silliness! *[He walks off towards the Strand].*

The Sarcastic Bystander: I can tell where you come from. You come from Anwell. Go back there.

The Note Taker: *[helpfully]* Hanwell.

The Sarcastic Bystander: *[affecting great distinction of speech]* Thenk you, teacher. Haw haw! So long *[he touches his hat with mock respect and strolls off].*

The Flower Girl: Frightening people like that! How would he like it himself.

The Mother: It's quite fine now, Clara. We can walk to a motor bus. Come. *[She gathers her skirts above her ankles and hurries off towards the Strand].*

The Daughter: But the cab—*[her mother is out of hearing].* Oh, how tiresome! *[She follows angrily].*

All the rest have gone except the note taker, the gentleman, and the flower girl, who sits arranging her basket, and still pitying herself in murmurs.

The Flower Girl: Poor girl! Hard enough for her to live without being worried and chivied.

The Gentleman: *[returning to his former place on the note taker's left]* How do you do it, if I may ask?

The Note Taker: Simply phonetics. The science of speech. Thats my profession: also my hobby. Happy is the man who can make a living by his hobby! You can spot an Irishman or a Yorkshireman by his brogue. I can place any man within six miles. I can place him within two miles in London. Sometimes within two streets.

The Flower Girl: Ought to be ashamed of himself, unmanly coward!

The Gentleman: But is there a living in that?

The Note Taker: Oh yes. Quite a fat one. This is an age of upstarts. Men begin in Kentish Town with £80 a year, and end in Park Lane with a hundred thousand. They want to drop Kentish Town; but they give themselves away every time they open their mouths. Now I can teach them —

The Flower Girl: Let him mind his own business and leave a poor girl —

The Note Taker: *[explosively]* Woman: cease this detestable boohooing instantly; or else seek the shelter of some other place of worship.

The Flower Girl: *[with feeble defiance]* Ive a right to be here if I like, same as you.

The Note Taker: A woman who utters such depressing and disgusting sounds has no right to be anywhere—no right to live. Remember that you are a human being with a soul and the divine gift of articulate speech: that your native language is the language of Shakespeare and Milton and The Bible; and dont sit there crooning like a bilious pigeon.

The Flower Girl: *[quite overwhelmed, and looking up at him in mingled wonder and deprecation without daring to raise her head]* Ah-ah-ah-ow-ow-ow-oo!

The Note Taker: *[whipping out his book]* Heavens! what a sound! *[He writes; then holds out the book and reads, reproducing her vowels exactly]* Ah-ah-ah-ow-ow-ow-oo!

The Flower Girl: *[tickled by the performance, and laughing in spite of herself]* Garn!

The Note Taker: You see this creature with her kerbstone English: the English that will keep her in the gutter to the end of her days. Well, sir, in three months I could pass that girl off as a duchess at an ambassador's garden party. I could even get her a place as lady's maid or shop assistant, which requires better English.

The Flower Girl: Whats that you say?

The Note Taker: Yes, you squashed cabbage leaf, you disgrace to the noble architecture of these columns, you incarnate insult to the English language: I could pass you off as the Queen of Sheba. *[To the Gentleman]* Can you believe that?

The Gentleman: Of course I can. I am myself a student of Indian dialects; and —

The Note Taker: *[eagerly]* Are you? Do you know Colonel Pickering, the author of Spoken Sanscrit?

The Gentleman: I am Colonel Pickering. Who are you?

The Note Taker: Henry Higgins, author of Higgins's Universal Alphabet.

Pickering: *[with enthusiasm]* I came from India to meet you.

Higgins: I was going to India to meet you.

Pickering: Where do you live?

Higgins: 27A Wimpole Street. Come and see me tomorrow.

Pickering: I'm at the Carlton. Come with me now and lets have a jaw over some supper.

Higgins: Right you are.

The Flower Girl: *[to Pickering, as he passes her]* Buy a flower, kind gentleman. I'm short for my lodging.

Pickering: I really havnt any change. I'm sorry *[he goes away]*.

Higgins: *[shocked at girl's mendacity]* Liar. You said you could change half-a-crown.

The Flower Girl: *[rising in desperation]* You ought to be stuffed with nails, you ought. *[Flinging the basket at his feet]* Take the whole blooming basket for sixpence.

The church clock strikes the second quarter.

Higgins: *[hearing in it the voice of God, rebuking him for his Pharisaic want of charity to the poor girl]* A reminder. *[He raises his hat solemnly; then throws a handful of money into the basket and follows Pickering]*.

The Flower Girl: *[picking up a half-crown]* Ah-ow-ooh! *[Picking up a couple of florins]* Aaah-ow-ooh! *[Picking up several coins]* Aaaaaah-ow-ooh! *[Picking up a half-sovereign]* Aaaaaaaaaaaaah-ow-ooh!!!

Freddy: *[springing out of a taxicab]* Got one at last. Hallo! *[To the girl]* Where are the two ladies that were here?

The Flower Girl: They walked to the bus when the rain stopped.

Freddy: And left me with a cab on my hands. Damnation!

The Flower Girl: *[with grandeur]* Never you mind, young man. I'm going home in a taxi. *[She sails off to the cab. The driver puts his hand behind him and holds the door firmly shut against her. Quite understanding his mistrust, she shews him her handful of money.]* A taxi fare aint no object to me, Charlie. *[He grins and opens the door]*. Here. What about the basket?

The Taximan: Give it here. Tuppence extra.

Liza: No: I dont want nobody to see it. *[She crushes it into the cab and gets in continuing the conversation through the window]* Goodbye, Freddy.

Freddy: *[dazedly raising his hat]* Goodbye.

Taximan: Where to?

Liza: Bucknam Pellis *[Buckingham Palace]*.

The Taximan: What d'ye mean—Bucknam Pellis?

Liza: Dont you know where it is? In the Green Park, where the King lives. Goodbye, Freddy. Dont let me keep you standing there. Goodbye.

Freddy: Goodbye. *[He goes].*

The Taximan: Here? Whats this about Bucknam Pellis? What business have you at Bucknam Pellis?

Liza: Of course I havnt none. But I wasnt going to let him know that. You drive me home.

The Taximan: And wheres home?

Liza: Angel Court, Drury Lane, next Meiklejohn's oil shop.

Taximan: That sounds more like it, Judy. *[He drives off].*

Let us follow the taxi to the entrance of Angel Court, a narrow little archway between two shops, one of them Meiklejohn's oil shop. When it stops there, Eliza gets out, dragging her basket with her.

Liza: How much?

Taximan: *[indicating the taximeter]* Cant you read? A shilling.

Liza: A shilling for two minutes!!

Taximan: Two minutes or ten: it's all the same.

Liza: Well, I dont call it right.

Taximan: Ever been in a taxi before?

Liza: *[with dignity]* Hundreds and thousands of times, young man.

Taximan: *[laughing at her]* Good for you, Judy. Keep the shilling, darling, with best love from all at home. Good luck! *[He drives off].*

Liza: *[humiliated]* Impidence!

She picks up the basket and trudges up the alley with it to her lodging: a small room with very old wall paper hanging loose in the damp places. A broken pane in the window is mended with paper. A portrait of a popular actor and a fashion plate of ladies' dresses, all wildly beyond poor Eliza's means, both torn from newspapers, are pinned up on the wall. A birdcage hangs in the window; but its tenant died long ago: it remains as a memorial only.

These are the only visible luxuries: the rest is the irreducible minimum of poverty's needs: a wretched bed heaped with all sorts of coverings that have any warmth in them, a draped packing case with a basin and jug on it and a little looking glass over it, a chair and table, the refuse of some suburban kitchen, and an American alarm clock on the shelf above the unused fireplace: the whole lighted with a gas lamp with a penny in the slot meter. Rent: four shillings a week.

Here Eliza, chronically weary, but too excited to go to bed, sits, counting her new riches and dreaming and planning what to do with them, until the gas goes out, when she enjoys for the first time the sensation of being able to put in another penny without grudging it. This prodigal mood does not extinguish her gnawing sense of the need for economy sufficiently to prevent her from calculating that she can dream and plan in bed more cheaply and warmly than sitting up without a fire. So she takes off her shawl and skirt and adds them to the miscellaneous bedclothes. Then she kicks off her shoes and gets into bed without any further change.

ACT II

Next day at 11 a.m. Higgins's laboratory in Wimpole Street. It is a room on the first floor, looking on the street, and was meant for the drawing room. The double doors are in the middle of the back wall; and persons entering find in the corner to their right two tall file cabinets at right angles to one another against the walls. In this corner stands a flat writing-table, on which are a phonograph, a laryngoscope, a row of tiny organ pipes with a bellows, a set of lamp chimneys for singing flames with burners attached to a gas plug in the wall by an indiarubber tube, several tuning-forks of different sizes, a life-size image of half a human head, shewing in section the vocal organs, and a box containing a supply of wax cylinders for the phonograph.

Further down the room, on the same side, is a fireplace, with a comfortable leather-covered easy-chair at the side of the hearth nearest the door, and a coal-scuttle. There is a clock on the mantelpiece. Between the fireplace and the phonograph table is a stand for newspapers.

On the other side of the central door, to the left of the visitor, is a cabinet of shallow drawers. On it is a telephone and the telephone directory. The corner beyond, and most of the side wall, is occupied by a grand piano, with the keyboard at the end furthest from the door, and a bench for the player extending the full length of the keyboard. On the piano is a dessert dish heaped with fruit and sweets, mostly chocolates.

The middle of the room is clear. Besides the easy-chair, the piano bench, and two chairs at the phonograph table, there is one stray chair. It stands near the fireplace. On the walls, engravings; mostly Piranesis and mezzotint portraits. No paintings.

Pickering is seated at the table, putting down some cards and a tuning-fork which he has been using. Higgins is standing up near him, closing two or three file drawers which are hanging out. He appears in the morning light as a robust, vital, appetizing sort of man of forty or thereabouts, dressed in a professional-looking black frock-coat with a white linen collar and black silk tie. He is of the energetic, scientific type, heartily, even violently interested in everything that can be studied as a scientific subject, and careless about himself and other people, including their feelings. He is, in fact, but for his years and size, rather like a very impetuous baby "taking notice" eagerly and loudly, and requiring almost as much watching to keep him out of unintended mischief. His manner varies from genial bullying when he is in a good humor to stormy petulance when anything goes wrong; but he is so entirely frank and void of malice that he remains likeable even in his least reasonable moments.*

Higgins: *[as he shuts the last drawer]* Well, I think thats the whole show.

Pickering: It's really amazing. I havnt taken half of it in, you know.

Higgins: Would you like to go over any of it again?

Pickering: *[rising and coming to the fireplace, where he plants himself with his back to the fire]* No, thank you; not now. I'm quite done up for this morning.

Higgins: *[following him, and standing beside him on his left]* Tired of listening to sounds?

Pickering: Yes. It's a fearful strain. I rather fancied myself because I can pronounce twenty-four distinct vowel sounds; but your hundred and thirty beat me. I cant hear a bit of difference between most of them.

Higgins: *[chuckling, and going over to the piano to eat sweets]* Oh, that comes with practice. You hear no difference at first; but you keep on listening, and presently you find theyre all as different as A from B. *[Mrs. Pearce looks in: she is Higgins's housekeeper]* Whats the matter?

Mrs. Pearce: *[hesitating, evidently perplexed]* A young woman wants to see you, sir.

Higgins: A young woman! What does she want?

Mrs. Pearce: Well, sir, she says youll be glad to see her when you know what shes come about. Shes quite a common girl, sir. Very common indeed. I should have sent her away, only I thought perhaps you wanted her to talk into your machines. I hope Ive not done wrong; but really you see such queer people sometimes—youll excuse me, I'm sure, sir —

Higgins: Oh, thats all right, Mrs. Pearce. Has she an interesting accent?

Mrs. Pearce: Oh, something dreadful, sir, really. I dont know how you can take an interest in it.

Higgins: *[to Pickering]* Lets have her up. Shew her up, Mrs. Pearce *[he rushes across to his working table and picks out a cylinder to use on the phonograph]*.

Mrs. Pearce: *[only half resigned to it]* Very well, sir. It's for you to say. *[She goes downstairs]*.

Higgins: This is rather a bit of luck. I'll shew you how I make records. We'll set her talking; and I'll take it down first in Bell's Visible Speech; then in broad Romic; and then we'll get her on the phonograph so that you can turn her on as often as you like with the written transcript before you.

Mrs. Pearce: *[returning]* This is the young woman, sir.

The flower girl enters in state. She has a hat with three ostrich feathers, orange, sky-blue, and red. She has a nearly clean apron, and the shoddy coat has been tidied a little. The pathos of this deplorable figure, with its innocent vanity and consequential air, touches Pickering, who has already straightened himself in the presence of Mrs. Pearce. But as to Higgins, the only distinction he makes between men and women is that when he is neither bullying nor exclaiming to the heavens against some feather-weight cross, he coaxes women as a child coaxes its nurse when it wants to get anything out of her.

Higgins: *[brusquely, recognizing her with unconcealed disappointment, and at once, babylike, making an intolerable grievance of it]* Why, this is the girl I jotted down last night. Shes no use: Ive got all the records I want of the Lisson Grove lingo; and I'm not going to waste another cylinder on it. *[To the girl]* Be off with you: I dont want you.

The Flower Girl: Dont you be so saucy. You aint heard what I come for yet. *[To Mrs. Pearce, who is waiting at the door for further instruction]* Did you tell him I come in a taxi?

Mrs. Pearce: Nonsense, girl! what do you think a gentleman like Mr. Higgins cares what you came in?

The Flower Girl: Oh, we are proud! He aint above giving lessons, not him: I heard him say so. Well, I aint come here to ask for any compliment; and if my money's not good enough I can go elsewhere.

Higgins: Good enough for what?

The Flower Girl: Good enough for yə-oo. Now you know, dont you? I'm come to have lessons, I am. And to pay for em t -oo: make no mistake.

Higgins: *[stupent]* Well ! ! ! *[Recovering his breath with a gasp]* What do you expect me to say to you?

The Flower Girl: Well, if you was a gentleman, you might ask me to sit down, I think. Dont I tell you I'm bringing you business?

Higgins: Pickering: shall we ask this baggage to sit down or shall we throw her out of the window?

The Flower Girl: *[running away in terror to the piano, where she turns at bay]* Ah-ah-ah-ow-ow-ow-oo! *[Wounded and whimpering]* I wont be called a baggage when Ive offered to pay like any lady.

Motionless, the two men stare at her from the other side of the room, amazed.

Pickering: *[gently]* What is it you want?

The Flower Girl: I want to be a lady in a flower shop stead of sellin at the corner of Tottenham Court Road. But they wont take me unless I can talk more genteel. He said he could teach me. Well, here I am ready to pay him—not asking any favor—and he treats me as if I was dirt.

Mrs. Pearce: How can you be such a foolish ignorant girl as to think you could afford to pay Mr. Higgins?

The Flower Girl: Why shouldnt I? I know what lessons cost as well as you do; and I'm ready to pay.

Higgins: How much?

The Flower Girl: [coming back to him, triumphant] Now youre talking! I thought youd come off it when you saw a chance of getting back a bit of what you chucked at me last night. [Confidentially] Youd had a drop in, hadnt you?

Higgins: [peremptorily] Sit down.

The Flower Girl: Oh, if youre going to make a compliment of it —

Higgins: [thundering at her] Sit down.

Mrs. Pearce: [severely] Sit down, girl. Do as youre told.

The Flower Girl: Ah-ah-ah-ow-ow-oo! [She stands, half rebellious, half bewildered].

Pickering: [very courteous] Wont you sit down? [He places the stray chair near the hearthrug between himself and Higgins.]

Liza: [coyly] Dont mind if I do. [She sits down. Pickering returns to the hearthrug].

Higgins: Whats your name?

The Flower Girl: Liza Doolittle.

Higgins: [declaiming gravely] Eliza, Elizabeth, Betsy and Bess, They went to the woods to get a bird nes':

Pickering: They found a nest with four eggs in it:

Higgins: They took one apiece, and left three in it.

They laugh heartily at their own fun.

Liza: Oh, dont be silly.

Mrs. Pearce: [placing herself behind Eliza's chair] You mustnt speak to the gentleman like that.

Liza: Well, why wont he speak sensible to me?

Higgins: Come back to business. How much do you propose to pay me for the lessons?

Liza: Oh, I know whats right. A lady friend of mine gets French lessons for eighteenpence an hour from a real French gentleman. Well, you wouldnt have the face to ask me the same for teaching me my own language as you would for French; so I wont give more than a shilling. Take it or leave it.

Higgins: [walking up and down the room, rattling his keys and his cash in his pockets] You know, Pickering, if you consider a shilling, not as a simple shilling, but as a percentage of this girl's income, it works out as fully equivalent to sixty or seventy guineas from a millionaire.

Pickering: How so?

Higgins: Figure it out. A millionaire has about £150 a day. She earns about half-a-crown.

Liza: [haughtily] Who told you I only —

Higgins: [continuing] She offers me two-fifths of her day's income for a lesson. Two-fifths of a millionaire's income for a day would be somewhere about £60. It's handsome. By George, it's enormous! it's the biggest offer I ever had.

Liza: [rising, terrified] Sixty pounds! What are you talking about? I never offered you sixty pounds. Where would I get—

Higgins: Hold your tongue.

Liza: [weeping] But I aint got sixty pounds. Oh —

Mrs. Pearce: Dont cry, you silly girl. Sit down. Nobody is going to touch your money.

Higgins: Somebody is going to touch you, with a broomstick, if you dont stop snivelling. Sit down.

Liza: [obeying slowly] Ah-ah-ah-ow-oo-o! One would think you was my father.

Higgins: If I decide to teach you, I'll be worse than two fathers to you. Here [he offers her his silk handkerchief]!

Liza: Whats this for?

Higgins: To wipe your eyes. To wipe any part of your face that feels moist. Remember: thats your handkerchief; and thats your sleeve. Dont mistake the one for the other if you wish to become a lady in a shop.

Liza, utterly bewildered, stares helplessly at him.

Mrs. Pearce: It's no use talking to her like that, Mr. Higgins: she doesnt understand you. Besides, youre quite wrong: she doesnt do it that way at all [she takes the handkerchief].

Liza: [snatching it] Here! You give me that handkerchief. He gev it to me, not to you.

Pickering: [laughing] He did. I think it must be regarded as her property, Mrs. Pearce.

Mrs. Pearce: [resigning herself] Serve you right, Mr. Higgins.

Pickering: Higgins: I'm interested. What about the ambassador's garden party? I'll say youre the greatest teacher alive if you make that good. I'll bet you all the expenses of the experiment you cant do it. And I'll pay for the lessons.

Liza: Oh, you are real good. Thank you, Captain.

Higgins: [tempted, looking at her] It's almost irresistible. She's so deliciously low—so horribly dirty —

Liza: [protesting extremely Ah-ah-ah-ah-ow-ow-oo-oo!!!

Pickering: Oh come, Higgins! be reasonable.

Mrs. Pearce: [resolutely] You must be reasonable, Mr. Higgins: really you must. You cant walk over everybody like this.

Higgins, thus scolded, subsides. The hurricane is succeeded by a zephyr of amiable surprise.

Higgins: [with professional exquisiteness of modulation] I walk over everybody! My dear Mrs. Pearce, my dear Pickering, I never had the slightest intention of walking over anyone. All I propose is that we should be kind to this poor girl. We must help her to prepare and fit herself for her new station in life. If I did not express myself clearly it was because I did not wish to hurt her delicacy, or yours.

Eliza, reassured, steals back to her chair.

Mrs. Pearce: [to Pickering] Well, did you ever hear anything like that, sir?

Pickering: [laughing heartily] Never, Mrs. Pearce: never.

Higgins: [patiently] Whats the matter?

Mrs. Pearce: Well, the matter is, sir, that you cant take a girl up like that as if you were picking up a pebble on the beach.

Higgins: Why not?

Mrs. Pearce: Why not! But you dont know anything about her. What about her parents? She may be married.

Liza: Garn!

Higgins: There! As the girl very properly says, Garn! Married indeed! Dont you know that a woman of that class looks a worn out drudge of fifty a year after shes married.

Liza: Whood marry me?

Higgins: [suddenly resorting to the most thrillingly beautiful low tones in his best elocutionary style] By George, Eliza, the streets will be strewn with the bodies of men shooting themselves for your sake before Ive done with you.

UNIT
6

Mrs. Pearce: Nonsense, sir. You mustnt talk like that to her.

Liza: [rising and squaring herself determinedly] I'm going away. He's off his chump, he is. I dont want no balmies teaching me.

Higgins: [wounded in his tenderest point by her insensibility to his elocution] Oh, indeed! I'm mad, am I? Very well, Mrs. Pearce:...Throw her out.

Liza: [whimpering] Nah-ow. You got no right to touch me.

Mrs. Pearce: You see now what comes of being saucy. [Indicating the door] This way, please.

Liza: [almost in tears] I didnt want no clothes. I wouldnt have taken them [she throws away the handkerchief]. I can buy my own clothes.

Higgins: [deftly retrieving the handkerchief and intercepting her on her reluctant way to the door] Youre an ungrateful wicked girl. This is my return for offering to take you out of the gutter and dress you beautifully and make a lady of you.

Mrs. Pearce: Stop, Mr. Higgins. I wont allow it. It's you that are wicked. Go home to your parents, girl; and tell them to take better care of you.

Liza: I aint got no parents. They told me I was big enough to earn my own living and turned me out.

Mrs. Pearce: Wheres your mother?

Liza: I aint got no mother. Her that turned me out was my sixth stepmother. But I done without them. And I'm a good girl, I am.

Higgins: Very well, then, what on earth is all this fuss about? The girl doesnt belong to anybody—is no use to anybody but me. [He goes to Mrs. Pearce and begins coaxing]. You can adopt her, Mrs. Pearce: I'm sure a daughter would be a great amusement to you. Now dont make any more fuss. Take her downstairs; and —

Mrs. Pearce: But whats to become of her? Is she to be paid anything? Do be sensible, sir.

Higgins: Oh, pay her whatever is necessary: put it down in the housekeeping book. [Impatiently] What on earth will she want with money? She'll have her food and her clothes. She'll only drink if you give her money.

Liza: [turning on him] Oh you are a brute. It's a lie: nobody ever saw the sign of liquor on me. [To Pickering] Oh sir: youre a gentleman: dont let him speak to me like that.

Pickering: [in good-humored remonstrance] Does it occur to you, Higgins, that the girl has some feelings?

Higgins: [looking critically at her] Oh no, I dont think so. Not any feelings that we need bother about. [Cheerily] Have you, Eliza?

Liza: I got my feelings same as anyone else.

Higgins: [to Pickering, reflectively] You see the difficulty?

Pickering: Eh? What difficulty?

Higgins: To get her to talk grammar. The mere pronunciation is easy enough.

Liza: I dont want to talk grammar. I want to talk like a lady in a flower-shop.

Mrs. Pearce: Will you please keep to the point, Mr. Higgins. I want to know on what terms the girl is to be here. Is she to have any wages? And what is to become of her when youve finished your teaching? You must look ahead a little.

Higgins: [impatiently] Whats to become of her if I leave her in the gutter? Tell me that, Mrs. Pearce.

Mrs. Pearce: Thats her own business, not yours, Mr. Higgins.

Higgins: Well, when Ive done with her, we can throw her back into the gutter; and then it will be her own business again; so thats all right.

Liza: Oh, youve no feeling heart in you: you dont care for nothing but yourself. [She rises and takes the floor resolutely]. Here! Ive had enough of this. I'm going [making for the *door].* You ought to be ashamed of yourself, you ought.

Higgins: *[snatching a chocolate cream from the piano, his eyes suddenly beginning to twinkle with mischief]* Have some chocolates, Eliza.

Liza: *[halting, tempted]* How do I know what might be in them? Ive heard of girls being drugged by the like of you.

Higgins whips out his penknife; cuts a chocolate in two; puts one half into his mouth and bolts it; and offers her the other half.

Higgins: Pledge of good faith, Eliza. I eat one half: you eat the other. *[Liza opens her mouth to retort: he pops the half chocolate into it].* You shall have boxes of them, barrels of them, every day. You shall live on them. Eh?

Liza: *[who has disposed of the chocolate after being nearly choked by it]* I wouldnt have ate it, only I'm too ladylike to take it out of my mouth.

Higgins: Listen, Eliza. I think you said you came in a taxi.

Liza: Well, what if I did? Ive as good a right to take a taxi as anyone else.

Higgins: You have, Eliza; and in future you shall have as many taxis as you want. You shall go up and down and round the town in a taxi every day. Think of that, Eliza.

Mrs. Pearce: Mr. Higgins: youre tempting the girl. It's not right. She should think of the future.

Higgins: At her age! Nonsense! Time enough to think of the future when you havnt any future to think of. No, Eliza: do as this lady does: think of other people's futures; but never think of your own. Think of chocolates, and taxis, and gold, and diamonds.

Liza: No: I dont want no gold and no diamonds. I'm a good girl, I am. *[She sits down again, with an attempt at dignity].*

Higgins: You shall remain so, Eliza, under the care of Mrs. Pearce. And you shall marry an

officer in the Guards, with a beautiful moustache: the son of a marquis, who will disinherit him for marrying you, but will relent when he sees your beauty and goodness —

Pickering: Excuse me, Higgins; but I really must interfere. Mrs. Pearce is quite right. If this girl is to put herself in your hands for six months for an experiment in teaching, she must understand thoroughly what she's doing.

Higgins: How can she? She's incapable of understanding anything. Besides, do any of us understand what we are doing? If we did, would we ever do it?

Pickering: Very clever, Higgins; but not to the present point. *[To Eliza]* Miss Doolittle —

Liza: *[overwhelmed]* Ah-ah-ow-oo!

Higgins: There! Thats all youll get out of Eliza. Ah-ah-ow-oo! No use explaining. As a military man you ought to know that. Give her her orders: thats enough for her. Eliza: you are to live here for the next six months, learning how to speak beautifully, like a lady in a florist's shop. If youre good and do whatever youre told, you shall sleep in a proper bedroom, and have lots to eat, and money to buy chocolates and take rides in taxis. If youre naughty and idle you will sleep in the back kitchen among the black beetles, and be walloped by Mrs. Pearce with a broomstick. At the end of six months you shall go to Buckingham Palace in a carriage, beautifully dressed. If the King finds out youre not a lady, you will be taken by the police to the Tower of London, where your head will be cut off as a warning to other presumptuous flower girls. If you are not found out, you shall have a present of seven-and-sixpence to start life with as a lady in a shop. If you refuse this offer you will be a most ungrateful and wicked girl; and the angels will weep for you. *[To Pickering]* Now are you satisfied, Pickering? *[To Mrs. Pearce]* Can I put it more plainly and fairly, Mrs. Pearce?

Mrs. Pearce: *[patiently]* I think youd better let me speak to the girl properly in private. I dont know that I can take charge of her or consent to the arrangement at all. Of course I know you dont mean her any harm; but when you

get what you call interested in people's accents, you never think or care what may happen to them or you. Come with me, Eliza.

Higgins: Thats all right. Thank you, Mrs. Pearce. Bundle her off to the bathroom.

Liza: [rising reluctantly and suspiciously] Youre a great bully, you are. I wont stay here if I dont like. I wont let nobody wallop me. I never asked to go to Bucknam Palace, I didnt. I was never in trouble with the police, not me. I'm a good girl —

Mrs. Pearce: Dont answer back, girl. You dont understand the gentleman. Come with me.

[She leads the way to the door, and holds it open for Eliza].

Liza: [as she goes out] Well, what I say is right. I wont go near the king, not if I'm going to have my head cut off. If I'd known what I was letting myself in for, I wouldnt have come here. I always been a good girl; and I never offered to say a word to him; and I dont owe him nothing; and I dont care; and I wont be put upon; and I have my feelings the same as anyone else —

Mrs. Pearce shuts the door; and Eliza's plaints are no longer audible.

Eliza is taken upstairs to the third floor greatly to her surprise; for she expected to be taken down to the scullery. There Mrs Pearce opens a door and takes her into a spare bedroom.

Mrs. Pearce: I will have to put you here. This will be your bedroom.

Liza: O-h, I couldnt sleep here, missus. It's too good for the likes of me. I should be afraid to touch anything. I aint a duchess yet, you know.

Mrs. Pearce: You have got to make yourself as clean as the room: then you wont be afraid of it. And you must call me Mrs Pearce, not missus. [She throws open the door of the dressing-groom, now modernized as a bathroom].

Liza: Gawd! whats this? Is this where you wash clothes? Funny sort of copper I call it.

Mrs. Pearce: It is not a copper. This is where we wash ourselves, Eliza, and where I am going to wash you.

Liza: You expect me to get into that and wet myself all over! Not me. I should catch my death. I knew a woman did it every Saturday night; and she died of it.

Mrs. Pearce: Mr Higgins has the gentleman's bathroom downstairs; and he has a bath every morning, in cold water.

Liza: Ugh! He's made of iron, that man.

Mrs. Pearce: If you are to sit with him and the Colonel and be taught you will have to do the same. They won't like the smell of you if you dont. But you can have the water as hot as you like it. There are two taps: hot and cold.

Liza: [weeping] I couldnt. I dursnt. It's not natural: it would kill me. Ive never had a bath in my life: not what youd call a proper one.

Mrs. Pearce: Well, don't you want to be clean and sweet and decent, like a lady? You know you cant be a nice girl inside if youre a dirty [one] outside.

Liza: Boohoo!!!!

Mrs. Pearce: Now stop crying and go back into your room and take off all your clothes. Then wrap yourself in this [Taking down a gown from its peg and handing it to her] and come back to me. I will get the bath ready.

Liza: [all tears] I cant. I wont. I'm not used to it. Ive never took off all my clothes before. It's not right: it's not decent.

Mrs. Pearce: Nonsense, child. Dont you take off all your clothes every night when you go to bed?

Liza: [amazed] No. Why should I? I should catch my death. Of course I take off my skirt.

Mrs. Pearce: Do you mean then you sleep in the underclothes you wear in the daytime?

Liza: What else have I to sleep in?

Mrs. Pearce: You will never do that again as long as you live here. I will get you a proper nightdress.

Liza: Do you mean change into cold things and lie awake shivering half the night? You want to kill me, you do.

Mrs. Pearce: I want to change you from a frowzy *[girl]* to a clean respectable girl fit to sit with the gentlemen in the study. Are you going to trust me and do what I tell you or be thrown out and sent back to your flower basket?

Liza: But you dont know what the cold is to me. You dont know how I dread it.

Mrs. Pearce: Your bed wont be cold here: I will put a hot water bottle in it. *[Pushing her into the bedroom]* Off with you and undress.

Liza: Oh, if only I'd known what a dreadful thing it is to be clean I'd never have come. I didnt know when I was well off. I—*[Mrs. Pearce pushes her through the door, but leaves it partly open lest her prisoner should take to flight]*.

Mrs Pearce puts on a pair of white rubber sleeves, and fills the bath, mixing hot and cold, and testing the result with the bath thermometer. She perfumes it with a handful of bath salts and adds a palmful of mustard. She then takes a formidable looking long handled scrubbing brush and soaps it profusely with a ball of scented soap.

Eliza comes back with nothing on but the bath gown huddled tightly round her, a piteous spectacle of abject terror.

Mrs. Pearce: Now come along. Take that thing off.

Liza: Oh I couldnt, Mrs Pearce: I reely couldnt. I never done such a thing.

Mrs. Pearce: Nonsense. Here: step in and tell me whether it's hot enough for you.

Liza: Ah-oo! Ah-oo! It's too hot.

Mrs. Pearce: *[deftly snatching the gown away and throwing Eliza down on her back]* It wont hurt you. *[She sets to work with the scrubbing brush]*.

Eliza's screams are heartrending.

Meanwhile the Colonel has been having it out with Higgins about Eliza. Pickering has come from the hearth to the chair and seated himself astride of it with his arms on the back to cross-examine him.

Pickering: Excuse the straight question, Higgins. Are you a man of good character where women are concerned?

Higgins: *[moodily]* Have you ever met a man of good character where women are concerned?

Pickering: Yes: very frequently.

Higgins: *[dogmatically, lifting himself on his hands to the level of the piano, and sitting on it with a bounce]* Well, I havnt. I find that the moment I let a woman make friends with me, she becomes jealous, exacting, suspicious,

and a damned nuisance. I find that the moment I let myself make friends with a woman, I become selfish and tyrannical. Women upset everything. When you let them into your life, you find that the woman is driving at one thing and youre driving at another.

Pickering: At what, for example?

Higgins: *[coming off the piano restlessly]* Oh, Lord knows! I suppose the woman wants to live her own life; and the man wants to live his; and each tries to drag the other on to the wrong track. One wants to go north and the other south; and the result is that both have to go east, though they both hate the east wind. *[He sits down on the bench at the keyboard]*. So here I am, a confirmed old bachelor, and likely to remain so.

Pickering: *[rising and standing over him gravely]* Come, Higgins! You know what I mean. If I'm to be in this business I shall feel responsible for that girl. I hope it's understood that no advantage is to be taken of her position.

Higgins: What! That thing! Sacred, I assure you. *[Rising to explain]* You see, she'll be a pupil; and teaching would be impossible unless pupils were sacred. Ive taught scores of American millionairesses how to speak English: the best looking women in the world. I'm seasoned. They might as well be blocks of wood. I might as well be a block of wood. It's —

Mrs. Pearce opens the door. She has Eliza's hat in her hand. Pickering retires to the easy-chair at the hearth and sits down.

Higgins: *[eagerly]* Well, Mrs. Pearce: is it all right?

Mrs. Pearce: *[at the door]* I just wish to trouble you with a word, if I may, Mr. Higgins.

Higgins: Yes, certainly. Come in. *[She comes forward]*. Dont burn that, Mrs. Pearce. I'll keep it as a curiosity. *[He takes the hat]*.

Mrs. Pearce: Handle it carefully, sir, please. I had to promise her not to burn it; but I had better put it in the oven for a while.

Higgins: *[putting it down hastily on the piano]* Oh! thank you. Well, what have you to say to me?

Pickering: Am I in the way?

Mrs. Pearce: Not at all, sir. Mr. Higgins: will you please be very particular what you say before the girl?

Higgins: *[sternly]* Of course. I'm always particular about what I say. Why do you say this to me?

Mrs. Pearce: *[unmoved]* No, sir: youre not at all particular when youve mislaid anything or when you get a little impatient. Now it doesnt matter before me: I'm used to it. But you really must not swear before the girl.

Higgins: *[indignantly]* I swear! *[Most emphatically]* I never swear. I detest the habit. What the devil do you mean?

Mrs. Pearce: *[stolidly]* Thats what I mean, sir. You swear a great deal too much. I dont mind your damning and blasting, and what the devil and where the devil and who the devil —

Higgins: Mrs. Pearce: this language from your lips! Really!

Mrs. Pearce: *[not to be put off]*—but there is a certain word I must ask you not to use. The girl used it herself when she began to enjoy the bath. It begins with the same letter as bath. She knows no better: she learnt it at her mother's knee. But she must not hear it from your lips.

Higgins: *[loftily]* I cannot charge myself with having ever uttered it, Mrs. Pearce. *[She looks at him steadfastly. He adds, hiding an uneasy conscience with a judicial air]* Except perhaps in a moment of extreme and justifiable excitement.

Mrs. Pearce: Only this morning, sir, you applied it to your boots, to the butter, and to the brown bread.

Higgins: Oh, that! Mere alliteration, Mrs. Pearce, natural to a poet.

Mrs. Pearce: Well, sir, whatever you choose to call it, I beg you not to let the girl hear you repeat it.

Higgins: Oh, very well, very well. Is that all?

Mrs. Pearce: No, sir. We shall have to be very particular with this girl as to personal cleanliness.

Higgins: Certainly. Quite right. Most important.

Mrs. Pearce: I mean not to be slovenly about her dress or untidy in leaving things about.

Higgins: *[going to her solemnly]* Just so. I intended to call your attention to that. *[He passes on to Pickering, who is enjoying the conversation immensely]*. It is these little things that matter, Pickering. Take care of the pence and the pounds will take care of themselves is as true of personal habits as of money. *[He comes to anchor on the hearthrug with the air of a man in an unassailable position.]*

Mrs. Pearce: Yes, sir. Then might I ask you not to come down to breakfast in your dressing-gown, or at any rate not to use it as a napkin to the extent you do, sir. And if you would be so good as not to eat everything off the same plate, and to remember not to put the porridge saucepan out of your hand on the clean table-cloth, it would be a better example to the girl. You know you nearly choked yourself with a fishbone in the jam only last week.

Higgins: *[routed from the hearthrug and drifting back to the piano]* I may do these things sometimes in absence of mind; but surely I dont do them habitually. *[Angrily]* By the way: my dressing-gown smells most damnably of benzine.

Mrs. Pearce: No doubt it does, Mr. Higgins. But if you will wipe your fingers —

Higgins: *[yelling]* Oh very well, very well: I'll wipe them in my hair in future.

Mrs. Pearce: I hope youre not offended, Mr. Higgins.

Higgins: *[shocked at finding himself thought capable of an unamiable sentiment]* Not at all, not at all. Youre quite right, Mrs. Pearce: I shall be particularly careful before the girl. Is that all?

Mrs. Pearce: No, sir. Might she use some of those Japanese dresses you brought from abroad? I really cant put her back into her old things.

Higgins: Certainly. Anything you like. Is that all?

Mrs. Pearce: Thank you, sir. Thats all. *[She goes out].*

Higgins: You know, Pickering, that woman has the most extraordinary ideas about me. Here I am, a shy, diffident sort of man. Ive never been able to feel really grown-up and tremendous, like other chaps. And yet she's

firmly persuaded that I'm an arbitrary over-bearing bossing kind of person. I cant account for it.

Mrs. Pearce returns.

Mrs. Pearce: If you please, sir, the trouble's beginning already. Theres a dustman downstairs, Alfred Doolittle, wants to see you. He says you have his daughter here.

Pickering: *[rising]* Phew! I say!

Higgins: *[promptly]* Send the blackguard up.

Mrs. Pearce: Oh, very well, sir. *[She goes out].*

Pickering: He may not be a blackguard, Higgins.

Higgins: Nonsense. Of course he's a blackguard.

Pickering: Whether he is or not, I'm afraid we shall have some trouble with him.

Higgins: *[confidently]* Oh no: I think not. If theres any trouble he shall have it with me, not I with him. And we are sure to get something interesting out of him.

Pickering: About the girl?

Higgins: No. I mean his dialect.

Pickering: Oh!

Mrs. Pearce: *[at the door]* Doolittle, sir. *[She admits Doolittle and retires].*

Alfred Doolittle is an elderly but vigorous dustman, clad in the costume of his profession, including a hat with a back brim covering his neck and shoulders. He has well marked and rather interesting features, and seems equally free from fear and conscience. He has a remarkably expressive voice, the result of a habit of giving vent to his feelings without reserve. His present pose is that of wounded honor and stern resolution.

Doolittle: *[at the door, uncertain which of the two gentlemen is his man]* Professor Iggins?

Higgins: Here. Good morning. Sit down.

Doolittle: Morning, Governor. *[He sits down magisterially]* I come about a very serious matter, Governor.

Higgins: *[to Pickering]* Brought up in Hounslow. Mother Welsh, I should think. *[Doolittle opens his mouth, amazed. Higgins continues]* What do you want, Doolittle?

Doolittle: *[menacingly]* I want my daughter: thats what I want. See?

Higgins: Of course you do. Youre her father, arnt you? You dont suppose anyone else wants her, do you? I'm glad to see you have some spark of family feeling left. Shes upstairs. Take her away at once.

Doolittle: *[rising, fearfully taken aback]* What!

Higgins: Take her away. Do you suppose I'm going to keep your daughter for you?

Doolittle: *[remonstrating]* Now, now, look here, Governor. Is this reasonable? Is it fairity to take advantage of a man like this? The girl belongs to me. You got her. Where do I come in? *[He sits down again]*.

Higgins: Your daughter had the audacity to come to my house and ask me to teach her how to speak properly so that she could get a place in a flower-shop. This gentleman and my housekeeper have been here all the time. *[Bullying him]* How dare you come here and attempt to blackmail me? You sent her here on purpose.

Doolittle: *[protesting]* No, Governor.

Higgins: You must have. How else could you possibly know that she is here?

Doolittle: Dont take a man up like that, Governor.

Higgins: The police shall take you up. This is a plant—a plot to extort money by threats. I shall telephone for the police *[he goes resolutely to the telephone and opens the directory]*.

Doolittle: Have I asked you for a brass farthing? I leave it to the gentleman here: have I said a word about money?

Higgins: *[throwing the book aside and marching down on Doolittle with a poser]* What else did you come for?

Doolittle: *[sweetly]* Well, what would a man come for? Be human, Governor.

Higgins: *[disarmed]* Alfred: did you put her up to it?

Doolittle: So help me, Governor, I never did. I take my Bible oath I aint seen the girl these two months past.

Higgins: Then how did you know she was here?

Doolittle: *["most musical, most melancholy"]* I'll tell you, Governor, if youll only let me get a word in. I'm willing to tell you. I'm wanting to tell you. I'm waiting to tell you.

Higgins: Pickering: this chap has a certain natural gift of rhetoric. Observe the rhythm of his native woodnotes wild. "I'm willing to tell you: I'm wanting to tell you: I'm waiting to tell you." Sentimental rhetoric! thats the Welsh strain in him. It also accounts for his mendacity and dishonesty.

Pickering: Oh, please, Higgins: I'm west country myself. *[To Doolittle]* How did you know the girl was here if you didnt send her?

Doolittle: It was like this, Governor. The girl took a boy in the taxi to give him a jaunt. Son of her landlady, he is. He hung about on the chance of her giving him another ride home. Well, she sent him back for her luggage when she heard you was willing for her to stop here. I met the boy at the corner of Long Acre and Endell Street.

Higgins: Public house. Yes?

Doolittle: The poor man's club, Governor: why shouldnt I?

Pickering: Do let him tell his story, Higgins.

Doolittle: He told me what was up. And I ask you, what was my feelings and my duty as a father? I says to the boy, "You bring me the luggage," I says —

Pickering: Why didnt you go for it yourself?

Doolittle: Landlady wouldnt have trusted me with it, Governor. Shes that kind of woman: you know. I had to give the boy a penny afore he trusted me with it, the little swine. I brought it to her just to oblige you like, and make myself agreeable. Thats all.

Higgins: How much luggage?

Doolittle: Musical instrument, Governor. A few pictures, a trifle of jewelry, and a bird-cage. She said she didnt want no clothes. What was I to think from that, Governor? I ask you as a parent what was I to think?

Higgins: So you came to rescue her from worse than death, eh?

Doolittle: [appreciatively: relieved at being so well understood] Just so, Governor. Thats right.

Pickering: But why did you bring her luggage if you intended to take her away?

Doolittle: Have I said a word about taking her away? Have I now?

Higgins: [determinedly] Youre going to take her away, double quick. [He crosses to the hearth and rings the bell].

Doolittle: [rising] No, Governor. Dont say that. I'm not the man to stand in my girl's light. Heres a career opening for her, as you might say; and —

Mrs. Pearce opens the door and awaits orders.

Higgins: Mrs. Pearce: this is Eliza's father. He has come to take her away. Give her to him. [He goes back to the piano, with an air of washing his hands of the whole affair].

Doolittle: No. This is a misunderstanding. Listen here —

Mrs. Pearce: He cant take her away, Mr. Higgins: how can he? You told me to burn her clothes.

Doolittle: Thats right. I cant carry the girl through the streets like a blooming monkey, can I? I put it to you.

Higgins: You have put it to me that you want your daughter. Take your daughter. If she has no clothes go out and buy her some.

Doolittle: [desperate] Wheres the clothes she come in? Did I burn them or did your missus here?

Mrs. Pearce: I am the housekeeper, if you please. I have sent for some clothes for your girl. When they come you can take her away. You can wait in the kitchen. This way, please.

Doolittle, much troubled, accompanies her to the door; then hesitates; finally turns confidentially to Higgins.

Doolittle: Listen here, Governor. You and me is men of the world, aint we?

Higgins: Oh! Men of the world, are we? Youd better go, Mrs. Pearce.

Mrs. Pearce: I think so, indeed, sir. [She goes, with dignity].

Pickering: The floor is yours, Mr. Doolittle.

Doolittle: [to Pickering] I thank you, Governor. [To Higgins, who takes refuge on the piano bench, a little overwhelmed by the proximity of his visitor; for Doolittle has a professional flavor of dust about him]. Well, the truth is, Ive taken a sort of fancy to you, Governor; and if you want the girl, I'm not so set on having her back home again but what I might be open to an arrangement. Regarded in the light of a young woman, shes a fine handsome girl. As a daughter she's not worth her keep; and so I tell you straight. All I ask is my rights as a father; and youre the last man alive to expect me to let her go for nothing; for I can see youre one of the straight sort, Governor. Well, whats a five pound note to you? And whats Eliza to me? [He returns to his chair and sits down judicially].

Pickering: I think you ought to know, Doolittle, that Mr. Higgins's intentions are entirely honorable.

Doolittle: Course they are, Governor. If I thought they wasnt, I'd ask fifty.

Higgins: [revolted] Do you mean to say, that you would sell your daughter for £50?

Doolittle: Not in a general way I wouldnt; but to oblige a gentleman like you I'd do a good deal, I do assure you.

Pickering: Have you no morals, man?

Doolittle: *[unabashed]* Cant afford them, Governor. Neither could you if you was as poor as me. Not that I mean any harm, you know. But if Liza is going to have a bit out of this, why not me too?

Higgins: *[troubled]* I dont know what to do, Pickering. There can be no question that as a matter of morals it's a positive crime to give this chap a farthing. And yet I feel a sort of rough justice in his claim.

Doolittle: Thats it, Governor. Thats all I say. A father's heart, as it were.

Pickering: Well, I know the feeling; but really it seems hardly right —

Doolittle: Dont say that, Governor. Dont look at it that way. What am I, Governors both? I ask you, what am I? I'm one of the undeserving poor: thats what I am. Think of what that means to a man. It means that hes up agen middle class morality all the time. If theres anything going, and I put in for a bit of it, it's always the same story: "Youre undeserving; so you cant have it." But my needs is as great as the most deserving widow's that ever got money out of six different charities in one week for the death of the same husband. I dont need less than a deserving man: I need more. I dont eat less hearty than him; and I drink a lot more. I want a bit of amusement, cause I'm a thinking man. I want cheerfulness and a song and a band when I feel low. Well, they charge me just the same for everything as they charge the deserving. What is middle class morality? Just an excuse for never giving me anything. Therefore, I ask you, as two gentlemen, not to play that game on me. I'm playing straight with you. I aint pretending to be deserving. I'm undeserving; and I mean to go on being undeserving. I like it; and thats the truth. Will you take advantage of a man's nature to do him out of the price of his own daughter what he's brought up and fed and clothed by the sweat of his brow until shes growed big enough to be interesting to you two gentlemen?

Is five pounds unreasonable? I put it to you; and I leave it to you.

Higgins: *[rising, and going over to Pickering]* Pickering: if we were to take this man in hand for three months, he could choose between a seat in the Cabinet and a popular pulpit in Wales.

Pickering: What do you say to that, Doolittle?

Doolittle: Not me, Governor, thank you kindly. Ive heard all the preachers and all the prime ministers—for I'm a thinking man and game for politics or religion or social reform same as all the other amusements—and I tell you it's a dog's life anyway you look at it. Undeserving poverty is my line. Taking one station in society with another, it's—it's—well, it's the only one that has any ginger in it, to my taste.

Higgins: I suppose we must give him a fiver.

Pickering: He'll make a bad use of it, I'm afraid.

Doolittle: Not me, Governor, so help me I wont. Dont you be afraid that I'll save it and spare it and live idle on it. There wont be a penny of it left by Monday: I'll have to go to work same as if I'd never had it. It wont pauperize me, you bet. Just one good spree for myself and the missus, giving pleasure to ourselves and employment to others, and satisfaction to you to think it's not been throwed away. You couldnt spend it better.

Higgins: *[taking out his pocket book and coming between Doolittle and the piano]* This is irresistible. Lets give him ten. *[He offers two notes to the dustman].*

Doolittle: No, Governor. She wouldnt have the heart to spend ten; and perhaps I shouldnt neither. Ten pounds is a lot of money: it makes a man feel prudent like; and then goodbye to happiness. You give me what I ask you, Governor: not a penny more, and not a penny less.

Pickering: Why dont you marry that missus of yours? I rather draw the line at encouraging that sort of immorality.

Doolittle: Tell her so, Governor: tell her so. I'm willing. It's me that suffers by it. Ive no hold on her. I got to be agreeable to her. I got to give her presents. I got to buy her clothes something sinful. I'm a slave to that woman, Governor, just because I'm not her lawful husband. And she knows it too. Catch her marrying me! Take my advice, Governor: marry Eliza while shes young and dont know no better. If you dont youll be sorry for it after. If you do, she'll be sorry for it after; but better you than her, because youre a man, and shes only a woman and dont know how to be happy anyhow.

Higgins: Pickering: if we listen to this man another minute, we shall have no convictions left. *[To Doolittle]* Five pounds I think you said.

Doolittle: Thank you kindly, Governor.

Higgins: You're sure you wont take ten?

Doolittle: Not now. Another time, Governor.

Higgins: *[handing him a five-pound note]* Here you are.

Doolittle: Thank you, Governor. Good morning. *[He hurries to the door, anxious to get away with his booty. When he opens it he is confronted with a dainty and exquisitely clean young Japanese lady in a simple blue cotton kimono printed cunningly with small white jasmine blossoms. Mrs. Pearce is with her. He gets out of her way deferentially and apologizes].* Beg pardon, miss.

The Japanese Lady: Garn! Dont you know your own daughter?

Doolittle: *[exclaiming]* Bly me! it's Eliza!

Higgins: *[simultaneously]* Whats that! This!

Pickering: By Jove!

Liza: Dont I look silly?

Higgins: Silly?

Mrs. Pearce: *[at the door]* Now, Mr. Higgins, please dont say anything to make the girl conceited about herself.

Higgins: *[conscientiously]* Oh! Quite right, Mrs. Pearce. *[To Eliza]* Yes: damned silly.

Mrs. Pearce: Please, sir.

Higgins: *[correcting himself]* I mean extremely silly.

Liza: I should look all right with my hat on. *[She takes up her hat; puts it on; and walks across the room to the fireplace with a fashionable air].*

Higgins: A new fashion, by George! And it ought to look horrible!

Doolittle: *[with fatherly pride]* Well, I never thought she'd clean up as good looking as that, Governor. She's a credit to me, aint she?

Liza: I tell you, it's easy to clean up here. Hot and cold water on tap, just as much as you like, there is. Woolly towels, there is; and a towel horse so hot, it burns your fingers. Soft brushes to scrub yourself, and a wooden bowl of soap smelling like primroses. Now I know why ladies is so clean. Washing's a treat for them. Wish they saw what it is for the like of me!

Higgins: I'm glad the bathroom met with your approval.

Liza: It didnt: not all of it; and I dont care who hears me say it. Mrs. Pearce knows.

Higgins: What was wrong, Mrs. Pearce?

Mrs. Pearce: *[blandly]* Oh, nothing, sir. It doesnt matter.

Liza: I had a good mind to break it. I didnt know which way to look. But I hung a towel over it, I did.

Higgins: Over what?

Mrs. Pearce: Over the looking-glass, sir.

Higgins: Doolittle: you have brought your daughter up too strictly.

Doolittle: Me! I never brought her up at all, except to give her a lick of a strap now and again. Dont put it on me, Governor. She aint accustomed to it, you see: thats all. But she'll soon pick up your free-and-easy ways.

Liza: I'm a good girl, I am; and I wont pick up no free and easy ways.

Higgins: Eliza: if you say again that youre a good girl, your father shall take you home.

Liza: Not him. You dont know my father. All he come here for was to touch you for some money to get drunk on.

Doolittle: Well, what else would I want money for? To put into the plate in church, I suppose. *[She puts out her tongue at him. He is so incensed by this that Pickering presently finds it necessary to step between them].* Dont you give me none of your lip; and dont let me hear you giving this gentleman any of it neither, or youll hear from me about it. See?

Higgins: Have you any further advice to give her before you go, Doolittle? Your blessing, for instance.

Doolittle: No, Governor: I aint such a mug as to put up my children to all I know myself. Hard enough to hold them in without that. If you want Eliza's mind improved, Governor, you do it yourself with a strap. So long, gentlemen. *[He turns to go].*

Higgins: *[impressively]* Stop. Youll come regularly to see your daughter. It's your duty, you know. My brother is a clergyman; and he could help you in your talks with her.

Doolittle: *[evasively]* Certainly, I'll come, Governor. Not just this week, because I have a job at a distance. But later on you may depend on me. Afternoon, gentlemen. Afternoon, maam. *[He takes off his hat to Mrs. Pearce, who disdains the salutation and goes out. He winks at Higgins, thinking him probably a fellow-sufferer from Mrs. Pearce's difficult disposition, and follows her].*

Liza: Dont you believe the old liar. He'd as soon you set a bulldog on him as a clergyman. You wont see him again in a hurry.

Higgins: I dont want to, Eliza. Do you?

Liza: Not me. I dont want never to see him again, I dont. He's a disgrace to me, he is, collecting dust, instead of working at his trade.

Pickering: What is his trade, Eliza?

Liza: Talking money out of other people's pockets into his own. His proper trade's a navvy; and he works at it sometimes too—for exercise—and earns good money at it. Aint you going to call me Miss Doolittle any more?

Pickering: I beg your pardon, Miss Doolittle. It was a slip of the tongue.

Liza: Oh, I dont mind; only it sounded so genteel. I should just like to take a taxi to the corner of Tottenham Court Road and get out there and tell it to wait for me, just to put the girls in their place a bit. I wouldnt speak to them, you know.

Pickering: Better wait til we get you something really fashionable.

Higgins: Besides, you shouldnt cut your old friends now that you have risen in the world. Thats what we call snobbery.

Liza: You dont call the like of them my friends now, I should hope. Theyve took it out of me often enough with their ridicule when they had the chance; and now I mean to get a bit of my own back. But if I'm to have fashionable clothes, I'll wait. I should like to have some. Mrs. Pearce says youre going to give me some to wear in bed at night different to what I wear in the daytime; but it do seem a waste of money when you could get something to shew. Besides, I never could fancy changing into cold things on a winter night.

Mrs. Pearce: *[coming back]* Now, Eliza. The new things have come for you to try on.

Liza: Ah-ow-oo-ooh! *[She rushes out].*

Mrs. Pearce: *[following her]* Oh, dont rush about like that, girl *[She shuts the door behind her].*

Higgins: Pickering: we have taken on a stiff job.

Pickering: *[with conviction]* Higgins: we have.

There seems to be some curiosity as to what Higgins's lessons to Eliza were like. Well, here is a sample: the first one.

Picture Eliza, in her new clothes, and feeling her inside put out of step by a lunch, dinner, and breakfast of a kind to which it is unaccustomed, seated with Higgins and the Colonel in the study, feeling like a hospital out-patient at a first encounter with the doctors.

Higgins, constitutionally unable to sit still, discomposes her still more by striding restlessly about. But for the reassuring presence and quietude of her friend the Colonel she would run for her life, even back to Drury Lane.

Higgins: Say your alphabet.

Liza: I know my alphabet. Do you think I know nothing? I dont need to be taught like a child.

Higgins: *[thundering]* Say your alphabet.

Pickering: Say it, Miss Doolittle. You will understand presently. Do what he tells you; and let him teach you in his own way.

Liza: Oh well, if you put it like that—Ahyee, bəyee, cəyee, dəyee—

Higgins: *[with the roar of a wounded lion]* Stop. Listen to this, Pickering. This is what we pay for as elementary education. This unfortunate animal has been locked up for nine years in school at our expense to teach her to speak and read the language of Shakespeare and Milton. And the result is Ahyee, Bə-yee, Cə-yee, Dəyee. *[To Eliza]* Say A, B, C, D.

Liza: *[almost in tears]* But I'm saying it. Ahyee, Bəyee, Cəyee —

Higgins: Stop. Say a cup of tea.

Liza: A cappətə-ee.

Higgins: Put your tongue forward until it squeezes against the top of your lower teeth. Now say cup.

Liza: C-c-c – I cant. C-Cup.

Pickering: Good. Splendid, Miss Doolittle.

Higgins: By Jupiter, she's done it the first shot. Pickering: we shall make a duchess of her. *[To Eliza]* Now do you think you could possibly say tea? Not tə-yee, mind: if you ever say bə-yee cə-yee də-yee again you shall be dragged round the room three times by the hair of your head. *[Fortissimo]* T, T, T, T.

Liza: *[weeping]* I cant hear no difference cep that it sounds more genteel-like when you say it.

Higgins: Well, if you can hear that difference, what the devil are you crying for? Pickering: give her a chocolate.

Pickering: No, no. Never mind crying a little, Miss Doolittle: you are doing very well; and the lessons wont hurt. I promise you I wont let him drag you round the room by your hair.

Higgins: Be off with you to Mrs. Pearce and tell her about it. Think about it. Try to do it by yourself: and keep your tongue well forward in your mouth instead of trying to roll it up and swallow it. Another lesson at half-past four this afternoon. Away with you.

Eliza, still sobbing, rushes from the room.

And that is the sort of ordeal poor Eliza has to go through for months before we meet her again on her first appearance in London society of the professional class.

Shaw, George Bernard. *Pygmalion*. New York: Simon & Schuster, 1973. (Original copyright 1916 by George Bernard Shaw).

LEADERSHIP PROFILE

Frederick Douglass (1817?–1895)

American Abolitionist, Orator, and Journalist
Narrative of the Life of Frederick Douglass

Introduction and Historical Background

Frederick Douglass was born a slave—the son of a slave and a white father. He escaped to the North in 1838. He made a speech at an antislavery convention in Nantucket in 1841, and attracted such attention from his speaking talents there that he was soon in great demand as a speaker. When critics questioned how a former slave could be so eloquent and clearly educated, Douglass determined to give a full accounting of his slave years and escape from slavery, including the names of his masters and places where he worked. He published his autobiography, *Narrative of the Life of Frederick Douglass*, in 1845. The work is not long, describing the major events of his life, including how he secretly learned to read and write (from the mistress of the plantation until her husband stopped the lessons and then Douglass "tricked" others into teaching him some things), and the cruelty of the master. It details the restricted, harsh life of the slaves and the ways in which slaves sought to overcome their plight through spirituality and a deep sense of community.

Douglass spent two years in Great Britain earning money to officially buy his freedom. Upon his return to the United States, he started a newspaper, *The North Star*. Douglass quickly became the most famous African American of his day and a prominent abolitionist. When the Civil War began, he advocated using black troops and worked for civil rights for freedmen. After the Civil War, he continued advocating for civil rights and an end to institutionalized inequality for blacks.

The portion of Douglass' autobiography excerpted here details his escape from Maryland and the subsequent years in which he sought to gain both security and freedom through marrying, establishing a home, working, and finally speaking for the cause of abolition.

Points to Consider

1. Reflect on a situation where the fear of failure prevented you from taking on a task and/or achieving a goal. What are some strategies for getting past the fear of failure in the effort to achieve a goal?

2. When Master Hugh agrees to allow Douglass to hire his time, in some ways it seems like a step backward: "He received all the benefits of slaveholding without its evils; while I endured all the evils of a slave, and suffered all the care and anxiety of a freeman." Can you think of experiences where you (alone or as part of a group) have had to take a step backward in order to achieve a long-range goal?

3. What are some strategies for helping an organization recognize the need for patience and the achievement of short-term goals, en route to a larger vision?

4. How does Douglass rationalize setting a goal that violates existing laws? Can you think of contemporary examples of an individual, group, or organization setting a goal that violates existing laws?

Narrative of the Life of Frederick Douglass

(Excerpt)
By Frederick Douglass

Chapter XI

I now come to that part of my life during which I planned, and finally succeeded in making, my escape from slavery. But before narrating any of the peculiar circumstances, I deem it proper to make known my intention not to state all the facts connected with the transaction. My reasons for pursuing this course may be understood from the following: First, were I to give a minute statement of all the facts, it is not only possible, but quite probable, that others would thereby be involved in the most embarrassing difficulties. Secondly, such a statement would most undoubtedly induce greater vigilance on the part of slaveholders than has existed heretofore among them; which would, of course, be the means of guarding a door whereby some dear brother bondman might escape his galling chains. I deeply regret the necessity that impels me to suppress any thing of importance connected with my experience in slavery. It would afford me great pleasure indeed, as well as materially add to the interest of my narrative, were I at liberty to gratify a curiosity, which I know exists in the minds of many, by an accurate statement of all the facts pertaining to my most fortunate escape. But I must deprive myself of this pleasure, and the curious of the gratification which such a statement would afford. I would allow myself to suffer under the greatest imputations which evil-minded men might suggest, rather than exculpate myself, and thereby run the hazard of closing the slightest avenue by which a brother slave might clear himself of the chains and fetters of slavery.

Library of Congress,
Prints and Photographs Division,
LC-USZ62-15887

I have never approved of the very public manner in which some of our western friends have conducted what they call the *underground railroad*, but which, I think, by their open declarations, has been made most emphatically the *upperground railroad*. I honor those good men and women for their noble daring, and applaud them for willingly subjecting themselves to bloody persecution, by openly avowing their participation in the escape of slaves. I, however, can see very little good resulting from such a course, either to themselves or the slaves escaping; while, upon the other hand, I see and feel assured that those open declarations are a positive evil to the slaves remaining, who are seeking to escape. They do nothing towards enlightening the slave, whilst they do much towards enlightening the master. They stimulate him to greater watchfulness, and enhance his power to capture his slave. We owe something to the slaves south of the line as well as to those north of it; and in aiding the latter on their way to freedom, we should be careful to do nothing which would be likely to hinder the former from escaping from slavery. I would keep the merciless slaveholder profoundly ignorant of the means of flight adopted by the slave. I would leave him to imagine himself surrounded by myriads of invisible tormentors, ever ready to snatch from his infernal grasp his trembling prey. Let him be left to feel his way in the dark; let darkness commensurate with his crime hover over him; and let him feel that at every step he takes, in pursuit of the flying bondman, he is running the frightful risk of having his hot brains dashed out by an invisible agency. Let us render the tyrant no aid; let us not hold the light by which he can trace the footprints of our flying brother. But enough of this. I will now proceed to the statement of those facts, connected with my escape, for which I am alone responsible, and for which no one can be made to suffer but myself.

In the early part of the year 1838, I became quite restless. I could see no reason why I should, at the end of each week, pour the reward of my toil into the purse of my master. When I carried to him my weekly wages, he would, after counting the money, look me in the face with a robber-like fierceness, and ask, "Is this all?" He was satisfied with nothing less than the last cent. He would, however, when I made him six dollars, sometimes give me six cents, to encourage me. It had the opposite effect. I regarded it as a sort of admission of my right to the whole. The fact that he gave me any part of my wages was proof, to my mind, that he believed me entitled to the whole of them. I always felt worse for having received any thing; for I feared that the giving me a few cents would ease his conscience, and make him feel himself to be a pretty honorable sort of robber. My discontent grew upon me. I was ever on the look-out for means of my escape; and, finding no direct means, I determined to try to hire my time, with a view of getting money with which to make my escape. In the spring of 1838, when Master Thomas came to Baltimore to purchase his spring goods, I got an opportunity, and applied to him to allow me to hire my time. He unhesitatingly refused my request, and told me this was another stratagem by which to escape. He told me I could go nowhere but that he could get me; and that, in the event of my running away, he should spare no pains in his efforts to catch me. He exhorted me to content myself, and be obedient. He told me, if I would be happy, I must lay out no plans for the future. He said, if I behaved myself properly, he would take care of me. Indeed, he advised me to complete thoughtlessness of the future, and taught me to depend solely upon him for happiness. He seemed to see fully the pressing necessity of setting aside my intellectual nature, in order to have contentment in slavery. But in spite of him, and even in spite of myself, I continued to think, and to think about the injustice of my enslavement, and the means of escape.

About two months after this, I applied to Master Hugh for the privilege of hiring my time. He was not acquainted with the fact that I had applied to Master Thomas, and had been refused. He too, at first, seemed disposed to refuse; but after some reflection, he granted me the privilege, and proposed the following terms: I was to be allowed all my time, make all contacts with those for whom I worked, and find my own employment; and, in return for this liberty, I was to pay him three dollars at the end of each week; find myself in calking tools, and in board and clothing. My board was two dollars and a half per week. This, with the wear and tear of clothing and calking tools, made my regular expenses about six dollars per week. This amount I was compelled to make up, or relinquish the privilege of hiring my time. This arrangement, it will be perceived, was decidedly in my master's favor. It relieved him of all need of looking after me. His money was sure. He received all the benefits of slaveholding without its evils; while I endured all the evils of a slave, and suffered all the care and anxiety of a freeman. I found it a hard bargain. But, hard as it was, I thought it better than the old mode of getting along. It was a step towards freedom to be allowed to bear the responsibilities of a freeman, and I was determined to hold on upon it. I bent myself to the work of making money. I was ready to work at night as well as day, and by the most untiring perseverance and industry, I made enough to meet my expenses, and lay up a little money every week. I went on thus from May till August. Master Hugh then refused to allow me to hire my time longer. The ground for his refusal was a failure on my part, one Saturday night, to pay him for my week's time. This failure was occasioned by my attending a camp meeting about ten miles from Baltimore. During the week, I had entered into an engagement with a number of young friends to start from Baltimore to the camp ground early Saturday evening; and being detained by my employer, I was unable to get down to Master Hugh's without disappointing the company. I knew that Master Hugh was in no special need of the money that night. I therefore decided to go to camp meeting, and upon my return pay him the three dollars. I staid at the camp meeting one day longer than I intended when I left. But as soon as I returned, I called upon him to pay him what he considered his due. I found him very angry; he could scarce restrain his wrath. He said he had a great mind to give me a severe whipping. He wished to know how I dared go out of the city without asking permission. I told him I hired my time, and while I paid him the price which he asked for it, I did not know that I was bound to ask him when and where I should go. This reply troubled him; and, after reflecting a few moments, he turned to me, and said I should hire my time no longer; that the next thing he should know of, I would be running away. Upon the same plea, he told me to bring my tools and clothing home forthwith. I did so; but instead of seeking work, as I had been accustomed to do previously to hiring my time, I spent the whole week without the performance of a single stroke of work. I did this in retaliation. Saturday night, he called upon me as usual for my week's wages. I told him I had no wages; I had done no work that week. Here we were upon the point of coming to blows. He raved, and swore his determination to get hold of me. I did not allow myself a single word; but was resolved, if he laid the weight of his hand upon me, it should be blow for blow. He did not strike me, but told me that he would find me in constant employment in future. I thought the matter over during the day, Sunday, and finally resolved upon the third day of September, as the day upon which I would make a second attempt to secure my freedom. I now had three weeks during which to prepare for my journey. Early on Monday morning, before Master Hugh had time to make any engagement for me, I went out and got employment of Mr. Butler, at his ship-yard near the draw-bridge, upon what is called the City Block, thus making it unnecessary for him to seek employment for me. At the end of the week, I brought him between eight and nine dollars. He seemed very well pleased, and asked me why I did not do the same the week before. He little knew what my plans were. My object in working steadily was to remove any suspicion he might entertain of my intent to run away; and in this I succeeded admirably. I suppose he thought I was never better satisfied with my condition than at the very time during which I was planning my escape. The second week passed, and again I carried him my full wages; and so well pleased was he, that he gave me twenty-five cents, (quite a large sum for a slaveholder to give a slave), and bade me to make a good use of it. I told him I would.

Things went on without very smoothly indeed, but within there was trouble. It is impossible for me to describe my feelings as the time of my contemplated start drew near. I had a number of warm-hearted friends in Baltimore,—friends that I loved almost as I did my life,—and the thought of being separated from them forever was painful beyond expression. It is my opinion that thousands would escape from slavery, who now remain, but for the strong cords of affection that bind them to their friends. The thought of leaving my friends was decidedly the most painful thought with which I had to contend. The love of them was my tender point, and shook my decision more than all things else. Besides the pain of separation, the dread and apprehension of a failure exceeded what I had experienced at my first attempt. The appalling defeat I then sustained returned to torment me. I felt assured that, if I failed in this attempt, my case would be a hopeless one—it would seal my fate as a slave forever. I could not hope to get off with any thing less than the severest punishment, and being placed beyond the means of escape. It required no very vivid imagination to depict the most frightful scenes through which I should have to pass, in case I failed. The wretchedness of slavery, and the blessedness of freedom, were perpetually before me. It was life and death with me. But I remained firm, and, according to my resolution, on the third day of September, 1838, I left my chains, and succeeded in reaching New York without the slightest interruption of any kind. How I did so,—what means I adopted,—what direction I traveled, and by what mode of conveyance,—I must leave unexplained, for the reasons before mentioned.

I have been frequently asked how I felt when I found myself in a free State. I have never been able to answer the question with any satisfaction to myself. It was a moment of the highest excitement I ever experienced. I suppose I felt as one may imagine the unarmed mariner to feel when he is rescued by a friendly man-of-war from the pursuit of a pirate. In writing to a dear friend, immediately after my arrival at New York, I said I felt like one who had escaped a den of hungry lions. This state of mind, however, very soon subsided; and I was again seized with a feeling of great insecurity and loneliness. I was yet liable to be taken back, and subjected to all the tortures of slavery. This in itself was enough to damp the ardor of my enthusiasm. But the loneliness overcame me. There I was in the midst of thousands, and yet a perfect stranger; without home and without friends, in the midst of thousands of my own brethren—children of a common Father, and yet I dared not to unfold to anyone of them my sad condition. I was afraid to speak to any one for fear of speaking to the wrong one, and thereby falling into the hands of money-loving kidnappers, whose business it was to lie in wait for the panting fugitive, as the ferocious beasts of the forest lie in wait for their prey. The motto which I adopted when I started from slavery was this—"Trust no man!" I saw in every white man an enemy, and in almost every colored man cause for distrust. It was a most painful situation; and, to understand it, one must needs experience it, or imagine himself in similar circumstances. Let him be a fugitive slave in a strange land—a land given up to be the hunting-ground for slaveholders—whose inhabitants are legalized kidnappers—where he is every moment subjected to the terrible liability of being seized upon by his fellow-men, as the hideous crocodile seizes upon his prey! I say, let him place himself in my situation—without home or friends—without money or credit—wanting shelter, and no one to give it—wanting bread, and no money to buy it,—and at the same time let him feel that he is pursued by merciless men-hunters, and in total darkness as to what to do, where to go, or where to stay,—perfectly helpless both as to the means of defence and means of escape,—in the midst of plenty, yet suffering the terrible gnawings of hunger,—in the midst of houses, yet having no home,—among fellow-men, yet feeling as if in the midst of wild beasts, whose greediness to swallow up the trembling and half-famished fugitive is only equaled by that with which the monsters of the deep swallow up the helpless fish upon which they subsist,—I say, let him be placed in this most trying situation,—the situation in which I was placed,—then, and not till then, will he fully appreciate the hardships of, and know how to sympathize with, the toil-worn and whip-scarred fugitive slave.

Thank Heaven, I remained but a short time in this distressed situation. I was relieved from it by the humane hand of Mr. David Ruggles, whose vigilance, kindness, and perseverance, I shall never forget. I am glad of an opportunity to express, as far as words can, the love and gratitude I bear him. Mr. Ruggles is now afflicted with blindness, and is himself in need of the same kind offices which he was once so forward in the performance of toward others. I had been in New York but a few days, when Mr. Ruggles sought me out, and very kindly took me to his boarding-house at the corner of Church and Lespenard Streets. Mr. Ruggles was then very deeply engaged in the memorable Darg case, as well as attending to a number of other fugitive slaves, devising ways and means for their successful escape; and, though watched and hemmed in on almost every side, he seemed to be more than a match for his enemies.

Very soon after I went to Mr. Ruggles, he wished to know of me where I wanted to go; as he deemed it unsafe for me to remain in New York. I told him I was a calker, and should like to go where I could get work. I thought of going to Canada; but he decided against it, and in favor of my going to New Bedford, thinking I should be able to get work there at my trade. At this time, Anna, my intended wife, came on (she was free); for I wrote to her immediately after my arrival at New York, (notwithstanding my homeless, houseless, and helpless condition,) informing her of my successful flight, and wishing her to come on forthwith. In a few days after her arrival, Mr. Ruggles called in the Rev. J.W.C. Pennington, who, in the presence of Mr. Ruggles, Mrs. Michaels, and two or three others, performed the marriage ceremony, and gave us a certificate, of which the following is an exact copy:—

"This may certify, that I joined together in holy matrimony Frederick Johnson* and Anna Murray, as man and wife, in the presence of Mr. David Ruggles and Mrs. Michaels.

"James W.C. Pennington."

"New York, Sept 15, 1838"

(* I had changed my name from Frederick *Bailey* to that of *Johnson*.)

Upon receiving this certificate, and a five-dollar bill from Mr. Ruggles, I shouldered one part of our baggage, and Anna took up the other, and we set out forthwith to take passage on board of the steamboat John W. Richmond for Newport, on our way to New Bedford. Mr. Ruggles gave me a letter to a Mr. Shaw in Newport, and told me, in case my money did not serve me to New Bedford, to stop in Newport and obtain further assistance; but upon our arrival at Newport, we were so anxious to get to a place of safety, that, notwithstanding we lacked the necessary money to pay our fare, we decided to take seats in the stage, and promise to pay when we got to New Bedford. We were encouraged to do this by two excellent gentlemen, residents of New Bedford, whose names I afterward ascertained to be Joseph Ricketson and William C. Taber. They seemed at once to understand our circumstances, and gave us such assurance of their friendliness as put us fully at ease in their presence. It was good indeed to meet with such friends, at such a time. Upon reaching New Bedford, we were directed to the house of Mr. Nathan Johnson, by whom we were kindly received, and hospitably provided for. Both Mr. and Mrs. Johnson took a deep and lively interest in our welfare. They proved themselves quite worthy of the name of abolition- ists. When the stage-driver found us unable to pay our fare, he held … our baggage as security for the debt. I had but to mention the fact to Mr. Johnson, and he forthwith advanced the money.

We now began to feel a degree of safety, and to prepare ourselves for the duties and responsibili- ties of a life of freedom. On the morning after our arrival at New Bedford, while at the breakfast- table, the question arose as to what name I should be called by. The name given me by my mother was, "Frederick Augustus Washington Bailey." I, however, had dispensed with the two middle names long before I left Maryland, so that I was generally known by the name of "Stanley." When I got to New York, I again changed my name to "Frederick Johnson," and thought that would be the last change. But when I got to New Bedford, I found it necessary again to change my name. The reason of this necessity was, that there were so many Johnsons in New Bedford, it was already quite difficult to distinguish between them. I gave Mr. Johnson the privilege of choosing me a name, but told him he must not take from me the name of "Frederick." I must hold on to that, to preserve a sense of my identity. Mr. Johnson had just been reading the "Lady of the Lake," and at once suggested that my name be "Douglass." From that time until now I have been called "Frederick Douglass;" and as I am more widely known by that name than by either of the others, I shall continue to use it as my own.

I was quite disappointed at the general appearance of things in New Bedford. The impression which I had received respecting the character and condition of the people of the north, I found to be singularly erroneous. I had very strangely supposed, while in slavery, that few of the com- forts, and scarcely any of luxuries, of life were enjoyed at the north, compared with what were enjoyed by the slaveholders of the south. I probably came to this conclusion from the fact that northern people owned no slaves. I supposed that they were about upon a level with the non- slaveholding population of the south. I knew they were exceedingly poor, and I had been accus- tomed to regard their poverty as the necessary consequence of their being non-slaveholders. I had somehow imbibed the opinion that, in the absence of slaves, there could be no wealth, and very little refinement. And upon coming to the north, I expected to meet with a rough, hard-handed, and uncultivated population, living in the most Spartan-like simplicity, knowing nothing of the ease, luxury, pomp, and grandeur of southern slaveholders. Such being my conjectures, any one acquainted with the appearance of New Bedford may very readily infer how palpably I must have seen my mistake.

In the afternoon of the day when I reached New Bedford, I visited the wharves, to take a view of the shipping. Here I found myself surrounded with the strongest proofs of wealth. Lying at the wharves, and riding in the stream, I saw many ships of the finest model, in the best order, and of the largest size. Upon the right and the left, I was walled in by granite warehouses of the widest dimensions, stowed to their utmost capacity with the necessaries and comforts of life. Added to this, almost every body [sic] seemed to be at work, but noiselessly so, compared with what I had been accustomed to in Baltimore. There were no loud songs heard from those engaged in loading and unloading ships. I heard no deep oaths or horrid curses on the laborer. I saw no whipping of men; but all seemed to go smoothly on. Every man appeared to understand his work, and went at it with a sober, yet cheerful earnestness, which betokened the deep interest which he felt in what he was doing, as well as a sense of his own dignity as a man. To me this looked exceedingly strange. From the wharves I strolled around and over the town, gazing with wonder and admiration at the splendid churches, beautiful dwellings, and finely-cultivated gardens; evincing an amount of wealth, comfort, taste, and refinement, such as I had never seen in any part of slaveholding Maryland.

Every thing [sic] looked clean, new, and beautiful. I saw few or no dilapidated houses, with poverty-stricken inmates; no half-naked children and barefooted women, such as I had been accustomed to see in Hillsborough, Easton, St. Michael's, and Baltimore. The people looked more able, stronger, healthier, and happier, than those of Maryland. I was for once made glad by a view of extreme wealth, without being saddened by seeing extreme poverty. But the most astonishing as well as the most interesting thing to me was the condition of the colored people, a great many of whom, like myself, had escaped thither as a refuge from the hunters of men. I found many, who had not been seven years out of their chains, living in finer houses, and evidently enjoying more of the comforts of life, than the average of slaveholders in Maryland. I will venture to assert that my friend Mr. Nathan Johnson (of whom I can say with a grateful heart, "I was hungry, and he gave me meat; I was thirsty, and he gave me drink; I was a stranger, and he took me in") lived in a neater house; dined at a better table; took, paid for, and read, more newspapers; better understood the moral, religious, and political character of the nation,—than nine tenths of the slaveholders in Talbot county, Maryland. Yet Mr. Johnson was a working man. His hands were hardened by toil, and not his alone, but those also of Mrs. Johnson.

I found the colored people much more spirited than I had supposed they would be. I found among them a determination to protect each other from the blood-thirsty kidnapper, at all hazards. Soon after my arrival, I was told of a circumstance which illustrated their spirit. A colored man and fugitive slave were on unfriendly terms. The former was heard to threaten the latter with informing his master of his whereabouts. Straightway a meeting was called among the colored people, under the stereotyped notice, "Business of importance!" The betrayer was invited to attend. The people came at the appointed hour, and organized the meeting by appointing a very religious old gentleman as president, who, I believe, made a prayer, after which he addressed the meeting as follows: *"Friends, we have got him here, and I would recommend that you young men just take him outside the door, and kill him!"* With this, a number of them bolted at him; but they were intercepted by some more timid than themselves, and the betrayer escaped their vengeance, and has not been seen in New Bedford since. I believe there have been no more such threats, and should there be hereafter, I doubt not that death would be the consequence.

I found employment, the third day after my arrival, in stowing a sloop with a load of oil. It was new, dirty, and hard work for me; but I went at it with a glad heart and a willing hand. I was now my own master. It was a happy moment, the rapture of which can be understood only by those who have been slaves. It was the first work, the reward of which was to be entirely my own. There was no Master Hugh standing ready, the moment I earned the money, to rob me of it. I worked that day with a pleasure I had never before experienced. I was at work for myself and my newly-married wife. It was to me the starting-point of a new existence. When I got through with that job, I went in pursuit of a job of calking; but such was the strength of prejudice against color, among the white calkers, that they refused to work with me, and of course I could get no employment (I am told that colored persons can now get employment at calking in New Bedford—a result of anti-slavery effort.) Finding my trade of no immediate benefit, I threw off my calking habiliments, and prepared myself to do any kind of work I could get to do. Mr. Johnson kindly let me have his wood-horse and saw, and I very soon found myself a plenty of work. There was no work too hard—none too dirty. I was ready to saw wood, shovel coal, carry the hod, sweep the chimney, or roll oil casks,—all of which I did for nearly three years in New Bedford, before I became known to the anti-slavery world.

In about four months after I went to New Bedford, there came a young man to me, and inquired if I did not wish to take the "Liberator." I told him I did; but, just having made my escape from slavery, I remarked that I was unable to pay for it then. I, however, finally became a subscriber to it. The paper came, and I read it from week to week with such feelings as it would be quite idle for me to attempt to describe. The paper became my meat and drink. My soul was set all on fire. Its sympathy for my brethren in bonds—its scathing denunciations of slaveholders—its faithful exposures of slavery—and its powerful attacks upon the upholders of the institution—sent a thrill of joy through my soul, such as I had never felt before!

I had not long been a reader of the "Liberator," before I got a pretty correct idea of the principles, measures and spirit of the anti-slavery reform. I took right hold of the cause. I could do but little; but what I could, I did with a joyful heart, and never felt happier than when in an anti-slavery meeting. I seldom had much to say at the meetings, because what I wanted to say was said so much better by others. But, while attending an anti-slavery convention at Nantucket, on the 11th of August, 1841, I felt strongly moved to speak, and was at the same time much urged to do so by Mr. William C. Coffin, a gentleman who had heard me speak in the colored people's meeting at New Bedford. It was a severe cross, and I took it up reluctantly. The truth was, I felt myself a slave, and the idea of speaking to white people weighed me down. I spoke but a few moments, when I felt a degree of freedom, and said what I desired with considerable ease. From that time until now, I have been engaged in pleading the cause of my brethren—with what success, and with what devotion, I leave those acquainted with my labors to decide.

Douglass, F. (1845). *Narrative of the life of Frederick Douglass, an American slave*. Anti-Slavery Office.

"The progression of emancipation of any class usually, if not always, takes place through the efforts of individuals of that class."

—Harriet Martineau (1802–1876), English Writer

REFLECT & FOCUS

Tell Me

Why should it be my loneliness,
Why should it be my song,
Why should it be my dream
Deferred overlong?

What happens to a dream deferred?

—Langston Hughes (1902–1967), American Writer

READINGS

Man's Search for Meaning

By Viktor E. Frankl (1905–1997)
Austrian Author and Psychiatrist

Points to Consider

1. How strong is the connection between state of mind and state of body? What are some strategies that an individual can use to maintain a strong state of mind in difficult situations?

2. What strategies can an individual use to promote the mental health of team or group members in difficult situations?

3. Frankl states, "Any attempt to restore a man's inner strength in the camp had first to succeed in showing him some future goal." Frankl, of course, needed to find strength in some exceptionally trying circumstances. That said, does this statement have implications in an organizational setting?

4. Frankl quotes Nietzsche, stating, "He who has a why can bear with almost any how." Do you agree? Why do those engaged in leadership have an obligation to ensure that their followers have a clear understanding of why they are doing what they are doing?

Man's Search for Meaning

(Excerpt)

Experiences in a Concentration Camp

[In Auschwitz], the prisoner who had lost faith in the future—his future—was doomed. With the loss of belief in the future, he also lost his spiritual hold; he let himself decline and became subject to mental and physical decay. Usually this happened quite suddenly, in the form of a crisis, the symptoms of which were familiar to the experienced camp inmate. We all feared this moment—not for ourselves, which would have been pointless, but for our friends. Usually it began with the prisoner refusing one morning to get dressed and wash or to go out on the parade grounds. No entreaties, no blows, no threats had any effect. He just lay there, hardly moving. If this crisis was brought about by an illness, he refused to be taken to the sick-bay or to do anything to help himself. He simply gave up. There he remained lying in his own excreta, and nothing bothered him anymore.

I once had a dramatic demonstration of the close link between the loss of faith in the future and this dangerous giving up. F—, my senior block warden, a fairly well-known composer and librettist, confided in me one day: "I would like to tell you something, Doctor. I have had a strange dream. A voice told me that I could wish for something, that I should only say what I wanted to know, and all my questions would be answered. What do you think I asked? That I would like to know when the war would be over for me. You know what I mean, Doctor—for me! I wanted to know when we, when our camp, would be liberated and our sufferings come to an end."

"And when did you have this dream?" I asked.

"In February, 1945." he answered. It was then the beginning of March.

"What did your dream voice answer?"

Furtively he whispered to me, "March thirtieth."

When F— told me about his dream, he was still full of hope and convinced that the voice of his dream would be right. But as the promised day drew nearer, the war news which reached our camp made it appear very unlikely that we would be free on the promised date. On March twenty-ninth, F— suddenly became ill and ran a high temperature. On March thirtieth, the day his prophecy had told him that the war and suffering would be over for him, he became delirious and lost consciousness. On March thirty-first, he was dead. To all outward appearances, he had died of typhus.

Those who know how close the connection is between the state of mind of a man—his courage and hope, or lack of them—and the state of immunity of his body will understand that the sudden loss of hope and courage can have a deadly effect. The ultimate cause of my friend's death was that the expected liberation did not come and he was severely disappointed. This suddenly lowered his body's resistance against the latent typhus infection. His faith in the future and his will to live had become paralyzed and his body fell victim to illness—and thus the voice of his dream was right after all.

The observations of this one case and the conclusion drawn from them are in accordance with something that was drawn to my attention by the chief doctor of our concentration camp. The death rate in the week between Christmas, 1944, and New Year's, 1945, increased in camp beyond all previous experience. In his opinion, the explanation for this increase did not lie in the harder working conditions or the deterioration of our food supplies or a change of weather or new epidemics. It was simply that the majority of the prisoners had lived in the naïve hope that they would be home again by Christmas. As the time drew near and there was no encouraging news, the prisoners lost courage and disappointment overcame them. This had a dangerous influence on their powers of resistance and a great number of them died.

As we said before, any attempt to restore a man's inner strength in the camp had first to succeed in showing him some future goal. Nietzsche's words, "He who has a why can bear with almost any how," could be the guiding motto for all psychotherapeutic and psychohygienic efforts regarding prisoners. Whenever there was an opportunity for it, one had to give them a why—an aim—for their lives, in order to strengthen them to bear the terrible how of their existence. Woe to him who saw no more sense in his life, no aim, no purpose, and therefore no point in carrying on. He was soon lost. The typical reply with which such a man rejected all encouraging arguments was, "I have nothing to expect from life any more." What sort of answer can one give to that?

What was really needed was a fundamental change in our attitude toward life. We had to learn ourselves and, furthermore, we had to teach the despairing men, that it did not really matter what we expected from life, but rather what life expected from us. We needed to stop asking about the meaning of life, and instead to think of ourselves as those who were being questioned by life—daily and hourly. Our answer must consist, not in talk and meditation, but in right conduct. Life ultimately means taking the responsibility to find the right answer to its problems and to fulfill the tasks which it constantly sets for each individual.

These tasks, and therefore the meaning of life, differ from man to man, and from moment to moment. Thus it is impossible to define the meaning of life in a general way. Questions about the meaning of life can never be answered by sweeping statements. "Life" does not mean something vague, but something very real and concrete. They form man's destiny, which is different and unique for each individual. No man and no destiny can be compared with any other man or any other destiny. No situation repeats itself, and each situation calls for a different response. Sometimes the situation in which a man finds himself may require him to shape his own fate by action. At other times it is more advantageous for him to make use of an opportunity for contemplation and to realize assets in this way. Sometimes man may be required simply to accept fate, to bear his cross. Every situation is distinguished by its uniqueness, and there is always only one right answer to the problem posed by the situation at hand.

When a man finds that it is his destiny to suffer, he will have to accept his suffering as his task; his single and unique task. He will have to acknowledge the fact that even in suffering he is unique and alone in the universe. No one can relieve him of his suffering or suffer in his place. His unique opportunity lies in the way in which he bears his burden.

For us, as prisoners, these thoughts were not speculations far removed from reality. They were the only thoughts that could be of help to us. They kept us from despair, even when there seemed to be no chance of coming out of it alive. Long ago we had passed the stage of asking what was the meaning of life, a naïve query which understands life as the attaining of some aim through the active creation of something of value. For us, the meaning of life embraced the wider cycles of life and death, of suffering and of dying.

Once the meaning of suffering had been revealed to us, we refused to minimize or alleviate the camp's tortures by ignoring them or harboring false illusions and entertaining artificial optimism. Suffering had become a task on which we did not want to turn our backs. We had realized its hidden opportunities for achievement, the opportunities which caused the poet Rilke to write, "Wie viel ist aufzuleiden!" (How much suffering there is to get through!) Rilke spoke of "getting through work." There was plenty of suffering for us to get through. Therefore, it was necessary to face up to the full amount of suffering, trying to keep moments of weakness and furtive tears to a minimum. But there was no need to be ashamed of tears, for tears bore witness that a man had the greatest of courage, the courage to suffer. Only very few realized that. Shamefacedly some confessed occasionally that they had wept, like the comrade who answered my question of how he had gotten over his edema, by confessing, "I have wept it out of my system."

"The Power of Goals"

By Stephen R. Covey, A. Roger Merrill, and Rebecca R. Merrill

Introduction

Knowledge of Stephen Covey's work is helpful for a full understanding of the following reading. In his best seller *The Seven Habits of Highly Effective People* (1993), Covey explains his belief that habits are learned behavior patterns that can either assist us or prevent us from reaching our goals. In order to provide a blueprint for success he defined seven hallmark habits of successful people.

1. Be proactive: "The habit of being proactive . . . means taking responsibility for our attitudes and actions. It is instructive to break the word responsibility into two parts: response/ability. Proactive people develop the ability to choose their response, making them more a product of their values and decisions than their moods and conditions."

2. Begin with the end in mind: it is extremely important to visualize what the end product looks like, and how you and others will feel when it is completed. This visualization is your blueprint or frame of reference for making decisions that affect the attainment of goals.

3. Put first things first: in order to reach your goals, you must make countless decisions that will affect the success or failure of your goals. By understanding your priorities, you will give "less attention to activities that are urgent but not important and more time to those things that are important but not necessarily urgent."

4. Think win-win: the attitude of seeking mutual success with others. It is based on the idea of "abundance mentality" in which everyone stands to gain from the abundance of rewards that are the consequence of attaining mutual goals.

5. Seek first to understand, then be understood: by actively listening to others, you will find the "abundance of opportunities" for understanding others and being understood by others.

6. Synergize: "the habit of creative cooperation or teamwork" in which the whole is greater than the sum of the parts. Working together as a team is stronger than separate individual efforts.

7. Sharpen the saw: just as a carpenter must take time from a job to sharpen her saw in order to be more efficient, so too each of us needs to make time to practice self-renewal in the physical, mental, and emotional areas of our lives. Through self-renewal, we are able to lead balanced and fulfilling lives instead of chaotic stress-filled ones.

By developing these habits, Covey believes that you can visualize and realistically attain goals that you set for yourself or your group, team, or organization. In the following reading, Covey, Merrill, and Merrill provide you with a format for developing and attaining goals.

Points to Consider

1. What is the connection between self-awareness and integrity?

2. How can one help prevent a team or group from facing the two areas of pain described by the authors?

3. What does the phrase "ladders against the wrong wall" mean? Can you think of examples of groups or organizations that have fallen into this situation? What are some strategies to avoid setting ladders against the wrong wall?

4. How do Viktor Frankl's experiences in a concentration camp demonstrate Covey, Merrill, and Merrill's explanation that powerful goal setting accesses the "four human endowments"?

"The Power of Goals"

You can want to do the right thing,
And you can even want to do it for the right reasons.
But if you don't apply the right principles,
You can still hit a wall.

One of the most common elements of all self-help and management literature is the idea of the power of goals. We've been told to set long-term goals, short-term goals, daily goals, monthly goals, personal goals, organizational goals, ten-year goals, lifetime goals. The virtues of "measurable, specific, and time-bound" goals have been preached from the pulpit of self-help books for generations.

Goal setting is obviously a powerful process. It's based on the same principle of focus that allows us to concentrate rays of diffused sunlight into a force powerful enough to start a fire. It's the manifestation of creative imagination and independent will. It's the practicality of "eating our elephants one bite at a time," of translating vision into achievable, actionable doing. It's a common denominator of successful individuals and organizations.

But despite their obvious value, our experience with and feelings about goals are mixed. Some of us can set heroic goals, exercise tremendous discipline, and pay the price for incredible achievement. Others can't keep a New Year's resolution to pass up dessert two days in a row. Some see goals as the primary factor shaping the destiny of individuals and nations. Others see them as superficial, pie-in-the-sky idealism that has no staying power in the "real" world. Some of us stick to a goal, no matter what. And some goals stick to us, no matter what. Some authors tell us that if we think positively, we can do anything; others tell us to stop beating ourselves up when we find out we can't.

Two Areas of Pain

In all our experience around goal setting, there seem to be two major areas of pain: 1) the blow to our integrity and courage when we don't achieve our goals; and 2) the sometimes devastating results when we do.

Withdrawals from the "Personal Integrity Account"

As we said earlier, we each have what we might call a "Personal Integrity Account" that reflects the amount of trust we have in ourselves. When we make and keep commitments, such as setting and achieving goals, we make deposits. We increase our confidence in our own trustworthiness, in our ability to make and keep commitments to ourselves and to others. A high balance in this account is a great source of strength and security.

But when we don't achieve our goals, we make withdrawals, and this becomes a source of great pain. Over time, frequent withdrawals cause us to lose confidence in our ability to make and keep commitments and to trust ourselves and others. Cynicism and rationalization follow, and these attitudes sever us from the power of setting and achieving meaningful goals. Then, when we need strength of character to meet critical challenges in our lives, we find it just isn't there.

Stephen: Once I served as an assistant in a survival camp and led a group of students on an overnight hike. We ended up in a valley where we had to cross a river hand-over-hand on a rope. We were exhausted, fatigued, and dehydrated. We'd had no food or water for about twenty-four hours. But we knew that across that raging, forty-foot-wide river was breakfast.

As one of the leaders of the group, I was supposed to go first. I started out with determination and even a little arrogance. I started bouncing around on the rope and showing off. But by the time I got halfway over, I felt my strength starting to go. I tried every technique I knew—from sheer will power to visualizing myself making it across and eating that food—but I reached the point where I was afraid even to take my hand off the rope to move forward. I didn't have the confidence my other hand could continue to hold up my body weight.

Right in the middle of the river, I fell. The strength just wasn't there. I was dangling on my safety rope on top of this churning water. The students loved it! "Pride goeth before the fall." As it turned out, most of them had the same experience. Only a few had the strength to make it.

Building character strength is like building physical strength. When the test comes, if you don't have it, no cosmetics can disguise the fact that it just isn't there. You can't fake it. It takes strength to set a heroic goal, to work on chronic problems instead of going for the "quick fix," to stay with your commitments when the tide of popular opinion turns against you.

There are many reasons why we don't achieve our goals. Sometimes the goals we set are unrealistic. We create expectations that don't reflect any sense of self-awareness. New Year's resolutions are typical examples. Suddenly, we expect to change the way we eat, the way we exercise, or the way we treat people simply because the calendar has changed from December 31 to January 1. It's like expecting one of our children to learn to crawl, eat with a fork, and drive a car all in the same day. Our goals are based on illusion, with little self-awareness or regard for the principles of natural growth.

Sometimes we set goals and work to achieve them, but either the circumstances change or we change. A new opportunity surfaces; there's a shift in the economy; another person comes into the picture; we get a different perspective. If we hold on to our goals, they become masters instead of servants. But if we let them go, we often feel uneasy or guilty that we didn't keep our commitment. We find it hard to maintain a high balance in our Personal Integrity Account when we constantly change our goals or fail to achieve our goals.

Ladders Against the Wrong Wall

While failing to achieve our goals creates painful problems, accomplishing them can as well. Sometimes the goals we achieve are at the expense of other more important things in our lives. It's the "ladder against the wrong wall" syndrome, meaning we climb the proverbial ladder of success only to find that it's leaning against the wrong wall for us.

One of our associates shared this story:

Several years ago, a man announced to his friends and neighbors that his goal for the year was to earn a million dollars. He was an entrepreneur who believed, "Give me a good idea and I can sell a million." He developed and patented a state-of-the-art recreational product, and then drove around the country selling it.

Occasionally he would take one of his kids with him on the road for a week or so. His wife complained to him about taking the kids, saying, "When they come back, they stop saying their prayers and doing their homework. They just party the whole week. Don't take the kids if you aren't going to help them do the things they ought to be doing."

Well, at the end of the year, the man announced that he had met his goal: he made a million dollars. Shortly after, however, he and his wife divorced. A couple of his kids wound up on drugs. Another went off the deep end. Basically the whole family disintegrated.

This man was focused on a single goal and measured everything against it. But he failed to count the total cost. That million dollars cost him a lot more than it was worth.

When we become consumed by a single goal, we're like a horse with blinders, unable to see anything else. Sometimes our goals are "hit-and-run" goals that leave bodies strewn along the way. At other times, our goals may be well intended, but accomplishing them creates other undesirable results. A program participant from Russia shared this experience:

Gorbachev wanted to restrict the use of alcohol and not allow the Russian people to drink as much. It was like the American Prohibition, with similar results. Rather than turning to more productive activities, as was hoped, people went from drinking alcohol to using narcotics instead. The government achieved their goal of dramatically reducing the consumption of alcohol, but it didn't bring them what they wanted.

We typically set a goal with the expectation that meeting it will create positive change and quality-of-life results. But often the change isn't so positive. Accomplishing one goal impacts other areas of life in a negative way. When we come face-to-face with the results, we become disillusioned.

In light of this "disillusioned if we do, and doomed if we don't" dilemma regarding goals, is it any wonder that many of us feel uncomfortable with the goal-setting process?

Is it possible to have the power without the problems? To build a strong Personal Integrity Account by setting and achieving meaningful goals on a regular basis? To be able to let go of or change or even partly reach a goal and still maintain, or even add to, our Personal Integrity Account? To ensure that our ladders are leaning against the right walls?

We affirm that it is possible—even that we can access a significant increase in the power of goal setting. The key is in using our four human endowments in a synergistic way in setting and achieving principle-based goals.

Using Our Four Human Endowments

Done well, traditional goal setting is powerful because it accesses the power of two of our unique endowments: *creative imagination and independent will.*

We use our creative imagination to visualize, to conceive of possibilities beyond our direct experience. We use our independent will to make choices, to transcend background, scripting, and circumstance. When we set a goal, we're saying, "I can envision something different from what is, and I choose to focus my efforts to create it." We use our imagination to keep the goal in mind, and our independent will to pay the price to achieve it.

The power of these two endowments is formidable—it's the power of purposeful living, the fundamental process of conscious change. But it's only a small part of the power available to us.

What's often missing in the goal-setting process is the power of two other endowments:

- Conscience—the deep connection of goals to mission, needs and principles; and

- Self-awareness—the accurate assessment of our capacity and the balance in our Personal Integrity Account.

Let's take a closer look at these two endowments to see how they can empower us to set and achieve meaningful goals.

Conscience Creates Alignment with Mission and Principles

Conscience is powerful because it creates alignment between mission and principles and gives guidance in the moment of choice. The moment we set a goal—the moment we consciously decide to focus our time and energy toward a particular purpose—is a moment of choice. What determines that choice? Is it the social mirror, the agendas of others, values that are truncated from fundamental principles, needs, and capacities? Or is it a deep, principle-based, conscience-connected, contribution-focused fire within?

Goals that are connected to our inner life have the power of passion and principle. They're fueled by the fire within and based on "true north" principles that create quality-of-life results.

One of the best ways to access this power is to ask three vital questions: what? why? and how?

What?

What do I desire to accomplish? What is the contribution I want to make? What is the end I have in mind?

A principle-based "what" focuses on growth and contribution. It isn't just setting and achieving goals that creates quality of life. Hitler set and achieved goals. So did Gandhi. The difference is what they chose to focus on. What we seek, we generally find. When we set goals that are in harmony with conscience and the principles that create quality of life, we seek—and find—the best.

Why?

Why do I want to do it? Does my goal grow out of mission, needs, and principles? Does it empower me to contribute through my roles?

In the context of mission and vision, the "what" may be easier to identify than the "why" and "how."

Roger: After speaking on the importance of mission and roles in a recent seminar, I asked one of the participants if he would be willing to go through the goal-setting process with me in front of the group. He agreed.

I said, "Okay, choose a role—any role you'd like."

"Father."

"What do you feel is the most important goal you could work on in this role?"

"To improve my relationship with my fourteen-year-old son."

"Why?"

"Well, our relationship's not that good."

"So why do you want to improve it?"

"He's having a lot of challenges at school with friends and peer pressure. He's being pulled in directions that are not productive. I feel it's important to be close to him at this time in his life."

"Why?"

"So I can help him stay on the right path and be productive."

"Why?"

"Because he needs it."

"So why do you want to do it?"

"To help him."

"Why?"

He was beginning to get a little flustered. "Because I'm his father! It's my responsibility!"

"So why do you want to do it?"

Frustration was evident on his face. "Well, because . . . because. . ."

There were two people at his table who absolutely could not sit still a minute longer. At the same instant, they both almost shouted, "Because you love him!"

It was written all over his face. It was reflected in his words. It was so evident that people around him could sense the deep love he had for his son. Maybe he couldn't say it because of the seminar environment, or maybe he hadn't made the connection with that fire within.

The moment these two people said the words, his face broke into a sheepish grin. "That's right!" he said. "I love him." Everyone could feel the strength and peace that flooded over him.

Without this deep connection, we go through life feeling duty-bound to develop sufficient self-control to achieve our goals, to endure to the end, to crawl battered and bruised over the finish line, if it's the last thing we do. There's no connection to our deep energy sources, our convictions, our experiences. We're working against ourselves, not sure why (or even if) we want to accomplish a particular goal. The commitments we make in a moment of enthusiasm don't have the sustaining power to carry us all the way to successful achievement of our goals.

The key to motivation is motive. It's the "why." It's what gives us the energy to stay strong in hard moments. It gives us the strength to say "no" because we connect with a deeper "yes!" burning inside.

If a goal isn't connected to a deep "why," it may be good, but it usually isn't best. We need to question the goal. If it is connected, we need to push our thinking and feeling until we break through and create an open flow between the passion of vision and the goal. The stronger the connection, the stronger and more sustained the motivation.

How?

How am I going to do it? What are the key principles that will empower me to achieve my purpose? What strategies can I use to implement these principles?

Once we create alignment between the "what" and the "why," we're ready to look at the "how." The choice of how often boils down to a choice between "control" and "release" styles of thinking and managing. If our paradigm is one of control, we assume that people have to be tightly supervised if they're going to produce or perform well. If our paradigm is one of release, our assumption is that, given the freedom, opportunity, and support, people will bring out the highest and best within them and accomplish great things.

The way we see others in terms of control or release generally reflects the way we see ourselves. If we have a control perspective, we assume we have to exercise strict control over ourselves if we want to accomplish anything. If we have release perspective, we see our primary leadership task as creating optimal conditions for releasing inner capacities. If our focus in goal setting is on the endowment of independent will—gut it out, discipline ourselves, do it no matter what—that's a good indication that our basic paradigm is one of control.

Roger: I said, "Okay, how are you going to show your love?"

"I don't know. I guess I'll just look for opportunities."

"How else?"

"I'm going to invest the time."

"How else?"

He sighed. "I don't know. To tell you the truth, I'm scared. I've tried before, and it hasn't worked. Sometimes it seems like the harder I try, the worse it gets."

We then began to talk about some of the principles that could be applied in his relationship with his son. We talked about trustworthiness—if you want to build a trusting relationship, be trustworthy. Make and keep commitments. Be loyal to those not present. We talked about empathy—seek first to understand. Give respect.

He began to realize that, no matter how desperately he wanted to help his son, his efforts would never be effective as long as he was building the relationship on the illusion that he could control him with good intent—not on the reality that he could release him with principle-centered leadership and love.

Often in a seminar situation, people choose a business instead of a family role. Most have an immediate sense of "what" they feel they should do:

"Increase sales 5 percent this month."

"Reduce operating costs 3 percent by the end of the quarter."

"Improve office morale."

But when we go through the "why" process, the motivations people recognize at first are usually negative, economic, extrinsically focused, or urgent:

"If I don't do it I'm going to lose my job."

"If I don't accomplish it, I'm going to lose credibility, and I'll feel terrible."

"We have a real problem here that has to be fixed before it spreads."

As we press for deeper answers, we often begin to hear a different story:

"If I do it, I'm going to feel like I really did my job and earned my pay."

"I enjoy feeling like I did something and provided a quality service to the customer."

"I really care about trying to make this world a better place."

Many businesses are so focused on the economic or physical dimension that they never tap into the deeper motivations. They fail to recognize or address social, mental, and spiritual needs. They don't let people connect naturally with what they feel in their hearts—their need to love, to learn, to live for something higher than self. And yet this connection is the very source of the energy, the creativity, the loyalty employers seek.

When we get to the "how," people who choose a business role usually think they just have to "gut it out."

"I just have to get in there and do it."

"Have you tried that before?"

"Yes."

"Did it work?"

"No."

We then talk together about some of the "true north" principles that could make a difference. We look at principles of interdependence—empathy, honesty, making and keeping commitments, building relationships. We look at principles of shared vision, win-win agreements, and systems alignment. It soon becomes apparent that knowing what to do and even deeply wanting to do it are not enough. The doing has to be based on the principles that create quality of life.

Doing the right thing for the right reason in the right way is the key to quality of life, and that can only come through the power of an educated conscience that aligns us with vision, mission, and true north.

Self-Awareness Empowers Us to Build Integrity

Our trustworthiness is only as high as the balance in our Personal Integrity Account. Because our integrity is the basis of our confidence in ourselves and the confidence we inspire in others, one of the greatest manifestations of effective personal leadership is the exercise of care and wisdom in building a high positive balance in that account.

Primarily, we build it through the exercise of independent will in making and keeping commitments. But without self-awareness, we don't have the wisdom necessary to manage such an account. We may set our goals too high, turning potential deposits into huge withdrawals when we fail to achieve them. We may set our goals too low, depositing pennies when we could be depositing dollars. We may pass up daily, weekly, moment-by-moment opportunities to make deposits because we're too busy blaming circumstances or other people for our own failure to achieve our goals.

Self-awareness involves deep personal honesty. It comes from asking and answering hard questions:

Do I really want to do it?

Am I willing to pay the price?

Do I have enough strength to do it?

Do I accept the responsibility for my own growth?

Am I settling for mediocrity when I could be achieving excellence?

Am I blaming and accusing others for my own inability to set and achieve goals?

Self-awareness prompts us to start where we are—no illusions, no excuses—and helps us to set realistic goals. On the other hand, it also doesn't allow us to cop out with mediocrity. It helps us recognize and respect our need to stretch, to push the limits, to grow. Since much of our frustration in life comes as a result of unmet expectations, the ability to set goals that are both realistic and challenging goes a long way toward empowering us to create peace and positive growth in our lives.

Self-awareness is ear to the voice of conscience. It helps us to recognize that there are principles independent of us, to understand the futility of trying to become a law unto ourselves. It helps us to be humble and open to growth and change, to realize that we are neither omniscient nor omnipotent when we set a goal. To the best of our awareness at the time, out of all the good things we could do, we choose the best thing, for the best reason, and we plan to do it in the best way.

But the situation may change. We may change. And we can't act with integrity without being open to that change.

Self-awareness empowers us to ask: Am I allowing the good to take the place of the best? The best may be the goal we set. The best may be in the unexpected opportunity, the new knowledge, the new options created by increased understanding. If change is driven primarily by urgency, mood, or opposition, it takes us away from the best. If change is driven by mission, conscience, and principles, it moves us toward the best. To have the self-awareness to know the difference between the good and the best and to act based on mission, conscience, and principles is to make the most significant deposits in our Personal Integrity Account.

Integrity means more than sticking to a goal, no matter what. It's integrity of system, an integrated process that creates an open connection between the mission and the moment.

How to Set and Achieve Principle-Based Goals

Without principles, goals will never have the power to produce quality-of-life results. You can want to do the right thing, and you can even want to do it for the right reasons. But if you don't apply the right principles, you can still hit a wall. A principle-based goal is all three: **the right thing, for the right reason, in the right way**.

Principle-based goal setting involves the full, synergistic use of all four human endowments:

- Through conscience, we connect with the passion of vision and mission and the power of principles.

- Through creative imagination, we envision possibility and synergistic, creative ways to achieve it.

- Through self-awareness, we set goals with realistic stretch and stay open to conscience-driven change.

- Through independent will, we make purposeful choice and carry it out; we have the integrity to walk our talk.

The principle-based goal-setting process is most effective when it includes: 1) setting "context" goals, 2) keeping a "perhaps" list, and 3) setting weekly goals.

1. Setting Long-Term and "Context" Goals

Most people find it helpful to connect weekly goals with the context provided by their mission statement through the use of long-term and mid-range goals. But the terms "long-term" and "mid-range" put these goals into a chronos framework.

While timing may be an important issue, we suggest that other issues such as relationships with people and with other goals and events are better recognized through "context" goals. The term "context" reminds us that personal leadership is not just having a long-range view—it's having broad-range understanding.

If you organize around your roles, you could keep a page of context goals under each role in your organizer for easy access. The what/why/how format is an effective way to capture these goals. For example, a context goal in your "sharpen the saw" role might look like this:

What:
My goal is to maintain a healthy, well-disciplined body.

Why:
So that:

- I can have the strength, endurance, and physical presentation necessary to effectively fulfill my missions.

- I can be an example to my children and to others in effective health maintenance.

- I can build my personal character strength.

How:
- *Good Nutrition.* I will increase my intake of fresh fruits and vegetables, complex carbohydrates, whole grains, poultry, and fish; I will decrease my intake of sugars, fats, salt, and red meats; and I will eat smaller meals more frequently.

- *Physical maintenance.* I will do thirty minutes of aerobic exercise four times a week; I will join a basketball league; and I will get seven hours of sleep a night by retiring and rising early.

- *Mind/body connection.* I will think positive thoughts about my body and health; I will read and attend seminars and workshops to learn more about health.

- *Focus.* I will attend to specific health problems.

This "what/why/how" format creates an open connection between mission, principles, and goals. As you prepare to set your weekly goals, you can review these context goals to immediately tap into that connection and select a bite-sized actionable piece that will move you toward them.

Looking at a goal in this way reaffirms the interconnectedness of our lives. Although this goal might be considered a "physical" goal and filed under the "sharpen the saw" role, think of how interrelated it is with each of the other dimensions and with all other roles.

For example, most people report that one of the greatest benefits of regular physical exercise is not in the physical, but in the spiritual dimension—the increase in integrity and character strength. The mental dimension—learning about health, thinking healthy thoughts, and reducing stress—powerfully impacts the effectiveness of this "physical" goal. Exercising with friends or family members can create a rich social as well as physical experience. Increased health empowers us in the physical, mental, social, and spiritual dimensions of all our other roles.

An awareness of this interconnectedness keeps us open to abundance thinking and empowers us to create a powerful synergy among our goals.

2. Keeping a "Perhaps" List
One problem we have in dealing with goals is that often we read a book, attend a seminar, or have a conversation with someone and come away from the experience with an idea of something we really want to do. We're not ready to set a goal, but we don't want to lose the idea.

Most of the time, we let it wander around in an already overcluttered cerebral waiting room, floating in and out of awareness, distracting us from the task at hand and causing a vague uneasiness of something not yet done. Or we write it down on a generic "to do" list that collects items faster than they can ever be accomplished, mingles top-priority items with things that don't matter much, and constantly reminds us of all we haven't done.

Far more effective is the "perhaps" list, a list kept under each role of things you might want to do. Whenever an idea occurs to you, write it on the "perhaps" list under the appropriate role for future consideration. Writing it here does not mean it's a goal or a commitment. Perhaps you'll do it; perhaps you won't. It's simply input to be considered for future organizing. Your integrity is not on the line.

Noting ideas on a "perhaps" list diffuses the anxiety and distraction and makes them accessible for future consideration. During weekly organizing, you can look over the list, translate any item you wish to a goal for the week, keep it on the list for future reconsideration or discard it as not really that important.

3. Setting Weekly Goals
When we set our weekly goals, the "what/why/how" format becomes more a way of thinking about our roles and goals. As we set our goals, we look at each role, and then we pause in the space between stimulus and response to ask:

What are the one or two most important things I could do in this role this week that would have the greatest positive impact?

The answer to this question may be in a feeling or impression that comes as we review our mission and roles. One man shared this experience:

When I review my roles each week, I often get impressions of specific things I need to do, especially in my role as a father. Something will come to my mind regarding a particular child. I find I'm more aware of my children's individual needs, more sensitive and open to opportunities to make a difference.

The answer may come as a result of reviewing our context goals in each role, or from an insight or idea we put on our "perhaps" list in a particular role during the week. As we review these things, we create an open connection between our deep inner life and our current situation. We create the context that gives meaning to our goals.

Characteristics of Effective Weekly Goals

As you set your goals, keep in mind five characteristics of effective weekly goals:

1. They're driven by conscience.

An effective goal is in harmony with our inner imperatives. It's not driven by urgency or reaction. It's not a reflection of the social mirror. It's something we feel, deep inside, we need to do, and it's in harmony with our mission and with true north principles. We need to be sensitive to our inner voice of conscience, especially as we select goals in our most unique roles, where we can have the greatest influence. We also need to maintain balance. It's important to remember that we don't necessarily need to set a goal in each role each week. There are times of short-term imbalance when wisdom suggests that we make the conscious choice not to set goals in some roles.

2. They're often Quadrant II goals.

The Quadrant II organizing process automatically creates a connection between the "what" and the "why." As a result, the goals that we select are typically important, but not necessarily urgent. We may also select some Quadrant I goals that are both urgent and important, but we select them primarily because they're important (for further explanation, see First Things First).

3. They reflect our four basic needs and capacities.

Good goals can be about doing in the physical dimension but they can also be about understanding and being (the spiritual dimension), relating (the social dimension), and growing or learning (the mental dimension). Many of us feel dissatisfied and imbalanced because the goals we pursue are essentially time-bound and physical. To ignore the reality of other vital dimensions is to severely limit our capacity to create meaningful quality of life. It's also to deprive ourselves of the incredible synergy that can be created among goals.

4. They're in our Center of Focus.

We each have what we call a Circle of Concern that encompasses everything we're concerned about—our health, a meeting with the boss, a teenage son's plans for the weekend, offensive magazines on display in a neighborhood convenience store, the President's foreign policy decisions, the threat of nuclear war. We also have another circle that usually falls within this Circle of Concern called the Circle of Influence. This circle defines the area of concern where we can actually make a difference. We may not be able to influence the President's foreign policy decisions or the threat of nuclear war, but we can do something about our health. We may also be

UNIT
6

able to influence our son's weekend plans or the neighborhood store's magazine display. But the most effective use of our time and energy is generally in a third circle—the Center of Focus. In this circle are the things we're concerned about, that are within our ability to influence, that are aligned with our mission, and are timely. To spend time and effort in any other circle diminishes our effectiveness. When we operate in our Circle of Concern, we basically waste effort on things we have no ability to control or affect. When we operate within our Circle of Influence, we do some good, but what we do may be at the expense of something better. When we set and achieve goals that are in our Center of Focus, we maximize the use of our time and effort. Interestingly, we find that as we do this over time, our Circle of Influence automatically increases. We find positive ways to influence more people and circumstances.

5. They're either determinations or concentrations.

You may find it helpful to distinguish between determinations—things you're determined to do, no matter what—and concentrations, areas of pursuit you focus your efforts around. When you set a determination, you put your integrity on the line. This is when it's vital to follow through, to keep our commitment, to do what you said you were going to do. The only valid reason for not sticking to a determination would be if you became thoroughly convinced—through conscience and deep self-awareness—that the "best" goal you set had for some reason become only "good." Then, and only then, could you change with integrity. When you set a concentration, you identify an area where you desire to focus time and energy. You seek opportunities to do it. You move toward it. But you don't risk your integrity. If you don't do it, you lose the benefit of the time and energy you invested, but you don't make withdrawals from your Personal Integrity Account. Remember, you don't have to put your integrity on the line every time you set a weekly goal. In fact, it's important to manage your actual commitments with great care, being sensitive and wise in building the balance in your Personal Integrity Account. But your caution should not keep you from moving forward with purpose.

Confidence and Courage

To set and work toward any goal is an act of courage. When we exercise the courage to set and act on goals that are connected to principles and conscience, we tend to achieve positive results. Over time, we create an upward spiral of confidence and courage. Our commitment becomes stronger than our moods. Eventually, our integrity is not even an issue. We build the courage to set increasingly challenging, even heroic goals. This is the process of growth, of becoming all we can become.

On the other hand, when we exercise courage in setting goals that are not deeply connected to principles and conscience, we often get undesirable results that lead to discouragement and cynicism. The cycle is reversed. Eventually, we find ourselves without the courage to set even small goals.

The power of principle-based goal setting is the power of principles—the confidence that the goals we set will create quality-of-life results, that our ladders are leaning against the right walls. It's the power of integrity—the ability to set and achieve meaningful goals regularly, the ability to change with confidence when the "best" becomes the "good." It's the power of the four human endowments working together to create the passion, vision, awareness, creativity, and character strength that nurture growth.

To access this power is to create the upward spiral that empowers us to continually put first things first in our lives.

Quadrant II Ideas to Nurture the Power of Goals

• Use the what/why/how format to set context goals in each of your roles.

• Set up a "perhaps" list under each role in your organizer. During the week, write down ideas that come to you for goals you may want to set under the appropriate role. Notice how you feel about putting these ideas on "perhaps" lists. As you plan your next week, refer to the lists for goal ideas.

• As you set your weekly goals, pause and connect with conscience. Act on what you feel is most important for you to do in each role.

• Think about how you're using each of your endowments as you set and achieve goals for the week.

• Identify each of your goals for the week as a "determination" or "concentration." At the end of the week, analyze how this differentiation affected your attitude toward the goal, your progress in achieving it, and the balance in your Personal Integrity Account.

Covey, S., Merrill, A. R., & Merrill, R. (1994). The Power of Goals. In *First Things First*. Used by permission of Franklin Covey.

"Seven Reasons Carrots and Sticks (Often) Don't Work"

By Daniel H. Pink

Introduction

This is Chapter 2 in Pink's book, *Drive: The Surprising Truth About What Motivates Us*. In the book's Introduction and first chapter, Pink provides information or explanations that will help you as you read the following excerpt from the book:

Historically, psychologists understood two motivational drives—biological needs, and external rewards and punishments. Harry F. Harlow's research in the 1940s resulted in his proposal of a new theory, postulating a third drive—intrinsic reward in which the internal joy of a task was its own reward. Pink explains that all animals have the biological drive as their "operating system," which he calls Motivation 1.0. As humans developed increasingly complex societies, a new "operating system" emerged that acknowledged biological drive but also included "cultural engineering" related to rewards and punishments. Pink calls this "operating system" Motivation 2.0. Motivation 2.0 has been around a long time, and there have been adjustments and "bug-fixes" (resulting in Motivation 2.1, and 2.2, etc.), but the premise of Pink's book is that Motivation 2.0—which is all about extrinsic rewards and punishments—is unreliable and doesn't always work to explain human behavior. He writes:

Motivation 2.0 suffers from three compatibility problems. It doesn't mesh with the way many new business models are organizing what we do—because we're intrinsically motivated purpose maximizers, not only extrinsically motivated profit maximizers. It doesn't comport with the way that twenty-first-century economics thinks about what we do—because economists are finally realizing that we're full-fledged human beings, not single-minded economic robots. And perhaps most important, it's hard to reconcile

with much of what we actually do at work—because for growing numbers of people, work is often creative, interesting, and self-directed rather than unrelentingly routine, boring, and other-directed. Taken together, these compatibility problems warn us that something's gone awry in our motivational operating system. (pp. 32–33).

The following chapter from Pink's book takes a closer look at the "bugs" in the system.

Points to Consider

1. Pink describes self-set goals that are devoted to achieving mastery as typically healthy. Can you think of examples of self-set goals that are unhealthy? How can you make sure that the goals you set are intrinsically focused and healthy?

2. How can one ensure that the goals developed for a group won't result in the negative behaviors described in this reading?

3. How can an organization ensure that any extrinsic motivators used are balanced by substantial intrinsic motivation?

4. In what ways is it ethical or unethical to create competition for extrinsic rewards?

5. How can the risk of goals that unintentionally encourage unethical actions be minimized?

"Seven Reasons Carrots and Sticks (Often) Don't Work"

Editors' Note: End notes are not included.

An object in motion will stay in motion, and an object at rest will stay at rest, unless acted on by an outside force.

That's Newton's first law of motion. Like Newton's other laws, this one is elegant and simple—which is part of its power. Even people like me, who bumbled through high school physics, can understand it and can use it to interpret the world.

Motivation 2.0 is similar. At its heart are two elegant and simple ideas:

Rewarding an activity will get you more of it. Punishing an activity will get you less of it.

And just as Newton's principles can help us explain our physical environment or chart the path of a thrown ball, Motivation 2.0's principles can help us comprehend our social surroundings and predict the trajectory of human behavior.

But Newtonian physics runs into problems at the subatomic level. Down there—in the land of hadrons, quarks, and Schrödinger's cat—things get freaky. The cool rationality of Isaac Newton gives way to the bizarre unpredictability of Lewis Carroll. Motivation 2.0 is similar in this regard too. When rewards and punishments encounter our third drive, something akin to behavioral quantum mechanics seems to take over and strange things begin to happen.

Of course, the starting point for any discussion of motivation in the workplace is a simple fact of life: People have to earn a living. Salary, contract payments, some benefits, a few perks are what I call "baseline rewards." If someone's baseline rewards aren't adequate or equitable, her focus will be on the unfairness of her situation and the anxiety of her circumstance. You'll get neither the predictability of extrinsic motivation nor the weirdness of intrinsic motivation. You'll get very little motivation at all.

But once we're past that threshold, carrots and sticks can achieve precisely the *opposite* of their intended aims. Mechanisms designed to increase motivation can dampen it. Tactics aimed at boosting creativity can reduce it. Programs to promote good deeds can make them disappear. Meanwhile, instead of restraining negative behavior, rewards and punishments can often set it loose—and give rise to cheating, addiction, and dangerously myopic thinking.

This is weird. And it doesn't hold in all circumstances (about which more after this chapter). But as Edward Deci's Soma puzzle experiment demonstrates, many practices whose effectiveness we take for granted produce counterintuitive results. They can give us less of what we want—and more of what we don't want. These are the bugs in Motivation 2.0. And they rise to the surface whether we're promising rupees in India, charging shekels in Israel, drawing blood in Sweden, or painting portraits in Chicago.

Less of What We Want

One of the most enduring scenes in American literature offers an important lesson in human motivation. In Chapter 2 of Mark Twin's *The Adventures of Tom Sawyer*, Tom faces the dreary task of whitewashing Aunt Polly's 810-square-foot fence. He's not exactly thrilled with the assignment. "Life to him seemed hollow, and existence but a burden," Twain writes.

But just when Tom has nearly lost hope, "nothing less than a great, magnificent inspiration" bursts upon him. When his friend Ben ambles by and mocks Tom for his sorry lot, Tom acts confused. Slapping paint on a fence isn't a grim chore he says. It's a fantastic privilege—a source of, ahem, intrinsic motivation. The job is so captivating that when Ben asks to try a few brush-strokes himself, Tom refuses. He doesn't relent until Ben gives up his apple in exchange for the opportunity.

Soon more boys arrive, all of whom tumble into Tom's trap and end up whitewashing the fence—several times over—on his behalf. From this episode, Twain extracts a key motivational principle, namely "that Work consists of whatever a body is OBLIGED to do, and the Play consists of whatever a body is not obliged to do." He goes on to write:

> There are wealthy gentlemen in England who drive four-horse passenger-coaches twenty or thirty miles on a daily line, in the summer, because the privilege costs them considerable money; but if they were offered wages for the service, that would turn it into work and then they would resign.

In other words, rewards can perform a weird sort of behavioral alchemy: They can transform an interesting task into a drudge. They can turn play into work. And by diminishing intrinsic motivation, they can send performance, creativity, and even upstanding behavior toppling like dominoes. Let's call this the Sawyer Effect. (Here's the two-sided definition of the Sawyer Effect: practices that can either turn play into work or turn work into play.) A sampling of intriguing experiments around the world reveals the four realms where this effect kicks in—and shows yet again the mismatch between what science knows and what business does.

Intrinsic Motivation

Behavioral scientists like Deci began discovering the Sawyer Effect nearly forty years ago, although they didn't use that term. Instead, they referred to the counterintuitive consequences of extrinsic incentives as "the hidden costs of rewards." That, in fact, was the title of the first book on the subject—a 1978 research volume that was edited by psychologists Mark Lepper and David Greene.

One of Lepper and Greene's early studies (which they carried out with a third colleague, Robert Nisbett) has become a classic in the field and among the most cited articles in the motivation literature. The three researchers watched a classroom of preschoolers for several days and identified the children who chose to spend their "free play" time drawing. Then they fashioned an experiment to test the effect of rewarding an activity these children clearly enjoyed.

The researchers divided the children into three groups. The first was the "expected-award" group. They showed each of these children a "Good Player" certificate—adorned with a blue ribbon and featuring the child's name—and asked if the child wanted to draw in order to receive the award. The second group was the "unexpected-award" group. Researchers asked these children simply if they wanted to draw. If they decided to, when the session ended, the researchers handed each child one of the "Good Player" certificates. The third group was the "no-award" group. Researchers asked these children if they wanted to draw, but neither promised them a certificate at the beginning nor gave them one at the end.

Two weeks later, back in the classroom, teachers set out paper and markers during the preschool's free play period while the researchers secretly observed the students. Children previously in the "unexpected-award" and "no-award" groups drew just as much, and with the same relish, as they had before the experiment. But children in the first group—the ones who'd expected and then received an award—showed much less interest and spent much less time drawing. The Sawyer Effect had taken hold. Even two weeks later, those alluring prizes—so common in classrooms and cubicles—had turned play into work.

To be clear, it wasn't necessarily the rewards themselves that dampened the children's interest. Remember: When children didn't expect a reward, receiving one had little impact on their intrinsic motivation. Only *contingent* rewards—if you do this, then you'll get that—had the negative effect. Why? "If–then" rewards require people to forfeit some of their autonomy. Like the gentlemen driving carriages for money instead of fun, they're no longer fully controlling their lives. And that can spring a hole in the bottom of their motivational bucket, draining an activity of its enjoyment.

Lepper and Greene replicated these results in several subsequent experiments with children. As time went on, other researchers found similar results with adults. Over and over again, they discovered that extrinsic rewards—in particular, contingent, expected, "if–then" rewards—snuffed out the third drive.

These insights proved so controversial—after all, they called into question a standard practice of most companies and schools—that in 1999 Deci and two colleagues reanalyzed nearly three decades of studies on the subject to confirm the findings. "Careful consideration of reward effects reported in 128 experiments lead to the conclusion that tangible rewards tend to have a substantially negative effect on intrinsic motivation," they determined. "When institutions—families, schools, businesses, and athletic teams, for example—focus on the short-term and opt for controlling people's behavior," they do considerable long-term damage.

Try to encourage a kid to learn math by paying her for each workbook page she completes—and she'll almost certainly become more diligent in the short term and lose interest in math on the long term. Take an industrial designer who loves his work and try to get him to do better by making his pay contingent on a hit product—and he'll almost certainly work like a maniac in the short term, but become less interested in his job in the long term. As one leading behavioral science textbook puts it, "People use rewards expecting to gain the benefit of increasing another person's motivation and behavior, but in so doing, they often incure [sic] the unintentional and hidden cost of undermining that person's intrinsic motivation toward the activity."

This is one of the most robust findings in social science—and also one of the most ignored. Despite the work of a few skilled and passionate popularizers—in particular, Alfie Kohn, whose prescient 1993 book, *Punished by Rewards*, lays out a devastating indictment of extrinsic incentives—we persist in trying to motivate people this way. Perhaps we're scared to let go of Motivation 2.0, despite its obvious downsides. Perhaps we can't get our minds around the peculiar quantum mechanics of intrinsic motivation.

Or perhaps there's a better reason. Even if those controlling "if–then" rewards activate the Sawyer Effect and suffocate the third drive, maybe they actually get people to perform better. If that's the case, perhaps they're not so bad. So let's ask: Do extrinsic rewards boost performance? Four economists went to India to find out.

High Performance

One of the difficulties of Laboratory experiments that test the impact of extrinsic motivators like cash is the cost. If you're going to pay people to perform, you have to pay them a meaningful amount. And in the United States or Europe, where standards of living are high, an individually meaningful amount multiplied by dozens of participants can rack up unsustainably large bills for behavioral scientists.

In part to circumvent this problem, a quartet of economists—including Dan Ariely, whom I mentioned in the last chapter—set up shop in Madurai, India, to gauge the effects of extrinsic incentives on performance. Because the cost of living in rural India is much lower than in North America, the researchers could offer large rewards without breaking their own banks.

They recruited eighty-seven participants and asked them to play several games—for example, tossing tennis balls at a target, unscrambling anagrams, recalling a string of digits—that required motor skills, creativity or concentration. To test the power of incentives, the experimenters offered three types of rewards for reaching certain performance levels.

One-third of the participants could earn a small reward—4 rupees (at the time worth around 50 U.S. cents and equal to about a day's pay in Madurai) for reaching their performance targets. One-third could earn a medium reward—40 rupees (about $5, or two weeks' pay). And one-third could earn a very large reward—400 rupees (about $50, or nearly five months' pay).

What happened? Did the size of the reward predict the quality of the performance?

Yes. But not in the way you might expect. As it turned out, the people offered the medium-sized bonus didn't perform any better than those offered the small one. And those in the 400-rupee super-incentivized group? They fared worst of all. By nearly every measure, they lagged behind both the low-reward and medium-reward participants. Reporting the results for the Federal Reserve Bank of Boston, the researchers wrote, "In eight of the nine tasks we examined across the three experiments, higher incentives led to *worse* performance."

Let's circle back to this conclusion for a moment. Four economists—two from MIT, one from Carnegie Melon, and one from the University of Chicago—undertake research for the Federal Reserve System, one of the most powerful economic actors in the world. But instead of affirming a simple business principle—higher rewards lead to higher performance—they seem to refute it. And it's not just American researchers reaching these counterintuitive conclusions. In 2009, scholars at the London School of Economics—alma mater of eleven Nobel laureates in economics—analyzed fifty-one studies of corporate pay-for-performance plans. These economists' conclusion: "We find that financial incentives...can result in a negative impact on overall performance."[6] On both sides of the Atlantic, the gap between what science is learning and what business is doing is wide.

"Many existing institutions provide very large incentives for exactly the type of tasks we used here," Ariely and his colleagues wrote. "Our results challenge [that] assumption. Our experiment suggests…that one cannot assume that introducing or raising incentives always improves performance." Indeed, in many instances, contingent incentives—that cornerstone of how businesses attempt to motivate employees—may be "a losing proposition."

Of course, procrastinating writers notwithstanding, few of us spend our working hours flinging tennis balls or doing anagrams. How about the more creative tasks that are more akin to what we actually do on the job?

Creativity

For a quick test of problem-solving prowess, few exercises are more useful than the "candle problem." Devised by psychologist Karl Duncker in the 1930s, the candle problem is used in a wide variety of experiments in behavioral science. Follow along and see how you do.

You sit at a table next to a wooden wall and the experimenter gives you materials shown below: a candle, some tacks, and a book of matches.

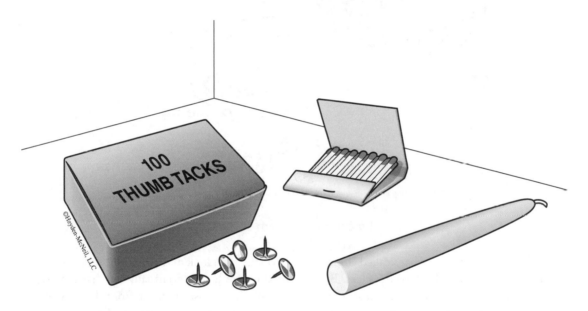

The candle problem presented.

Your job is to attach the candle to the wall so that the wax doesn't drip on the table. Think for a moment about how you'd solve the problem. Many people begin by trying to tack the candle to the wall. But that doesn't work. Some light a match, melt the side of the candle, and try to adhere it to the wall. That doesn't work either. But after five or ten minutes, most people stumble onto the solution, which you can see below.

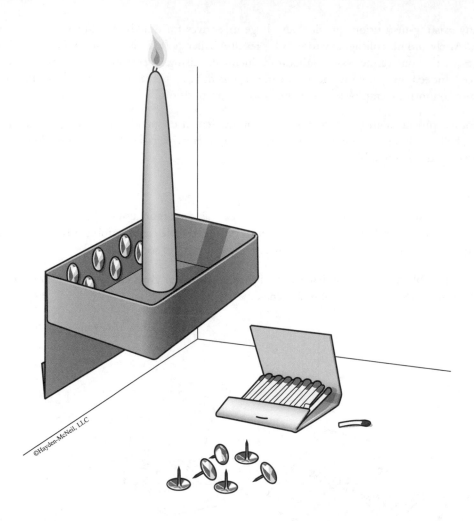

©Hayden-McNeil, LLC

The candle problem solved.

The key is to overcome what's called "functional fixedness." You look at the box and see only one function—as a container for the tacks. But by thinking afresh, you eventually see that the box can have another function—as a platform for the candle. To reprise language from the previous chapter, the solution isn't algorithmic (following a set path) but heuristic (breaking from the path to discover a novel strategy).

What happens when you give people a conceptual challenge like this and offer them rewards for speedy solution? Sam Glucksberg, a psychologist now at Princeton University, tested this a few decades ago by timing how quickly two groups of participants solved the candle problem. He told the first group that he was timing their work merely to establish norms for how long it typically took someone to complete this sort of puzzle. To the second group he offered incentives. If a participant's time was among the fastest 25 percent of all the people being tested, that participant would receive $5. If the participant's time was the fastest of all, the reward would be $20. Adjusted for inflation, those are decent sums of money for a few minutes of effort—a nice motivator.

How much faster did the incentivized group come up with a solution? On average, it took them nearly three and a half minutes *longer*. Yes, three and a half minutes longer. (Whenever I've relayed these results to a group of businesspeople, the reaction is almost always a loud, pained, involuntary gasp.) In direct contravention to the core tenets of Motivation 2.0, an incentive designed to clarify thinking and sharpen creativity ended up clouding thinking and dulling creativity. Why? Rewards, by their very nature, narrow our focus. That's helpful when there's a clear path to a solution. They help us stare ahead and race faster. But "if–then" motivators are terrible for challenges like the candle problem. As this experiment shows, the rewards narrowed people's focus and blinkered the wide view that might have allowed them to see new uses for old objects.

Something similar seems to occur for challenges that aren't so much about cracking an existing problem but about iterating something new. Teresa Amabile, the Harvard Business School professor and one of the world's leading researchers on creativity, has frequently tested the effects of contingent rewards on the creative process. In one study, she and two colleagues recruited twenty-three professional artists from the United States who had produced both commissioned and noncommissioned artwork. They asked the artists to randomly select ten commissioned works and ten noncommissioned works. Then Amabile and her team gave the works to a panel of accomplished artists and curators, who knew nothing about the study, and asked the experts to rate the pieces on creativity and technical skill.

"Our results were quite startling," the researchers wrote. "The commissioned works were rated as significantly less creative than the non-commissioned works, yet they were not rated as different in technical quality. Moreover, the artists reported feeling significantly more constrained when doing commissioned works than when doing non-commissioned works." One artist whom they interviewed describes the Sawyer Effect in action:

> Not always, but a lot of the time, when you are doing a piece for someone else it becomes more "work" than joy. When I work for myself there is the pure joy of creating and I can work through the night and not even know it. On a commissioned piece you have to check yourself—be careful to do what the client wants.

Another study of artists over a longer period shows that a concern for outside rewards might actually hinder eventual success. In the early 1960s, researchers surveyed sophomores and juniors at the School of the Art Institute of Chicago about their attitudes toward work and whether they were more intrinsically or extrinsically motivated. Using these data as a benchmark, another researcher followed up with these students in the early 1980s to see how their careers were progressing. Among the starkest findings, especially for men: "The less evidence of extrinsic motivation during art school, the more success in professional art both several years after graduation and nearly twenty years later." Painters and sculptors who were intrinsically motivated, those for whom the joy of discovery and the challenge of creation were their own rewards, were able to weather the tough times—and the lack of remuneration and recognition—that inevitably accompany artistic careers. And that led to yet another paradox in the Alice in Wonderland world of the third drive. "Those artists who pursued their painting and sculpture more for the pleasure of the activity itself than for extrinsic rewards have produced art that has been socially recognized as superior," the study said. "It is those who are least motivated to pursue extrinsic rewards who eventually receive them."

This result is not true across all tasks, of course. Amabile and others have found that extrinsic rewards can be effective for algorithmic tasks—those that depend on following an existing formula to its logical conclusion. But for more right-brain undertakings—those that demand flexible problem-solving, inventiveness, or conceptual understanding—contingent rewards can be dangerous. Rewarded subjects often have a harder time seeing the periphery and crafting original solutions. This, too, is one of the sturdiest findings in social science—especially as Amabile and others have refined it over the years. For artists, scientists, inventors, schoolchildren, and the rest of us, intrinsic motivation—the drive to do something because it is interesting, challenging, and absorbing—is essential for high levels of creativity. But the "if–then" motivators that are the staple of most businesses often stifle, rather than stir, creative thinking. As the economy moves toward more right-brain, conceptual work—as more of us deal with our own versions of the candle problem—this might be the most alarming gap between what science knows and what business does.

Good Behavior

Philosophers and medical professionals have long debated whether blood donors should be paid. Some claim that blood, like human tissue or organs, is special—that we shouldn't be able to buy and sell it like a barrel of crude oil or a crate of ball bearings. Others argue that we should shelve our squeamishness, because paying for this substance will ensure an ample supply.

But in 1970, British sociologist Richard Titmuss, who had studied blood donation in the United Kingdom, offered a bolder speculation. Paying for blood wasn't just immoral, he said. It was also inefficient. If Britain decided to pay citizens to donate, that would actually reduce the country's blood supply. It was an oddball notion, to be sure. Economists snickered. And Titmuss never tested the idea; it was merely a philosophical hunch.

But a quarter-century later, two Swedish economists decided to see if Titmuss was right. In an intriguing field experiment, they visited a regional blood center in Gothenburg and found 153 women who were interested in giving blood. Then—as seems to be the custom among motivation researchers—they divided the women into three groups. Experimenters told those in the first group that blood donation was voluntary. These participants could give blood, but they wouldn't receive a payment. The experimenters offered the second group a different arrangement. If these participants gave blood, they'd each receive 50 Swedish kronor (about $7). The third group received a variation on that second offer: a 50-kronor payment with an immediate option to donate the amount to a children's cancer charity.

Of the first group, 52 percent of the women decided to go ahead and donate blood. They were altruistic citizens apparently, willing to do a good deed for their fellow Swedes even in the absence of compensation.

And the second group? Motivation 2.0 would suggest that this group might be a bit more motivated to donate. They'd shown up, which indicated intrinsic motivation. Getting a few kronor on top might give that impulse a boost. But—as you might have guessed by now—that's not what happened. In this group, only 30 percent of the women decided to give blood. Instead of increasing the number of blood donors, offering to pay people *decreased* the number by nearly half.

Meanwhile, the third group—which had the option of donating the fee directly to charity—responded much the same as the first group. Fifty-three percent became blood donors.*

Titmuss' hunch might have been right, after all. Adding a monetary incentive didn't lead to more of the desired behavior. It led to less. The reason: It tainted an altruistic act and "crowded out" the intrinsic desire to do something good. Doing good is what blood donation is all about. It provides what the American Red Cross brochures say is "a feeling that money can't buy." That's why voluntary blood donations invariably increase during natural disasters and other calamities. But if governments were to pay people to help their neighbors during these crises, donations might decline.

---

* The results for the 119 men in the experiment were somewhat different. The payment had no statistically significant effect, positive or negative, on the decision to give blood.

That said, in the Swedish example, the reward itself wasn't inherently destructive. The immediate option to donate the 50-kronor payment rather than pocket it seemed to negate the effect. This too, is extremely important. It's not that all rewards at all times are bad. For instance, when the Italian government gave blood donors paid time off work, donation increased. The law removed an obstacle to altruism. So while a few advocates would have you believe in the basic evil of extrinsic incentives, that's just not empirically true. What is true is that mixing rewards with inherently interesting, creative, or noble tasks—deploying them without understanding the peculiar science of motivation—is a very dangerous game. When used in these situations, "if–then" rewards usually do more harm than good. By neglecting the ingredients of genuine motivation—autonomy, master, and purpose—they limit what each of us can achieve.

More of What We Don't Want
In the upside-down universe of the third drive, rewards can often produce less of the very things they're trying to encourage. But that's not the end of the story. When used improperly, extrinsic motivators can have another unintended collateral consequence: They can give us more of what we don't want. Here, again, what business does hasn't caught up with what science knows. And what science is revealing is that carrots and sticks can promote bad behavior, create addiction, and encourage short-term thinking at the expense of the long view.

Unethical Behavior
What could be more valuable than having a goal? From our earliest days, teachers, coaches, and parents advise us to set goals and to work mightily to achieve them—and with good reason. Goals work. The academic literature shows that by helping us tune out distractions, goals can get us to try harder, work longer, and achieve more.

But recently a group of scholars from the Harvard Business School, Northwestern University's Kellogg School of Management, and University of Arizona's Eller College of Management, and the University of Pennsylvania's Wharton School questioned the efficacy of this broad prescription. "Rather than being offered as an 'over-the-counter' salve for boosting performance, goal setting should be prescribed selectively, presented with a warning label, and closely monitored," they wrote. Goals that people set for themselves and that are devoted to attaining mastery are usually healthy. But goals imposed by others—sales targets, quarterly returns, standardized test scores, and so on—can sometimes have dangerous side effects.

Like all extrinsic motivators, goals narrow our focus. That's one reason they can be effective; they concentrate the mind. But as we've seen, a narrowed focus exacts a cost. For complex or conceptual tasks, offering a reward can blinker the wide-ranging thinking necessary to come up with an innovative solution. Likewise, when an extrinsic goal is paramount—particularly a short-term, measurable one whose achievement delivers a big payoff—its presence can restrict our view of the broader dimensions of our behavior. As the cadre of business school professors write, "Substantial evidence demonstrates that in addition to motivating constructive effort, goal setting can induce unethical behavior."

The examples are legion, the researchers note. Sears imposes a sales quota on its auto repair staff—and workers respond by over-charging customers and completing unnecessary repairs. Enron sets lofty revenue goals—and the race to meet them by any means possible catalyzes the company's collapse. Ford is so intent on producing a certain car at a certain weight at a certain price by a certain date that it omits safety checks and unleashes the dangerous Ford Pinto.

The problem with making an extrinsic reward the only destination that matters is that some people will choose the quickest route there, even if it means taking the low road.

Indeed, most of the scandals and misbehavior that have seemed endemic to modern life involve shortcuts. Executives game their quarterly earnings so they can snag a performance bonus. Secondary school counselors doctor student transcripts so their seniors can get into college.[17] Athletes inject themselves with steroids to post better numbers and trigger lucrative performance bonuses.

Contrast that approach with behavior sparked by intrinsic motivation. When the reward is the activity itself—deepening learning, delighting customers, doing one's best—there are no shortcuts. The only route to the destination is the high road. In some sense, it's impossible to act unethically because the person who's disadvantaged isn't a competitor but yourself.

Of course, all goals are not created equal. And—let me emphasize this point—goals and extrinsic rewards aren't inherently corrupting. But goals are more toxic than Motivation 2.0 recognizes. In fact, the business school professors suggest they should come with their own warning label: *Goals may cause systematic problems for organizations due to narrowed focus, unethical behavior, increased risk taking, decreased cooperation, and decreased intrinsic motivation. Use care when applying goals in your organization.*

If carrots-as-goals sometimes encourage unworthy behavior, then sticks-as punishment should be able to halt it, right? Not so fast. The third drive is less mechanistic and more surprising than that, as two Israeli economists discovered at some day care centers.

In 2000, economists Uri Gneezy and Aldo Rustichini studied a group of child care facilities in Haifa, Israel, for twenty weeks. The centers opened at 7:30 a.m. and closed at 4:00 p.m. Parents had to retrieve their children by the closing time or a teacher would have to stay late.

During the first four weeks of the experiment, the economists recorded how many parents arrived late each week. Then, before the fifth week, with the permission of the day care centers, they posted the following sign:

Announcement:

Fine for coming late

> *As you all know, the official closing time of the day care center is 1600 every day. Since some parents have been coming late, we (with the approval of the Authority for Private Day-Care Centers in Israel) have decided to impose a fine on parents who come late to pick up their children.*

> *As of next Sunday a fine of NS 10* will be charged every time a child is collected after 1610. This fine will be calculated monthly, it is to be paid together with the regular monthly payment.*

> *Sincerely,*

> *The manager of the day-care center*

(* The fine was per child, so a parent with two children would have to pay twenty Israeli shekels (NS20) for each instance of tardiness. When the experiment was conducted, ten Israeli shekels was equivalent to about three U.S. dollars.)

The theory underlying the fine, said Gneezy and Rustichini, was straightforward: "When negative consequences are imposed on a behavior, they will produce a reduction of that particular response." In other words, thwack the parents with a fine, and they'll stop showing up late.

But that's not what happened. "After the introduction of the fine we observed a steady *increase* in the number of parents coming late," the economists wrote. "The rate finally settled, at a level that was higher, and *almost twice as large* as the initial one." And in language reminiscent of Harry Harlow's head scratching, they write that the existing literature didn't account for such a result. Indeed, the "possibility of an increase in the behavior being punished was not even considered."

Up pops another bug in Motivation 2.0. One reason most parents showed up on time is that they had a relationship with the teachers—who, after all, were caring for their precious sons and daughters—and wanted to treat them fairly. Parents had an intrinsic desire to be scrupulous about punctuality. But the threat of a fine—like the promise of the kronor in the blood experiment—edged aside that third drive. The fine shifted the parents' decision from a partly moral obligation (be fair to my kids' teachers) to a pure transaction (I can buy extra time). There wasn't room for both. The punishment didn't promote good behavior; it crowded it out.

Addiction

If some scientists believe that "if–then" motivators and other extrinsic rewards resemble prescription drugs that carry potentially dangerous side effects, others believe they're more like illegal drugs that foster a deeper and more pernicious dependency. According to these scholars, cash rewards and shiny trophies can provide a delicious jolt of pleasure at first, but the feeling soon dissipates—and to keep it alive, the recipient requires ever larger and more frequent doses.

The Russian economist Anton Suvorov has constructed an elaborate econometric model to demonstrate this effect, configured around what's called "principal-agent theory." Think of the principal as the motiva*tor*—the employer, the teacher, the parent. Think of the agent as the motiva*tee*—the employee, the student, the child. A principal essentially tries to get the agent to do what the principal wants, while the agent balances his own interests with whatever the principal is offering. Using a blizzard of complicated equations that test a variety of scenarios between principal and agent, Suvorov has reached conclusions that make intuitive sense to any parent who's tried to get her kids to empty the garbage.

By offering a reward, a principal signals to the agent that the task is undesirable. (If the task were desirable, the agent wouldn't need a prod.) But that initial signal, and the reward that goes with it, forces the principal onto a path that's difficult to leave. Offer too small a reward and the agent won't comply. But offer a reward that's enticing enough to get the agent to act the first time, and the principal "is doomed to give it again in the second." There's no going back. Pay your son to take out the trash—and you've pretty much guaranteed the kid will never do it again for free. What's more, once the initial money buzz tapers off, you'll likely have to increase the payment to continue compliance.

As Suvorov explains, "Rewards are addictive in that once offered, a contingent reward makes an agent expect it whenever a similar task is faced, which in turn compels the principal to use rewards over and over again." And before long, the existing reward may no longer suffice. It will quickly feel less like a bonus and more like the status quo—which then forces the principal to offer larger rewards to achieve the same effect.

This addictive pattern is not merely blackboard theory. Brian Knutson, then a neuroscientist at the National Institute on Alcohol Abuse and Alcoholism, demonstrated as much in an experiment using the brain scanning technique known as functional magnetic resonance imaging (fMRI). He placed healthy volunteers into a giant scanner to watch how their brains responded during a game that involved the prospect of either winning or losing money. When participants knew they had a chance to win cash, activation occurred in the part of the brain called the nucleus accumbens. That is, when the participants anticipated getting a reward (but not when they anticipated losing one), a burst of the brain chemical dopamine surges to this part of the brain. Knutson, who is now at Stanford University, has found similar results in subsequent studies where people anticipated rewards. What makes this response interesting for our purposes is that the same basic physiological process—this particular brain chemical surging to this particular part of the brain—is what happens in addiction. The mechanism of most addictive drugs is to send a fusillade of dopamine to the nucleus accumbens. The feeling delights, then dissipates, then demands another dose. In other words, if we watch how people's brains respond, promising them monetary rewards and giving them cocaine, nicotine, or amphetamines look disturbingly similar. This could be one reason that paying people to stop smoking often works in the short run. It replaces one (dangerous) addiction with another (more benign) one.

Rewards' addictive qualities can also distort decision-making. Knutson has found that activation in the nucleus accumbens seems to predict "both risky choices and risk-seeking mistakes." Get people fired up with the prospect of rewards, and instead of making better decisions, as Motivation 2.0 hopes, they can actually make worse ones. As Knutson writes, "This may explain why casinos surround their guests with reward cues (e.g., inexpensive food, free liquor, surprise gifts, potential jackpot prizes)—anticipation of rewards activates the [nucleus accumbens], which may lead to an increase in the likelihood of individuals switching from risk-averse to risk-seeking behavior."

In short, while that dangled carrot isn't all bad in all circumstances, in some instances it operates similar to a rock of crack cocaine and can induce behavior similar to that found around the craps table or roulette wheel—not exactly what we hope to achieve when we "motivate" our teammates and coworkers.

Short-Term Thinking

Think back to the candle problem again. The incentivized participants performed worse than their counterparts because they were so focused on the prize that they failed to glimpse a novel solution on the periphery. Rewards, we've seen, can limit the *breadth* of our thinking. They can focus our sights on only what's immediately before us rather than what's off in the distance.

Many times a concentrated focus makes sense. If your office building is on fire, you want to find an exit immediately rather than ponder how to rewrite the zoning regulations. But in less dramatic circumstances, fixating on an immediate reward can damage performance over time. Indeed, what our earlier examples—unethical actions and addictive behavior—have in common, perhaps more than anything else, is that they're entirely short-term. Addicts want the quick fix regardless of the eventual harm. Cheaters want the quick win—regardless of the lasting consequences. Yet even when the behavior doesn't devolve into shortcuts or addiction, the near-term allure of rewards can be harmful in the long run. Consider publicly held companies. Many such companies have existed for decades and hope to exist for decades more. But much of what their executives and middle managers do each day is aimed single-mindedly at the corporation's performance over the next three months. At these companies, quarterly earnings are an obsession. Executives devote substantial resources to making sure the earnings come out just right. And they spend considerable time and brain-power offering guidance to stock analysts so that the market knows what to expect and therefore responds favorably. This laser focus on a narrow, near-term slice of corporate performance is understandable. It's a rational response to stock markets that reward or punish tiny blips in those numbers, which, in turn, affect executives' compensation.

But companies pay a steep price for not extending their gaze beyond the next quarter. Several researchers have found that companies that spend the most time offering guidance on quarterly earnings deliver significantly lower long-term growth rates than companies that offer guidance less frequently. (One reason: The earnings-obsessed companies typically invest less in research and development.) They successfully achieve their short-term goals, but threaten the health of the company two or three years hence. As the scholars who warned about goals gone wild put it, "The very presence of goals may lead employees to focus myopically on short-term gains and to lose sight of the potential devastating long-term effects on the organization."

Perhaps nowhere is this clearer than in the economic calamity that gripped the world economy in 2008 and 2009. Each player in the system focused only on the short-term reward—the buyer who wanted a house, the mortgage broker who wanted a commission, the Wall Street trader who wanted new securities to sell, the politician who wanted a buoyant economy during reelection—and ignored the long-term effects of their actions on themselves or others. When the music stopped, the entire system nearly collapsed. This is the nature of economic bubbles: What seems to be irrational exuberance is ultimately a bad case of extrinsically motivated myopia.

By contrast, the elements of genuine motivation that we'll explore later, by their very nature, defy a short-term view. Take mastery. The objective itself is inherently long-term because complete mastery, in a sense, is unattainable. Even Roger Federer, for instance, will never fully "master" the game of tennis. But introducing an "if–then" reward to help develop mastery usually backfires. That's why schoolchildren who are paid to solve problems typically choose easier problems and therefore learn less.[25] The short-term prize crowds out the long-term learning.

In environments where extrinsic rewards are most salient, many people work only to the point that triggers the reward—and no further. So if students get a prize for reading three books, many won't pick up a fourth, let alone embark on a lifetime of reading—just as executives who hit their quarterly numbers often won't boost earnings a penny more, let alone contemplate the long-term health of their company. Likewise, several studies show that paying people to exercise, stop smoking, or take their medicines produces terrific results at first—but the healthy behavior disappears once the incentives are removed. However, when contingent rewards aren't involved, or when incentives are used with the proper deftness, performance improves and understanding deepens. Greatness and nearsightedness are incompatible. Meaningful achievement depends on lifting one's sights and pushing toward the horizon.

CARROTS AND STICKS: The Seven Deadly Flaws

1. They can extinguish intrinsic motivation.
2. They can diminish performance.
3. They can crush creativity.
4. They can crowd out good behavior.
5. They can encourage cheating, shortcuts, and unethical behavior.
6. They can become addictive.
7. They can foster short-term thinking.

Pink, Daniel H. "Seven Reasons Carrots and Sticks (Often) Don't work." In *Drive: The Surprising Truth About What Motivates Us*. New York: Riverhead Books, 2009. pp. 34–59. Reprinted by permission.

FILM STUDIES

Mr. Smith Goes to Washington (1939)

Story by Lewis R. Foster
Screenplay by Sidney Buchman
Directed by Frank Capra

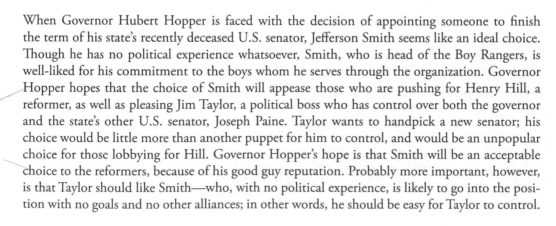

Character Guide

Clarissa Saunders	Jean Arthur
Jefferson Smith	James Stewart
Sen. Joseph Harrison Paine	Claude Rains
Jim Taylor	Edward Arnold
Gov. Hubert Hopper	Guy Kibbee
Diz Moore	Thomas Mitchell
Chick McGann	Eugene Pallette
President of the Senate Henry	Harry Carey

Introduction

When Governor Hubert Hopper is faced with the decision of appointing someone to finish the term of his state's recently deceased U.S. senator, Jefferson Smith seems like an ideal choice. Though he has no political experience whatsoever, Smith, who is head of the Boy Rangers, is well-liked for his commitment to the boys whom he serves through the organization. Governor Hopper hopes that the choice of Smith will appease those who are pushing for Henry Hill, a reformer, as well as pleasing Jim Taylor, a political boss who has control over both the governor and the state's other U.S. senator, Joseph Paine. Taylor wants to handpick a new senator; his choice would be little more than another puppet for him to control, and would be an unpopular choice for those lobbying for Hill. Governor Hopper's hope is that Smith will be an acceptable choice to the reformers, because of his good guy reputation. Probably more important, however, is that Taylor should like Smith—who, with no political experience, is likely to go into the position with no goals and no other alliances; in other words, he should be easy for Taylor to control.

UNIT
6

Smith does, however, have one modest goal—to establish a national boys camp in his home state. That goal puts Smith at odds with Taylor and the goal for a dam project filled with political graft.

Dialogue Questions

1. Regarding the appointment of a new senator, Governor Hopper found himself in the middle of factions with contradictory goals. What was the goal of Jim Taylor and Senator Paine? What was the goal of the committees? How did Hopper resolve the issue?

2. What are some strategies for managing a situation like the one Hopper was in, where different groups had conflicting goals?

3. What did Jefferson Smith mean when he said, in reference to his goal to accomplish something as senator, "Otherwise, I'm just a Christmas tiger"? How did Paine respond to this and why?

4. Smith recognizes that help from Saunders is key if he is to achieve his goal of passing a bill for a national boys camp. How does Saunders initially respond to Smith regarding his goal? What are some ways of achieving buy-in for a goal that seems to others to be out of reach?

Argo (2012)

Screenplay by Chris Terrio
Directed by Ben Affleck

Character Guide

Tony Mendez	Ben Affleck
Jack O'Donnell	Bryan Cranston
Lester Siegel	Alan Arkin
John Chambers	John Goodman
Ken Talor	Victor Garber
Bob Anders	Tate Donovan
Cora Lijek	Clea DuVall
Jo Stafford	Scoot McNairy
Lee Schatz	Rory Cochrane
Mark Lijek	Christopher Denham
Kathy Stafford	Kerry Bishé

Introduction

In November 1979, a mob of Iranian supporters of Ayatollah Khomeini made their way over the wall surrounding the U.S. Embassy in Tehran. Most of those in the embassy were captured and held as hostages for 444 days, in what became known as the Iran Hostage Crisis. Six people in the embassy, however, were able to escape the compound. These six were granted shelter by Ken Taylor, the Canadian ambassador in Iran. While the Canadians were able to provide the six with temporary safety, getting them out of Tehran alive was another matter. Ultimately, the orchestration of their escape required the cooperation of multiple agencies and countries.

Tony Mendez was the CIA agent sent to escort the six safely out of Tehran. Operating under the guise of a Canadian film crew, Mendez and the 6 escapees would be issued Canadian passports and would take on the role of filmmakers scouting Tehran as a potential location for a film; the plan required them to be convincing enough that the group would be able to stage an uneventful exit from Iran at the conclusion of their scouting trip.

Argo focuses primarily on agent Mendez and the execution of the film crew plan, with the goal of safely escorting the six out of the country.

Dialogue Questions

1. How did the six escapees react to the plan set forth by Mendez? Why do you think they react this way?

2. How important was it to have the buy-in of all involved parties in achieving the goal of leaving Tehran in the guise of a Canadian film crew? How can one effectively achieve consensus in such circumstances?

3. In an exchange with O'Donnell over the cancelling of the escape plan, Mendez states, "We're responsible for those people!" O'Donnell replies, "What we are is required to follow orders." How does one function in a situation where the individual or group goal is at odds with the goal of the organization?

4. Ultimately, Mendez chooses to finish the mission without the approval of his superiors. Besides the obvious risks of life endangerment, what additional risks does Mendez take on with this decision? Are there generalizations you can make about when it is appropriate to take action that is directly contrary to one's orders?

EXERCISE

Setting Goals for Your Community

Introduction

This exercise will allow you to experience goal setting in a group. It also provides you with an opportunity to get better acquainted with your classmates and identify and learn about issues of concern within your community.

Instructions

Your Instructor will provide you with the instructions and handouts for this exercise.

SUGGESTED READING

This selected bibliography is intended to supplement the excerpts and articles of authors included in this Unit. There is an emphasis on books that are pivotal and recent publications. Numerous journals regularly offer articles related to these topics, but are not included in this selected bibliography. For further research, you may wish to include searches of the following journals: (alphabetically) *Academy of Management Executive, Academy of Management Journal, Harvard Business Review, Journal of Leadership Studies, Leadership in Action, Leadership Quarterly,* and *Leader To Leader.*

This list is organized by author's last name using Modern Language Association-style citations.

Amabile, Teresa, and Steven Kramer. *The Progress Principle: Using Small Wins to Ignite Joy, Engagement, and Creativity at Work.* **Boston: Harvard Business Press, 2011.**
Amabile and Kramer demonstrate how seemingly mundane workday events can make or break employees' inner work lives. The book is based on a large qualitative study of thousands of employee journal entries.

Covey, Stephen R. *Seven Habits of Highly Effective People.* **Revised ed. New York: Free Press, 2004.**
Covey defines "habit" as a combination of knowledge, skill, and desire, or the what to do, why, how, and want to do. His seven habits are based on the fundamental principles of human effectiveness.

Covey, Stephen R. *The 8th Habit: From Effectiveness to Greatness.* **New York: Free Press, 2005.**
Covey adds to the seven habits that it is important to find one's voice and help others find theirs.

Goleman, Daniel. *Focus: The Hidden Driver of Excellence.* **New York: Harper Collins, 2013.**
Goleman contends that the science of attention provides the key to success in a complex world. He presents many studies related to the science of attention.

Holroyd, Michael. *George Bernard Shaw: The One-Volume, Definitive Edition.* **New York: W. W. Norton, 2005.**
A comprehensive biography of George Bernard Shaw.

Huggins, Nathan Irvin. *Slave and Citizen: The Life of Frederick Douglass.* **Boston: Little, Brown, 1980.**
A comprehensive biography of Frederick Douglass.

Kouzes, James, and Barry Posner. *The Leadership Challenge: How to Make Extraordinary Things Happen in Organizations.* **5th ed. San Francisco: Jossey-Bass 2012.**
This revision includes recent examples of tough organizational challenges and the leadership practices that help overcome them.

Mintzberg, Henry. *The Rise and Fall of Strategic Planning: Reconceiving Roles for Planning, Plans, Planners.* **New York: Free Press, 1994.**
A contrary view of planning (goal setting) and the dangers it presents when it destroys commitment and leads to political maneuvering in an organization.

Moskowitz, Gordon B., and Heidi Grant, eds. *The psychology of goals.* **New York: Guilford Press, 2009.**
This is an edited volume that brings together leading authorities on the psychology of goals.

UNIT 7

MAKING DECISIONS

INTRODUCTION

Although no leader is a perfect decision maker all of the time, there is enough concrete information about the decision-making process to improve a leader's batting average. Unit Seven investigates decision making—the process of identifying and then selecting a course of action to solve a specific problem or meet a specific goal. This process should be rational, intelligent, and systematic. Each component of the Unit contributes to an understanding of learnable steps that can enhance the process of decision making, whether a personal decision, a group decision, or a decision with implications for an entire organization.

The Classic Case from *Huckleberry Finn* examines the importance of searching for one's values and making decisions that are true to those personal values. The Leadership Profile of Chief Joseph allows for an examination of the different styles of leadership and the decision-making processes in play among the leaders seeking to decide the destiny of a people. "The Road Not Taken," by Robert Frost, is a well-known, often-quoted poem appearing on the Reflect & Focus page. This poem is usually interpreted as a message to follow the less-traveled path and experience life differently than those who travel the beaten path. However, it also deals with the difficulty for us in deciding courses of action when we realize that making the decision means we will never know how things would have turned out if we had made a different choice.

Another humanities selection, "Shooting an Elephant," by George Orwell, illustrates how difficult it sometimes is for us to make the right decision when we are overly concerned with the image the decision will project, rather than the desired result for the long term. A decision maker's ability to develop several alternative ways to solve a problem is a crucial leadership skill. Yet, generating alternatives frequently involves "thinking outside the box" and thinking creatively is crucial. Many leaders are less comfortable with creativity than with rational objectivity, and thus limit options this way, too. David A. Garvin and Michael A. Roberto provide suggestions to overcome the discomfort and use alternative ways to develop a variety of ideas such as "structured debate." Their article "What You Don't Know About Making Decisions" also examines how leaders must encourage healthy conflict during the decision-making process. "A Question of Leadership: What Can Leaders Do to Avoid Groupthink?," by Wynne Whyman and Robert Ginnett, explores what leaders can do to avoid the phenomenon of "groupthink," which can significantly inhibit making the best, most effective decisions.

The classic Film Study, *To Kill a Mockingbird*, focuses on the decision of Atticus Finch, an attorney in an Alabama town in the 1930s, to defend a black man accused of raping a white woman. The contemporary Film Study, *Milk*, focuses on Harvey Milk's decisions to seek political office and to work as a gay rights activist.

Learning Objectives

- Identify effective personal decision-making strategies

- Recognize the role of leadership in effective group decision making

- Recognize the roles of cooperation and debate in the decision making process

- Understand the impact of perspective and advocacy in decision making

- Apply techniques that facilitate effective decision-making and avoid groupthink

- Appreciate the contributions made by the Classic Case and Leadership Profile in this Unit toward understanding personal responsibility

CLASSIC CASE

The Adventures of Huckleberry Finn

By Mark Twain (1835–1910)
American Novelist

Introduction and Historical Background

Samuel Langhorne Clemens, better known as Mark Twain, was born in 1835 in Florida, Missouri and moved with his family to the Mississippi River town of Hannibal, Missouri, when he was four years old. There he grew up in pre-Civil War southern society and absorbed the values and traditions of this world. His experience in and around the Mississippi River left him with a tumult of conflicting feelings and loyalties. He returned to the world of his childhood for the raw materials of his masterpiece, *The Adventures of Huckleberry Finn*, and was able to write a book that is a wonderful adventure story even while it provides a powerful commentary of social criticism. When he finished *Huckleberry Finn* and published it in 1885, it was widely read and loved, but even Twain might have been surprised to know that it was to become recognized as one of the world's great books and a central document of American literature.

In the story, Huck and Jim, a slave, are more than footloose wanderers; they are escaping from their respective forms of bondage—forms imposed by their society. They escape their hometown aboard a raft on the Mississippi River. The river plays a central role throughout the book: it is the timeless force, different from the fixed order of the land, an image of freedom and regeneration, and a life-giving force that provides renewal for Huck and Jim. Each time Huck and Jim venture to land, they are reminded of the cruelty, stupidity, greed, and vulnerability prevalent among mankind. They often witness man's inhumanity to man firsthand. Upon each return from the shore, Huck and Jim express their relief and thanksgiving to be back on the river. Huck and Jim form a family aboard the raft, a community of equals unconcerned with society's rules about master and slave and all the lies that society tells to justify its values. But it is not easy to throw away this code that society and Sunday school have taught, and Huck struggles with seeking to do the right thing. The journey down the river for Jim is a quest for freedom from the bondage of slavery, and for Huck it is a quest for spiritual freedom.

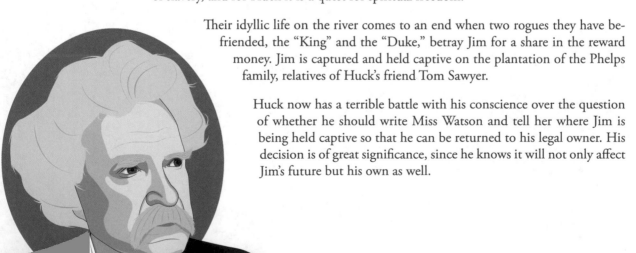

Their idyllic life on the river comes to an end when two rogues they have befriended, the "King" and the "Duke," betray Jim for a share in the reward money. Jim is captured and held captive on the plantation of the Phelps family, relatives of Huck's friend Tom Sawyer.

Huck now has a terrible battle with his conscience over the question of whether he should write Miss Watson and tell her where Jim is being held captive so that he can be returned to his legal owner. His decision is of great significance, since he knows it will not only affect Jim's future but his own as well.

Points to Consider

1. What alternatives does Huck explore in making his decision? Can you think of a situation where you had to explore multiple alternatives, each with positive and negative aspects?

2. What are some strategies for moderating a group discussion so the group can make a decision when the topic is difficult and/or uncomfortable?

3. How would you communicate views that go against the prevailing beliefs of a group or organization?

4. At what point is addressing a difficult issue counterproductive to the group's goals and operation? What can one do if such a situation occurs?

UNIT
7

The Adventures of Huckleberry Finn

(Excerpt)

...for I see our chance; and I made up my mind that it would be a long day before they ever see me and Jim again. I got down there all out of breath but loaded up with joy, and sung out—"Set her loose, Jim, we're all right now!"

But there warn't no answer, and nobody come out of the wigwam. Jim was gone! I set up a shout,—and then another—and then another one; and run this way and that in the woods, whooping and screeching; but it warn't no use—old Jim was gone. Then I set down and cried; I couldn't help it. But I couldn't set still long. Pretty soon I went out on the road, trying to think what I better do, and I run across a boy walking, and asked him if he'd seen a strange nigger, dressed so and so, and he says:

"Yes."

"Whereabouts?" says I.

"Down to Silas Phelps's place, two mile below here. He's a runaway nigger, and they've got him. Was you looking for him?"

"You bet I ain't! I run across him in the woods about an hour or two ago, and he said if I hollered he'd cut my livers out—and told me to lay down and stay where I was; and I done it. Been there ever since; afeard to come out."

"Well," he says, "you needn't be afeard no more, becuz they've got him. He run off f'm down south, som'ers."

"It's a good job they got him."

"Well, I *reckon*! There's two hunderd dollars reward on him. It's like picking up money out'n the road."

"Yes, it is—and I could a had it if I'd been big enough: I see him *first*. Who nailed him?"

"It was an old fellow—a stranger—and he sold out his chance in him for forty dollars, becuz he's got to go up the river and can't wait. Think o'that, now! You bet *I'd* wait, if it was seven year."

"That's me, every time," says I. "But maybe his chance ain't worth no more than that, if he'll sell it so cheap. Maybe there's something ain't straight about it."

"But it *is*, though—straight as a string. I see the handbill myself. It tells all about him, to a dot—paints him like a picture, and tells that plantation he's frum, below Newr*leans*. No-sir-ree-*bob*, they ain't no trouble 'bout *that* speculation, you bet you. Say, gimme a chaw tobacker, won't ye?"

I didn't have none, so he left. I went to the raft, and set down in the wigwam to think. But I couldn't come to nothing. I thought till I wore my head sore, but I couldn't see no way out of the trouble. After all this long journey, and after all we'd done for them scoundrels, here it was all come to nothing, everything all busted up and ruined, because they could have the heart to serve Jim such a trick as that, and make him a slave again all his life, and amongst strangers, too, for forty dirty dollars.

Once I said to myself it would be a thousand times better for Jim to be a slave at home where his family was, as long as he'd *got* to be a slave, and so I'd better write a letter to Tom Sawyer and tell him to tell Miss Watson where he was. But I soon give up the notion, for two things: she'd be mad and disgusted at his rascality and ungratefulness for leaving her, and so she'd sell him straight down the river again; and if she didn't everybody naturally despises an ungrateful nigger, and they'd make Jim feel it all the time, and so he'd feel ornery and disgraced. And then think of *me*! It would get all around, that Huck Finn helped a nigger to get his freedom; and if I was to ever see anybody from that town again, I'd be ready to get down and lick his boots for shame. That's just the way: a person does a low-down thing, and then he don't want to take no consequences of it. Thinks as long as he can hide it, it ain't no disgrace. That was my fix exactly. The more I studied about this, the more my conscience went to grinding me, and the more wicked, and low-down and ornery I got to feeling. And at last, when it hit me all of a sudden that here was the plain hand of Providence slapping me in the face and letting me know my wickedness was being watched all the time from up there in heaven, whilst I was stealing a poor old woman's nigger that hadn't ever done me no harm, and now was showing me there's One that's always on the lookout, and ain't agoing to allow no such miserable doings to go only just so fur and no further, I most dropped in my tracks I was so scared. Well, I tried the best I could to kinder soften it up somehow for myself, by saying I was brung up wicked,

and so I warn't so much to blame; but something inside of me kept saying, "There was the Sunday School, you could a gone to it; and if you'd a done it they'd a learnt you, there, that people that acts as I'd been acting about the nigger goes to everlasting fire."

It made me shiver. And I about made up my mind to pray; and see if I couldn't try to quit being the kind of a boy I was, and be better. So I kneeled down. But the words wouldn't come. Why wouldn't they? It warn't no use to try and hide it from Him. Nor from *me*, neither. I knowed very well why they wouldn't come. It was because my heart warn't right; it was because I warn't square; it was because I was playing double. I was letting *on* to give up sin, but away inside of me I was holding on to the biggest one of all. I was trying to make my mouth *say* I would do the right thing and the clean thing, and go and write to the nigger's owner and tell where he was; but deep down in me I knowed it was a lie—and He knowed it. You can't pray a lie—I found that out.

So I was full of trouble, full as I could be; and didn't know what to do. At last I had an idea; and I says, I'll go and write the letter—and then see if I can pray. Why, it was astonishing, the way I felt as light as a feather, right straight off, and my troubles all gone. So I got a piece of paper and a pencil, all glad and excited, and set down and wrote:

Miss Watson, your runaway nigger Jim is down here two mile below Pikesville and Mr. Phelps has got him and he will give him up for the reward if you send. HUCK FINN.

I felt good and all washed clean of sin for the first time I had ever felt so in my life, and I knowed I could pray, now. But I didn't do it straight off, but laid the paper down and set there thinking; thinking how good it was all this happened so, and how near I come to being lost and going to hell. And went on thinking. And got to thinking over our trip down the river; and I see Jim before me, all the time, in the day, and in the night-time, sometimes moonlight, sometimes storms, and we a floating along, talking, and singing, and laughing. But somehow I couldn't seem to strike no places to harden me against him, but only the other kind. I'd see him standing my watch on top of his'n, stead of calling me—so I could go on sleeping; and see him how glad he was when I come back out of the fog; and when I come to him again in the swamp, up there where the feud was; and such-like times; and would always call me honey, and pet me, and do everything he could think of for me, and how good he always was; and at last I struck the time I saved him by telling the men we had small-pox aboard, and he was so grateful, and said I was the best friend old Jim ever had in the world, and the *only* one he's got now; and then I happened to look around, and see that paper.

It was a close place. I took it up, and held it in my hand. I was a trembling, because I'd got to decide, forever, betwixt two things, and I knowed it. I studied a minute, sort of holding my breath, and then says to myself: "All right, then, I'll go to hell"—and tore it up.

[Huck then resolves to help Jim escape from the Phelps'.]

Twain, M. (1885). *The adventures of Huckleberry Finn.*

UNIT

7

LEADERSHIP PROFILE

Chief Joseph (1840–1904)

Head of the Wallowa Band of Nez Percés
"An Indian's View of Indian Affairs"
(A speech delivered in Washington, D.C., 1879)

Introduction and Historical Background

Chief Joseph is well-known for his resistance in the late-1800s to the U.S. government's attempts to force his Wallowa Band of Nez Percés onto reservations. Their name means "nose-pierced" in French, a name that stuck after their earliest encounters with French fur traders. The Nez Percés were a large, loosely organized Native American cultural group that inhabited an area of approximately 70,200 square miles in what is now northern Idaho, eastern Oregon, and Washington. For thousands of years, the Nez Percés were semi-nomadic. They moved within their territory to harvest different resources at different times of the year. In the 1700s, the Nez Percés began to amass huge herds of horses. Horses allowed them to travel further for hunting, harvesting, trading, and raiding other Native American villages—a practice adopted from the Plains Indians that was the method for acquiring additional hors-

National Archives and
Records Administration

es and honor and recognition for young warriors. The Nez Percés maintained good relations with the fur traders, the Lewis and Clark Expedition, and the settlers that began moving into the area in the first half of the 1800s.

In 1855, Governor Isaac Stevens of Washington called the Nez Percés to a treaty meeting. As a result of the Walla Walla Council, the Nez Percés were granted a reservation of five thousand square miles and some monies for improvements and annuities. Before the U.S. government ratified the treaty, however, gold was discovered on the land and new treaties that significantly reduced the size of the Nez Percés reservation were negotiated in 1863 and 1868. Not all of the Nez Percés agreed to the new treaties, and they split into two groups known as the "treaty-" and the "non-treaty-Indians." The former moved onto Lapwai Reservation and became "civilized" agriculturalists, while the latter remained hunters and stockmen. Chief Joseph's father, Old Chief Joseph, refused to sign the treaties, and as his health failed he urged his son not to sell their homeland.

Chief Joseph became the leader of the Wallowa Band of the Nez Percés in 1871 upon the death of his father. Relations between the non-treaty Indians and the U.S. government came to a head in May 1877, when General Howard issued an ultimatum that they had thirty days to gather their stock and move to the Lapwai Reservation or the United States government would move them by force. In addition to the ultimatum, the Nez Percés had fresh memories of unfair treatment, encroachment of white settlers, and a Nez Percés murder by white settlers. In response to these things, a group of young warriors conducted a series of raids against white settlers. The raids precipitated the Nez Percés War, lasting eleven weeks. During the war, the Nez Percés were faced with increasingly narrow options for decisions of greater and greater importance to the band.

After surrendering in order to prevent further bloodshed, and agreeing to terms of surrender stating that they would return to the Lapwai Reservation, the non-treaty Nez Percés were moved to Kansas and then finally to Indian Territory (Oklahoma). Chief Joseph continued to work for the return of his people to their homeland, and in 1879 the U.S. government allowed him to travel to Washington, D.C. where he made the speech reproduced for this Leadership Profile. Finally, in 1885 the remnants of his band were allowed to return to the Nez Percés reservation in Idaho. Chief Joseph, however, never gave up fighting for the return of his people to the Wallowa Valley. He never succeeded.

Chief Joseph's speech, "An Indian's View of Indian Affairs," is an eloquent and sometimes moving account of the relationships among his tribe, the Wallowa Nez Percés, the Euro-American settlers, and the U.S. government. It relates the decisions that Chief Joseph faced in the heroic struggle of the Nez Percés to maintain their own identity and homeland against almost insurmountable odds. It speaks of misunderstandings and failures of communication that had tragic consequences. It recounts the tales of heroic resistance, of victory in battle, and of terms of surrender that were not met. In the end, it offers a vision of the human condition in which diversity and complexity are acknowledged, valued, and celebrated.

UNIT 7

Points to Consider

1. When division occurs within a group, what is a leader's role?

2. How can a leader discern what is best or right for a group?

3. How do the Nez Percés and the U.S. government differ as "organizations"? How does each type of organization make decisions?

4. At the end of his speech, Chief Joseph pleas for fair treatment for his people. How does the way that the Nez Percés view the concept of fairness differ from that of the U.S. government?

Significant People Mentioned in Chief Joseph's Speech

Mr. Chapman
Friend and advisor to Chief Joseph

Old Chief Joseph
Leader of the non-treaty Nez Percés

Chief Joseph
Leader of the non-treaty Nez Percés after the death of his father

Lawyer
Chief who signed away nearly all of the lands of the Nez Percés in the second council in 1863

General Howard
General whose ultimatum was instrumental in precipitating war between the U.S. government and the Nez Percés

General Miles
General who convinced the Nez Percés to surrender with the promise that they could return to their native lands

Governor Stevens
Governor of Washington Territory in the 1850s

Rev. Spaulding
Christian missionary (also referred to as Mr. Spaulding)

Too-hool-hool-suit
Leader and orator picked by the Nez Percés to plead their case before General Howard

"An Indian's View of Indian Affairs"

By Chief Joseph

My friends, I have been asked to show you my heart. I am glad to have a chance to do so. I want the white people to understand my people. Some of you think an Indian is like a wild animal. This is a great mistake. I will tell you all about our people, and then you can judge whether an Indian is a man or not. I believe much trouble and blood would be saved if we opened our hearts more. I will tell you in my way how the Indian sees things. The white man has more words to tell you how they look to him, but it does not require many words to speak the truth. What I have to say will come from my heart, and I will speak with a straight tongue. Ah-cum-kin-i-ma-me-hut (the Great Spirit) is looking at me, and will hear me.

My name is In-mut-too-yah-lat-lat (Thunder traveling over the Mountains). I am chief of the Wal-lam-wat-kin band of Chute-pa-lu, or Nez Percés (nose pierced Indians). I was born in eastern Oregon, thirty-eight winters ago. My father was chief before me. When a young man, he was called Joseph by Mr. Spaulding, a missionary. He died a few years ago. He left a good name on earth. He advised me well for my people.

Our fathers gave us many laws, which they had learned from their fathers. These laws were good. They told us to treat all men as they treated us; that we should never be the first to break a bargain; that it was a disgrace to tell a lie; that we should speak only the truth; that it was a shame for one man to take from another his wife, or his property without paying for it. We were taught to believe that the Great Spirit sees and hears everything, and that he never forgets; that hereafter he will give every man a spirit-home according to his desserts [sic]: if he has been a good man, he will have a good home; if he has been a bad man, he will have a bad home. This I believe, and all my people believe the same.

We did not know there were other people besides the Indian until about one hundred winters ago, when some men with white faces came to our country. They brought many things with them to trade for furs and skins. They brought tobacco, which was new to us. They brought guns with flint stones on them, which frightened our women and children. Our people could not talk with these white-faced men, but they used signs which all people understand. These men were Frenchmen, and they called our people "Nez Percés," because they wore rings in their noses for ornaments. Although very few of our people wear them now, we are still called by the same name. These French trappers said a great many things to our fathers, which have been planted in our hearts. Some were good for us, but some were bad. Our people were divided in opinion about these men. Some thought they taught more bad than good. An Indian respects a brave man, but he despises a coward. He loves a straight tongue, but he hates a forked tongue. The French trappers told us some truths and some lies.

The first white men of your people who came to our country were named Lewis and Clarke [sic]. They also brought many things that our people had never seen. They talked straight, and our people gave them a great feast, as a proof that their hearts were friendly. These men were very kind. They made presents to our chiefs and our people made presents to them. We had a great many horses, of which we gave them what they needed, and they gave us guns and tobacco in return. All the Nez Percés made friends with Lewis and Clarke [sic], and agreed to let them pass through their country, and never to make war on white men. This promise the Nez Percés have never broken. No white man can accuse them of bad faith, and speak with a straight tongue. It has always been the pride of the Nez Percés that they were the friends of the white men. When my father was a young man there came to our country a white man (Rev. Mr. Spaulding) who talked the spirit law. He won the affections of our people because he spoke good things to them. At first he did not say anything about white men wanting to settle our lands. Nothing was said about that until about twenty winters ago, when a number of white people came into our country and built houses and made farms. At first our people made no complaint. They thought there was room enough for all to live in peace, and they were learning many things from the white man that seemed to be good. But we soon found that the white men were growing rich very fast and were greedy to possess everything the Indian had. My father was the first to see through the schemes of the white men, and he warned his tribe to be careful about trading with them. He had suspicion of men who seemed anxious to make money. I was a boy then, but I remember well my father's caution. He had sharper eyes than the rest of our people.

Next there came a white officer (Governor Stevens), who invited all the Nez Percés to a treaty council. After the council was opened he made known his heart. He said there were a great many white people in our country, and many more would come; that he wanted the land marked out so that the Indians and white men could be separated. If they were to live in peace it was necessary, he said, that the Indians should have a country set apart for them, and in that country they must stay. My father, who represented his band, refused to have anything to do with the council, because he wished to be a free man. He claimed that no man owned any part of the earth, and a man could not sell what he did not own.

Mr. Spaulding took hold of my father's arm and said, "Come and sign the treaty." My father pushed him away and said: "Why do you ask me to sign away my country? It is your business to talk to us about spirit matters and not to talk to us about parting with our land." Governor Stevens urged my father to sign his treaty, but he refused. "I will not sign your paper," he said; "you go where you please, so do I; you are not a child, I am no child; I can think for myself. No man can think for me. I have no other home than this. I will not give it up to any man. My people would have no home. Take away your paper. I will not touch it with my hand."

My father left the council. Some of the chiefs of the other bands of the Nez Percés signed the treaty [The Walla Walla Council of 1855], and then Governor Stevens gave them presents of blankets. My father cautioned his people to take no presents, for "after a while," he said, "they will claim that you have accepted pay for your country." Since that time four bands of the Nez Percés have received annuities from the United States. My father was invited to many councils, and they tried hard to make him sign the treaty, but he was firm as the rock, and would not sign away his home. His refusal caused a difference among the Nez Percés.

Eight years later (1863) was the next treaty council. A chief called Lawyer, because he was a great talker, took the lead in this council, and sold nearly all the Nez Percés country. My father was not there. He said to me: "When you go into council with the white man, always remember your country. Do not give it away. The white man will cheat you out of your home. I have taken no pay from the United States. I have never sold our land." In this treaty Lawyer acted without authority from our band. He had no right to sell the Wallowa (winding water) country. That had always belonged to my father's own people, and the other bands had never disputed our right to it. No other Indians ever claimed Wallowa.

In order to have all people understand how much land we owned, my father planted poles around it and said:

"Inside is the home of my people—the white man may take the land outside. Inside this boundary all our people were born. It circles around the graves of our fathers, and we will never give up these graves to any man."

The United States claimed that they had bought all the Nez Percés country outside the Lapwai Reservation, from Lawyer and other chiefs, but we continued to live on this land in peace until eight years ago, when white men began to come inside the bounds my father had set. We warned them against this great wrong, but they would not leave our land, and some bad blood was raised. The white men represented that we were going upon the warpath. They reported many things that were false.

The United States Government asked again for a treaty council. My father had become blind and feeble. He could no longer speak for his people. It was then that I took my father's place as chief. In this council I made my first speech to white men. I said to the agent who held the council:

"I did not want to come to this council, but I came hoping that we could save blood. The white man has no right to come here and take our country. We have never accepted any presents from the Government. Neither Lawyer nor any other chief had authority to sell this land. It has always belonged to my people. It came unclouded to them from our fathers, and we will defend this land as long as a drop of Indian blood warms the hearts of our men."

The agent said he had orders, from the Great White Chief at Washington, for us to go upon the Lapwai Reservation, and that if we obeyed he would help us in many ways. "You must move to the agency," he said. I answered him: "I will not. I do not need your help; we have plenty, and we are contented and happy if the white man will let us alone. The reservation is too small for so many people with all their stock. You can keep your presents; we can go to your towns and pay for all we need; we have plenty of horses and cattle to sell, and we won't have any help from you; we are free now; we can go where we please. Our fathers were born here. Here they lived, here they died, here are their graves. We will never leave them." The agent went away, and we had peace for a little while.

Soon after this my father sent for me. I saw he was dying. I took his hand in mine. He said: "My son, my body is returning to my mother earth, and my spirit is going very soon to see the Great Spirit Chief. When I am gone, think of your country. You are the chief of these people. They look to you to guide them. Always remember that your father never sold this country. You must stop your ears whenever you are asked to sign a treaty selling your home. A few years more, and white men will be all around you. They have their eyes on this land. My son, never forget my dying words. This country holds your father's body. Never sell the bones of your father and your mother." I pressed my father's hand and told him I would protect his grave with my life. My father smiled and passed away to the spirit land.

I buried him in that beautiful valley of winding waters. I love that land more than all the rest of the world. A man who would not love his father's grave is worse than a wild animal.

For a short time we lived quietly. But this could not last. White men had found gold in the mountains around the land of winding water. They stole many horses from us, and we could not get them back because we were Indians. The white men told lies for each other. They drove off a great many of our cattle. Some white men branded our young cattle so they could claim them. We had no friend who would plead our cause before the law councils. It seemed to me that some of the white men in Wallowa were doing these things on purpose to get up a war. They knew that we were not strong enough to fight them. I labored hard to avoid trouble and bloodshed. We gave up some of our country to the white men, thinking that then we could have peace. We were mistaken. The white man would not let us alone. We could have avenged our wrongs many times, but we did not. Whenever the Government asked us to help them against other Indians, we have never refused. When the white men were few and we were strong we could have killed them all off, but the Nez Percés wished to live at peace.

If we have not done so, we have not been to blame. I believe that the old treaty has never been correctly reported. If we ever owned land we own it still, for we never sold it. In the treaty councils the commissioners have claimed that our country had been sold to the Government. Suppose a white man should come to me and say, "Joseph, I like your horses, and I want to buy them." I say to him, "No, my horses suit me, I will not sell them." Then he goes to my neighbor, and says to him: "Joseph has some good horses. I want to buy them, but he refuses to sell." My neighbor answers, "Pay me the money, and I will sell you Joseph's horses." The white man returns to me, and says, "Joseph, I have bought your horses, and you must let me have them." If we sold our lands to the Government, this is the way they were bought.

On account of the treaty made by the other bands of the Nez Percés, the white men claimed my lands. We were troubled greatly by white men crowding over the line. Some of these were good men, and we live on peaceful terms with them, but they were not all good.

Nearly every year the agent came over from Lapwai and ordered us on to the reservation. We always replied that we were satisfied to live in Wallowa. We were careful to refuse presents or annuities which he offered.

Through all the years since the white men came to Wallowa we have been threatened and taunted by them and the treaty Nez Percés. They have given us no rest. We have had a few good friends among white men, and they have always advised my people to bear these taunts without fighting. Our young men were quick-tempered, and I have had great trouble in keeping them from doing rash things. I have carried a heavy load on my back ever since I was a boy. I learned then that we were but few, while the white men were many, and that we could not hold our own with them. We were like deer. They were like grizzly bears. We had a small country. Their country was large. We were contented to let things remain as the Great Spirit Chief made them. They were not; and would change the rivers and mountains if they did not suit them.

Year after year we have been threatened, but no war was made upon my people until General Howard came to our country two years ago and told us he was the white war-chief of all that country. He had one house full of troops all the time at Fort Lapwai. The next spring the agent at Umatilla agency sent an Indian runner to tell me to meet General Howard at Walla Walla. I could not go myself, but I sent my brother and five other head men to meet him, and they had a long talk.

General Howard said: "You have talked straight, and it is all right. You can stay in Wallowa." He insisted that my brother should go with him to Fort Lapwai. When the party arrived there General Howard sent out runners and called all the Indians in a grand council. I was in that council. I said to General Howard, "We are ready to listen." He answered that he would not talk then, but would hold a council next day, when he would talk plainly. I said to General Howard: "I am ready to talk today. I have been in a great many councils, but I am no wiser. We are all sprung from a woman, although we are unlike in many things. We cannot be made over again.

You are as you were made, and as you were made you can remain. We are just as we were made by the Great Spirit, and you cannot change us; then why should children of one mother and father quarrel—why should one try to cheat the other? I do not believe that the Great Spirit Chief gave one kind of men the right to tell another kind of men what they must do."

General Howard replied: "You deny my authority, do you? You want to dictate to me, do you?"

Then one of my chiefs—Too-hool-hool-suit—rose in the council and said to General Howard: "The Great Spirit Chief made the world as it is, and as he wanted it, and he made a part of it for us to live upon. I do not see where you get authority to say that we shall not live where he placed us."

General Howard lost his temper and said: "Shut up! I don't want to hear any more of such talk. The law says you shall go upon the reservation to live, and I want you to do so, but you persist in disobeying the law" (meaning the treaty). "If you do not move, I will take the matter into my own hand, and make you suffer for your disobedience."

Too-hool-hool-suit answered: "Who are you, that you ask us to talk, and then tell me I sha'n't talk? Are you the Great Spirit? Did you make the world? Did you make the sun? Did you make the rivers to run for us to drink? Did you make the grass to grow? Did you make all these things, that you talk to us as though we were boys? If you did, then you have the right to talk as you do."

General Howard replied, "You are an impudent fellow, and I will put you in the guard house," and then ordered a soldier to arrest him.

Too-hool-hool-suit made no resistance. He asked General Howard: "Is that your order? I don't care. I have expressed my heart to you. I have nothing to take back. I have spoken for my country. You can arrest me, but you cannot change me or make me take back what I have said."

The soldiers came forward and seized my friend and took him to the guard house. My men whispered among themselves whether they should let this thing be done. I counseled them to submit. I knew if we resisted that all the white men present, including General Howard, would be killed in a moment, and we would be blamed. If I had said nothing, General Howard would never have given another unjust order against my men. I saw the danger, and, while they dragged Too-hool-hool-suit to prison, I arose and said: "I am going to talk now. I don't care whether you arrest me or not." I turned to my people and said: "The arrest of Too-hool-hool-suit was wrong, but we will not resent the insult. We were invited to this council to express our hearts, and we have done so." Too-hool-hool-suit was prisoner for five days before he was released.

The council broke up for the day. On the next morning General Howard came to my lodge, and invited me to go with him and White-Bird and Looking-Glass, to look for land for my people. As we rode along, we came to some good land that was already occupied by Indians and white people. General Howard, pointing to this land, said: "If you will come on to the reservation, I will give you these lands and move these people off."

I replied: "No. It would be wrong to disturb these people. I have no right to take their homes. I have never taken what did not belong to me. I will not now."

We rode all day upon the reservation, and found no good land unoccupied. I have been informed by men who do not lie that General Howard sent a letter that night, telling the soldiers at Walla Walla to go to Wallowa Valley, and drive us out upon our return home.

In the council, next day, General Howard informed me, in a haughty spirit, that he would give my people thirty days to go back home, collect all their stock, and move on to the reservation, saying, "If you are not here in that time, I shall consider that you want to fight, and will send my soldiers to drive you on."

I said: "War can be avoided, and it ought to be avoided. I want no war. My people have always been the friends of the white man. Why are you in such a hurry? I cannot get ready and move in thirty days. Our stock is scattered, and Snake River is very high. Let us wait until fall, then the river will be low. We want time to hunt up our stock and gather supplies for winter."

General Howard replied: "If you let the time run over one day, the soldiers will be there to drive you on to the reservation, and all your cattle and horses outside of the reservation at that time will fall into the hands of the white men."

UNIT
7

I knew I had never sold my country, and that I had no land in Lapwai; but I did not want blood-shed. I did not want my people killed. I did not want anybody killed. Some of my people had been murdered by white men, and the white murderers were never punished for it. I told General Howard about this, and again said I wanted no war. I wanted the people who lived upon the lands I was to occupy at Lapwai to have time to gather their harvest.

I said in my heart that, rather than have war, I would give up my country. I would give up my father's grave. I would give up everything rather than have the blood of white men upon the hands of my people.

General Howard refused to allow me more than thirty days to move my people and their stock. I am sure that he began to prepare for war at once.

When I returned to Wallowa I found my people very much excited upon discovering that the soldiers were already in the Wallowa valley. We held a council and decided to move immediately, to avoid bloodshed.

Too-hool-hool-suit, who felt outraged by his imprisonment, talked for war, and made many of my young men willing to fight rather than be driven like dogs from the land where they were born. He declared that blood alone would wash out the disgrace General Howard had put upon him. It required a strong heart to stand up against such talk, but I urged my people to be quiet, and not to begin a war.

We gathered all the stock we could find, and made an attempt to move. We left many of our horses and cattle in Wallowa, and we lost several hundred in crossing the river. All of my people succeeded in getting across in safety. Many of the Nez Percés came together in Rocky Cañon to hold a grand council. I went with all my people. This council lasted ten days. There was a great deal of war talk, and a great deal of excitement. There was one young brave present whose father had been killed by a white man five years before. This man's blood was bad against white men, and he left the council calling for revenge. Again I counseled peace, and I thought the danger was past. We had not complied with General Howard's order because we could not, but we intended to do so as soon as possible. I was leaving the council to kill beef for my family, when news came that the young man whose father had been killed had gone out with several other hot-blooded young braves and killed four white men. He rode up to the council and shouted: "Why do you sit here like women? The war has begun already." I was deeply grieved. All the lodges were moved except my brother's and my own. I saw clearly that the war was upon us when I learned that my young men had been secretly buying ammunition. I heard then that Too-hool-hool-suit, who had been imprisoned by General Howard, had succeeded in organizing a war party. I knew that their acts would involve all my people. I saw that the war could not be prevented. The time had passed. I counseled peace from the beginning. I knew that we were too weak to fight the United States. We had many grievances, but I knew that war would bring more. We had good white friends, who advised us against taking the war path. My friend, and brother, Mr. Chapman, who has been with us since the surrender, told us just how the war would end. Mr. Chapman took sides against us, and helped General Howard. I do not blame him for doing so. He tried hard to prevent bloodshed. We hoped the white settlers would not join the soldiers. Before the war commenced we had discussed this matter all over, and many of my people were in favor of warning them that if they took no part against us they should not be molested in the event of war being begun by General Howard. This plan was voted down in the war council.

There were bad men among my people who had quarreled with white men, and they talked of their wrongs until they roused all the bad hearts in the council. Still I could not believe that they would begin the war. I know that my young men did a great wrong, but I ask, Who was first to blame? They had been insulted a thousand times; their fathers and brothers had been killed; their mothers and wives had been disgraced; they had been driven to madness by whisky sold to them by white men; they had been told by General Howard that all their horses and cattle which they had been unable to drive out of Wallowa were to fall into the hands of white men; and, added to all this, they were homeless and desperate.

I would have given my own life if I could have undone the killing of white men by my people. I blame my young men and I blame the white men. I blame General Howard for not giving my people time to get their stock away from Wallowa. I do not acknowledge that he had the right to order me to leave Wallowa at any time. I deny that either my father or myself ever sold that land. It is still our land. It may never again be our home, but my father sleeps there, and I love it as I love my mother. I left there, hoping to avoid bloodshed.

If General Howard had given me plenty of time to gather up my stock, and treated Too-hool-hool-suit as a man should be treated, there would have been no war.

My friends among white men have blamed me for the war. I am not to blame. When my young men began the killing, my heart was hurt. Although I did not justify them, I remembered all the insults I had endured, and my blood was on fire. Still I would have taken my people to the buffalo country without fighting, if possible.

I could see no other way to avoid a war. We moved over to White Bird Creek, sixteen miles away, and there encamped, intending to collect our stock before leaving; but the soldiers attacked us, and the first battle was fought. [The Battle of White Bird Canyon] We numbered in that battle sixty men, and the soldiers numbered a hundred. The fight lasted a few minutes, when the soldiers retreated before us for twelve miles. They lost thirty-three killed, and had seven wounded. When an Indian fights, he only shoots to kill; but soldiers shoot at random. None of the soldiers were scalped. We do not believe in scalping or in killing wounded men. Soldiers do not kill many Indians unless they are wounded and left upon the battle field. Then they kill Indians.

Seven days after the first battle, General Howard arrived in the Nez Percés country, bringing seven hundred more soldiers. It was now war in earnest. We crossed the Salmon River, hoping General Howard would follow. We were not disappointed. He did follow us, and we got back between him and his supplies, and cut him off for three days. He sent out two companies to open the way. We attacked them, killing one officer, two guides and ten men.

We withdrew, hoping the soldiers would follow, but they had got fighting enough for that day. They entrenched themselves, and next day we attacked them again. The battle lasted all day, and was renewed next morning. We killed four and wounded seven or eight.

About this time General Howard found out that we were in his rear. Five days later he attacked us with three hundred and fifty warriors. The fight lasted twenty-seven hours. We lost four killed and several wounded. General Howard's loss was twenty-nine men killed and sixty wounded.

The following day the soldiers charged upon us, and we retreated with our families and stock a few miles, leaving eighty lodges to fall into General Howard's hands. [The Battle of Clearwater]

Finding that we were outnumbered, we retreated to Bitter Root Valley. Here another body of soldiers came upon us and demanded our surrender. We refused. They said, "You can not get by us." We answered, "We are going by you without fighting if you will let us, but we are going by you anyhow." [The Battle of Fort Fizzle] We then made a treaty with these soldiers. We agreed not to molest any one, and they agreed that we might pass through the Bitter Root country in peace. We bought provisions and traded stock with white men there.

We understood that there was to be no more war. We intended to go peaceably to the buffalo country, and leave the question of returning to our country to be settled afterward.

With this understanding we traveled on for four days, and, thinking that the trouble was all over, we stopped and prepared tent poles to take with us. We started again, and at the end of two days we saw three white men passing our camp. Thinking that the peace had been made, we did not molest them. We could have killed them or taken them prisoners, but we did not suspect them of being spies, which they were.

That night the soldiers surrounded our camp. About daybreak one of my men went out to look after his horses. The soldiers saw him and shot him down like a coyote. I have since learned that these soldiers were not those we had left behind. They had come upon us from another direction. The new white war chief's name was Gibbon. He charged upon us while some of my people were still asleep. We had a hard fight. Some of my men crept around and attacked the soldiers from the rear. In this battle, we lost nearly all our lodges, but we finally drove General Gibbon back. [The Battle of the Big Hole]

Finding that he was not able to capture us, he sent to his camp a few miles away for his big guns (cannons), but my men had captured them and all the ammunition. We damaged the big guns all we could, and carried away the powder and lead. In the fight with General Gibbon we lost fifty women and children and thirty fighting men. We remained long enough to bury our dead. The Nez Percés never make war on women and children; we could have killed a great many women and children while the war lasted, but we would feel ashamed to do so cowardly an act.

We never scalp our enemies, but when General Howard came up and joined General Gibbon, their Indian scouts dug up our dead and scalped them. I have been told that General Howard did not order this great shame to be done.

We retreated as rapidly as we could toward the buffalo country. After six days General Howard came close to us, and we went out and attacked him, and captured nearly all his horses and mules (about two hundred and fifty head). [The Battle of Camas Meadows] We then marched on to the Yellowstone Basin.

On the way we captured one white man and two white women. We released them at the end of three days. They were treated kindly. The women were not insulted. Can the white soldiers tell me of one time when Indian women were taken prisoners, and held three days and then released without being insulted? Were the Nez Percés women who fell into the hands of General Howard's soldiers treated with as much respect? I deny that a Nez Percés was ever guilty of such a crime.

A few days later we captured two more white men. One of them stole a horse and escaped. We gave the other a poor horse and told him he was free.

Nine days' march brought us to the mouth of Clarke's [sic] Fork of the Yellowstone. We did not know what had become of General Howard, but we supposed that he had sent for more horses and mules. He did not come up, but another new war chief (General Sturgis) attacked us. [The Battle of Canyon Creek] We held him in check while we moved all our women and children and stock out of danger, leaving a few men to cover our retreat.

Several days passed, and we heard nothing of General Howard, or Gibbon, or Sturgis. We had repulsed each in turn, and began to feel secure, when another army, under General Miles, struck us. [The Battle of Bear Paws] This was the fourth army, each of which outnumbered our fighting force, that we had encountered within sixty days.

We had no knowledge of General Miles' army until a short time before he made a charge upon us, cutting our camp in two, and capturing nearly all of our horses. About seventy men, myself among them, were cut off. My little daughter, twelve years old, was with me. I gave her a rope, and told her to catch a horse and join the others who were cut off from the camp. I have not seen her since, but I have learned that she is alive and well.

I thought of my wife and children, who were now surrounded by soldiers, and I resolved to go to them or die. With a prayer in my mouth to the Great Spirit Chief who rules above, I dashed unarmed through the line of soldiers. It seemed to me that there were guns on every side, before and behind me. My clothes were cut to pieces and my horse was wounded, but I was unhurt. As I reached the door of my lodge, my wife handed me my rifle, saying: "Here's your gun. Fight!"

The soldiers kept up a continuous fire. Six of my men were killed in one spot near me. Ten or twelve soldiers charged into our camp and got possession of two lodges, killing three Nez Percés and losing three of their men, who fell inside our lines. I called my men to drive them back. We fought at close range, not more than twenty steps apart, and drove the soldiers back upon their main line, leaving their dead in our hands. We secured their arms and ammunition. We lost, the first day and night, eighteen men and three women. General Miles lost twenty-six killed and forty wounded. The following day General Miles sent a messenger into my camp under protection of a white flag. I sent my friend Yellow Bull to meet him.

Yellow Bull understood the messenger to say that General Miles wished me to consider the situation; that he did not want to kill my people unnecessarily. Yellow Bull understood this to be a demand for me to surrender and save blood. Upon reporting this message to me, Yellow Bull said he wondered whether General Miles was in earnest. I sent him back with my answer, that I had made up my mind, but would think about it and send word soon. A little later he sent some Cheyenne scouts with another message. I went out to meet them. They said they believed that General Miles was sincere and really wanted peace. I walked on to General Miles' tent. He met me and we shook hands. He said, "Come, let us sit down by the fire and talk this matter over." I remained with him all night; next morning Yellow Bull came over to see if I was alive, and why I did not return. General Miles would not let me leave the tent to see my friend alone.

Yellow Bull said to me: "They have got you in their power, and I am afraid they will never let you go again. I have an officer in our camp, and I will hold him until they let you go free."

I said: "I do not know what they mean to do with me, but if they kill me you must not kill the officer. It will do no good to avenge my death by killing him."

Yellow Bull returned to my camp. I did not make any agreement that day with General Miles. The battle was renewed while I was with him. I was very anxious about my people. I knew that we were near Sitting Bull's camp in King George's land, and I thought maybe the Nez Percés who had escaped would return with assistance. No great damage was done to either party during the night.

On the following morning I returned to my camp by agreement, meeting the officer who had been held a prisoner in my camp by the flag of truce. My people were divided about surrendering. We could have escaped from Bear Paw Mountain if we had left our wounded, old women, and children behind. We were unwilling to do this. We had never heard of a wounded Indian recovering while in the hands of white men.

On the evening of the fourth day General Howard came in with a small escort, together with my friend Chapman. We could now talk understandingly. General Miles said to me in plain words, "If you will come out and give up your arms, I will spare your lives and send you to your reservation." I do not know what passed between General Miles and General Howard.

I could not bear to see my wounded men and women suffer any longer; we had lost enough already. General Miles had promised that we might return to our own country with what stock we had left. I thought we could start again. I believed General Miles, or I never would have surrendered. I have heard that he has been censured for making the promise to return us to Lapwai. He could not have made any other terms with me at that time. I would have held him in check until my friends came to my assistance, and then neither of the generals nor their soldiers would have ever left Bear Paw Mountain alive.

On the fifth day I went to General Miles and gave up my gun, and said, "From where the sun now stands I will fight no more." My people needed rest—we wanted peace.

I was told we could go with General Miles to Tongue River and stay there until spring, when we would be sent back to our country. Finally it was decided that we were be taken to Tongue River. We had nothing to say about it. After our arrival at Tongue River, General Miles received orders to take us to Bismarck. The reason given was, that subsistence would be cheaper there.

General Miles was opposed to this order. He said: "You must not blame me. I have endeavored to keep my word, but the chief who is over me has given the order that I must obey or resign. That would do you no good. Some other officer would carry out the order."

I believe General Miles would have kept his word if he could have done so. I do not blame him for what we have suffered since the surrender. I do not know who is to blame. We gave up all our horses—over eleven hundred—and all our saddles—over one hundred—and we have not heard from them since. Somebody has got our horses.

General Miles turned my people over to another soldier, and we were taken to Bismarck. Captain Johnson, who now had charge of us, received an order to take us to Fort Leavenworth. At Leavenworth we were placed on a low river bottom, with no water except river water to drink and cook with. We had always lived in a healthy country, where mountains were high and the water was cold and clear. Many of my people sickened and died, and we buried them in this strange land. I can not tell how much my heart suffered for my people while at Leavenworth. The Great Spirit Chief who rules above seemed to be looking some other way, and did not see what was being done to my people.

During the hot days (July, 1878) we received notice that we were to be moved farther away from our own country. We were not asked if we were willing to go. We were ordered to get into railroad cars. Three of my people died on the way to Baxter Springs. It was worse to die there than to fight in the mountains.

We were moved from Baxter Springs (Kansas) to the Indian Territory, and set down without our lodges. We had but little medicine, and we were nearly all sick. Seventy of my people have died since we moved there.

We have had a great many visitors who have talked many ways. Some of the chiefs (General Fish and Colonel Stickney) from Washington came to see us, and selected land for us to live upon. We have not moved to that land, for it is not a good place to live.

The Commissioner Chief (E.A. Hayt) came to see us. I told him, as I told every one, that I expected General Miles' word to be carried out. He said it "could not be done; that white men now lived in my country and all the land was taken up; that, if I returned to Wallowa, I could not live in peace; that law-papers were out against my young men who began the war, and that the Government could not protect my people." This talk fell like a heavy stone upon my heart. I saw that I could not gain anything by talking to him. Other law chiefs (Congressional Committee) came to see me and said they would help me to get to a healthy country. I did not know who to believe. The white people have too many chiefs. They do not understand each other. They do not all talk alike.

The Commissioner Chief (Mr. Hayt) invited me to go with him and hunt for a better home than we have now. I like the land we found (west of the Osage Reservation) better than any place I have seen in that country; but it is not a healthy land. There are no mountains and rivers. The water is warm. It is not good country for stock. I do not believe my people can live there. I am afraid they will all die. The Indians who occupy that country are dying off. I promised Chief Hayt to go there, and do the best I could until the Government got ready to make good General Miles' word. I was not satisfied, but I could not help myself.

Then the Inspector Chief (General McNiel) came to my camp and we had a long talk. He said I ought to have a home in the mountain country north, and that he would write a letter to the Great Chief at Washington. Again the hope of seeing the mountains of Idaho and Oregon grew up in my heart.

At last I was granted permission to come to Washington and bring my friend Yellow Bull and our interpreter with me. I am glad we came. I have shaken hands with a great many friends, but there are some things I want to know which no one seems able to explain. I can not understand how the Government sends a man out to fight us, as it did General Miles, and then breaks his word. Such a government has something wrong about it. I can not understand why so many chiefs are allowed to talk so many different ways, and promise so many different things. I have seen the Great Father Chief (the President), the next Great Chief (Secretary of the Interior), the Commissioner Chief (Hayt), the Law Chief (General Butler), and many other law chiefs (Congressmen), and they all say they are my friends, and that I shall have justice, but while their mouths all talk right I do not understand why nothing is done for my people. I have heard talk and talk, but nothing is done. Good words do not last long unless they amount to something. Words do not pay for my dead people. They do not pay for my country, now overrun by white men. They do not protect my father's grave. They do not pay for all my horses and cattle. Good words will not give me back my children. Good words will not make good the promise of your War Chief General Miles. Good words will not give my people good health and stop them from dying. Good words will not get my people a home where they can live in peace and take care of themselves. I am tired of talk that comes to nothing. It makes my heart sick when I remember all the good words and all the broken promises. There has been too much talking by men who had no right to talk. Too many misrepresentations have been made, too many misunderstandings have come up between the white men about the Indians.

If the white man wants to live in peace with the Indian he can live in peace. There need be no trouble. Treat all men alike. Give them the same law. Give them all an even chance to live and grow. All men were made by the same Great Spirit Chief. They are all brothers. The earth is the mother of all people, and all people should have equal rights upon it. You might as well expect the rivers to run backward as that any man who was born a free man should be contented when penned up and denied liberty to go where he pleases. If you tie a horse to a stake, do you expect he will grow fat? If you pen an Indian up on a small spot of earth, and compel him to stay there, he will not be contented, nor will he grow and prosper. I have asked some of the great white chiefs where they got their authority to say to the Indian that he shall stay in one place, while he sees white men going where they please. They can not tell me.

I only ask of the Government to be treated as all other men are treated. If I can not go to my own home, let me have a home in some country where my people will not die so fast. I would like to go to Bitter Root Valley. There my people would be healthy; where they are now they are dying. Three have died since I left my camp to come to Washington.

When I think of our condition my heart is heavy. I see men of my race treated as outlaws and driven from country to country, or shot down like animals.

I know that my race must change. We can not hold our own with the white men as we are. We only ask an even chance to live as other men live. We ask to be recognized as men. We ask that the same law shall work alike on all men. If the Indian breaks the law, punish him by the law. If the white man breaks the law, punish him also.

Let me be a free man—free to travel, free to stop, free to work, free to trade where I choose, free to choose my own teachers, free to follow the religion of my fathers, free to think and talk and act for myself—and I will obey every law, or submit to the penalty.

Whenever the white man treats an Indian as they treat each other, then we will have no more wars. We shall all be alike—brothers of one father and one mother, with one sky above us and one country around us, and one government for all. Then the Great Spirit Chief who rules above will smile upon this land, and send rain to wash out the bloody spots made by brothers' hands from the face of the earth. For this time the Indian race are waiting and praying. I hope that no more groans of wounded men and women will ever go to the ear of the Great Spirit Chief above, and that all people may be one people.

In-mut-too-yah-lat-lat has spoken for his people.

Chief Joseph. (1879/1971). An Indian's view of Indian affairs. In W.C. Vanderwerth, *Indian Oratory: Famous Speeches by Noted Indian Chieftains.* Copyright © 1979. Used by permission of University of Oklahoma Press.

The Introduction and Historical Background for the "Leadership Profile: The Nez Percés' Chief Joseph" is adapted from sections of a Hartwick Classic Leadership Case™ entitled "Chief Joseph: 'An Indian's View of Indian Affairs'" by Michael K. Green (State University of New York at Oneonta) and Roy Savoian (Lynchburg College, Virginia), edited by Jerrold C. Brown (The Hartwick Humanities in Management Institute, Hartwick College, Oneonta, New York).

UNIT

7

REFLECT & FOCUS

The Road Not Taken

Two roads diverged in a yellow wood,
And sorry I could not travel both
And be one traveler, long I stood
And looked down one as far as I could
To where it bent in the undergrowth;

Then took the other, as just as fair,
And having perhaps the better claim,
Because it was grassy and wanted wear;
Though as for that, the passing there
Had worn them really about the same,

And both that morning equally lay
In leaves no step had trodden black.
Oh, I kept the first for another day!
Yet knowing how way leads on to way,
I doubted if I should ever come back.

I shall be telling this with a sigh
Somewhere ages and ages hence:
Two roads diverged in a wood, and I —
I took the one less traveled by,
And that has made all the difference.

—Robert Frost (1874–1963),
American Poet

Frost, R. (1920). *The Road Not Taken*.

READINGS

"Shooting an Elephant"

By George Orwell (1903–1950)
English Writer

Points to Consider

1. How can one overcome the pressure to make a decision that he or she knows is not the best decision?

2. How have Orwell's assumptions about the group he is a part of (although temporarily) affected his decision-making process? His effectiveness as a leader?

3. What allegiance does a leader owe to a larger organization (in this instance, the British Empire) when he or she doesn't share the same vision, mission, and goals?

4. To what extent can one lead effectively when her or his convictions are compromised?

"Shooting an Elephant"

In Moulmein, in lower Burma, I was hated by large numbers of people—the only time in my life that I have been important enough for this to happen to me. I was sub-divisional police officer of the town, and in an aimless, petty kind of way anti-European feeling was very bitter. No one had the guts to raise a riot, but if a European woman went through the bazaars alone somebody would probably spit betel juice over her dress. As a police officer I was an obvious target and was baited whenever it seemed safe to do so. When a nimble Burman tripped me up on the football field and the referee (another Burman) looked the other way, the crowd yelled with hideous laughter. This happened more than once. In the end the sneering yellow faces of young men that met me everywhere, the insults hooted after me when I was at a safe distance, got badly on my nerves. The young Buddhist priests were the worst of all. There were several thousands of them in the town and none of them seemed to have anything to do except stand on street corners and jeer at Europeans.

All this was perplexing and upsetting. For at that time I had already made up my mind that imperialism was an evil thing and the sooner I chucked up my job and got out of it the better. Theoretically—and secretly, of course—I was all for the Burmese and all against their oppressors, the British. As for the job I was doing, I hated it more bitterly than I can perhaps make clear. In a job like that you see the dirty work of Empire at close quarters. The wretched prisoners huddling in the stinking cages of the lock-ups, the grey, cowed faces of the long-term convicts, the scarred buttocks of the men who had been flogged with bamboos—all these oppressed me with an intolerable sense of guilt. But I could get nothing into perspective. I was young and ill-educated and I had had to think out my problems in the utter silence that is imposed on every Englishman in the East. I did not even know that the British Empire is dying, still less did I know that it is a great deal better than the younger empires that are going to supplant it. All I knew was that I was stuck between my hatred of the empire I served and my rage against the evil-spirited little beasts who tried to make my job impossible. With one part of my mind I thought of the British Raj as an unbreakable tyranny, as something clamped down, in *saecula saeculorum*, upon the will of prostrate peoples; with another part I thought that the greatest joy in the world would be to drive a bayonet into a Buddhist priest's guts. Feelings like these are the normal by-products of imperialism; ask any Anglo-Indian official, if you can catch him off duty.

One day something happened which in a roundabout way was enlightening. It was a tiny incident in itself, but it gave me a better glimpse than I had had before of the real nature of imperialism—the real motives for which despotic governments act. Early one morning the sub-inspector at a police station the other end of the town rang me up on the 'phone and said that an elephant was ravaging the bazaar. Would I please come and do something about it? I did not know what I could do, but I wanted to see what was happening and I got on to a pony and started out. I took my rifle, an old .44 Winchester and much too small to kill an elephant, but I thought the noise might be useful *in terrorem*. Various Burmans stopped me on the way and told me about the elephant's doings. It was not, of course, a wild elephant, but a tame one which had gone "must." It had been chained up, as tame elephants always are when their attack of "must" is due, but on the previous night it had broken its chain and escaped. Its mahout, the only person who could manage it when it was in that state, had set out in pursuit, but had taken the wrong direction and was now twelve hours' journey away, and in the morning the elephant had suddenly reappeared in the town. The Burmese populations had no weapons and were quite helpless against it. It had already destroyed somebody's bamboo hut, killed a cow and raided some fruit-stalls and devoured the stock; also it had met the municipal rubbish van and, when the driver jumped out and took to his heels, had turned the van over and inflicted violences upon it.

The Burmese sub-inspector and some Indian constables were waiting for me in the quarter where the elephant had been seen. It was a very poor quarter, a labyrinth of squalid bamboo huts, thatched with palm-leaf, winding all over a steep hillside. I remember that it was a cloudy, stuffy morning at the beginning of the rains. We began questioning the people as to where the elephant had gone and, as usual, failed to get any definite information. That is invariably the case in the East; a story always sounds clear enough at a distance, but the nearer you get to the scene of events the vaguer it becomes. Some of the people said that the elephant had gone in one direction, some said that he had gone in another, some professed not even to have heard of any elephant. I had almost made up my mind that the whole story was a pack of lies, when we heard yells a little distance away. There was a loud, scandalized cry of "Go away, child! Go away this instant!" and an old woman with a switch in her hand came round the corner of a hut, violently shooing away a crowd of naked children. Some more women followed, clicking their tongues and exclaiming; evidently there was something that the children ought not to have seen. I rounded the hut and saw a man's dead body sprawling in the mud. He was an Indian, a black Dravidian coolie, almost naked, and he could not have been dead many minutes. The people said that the elephant had come suddenly upon him round the corner of the hut, caught him with its trunk, put its foot on his back and ground him into the earth. This was the rainy season and the ground was soft, and his face had scored a trench a foot deep and a couple of yards long. He was lying on his belly with arms crucified and head sharply twisted to one side. His face was coated with mud, the eyes wide open, the teeth bared and grinning with an expression of unendurable agony. (Never tell me, by the way, that the dead look peaceful. Most of the corpses I have seen looked devilish.) The friction of the great beast's foot had stripped the skin from his back as neatly as one skins a rabbit. As soon as I saw the dead man I sent an orderly to a friend's house nearby to borrow an elephant rifle. I had already sent back the pony, not wanting it to go mad with fright and throw me if it smelt the elephant.

The orderly came back in a few minutes with a rifle and five cartridges, and meanwhile some Burmans had arrived and told us that the elephant was in the paddy fields below, only a few hundred yards away. As I started forward practically the whole population of the quarter flocked out of the houses and followed me. They had seen the rifle and were all shouting excitedly that I was going to shoot the elephant. They had not shown much interest in the elephant when he

UNIT

7

was merely ravaging their homes, but it was different now that he was going to be shot. It was a bit of fun to them, as it would be to an English crowd; besides they wanted the meat. It made me vaguely uneasy. I had no intention of shooting the elephant—I had merely sent for the rifle to defend myself if necessary—and it is always unnerving to have a crowd following you. I marched down the hill, looking and feeling a fool, with the rifle over my shoulder and an ever-growing army of people jostling at my heels. At the bottom, when you got away from the huts, there was a metalled road and beyond that a miry waste of paddy fields a thousand yards across, not yet ploughed but soggy from the first rains and dotted with coarse grass. The elephant was standing eight yards from the road, his left side towards us. He took not the slightest notice of the crowd's approach. He was tearing up bunches of grass, beating them against his knees to clean them and stuffing them into his mouth.

I had halted on the road. As soon as I saw the elephant I knew with perfect certainty that I ought not to shoot him. It is a serious matter to shoot a working elephant—it is comparable to destroying a huge and costly piece of machinery—and obviously one ought not to do it if it can possibly be avoided. And at that distance, peacefully eating, the elephant looked no more dangerous than a cow. I thought then and I think now that his attack of "must" was already passing off in which case he would merely wander harmlessly about until the mahout came back and caught him. Moreover, I did not in the least want to shoot him. I decided that I would watch him for a little while to make sure that he did not turn savage again, and then go home.

But at that moment I glanced round at the crowd that had followed me. It was an immense crowd, two thousand at the least and growing every minute. It blocked the road for a long distance on either side. I looked at the sea of yellow faces above the garish clothes—faces all happy and excited over this bit of fun, all certain that the elephant was going to be shot. They were watching me as they would watch a conjurer about to perform a trick. They did not like me, but with the magical rifle in my hands I was momentarily worth watching. And suddenly I realized that I should have to shoot the elephant after all. The people expected it of me and I had got to do it; I could feel their two thousand wills pressing me forward, irresistibly. And it was at this moment, as I stood there with the rifle in my hands, that I first grasped the hollowness, the futility of the white man's dominion in the East. Here was I, the white man with his gun, standing in front of the unarmed native crowd seemingly the leading actor of the piece; but in reality I was only an absurd puppet pushed to and fro by the will of those yellow faces behind. I perceived in this moment that when the white man turns tyrant it is his own freedom that he destroys. He becomes a sort of hollow, posing dummy, the conventionalized figure of a sahib. For it is the condition of his rule that he shall spend his life in trying to impress the "natives," and so in every crisis he has got to do what the "natives" expect of him. He wears a mask, and his face grows to let it. I had got to shoot the elephant. I had committed myself to doing it when I sent for the rifle. A sahib has got to act like sahib; he has got to appear resolute, to know his own mind and do definite things. To come all that way, rifle in hand, with two thousand people marching at my heels, and then to trail feebly away, having done nothing—no, that was impossible. The crowd would laugh at me. And my whole life, every white man's life in the East, was one long struggle not to be laughed at.

But I did not want to shoot the elephant. I watched him beating his bunch of grass against his knees, with that preoccupied grandmotherly air that elephants have. It seemed to me that it would be murder to shoot him. At that age I was not squeamish about killing animals, but I had never shot an elephant and never wanted to. (Somehow it always seems worse to kill a large animal.) Besides, there was the beast's owner to be considered. Alive, the elephant was worth at least a hundred pounds; dead, he would only be worth the value of his tusks, five pounds, possibly. But I had got to act quickly. I turned to some experienced-looking Burmans who had been there when we arrived, and asked them how the elephant had been behaving. They all said the same thing: he took no notice of you if you left him alone, but he might charge if you went too close to him.

It was perfectly clear to me what I ought to do. I ought to walk up to within, say, twenty-five yards of the elephant and test his behavior. If he charged, I could shoot; if he took no notice of me, it would be safe to leave him until the mahout came back. But also I knew that I was going to do no such thing. I was a poor shot with a rifle and the ground was soft mud into which one would sink at every step. If the elephant charged and I missed him, I should have about as much chance as a toad under a steam-roller. But even then I was not thinking particularly of my own skin, only of the watchful yellow faces behind. For at that moment, with the crowd watching me, I was not afraid in the ordinary sense, as I would have been if I had been alone. A white man mustn't be frightened in front of "natives"; and so, in general, he isn't frightened. The sole thought in my mind was that if anything went wrong those two thousand Burmans would see me pursued, caught, trampled on and reduced to a grinning corpse like that Indian up the hill. And if that happened it was quite probable that some of them would laugh. That would never do. There was only one alternative. I shoved the cartridges into the magazine and lay down on the road to get a better aim.

The crowd grew very still, and a deep, low, happy sigh, as of people who see the theatre curtain go up at last, breathed from innumerable throats. They were going to have their bit of fun after all. The rifle was a beautiful German thing with cross-hair sights. I did not then know that in shooting an elephant one should shoot to cut an imaginary bar running from ear-hole to ear-hole. I ought, therefore, as the elephant was sideways on, to have aimed straight at his ear-hole; actually I aimed several inches in front of this, thinking the brain would be further forward.

When I pulled the trigger I did not hear the bang or feel the kick—one never does when a shot goes home—but I heard the devilish roar of glee that went up from the crowd. In that instant, in too short a time, one would have thought, even for the bullet to get there, a mysterious, terrible change had come over the elephant. He neither stirred nor fell, but every line of his body had altered. He looked suddenly stricken, shrunken, immensely old, as though the frightful impact of the bullet had paralysed him without knocking him down. At last, after what seemed a long time—it might have been five seconds, I dare say—he sagged flabbily to his knees. His mouth slobbered. An enormous senility seemed to have settled upon him. One could have imagined him thousands of years old. I fired again into the same spot. At the second shot he did not collapse but climbed with desperate slowness to his feet and stood weakly upright, with legs sagging and head drooping. I fired a third time. That was the shot that did for him. You can see the agony of it jolt his whole body and knock the last remnant of strength from his legs. But in falling he seemed for a moment to rise, for as his hind legs collapsed beneath him he seemed to tower upward like a huge rock toppling, his trunk reaching skywards like a tree. He trumpeted, for the first and only time. And then down he came, his belly towards me, with a crash that seemed to shake the ground even where I lay. I got up. The Burmans were already racing past me across the mud. It was obvious that the elephant would never rise again, but he was not dead. He was breathing very rhythmically with long rattling gasps, his great mound of a side painfully rising and falling. His mouth was wide open—I could see far down into caverns of pale pink throat. I waited a long time for him to die, but his breathing did not weaken. Finally, I fired my two remaining shots into the spot where I thought his heart must be. The thick blood welled out of him like red velvet, but still he did not die. His body did not even jerk when the shots hit him, the tortured breathing continued without a pause. He was dying, very slowly and in great agony, but in some world remote from me where not even a bullet could damage him further. I felt that I had got to put an end to the dreadful noise. It seemed dreadful to see the great beast lying there, powerless to move and yet powerless to die, and not even to be able to finish him. I sent back for my small rifle and poured shot after shot into his heart and down his throat. They seemed to make no impression. The tortured gasps continued as steadily as the ticking of a clock.

In the end I could not stand it any longer and went away. I heard later that it took him half an hour to die. Burmans were bringing dahs and baskets even before I left, and I was told they had stripped his body almost to the bones by the afternoon.

Afterwards, of course, there were endless discussions about the shooting of the elephant. The owner was furious, but he was only an Indian and could do nothing. Besides, legally I had done the right thing, for a mad elephant has to be killed, like a mad dog, if its owner fails to control it. Among the Europeans opinion was divided. The older men said I was right, the younger men said it was a damn shame to shoot an elephant for killing a coolie, because an elephant was worth more than any damn Coringhee coolie. And afterwards I was very glad that the coolie had been killed; it put me legally in the right and it gave me a sufficient pretext for shooting the elephant. I often wondered whether any of the others grasped that I had done it solely to avoid looking a fool.

"Shooting an Elephant" from COLLECTIONS OF ESSAYS by George Orwell. Copyright 1950 by Sonia Brownell Orwell. Copyright © renewed 1978 by Sonia Pitt-Rivers. Reprinted by permission of Houghton Mifflin Harcourt Publishing Company. All rights reserved.

UNIT 7

"What You Don't Know About Making Decisions"

By David A. Garvin and Michael A. Roberto

Points to Consider

1. How can one effectively balance the need for open discourse early in the decision-making process, and the need for unity at the end of the process?

2. To what degree are uncertainty and vulnerability important characteristics for small group leadership?

3. How important is goal setting when conflicts arise in large organizations? Why?

4. In many cases, a leader's profound influence can be seen as beneficial. When, however, does that influence become a liability, and how can leaders ensure that it won't hamper the decision-making process?

"What You Don't Know About Making Decisions"

Leaders show their mettle in many ways—setting strategy and motivating people, just to mention two—but above all else leaders are made or broken by the quality of their decisions. That's a given, right? If you answered yes, then you would probably be surprised by how many executives approach decision making in a way that neither puts enough options on the table nor permits sufficient evaluation to ensure that they can make the best choice. Indeed, our research over the past several years strongly suggests that, simply put, most leaders get decision making all wrong.

The reason: Most businesspeople treat decision making as an event—a discrete choice that takes place at a single point in time, whether they're sitting at a desk, moderating a meeting, or staring at a spreadsheet. This classic view of decision making has a pronouncement popping out of a leader's head, based on experience, gut, research, or all three. Say the matter at hand is whether to pull a product with weak sales off the market. An "event" leader would mull in solitude, ask for advice, read reports, mull some more, then say yea or nay and send the organization off to make it happen. But to look at decision making that way is to overlook larger social and organizational contexts, which ultimately determine the success of any decision.

The fact is, decision making is not an event. It's a process, one that unfolds over weeks, months, or even years; one that's fraught with power plays and politics and is replete with personal nuances and institutional history; one that's rife with discussion and debate; and one that requires support at all levels of the organization when it comes time for execution. Our research shows that the difference between leaders who make good decisions and those who make bad ones is striking. The former recognize that all decisions are processes, and they explicitly design and manage them as such. The latter persevere in the fantasy that decisions are events they alone control.

In the following pages, we'll explore how leaders can design and manage a sound, effective decision-making process—an approach we call inquiry—and outline a set of criteria for assessing the quality of the decision-making process. First, a look at the process itself.

Decisions as Process: Inquiry versus Advocacy

Not all decision-making processes are equally effective, particularly in the degree to which they allow a group to identify and consider a wide range of ideas. In our research, we've seen two broad approaches. Inquiry, which we prefer, is a very open process designed to generate multiple alternatives, foster the exchange of ideas, and produce a well-tested solution. Unfortunately, this approach doesn't come easily or naturally to most people. Instead, groups charged with making a decision tend to default to the second mode, one we call advocacy. The two look deceptively similar on the surface: groups of people, immersed in discussion and debate, trying to select a course of action by drawing on what they believe is the best available evidence. But despite their similarities, inquiry and advocacy produce dramatically different results.

When a group takes an advocacy perspective, participants approach decision making as a contest, although they don't necessarily compete openly or even consciously. Well-defined groups with special interests—dueling divisions in search of budget increases, for example—advocate for particular positions. Participants are passionate about their preferred solutions and therefore stand firm in the face of disagreement. That level of passion makes it nearly impossible to remain objective, limiting people's ability to pay attention to opposing arguments. Advocates often present information selectively, buttressing their arguments while withholding relevant conflicting data. Their goal, after all, is to make a compelling case, not to convey an evenhanded or balanced view. Two different plant managers pushing their own improvement programs, for example, may be wary of reporting potential weak points for fear that full disclosure will jeopardize their chances of winning the debate and gaining access to needed resources.

What's more, the disagreements that arise are frequently fractious and even antagonistic. Personalities and egos come into play, and differences are normally resolved through battles of wills and behind-the-scenes maneuvering. The implicit assumption is that a superior solution will emerge from a test of strength among competing positions. But in fact this approach typically suppresses innovation and encourages participants to go along with the dominant view to avoid further conflict.

By contrast, an inquiry-focused group carefully considers a variety of options and works together to discover the best solution. While people naturally continue to have their own interests, the goal is not to persuade the group to adopt a given point of view but instead to come to agreement on the best course of action. People share information widely, preferably in raw form, to allow participants to draw their own conclusions. Rather than suppressing dissension, an inquiry process encourages critical thinking. All participants feel comfortable raising alternative solutions and asking hard questions about the possibilities already on the table.

People engaged in an inquiry process rigorously question proposals and the assumptions they rest on, so conflict may be intense—but it is seldom personal. In fact, because disagreements revolve around ideas and interpretations rather than entrenched positions, conflict is generally healthy, and team members resolve their differences by applying rules of reason. The implicit assumption is that a consummate solution will emerge from a test of strength among competing ideas rather than dueling positions. Recent accounts of GE's succession process describe board members pursuing just such an open-minded approach. All members met repeatedly with the major candidates and gathered regularly to review their strengths and weaknesses—frequently without Jack Welch in attendance—with little or no attempt to lobby early for a particular choice.

A process characterized by inquiry rather than advocacy tends to produce decisions of higher quality—decisions that not only advance the company's objectives but also are reached in a timely manner and can be implemented effectively. Therefore, we believe that leaders seeking to improve their organization's decision-making capabilities need to begin with a single goal: moving as quickly as possible from a process of advocacy to one of inquiry. That requires careful attention to three critical factors, the "three C's" of effective decision making: conflict, consideration, and closure. Each entails a delicate balancing act.

UNIT
7

Constructive Conflict

Critical thinking and rigorous debate invariably lead to conflict. The good news is that conflict brings issues into focus, allowing leaders to make more informed choices. The bad news is that the wrong kind of conflict can derail the decision-making process altogether.

Indeed, conflict comes in two forms—cognitive and affective. Cognitive, or substantive, conflict relates to the work at hand. It involves disagreements over ideas and assumptions and differing views on the best way to proceed. Not only is such conflict healthy, it's crucial to effective inquiry. When people express differences openly and challenge underlying assumptions, they can flag real weaknesses and introduce new ideas. Affective, or interpersonal, conflict is emotional. It involves personal friction, rivalries, and clashing personalities, and it tends to diminish people's willingness to cooperate during implementation, rendering the decision-making process less effective. Not surprisingly, it is a common feature of advocacy processes.

On examination, the two are easy to distinguish. When a team member recalls "tough debates about the strategic candidates," she is referring to cognitive conflict. When a team member comments on "heated arguments that degenerated into personal attacks," he means affective conflict. But in practice the two types of conflict are surprisingly hard to separate. People tend to take any criticism personally and react defensively. The atmosphere quickly becomes charged, and even if a high-quality decision emerges, the emotional fallout tends to linger, making it hard for team members to work together during implementation.

The challenge for leaders is to increase cognitive conflict while keeping affective conflict low—no mean feat. One technique is to establish norms that make vigorous debate the rule rather than the exception. Chuck Knight, for 27 years the CEO of Emerson Electric, accomplished this by relentlessly grilling managers during planning reviews, no matter what he actually thought of the proposal on the table, asking tough, combative questions and expecting well-framed responses. The process—which Knight called the "logic of illogic" because of his willingness to test even well-crafted arguments by raising unexpected, and occasionally fanciful, concerns—was undoubtedly intimidating. But during his tenure it produced a steady stream of smart investment decisions and an unbroken string of quarterly increases in net income.

Bob Galvin, when he was CEO of Motorola in the 1980s took a slightly different approach. He habitually asked unexpected hypothetical questions that stimulated creative thinking. Subsequently, as chairman of the board of overseers for the Malcolm Baldrige National Quality

Program, Galvin took his colleagues by surprise when, in response to pressure from constituents to broaden the criteria for the award, he proposed narrowing them instead. In the end, the board did in fact broaden the criteria, but his seemingly out-of-the-blue suggestion sparked a creative and highly productive debate.

Another technique is to structure the conversation so that the process, by its very nature, fosters debate. This can be done by dividing people into groups with different, and often competing, responsibilities. For example, one group may be asked to develop a proposal while the other generates alternative recommendations. Then the groups would exchange proposals and discuss the various oppositions. Such techniques virtually guarantee high levels of cognitive conflict. (The exhibit "Structuring the Debate" outlines two approaches for using different groups to stimulate creative thinking.)

But even if you've structured the process with an eye toward encouraging cognitive conflict, there's always a risk that it will become personal. Beyond cooling the debate with "time-outs," skilled leaders use a number of creative techniques to elevate cognitive debate while minimizing affective conflict.

First, adroit leaders pay careful attention to the way issues are framed, as well as to the language used during discussions. They preface contradictory remarks or questions with phrases that remove some of the personal sting ("Your arguments make good sense, but let me play devil's advocate for a moment"). They also set ground rules about language, insisting that team members avoid words and behavior that trigger defensiveness. For instance, in the U.S. Army's after-action reviews, conducted immediately after missions to identify mistakes so they can be avoided next time, facilitators make a point of saying, "We don't use the 'b' word, and we don't use the 'f' word. We don't place blame, and we don't find fault."

Second, leaders can help people step back from their pre-established positions by breaking up natural coalitions and assigning people to tasks on some basis other than traditional loyalties. At a leading aerospace company, one business unit president had to deal with two powerful coalitions within his organization during a critical decision about entering into a strategic alliance. When he set up two groups to consider alternative alliance partners, he interspersed the groups with members of each coalition, forcing people with different interests to work with one another. He then asked both groups to evaluate the same wide range of options using different criteria (such as technological capability, manufacturing prowess, or project management skills). The two groups then shared their evaluations and worked together to select the best partner. Because nobody had complete information, they were forced to listen closely to one another.

Third, leaders can shift individuals out of well-grooved patterns, where vested interests are highest. They can, for example, ask team members to research and argue for a position they did not endorse during initial discussions. Similarly, they can assign team members to play functional or managerial roles different from their own, such as asking an operations executive to take the marketing view or asking a lower-level employee to assume the CEO's strategic perspective.

Finally, leaders can ask participants locked in debate to revisit key facts and assumptions and gather more information. Often, people become so focused on the differences between opposing positions that they reach a stalemate. Emotional conflict soon follows. Asking people to examine underlying presumptions can defuse the tension and set the team back on track. People quickly recognize areas of agreement, discover precisely how and why they disagree, and then focus their debate on specific issues.

Consideration

Once a decision's been made and the alternative dismissed, some people will have to surrender the solution they preferred. At times, those who are overruled resist the outcome; at other times, they display grudging acceptance. What accounts for the difference? The critical factor appears to be the perception of fairness—what scholars call "procedural justice." The reality is that the leader will make the ultimate decision, but the people participating in the process must believe that their views were considered and that they had a genuine opportunity to influence the final decision. Researchers have found that if participants believe the process was fair, they are far more willing to commit themselves to the resulting decision even if their views did not prevail. (For a detailed discussion of this phenomenon, see W. Chan Kim and Renée Mauborgne, "Fair Process: Managing in the Knowledge Economy," *Harvard Business Review* July–August 1997).

Many managers equate fairness with voice—with giving everyone a chance to express his or her own views. They doggedly work their way around the table, getting everyone's input. However, voice is not nearly as important as consideration—people's belief that the leader actively listened to them during the discussions and weighed their views carefully before reaching a decision. In his 1999 book, *Only the Paranoid Survive*, Intel's chairman Andy Grove describes how he explains the distinction to his middle managers: "Your criterion for involvement should be that you're heard and understood...All sides cannot prevail in the debate, but all opinions have value in shaping the right answer."

In fact, voice without consideration is often damaging; it leads to resentment and frustration rather than to acceptance. When the time comes to implement the decision, people are likely to drag their feet if they sense that the decision-making process has been a sham—an exercise in going through the motions designed to validate the leader's preferred solution. This appears to have been true of the Daimler-Chrysler merger. Daimler CEO Jurgen Schrempp asked for extensive analysis and assessment of potential merger candidates but had long before settled on Chrysler as his choice. In fact, when consultants told him that his strategy was unlikely to create shareholder value, he dismissed the data and went ahead with his plans. Schrempp may have solicited views from many parties, but he clearly failed to give them much weight.

Leaders can demonstrate consideration throughout the decision-making process. At the outset, they need to convey openness to new ideas and a willingness to accept views that differ from their own. In particular, they must avoid suggesting that their minds are already made up. They should avoid disclosing their personal preferences early in the process, or they should clearly state that any initial opinions are provisional and subject to change. Or they can absent themselves from early deliberations.

During the discussions, leaders must take care to show that they are listening actively and attentively. How? By asking questions, probing for deeper explanations, echoing comments, making eye contact, and showing patience when participants explain their positions. Taking notes is an especially powerful signal, since it suggests that the leader is making a real effort to capture, understand, and evaluate people's thoughts.

And after they make the final choice, leaders should explain their logic. They must describe the rationale for their decision, detailing the criteria they used to select a course of action. Perhaps more important, they need to convey how each participant's arguments affected the final decision or explain clearly why they chose to differ with those views.

UNIT

7

Closure

Knowing when to end deliberations is tricky; all too often decision-making bodies rush to a conclusion or else dither endlessly and decide too late. Deciding too early is as damaging as deciding too late, and both problems can usually be traced to unchecked advocacy.

Deciding Too Early. Sometimes people's desire to be considered team players overrides their willingness to engage in critical thinking and thoughtful analysis, so the group readily accepts the first remotely plausible option. Popularly known as "groupthink," this mind-set is prevalent in the presence of strong advocates, especially in new teams, whose members are still learning the rules and may be less willing to stand out as dissenters.

The danger of groupthink is not only that it suppresses the full range of options but also that unstated objections will come to the surface at some critical moment—usually at a time when aligned, cooperative action is essential to implementation. The leader of a large division of a fast-growing retailer learned this the hard way. He liked to work with a small subset of his senior team to generate options, evaluate the alternatives, and develop a plan of action, and then bring the proposal back to the full team for validation. At that point, his managers would feel they had been presented with a fait accompli and so would be reluctant to raise their concerns. As one of them put it: "Because the meeting is the wrong place to object, we don't walk out of the room as a unified group." Instead, they would reopen the debate during implementation, delaying important initiatives by many months.

As their first line of defense against groupthink, leaders need to learn to recognize latent discontent, paying special attention to body language: furrowed brows, crossed arms, or curled-up defiance. To bring disaffected people back into the discussion, it may be best to call for a break, approach dissenters one by one, encourage them to speak up, and then reconvene. GM's Alfred Sloan was famous for this approach, which he would introduce with the following speech: "I take it we are all in complete agreement on the decision here. Then I propose we postpone further discussion of the matter until our next meeting to give ourselves time to develop disagreement and perhaps gain some understanding of what the decision is all about."

Another way to avoid early closure is to cultivate minority views either through norms or through explicit rules. Minority views broaden and deepen debate; they stretch a group's thinking, even though they are seldom adopted intact. It is for this reason that Andy Grove routinely seeks input from "helpful Cassandras," people who are known for raising hard questions and offering fresh perspectives about the dangers of proposed policies.

Deciding Too Late. Here, too, unchecked advocacy is frequently the source of the problem, and in these instances it takes two main forms. At times, a team hits gridlock: Warring factions refuse to yield, restating their positions over and over again. Without a mechanism for breaking the deadlock, discussions become an endless loop. At other times, people bend over backward to ensure evenhanded participation. Striving for fairness, team members insist on hearing every view and resolving every question before reaching a conclusion. This demand for certainty—for complete arguments backed by unassailable data—is its own peculiar form of advocacy. Once again, the result is usually an endless loop, replaying the same alternatives, objections, and requests for further information. Any member of the group can unilaterally derail the discussion by voicing doubts. Meanwhile, competitive pressures may be demanding an immediate response, or participants may have tuned out long ago, as the same arguments are repeated ad nauseam.

At this point, it's the leader's job to "call the question." Jamie Houghton, the longtime CEO of Corning, invented a vivid metaphor to describe this role. He spoke of wearing two hats when working with his senior team: He figuratively put on his cowboy hat when he wanted to debate with members as an equal, and he donned a bowler when, as CEO, he called the question and announced a decision. The former role allowed for challenges and continued discussion; the latter signaled an end to the debate.

The message here is that leaders—and their teams—need to become more comfortable with ambiguity and be willing to make speedy decisions in the absence of complete, unequivocal data or support. As Dean Stanley Teele of Harvard Business School was fond of telling students: "The art of management is the art of making meaningful generalizations out of inadequate facts."

A Litmus Test

Unfortunately, superior decision making is distressingly difficult to assess in real time. Successful outcomes—decisions of high quality, made in a timely manner and implemented effectively—can be evaluated only after the fact. But by the time the results are in, it's normally too late to take corrective action. Is there any way to find out earlier whether you're on the right track?

There is indeed. The trick, we believe, is to periodically assess the decision-making process, even as it is under way. Scholars now have considerable evidence showing that a small set of process traits is closely linked with superior outcomes. While they are no guarantee of success, their combined presence sharply improves the odds that you'll make a good decision.

Multiple Alternatives. When groups consider many alternatives, they engage in more thoughtful analysis and usually avoid settling too quickly on the easy, obvious answer. This is one reason techniques like point-counterpoint, which requires groups to generate at least two alternatives, are so often associated with superior decision making. Usually, keeping track of the number of options being considered will tell if this test has been met. But take care not to double count. Go/no-go choices involve only one option and don't qualify as two alternatives.

Assumption Testing. "Facts" come in two varieties: those that have been carefully tested and those that have been merely asserted or assumed. Effective decision-making groups do not confuse the two. They periodically step back from their arguments and try to confirm their assumptions by examining them critically. If they find that some still lack hard evidence, they may elect to proceed, but they will at least know they're venturing into uncertain territory. Alternatively, the group may designate "intellectual watchdogs" who are assigned the task of scrutinizing the process for unchecked assumptions and challenging them on the spot.

Well-Defined Criteria. Without crisp, clear goals, it's easy to fall into the trap of comparing apples with oranges. Competing arguments become difficult to judge, since advocates will suggest using those measures (net income, return on capital, market presence, share of mind, and so on) that favor their preferred alternative. Fuzzy thinking and long delays are the likely result.

To avoid the problem, the team should specify goals up front and revisit them repeatedly during the decision-making process. These goals can be complex and multifaceted, quantitative and qualitative, but whatever form they take, they must remain at the fore. Studies of merger decisions have found that as the process reaches its final stages and managers feel the pressure of deadlines and the rush to close, they often compromise or adjust the criteria they originally created for judging the appropriateness of the deal.

Dissent and Debate. David Hume, the great Scottish philosopher, argued persuasively for the merits of debate when he observed that the "truth springs from arguments amongst friends." There are two ways to measure the health of a debate: the kinds of questions being asked and the level of listening.

Some questions open up discussion; others narrow it and end deliberations. Contrarian hypothetical questions usually trigger healthy debate. A manager who worked for former American Express CEO Harvey Golub points to a time when the company was committed to lowering credit card fees, and Golub unexpectedly proposed raising fees instead. "I don't think he meant it seriously," says the manager. "But he certainly taught us how to think about fees."

The level of listening is an equally important indicator of a healthy decision-making process. Poor listening produces flawed analysis as well as personal friction. If participants routinely interrupt one another or pile on rebuttals before digesting the preceding comment, affective conflict is likely to materialize. Civilized discussions quickly become impossible, for collegiality and group harmony usually disappear in the absence of active listening.

Perceived Fairness. A real-time measure of perceived fairness is the level of participation that's maintained after a key midpoint or milestone has been reached. Often, a drop in participation is an early warning of problems with implementation since some members of the group are already showing their displeasure by voting with their feet.

In fact, keeping people involved in the process is, in the end, perhaps the most crucial factor in making a decision—and making it stick. It's a job that lies at the heart of leadership and one that uniquely combines the leader's numerous talents. It requires the fortitude to promote conflict while accepting ambiguity, the wisdom to know when to bring conversations to a close, the patience to help others understand the reasoning behind your choice, and, not least, a genius for balance—the ability to embrace both the divergence that may characterize early discussions and the unity needed for effective implementation. Cyrus the Great, the founder of the Persian Empire and a renowned military leader, understood the true hallmark of leadership in the sixth century BC, when he attributed his success to "diversity in counsel, unity in command."

Two Approaches to Decision Making

	Advocacy	Inquiry
Concept of decision making	a contest	collaborative problem solving
Purpose of discussion	persuasion and lobbying	testing and evaluation
Participants' role	spokespeople	critical thinkers
Patterns of behavior	strive to persuade others, defend your position, downplay weaknesses	present balanced arguments, remain open to alternatives, accept constructive criticism
Minority views	discouraged or dismissed	cultivated and valued
Outcome	winners and losers	collective ownership

Structuring the Debate

By breaking a decision-making body into two subgroups, leaders can often create an environment in which people feel more comfortable engaging in debate. Scholars recommend two techniques in particular, which we call the "point-counterpoint" and "intellectual watchdog" approaches. The first three steps are the same for both techniques: Point-Counterpoint and Intellectual Watchdog.

Point-Counterpoint	Intellectual Watchdog
The team divides into two subgroups.	The team divides into two subgroups.
Subgroup A develops a proposal fleshing out the recommendation, the key assumptions, and the critical supporting data.	Subgroup A develops a proposal fleshing out the recommendation, the key assumptions, and the critical supporting data.
Subgroup A presents the proposal to Subgroup B in written and oral forms.	Subgroup A presents the proposal to Subgroup B in written and oral forms.
Subgroup B generates one or more alternative plans of action.	Subgroup B develops a detailed critique of these assumptions and recommendations. It presents this critique in written and oral forms. Subgroup A revises its proposal based on this feedback.
The subgroups come together to debate the proposals and seek agreement on a common set of assumptions.	The subgroups continue in this revision-critique-revision cycle until they converge on a common set of assumptions.
Based on these assumptions the subgroups continue to debate various options and strive to agree on a common set of recommendations.	Then, the subgroups work together to develop a common set of recommendations.

UNIT
7

Advocacy versus Inquiry in Action: The Bay of Pigs and the Cuban Missile Crisis

Perhaps the best demonstration of advocacy versus inquiry comes from the administration of President John F. Kennedy. During his first two years in office, Kennedy wrestled with two critical foreign policy decisions: the Bay of Pigs invasion and the Cuban Missile Crisis. Both were assigned to cabinet-level task forces, involving many of the same players, the same political interests, and extremely high stakes. But the results were extraordinarily different, largely because the two groups operated in different modes.

The first group, charged with deciding whether to support an invasion of Cuba by a small army of U.S.-trained Cuban exiles, worked in advocacy mode, and the outcome is widely regarded as an example of flawed decision making. Shortly after taking office, President Kennedy learned of the planned attack on Cuba developed by the CIA during the Eisenhower administration. Backed by the Joint Chiefs of Staff, the CIA argued forcefully for the invasion and minimized the risks, filtering the information presented to the president to reinforce the agency's position. Knowledgeable individuals on the State Department's Latin America desk were excluded from deliberations because of their likely opposition.

Some members of Kennedy's staff opposed the plan but held their tongues for fear of appearing weak in the face of strong advocacy by the CIA. As a result, there was little debate, and the group failed to find out whether the exiles could fade into the mountains (which were 80 miles from the landing site) should they meet with strong resistance. The resulting invasion is generally considered to be one of the low points of the Cold War. About 100 lives were lost, and the rest of the exiles were taken hostage. The incident was a major embarrassment to the Kennedy administration and dealt a blow to America's global standing.

After the botched invasion, Kennedy conducted a review of the foreign policy decision-making process and introduced five major changes, essentially transforming the process into one of inquiry. First, people were urged to participate in discussions as "skeptical generalists"—that is, as disinterested critical thinkers rather than as representatives of particular departments. Second, Robert Kennedy and Theodore Sorensen were assigned the role of intellectual watchdogs, expected to pursue every possible point of contention, uncovering weaknesses and untested assumptions. Third, task forces were urged to abandon the rules of protocol, eliminating formal agendas and deference to rank. Fourth, participants were expected to split occasionally into subgroups to develop a broad range of options. And finally, President Kennedy decided to absent himself from some of the early task force meetings to avoid influencing other participants and slanting the debate.

The inquiry mode was used to great effect when in October 1962 President Kennedy learned that the Soviet Union had placed nuclear missiles on Cuban soil, despite repeated assurances from the Soviet ambassador that this would not occur. Kennedy immediately convened a high-level task force, which contained many of the same men responsible for the Bay of Pigs invasion, and asked them to frame a response. The group met night and day for two weeks, often inviting additional members to join in their deliberations to broaden their perspective. Occasionally, to encourage the free flow of ideas, they met without the president. Robert Kennedy played his new role thoughtfully, critiquing options frequently and encouraging the group to develop additional alternatives. In particular, he urged the group to move beyond a simple go/no-go decision on a military air strike.

Ultimately, subgroups developed two positions, one favoring a blockade and the other an air strike. These groups gathered information from a broad range of sources, viewed and interpreted the same intelligence photos, and took great care to identify and test underlying assumptions, such as whether the Tactical Air Command was indeed capable of eliminating all Soviet missiles in a surgical air strike. The subgroups exchanged position papers, critiqued each other's proposals, and came together to debate the alternatives. They presented Kennedy with both options, leaving him to make the final choice. The result was a carefully framed response, leading to a successful blockade and a peaceful end to the crisis.

Garvin, David A. and Michael A. Roberto. "What You Don't Know About Making Decisions." *The Harvard Business Review*, September, (2001): Used by permission of Harvard Business School Publishing.

"A Question of Leadership:
What Can Leaders Do to Avoid Groupthink?"

By Wynne Whyman and Robert Ginnett

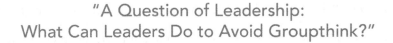

Points to Consider

1. Which technique for avoiding groupthink would you be most comfortable using? Why?

2. To what extent does the size of the group affect groupthink?

3. How can one distinguish between groupthink and shared opinion that is not the result of groupthink?

4. Is it necessarily unethical for a group leader to attempt to guide a group to a particular decision?

"A Question of Leadership:
What Can Leaders Do to Avoid Groupthink?"

From Wynne Whyman

Whyman is a design faculty member at The Center for Creative Leadership, managing the Blended Learning Solutions project, which integrates learning technology with face-to-face training. She holds master's degrees from the University of Colorado at Denver and Denver University.

The pressure is on. A decision needs to be made, on a short timeline. The solution? The executive quickly calls a meeting, soliciting a small group of people familiar with the problem.

Let's keep it simple, he thinks. When the group members assemble in the conference room, he thanks them all for their time, briefly talks about the problem, and calls for a straw vote. "Let's quickly see where we all stand," he says. The results: one person for option A, four people for option B, and one person for option C. "It's obvious the majority thinks option B is the best," the executive says. "Any objections? Thanks, everyone, for a short meeting."

Because we live in a democratic society, we tend to act in accordance with one of democracy's major values: the majority is right. Sometimes, however, the majority may not provide the solution needed. Instead, this rationalization of the decision-making process can contribute to groupthink.

How can a group avoid groupthink? One way is to use a process that involves more than one technique for making a decision.

Take time at the beginning of the meeting to have a dialogue about the problem. Perhaps the four people who voted for option B are from the same department and thus share the same perspective. Maybe they have not heard the perspectives of people from other areas of the organization. Drawing out different perspectives on the problem, and perhaps recording them on a flip chart, helps the group to develop shared meaning. Members of the group can begin to see the whole problem and not just their individual experience with it.

Clarify the goal. The purpose of the meeting in the opening example may not have been to find the best decision but to have a short meeting. The group deferred to the quickest agreement, kept the meeting short, and the goal was reached. To avoid such problems, the leader needs to describe the authentic purpose of the meeting and then align the subsequent process to support that goal.

Make a list of criteria for the decision. Each person in the straw vote used his or her own criteria for selecting one of the three options. If the group's criteria are identified in the meeting, unrecognized criteria may surface, providing a new perspective on the problem. The next step is to identify the two or three essential criteria that everyone can agree on. This helps to minimize voting ties and to build unity among the group.

Use straw votes as initial polls, not as final decision makers. Short-story writer O. Henry wrote, "A straw vote only shows which way the hot air blows." When an initial straw vote is taken, people should explain why they voted for their option. They should be asked to focus on sharing perspectives in alignment with the agreed-upon criteria, not to defend their vote.

Ask probing questions. Good leaders ask open-ended questions. Instead of asking, "Any objections?" the executive in the example could have asked, "What are the short- and long-term risks of this solution?" or, "What have we learned in the past from implementing similar solutions?"

To avoid the groupthink sand trap, leaders must develop techniques and processes to help members of groups understand perspectives and patterns.

From Robert Ginnett
Ginnett is a senior fellow at The Center for Creative Leadership in Colorado Springs. He holds an M.B.A. and a Ph.D. degree from Yale University.

Eons ago, when I was a doctoral student at Yale, groupthink was a commonly bantered and frequently cited term. This bandwagon was driven not so much by Yale's practice of the concept (although the students often accused the administration of exactly that sin) as by the fact that the founder of the *groupthink* concept, Irving Janis, was a member of the Yale faculty. Janis defined *groupthink* as "a mode of thinking that people engage in when they are deeply involved in a cohesive in-group, when the members' strivings for unanimity override their motivation to realistically appraise alternative courses of action." Back then, you could hardly grade an MBA student's paper without finding some reference to groupthink.

Unfortunately, the phenomenon of groupthink has apparently not lost any of its nefarious power today. Enron, Tyco, Qwest, WorldCom—the list goes on and on. On the brighter side, Janis' suggestions for preventing groupthink are as relevant today as they were when I was at Yale. Here is a selected list:

- Use a policy-forming group that reports to the larger group.
- Let all members of the group voice an opinion before the leader expresses an opinion.
- Discuss within subgroups, then report back.
- Divide into subgroups, then discuss differences.
- Bring in outside experts.
- Use a devil's advocate to question the group's ideas.
- Hold a second-chance meeting to offer a last opportunity to choose another course of action.

Perhaps the easiest of these guidelines to implement, because it requires merely an assigned role, is the use of a devil's advocate. The term devil's advocate comes from the Roman Catholic Church. When the church hierarchy was debating whether a person should be sainted, a devil's advocate used to be appointed to present the argument against doing so. In essence, the role of the devil's advocate was to keep the entire group from engaging in groupthink.

Which kinds of leaders should be particularly vigilant about groupthink? From my experience in working with groups and teams, I would suggest two: members of senior executive teams and members of boards. Why? Because both of these groups typically possess the underlying characteristic that allows the groupthink phenomenon to occur: high cohesion. Think about it. Once you work your way up the ladder and finally make the executive team or the board, do you want to do something that might get you kicked out? Of course not. So expecting members of executive teams or boards to speak out against a decision that is apparently gaining support among others in the group or on the team is not very realistic.

But when, for each big, important decision, a devil's advocate is appointed and that role is taken seriously, with considerable expectation that this person will find the flaws and downsides of a potential decision, then speaking out not only becomes appropriate but can also be rewarded because it helps the group avoid potential catastrophe.

F. Scott Fitzgerald once said, "The test of a first-rate intelligence is the ability to hold two opposed ideas in the mind at the same time, and still retain the ability to function." I think it is safe to extrapolate that concept to a first-rate team. By deliberately bringing in contrary ideas through devil's advocates and outside experts, an executive team or board will be far less likely to fall into the illusion of unanimity that is characteristic of groupthink.

Whyman, W. & Ginnett, R. (2005). A question of leadership: What can leaders do to avoid groupthink? *Leadership in Action* 25(2), 12-13. Used by permission of Center for Creative Leadership.

FILM STUDIES

To Kill a Mockingbird (1962)

Screenplay by Horton Foote
Directed by Robert Mulligan

Character Guide

Atticus Finch . . . . Gregory Peck

Dill Harris . . . . John Megna

Sheriff Heck Tate . . . . Frank Overton

Maudie Atkinson . . . . Rosemary Murphy

Mrs. Dubose . . . . Ruth White

Tom Robinson . . . . Brock Peters

Judge Taylor . . . . Paul Fix

Introduction

This film, based on the Pulitzer Prize-winning novel by Harper Lee, offers a look at racial tensions in the southern United States in the 1930s. The story takes place in Maycomb, Alabama, where Atticus Finch, a local attorney, is asked to defend Tom Robinson, a black man accused of raping a white woman. Lee, herself, was raised in Alabama during the Great Depression and was the daughter of an attorney. *To Kill a Mockingbird* was published in 1960, coinciding with the quickly escalating Civil Rights Movement in the United States.

Finch quickly accepts the case, and, to the chagrin of some in the community, he makes it clear that he intends to do his very best to free Robinson, whom he believes is innocent. His decision results in physical threats and verbal attacks—both on Finch and his two children, Jem and Scout. Finch shows no regret for his decision, and uses the opportunity to show Jem and Scout that while there is bad in the world, it is important to see through the bad and live a life of integrity.

Dialogue Questions

1. Why did Atticus accept the Tom Robinson case so quickly? Was he aware of the potential impact his decision would have on himself and his children?

2. After returning from the Robinson home, Atticus tells Jem, "There's a lot of ugly things in this world, son, and I wish I could keep them all away from you; that's never possible." To what extent can/should one in a leadership role protect followers from some of the "ugly things" that can go on? Can you think of examples of this in a group or organizational setting?

3. Both Atticus and his children experience a lot of anguish as a result of his decision to defend Robinson. Despite that, when Scout asks Atticus why he took the case, he says, "If I didn't, I couldn't hold my head up in town." What does he mean by this statement, which affirms his decision to defend Robinson?

4. What characteristics of a servant leader can you see in Atticus in his interactions with his children? His client? Other members of the community?

UNIT
7

Milk (2008)

Written by Dustin Lance Black
Directed by Gus Van Sant

Character Guide

Harvey Milk . . . . Sean Penn

Cleve Jones . . . . Emile Hirsch

Dan White . . . . Josh Brolin

Scott Smith . . . . James Franco

Anne Kronenberg . . . . Alison Pill

Introduction

Harvey Milk changed the political landscape when he became, arguably, the first openly gay man to be elected to major public office. Milk ran for office, unsuccessfully, multiple times before being elected in 1977. In the process, he experienced pressures on his personal and professional relationships, as well as threats to his own well-being.

Milk grew up in Woodmere, New York, part of a middle-class Jewish family. He played football and sang opera in high school, and worked at his family's department store. After high school, he served in the U.S. Navy from 1951–55. From there, he moved to New York City, working a variety of jobs.

Feeling unsatisfied with his life in New York, Milk moved to San Francisco in 1972, where he opened a camera shop. There, he became a vocal member of the business community and a leader in the local gay rights movement. He made his first run for the San Francisco Board of Supervisors in 1973, losing the election but not his determination. He tried again two years later, losing again—but by a narrower margin. In 1977, he finally won a seat on the board. In 1978, Dan White, who had recently resigned from a position as one of Milk's colleagues on the board, entered City Hall and murdered both Milk and San Francisco Mayor George Moscone.

Milk's decision to become a part of the public dialogue on gay rights and his decisions to run for public office multiple times, along with the motivation and risk behind those decisions, are highlighted in the film, *Milk*.

Dialogue Questions

1. What are the unique risks that Milk assumed as a candidate for public office? What are the common risks that any candidate for public office faces? Does the decision to become a public figure necessitate taking on a certain amount of potential risk?

2. What strategies does Milk use to motivate others? How does he handle encounters with those who oppose him and/or his positions? What strategies have you used/observed for effectively dealing with people who show open (or even hostile) opposition to an idea or plan?

3. How do members of Milk's team react to his decision to bring in a woman to manage his campaign? Why does Milk make this decision? What are the risks and rewards of introducing diversity into a group or organization?

4. How does Milk "control" the reaction in San Francisco to the repeal of the Gay Rights Ordinance in Dade County, Florida? Why does he make this decision?

5. Why does Milk decide to make a third run for the San Francisco Board of Supervisors, after having already suffered two defeats? Can you think of other examples of individuals who have continued to persevere after multiple failures? How does one maintain a sense of hope in such circumstances?

EXERCISE

Decision Making in *Twelve Angry Men* (1957)

Screenplay by Reginald Rose
Directed by Sidney Lumet

UNIT

7

Character Guide
(clockwise from foreman's position by actor's name)

Martin Balsam . . . .Foreman, head of table, football coach

John Fiedler . . . . .Right side of table, 1st back from foreman, balding, glasses, pipe, works at a bank

Lee J. Cobb . . . . .Runs "Beck and Call Company" messenger service, right side of table, 2nd back from foreman, frequently paces the room

E.G. Marshall . . . .Right side of table, 3rd back from foreman, broker, light suit

Jack Klugman . . . .Right side of table, 4th seat back from foreman

Edward Binns . . . .Short-sleeved sport shirt with open collar, right side of table, 5th back from foreman, working man, paints apartments

Jack Warden . . . . .End of table, straw hat, has tickets to ball game, impatient to go, striped sport coat which he removes, marmalade salesman

Henry Fonda. . . . .Architect, left side of table, 5th back from foreman

Joseph Sweeney. . . .Left side of table, 4th back from foreman

Ed Begley . . . . . .Left side of table, 3rd back from foreman, has summer cold, carries handkerchief

George Voskovec . . .Mustache, left side of table, 2nd back from foreman, foreign accent, suspenders, watchmaker

Robert Webber . . . .Advertising agency executive in suit, left of table, 1st back from foreman, doodles to think clearly

Introduction

This film depicts the deliberations of a jury at the end of a murder trial. Each juror must decide whether the accused is guilty or innocent. The decision of the jury must be unanimous. The initial vote of the jury is eleven "guilty" to one "not guilty." As the film unfolds, an effective leader emerges—the juror who votes "not guilty" from the first vote. He believes strongly in his decision and does not fall victim to "groupthink" phenomena that are apparent at the start of the film, nor does he have any personal circumstances or prejudices that affect his decision. He variously engages each juror to employ rational problem-solving skills, creativity and intuition, and inference until they, one by one, change their decisions in favor of a "not guilty" verdict.

As you view the first part of the film, use your own decision-making skills to decide the sequence in which you think the jurors will change their votes. Observe behavioral clues of each juror as closely as possible. In particular, focus on each juror's degree of attitudinal and behavioral flexibility. Use the inferences you make from these behavioral and attitudinal clues to make decisions about the order in which they will change their votes and number the order in the "Your Order" column of the *Twelve Angry Men* Work Table. Be prepared to identify clues you used in making your decisions and to respond to the Dialogue Questions.

Dialogue Questions

1. The character played by Henry Fonda was not the "official" leader of the group, i.e., he was not elected foreman, yet he became the real leader of the group. What characteristics did he exhibit that allowed him to assume the leadership role?

2. Have you participated in a group in which the person who held the title of leader was not the real leader? Did the group function smoothly? Did the presence of the "untitled leader" create conflict or make the group function more effectively?

3. Identify the different stages of problem solving that Fonda and the other characters exhibited in the film. How important were facts, creativity, and inference in each stage?

4. Identify the different stages of problem solving you used in attempting to predict the behavior of the jurors. How important were facts, creativity, and influence in each stage?

Twelve Angry Men Work Table

Juror	Your Order	Correct Order	Absolute Difference
Martin Balsam, foreman			
John Fiedler, right side of table, 1st back from foreman, balding, glasses, pipe, works at a bank			
Lee J. Cobb, runs "Beck and Call Company" messenger service, right side of table, 2nd back from foreman, frequently paces the room			
E.G. Marshall, right side of table, 3rd back from foreman, broker, light suit			
Jack Klugman, right side of table, 4th seat back from foreman			
Edward Binns, short-sleeved sport shirt with open collar, right side of table, 5th back from foreman, working man, paints apartments			
Jack Warden, end of table, straw hat, has tickets to ball game, impatient to go, striped sport coat which he removes, marmalade salesman			
Joseph Sweeney, left side of table, 4th back from foreman			
Ed Begley, left side of table, 3rd back from foreman, has summer cold, carries handkerchief			
George Voskovec, mustache, left side of table, 2nd back from foreman, foreign accent, suspenders, watchmaker			
Robert Webber, advertising agency executive in suit, left side of table, 1st back from foreman, doodles to think			
Totals			

UNIT
7

SUGGESTED READING

This selected bibliography is intended to supplement the excerpts and articles of authors included in this Unit. There is an emphasis on books that are pivotal and recent publications. Numerous journals regularly offer articles related to these topics, but are not included in this selected bibliography. For further research, you may wish to include searches of the following journals: (alphabetically) *Academy of Managem ent Executive, Academy of Management Journal, Harvard Business Review, Journal of Leadership Studies, Leadership in Action, Leadership Quarterly,* and *Leader To Leader.*

This list is organized by author's last name using Modern Language Association-style citations.

Bolman, Lee G., and Terrence E. Deal. *Reframing Organizations: Artistry, Choice, and Leadership.* **5th ed. San Francisco: Jossey-Bass, 2011.**
The authors present a simple four-frame model for understanding organizations. When leaders examine issues through all four frames, they broaden their options.

Byrnes, James. *The Nature and Development of Decision Making: A Self-Regulation Model.* **New York: Routledge, 2011.**
Byrnes' model explains the origin and nature of individual differences in decision-making competence. He also summarizes other models of decision making and risk taking.

Hammond, John, Ralph Keeney, and Howard Raiffa. *Smart Choices: A Practical Guide to Making Better Life Decisions.* **New York: Broadway Books, 2002.**
The authors combine research and experience to make recommendations for approaching difficult decisions, such as those involving tradeoffs or uncertainty.

Manktelow, Ken. *Thinking and Reasoning: An Introduction to the Psychology of Reason, Judgment and Decision Making.* **New York: Psychology Press, 2012.**
This new textbook includes the latest research and changes in the field.

Marquardt, Michael. *Leading with Questions: How Leaders Find the Right Solutions By Knowing What to Ask.* **San Francisco: Jossey-Bass, 2005.**
Learn about framing questions and their power to foster teamwork and engagement, solve problems, and more.

Mitroff, Ian I. *Smart Thinking for Crazy Times: The Art of Solving the Right Problems.* **San Francisco: Berrett-Koehler, 1998.**
This book emphasizes the development of critical thinking skills to avoid what Mitroff says is a common error: solving the wrong problem precisely.

Von Oech, Roger. *A Whack on the Side of the Head: How You Can Be More Creative.* **Revised ed. New York: Warner Books, 2008.**
Fully illustrated; filled with provocative puzzles, anecdotes, exercises, metaphors, and tips. This book systematically breaks through your mental blocks and unlocks your mind for creative thinking.

UNIT 8

GUIDING THROUGH CONFLICT

INTRODUCTION

We can broadly define conflict as what happens when there are incompatible goals, thoughts, beliefs, or emotions between or within individuals or groups that lead to opposition or differences in opinion. As such, it is almost ever-present. Dealing with it effectively is one of the things that separates those who exercise leadership effectively from the also-rans. There are two basic approaches to dealing with conflict. One relies on organizational structure: things such as policies, procedures, and job descriptions which make sure that each person in the organization knows what his or her job is, its limits, and its responsibilities. The conventional wisdom here is that if everyone knows what's expected of him or her, the possibilities of conflict are significantly reduced. Unfortunately, human nature is never quite so simple. Humans, to paraphrase Sigmund Freud, are not termites working selflessly for the good of the organization. Freud went on: "No doubt [man] will always defend his claim to individual liberty against the will of the group." Freud was right. Individual needs are frequently in conflict with the needs of the organization. This Unit's Classic Case, excerpts from *The Iliad* of Homer, looks squarely at the conflict between two Greek leaders, Agamemnon and Achilles, to identify the kind of counter-productive, interpersonal conflict that can bring organizations down. Each of these leaders allowed his personal needs or desires to supersede the organizational goals.

There was a time when leaders thought of *all* conflict as corrosive to an organization's well-being. Leaders expected people to fall into line, agree not to disagree, and be good "organizational men and women." Many thought that whenever conflict in an organization did occur, it was a sure signal that something was wrong—that leadership had failed somehow. The belief was that effective leadership resulted in an agreeable, "happy" organization. Nothing other than peace and tranquility was positive. The problem, of course, was that frequently this meant an organization full of "yes-men" and "yes-women."

A more contemporary and realistic view suggests something quite different. Leaders expect, even desire, conflict. It is human nature to disagree. Much of what we think of as destructive conflict is, in fact, constructive and just what an organization needs if it is to be creative, innovative, and adaptable—exactly what David Garvin and Michael Roberto explained in their article presented in the previous Unit on Making Decisions. Therefore, a leader should go further than merely tolerating conflict, and actually stimulate it, then guide it through to ensure that it is a positive force in an organization. It is the leader's responsibility to analyze, and then use conflict carefully. If organizational conflict becomes counter-productive, it is up to the leader to redirect the energy in productive directions.

The Leadership Profiles of Maureen Dowd, the only female Op-Ed columnist for *The New York Times*, and Dr. Jehan Sadat, the former First Lady of Egypt, peace activist and professor, highlight their civil conflict about the role of women in the Middle East. William Langeweische's observations of the factionalism that developed at the site of the World Trade Center destruction provide a contemporary case study. "The Federalist: Number 10" by James Madison offers profound insight regarding the corrosive effects of organizational conflict and makes specific recommendations for avoiding negative factionalism. David Rock explores conflict and cooperation through brain science in an excerpt from his essay, "SCARF: A Brain-Based Model for Collaborating with and Influencing Others." And in an excerpt from their book, *Difficult Conversations*, Douglas Stone, Bruce Patton and Sheila Heen discuss three types of conversations that lead to misunderstandings between individuals and among groups and offer ways to use understanding of those conversation types to mediate conflict. The Film Studies of *All the President's Men* and *Freedom Writers* illustrate examples of interpersonal and organizational conflict and the intersections between them that develop because people bring lots of "baggage"—past experiences, beliefs, prejudices—to interactions with others, relationships, and their organizations. The Exercise for the Unit allows for further exploration of the conflict portrayed in *The Iliad* and is an opportunity to think of analogous situations in modern times and the possible solutions to such destructive conflict.

Learning Objectives

- Recognize the importance of a leader's role in guiding through conflict

- Understand that conflict is an ever-present element in most organizations

- Differentiate between dysfunctional, destructive conflict and functional, constructive or creative conflict

- Identify various types of interpersonal conflict

- Identify practical approaches and techniques for guiding through conflict

- Appreciate the contributions made by the Classic Case and Leadership Profile in the Unit toward learning about guiding through conflict

UNIT

8

CLASSIC CASE

The Iliad

Attributed to Homer (9th Century [?] B.C.E.)
Ancient Greek Epic Poet

Introduction and Historical Background

Homer was a bard, a storyteller who performed the multiple roles of raconteur, actor, historian, news reporter, and teacher. He is also traditionally, but controversially, credited as the author of *The Iliad* and *The Odyssey*. These two major Greek epics, created in the ninth century, or perhaps the eighth century B.C.E., from many historical stories and legends told for generations (and revised extensively in the sixth century B.C.E. and again in the second century B.C.E. by Aristarchus), were based on events that occurred approximately five hundred years earlier. While both epics are written in impersonal and formal verse as opposed to language used for daily or ordinary conversation, they are very different. *The Iliad* deals with passion and insoluble dilemmas. It is basically without real villains, just victims of a cruel and ultimately tragic universe. However, in *The Odyssey* the wicked are destroyed and right prevails. These epics are not only historically significant but are also filled with leadership insight.

It was businessman-turned-archaeologist Heinrich Schliemann who kindled renewed interest in Homer. Schliemann went to Turkey in 1870 to find Troy and, against all expert opinion, began excavations under a hill named Hissarlik. After a year, he made one of the most important finds in history: the remnants of the Troy described in Homer's *Iliad*. Further evidence was found of a battle fought at the site at approximately the time reported in the epic. Six years later, in an effort to discover Agamemnon's home, Schliemann began excavations at Mycenae. Once again, he discovered artifacts that confirmed the reliability of the epics.

The Iliad is set in the final and tenth year of the Trojan War. The entire Greek expeditionary force has been encamped for years outside the walls of Troy, trying valiantly to conquer this tiny town located on a small hill in what is now northwestern Turkey. With the men wanting to return home, the supply lines overtaxed, and the costs mounting, the situation is becoming intolerable.

The major characters are Agamemnon, the arrogant and autocratic commander-in-chief, and Achilles, the Greeks' best field commander. Insulted by Agamemnon, Achilles withdraws from the war, leaving his fellow Greeks to suffer at the hands of the Trojans. At first Achilles rejects the Greeks' attempts at reconciliation. Eventually, however, he allows his companion Patroclus to lead his troops in his place. When Patroclus is slain, Achilles rejoins the effort, turning his full wrath against the Trojans.

The Iliad is much more than just a war story, however. It is the dramatic tale of how conflict can destroy an enterprise, and it is an excellent study of what happens when the needs of the individual and the organization are out of balance.

Points to Consider

1. In what ways did Achilles and Agamemnon experience the conflict between them differently? What are the different ways that their conflict affected the people around them?

2. Who is exercising leadership the most effectively: Achilles, Agamemnon, or perhaps Nestor, the mediator, or someone else? How is this person exercising leadership the most effectively?

3. In what ways does the conflict between Achilles and Agamemnon prevent the Greeks from achieving their ultimate goals? How could conflict have been resolved or avoided?

Character Guide

Agamemnon . . . The commander-in-chief of the Greek army

Achilles . . . . . Greek field commander for the Myrmidons and the very best warrior of the Greeks

Calchas . . . . . Prophet and truth-teller

Nestor. . . . . . Elder statesman and advisor; also commander of a group of Greek soldiers fighting at Troy

Odysseus. . . . . Commander of a group of Greek soldiers; an excellent warrior

Ajax. . . . . . . Another commander of a group of Greek soldiers, another excellent warrior

Briseis . . . . . . Woman whom Achilles has taken as a war prize

UNIT

8

The Iliad

(Excerpts)
Translated by Robert Fagles

Book I, 1–358

Rage—Goddess, sing the rage of Peleus' son Achilles, murderous, doomed, that cost the Achaeans countless losses, hurling down to the House of Death so many sturdy souls, great fighters' souls, but made their bodies carrion, feasts for the dogs and birds, and the will of Zeus was moving toward its end. Begin, Muse, when the two first broke and clashed, Agamemnon lord of men and brilliant Achilles.

What god drove them to fight with such a fury? Apollo the son of Zeus and Leto. Incensed at the king he swept a fatal plague through the army—men were dying and all because Agamemnon spurned Apollo's priest.

Yes, Chryses approached the Achaeans' fast ships to win his daughter back, bringing a priceless ransom and bearing high in hand, wound on a golden staff, the wreaths of the god, the distant deadly Archer. He begged the whole Achaean army but most of all the two supreme commanders, Atreus' two sons, "Agamemnon, Menelaus—all Argives geared for war! May the gods who hold the halls of Olympus give you Priam's city to plunder, then safe passage home. Just set my daughter free, my dear one… here, accept these gifts, this ransom. Honor the god who strikes from worlds away—the son of Zeus, Apollo!"

And all ranks of Achaeans cried out their assent: "Respect the priest, accept the shining ransom!" But it brought no joy to the heart of Agamemnon. The king dismissed the priest with a brutal order ringing in his ears: "Never again, old man, let me catch sight of you by the hollow ships! Not loitering now, not slinking back tomorrow. The staff and the wreaths of god will never save you then. The girl—I won't give up the girl. Long before that, old age will overtake her in my house, in Argos, far from her fatherland, slaving back and forth at the loom, forced to share my bed. Now go, don't tempt my wrath—and you may depart alive."

The old man was terrified. He obeyed the order, turning, trailing away in silence down the shore where the roaring battle lines of breakers crash and drag. And moving off to a safe distance, over and over the old priest prayed to the son of sleek-haired Leto, lord Apollo, "Hear me, Apollo! God of the silver bow who strides the walls of Chryse and Cilla sacrosanct—lord in power of Tenedos—Smintheus, god of the plague! If I ever roofed a shrine to please your heart, ever burned the long rich bones of bulls and goats on your holy altar, now, now bring my prayer to pass. Pay the Danaans back—your arrows for my tears!"

His prayer went up and Phoebus Apollo heard him. Down he strode from Olympus' peaks, storming at heart with his bow and hooded quiver slung across his shoulders. The arrows clanged at his back as the god quaked with rage, the god himself on the march and down he came like night. Over against the ships he dropped to a knee, let fly a shaft and a terrifying clash rang out from the great silver bow. First he went for the mules and circling dogs but then, launching a piercing shaft at the men themselves, he cut them down in droves—and the corpse-fires burned on, night and day, no end in sight.

Nine days the arrows of god swept through the army. On the tenth Achilles called all ranks to muster—the impulse seized him, sent by white-armed Hera grieving to see Achaean fighters drop and die. Once they'd gathered, crowding the meeting grounds, the swift runner Achilles rose and spoke among them: "Son of Atreus, now we are beaten back, I fear, the long campaign is lost. So home we sail…if we can escape our death—if war and plague are joining forces now to crush the Argives. But wait: let us question a holy man, a prophet, even a man skilled with dreams—dreams as well can come our way from Zeus—come, someone to tell us why Apollo rages so, whether he blames us for a vow we failed, or sacrifice. If only the god would share the smoky savor of lambs and full-grown goats, Apollo might be willing, still, somehow, to save us from this plague."

The Prophet Speaks

So he proposed and down he sat again as Calchas rose among them, Thestor's son, the clearest by far of all the seers who scan the flight of birds. He knew all things that are, all things that are past and all that are to come, the seer who had led the Argive ships to Troy with the second sight that god Apollo gave him. For the armies' good the seer began to speak: "Achilles, dear to Zeus…you order me to explain Apollo's anger, the distant deadly Archer? I will tell it all. But strike a pact with me, swear you will defend me with all your heart, with words and strength of hand. For there is a man I will enrage—I see it now—a powerful man who lords it over all the Argives, one the Achaeans must obey…. A mighty king, raging against an inferior, is too strong. Even if he can swallow down his wrath today, still he will nurse the burning in his chest until, sooner or later, he sends it bursting forth. Consider it closely, Achilles. Will you save me?"

And the matchless runner reassured him: "Courage! Out with it now, Calchas. Reveal the will of god, whatever you may know. And I swear by Apollo dear to Zeus, the power you pray to, Calchas, when you reveal god's will to the Argives—no one, not while I am alive

and see the light on earth, no one will lay his heavy hands on you by the hollow ships. None among all the armies. Not even if you mean Agamemnon here who now claims to be, by far, the best of the Achaeans."

The seer took heart and this time he spoke out, bravely: "Beware—he casts no blame for a vow we failed, a sacrifice. The god's enraged because Agamemnon spurned his priest, he refused to free his daughter, he refused the ransom. That's why the Archer sends us pains and he will send us more and never drive this shameful destruction from the Argives, not till we give back the girl with the sparkling eyes to her loving father—no price, no ransom paid—and carry her a sacred hundred bulls to Chryse town. Then we can calm the god, and only then appease him."

So he declared and sat down. But among them rose the fighting son of Atreus, lord of the far-flung kingdoms, Agamemnon—furious, his dark heart filled to the brim, blazing with anger now, his eyes like searing fire. With a sudden, killing look he wheeled on Calchas first: "Seer of misery! Never a word that works to my advantage! Always misery warms your heart, your prophecies—never a word of profit said or brought to pass. Now, again, you divine god's will for the armies, bruit it about, as fact, why the deadly Archer multiplies our pains: because I, I refused that glittering price for the young girl Chryseis. Indeed, I prefer *her* by far, the girl herself, I want her mine in my own house! I rank her higher than Clytemnestra, my wedded wife—she's nothing less in build or breeding, in mind or works of hand. But I am willing to give her back, even so, if that is best for all. What I really want is to keep my people safe, not see them dying. But fetch me another prize, and straight off too, else I alone of the Argives go without my honor. That would be a disgrace. You are all witness, look—*my* prize is snatched away!"

UNIT
8

Achilles Requests

But the swift runner Achilles answered him at once, "Just how, Agamemnon, great field marshal,…most grasping man alive, how can the generous Argives give you prizes now? I know of no troves of treasure, piled, lying idle, anywhere. Whatever we dragged from towns we plundered, all's been portioned out. But collect it, call it back from the rank and file? That would be the disgrace. So return the girl to the god, at least for now. We Achaeans will pay you back, three, four times over, if Zeus will grant us the gift, somehow, someday, to raze Troy's massive ramparts to the ground."

But King Agamemnon countered, "Not so quickly, brave as you are, godlike Achilles—trying to cheat me. Oh no, you won't get past me, take me in that way! What do you want? To cling to your own prize while I sit calmly by—empty-handed here? Is that why you order me to give her back? No—if our generous Argives will give me a prize, a match for my desires, equal to what I've lost, well and good. But if they give me nothing I will take a prize myself—your own, or Ajax' or Odysseus' prize—I'll commandeer her myself and let that man I go to visit choke with rage! Enough. We'll deal with all this later, in due time. Now come, we haul a black ship down to the bright sea, gather a decent number of oarsmen along her locks and put aboard a sacrifice, and Chryseis herself, in all her beauty… we embark her too. Let one of the leading captains take command. Ajax, Idomeneus, trusty Odysseus or you, Achilles, you—the most violent man alive—so you can perform the rites for us and calm the god yourself."

A dark glance and the headstrong runner answered him in kind: "Shameless—armored in shamelessness—always shrewd with greed! How could any Argive soldier obey your orders, freely and gladly do your sailing for you or fight your enemies, full force? Not I, no. It wasn't Trojan spearmen who brought me here to fight. The Trojans never did me damage, not in the least, they never stole my cattle or my horses, never in Phthia where the rich soil breeds strong men did they lay waste my crops. How could they? Look at the endless miles that lie between us… shadowy mountain ranges, seas that surge and thunder. No, you colossal, shameless—we all followed you, to please you, to fight you, to win your honor back from the Trojans—Menelaus and you, you dog-face! What do you care? Nothing. You don't look right or left. And now you threaten to strip me of my prize in person—the one I fought for long and hard, and sons of Achaea handed her to me.

My honors never equal yours, whenever we sack some wealthy Trojan stronghold—my arms bear the brunt of the raw, savage fighting, true, but when it comes to dividing up the plunder the lion's share is yours, and back I go to my ships, clutching some scrap, some pittance that I love, when I have fought to exhaustion.

No more now—back I go to Phthia. Better that way by far, to journey home in the beaked ships of war. I have no mind to linger here disgraced, brimming your cup and piling up your plunder."

Agamemnon Reacts

But the lord of men Agamemnon shot back, "Desert, by all means—if the spirit drives you home! I will never beg you to stay, not on my account. Never—others will take my side and do me honor, Zeus above all, whose wisdom rules the world. You—I hate you most of all the warlords loved by the gods. Always dear to your heart, strife, yes, and battles, the bloody grind of war. What if you are a great soldier? That's just a gift of god. Go home with your ships and comrades, lord it over your Myrmidons!

You are nothing to me—you and your overweening anger! But let this be my warning on your way: since Apollo insists on taking my Chryseis, I'll send her back in my own ships with my crew. But I, I will be there in person at your tents to take Briseis in all her beauty, your own prize—so you can learn just how much greater I am than you and the next man up may shrink from matching words with me, from hoping to rival Agamemnon strength for strength!"

He broke off and anguish gripped Achilles. The heart in his rugged chest was pounding, torn… Should he draw the long sharp sword slung at his hip, thrust through the ranks and kill Agamemnon now?—or check his rage and beat his fury down? As his racing spirit veered back and forth, just as he drew his huge blade from its sheath, down from the vaulting heavens swept Athena, the white-armed goddess Hera sped her down: Hera loved both men and cared for both alike. Rearing behind him Pallas seized his fiery hair—only Achilles saw her, none of the other fighters—struck with wonder he spun around, he knew her at once, Pallas Athena! the terrible blazing of those eyes, and his winged words went flying: "Why, why now? Child of Zeus with the shield of thunder, why come now? To witness the outrage Agamemnon just committed? I tell you this, and so help me it's the truth—he'll soon pay for his arrogance with his life!"

Athena Intervenes

Her gray eyes clear, the goddess Athena answered, "Down from the skies I come to check your rage if only you will yield. The white-armed goddess Hera sped me down: she loves you both, she cares for you both alike. Stop this fighting, now. Don't lay hand to sword. Lash him with threats of the price that he will face. And I tell you this—and I *know* it is the truth—one day glittering gifts will lie before you, three times over to pay for all his outrage. Hold back now. Obey us both."

So she urged and the swift runner complied at once: "I must—when the two of you hand down commands, Goddess, a man submits though his heart breaks with fury. Better for him by far. If a man obeys the gods they're quick to hear his prayers."

And with that Achilles stayed his burly hand on the silver hilt and slid the huge blade back in its sheath. He would not fight the orders of Athena. Soaring home to Olympus, she rejoined the gods aloft in the halls of Zeus whose shield is thunder.

But Achilles rounded on Agamemnon once again, lashing out at him, not relaxing his anger for a moment: "Staggering drunk, with your dog's eyes, your fawn's heart! Never once did you arm with the troops and go to battle or risk an ambush packed with Achaea's picked men—you lack the courage, you can see death coming. Safer by far, you find, to foray all through camp, commandeering the prize of any man who speaks against you. King who devours his people! Worthless husks, the men you rule—if not, Atrides, this outrage would have been your last. I tell you this, and I swear a mighty oath upon it…. by this, this scepter, look, that never again will put forth crown and branches, now it's left its stump on the mountain ridge forever, nor will it sprout new green again, now the brazen ax has stripped its bark and leaves, and now the sons of Achaea pass it back and forth as they hand their judgments down, upholding the honored customs whenever Zeus commands —. This scepter will be the mighty force behind my oath: someday, I swear, a yearning for Achilles will strike Achaea's sons and all your armies! But then, Atrides, harrowed as you will be, *nothing* you do can save you—not when your hordes of fighters drop and die, cut down by the hands of man-killing Hector! Then—then you will tear your heart out, desperate, raging that you disgraced the best of the Achaeans!"

UNIT

8

Nestor Mediates

Down on the ground he dashed the scepter studded bright with golden nails, then took his seat again. The son of Atreus smoldered, glaring across at him, but Nestor rose between them, the man of winning words, the clear speaker of Pylos…Sweeter than honey from his tongue the voice flowed on and on.

Two generations of mortal men he had seen go down by now, those who were born and bred with him in the old days, in Pylos' holy realm, and now he ruled the third. He pleaded with both kings, with clear good will, "No more— or enormous sorrow comes to all Achaea! How they would exult, Priam and Priam's sons and all the Trojans. Oh they'd leap for joy to hear the two of you battling on this way, you who excel us all, first in Achaean councils, first in the ways of war.

Stop. Please. Listen to Nestor. You are both younger than I, and in my time I struck up with better men than you, even you, but never once did they make light of me. I've never seen such men, I never will again…men like Pirithous, Dryas, that fine captain, Caeneus and Exadius, and Polyphemus, royal prince, and Theseus, Aegeus' boy, a match for the immortals. They were the strongest mortals ever bred on earth, the strongest, and they fought against the strongest too, shaggy Centaurs, wild brutes of the mountains—they hacked them down, terrible, deadly work. And I was in their ranks, fresh out of Pylos, far away from home—they enlisted me themselves and I fought on my own—a free lance, single-handed. And none of the men who walk the earth these days could battle with those fighters, none, but they, they took to heart my counsels, marked my words. So now you listen too. Yielding is far better…. Don't seize the girl, Agamemnon, powerful as you are—leave her, just as the sons of Achaea gave her, his prize from the very first. And you, Achilles, never hope to fight it out with your king, pitting force against his force: no one can match the honors dealt a king, you know, a sceptered king to whom great Zeus gives glory. Strong as you are—a goddess was your mother—he has more power because he rules more men. Atrides, end your anger—look, it's Nestor! I beg you, cool your fury against Achilles. Here the man stands over all Achaea's armies, our rugged bulwark braced for shocks of war."

But King Agamemnon answered him in haste, "True old man—all you say is fit and proper—but this soldier wants to tower over the armies, he wants to rule over all, to lord it over all, give out orders to every man in sight. Well, there's one, I trust, who will never yield to *him*! What if the everlasting gods have made a spearman of him? Have they entitled him to hurl abuse at *me*?"

"Yes!"—blazing Achilles broke in quickly—"What a worthless, burnt-out coward I'd be called if I would submit to you and all your orders, whatever you blurt out. Fling them at others, don't give me commands! Never again, I trust, will Achilles yield to *you*. And I tell you this—take it to heart, I warn you—my hands will never do battle for that girl, neither with you, King, nor any man alive. You Achaeans gave her, now you've snatched her back. But all the rest I possess beside my fast black ship—not one bit of it can you seize against my will, Atrides. Come, try it! So the men can see, that instant, your black blood gush and spurt around my spear!"

Once the two had fought it out with words, battling face-to-face, both sprang to their feet and broke up the muster beside the Argive squadrons.

[*During the argument with Agamemnon, Achilles says that he would no longer fight against the Trojans and declares that he intended to return home. After the assembly breaks up, Achilles withdraws from all contact with the Greeks, retires to his tent and sulks. Agamemnon in the meantime sends a mission to the god Apollo to appease him with sacrifices. He further enjoins a group of soldiers to go to Achilles' quarters and to take the girl Briseis from him. Thus Agamemnon carries out the threat which he made in the assembly.*

When Achilles' mother, the sea goddess Thetis, learns that he has been dishonored by Agamemnon and that he is very unhappy, she visits Zeus and pleads with him to turn the tide of the war in favor of the Trojans. With such stress put upon the Greeks, the importance of Achilles' contribution to their cause will be made evident by his absence; before this moment in the war the Trojans have scarcely dared to venture beyond their own walls.

Zeus agrees to the request of Thetis and alters the direction of the war. The Trojans and especially their leader Hector become increasingly emboldened by their success in battle and now begin to exert considerable pressure on the demoralized Greeks. In the next selection, Agamemnon and the council of other leaders discuss several courses of action before deciding upon the embassy of Achilles.]

Book IX, 103–522

Meanwhile marshal Agamemnon led his commanders, a file of senior chiefs, toward his own lodge and set before them a feast to please their hearts. They reached out for the good things that lay at hand but when they had put aside desire for food and drink the old man began to weave his counsel among them: Nestor was first to speak—from the early days his plans and tactics always seemed the best. With good will to the chiefs he rose and spoke, "Great marshal

Atrides, lord of men Agamemnon…with you I will end, my King, with you I will begin, since you hold sway over many warriors, vast armies, and Zeus has placed in your hands the royal scepter and time-honored laws, so you will advise them well. So you above all must speak your mind, and listen, and carry out the next man's counsel too, whenever his spirit leads him on to speak for the public good. Credit will go to you for whatever he proposes. Now I will tell you what seems best to me. No one will offer a better plan than this… the plan I still retain, and I've been forming, well, for a good long while now, from the very day that you, my illustrious King, infuriated Achilles—you went and took from his tents the girl Briseis, and not with any applause from us, far from it: I for one, I urged you against it, strenuously. But you, you gave way to your overbearing anger, disgraced a great man the gods themselves esteem—you seized his gift of honor and keep her still. But even so, late as it is, let us contrive to set all this to rights, to bring him round with gifts of friendship and warm, winning words."

Agamemnon Offers Gifts

And Agamemnon the lord of men consented quickly: "That's no lie, old man—a full account you give of all my acts of madness. Mad, blind I was! Not even I would deny it. Why look, that man is worth an entire army, the fighter Zeus holds dear with all his heart—how he exalts him now and mauls Achaea's forces! But since I was blinded, lost in my own inhuman rage, now, at last, I am bent on setting things to rights: I'll give a priceless ransom paid for friendship.

"Here, before you all, I'll name in full the splendid gifts I offer. Seven tripods never touched by fire, ten bars of gold, twenty burnished cauldrons, a dozen massive stallions, racers who earned me trophies with their speed. He is no poor man who owns what they have won, not strapped for goods with all that lovely gold—what trophies those high-strung horses carried off for me! Seven women I'll give him, flawless, skilled in crafts, women of Lesbos—the ones I chose, my privilege, that day he captured the Lesbos citadel himself: they outclassed the tribes of women in their beauty. These I will give, and along with them will go the one I took away at first, Briseus' daughter and I will swear a solemn, binding oath in the bargain: I never mounted her bed, never once made love with her   the natural thing for mankind, men and women joined. Now all these gifts will be handed him at once. But if, later, the gods allow us to plunder the great city of Priam, let him enter in when we share the spoils, load the holds of his ship with gold and bronze—as much as his heart desires—and choose for his pleasure twenty Trojan women second only to Argive Helen in their glory. And then, if we can journey home to Achaean Argos, pride of the breasting earth, he'll be my son-by-marriage! I will even honor him on a par with my Orestes, full-grown by now, reared in the lap of luxury. Three daughters are mine in my well-built halls—Chrysothemis and Laodice and Iphianassa—and he may lead away whichever one he likes, with no bride-price asked, home to Peleus' house. And I will add a dowry, yes, a magnificent treasure the likes of which no man has ever offered with his daughter! Seven citadels I will give him, filled with people, Cardamyle, Enope, and the grassy slopes of Hire, Pherae the sacrosanct, Anthea deep in the meadows, rolling Aepea and Pedasus green with vineyards. All face the sea at the far edge of sandy Pylos and the men who live within them, rich in sheep-flocks, rich in shambling cattle, will honor him like a god with hoards of gifts and beneath his scepter's sway live out his laws in sleek and shining peace.

"All this—I would extend to him if he will end his anger. Let him submit to me! Only the god of death is so relentless, Death submits to no one—so mortals hate him most of all the gods. Let him bow down to me! I am the greater king, I am the elder-born, I claim—the greater man."

Nestor the noble charioteer embraced his offer: "Generous marshal Atrides, lord of men Agamemnon! No one could underrate these gifts of yours, not now, the treasure trove you offer Prince Achilles. Come—we'll send a detail of picked men. They'll go to Achilles' tent with all good speed. Quick, whomever my eye will light on in review, the mission's theirs. And old Phoenix first—Zeus loves the man, so let him lead the way. Then giant Ajax and tactful royal Odysseus. Heralds? Odius and Eurybates, you escort them. Water for their hands! A reverent silence now…a prayer to Zeus. Perhaps he'll show us mercy."

The brisk commands he issued pleased them all. Heralds brought the water at once and rinsed their hands, and the young men brimmed the mixing bowls with wine and tipping first drops for the god in every cup they poured full rounds for all. Libations finished, each envoy having drunk to his heart's content, the party moved out from Atrides' shelters. Nestor the old driver gave them marching orders—a sharp glance at each, Odysseus most of all: "Try hard now, bring him round—invincible Achilles!"

Achilles Welcomes the Embassy

So Ajax and Odysseus made their way at once where the battle lines of breakers crash and drag, praying hard to the god who moves and shakes the earth that they might bring the proud heart of Achilles round with speech and ease.

Reaching the Myrmidon shelters and their ships, they found him there, delighting his heart now, plucking strong and clear on the fine lyre—beautifully carved, its silver bridge set firm—he won from the spoils when he razed Eetion's city. Achilles was lifting his spirits with it now, singing the famous deeds of fighting heroes….Across from him Patroclus sat alone, in silence waiting for Aeacus' son to finish with his song. And on they came, with good Odysseus in the lead, and the envoys stood before him. Achilles, startled, sprang to his feet, the lyre still in his hands, leaving the seat where he had sat in peace. And seeing the men, Patroclus rose up too as the famous runner called and waved them on: "Welcome! Look, dear friends have come our way—I must be sorely needed now—my dearest friends in all the Achaean armies, even in my anger."

So Prince Achilles hailed and led them in, sat them down on settles with purple carpets and quickly told Patroclus standing by, "Come, a bigger winebowl, son of Menoetius, set it here. Mix stronger wine. A cup for the hands of each guest—here beneath my roof are the men I love the most."

He paused. Patroclus obeyed his great friend, who put down a heavy chopping block in the firelight and across it laid a sheep's chine, a fat goat's and the long back-cut of a full-grown pig, marbled with lard. Automedon held meats while lordly Achilles carved them into quarters, cut them well into pieces, pierced them with spits and Patroclus raked the hearth, a man like a god making the fire blaze. Once it had burned down and the flames died away, he scattered the coals and stretching the spitted meats across the embers, raised them onto supports and sprinkled clean pure salt. As soon as the roasts were done and spread on platters, Patroclus brought the bread, set it out on the board in ample wicker baskets. Achilles served the meat. Then face-to-face with his noble guest Odysseus he took his seat along the farther wall, he told his friend to sacrifice to the gods and Patroclus threw the first cuts in the fire. They reached out for the good things that lay at hand and when they had put aside desire for food and drink, Ajax nodded to Phoenix. Odysseus caught the signal, filled his cup and lifted it toward Achilles, opening with this toast: "Your health, Achilles! We have no lack of a handsome feast, I see that, either in Agamemnon's tent, the son of Atreus, or here and now, in yours. We can all banquet here to our heart's content.

But it's not the flowing feast that is on our minds now—no, a stark disaster, too much to bear, Achilles bred by the gods, that is what we are staring in the face and we are afraid. All hangs in the balance now: whether we save our beached ships or they're destroyed, unless, of course, you put your fighting power in harness. They have pitched camp right at our ships and rampart, those brazen Trojans, they and their far-famed allies, thousands of fires blaze throughout their armies…. Nothing can stop them now—that's their boast—they'll hurl themselves against our blackened hulls. And the son of Cronus sends them signs on the right, Zeus's firebolts flashing. And headlong Hector, delirious with his strength, rages uncontrollably, trusting to Zeus—no fear of man or god, nothing—a powerful rabid frenzy has him in its grip! Hector prays for the sacred Dawn to break at once, he threatens to lop the high horns of our sterns and gut our ships with fire, and all our comrades pinned against the hulls, panicked by thick smoke, he'll rout and kill in blood! A nightmare—I fear it, with all my heart—I fear the gods will carry out his threats and then it will be our fate to die in Troy, far from the stallion-land of Argos….

Up with you—now, late as it is, if you want to pull our Argives, our hard-hit armies, clear of the Trojan onslaught. Fail us now? What a grief it will be to you through all the years to come. No remedy, no way to cure the damage once it's done. Come, while there's still time, think

hard: how can you fight off the Argives' fatal day? Oh old friend, surely your father Peleus urged you, that day he sent you out of Phthia to Agamemnon, 'My son, victory is what Athena and Hera will give, if they so choose. But you, you hold in check that proud, fiery spirit of yours inside your chest! Friendship is much better. Vicious quarrels are deadly—put an end to them, at once. Your Achaean comrades, young and old, will exalt you all the more.' That was your aged father's parting advice. It must have slipped your mind.

But now at last, stop, Achilles—let your heart-devouring anger go! The king will hand you gifts to match his insults if only you'll relent and end your anger…. So come then, listen as I count out the gifts, the troves in his tents that Agamemnon vows to give you.

[Odysseus now repeats the long list of gifts which were proposed earlier by Agamemnon; he omits Agamemnon's request for Achilles to submit.]

"All this…he would extend to you if you will end your anger. But if you hate the son of Atreus all the more, him and his troves of gifts, at least take pity on all our united forces mauled in battle here—they will honor you, honor you like a god. Think of the glory you will gather in their eyes! Now you can kill Hector—seized with murderous frenzy, certain there's not a single fighter his equal, no Achaean brought to Troy in the ships—now, for once, you can meet the man head-on!"

Achilles Responds

The famous runner Achilles rose to his challenge: "Royal son of Laertes, Odysseus, great tactician…. I must say what I have to say straight out, must tell you how I feel and how all this will end—so you won't crowd around me, one after another, coaxing like a murmuring clutch of doves. I hate that man like the very Gates of Death who says one thing but hides another in his heart. I will say it outright. That seems best to me. Will Agamemnon win me over? Not for all the world, I swear it—nor

will the rest of the Achaeans. No, what lasting thanks in the long run for warring with our enemies, on and on, no end? One and the same lot for the man who hangs back and the man who battles hard. The same honor waits for the coward and the brave. They both go down to Death, the fighter who shirks, the one who works to exhaustion. And what's laid up for me, what pittance? Nothing—and after suffering hardships, year in, year out, staking my life on the mortal risks of war.

"Like a mother bird hurrying morsels back to her wingless young ones—whatever she can catch—but it's all starvation wages for herself.

"So for me. Many a sleepless night I've bivouacked in harness, day after bloody day I've hacked my passage through, fighting other soldiers to win their wives as prizes. Twelve cities of men I've stormed and sacked from shipboard, eleven I claim by land, on the fertile earth of Troy. And from all I dragged off piles of splendid plunder, hauled it away and always gave the lot to Agamemnon, that son of Atreus—always skulking behind the lines, safe in his fast ships—and he would take it all, he'd parcel out some scraps but keep the lion's share. Some he'd hand to the lords and kings—prizes of honor—and they, they hold them still. From me alone, Achilles of all Achaeans, he seizes, he keeps the wife I love…. Well *let* him bed her now—enjoy her to the hilt!

"Why must we battle Trojans, men of Argos? Why did he muster an army, lead us here, that son of Atreus? Why, why in the world if not for Helen with her loose and lustrous hair? Are *they* the only men alive who love their wives, those sons of Atreus? Never! Any decent man, a man with sense, loves his own, cares for his own as deeply as I, I loved that woman with all my heart, though I won her like a trophy with my spear…. But now that he's torn my honor from my hands, robbed me, lied to me—don't let him try me now. I know *him* too well—he'll never win me over!

"No, Odysseus, let him rack his brains with you and the other captains how to fight the raging fire off the ships. Look—what a mighty piece of work he's done without *me*! Why, he's erected a rampart, driven a trench around it, broad, enormous, and planted stakes to guard it. No use! He still can't block the power of man-killing Hector! No, though as long as *I* fought on Achaea's lines Hector had little lust to charge beyond his walls, never ventured beyond the Scaean Gates and oak tree. There he stood up to me alone one day—and barely escaped my onslaught.

"Ah but now, since I have no desire to battle glorious Hector, tomorrow at daybreak, once

I have sacrificed to Zeus and all the gods and loaded up my holds and launched out on the breakers—watch, my friend, if you'll take the time and care to see me off, and you will see my squadrons sail at dawn, fanning out on the Hellespont that swarms with fish, my crews manning the oarlocks, rowing out with a will, and if the famed god of the earthquake grants us safe passage, the third day out we raise the dark rich soil of Phthia. There lies my wealth, hoards of it, all I left behind when I sailed to Troy on this, this insane voyage—and still more hoards from here: gold, ruddy bronze, women sashed and lovely, and gleaming gray iron, and I will haul it home, all I won as plunder. All but my prize of honor…he who gave that prize has snatched it back again—what outrage! That high and mighty King Agamemnon, that son of Atreus!

"Go back and tell them all, all I say—out in the open too—so other Achaeans can wheel on him in anger if he still hopes—who knows?—to deceive some other comrade.

"Shameless, inveterate—armored in shamelessness! Dog that he is, he'd never dare to look me straight in the eyes again. No, I'll never set heads together with that man—no planning in common, no taking common action. He cheated me, did me damage, wrong! But never again, he'll never rob me blind with his twisting words again! Once is enough for him. Die and be damned for all I care! Zeus who rules the world has ripped his wits away. His gifts, I loathe his gifts…. I wouldn't give you a splinter for that man! Not if he gave me ten times as much, twenty times over, all he possesses now, and all that could pour in from the world's end—not all the wealth that's freighted into Orchomenos, even into Thebes, Egyptian Thebes where the houses overflow with the greatest troves of treasure, Thebes with the hundred gates and through each gate battalions, two hundred fighters surge to war with teams and chariots—no, not if his gifts outnumbered all the grains of sand and dust in the earth—no, not even then could Agamemnon bring my fighting spirit round until he pays me back, pays full measure for all his heartbreaking outrage!

"His daughter...I will marry no daughter of Agamemnon. Not if she rivaled Aphrodite in all her golden glory, not if she matched the crafts of clear-eyed Athena, not even then would I make *her* my wife! No, let her father pitch on some other Argive—one who can please *him*, a greater king than I. If the gods pull me through and I reach home alive, Peleus needs no help to fetch a bride for me himself. Plenty of Argive women wait in Hellas and in Phthia, daughters of lords who rule their citadels in power. Whomever I want I'll make my cherished wife—at home. Time and again my fiery spirit drove me to win a wife, a fine partner to please my heart, to enjoy with her the treasures my old father Peleus piled high. I say no wealth is worth my life! Not all they claim was stored in the depths of Troy, that city built on riches, in the old days of peace before the sons of Achaea came—not all the gold held fast in the Archer's rocky vaults, in Phoebus Apollo's house on Pytho's sheer cliffs! Cattle and fat sheep can all be had for the raiding, tripods all for the trading, and tawny-headed stallions. But a man's life breath cannot come back again—no raiders in force, no trading brings it back, once it slips through a man's clenched teeth.

"Mother tells me, the immortal goddess Thetis with her glistening feet, that two fates bear me on to the day of death. If I hold out here and I lay siege to Troy, my journey home is gone, but my glory never dies. If I voyage back to the fatherland I love, my pride, my glory dies... true, but the life that's left me will be long, the stroke of death will not come on me quickly.

"One thing more. To the rest I'd pass on this advice: sail home now! You will never set your eyes on the day of doom that topples looming Troy. Thundering Zeus has spread his hands above her—her armies have taken heart!

"So you go back to the great men of Achaea. You report my message—since this is the privilege of senior chiefs—let *them* work out a better plan of action, use their imaginations now to save the ships and Achaea's armies pressed to their hollow hulls. This maneuver will never work for them, this scheme they hatched for the moment as I raged on and on. But Phoenix can stay and rest the night with us, so he can voyage home, home in the ships with me to the fatherland we love. Tomorrow at dawn. But only if Phoenix wishes. I will never force the man to go." [*Phoenix's speech and Achilles' response are here omitted.*]

Book IX, 760–805

Ajax Speaks

Giant Ajax rose to his feet, the son of Telamon, tall as a god, turned and broke his silence: "Ready Odysseus? Royal son of Laertes, great tactician—come, home we go now. There's no achieving our mission here, I see, not with this approach. Best to return at once, give the Achaeans a full report, defeating as it is. They must be sitting there, waiting for us now.

"Achilles—he's made his own proud spirit so wild in his chest, so savage, not a thought for his comrades' love—we honored him past all others by the ships. Hard, ruthless man.... Why, any man will accept the blood-price paid for a brother murdered, a child done to death. And the murderer lives on in his own country—the man has paid enough, and the injured kinsman curbs his pride, his smoldering, vengeful spirit, once he takes the price.

"You—the gods have planted a cruel, relentless fury in your chest! All for a girl, just one, and here we offer you seven—outstanding beauties—that, and a treasure trove besides. Achilles, put some human kindness in your heart. Show some respect for your own house. Here we are, under your roof, sent from the whole Achaean force! Past all other men, all other Achaean comrades, we long to be your closest, dearest friends."

Achilles Answers

And the swift runner Achilles answered warmly, "Ajax, royal son of Telamon, captain of armies, all well said, after my own heart, or mostly so. But my heart still heaves with rage whenever I call to mind that arrogance of his—how he mortified me, right in front of the Argives—that son of Atreus treating me like some vagabond, like some outcast stripped of all my rights! You go back to him and declare my message: I will not think of arming for bloody war again, not till the son of wise King Priam, dazzling Hector batters all the way to the Myrmidon ships and shelters, slaughtering Argives, gutting the hulls with fire. But round my own black ship and camp this Hector will be stopped, I trust, blazing for battle as he goes—stopped dead in his tracks!"

So he finished. Then each man, lifting his own two-handled cup, poured it out to the gods, and back they went along the ships, Odysseus in the lead.

[In the next passages, Achilles remains near his tent and feeds upon his anger. The situation of the Greeks continues to deteriorate until the Trojans are close to setting fire to the ships of the Greeks. In Book XVI, Patroclus borrows the armor of his best friend Achilles and in this disguise drives the Trojans away from the ships. He does not, however, pay attention to the warning of Achilles to stay away from the walls of Troy and to avoid trying to capture the city of their enemy. With help from others, including the god Apollo, Hector kills Patroclus and strips off the armor as a prize of honor for himself.]

LEADERSHIP PROFILES

Maureen Dowd (b. 1952)

New York Times Columnist

Jehan Sadat (b. 1933)

Educator, Peace Activist and Former Egyptian First Lady

Introduction and Historical Background

Maureen Dowd was born in Washington, D.C. and earned an English degree from The Catholic University of America. She is a former columnist for *Time* and the *Washington Star* and became a best-selling author of such works as *Are Men Necessary: When Sexes Collide* (2005). Dowd won the Pulitzer Prize in 1999 for a series of columns about the Monica Lewinsky scandal during the Clinton Administration. In 1995, she became a columnist for the Op-Ed page at the *New York Times*. In a 2010 piece about Dowd for *New York* magazine, Ariel Levy wrote that Dowd said she is "'not temperamentally suited to'" her post as the only female Op-Ed columnist at the *Times*, "despite the fact she's been doing it for ten years and has won a Pulitzer and a passionate army of fans in the process, because Dowd doesn't like 'a lot of angst in my life,' and it is specifically her job to provoke. Her natural inclination—her fundamental drive—is, rather, to seduce. But then those two things are not entirely unrelated."

Maureen Dowd
© Bob Daemmrich/Corbis

One of Dowd's 2001 Op-Ed pieces, "Cleopatra and Osama," caught Jehan Sadat's attention. In the *Times* column Dowd mused, "It is hard to fathom how a part of the world that produced Cleopatra…could two millenniums later produce societies where women are swaddled breeders under house arrest." Sadat, who in the 1970s worked to change the image of Muslim women in the West, responded to Dowd's column in her 2009 book, *My Hope for Peace*. These two educated, accomplished women, both of whom have worked throughout their careers to foster women's rights, had conflicting views of what the term "women's rights" meant. Their conflict, conducted with civility, started important dialogue about the meaning of freedom and conflicting views about women's places in the world.

Jehan Sadat was born in Cairo, Egypt to an upper-middle-class family. Her father was Egyptian and a surgeon. Her mother was English and a music teacher. She was raised a Muslim at the request of her father. She first met her future husband, Anwar al-Sadat, at a birthday party when she was fifteen years old. He was thirty, a local hero for his political activities, and had just been released from prison. Jehan was intrigued with him, and they married in 1949, over the objections of her parents, when she was just shy of her sixteenth birthday. They were married for

thirty-two years and raised four children. Anwar Sadat became President of Egypt in October 1970 and served in that role for eleven years before being assassinated for his role in peace negotiations with Israel. As First Lady of Egypt, Sadat was known for her work on behalf of Arab women as well as for her dedication to fostering peace. During her time as First Lady, Sadat earned her B.A. degree in Arab literature and her M.A. degree in comparative literature from Cairo University. After her husband's death, she earned a Ph.D. in comparative literature, also from Cairo University, and went on to teach as a visiting professor at American University, the University of South Carolina, and Radford University. She is the author of *A Woman of Egypt* (2002) and *My Hope for Peace* (2009).

Jehan Sadat
National Archives and
Records Administration

Points to Consider

1. How and why do you think Jehan Sadat and Maureen Dowd developed differing views of women's rights?

2. To what extent can women from different cultures fully understand each other's views about the roles of women in the world?

3. Why does Dowd implore Laura Bush to expand the First Lady's work on behalf of women beyond Afghanistan?

4. To what extent does Sadat agree with Dowd? In what ways do Sadat's views about women's rights conflict with Dowd's views? To what degree is there common ground between their views? How might their views be reconciled?

5. Why does Sadat see women's roles in the world as significant to her hope for peace? Do you agree or disagree? Why?

"Cleopatra and Osama"

By Maureen Dowd

It is hard to fathom how a part of the world that produced Cleopatra—who perfumed the sails of her boat so men would know she was coming and ruled with elegant authority, signing one tax decree "Make it happen"—could two millenniums later produce societies where women are swaddled breeders under house arrest.

When civilization rose in the East, it was scientific and sensual, embracing the possibilities and pleasures of life from mathematics to literature, art and fashion.

There have been many repressive regimes throughout history. But the Taliban were obsessively focused on denying gender, sexuality and the forces at the very gut of life.

When the barbarian puritans running Afghanistan began to scurry away last week, men raced to buy pin-ups of beautiful girls. And, in a moving and amazing tableau, some women unwrapped themselves, letting the sun shine on their faces as they smiled shyly and delightedly. A few dared to show a little ankle or put on high heels.

"Your head hurts and your eyes hurt from the limited vision," one young woman in Kabul told a reporter, discarding her despised burka. "It was very difficult to walk without falling over." (Most have held off burning burkas because, as one woman put it, "They say the Taliban beat first and asked questions afterward. They say the Northern Alliance asks questions first and beats afterward.")

In a real version of Margaret Atwood's creepy "Handmaid's Tale," the Taliban reduced women to vessels designed to serve the needs and bolster the status of men.

"I agree that a kind of religion motivates the Taliban, but the religion in question, I'd say, is not Islam," Robert McElvaine, a history professor, wrote in *The Washington Post*. It is "insecure masculinity. These men are terrified of women."

Afghan warlords have long used castration to torture foes. The hijackers were haywire about women. Some draped towels over the prints of 20's bathing beauties in pantaloons in a Florida motel room; others indulged in lap dances, strip clubs and prostitutes, keeping busy until they got their bounty of 70 virgins.

Mohamed Atta's will had loopy, misogynistic instructions: "I don't want a pregnant woman or a person who is not clean to come and say goodbye to me" and "I don't want any women to go to my grave."

The White House, suddenly shocked by five-year-old Taliban excesses, began a campaign against their treatment of women. "Only the terrorists and the Taliban threaten to pull out women's fingernails for wearing nail polish," Laura Bush said, taking over her husband's weekly radio address.

Bush aides say the campaign will try to influence the Northern Alliance to restore women's rights and press for women in the Afghan government. Of course, they also want to impress U.S. women, who preferred Gore to Bush by 11 points. It's a freebie, an easy way to please feminists who got mad when the administration ended financing for international family-planning groups that support abortion.

This belated promotion of women as a moderating, modernizing force in the Islamic world sounds hollow.

Bush senior went to war to liberate Kuwait, yet America has not made a fuss over the fact that Kuwaiti women still can't vote or initiate divorce proceedings. We also turn a blind eye to Saudi Arabia's treating women like chattel. There are 5,000 Saudi princes, but where are the princesses?

The Saudi religious police, the matawain, use sticks to make sure women hide beneath their abayas, the long black cloaks.

Besides having to put up with polygamy, Saudi women cannot marry outside Islam, while men can. Or divorce without cause, as men can. Women also have to use separate banks and schools and obtain written permission from a male relative before traveling alone or going to a hospital. They must sit in the back seats of the cars they are not allowed to drive. (American military women stationed there are angry that they have to wear abayas and sit in the back seat when they leave the base.)

UNIT
8

But the Bushes love that royal family and its oil. What does it matter if Saudi women can drive, as long as American women can keep driving their S.U.V.'s?

Millions of Muslim women are still considered property. The first lady might think about extending her campaign beyond Afghanistan.

Dowd, M. (2001, November 18). Cleopatra and Osama. *The New York Times*. Retrieved from http://www.nytimes.com/2001/11/18/opinion/18DOWD.html.

"On Being a Muslim Woman"

(Excerpts from *My Hope for Peace*)
By Jehan Sadat

The U.S. invasion of Afghanistan focused the world's attention on the cruel practices of the Taliban, particularly their medieval attitudes toward women. Unfortunately, in the minds of many non-Muslims, the Taliban became synonymous with all of Islam. The burka-clad woman became a mute archetype for the Oppressed Muslim Woman, and thereafter, it was not too difficult to imagine that this entire benighted population was in need of rescuing—and not just from a corrupt and inhumane political regime that took hold as a result of the spectacular misery of recent Afghan history, but also from Islam itself. Western concern about the "plight of Muslim women," well meaning as it may be, has often played into stereotypical ideas that we are oppressed and intimidated, voiceless and victimized.

Examples are ubiquitous. They may be heavy-handed, like Christina Hoff Sommers's 2007 *Weekly Standard* article "The Subjection of Islamic Women." Sommers makes no apologies for sweeping generalizations about Muslim women and goes on to critique what she sees as the failure of American feminism not to confront the "condition of Muslim women," which is "the most pressing women's issue of our age":

> The subjection of women in Muslim societies—especially in Arab nations and in Iran—is today very much in the public eye. Accounts of lashings, stonings, and honor killings are regularly in the news, and searing memoirs by Ayaan Hirsi Ali and Azar Nafisi have become major best-sellers. One might expect by now American feminist groups would be organizing protests against such glaring injustices, joining forces with the valiant Muslim women who are working to change their societies. This is not happening.

Although I share Hoff's outrage at the incidents of violence against women, I do not agree with the analysis she lays out in her article: that Muslim women are universally oppressed, in crisis, and prisoners to their faith. She is, however, quite right about the fact that accounts of lashings, stonings, and honor killings dominate the news, to the complete exclusion of more common and less sensational tales of women for whom Islam does not mean brutality or subjugation. Similarly, albeit from a very different place on the ideological spectrum, *New York Times* columnist Maureen Dowd lets loose an equally sweeping generalization. In a 2001 piece, "Liberties: Cleopatra and Osama," she wrote, "It is hard to fathom how a part of the world that produced Cleopatra—who perfumed the sails of her boat so men would know she was coming and ruled with elegant authority, signing one tax decree 'Make it happen'—could two millenniums later produce societies where women are swaddled breeders under house arrest."

Dowd then dedicates her column to a legitimate targeting of the Taliban regime, but her confla-tion of ancient Egypt and twenty-first-century Afghanistan, not to mention the implication that Muslim women from this "part of the world" share the same appalling fate, is both ridiculous and deeply misleading. Indeed, many of the media depictions of Muslim women—whether in pieces aimed at improving cross-cultural understanding or fiery polemics that warn the West to remain vigilant against the Muslim threat—seem amazingly one-note. All reinforce the ideas that Muslim women need rescuing: rescue from the veil, rescue from forced marriage, rescue from barbarism, rescue from fanaticism. While many fine books have been published on women and Islam, and not all of them by escapees from fanatical or abusive Muslim men and societies (though this trope remains perennially popular), chances are good that the image of a heavily veiled woman will decorate their covers, even when such an image has little bearing on the sub-ject. Media professionals know that few images are more evocative to Western audiences than a shrouded woman, and so her eyes (for usually this is all that are showing) adorn the covers of literary anthologies, political polemics, popular histories, personal accounts, and everything in between. It galls me that people interested in Muslim women are invariably less interested in our achievements (for example, that four of the most populous Muslim majority nations have had women as leaders) than our so-called status as victims.

UNIT 8

While it is certainly true that many Muslim women wish to shake off the oppressive practices and ideologies that presuppose they are less worthy than men, Muslim women do not require, nor do they desire, liberation from Islam. Islam is a way of life entirely compatible with and sympathetic to satisfying the aspirations of most women. A noted Islamic scholar, Muhammad Abdul-Rauf, wrote in 1977, "Under Islam a woman, like a man, is a responsible free agent fully entitled to civil rights. When she becomes of age, her independence is fully recognized." People, not Islam, infringe on the rights of women. Muslim and non-Muslim alike have been too quick to use our faith as an excuse to perpetuate customs that radically depart from the Qur'an and the example set by the Prophet. Time, tradition, customary law, and the collusion of men unwilling to have their authority challenged have combined to undermine the status of women.

The great reformer and father of modern Turkey, Kamal Ataturk, said, "Nothing in our religion requires women to be inferior to men." In Islam, men and women are, by nature held to be dif-ferent and are given different roles to play, but neither is superior or more important than the other. In the Qur'an, God addresses women in the same manner as men, enjoining the same moral responsibilities and religious obligations upon them. Men and women are equal in human values, religious requirements, civil and criminal laws, and reward and punishment: "Those who surrender themselves to God and accept the true Faith; who are devout, sincere, patient, humble, charitable, and chaste; who fast and are ever mindful of God—on these, both men and women, God will bestow forgiveness and a rich reward" (Qur'an, 33:35).

In marked contrast to traditional Christian doctrine, Muslims do not hold Eve responsible for Adam's sin and the subsequent Fall. On the contrary, Eve is accountable only for her transgres-sion, and Adam only for his. Because both possessed free will, both were equally to blame for their disobedience. Moreover, Muslims believe that when Adam and Eve repented, God, who is ever merciful, forgave them. Thus, they were not cast out of Paradise for the Fall, but rather placed on earth in accordance with God's will. Islam has never entertained the idea of woman as "cursed" or morally inferior to men. Indeed, in Islam, Eve was not created as an afterthought or appendage from Adam's rib; rather, men and women were created from a "single soul" to comple-ment and give comfort to one another: "It is He Who created you from a single soul. From that being He created his spouse, so that he may find comfort in her (Qur'an, 7:189). Moreover, we matter equally in the eyes of God. "I will deny no man or woman among you the reward of their labors. You are the offspring of one another" (Qur'an, 3:195).

Historically, Muslim women have been socially active women and warrior women as far back as the time of the Prophet's wife, Khadija, a prominent businesswoman in her own right. Indeed, the examples of womanhood enshrined by Islam are not weak, oppressed or timid. Khadija's story is well known to all Muslims, so in citing her as an example, I need to resort to extraordinary acts of feminist revisionism.

Khadija was well respected in her community of the Quraysh, not only for her business acumen and wealth but also for her spotless character. It was unusual for a woman to enjoy such a high status: pre-Islamic Arabia was a cruel place for women. Before Islam, female infanticide was common practice, men could take as many wives as they wished, and most women were little better than chattel. Twice widowed as a result of the wars that plagued Arabia, she was reluctant to remarry. She had learned of Mohammed's reputation as an honest and upright young man and asked that he act as her agent and lead her caravan on a trade mission to Syria. His expedition was twice as successful as she had anticipated. Eventually her regard for Mohammed deepened into love, and despite the fact that she was his employer and fifteen years his senior—Khadija was forty and Mohammed twenty-five—she proposed marriage. Their twenty-five-year union was a happy one. That Mohammed loved her deeply there is no question, for he never took any other wives during her lifetime and was devastated when she died. Indeed, he continued to speak so reverently of his late wife that Aisha, whom he married after Khadija's death, grew jealous. According to the Hadith, she told Mohammed that Khadija "was only an old woman with red eyes, and Allah has compensated you with better and younger wife." He replied, "No, indeed; He has not compensated me with someone better than her. She believed in me when all others disbelieved; she held me truthful when others called me a liar; she sheltered me when others abandoned me; she comforted me when others shunned me; and Allah granted me children by her while depriving me of children by other women." Aisha regretted her outburst and promised never to speak ill of Khadija again. Indeed, it is by Aisha's own report that this Hadith was handed down.

Khadija enjoys the distinction of being, of all men and women, the first Muslim. It was she who consoled Mohammed when, after his encounter with the angel Gabriel, he returned to his home trembling uncontrollably. In response to his plea, "Cover me!" she wrapped him in a cloak and held him in her arms until he had grown calmer. When he confided that he feared he had gone mad, she comforted him: "Never! By Allah, Allah will never disgrace you. You keep good relations with your kinfolk, help the poor and the destitute, serve your guests generously and assist the deserving calamity-afflicted ones." In this fateful moment, and for the whole of their marriage, Khadija stood by the Prophet Mohammed spiritually, emotionally, and, with her considerable wealth, financially. Her fortune was spent in support of the nascent Muslim community, and she weathered persecution at the hands of her fellow Meccans with steadfastness and courage. Their union—a partnership based on love and mutual respect between two extraordinary individuals—was the first Muslim marriage. It could not be further from the stereotype of tyrannical Muslim husbands and their silent, subservient wives.

Aisha, who was certainly outspoken, is another beloved example of a powerful Muslim woman. It is thanks to her that Muslims have a significant portion of the Hadith, Islam's second most sacred text after the Qur'an. She recounted and corrected the stories of the Prophet Mohammed's words and deeds, including those, like the account of her jealousy of Khadija, that portray her in a very human light. This role alone gives her a preeminent place in Islam. In addition she was a person of formidable intelligence, resolve, and spirit.

In the years after Khadija's death, the Prophet remarried a number of times. Most of these wives were war widows, many with children, for whom marriage to the Prophet Mohammed meant the protection of his household. The exception, however, was Aisha, the young daughter of his close friend Abu Bakr. Intelligent, lovely, playful, and self-assured, she enjoyed the protection of

the Prophet's household when she was very young, but she and the Prophet Mohammed did not live together as man and wife until she was past puberty, and such early betrothals were not out of the ordinary in seventh-century Arabia. Aisha was in fact already betrothed to a non-Muslim when marriage to the Prophet Mohammed was suggested. Likewise, that the Prophet had many wives is no indication of moral laxity in Islam or disrespect for women. Polygamy was the norm then (and was practiced by many biblical patriarchs), and the Prophet Mohammed was deeply solicitous of his wives and helped with various domestic tasks in their households.

Aisha, for all her youth, was not timid or subservient, and certainly not silent. On the contrary, she did not hesitate to speak up: she questioned the Prophet carefully in order to better understand the revelations he received from God, and she could be sharp-tongued and critical, even of her husband. Aisha outlived the Prophet by fifty years—it was in her arms that he died—and in her lifetime, she was acclaimed as an expert in medicine, mathematics, poetry, and Islamic jurisprudence. She instructed both boys and girls in Qur'anic scholarship, and her advice was widely sought by all members of the Muslim community, men and women alike. Her eloquence and generosity of spirit were legendary. In addition, she was politically active, in peacetime and in war—first accompanying men to the battlefield, bringing them water, and attending the wounded, and, in 656, leading an army into battle.

What have these long-dead women to do with Muslim women today? A great deal. For Sunni Muslims in particular, Khadija and Aisha are not dimly recalled scriptural figures; they are revered as exemplars of Islam. Their strength and accomplishments make them twenty-first-century role models for Muslim women around the world. That Muslim women can find within our own tradition validation of our individual worth, intellectual abilities, spiritual development, and leadership potential has meant that Western-style feminism has held limited allure. Muslim women, by and large, are not interested in proving that men and women are the same, nor do we wish to denigrate a woman's role within the family. Motherhood and family are exalted in Islam, and so rejecting them makes little sense to us. In fact, it is difficult to overstate the revered place of motherhood in Islam—the adoration and respect that most Muslim mothers command from their children. A famous saying of the Prophet is, "Paradise is at the feet of mother." Another well-known Hadith (one cited by both Shih el-Bukhari and Imam Muslim, two of the six principal sources of Hadith), recounts the story of a man who asked the Prophet: "'Who among the people is the most worthy of my good company?' The Prophet said, 'Your mother.' The man said, 'Then who else?' The Prophet said, 'Your mother.' The man asked, 'Then who else?' Only then did the Prophet say, 'Your father.'"

This is not to say that the home is the only sphere in which Muslim women can or wish to function. Nor should a woman's desire to work outside the home be construed as a repudiation of her role within it. For example, I always had a burning desire to be someone in addition to, not rather than, Anwar Sadat's wife and the mother of his children, though I am immensely proud of being both. I do not consider my ambition as a contradiction but rather as an extension of who I am. Much as I treasured my marriage, I wanted my independence and separate identity; the same is true for many of my sisters. Although we belong to a faith with deeply egalitarian foundations, we unfortunately face many barriers to full civic and economic participation. We have a great distance to go before we realize the rights that God gave us and the Prophet recognized.

How can we reach this state? In the Islamic world as in the world in general, success, freedom, and equality have one common denominator: education. To all Muslims, male and female, the acquisition of education is a duty assigned to them by the teachings of the Prophet Mohammed and the Qur'an, which commands the faithful to think, reflect, and reason. Islam is not a faith of blind obedience—for men or women—but rather one of active intellectual engagement.

UNIT 8

Opponents of women's progress persist in the groundless claim that Muslim women do not require an education in order to be wives and mothers. This is absurd. How can a woman fulfill the Qur'anic requirement for all Muslims to educate themselves if she cannot go to school? How can a mother teach her children to participate in society if she herself is illiterate and ignorant?

…

There is a certain irony in noting that both "Islam" and "the West" seem to find each other's treatment of women objectionable. I suspect that both sides have valid complaints. After all, women the world over—whether they are Oriental or Occidental, inhabitants of the developing world or the industrialized—have yet to achieve the full measure of political, economic, or social equality that we deserve. The challenge of any global women's movements is to recognize the shared spirit of our efforts toward full participation in our societies while honoring the very real differences between those societies.

Sadat, Jehan. (2009). "On Being a Muslim Woman." In *My Hope for Peace*. Simon and Schuster. Pp. 129–137, 141.

REFLECT & FOCUS

"When you want to convert someone to your view, you go over to where he is standing, take him by the hand, and guide him. You don't stand across the room and shout at him; you don't order him to come over where you are. You start where he is and work from that position. That's the only way to make him to budge."

—Thomas Aquinas (1225–1274), Italian Theologian and Philosopher

READINGS

American Ground:
Unbuilding the World Trade Center

By William Langewiesche

Points to Consider

1. In what ways did individuals react to the World Trade Center Towers' collapse that contributed to the conflict between groups of first responders? To what extent could this conflict have been avoided?

2. What are the issues at the root of the clashes between the firefighters and the police?

3. What other groups clashed and why?

4. Why did it take so long for a sense of organization to develop at the site of the World Trade Center Towers' collapse?

5. What strategies did the key players employ to lead through the tension and conflict in these different clashes?

American Ground:
Unbuilding the World Trade Center

On the morning of Friday, November 2, 2001, seven weeks and three days after the Twin Towers collapsed, tribal fighting broke out at the World Trade Center site. The battle was brief and inconclusive. It occurred near the northwest corner of the ruins, when an emotionally charged demonstration turned violent, and firemen attacked the police. Within that intense inner world it came as no surprise. Resentments and jealousies among the various groups had been mounting for weeks, as the initial rush to find survivors had transmuted into a grim search for the dead, and as territoriality and the embrace of tragedy had crept in. The catalyst for the confrontation was a decision made several days earlier by Mayor Rudolph Giuliani to rein in the firemen, who for nearly two months had basked in overwhelming public sympathy and enjoyed unaccustomed influence and unlimited access to the site. In the interest of returning the city to normal life, Giuliani declared that the firemen now would have to participate in a joint command, with the New York and Port Authority police and the civilian heavy-construction managers in the DDC [Department of Design and Construction]. This did not sit well. Moreover, access would be restricted, new procedures would be imposed at the pile, and the number of searchers would be reduced by two thirds.

The reason given publicly for this new arrangement was "safety," a term so often used to mask other agendas in modern America that it caused an immediate, instinctive reaction of disbelief. Ordinary frontline firemen were the angriest. As many as 250 of their colleagues lay unaccounted for in the ruins, and they intended as a matter of honor to find every one of them. That week alone they had found fourteen. They were convinced that only they could sustain the necessary attention to detail on the pile, and that in his eagerness to "clean up" the site (a term they despised), Giuliani was willing to risk overlooking some of the dead, scooping them up with the steel and concrete and relying on the sorting process at Fresh Kills to separate their remains from the rubble.

UNIT

8

To a degree the firemen's suspicions may have been well founded. Certainly the unbuilders themselves, operating under the direction of Mike Burton, were pursuing the most aggressive possible schedule of demolition and debris removal. Even Sam Melisi had doubts about the city's motivations. To me he said, "If you do a good job, and you do it in record time—who knows what record time is, since nobody's ever dealt with this before—is there a bonus? Do you get to be a commissioner or something? I don't know. Burton's just hard to figure out. Sometimes he's very personable and human: 'Oh, geez, you found X amount of people. Oh, that's great.' And then other times: 'You're really taking way too much time to look at this stuff, and we've got to keep moving.' Putting his arm around me and winking. 'We really have to move on this.' But you know what? We're going to take as long as it has to take. We're not going to compromise on that. We just can't do it. I don't have an allegiance to any construction company, or even to the City of New York. My only allegiance is to the people who lost their lives—to their families. The best we can do is try to retrieve as many people as we can in the most humane fashion. And then when all this is over, I can just go back to doing what I do."

Melisi was the reasonable one, and the most broadly involved of any person at the Trade Center site. By comparison, the ordinary firemen were narrowly focused on the rubble underfoot, where the remains of civilians and police officers were regularly discovered, but only the recovery of their own people seemed genuinely to interest them. Though their attitude was sometimes offensive to others working on the pile, it was not difficult to understand: the firemen were straightforward guys, initiates in a closed and fraternal society who lived and ate together at the station houses, and shared the drama of responding to emergencies. Some had lost family when the Trade Center fell, and nearly all had lost friends. Their bereavement was real. Still, for nearly two months they had let their collective emotions run unchecked, and they had been indulged and encouraged in this by society at large—the presumption being something like, "It helps to cry." The effect had turned out to be quite the opposite: rather than serving a cathartic purpose, the emotionalism seemed to have heightened the firemen's sense of righteousness and loss. Now, with the city ordering cutbacks in the firemen's presence on the pile, the agitation among the rank and file was so great that the firefighter's unions warned the city that they had lost control, and would have to organize a protest to avoid a break with their own membership.

None of this was conductive to clear, calm thought though. Two days before the fighting broke out, a fire captain and union trustee named Matty James presented the situation starkly to the *Daily News*, as if retrieval of the bodies were an all-or-nothing affair. He said, "The city may be ready to turn this into a construction job, but we're not. We want our brothers back. By doing this, the city is taking away from these families, these widows, these mothers and fathers, any chance for closure. What are we supposed to do? Go to the Fresh Kills landfill to look for our people?" In a similar style, the mother of a dead fireman whose body had been found said, "Our memorial Mass became a funeral. It gave me an opportunity to hug the casket and to say good-bye. It's just awful, what they are trying to do…to deprive other women of that wonderful feeling."

Such was the rhetoric during the days leading up to that Friday morning, when hundreds of firemen began to assemble at the corner of Chambers and West Streets, by the red-brick walls of PS 89 [Public School Number 89]. In the emergency command center on the second floor, most of the site-management team from the DDC made plans to stay inside and out of sight. Mike Burton looked worriedly down at the scene on the street—at the slowly growing crowd, the opposing lines of blue-uniformed police officers, the television crews that were just then arriving. As if to himself he said, "These guys are not happy…not happy at all."

Earlier that morning Burton had led the first "combined" site-management meeting, at which the Fire Department, the police, and the DDC had been required to share the stage. It had taken place down the hallway, in the school auditorium. The various tribes had eyed one another with frank distrust, but had spoken in veiled terms to keep conflicts from breaking out into the open. Burton had said, "The DDC will have oversight (Meaning: control) over all recovery efforts on the pile," in a tone that somehow implied that this was a decision imposed on him from far above. He had also said, "We're making a push for increased safety. There may be some negative consequences. The police will not let anyone in or out of this building after 10 A.M." (Meaning: The firemen are being hysterical.) A fire chief in a white uniform shirt seemed not to have heard a word. He said, "We're trying to hammer out a plan for the removal of victims and uniformed personnel. We've just located fourteen Fire Department members near the South Tower." (Meaning: We're not going to make this easy.)

In the kindergarten room Holden decided that he needed to go to the pile to keep a close watch on the situation himself. Peter Rinaldi expressed concern for Holden's safety. Holden said, "I'm going to wear a sign saying, 'I don't know Mike Burton.'" Burton smiled humorlessly. His relationship with Holden was increasingly strained. There was another Port Authority man in the room, a strapping ex-Marine named Tom O'Connor, whose wife had worked in a neighboring building. She had survived, but they had lost many friends in the attack. He said, "We are now viewed as monsters." His manner was matter-of-fact.

Becky Clough, a pugnacious DDC manager and one of the few women active on the ground at the heart of the site, said, "What are we afraid of? We're doing the right thing."

Burton said, "It had to happen sometime anyway. Maybe there are some positive sides."

O'Connor said, "So when are you losing your job?"

I slipped outside before the building was locked down, and walked through the demonstration. The crowd by then had grown to perhaps five hundred off-duty firemen, and it was continuing to expand as others streamed in from the subways and parking lots. Some were dressed in civilian clothes, but most wore the standard protective "turnout coats," black with yellow reflector stripes and FDNY [Fire Department New York] written in block letters across the back. Most were bareheaded. As protesters, they seemed awkward and self-conscious at first, and unsure of how to proceed, but they were also genuinely angry. Encouraged by a union official with a bullhorn, they raised their fists and chanted, "Bring our brothers home!" They waved a union banner and American flags. The TV crews moved in tightly, and found firemen for one-on-one interviews. A retired fire captain said, "My son Tommy is still in that building, and we haven't gotten him yet." The firemen began shouting, "Bring Tommy home! Bring Tommy home!" The unions had promised City Hall that the demonstration would be orderly, and that it would remain outside the site's perimeter—that it would amount to little more than a show for the cameras. But the firemen proved difficult to control. As the crowd swelled to nearly a thousand, it grew louder and more confident, and suddenly surged south through the first police barricades toward the Trade Center ruins.

The TV crews followed eagerly. To the police demonstrators shouted, "Walk with us!" and "Shut 'em down!" But the police were on duty, and after weeks of growing resentments on the pile they were not inclined to sympathize. As the demonstrators shoved through a second line of defense, the police shoved back, and some of the firemen started to swing. I saw one policeman go down with a roundhouse punch to the face; and others responded, tackling and cuffing the offender. The crowd kept pushing through, with fights breaking out where the two groups met. These were big, physical guys on both sides, and they grappled in ungainly dances, straining hard, cursing each other, and toppling to the ground in aggressive embraces. Five policemen were injured. On the periphery the protesters who were arrested—twelve in all—were hustled into police vans.

One was a tough-looking old man in a fireman's uniform, who kept bellowing, "My son's in there! My son's in there!" Firefighters shouted, "Let him go!" But like the others who had been arrested, the old man was hauled away.

The protesters gathered on West Street beside the ruins, where they were joined by a scattering of die-hard union sympathizers from the site—primarily a group of ironworkers who sauntered over out of curiosity, and got into the spirit of things. One in particular seemed to delight in showing the crowd how to go about making a TV appearance. He was the very image of a beefy construction worker, dressed in a hardhat and a soil-stained thermal undershirt. He climbed onto a diesel excavator and for several minutes mugged wordlessly for the cameras, waving an American flag and pumping his fist in the air. It was not clear that he knew or cared what the protest was about.

The same was obviously not true of the firefighters' union official, who climbed onto the excavator and used his bullhorn again, repeating his cry of "Bring our brothers home!" and threatening to find reinforcements by the thousands, including "brothers" from other cities, if Giuliani did not back down. Exhibiting more bravado than political sensitivity, he called on the police to release the men who had been arrested, and to march with the demonstrators on City Hall. But of course the police were angry at having been attacked—all the more so because they, too, had tribal allegiances, and had lost twenty-three colleagues in the Trade Center collapse. The firemen marched to City Hall, where they chanted, "Rudy must go!" This was somewhat gratuitous, since Giuliani was only two months from the end of his tenure. They also chanted for the ouster of their fire commissioner, Thomas Von Essen, who for years had been a well-liked New York fireman and union leader, but who now was going around quietly making the point that by far the greatest loss of life had been civilian, and that the Trade Center tragedy was larger than just firefighters' or even a New Yorkers' affair.

Giuliani was infuriated by what he viewed as an assault on the city's all-important process of recovery, and he lashed out with the vindictiveness for which he was known. With the demonstration still going on, he called Holden on Holden's cell phone and demanded that he identify the ironworkers and fire them. This was only the second time in eight years that Holden had received a call from the mayor, and he was aghast at what he was hearing. Very few ironworkers had joined with the firemen, but those who had were likely to be union activists, and therefore just the sort of people who could rally sympathy across the pile. Any attempt to discipline them could easily backfire and lead to a full-scale rebellion. Moreover, for all he knew, the ironworkers were on their break (or could claim to be), and since they were not disrupting the work, they had every right to protest. This was the inner world of the Trade Center site, an emergency zone, yes, but not subject to martial law; if it was a turbulent and quarrelsome place, it was also courageous and creative, and an authentic piece of American ground. But Holden knew better than to argue with Giuliani, and he did not try. After ending the call, he dutifully had a DDC staffer at the scene take some pictures of the ironworkers. It was a particularly unpleasant moment: the workers had no idea what the snapshots were about, and some posed for them festively, as if they were on a weekend outing. Holden looked disgusted by the whole affair. He was irritable in a way I had not seen before. As the demonstration drifted away from the pile, he came upon a New York tabloid-TV crew that was setting up to interview a man in an FDNY T-shirt—presumably about the depths of his sorrow. Holden told me he was tired of all the exploitation. He walked up to the reporter and demanded that he take his camera and leave. The reporter said, "We just want to…"

"Out!" Holden snapped, pointing north.

The reported gave Holden a look of pure hatred. He said, "The man's got no heart."

"Out!"

By late afternoon Holden was sitting again in the kindergarten room of PS 89, thumbing glumly through pictures of the protesting ironworkers. He had no intention of following through with Giuliani's orders, but he knew that if he flaunted his disobedience, the repercussions would be swift and severe. He himself had told me earlier that the first lesson of "commissioner school" was "Don't contradict the mayor." The only alternative now was to procrastinate, and to hope that the idea would somehow go away. This was not the style of the Giuliani administration, in which the mayor's whims were treated as dictates. Indeed, during several phone calls that followed, one of Giuliani's deputy mayors, Tony Coles, continued to demand punishment for the ironworkers long after it could conceivably have served a useful purpose. But Holden held the line, in this case for inaction, and with defensive skills unheralded even within PS 89, he managed to protect Giuliani from himself, and the nation from Giuliani, and to keep the recovery effort on track.

It was a troubled time anyway, that first half of November, the low point in New York's response to the Trade Center attack. The Yankees had lost the World Series—and to Arizona, of all teams. The various groups at the Trade Center site were turning into warring camps. To make matters worse, Giuliani seemed to have lost control of his emotions. After the demonstration (soon known as "the firemen's riot") he continued for several days to rage about the protestors' distortions, and what he saw as their betrayal of the city's well-being. He did not seek conciliation—for instance, by forgiving those who were involved in the demonstration. Rather, the police hunted down another six firemen as culprits, and booked them on charges of criminal trespassing. Among these men were the presidents of both firefighters' unions: Captain Peter L. Gorman, of the 2,500-member Uniformed Fire Officers Association, and Kevin E. Gallagher, the protester with the bullhorn, who headed the 9,000-member Uniformed Firefighters Association.

These were honest union officials, expressing the legitimate if misguided dissent of their membership, and their arrest was unusual to say the least. It was also, of course, counterproductive. The firemen were outraged. Captain Gorman, who had worn the uniform for twenty-eight years, said, "They're putting me through the system like I'm a thug." He called the fire and police commissioners "Giuliani's goons," and Giuliani himself a "fascist." The unions had threatened privately to hold a news conference and accuse the mayor of being "anti-American," but apparently thought better of going public with such a foolish claim. Instead, more accurately, a union spokesman said to *The New York Times*, "The mayor fails to realize that New York City is not a dictatorship, where if you don't like what a union is doing you can just go and lock up a union's president. The message being sent from City Hall is that if you don't agree with this administration, we will get you." Outside the Trade Center site America bloomed with bumper stickers proclaiming UNITED WE STAND, a strangely forlorn slogan in a country that so obviously draws strength from disagreement. Drawing strength from disagreement is a trick that the attacking terrorists must certainly have discounted. But of course there are also limits to the creative power of disunity—and the Trade Center response seemed to be veering toward just the sort of social implosion that the terrorists may have had in mind.

The tribalism that grew up on the pile had origins so primitive that they can only be understood as instinctual. At the core was an us-versus-them mentality brought on by the mere act of donning a uniform. Whether as firefighters or as the two sorts of police (city and Port Authority), the uniformed personnel at the site were generally drawn from the same white "ethnic" outerborough neighborhoods and families, but as members of their respective organizations they had learned to distrust and resent the others. The hostility was historical, and because it was strongest on the lowest levels, among the rank and file, it had proved impossible to root out. People at the site referred to it alliteratively as the Battle of the Badges. Across the years it had led to frequent arguments over turf and occasional bouts of outright obstructionism at emergency scenes. At the Trade Center it had been a factor from the first moments after the attack, when the Police and

Fire Departments had set up separate command posts several blocks apart, and without communication between them. There were consequences to this: after the South Tower fell, police helicopter pilots took a close-up look at the fire in the North Tower, and twenty-one minutes before the final collapse they urged their own command to evacuate the building. The warning was radioed to the policemen inside the North Tower, most of whom escaped, but it was not relayed to the fire commands, or to the firemen in the building, only some of whom were able to hear independently radioed orders to evacuate, and more than 120 of whom subsequently died. The lack of communication was certainly no more the fault of one side than of the other, but it aggravated the divisions between them. Even during the initial desperate search for survivors the police and firemen quarreled over turf, and asserted their differences. By the end of the first day the bucket brigades had separated according to uniform. Throughout the months that followed, individual friendships and family ties cut across the lines. Nonetheless, the tribalism festered and soon infected the construction crews, too, who did not quarrel much among themselves but generally distrusted the police as ordinary citizens do, and who probably hadn't given firemen much thought before, but came now to resent their claims to special privilege on the pile.

UNIT
8

The firemen's claims were based on an unspoken tribal conceit: that the deaths of their own people were worthier than the deaths of others—and that they themselves, through association, were worthier too. This was difficult for the police and civilian workers at the site to accept. The collapse of the towers had been anything but certain. The firemen who had gone inside had been normally brave—as people are who are not cowards. They were not soldiers crossing the lip of a trench or assaulting a machine nest in battle; they were men with a job that demanded mental willingness and hard physical labor, and on that day they were climbing endless stairwells one flight at a time in the company of friends, and with little obvious purpose in mind beyond finding the civilians who must have been injured by the twin attacks. The firemen in the South Tower were killed without warning. They were unintentional martyrs, noncombatants, typical casualties of war. Those in the North Tower felt the rumble of the South Tower's collapse, but as best as is known, most did not understand what had happened or conclude that their own building soon would come down. Later on, as the precariousness of the North Tower became clearer, there were firemen who committed acts of extraordinary heroism—for instance, by lingering to help civilians, or remaining in the lower lobbies, desperately working the radios and calling for an emergency retreat. But the Fire Department had no monopoly on altruism that day, and terrible though its casualties were, the 343 dead, it did not suffer the greatest losses. As the workers on the pile knew all too well, that sad distinction went to Cantor Fitzgerald, where 658 people had died—some of them no doubt as altruists too. But what did such categories mean anyway? Nearly 3,000 people had been slaughtered here, nearly all of them on the job, and each of them at the last instant equally alone. Those who had not been vaporized lay scattered in the rubble's democratic embrace. The dead were dead now and didn't care. And it was absurd for the living to group and rank them.

Were it not for all the hype, this would hardly need saying. It's true that the United States was shaken, and that people in their insecurity felt the need for heroes. The dead firemen certainly fit the bill. They were seen as brawny, square-jawed men, with young wives and children—perfectly tragic figures, unreliant on microchips or machines, who seemed to have sprung from the American earth like valiant heroes from a simpler time. They had answered the call of history, rushed to the defense of the homeland, and unhesitatingly given their lives. They had died at the hands of barbarians, leaving behind widows who were helpless, or who were said to be. All this presented opportunities for image-making that neither the media nor the political system could resist. Progressives may have been shocked by the ease with which America slipped into patterns of the past—with women at the hearth, men as their protectors, and swarthy strangers at the gate. Rationalists may have worried about the wallowing in victimization, and the financial precedents being set by promises of payouts to the victims' families. As usual in America, there was reason for everyone to deplore the cynicism and crassness of the press. However, there would be time for refinements later. As an initial reaction to the first shock of war, the hero worship was probably a healthy thing, as long as it was confined to the dead.

But when it spilled over indiscriminately to the living, problems arose, particularly at the center of attention, on the Trade Center pile. The firemen now on the scene were by definition those who either had escaped from the Twin Towers before the collapses or, more likely, had not been inside them to start with—in most cases because they were somewhere else in the city at the time. They were not lesser men for this. But if the loss of the others was to mean anything beyond the waste of war, it had to be admitted that people on the pile since then, though ferociously dedicated to a grim and dangerous task, were simply not involved in heroics. Of course the situation was presented differently on the outside, where the public was led to believe that conditions on the pile were so difficult that merely by working there people were sacrificing themselves, and that the firemen in particular—anonymous figures who wore the same wide-brimmed helmets as their fallen brethren—deserved the nation's adoration. For many of the firemen, who tended to have led quiet lives until then, the sudden popularity became a disorienting thing. Even those with the strength to resist the publicity—who stayed off TV, and did not strut in public— seemed nonetheless to be influenced by this new external idea of themselves as tragic characters on a national stage. The image of "heroes" seeped through their ranks like a low-grade narcotic. It did not intoxicate them, but it skewed their view.

Strangely enough, it was this patriotic imagery that ultimately drove the disunity on the pile, and that by early November nearly caused the recovery effort to fall apart. The mechanisms were complex. On the one hand, there were some among the construction workers and the police who grew unreasonably impatient with the firemen, and became overeager to repeat the obvious—in polite terms, that these so-called heroes were just ordinary men. On the other hand, the firemen seemed to become steadily more self-absorbed and isolated from the larger cleanup efforts under way. The resentments rarely erupted into fistfights (though fistfights did occur) but increasingly were expressed in private conversations on the pile—often on the subject of the looting that for the first few months tarnished the Trade Center response.

The looting was shadowy, widespread, and unsurprising. The Trade Center was known to have been hit before by errant policemen and firemen, after the terrorist bombing of 1993. This time the thievery was less intense but longer-lived. It involved small numbers of construction workers and men from the same uniformed groups as did before, and it was shallow and opportunistic rather than deeply criminal in intent. It started in the shopping complex, with the innocuous filching of cigarettes and soda pop, and expanded into more ambitious acquisitions. As rumor had it, the tribalism at the site extended even to the choice of goods. Firemen were said to prefer watches from the Tourneau store, policemen to opt for kitchen appliances, and construction workers (who were at a disadvantage here) to enjoy picking through whatever leftovers they came upon—for instance, wine under the ruins of the Marriott hotel, and cases of contraband cigarettes that spilled from U.S. Customs vaults in the Building Six debris. No one, as far as I know, stole women's clothes, which hung on racks for months, or lifted books from the Borders bookstore, which were said to be contaminated with dangerous mold. After a few arrests were made, the filching shifted to the peripheral buildings, which were gradually thinned of computers until the authorities wised up and posted guards. It's important to realize that these transgressions occurred not in a normal part of the city but in a war zone, where standards had changed, food and supplies were provided free of charge, and a flood of donated goods (flashlights, gloves, Timberland boots) was believed to be backwashing onto the streets. It was also a place where the entire nation had been attacked and was responding as a collective, and where therefore, surprisingly for modern America, the meaning of individual property had diminished. In context the looting simply did not seem shocking.

Knowledge of it, however, cast a shadow on the use of the word "hero," and at least once became a source of embarrassment and bitter mockery. One autumn afternoon, at the base of the South Tower ruins, diesel excavators were digging into unexplored reaches of the Trade Center's foundation hole. Fifty feet below the level of the street they began to uncover the hulk of a fire truck that had been driven deep by the collapse. The work was being directed by the field superintendent for one of the major construction companies, a muscular and charismatic man who was widely admired (and to some extent feared) for his unabashed physicality and his manner of plunging unhesitatingly into battle with debris. If for no other reason than his confidence in the enormous mechanical power at his disposal, the superintendent believed in acting first and worrying about the consequences later. Early on he made it clear to me that were he in charge, he would clean up the site in no time flat, and that his first step would be to throw the firemen off the pile. Such was his disdain that he might even have included Sam Melisi in the toss, hard as that was to imagine. He assured me that he'd had nothing against firemen before (he shrugged and said, "Why would I?"), but he just couldn't stand this hero stuff anymore. He didn't like the moralistic airs these guys were putting on. He didn't like the way they treated the civilian dead. And he especially didn't like the fact that they kept forcing his operation to shut down—once for three days straight—while they worked by hand and poked through the rubble for their colleagues' remains.

UNIT
8

Imagine his delight, then, after the hulk of the fire truck appeared, that rather than containing bodies (which would have required decorum), its crew cab was filled with dozens of new pairs of jeans from a Trade Center store. When a grappler pulled off the roof, the jeans were strewn about for all to see. It was exactly the sort of evidence the field superintendent had been waiting for. While a crowd of initially bewildered firemen looked on, the construction workers went wild. "Jeans! Look at these! Fucking guys! Jeans!" In their eyes, it was hard to avoid the conclusion that the looting had begun even before the first tower fell, and that while hundreds of doomed firemen had climbed through the wounded buildings, this particular crew had been engaged in something else entirely, of course without the slightest suspicion that the South Tower was about to hammer down. This was not what the firemen wanted to hear. An angry fire chief tried to shut the construction workers up. He offered an explanation—that the jeans (tagged, folded, stacked by size) had been blown into the crew cab by the force of the collapse. The field superintendent, seeming not to hear, asked the fire chief to repeat what he had said. When he did, the construction workers only jeered louder.

Scattered jeans lay on the pile for several days. The story got around. For Ken Holden and Mike Burton, this and other incidents on the pile amounted to important lessons in their war's early months: the site would never stand united, as sloganeers said it should, so some other approach would have to be found.

Though the firemen who rioted on November 2 did not believe it, when Giuliani gave "safety" as the reason for reducing their presence on the pile, he was completely sincere. This was somewhat counterintuitive, since the safety record so far had been extraordinarily good: despite the fires, the instability of the ruins, and the crushing weight of the equipment and debris, not a single recovery worker had been killed, and only a few had been seriously injured. Indeed, discounting possible long-term respiratory problems, the injury rate was about half that of the construction-industry average. Some people claimed this as a sign of God's favor, but a more mundane explanation was that the inapplicability of ordinary rules and procedures to such a chaotic environment required workers there to think for themselves, which they proved very capable of doing. Nonetheless, the city had reason to be especially concerned about the firemen at the site, who formed maverick groups on the pile, prone to clustering too close to the diesel grapplers and to taking impetuous risks in the smoke and debris.

The lack of discipline was a well-known aspect of the firemen's culture. In some ways it was a necessary thing, hard to separate from their views of manliness and bravery and their eagerness to take on fires. It also, however, led to needless danger. After he left the service, in January of 2002, Commissioner Von Essen mentioned that as a longtime firefighter, he had often stood on floors among thirty others where only ten were needed. Indeed, on September 11 many of the firefighters who responded were off duty at the time, and many bypassed check-in procedures, or arrived by subway or car in violation of orders to stay away. Many also went into the towers unnecessarily and with little coordination, at a time when there were enough other firemen on duty to handle the evacuations, and when the Fire Department had decided that the fires were unfightable. Sixty off-duty firefighters died that day. "Courage is not enough," Von Essen later said. "The fact that the guys are so dedicated comes back to hurt them down the line." The police at the site were better disciplined—and, partly as a result, they suffered fewer casualties on the day of the attack. But nearly two months after the tragedy, with no conceivable justification for continuing to jump into voids or clamber across unstable cliffs, there were still firemen running wild.

Giuliani had good reason, therefore, to rein them in. Viewed from the outside, the plan seemed sensible: you scale back the searchers to three teams of twenty-five—one from each of the uniformed services: you allow only one spotter at a time to stand beside each diesel excavator on the pile; until human remains are found, you require the other team members to wait in designated "safe areas" nearby; you do not allow ordinary firemen to keep shutting down the site; you create a joint command to soothe people's egos but give practical control to the engineers and the construction types, who are businesslike and know how to finish the job; you shrink the perimeter, with the goal of returning even heavily damaged West Street as soon as possible to the city; you thin the crowds of hangers-on by requiring new badges for the inner and outer zones, and asking the Red Cross and the Salvation Army to consolidate and simplify their feeding operations; you scale back the public displays of mourning; you encourage people to get on with their lives.

The planners were not completely naïve about the transition: they suspected that they might have some difficulty in getting the firemen to comply. Mike Burton decided that the best approach would be to start with strict enforcement of the new rules, and loosen up later for the sake of efficiency. I was surprised by his confidence that anything here could go according to plan. And indeed, little did.

Questions of personality and professional formation were at play. The construction crews, like the DDC itself, were made up of hard-driving people, accustomed to shaving minutes in a time-obsessed industry. Though they understood the desirability of finding the human remains at the Trade Center site, they were not going to slow the excavation of the ruins just to ensure that the final inspections at the Fresh Kills landfill did not turn up body parts. Mike Burton in particular was pushing for speed, and was determined to finish the job below cost and ahead of schedule—however arbitrary those targets may have been. He was climbing his mountain of success, and was not about to let a gang of irrational firemen get in his way. In public and during the morning meetings he was gracious and respectful toward them, but in private—in the confines of the kindergarten rooms, or during long walks with me on the pile—he let his impatience show. On the evening after the riot we came upon one of the new search-team "safe areas" (a ten-foot square of Jersey barriers spray painted FDNY), and he shot me a hard little smile of victory. He used the firemen's term for it and said, "The penalty box." I assumed he was thinking about the attack on the police. He may have believed that the way forward was clear. He seemed not to notice that the penalty box was empty.

This was not a game. There were no rules. The firemen continued with their headstrong ways on the pile, refusing to submit to civilian authority. Five days after the riot, after the unions formally apologized to the police, Giuliani began a partial retreat. He said he would increase the size of the search teams to fifty. The firemen were unmollified. The place where their friends had been killed was still being turned into an unholy "construction site." Three days later, on November 10, charges were dropped against all but one of the arrested demonstrators. It did no good. The firemen pulled out the stops and demanded a meeting between the mayor and the dead firemen's families.

The meeting took place behind closed doors in a Sheraton hotel in midtown Manhattan, on the evening of November 12. It had been a rough day already: that morning an American Airlines flight departing for the Dominican Republic had crashed into a residential neighborhood in Queens, killing 265 people, and most of the officials at the meeting had visited the scene. Now they sat behind a table on a raised platform—the mayor, the medical examiner, the fire commissioner, and, from the Trade Center site, Mike Burton and Bill Cote. The crowd they faced consisted mostly of widows—an increasingly organized group that spoke for mothers, fathers, and children as well, and that after two months of national sympathy was gaining significant political strength. Payouts to the victims' families hadn't yet begun, and firemen's widows, not without reason, felt neglected and put-upon. They believed that the city was essentially giving up on the search for the dead. And they were angry about it.

The medical examiner was the first to come under fire. He had begun to talk about the procedures in place for handling remains when he made the mistake of mentioning that full or even partially intact corpses had not recently been found, and that they were unlikely to be found in the future. A woman stood up and yelled, "You're a liar! We know what you're finding! You're a liar!" Others chimed in, shouting that their husbands' bodies had been recovered in good condition. One woman yelled that when her husband was found, the searchers on the pile could even see the dimple on his chin. It was as if an emotional dam had burst in the crowd. The medical examiner listened somberly. When the crowd briefly quieted, he tried to explain his reasoning: the excavation had moved into the mid-levels of the ruins, where the debris was severely compacted and the dead had been shattered or vaporized; furthermore, from what was known of the pile's composition, along with the process of organic decay, there was little chance that whole bodies would be discovered in the future. The widows would have none of this. They continued to shout "Liar!" until the medical examiner sat down. The months ahead would show that the medical examiner was wrong—that the ruins were riddled with unexpected cavities deep down, and that nearly whole corpses, particularly of the heavily clad firemen, lay waiting to be found. However, this would have been impossible to predict at the time.

The mayor handled himself well that night. He was patient and compassionate, and he allowed the grieving crowd to rail, but he did not pander to it. About the medical examiner he simply said, "He's not lying. He's telling you what we know." Then it was Burton's time to talk.

Burton started gamely into an explanation of the transition on the pile, including the new placement of spotters, the "safe areas," and the handling and inspection of the debris. The crowd listened sullenly for a while, until a woman stood up and yelled, "We don't even want to hear from you! You're Mr. Scoop and Dump!"

Burton was flustered. He said, "Listen, this will only be a few more minutes. Just let me explain our thinking, so we're all on the same page and can have a rational conversation."

The woman shouted, "No! You're not the sort of person I want to talk to! You're the problem!"

Burton tried a soothing tone. He said, "We'll get through this, if you'll just…"

"No! You're Mr. Scoop and Dump!"

Others joined in, shouting, "Scoop and Dump! Scoop and Dump! Scoop and Dump!" Burton allowed a small, nervous smile to flicker across his face. His tormentor saw it. She yelled, "You're smirking? You're smirking at me? You think this is funny? This isn't funny!" Someone else shouted, "Yeah, he's smirking!" and again the whole crowd started in. Burton was mortified. He made a few weak attempts to speak, but the widows were relentless, and they overwhelmed him. For minutes he stood miserably on the platform, absorbing the abuse, unable to advance or retreat. Bill Cote felt terrible for him, and wanted to go to his rescue, but could not. Finally the mayor stepped in and got the crowd to simmer down. He told a little story and made a quip that caused Burton's tormentor to smile. The mayor noticed and said, "You see, you just smirked. When people are nervous, they smirk. So can we please put this behind us now? Let's just stop."

But the widows were too angry for that, and they soon widened their attacks. They had some legitimate complaints—for instance, that the Fire Department had never gotten around to contacting some of the women about their husbands' deaths, or to clarify the associated administrative financial details. A few of those whose husbands had yet to be identified were still having a hard time accepting their demises. And what about their paychecks? If a fireman remained trapped somewhere inside the pile, wouldn't he still be on duty and earning overtime? Conversely, was it correct to assume that all those who had disappeared had stopped working at the moment of the collapse? Unexpected though these questions seemed, they were obviously practical, and the fire commissioner admitted that the department had done a poor job of handling such things.

For the most part, though, the widows simply vented their emotions. They argued as much among themselves as with the officials at the head of the room. One woman kept insisting that her husband was still alive, because she could send signals to his beeper and it would respond. Others, who had accepted the reality of death, were infuriated by the possibility that any of the firemen's remains would not be found until they reached the landfill. Not surprisingly, this turned out to be the most difficult issue of the night. The crowd demanded to know why the final sifting operation could not be moved from the Fresh Kills to the Trade Center site or the streets nearby. There were many reasons why—including dust, noise, neighborhood opposition, and, most important, the complete lack of space in Lower Manhattan—but neither Burton nor Cote was about to say that now. They promised to look into the possibility. Of course the crowd did not believe them. At one point a woman came forward with her son, a boy of about seven, and started screaming, "You tell him! You tell him!" Burton and Cote looked at her without understanding. Tell him what? She continued, "You tell him his father's going to be found at the dump!" The crowd broke into applause. The woman began to cry. "Tell him! Tell him!" Her son watched her in apparent confusion. Friends came up, put their arms around her, and led her and the boy gently away.

Burton and Cote were badly shaken. When the meeting ended, after more than three hours of emotional storms, the two of them got into Burton's Jeep and drove away through the quiet streets. At first they did not speak, except briefly to agree that the experience had been the worst of their lives. In the theater district they found a bar, and went in for a drink. The other customers there—tourists pioneering a return to the city, lovers hunched together before bed, late-night regulars of various kinds—could never have guessed the role of these nondescript men, or the utter seriousness of their talk.

The widows' meeting turned out to be a watershed in the Trade Center recovery. Burton and Cote were tough guys, accustomed to seeing life as a struggle, and they would not have been unjustified had they responded impatiently to the encounter. This was dangerous to admit out loud, but it was on many people's minds: the firemen's widows were victims of victimization

itself, and in their agony and myopia they were starting to blunder around; moreover, they clearly did not represent the thousands of others who had lost family on September 11 and were coming to terms with the events more stoically. It would have been understandable, therefore, if Burton and Cote had mentally stiff-armed the widows, privately dismissing their emotions as overblown and rededicating themselves to the efficiency of the excavation. They had it within their power to do this—and had they been officials in many other parts of the world, they probably would have followed such a hard line. It was lucky for the ultimate success of the recovery effort that this was not the way they naturally reacted.

Instead, over a couple of beers they talked for the first time since September 11 about people's emotional reactions to the attack, and they questioned why they themselves had felt so little affected by the death and destruction at the site. Burton called Cote a "cold fish." Cote pointed out that neither of them had family or close friends who had died. It also had to be admitted that the project was going well, and that for both of them it was utterly consuming professionally, offering an emotional advantage that others did not have: they simply did not have time to dwell on the tragedy. Still, each had been moved that night by the suffering of the widows, and had been troubled by the realization that, though they had tried to do the best possible job, there were people who now believed that their actions were wrong, even wicked. It made them question the doggedness of their approach, and reminded them of a simple imperative that in the crush of daily decisions they were tending to forget: that the unbuilding was more than just a problem of deconstruction, and that for the final measure of success they would have to take emotions into account. They finished their beers, drove downtown, and walked through the site.

UNIT
8

In practice the firemen had lost the fight, but the terms of the peace would have to be generous. Burton knew this now, and Giuliani did too. The mayor increased the search teams' numbers back to seventy-five per shift, though they would have to proceed on a less ambitious basis than before: it was understood that beyond being allowed to search for their dead, they would in fact have little to say. The tensions never went away, and indeed escalated toward the very end. But already on the morning after the widows' night, at the joint meeting at PS 89, one of the fire chiefs unintentionally made a show of his loss of power when his only contribution was to ask for a moment of silence for the dead of the Queens airline crash—a strangely irrelevant request that emphasized the changes under way by signaling that he had little to say about the work at hand. The widows would be heard from again—but increasingly through formal channels created for them. Mike Burton was now unchallenged as the Trade Center Czar. But he seemed to understand that to succeed he would have to keep his ambitions in check, and that America does not function as a dictatorship of rationalists.

"The Federalist: Number 10"

By James Madison (1751–1836)
Member of the Continental Congress, the Virginia House of Delegates,
the Constitutional Convention, and Fourth President of the U.S., 1809–1817

Introduction and Historical Background

As a young man, James Madison, the son of a wealthy planter, was a 1771 graduate of what is now Princeton University, served in the Continental Congress during the American Revolution, and played a dominant role at the Constitutional Convention, which met in Philadelphia in May 1787. He was responsible for the creation of several major components of the Constitution. For instance, based on his views, the Constitution provided for a separation of powers with a system of checks and balances, the creation of a strong executive branch with veto power, and a judiciary branch with power to override state laws.

While the proposed Constitution provoked a number of profound writings, the most noted is a series of essays known as *The Federalist Papers*, published in 1787–88. Written by Alexander Hamilton, James Madison, and John Jay, but all signed *Publius*, the eighty-five essays appeared first in New York newspapers and later in many other journals and books. The essays were written in defense of the Constitution during the period of debate about its ratification and as a rebuttal to those fearful of centralized power. Opponents of the Constitution charged, among other things, that the Constitution failed to protect individual rights. As added protection for individual rights, in 1789, then a member of the United States House of Representatives, James Madison sponsored the first ten amendments to the Constitution to fulfill a pledge to these opponents that he made during the fight over ratification of the Constitution. These ten amendments are known as the Bill of Rights.

Following his career as a member of Congress, Madison served as Secretary of State under President Thomas Jefferson (1801–1809), and was elected fourth president of the United States (1809–1817).

The tenth essay of *The Federalist Papers*, by Madison, provides persuasive evidence that even large, disparate organizations can achieve stability and justice if they can manage factionalism. This essay offers profound insights regarding departmental suboptimization, the all-too-common situation in which subunits of an organization neutralize, or even sabotage, the efforts of others they view as enemies. Madison looks closely at the causes of this kind of corrosive factionalism and makes specific recommendations for correcting the situation.

Points to Consider

1. What danger does Madison see in allowing a majority faction to rule?

2. According to Madison, what role do factions play in a political system (or any organization)?

3. Madison writes that the dangers of factions can be ended by eliminating the causes of factions, or by controlling the effects. In what ways is this also true for any kind of conflict?

4. How does Madison say that a large organization can prevent factions from destroying it? Will this also work in conflicts among individuals?

"The Federalist: Number 10"

The Utility of the Union as a Safeguard Against Domestic Faction and Insurrection
Daily Advertiser, *November 22, 1787*

To the people of the State of New York:
Among the numerous advantages promised by a well-constructed Union, none deserves to be more accurately developed than its tendency to break and control the violence of faction. The friend of popular governments never finds himself so much alarmed for their character and fate as when he contemplates their propensity to this dangerous vice. He will not fail, therefore, to set a due value on any plan which, without violating the principles to which he is attached, provides a proper cure for it. The instability, injustice, and confusion introduced into the public councils, have, in truth, been the mortal diseases under which popular governments have everywhere perished; as they continue to be the favorite and fruitful topics from which the adversaries to liberty derive their most specious declamations. The valuable improvements made by the American constitution on the popular models, both ancient and modern, cannot certainly be too much admired; but it would be an unwarrantable partiality, to contend that they have as effectually obviated the danger on this side, as was wished and expected. Complaints are everywhere heard from our most considerate and virtuous citizens, equally the friends of public and private faith, and of public and personal liberty, that our governments are too unstable, that the public good is disregarded in the conflicts of rival parties, and that measures are too often decided, not according to the rules of justice and the rights of the minor party, but by the superior force of an interested and overbearing majority. However anxiously we may wish that these complaints had no foundation, the evidence of known facts will not permit us to deny that they are in some degree true. It will be found, indeed, on a candid review of our situation, that some of the distresses under which we labour have been erroneously charged on the operation of our governments; but it will be found, at the same time, that other causes will not alone account for many of our heaviest misfortunes; and, particularly, for that prevailing and increasing distrust of public engagements and alarm for private rights, which are echoed from one end of the continent to the other. These must be chiefly, if not wholly, effects of the unsteadiness and injustice with which a factious spirit has tainted our public administrations.

By a faction, I understand a number of citizens, whether amounting to a majority or minority of the whole, who are united and actuated by some common impulse of passion, or of interest, adverse to the rights of other citizens, or to the permanent and aggregate interests of the community.

There are two methods of curing the mischiefs of faction: the one, by removing its causes; the other, by controlling its effects.

There are again two methods of removing the causes of faction: the one by destroying the liberty which is essential to its existence; the other, by giving to every citizen the same opinions, the same passions, and the same interests.

It could never be more truly said than of the first remedy, that it was worse than the disease. Liberty is to faction what air is to fire, an ailment without which it instantly expires. But it could not be less folly to abolish liberty, which is essential to political life, because it nourishes faction, than it would be to wish the annihilation of air, which is essential to animal life, because it imparts to fire its destructive agency.

The second expedient is as impracticable as the first would be unwise. As long as the reason of man continues fallible, and he is at liberty to exercise it, different opinions will be formed. As long as the connection subsists between his reason and his self-love, his opinions and his passions will have a reciprocal influence on each other; and the former will be objects to which the latter will attach themselves. The diversity in the faculties of men, from which the rights of property originate, is not less an insuperable obstacle to a uniformity of interests. The protection of these faculties is the first object of government. From the protection of different and unequal faculties of acquiring property, the possession of different degrees and kinds of property immediately results; and from the influence of these on the sentiments and views of the respective proprietors, ensues a division of the society into different interests and parties.

The latent causes of faction are thus sown in the nature of man; and we see them everywhere brought into different degrees of activity, according to the different circumstances of civil society. A zeal for different opinions concerning religion, concerning government, and many other points, as well of speculation as of practice; an attachment of different leaders ambitiously contending for pre-eminence and power; or to persons of other descriptions whose fortunes have been interesting to the human passions, have in turn, divided mankind into parties, inflamed them with mutual animosity, and rendered them much more disposed to vex and oppress each other than to cooperate for their common good. So strong is this propensity of mankind to fall into mutual animosities, that where no substantial occasion presents itself, the most frivolous and fanciful distinctions have been sufficient to kindle their unfriendly passions and excite their most violent conflicts. But the most common and durable source of factions has been the various and unequal distribution of property. Those who hold and those who are without property have ever formed distinct interests in society. Those who are creditors, and those who are debtors, fall under a like discrimination. A landed interest, a manufacturing interest, a mercantile interest, with many lesser interests, grow up of necessity in civilized nations, and divide them into different classes, actuated by different sentiments and views. The regulation of these various and interfering interests forms the principal task of modern legislation, and involves the spirit of party and faction in the necessary and ordinary operations of the government.

No man is allowed to be a judge in his own cause, because his interest would certainly bias his judgment, and, not improbably, corrupt his integrity. With equal, nay, with greater reason, a body of men are unfit to be both judges and parties at the same time; yet what are many of the most important acts of legislation but so many judicial determinations, not indeed concerning the rights of single persons, but concerning the rights of large bodies of citizens? And what are the different classes of legislators but advocates and parties to the causes which they determine? Is a law proposed concerning private debts? It is a question to which the creditors are parties on one side and debtors on the other. Justice ought to hold the balance between them. Yet the parties are, and must be, themselves the judges; and the most numerous party, or, in other words, the most powerful faction must be expected to prevail. Shall domestic manufactures be encouraged, and in what degree, by restrictions on foreign manufactures? are questions which would be differently decided by the landed and the manufacturing classes, and probably by neither with a sole regard to justice and the public good. The apportionment of taxes on the various descriptions of property is an act which seems to require the most exact impartiality; yet there is, perhaps, no legislative act in which greater opportunity and temptation are given to a predominant party to trample on the rules of justice. Every shilling with which they overburden the inferior number is a shilling saved to their own pockets.

It is in vain to say that enlightened statesmen will be able to adjust these clashing interests, and render them all subservient to the public good. Enlightened statesmen will not always be at the helm. Nor, in many cases, can such an adjustment be made at all without taking into view indirect and remote considerations, which will rarely prevail over the immediate interests which one party may find in disregarding the rights of another or the good of the whole.

The inference to which we are brought is, that the *causes* of faction cannot be removed, and that relief is only to be sought in the means of controlling its *effects*.

If a faction consists of less than a majority, relief is supplied by the republican principle, which enables the majority to defeat its sinister views by regular vote. It may clog the administration, it may convulse the society; but it will be unable to execute and mask its violence under the forms of the Constitution. When a majority is included in a faction, the form of popular government, on the other hand, enables it to sacrifice to its ruling passion or interest both the public good and the rights of other citizens. To secure the public good and private rights against the danger of such a faction, and at the same time to preserve the spirit and the form of popular government, is then the great object to which our inquiries are directed. Let me add that it is the great desideratum by which this form of government can be rescued from the opprobrium under which it has so long laboured, and be recommended to the esteem and adoption of mankind.

By what means is this object obtainable? Evidently by one of two only. Either the existence of the same passion or interest in a majority at the same time must be prevented, or the majority, having such co-existent passion or interest, must be rendered, by their number and local situation, unable to concert and carry into effect schemes of oppression. If the impulse and the opportunity be suffered to coincide, we well know that neither moral nor religious motives can be relied on as an adequate control. They are not found to be such on the injustice and violence of individuals, and lose their efficacy in proportion to the number combined together, that is, in proportion as their efficacy becomes needful.

From this point of view of the subject it may be concluded that a pure democracy, by which I mean a society consisting of a small number of citizens, who assemble and administer the government in person, can admit of no cure for the mischiefs of faction. A common passion or interest will, in almost every case, be felt by a majority of the whole; a communication and concert result from the form of government itself; and there is nothing to check the inducements to sacrifice the weaker party or an obnoxious individual. Hence it is that such democracies have ever been spectacles of turbulence and contention; have ever been found incompatible with personal security or the rights of property; and have in general been as short in their lives as they have been violent in their deaths. Theoretic politicians, who have patronized this species of government, have erroneously supposed that by reducing mankind to a perfect equality in their political rights, they would, at the same time, be perfectly equalized and assimilated in their possessions, their opinions, and their passions.

A republic, by which I mean a government in which the scheme of representation takes place, opens a different prospect, and promises the cure for which we are seeking. Let us examine the points in which it varies from pure democracy, and we shall comprehend both the nature of the cure and the efficacy which it must derive from the Union.

Republics versus Democracies

The two great points of difference between a democracy and a republic are: first the delegation of the government, in the latter, to a small number of citizens elected by the rest; secondly, the greater number of citizens, and greater sphere of country, over which the latter may be extended.

The effect of the first difference is, on the one hand, to refine and enlarge the public views, by passing them through the medium of a chosen body of citizens, whose wisdom may best discern the true interest of their country, and whose patriotism and love of justice will be least likely to

UNIT
8

sacrifice it to temporary or partial considerations. Under such a regulation, it may well happen that the public voice, pronounced by the representatives of the people, will be more consonant to the public good than if pronounced by the people themselves, convened for the purpose. On the other hand, the effect may be inverted. Men of factious tempers, of local prejudices, or of sinister designs, may, by intrigue, by corruption, or by other means, first obtain the suffrages, and then betray the interests, of the people. The question resulting is, whether small or extensive republics are more favourable to the election of proper guardians of the public weal; and it is clearly decided in favour of the latter by two obvious considerations:

In the first place, it is to be remarked that, however small the republic may be, the representatives must be raised to a certain number, in order to guard against the cabals of a few; and that, however large it may be, they must be limited to a certain number, in order to guard against the confusion of a multitude. Hence the number of representatives in the two cases not being in proportion to that of the two constituents, and being proportionally greater in the small republic, it follows that, if the proportion of fit characters be not less in the large than in the small republic, the former will present a greater option, and consequently a greater probability of a fit choice.

In the next place, as each representative will be chosen by a greater number of citizens in the large than in the small republic, it will be more difficult for unworthy candidates to practice with success the vicious arts by which elections are too often carried; and the suffrages of the people being more free, will be more likely to centre in men who possess the most attractive merit and the most diffusive and established characters.

It must be confessed that in this, as in most other cases, there is a mean, on both sides of which inconveniences will be found to lie. By enlarging too much the number of electors, you render the representative too little acquainted with all their local circumstances and lesser interests; as by reducing it too much, you render him unduly attached to these, and too little fit to comprehend and pursue great and national objects. The federal Constitution forms a happy combination in this respect; the great and aggregate interests being referred to the national, the local and particular to the State legislatures.

The other point of difference is, the greater number of citizens and extent of territory which may be brought within the compass of republican than of democratic government; and it is this circumstance principally which renders factious combinations less to be dreaded in the former than in the latter. The smaller the society, the fewer probably will be the distinct parties and interests composing it; the fewer the distinct parties and interests, the more frequently will a majority be found of the same party; and the smaller the number of individuals composing a majority, and the smaller the compass within which they are placed, the more easily will they concert and execute their plans of oppression. Extend the sphere, and you take in a greater variety of parties and interests; you make it less probable that a majority of the whole will have a common motive to invade the rights of other citizens; or if such a common motive exists, it will be more difficult for all who feel it to discover their own strength, and to act in unison with each other. Besides other impediments, it may be remarked that, where there is a consciousness of injust or dishonourable purposes, communication is always checked by distrust in proportion to the number whose concurrence is necessary.

Hence, it clearly appears, that the same advantage which a republic has over a democracy, in controlling the effects of faction, is enjoyed by a large over a small republic—is enjoyed by the Union over the States composing it. Does the advantage consist in the substitution of representatives whose enlightened views and virtuous sentiments render them superior to local prejudices and to schemes of injustice? It will not be denied that the representation of the Union will be most likely to possess these requisite endowments. Does it consist in the greater security afforded by a greater variety of parties, against the event of any one party being able to outnumber and oppress the rest? In an equal degree does the increased variety of parties comprised within the Union increase this security? Does it, in fine, consist in the greater obstacles opposed to the concert and accomplishment of the secret wishes of an unjust and interested majority? Here, again, the extent of the Union gives it the most palpable advantage.

The influence of factious leaders may kindle a flame within their particular States, but will be unable to spread a general conflagration through the other States. A religious sect may degenerate into a political faction in a part of the Confederacy [the United States under The Articles of Confederation]; but the variety of sects dispersed over the entire face of it must secure the national councils against any danger from that source. A rage for paper money, for an abolition of debts, for an equal division of property, or for any other improper or wicked project, will be less apt to pervade the whole body of the Union than a particular member of it; in the same proportion as such a malady is more likely to taint a particular county or district, than an entire State.

In the extent and proper structure of the Union, therefore, we behold a republican remedy for the diseases most incident to republican government. And according to the degree of pleasure and pride we feel in being republicans, ought to be our zeal in cherishing the spirit and supporting the character of Federalists.

—*Publius*

UNIT
8

"SCARF: A Brain-Based Model for Collaborating with and Influencing Others"

By David Rock

Points to Consider

1. What, according to Rock, is the driving motivation for individuals' social behavior? Why is it important to understand this overarching principle when working with groups of people?

2. What are the five domains of human social experience? In what ways do these domains relate to the driving motivation for individuals' social behavior?

3. What role does status play in creating or easing conflict among individuals? In small groups? In organizations?

4. To what extent is it possible to increase the reward from fairness and decrease the threat of unfairness in ways that help individuals, groups or organizations successfully navigate conflict?

"SCARF: A Brain-Based Model for Collaborating with and Influencing Others"

In a world of increasing interconnectedness and rapid change, there is a growing need to improve the way people work together. Understanding the true drivers of human social behavior is becoming ever more urgent in this environment.

The study of the brain, particularly within the field of social, cognitive and affective neuroscience, is starting to provide some underlying brain insights that can be applied in the real world (Lieberman, 2007). Social neuroscience explores the biological foundations of the way humans relate to each other and to themselves and covers diverse topics that have a different degree to which they can be operationalized and unambiguously tested. Topics include: theory of mind, the self, mindfulness, emotional regulation, attitudes, stereotyping, empathy, social pain, status, fairness, collaboration, connectedness, persuasion, morality, compassion, deception, trust and goal pursuit.

From this diversity, two themes are emerging from social neuroscience. Firstly, that much of our motivation driving social behavior is governed by an overarching organizing principle of minimizing threat and maximizing reward (Gordon, 2000). Secondly, that several domains of social experience draw upon the same brain networks to maximize reward and minimize threat as the brain networks used for primary survival needs (Lieberman and Eisenberger, 2008). In other words, social needs are treated in much the same way in the brain as the need for food and water.

The SCARF model summarizes these two themes within a framework that captures the common factors that can activate a reward or threat response in social situations. This model can be applied (and tested) in any situation where people collaborate in groups, including all types of workplaces, educational environments, family settings and general social events.

The SCARF model involves five domains of human social experience: Status, Certainty, Autonomy, Relatedness and Fairness.

Status is about relative importance to others. Certainty concerns being able to predict the future. Autonomy provides a sense of control over events. Relatedness is a sense of safety with others, of friend rather than foe. And fairness is a perception of fair exchanges between people.

These five domains activate either the 'primary reward' or 'primary threat' circuitry (and associated networks) of the brain. For example, a perceived threat to one's status activates similar brain networks to a threat to one's life. In the same way, a perceived increase in fairness activates the same reward circuitry as receiving a monetary reward.

The model enables people to more easily remember, recognize, and potentially modify the core social domains that drive human behavior. Labelling and understanding these drivers draws conscious awareness to otherwise nonconscious processes, which can help in two ways. Firstly, knowing the drivers that can cause a threat response enables people to design interactions to minimize threats. For example, knowing that a lack of autonomy activates a genuine threat response, a leader or educator may consciously avoid micromanaging their employees or students. Secondly, knowing about the drivers that can activate a reward response enables people to motivate others more effectively by tapping into internal rewards, thereby reducing the reliance on external rewards such as money. For example, a line manager might grant more autonomy as a reward for good performance.

Before exploring the domains of SCARF individually a brief context of the underlying science of the SCARF model, namely, the approach (reward)–avoid (threat) response and the impact of this response on mental performance, is provided.

Foundations of the SCARF Model

The approach (reward)–avoid (threat) response: a survival instinct

According to Integrative Neuroscientist Evian Gordon, the 'minimize danger and maximize reward' principle is an overarching, organizing principle of the brain (Gordon, 2000). This central organizing principle of the brain is analogous to a concept that has appeared in the literature for a long time: the approach–avoid response. This principle represents the likelihood that when a person encounters a stimulus their brain will either tag the stimulus as 'good' and engage in the stimulus (approach), or their brain will tag the stimulus as 'bad' and they will disengage from the stimulus (avoid). If a stimulus is associated with positive emotions or rewards, it will likely lead to an approach response; if it is associated with negative emotions or punishments, it will likely lead to an avoid response. The response is particularly strong when the stimulus is associated with survival. Other concepts from the scientific literature are similar to approach and avoidance and are summarized in the chart below.

The approach–avoid response is a survival mechanism designed to help people stay alive by quickly and easily remembering what is good and bad in the environment. The brain encodes one type of memory for food that tasted disgusting in the past, and a different type of memory for food that was good to eat. The amygdala, a small almond-shaped object that is part of the limbic system, plays a central role in remembering whether something should be approached or avoided. The amygdala (and its associated networks) are believed to activate proportionally to the strength of an emotional response.

UNIT
8

The limbic system can process stimuli before it reaches conscious awareness. One study showed that subliminally presented nonsense words that were similar to threatening words, were still categorized as possible threats by the amygdala (Naccache et al, 2005). Brainstem–Limbic networks process threat and reward cues within a fifth of a second, providing you with ongoing nonconscious intuition of what is meaningful to you in every situation of your daily life (Gordon et al. Journal of Integrative Neuroscience, Sept 2008). Such studies show that the approach–avoid response drives attention at a fundamental level—nonconsciously, automatically and quickly. It is a reflexive activity.

It is easy to see that the ability to recognizing [sic] primary rewards and threats, such as good versus poisonous food, would be important to survival and thus a part of the brain. Social neuroscience shows us that the brain uses similar circuitry for interacting with the social world. Lieberman and Eisenberger explore this finding in detail in a paper in this journal entitled 'The Pains and Pleasures of Social Life' (Lieberman & Eisenberger, 2008).

The effects of approaching versus avoiding

The significance of the approach–avoid response becomes clearer when one discovers the dramatic effect that these states can have on perception and problem solving, and the implications of this effect on decision-making, stress-management, collaboration and motivation.

In one study, two groups of people completed a paper maze that featured a mouse in the middle trying to reach a picture on the outside. One group had a picture of cheese on the outside, the other a predator—an owl. After completing the maze both groups were given creativity tests. The group heading towards the cheese solved significantly more creative problems than those heading to the owl (Friedman and Foster, 2001). This study, supported by several other similar studies, shows that even subtle effects of this approach–avoid response can have a big impact on cognitive performance.

Translating this effect to the social world, someone feeling threatened by a boss who is undermining their credibility is less likely to be able to solve complex problems and more likely to make mistakes. This reduced cognitive performance is driven by several factors. Firstly, when a human being senses a threat, resources available for overall executive functions in the prefrontal cortex decrease. There is a strong negative correlation between the amount of threat activation, and the resources available for the prefrontal cortex (Arnsten, 1998). The result is literally less oxygen and glucose available for the brain functions involved in working memory, which impacts linear, conscious processing. When feeling threatened by one's boss, it is harder to find smart answers because of diminished cognitive resources. Secondly, when threatened, the increased overall activation in the brain inhibits people from perceiving the more subtle signals required for solving non-linear problems, involved in the insight or 'aha!' experience (Subramaniam et al., 2007). Thirdly, with the amygdala activated, the tendency is to generalize more, which increases the likelihood of accidental connections. There is a tendency to err on the safe side, shrinking from opportunities, as they are perceived to be more dangerous. People become more likely to react defensively to stimuli. Small stressors become more likely to be perceived as large stressors (Phelps, 2006). When the boss appears threatening, perhaps they [sic] just do not smile that day, suddenly a whole meeting can appear threatening and the tendency can be to avoid taking risks.

Response	Synonyms in literature	Which traditional primary factors activate the response	What social factors/situations activate the response
Approach	Advance, attack, reward, resource, expand, solution, strength, construct, engage.	Rewards in form of money, food, water, sex, shelter, physical assets for survival.	Happy, attractive faces. Rewards in the form of increasing status, certainty, autonomy, relatedness, fairness.
Avoid	Withdraw, retreat, danger, threat, contract, problem, weakness, deconstruct.	Punishment in the form of removal of money or other resources or threats like a large hungry predator or a gun.	Fearful, unattractive, unfamiliar faces. Threats in the form of decreasing status, certainty, autonomy, relatedness, fairness.

Clearly the threat or avoid response is not an ideal state for collaborating with and influencing others. However, this response is the default situation that often occurs in teams. Due to the overly vigilant amygdala, more tuned to threats than rewards, the threat response is often just below the surface and easily triggered. Just speaking to one's supervisor, or someone of higher status is likely to activate this response. Thus it is much easier to cause aggravation (activate an avoid response) than it is to help others think rationally and creatively (the approach response). Many psychological and brain studies now support this idea, showing that the avoid response generates far more arousal in the limbic system, more quickly and with longer lasting effects than an approach response (Beaumeister, 2001). This discovery that our brain is inherently attuned to threatening stimuli helps explain many disquieting parts of life, from why the media focuses on bad news to why people are self-critical. It also points to the need to understand the social nature of the brain and proactively minimize common social threats.

On the other hand, an approach response is synonymous with the idea of engagement. Engagement is a state of being willing to do difficult things, to take risks, to think deeply about issues and develop new solutions. An approach state is also closely linked to positive emotions. Interest, happiness, joy and desire are approach emotions. This state is one of increased dopamine levels, important for interest and learning. There is a large and growing body of research which indicates that people experiencing positive emotions perceive more options when trying to solve problems (Frederickson, 2001), solve more non-linear problems that require insight (Jung-Beeman, 2007), collaborate better and generally perform better overall.

In summary, the SCARF model is an easy way to remember and act upon the social triggers that can generate both the approach and avoid responses. The goal of this model is to help minimize the easily activated threat responses, and maximize positive engaged states of mind during attempts to collaborate with and influence others.

The SCARF Model

UNIT
8

While the five domains of the SCARF model appear to be interlinked in many ways, there is also value in separating out and understanding each domain individually. Let's look now at some of the supporting research for each domain, then explore how threats and rewards might be managed in each.

Status

In researcher Michael Marmot's book *The Status Syndrome: How Social Standing Affects our Health and Longevity*, Marmot makes the case that status is the most significant determinant of human longevity and health, even when controlling for education and income. This finding is supported by Sapolski's work with primates (Sapolski, 2002). Sapolski found that in primate communities, status equals survival: higher status monkeys have lower baseline cortisol levels, live longer and are healthier.

Status is about relative importance, 'pecking order' and seniority. Humans hold a representation of status in relation to others when in conversations, and this affects mental processes in many ways (Zink, 2008). The brain thinks about status using similar circuits for processing numbers (Chaio, 2003). One's sense of status goes up when one feels 'better than' another person. In this instance the primary reward circuitry is activated, in particular the striatum, which increases dopamine levels. One study showed that an increase in status was similar in strength to a financial windfall (Izuma et al., 2008). Winning a swimming race, a card game or an argument probably feels good because of the perception of increased status and the resulting reward circuitry being activated.

The perception of a potential or real reduction in status can generate a strong threat response. Eisenberger and colleagues showed that a reduction in status resulting from being left out of an activity lit up the same regions of the brain as physical pain (Eisenberger et al., 2003). While this study explores social rejection, it is closely connected to the experience of a drop in status.

Reducing status threat

It can be surprisingly easy to accidentally threaten someone's sense of status. A status threat can occur through giving advice or instructions, or simply suggesting someone is slightly ineffective at a task. Many everyday conversations devolve into arguments driven by a status threat, a desire to not be perceived as less than another. When threatened, people may defend a position that doesn't make sense, to avoid the perceived pain of a drop in status.

In most people, the question 'can I offer you some feedback' generates a similar response to hearing fast footsteps behind you at night. Performance reviews often generate status threats, explaining why they are often ineffective at stimulating behavioral change. If leaders want to change others' behavior, more attention must be paid to reducing status threats when giving feedback. One way to do this is by allowing people to give themselves feedback on their own performance.

Increasing status reward

Organizations know all about using status as a reward and many managers feel compelled to reward employees primarily via a promotion. This may have the unfortunate side effect of promoting people to the point of their incompetence. The research suggests that status can be increased in more sustainable ways. For example, people feel a status increase when they feel they are learning and improving and when attention is paid to this improvement. This probably occurs because individuals think about themselves using the same brain networks they use for thinking about others (Mitchell, 2006). For example, when beating one's own best time at a task or sporting activity, the reward circuitry from a sense of being 'better than' is activated, but in this case, the person one is 'better than' is oneself in the past.

> *Many everyday conversations devolve into arguments driven by a status threat, a desire to not be perceived as less than another.*

Status can go up when people are given positive feedback, especially public acknowledgment. One study showed activation of the reward circuitry in children being as strong as money as when told 'that's correct' by a repetitive computer voice. (Scott, Dapretto, et al., 2008, under review). Leaders can be afraid of praising their people for fear of the request for promotion. However, given the deeply rewarding nature of status, giving positive feedback may reduce the need for constant promotions, not increase it.

Finally, status is about one's relative position in a community of importance such as a professional group or social club based on what is valued. While society, especially advertising and the media, would have people spend money in order to be 'better than others', it doesn't have to be a zero-sum game. Status can be increased without cost to others or an effect on relatedness. As well as playing against oneself, one can also change the community one focuses on, as when a low level mailroom clerk becomes the coach of a junior baseball team. Or, one can change what is important, for example deciding that the quality of one's work is more important than the quantity of one's work.

Certainty

The brain is a pattern-recognition machine that is constantly trying to predict the near future. For example, the motor network is useless without the sensory system. To pick up a cup of coffee, the sensory system, sensing the position of the fingers at each moment, interacts dynamically with the motor cortex to determine where to move your fingers next. Your fingers don't draw on fresh data each time; the brain draws on the memory of what a cup is supposed to feel like in the hand, based on expectations drawn from previous experiences. If it feels different, perhaps slippery, you immediately pay attention (Hawkins, 2004). The brain likes to know the pattern occurring moment to moment, it craves certainty, so that prediction is possible. Without prediction, the brain must use dramatically more resources, involving the more energy-intensive prefrontal cortex, to process moment-to-moment experience.

Even a small amount of uncertainty generates an 'error' response in the orbital frontal cortex (OFC). This takes attention away from one's goals, forcing attention to the error (Hedden,

Garbrielli, 2006). If someone is not telling you the whole truth, or acting incongruously, the resulting uncertainty can fire up errors in the OFC. This is like having a flashing printer icon on your desktop when paper is jammed—the flashing cannot be ignored, and until it is resolved it is difficult to focus on other things. Larger uncertainties, like not knowing your boss' [sic] expectations or if your job is secure, can be highly debilitating.

The act of creating a sense of certainty is rewarding. Examples are everywhere in daily life: music that has simple repeating patterns is rewarding because of the ability to predict the flow of information. Meeting expectations generates an increase in dopamine levels in the brain, a reward response (Schultz, 1999). Going back to a well-known place feels good because the mental maps of the environment can be easily recalled.

Reducing the threat from uncertainty

Any kind of significant change generates uncertainty. Yet uncertainty can be decreased in many simple ways. This is a big part of the job of managers, consultants and leaders. As people build business plans, strategies, or map out an organization's structure, they feel increasing levels of clarity about how an organization might better function in the future. Even though it is unlikely things ever go as planned, people feel better because certainty has increased. Breaking a complex project down into small steps does the same. Another key tool involves establishing clear expectations of what might happen in any situation, as well as expectations of desirable outcomes.

UNIT
8

Increasing the reward from certainty

Some examples of how to increase certainty include making implicit concepts more explicit, such as agreeing verbally how long a meeting will run, or stating clear objectives at the start of any discussion. In learning situations, the old adage is 'tell people what you are going to tell them, tell them, then tell them what you told them', all of which increases certainty.

The perception of certainty can be increased even during deeply uncertain times. For example, when going through an organizational restructure, providing a specific date when people will know more information about a change may be enough to increase a sense of certainty. Much of the field of change management is devoted to increasing a sense of certainty where little certainty exists.

Autonomy

Autonomy is the perception of exerting control over one's environment; a sensation of having choices. Mieka (1985) showed that the degree of control organisms can exert over a stress factor determines whether or not the stressor alters the organism's functioning. Inescapable or uncontrollable stress can be highly destructive, whereas the same stress interpreted as escapable is significantly less destructive (Donny et al., 2006). The difference in some rodent studies was life and death (Dworkin et al., 1995).

An increase in the perception of autonomy feels rewarding. Several studies in the retirement industry find strong correlations between a sense of control and health outcomes (Rodin, 1986). People leave corporate life, often for far less income, because they desire greater autonomy.

A reduction in autonomy, for example when being micromanaged, can generate a strong threat response. When one senses a lack of control, the experience is of a lack of agency, or an inability to influence outcomes.

Reducing autonomy threat

Working in a team necessitates a reduction in autonomy. In healthy cultures, this potential threat tends to be counteracted with an increase in status, certainty and relatedness. With an autonomy threat just below the surface, it can be helpful to pay attention to this driver. The statement 'Here's two options that could work, which would you prefer?' will tend to elicit a better response than 'Here's what you have to do now'.

Increasing rewards from autonomy

Providing significant autonomy in an organization can be difficult. Yet even a subtle perception of autonomy can help, for example by having self-directed learning portals, where employees get to design their learning curriculum, and self-driven human resource systems.

Allowing people to set up their own desks, organize their workflow, even manage their working hours, can all be beneficial if done within agreed parameters. Sound policy establishes the boundaries within which individuals can exercise their creativity and autonomy. Sound policy should enable individual point-of-need decision-making without consultation with, or intervention by, leaders. In this regard, sound policy hardwires autonomy into the processes of an organization.

Relatedness

Relatedness involves deciding whether others are 'in' or 'out' of a social group. Whether someone is friend, or foe. Relatedness is a driver of behavior in many types of teams, from sports teams to organizational silos: people naturally like to form 'tribes' where they experience a sense of belonging. The concept of being inside or outside the group is probably a by-product of living in small communities for millions of years, where strangers were likely to be trouble and should be avoided.

> *In the absence of safe social interactions the body generates a threat response...*

The decision that someone is friend or foe happens quickly and impacts brain functioning (Carter & Pelphrey, 2008). For example, information from people perceived as 'like us' is processed using similar circuits for thinking one's own thoughts. When someone is perceived as a foe, different circuits are used (Mitchell, 2006). Also, when treating someone as a competitor, the capacity to empathise drops significantly (Singer et al., 2006).

Neuroscientist John Cacioppo talks about the need for safe human contact being a primary driver, like the need for food (Cacioppo, 2008). In the absence of safe social interactions the body generates a threat response, also known as feeling lonely. However, meeting someone unknown tends to generate an automatic threat response. This explains why one feels better at a party knowing three people rather than one. Alcohol helps to reduce this automatic social threat response, enabling strangers to communicate more easily, hence its use as a social lubricant the world over. In the absence of alcohol, getting from foe to friend can be helped by an oxytocin response, an experience of connecting with the other person. Oxytocin is a hormone produced naturally in the brain, and higher levels of this substance are associated with greater affiliative behavior (Domes et al., 2007). Studies have shown far greater collaboration when people are given a shot of oxytocin, through a nasal spray (Kosfield, 2005). A handshake, swapping names and discussing something in common, be it just the weather, may increase feeling of closeness by causing the release of oxytocin (Zak et al., 2005). The concept of relatedness is closely linked to trust. One trusts those who appear to be in your group, who one has connected with, generating approach emotions. And when someone does something untrustworthy, the usual response is to withdraw. The greater that people trust one another, the stronger the collaboration and the more information that is shared.

Reducing threats from lack of relatedness

Increasing globalization highlights the importance of managing relatedness threats. Collaboration between people from different cultures, who are unlikely to meet in person, can be especially hard work. The automatic foe response does not get diminished by social time together. This response can be mitigated by dedicating social time in other forms. For example, using video to have an informal meeting, or ensuring that people forming teams share personal aspects of themselves via stories, photos or even social-networking sites. In any workplace it appears to pay off well to encourage social connections. A Gallup report showed that organizations that encourage 'water cooler' conversations increased productivity (Gallup, November 2008).

Increasing the rewards from relatedness

Positive social connections are a primary need; however, the automatic response to new social connections involves a threat. To increase the reward response from relatedness, the key is to find ways to increase safe connections between people. Some examples include setting up clearly defined buddy systems, mentoring or coaching programs, or small action learning groups. Small groups appear to be safer than large groups. The Gallup organizations research on workplace engagement showed that the statement 'I have a best friend at work' was central to engagement in their 'Q12' assessment (Gallup organization). Perhaps even having one trusting relationship can have a significant impact on relatedness.

UNIT

8

Fairness

Studies by Golnaz Tabibnia and Matthew Lieberman at UCLA showed that 50 cents generated more of a reward in the brain than $10.00, when it was 50 cents out of a dollar, and the $10 was out of $50 (Tabibnia & Lieberman, 2007). This study and a number of others illustrate that fair exchanges are intrinsically rewarding, independent of other factors. The need for fairness may be part of the explanation as to why people experience internal rewards for doing volunteer work to improve their community; it is a sense of decreasing the unfairness in the world.

Unfair exchanges generate a strong threat response (Tabibnia & Lieberman, 2007). This sometimes includes activation of the insular, a part of the brain involved in intense emotions such as disgust. Unfair situations may drive people to die to right perceived injustices, such as in political struggles. People who perceive others as unfair don't feel empathy for their pain, and in some instances, will feel rewarded when unfair others are punished (Singer et al., 2006).

Reducing the threat from unfairness and increasing the reward from fairness

A threat response from a sense of unfairness can be triggered easily. The following statements are examples of what employees might say in reaction to a threat to fairness:

- 'He has a different set of rules for Mike and Sally than for the rest of us.'

- 'Management tells us that we need to lose headcount, but our sales are carrying the other division and they don't have to cut anyone.'

- 'They do all this talk about 'values' but it's business as usual at the top.'

The threat from perceived unfairness can be decreased by increasing transparency, and increasing the level of communication and involvement about business issues. For example, organizations that allow employees to know details about financial processes may have an advantage here.

Establishing clear expectations in all situations—from a one-hour meeting to a five-year contract—can also help ensure fair exchanges occur. A sense of unfairness can result from a lack of clear ground rules, expectations or objectives. Allowing teams to identify their own rules can also help. In an educational context, a classroom that creates the rules of what is accepted behavior is likely to experience less conflict. Examples of the success of self-directed teams in manufacturing abound (Semler, 1993). Much of what these self-driven teams do is ensure fairness in grass-roots decisions, such as how workloads are shared and who can do which tasks.

The issue of pay discrepancies in large organizations is a challenging one, and many employees are deeply unhappy to see another person working similar hours earning 100 times their salary. Interestingly, it is the perception of fairness that is key, so even a slight reduction in senior executive salaries during a difficult time may go a long way to reducing a sense of unfairness.

The Wider Implications of the SCARF Model

Managing oneself

The SCARF model helps individuals both minimize threats and maximize rewards inherent in everyday experience. For minimizing threats, knowing about the domains of SCARF helps one to label and reappraise experiences that might otherwise reduce performance. Labelling (Lieberman et al., 2007) and reappraisal (Ochsner & Gross, 2005) are cognitive tools that have been verified in brain studies to be effective techniques for reducing the threat response. These techniques have been shown to be more effective at reducing the threat response than the act of trying to suppress an emotion (Goldin et al., 2007). Knowing about the elements of SCARF helps one understand issues such as why you can't think clearly when someone has attacked your status, instead of just trying to push the feeling aside.

Knowing the domains of SCARF also allows an individual to design ways to motivate themselves more effectively. An example might be focusing attention on increasing one's sense of autonomy during a time of uncertainty, such as focusing on the thrill of doing whatever you like when suddenly out of work.

Education and training

Successful educators, trainers and facilitators intuitively use the SCARF model. They know that people learn best when they are interested in something. Interest is an approach state. Teaching children who feel threatened, disconnected, socially rejected or treated unfairly is an uphill battle. For example, educators can create a nurturing learning environment by pointing out specifically how people are improving, which increases a sense of status. This is particularly important when learning anything new, which can create a threat response. Educators can also create certainty by presenting clear outlines of what is being learned, and provide a perception of some autonomy by introducing choice into the classroom. The key here is for educators, trainers and coaches to value the approach state as the necessary state for learning, and to put effort and attention into maintaining this toward state.

Coaching

Personal and executive coaching can increase all five SCARF domains. Status can be increased through regular positive feedback, attention to incremental improvements, and the achievement of large goals. Certainty can be increased by identifying central goals, and subsequently reducing the uncertainty inherent in maintaining multiple focuses. Breaking down large goals into smaller steps increases certainty about how a goal can be reached. Finding ways to take action when challenges appear insurmountable can increase autonomy. Relatedness can be increased through the relationship with the coach. Fairness can be reduced through seeing situations from other perspectives. The SCARF model helps explain why coaching can be so effective at facilitating change, and points to ways of improving its delivery.

The SCARF model points to more creative ways of motivating that may not just be cheaper, but also stronger and more sustainable.

Leadership development

The SCARF model provides a robust scientific framework for building self-awareness and awareness of others amongst leaders. Many new leaders may negatively impact the domains of SCARF by accident. They may know how things should be done, and subsequently provide too much direction and not enough positive feedback, thereby affecting people's status. They often don't provide clear expectations, impacting certainty. They micromanage, impacting autonomy. They want to maintain a professional distance, impacting relatedness. And, they may impact fairness by not being transparent enough. When the opposite happens and you meet someone who makes you feel better about yourself, provides clear expectations, lets you make decisions, trusts you and is fair, you will probably work harder for them as you feel intrinsically rewarded by the relationship itself. Spending time around a leader like this activates an approach response and opens up people's thinking, allowing others to see information they wouldn't see in an avoid state.

UNIT 8

Organizational systems

SCARF has many implications for how organizations are structured, including reward systems, communications systems, decision processes, information flow and remuneration structures. In the space available in this article we will explore just one of these—reward systems. Techniques for motivating and rewarding staff are largely based on the carrot and stick principle, with the carrot mostly involving money or a promotion. The SCARF model points to more creative ways of motivating that may not just be cheaper, but also stronger and more sustainable. For example, success could be rewarded by increasing people's autonomy by allowing them to have greater flexibility in their work hours. Or, rewards could be provided via increasing the opportunity for learning new skills, which can increase a sense of status. Or, people could be rewarded through increasing relatedness through allowing more time to network with peers during work hours.

Summary

... [T]he five domains of SCARF reflect core brain networks of greatest significance when it comes to collaborating with and influencing others. Understanding these drivers can help individuals and organizations to function more effectively, reducing conflicts that occur so easily amongst people, and increasing the amount of time people spend in the approach state, a concept synonymous with good performance.

Understanding the domains in the SCARF model and finding personalized strategies to effectively use these brain insights, can help people become better leaders, managers, facilitators, coaches, teachers and even parents.

In the early 2000s, the philosopher Theodore Zeldin said, 'When will we make the same breakthroughs in the way we treat each other as we have made in technology?' These findings about the deeply social nature of the brain, and the deep relevance of the domains of SCARF in everyday life, may provide some small steps in the right direction.

Suggestions for future research

An abbreviated list of potential research issues includes the following questions:

Which of the domains of SCARF generate the strongest threats or rewards?

Which domains have the longest-term impact?

What are the links between the domains?

How can studies be designed to identify individual domains?

What are the best techniques for minimizing threat and maximizing reward in each of the domains?

Do people vary in the importance of the 5 domains, and if so are there patterns across men and women, age groups or cultures?

Is there value in assessing these domains in individuals or culturally in organizations?

What are the organizational implications of this model for how systems are set up?

Testing what aspects of the model are most effective to which individual leaders?

Acknowledgments

This article was written with the help of several reviewers, including Rachel Sheppard, Dr. Evian Gordon Joanne Capritti and Karen Jayne Eyre. I am grateful to the dozens of interviews with many of the scientists referenced for their input as well, with special thanks to Dr. Jeffrey M. Schwartz, Dr. Matthew Lieberman, Dr. Mark Jung-Beeman and Dr. Yi-Yuan Tang for their informal mentoring over recent years on these topics.

First published in the NeuroLeadership Journal
ISSUE ONE 2008

www.NeuroLeadership.org
SCARF: a brain-based model for collaborating with and influencing others
David Rock
CEO, Results Coaching Systems international, GPO Box 395, Sydney, NSW Australia 2001
Faculty, CIMBA
Co-founder, NeuroLeadership Institute
Editor, NeuroLeadership Journal
davidrock@workplacecoaching.com

References

Arnsten, A. F. T. (1998). The Biology of Being Frazzled. *Science, 280*, 1711–1712.

Baumeister, R. F., Bratslavsky, E., & Vohs, K.D. (2001). Bad Is Stronger Than Good. *Review of General Psychology, 5*(4), 323–370.

Baumeister, R. F. & Leary, M. R. (1995). The need to belong: Desire for interpersonal attachments as a fundamental human motivation. *Psychological Bulletin, 117*, 497–529.

Cacioppo, J. T., & Patrick, B. (2008). *Loneliness: Human nature and the need for social connection.* New York: W. W. Norton and Company.

Carter, E. J. & Pelphrey, K. A., (2008). Friend or foe? Brain systems involved in the perception of dynamic signals of menacing and friendly social approaches. *Journal Social Neuroscience, Volume 3, Issue 2 June 2008*, pages 151–163.

Chiao, J. Y., Bordeaux, A. R., Ambady, N. (2003). Mental representations of social status. *Cognition, 93*, 49–57.

Domes, G., Heinrichs, M., Glèscher J., B*f*chel, C., Braus, D., Herpertz, S. (2007). Oxytocin Attenuates Amygdala Responses to Emotional Faces Regardless of Valence. *Biological Psychiatry, 62*(10), 1187–1190.

Donny, E. C., Bigelow, G. E., & Walsh S. L. (2006). Comparing the physiological and subjective effects of self-administered vs yoked cocaine in humans. *Psychopharmacology, 186*(4), 544–52.

Dworkin, S I., Mirkis, S., Smith J. E. (1995). Response-dependent versus response-independent presentation of cocaine: differences in the lethal effects of the drug. *Psychopharmacology, 117*(3), 262–266.

Eisenberger, N. I., Lieberman, M. D., & Williams, K. D. (2003). Does rejection hurt? An fMRi study of social exclusion. *Science, 302*, 290–292.

Fredrickson, B. L. (2001). The Role of Positive Emotions in Positive Psychology: The Broaden-and-Build Theory of Positive Emotions. *American Psychologist, 56*, 218–226.

Friedman R. and Foster J. (2001). The effects of promotion and prevention cues on creativity. *Journal of Personality and Social Psychology, 81*, 1001–1013.

Gallup, 13 November 2008. Newsflash: Workplace Socializing Is Productive Gallup Organization. Employee Engagement. Retrieved November 20, 2009 *http://www.gallup.com/ consulting/52/employee-engagement.aspx*

Gilbert, D. (2006). *Stumbling upon happiness*. Knopf Publishing Group.

Goldin, P. R., McRae, K., Ramel, W., & Gross, J. J. (2007). The Neural Bases of Emotion Regulation: Reappraisal and Suppression of Negative Emotion. *Biological Psychiatry, 63*, 577–586.

Gordon, E. (2000). *Integrative Neuroscience: Bringing together biological, psychological and clinical models of the human brain*. Singapore: Harwood Academic Publishers.

Gordon, E. et al. (2008). *An Integrative Neuroscience platform: application to profiles of negativity and positivity bias.* Journal of Integrative Neuroscience.

Hawkins, J. & Blakeslee, S. (2004). *On Intelligence*. Times Books.

Hedden, T., & Gabrieli, J. D. E. (2006). The ebb and flow of attention in the human brain. *Nature Neuroscience, 9*, 863–865.

Izuma, K., Saito, D., Sadato, N. (2008). Processing of Social and Monetary Rewards in the Human Striatum. *Neuron, 58*(2), 284–294.

Kosfeld, M., Heinrichs, M., Zak, P. J., Fischbacher, U., & Fehr, E. (2005). Oxytocin increases trust in humans. *Nature, 435*, 673–676.

Lieberman, Eisenberger, Crockett, Tom, Pfeifer, & Way (2007). Putting Feelings into Words: Affect Labelling Disrupts Amygdala Activity in Response to Affective Stimuli. *Psychological Science, 18*(5), 421–428.

Lieberman & Eisenberg (2008) The pains and pleasures of social life. *NeuroLeadership Journal*, Edition 1.

Lieberman & Eisenberger (2004). Why it hurts to be left out: The neurocognitive overlap between physical and social pain. *Trends in Cognitive Sciences, 8*, 294–300.

Jung Beeman, M., (2007). Presented at the first NeuroLeadership Summit, Asolo, Italy.

Lieberman, M. D. (2007). Social Cognitive Neuroscience: A Review of Core Processes. *Annual Review of Psychology, 58*, 259–289.

Mason, M. F., Norton, M. I., Van Horn, J. D., Wegner, D. M., Grafton, S. T., & Macrae, C. N. (2007). Wandering minds: the default network and stimulus-independent thought. *Science, 315*, 393–395.

Mather, M., Mitchell, K. J., Raye, C. L., Novak, D. L., Greene, E.J., & Johnson, M. K. (2006). Emotional Arousal Can Impair Feature Binding in Working Memory. *Journal of Cognitive Neuroscience, 18*, 614–625.

Mineka, S. & Hendersen, R. W. (1985). Controllability and predictability in acquired motivation. *Annual Review of Psychology, 36*, 495–529.

Mitchell, J. P., Macrae, C. N., & Banaji, M. R. (2006). Dissociable Medial Prefrontal Contributions to Judgments of Similar and Dissimilar Others. *Neuron, 50*, 655–663.

Naccache, L., Gaillard, R.L., Adam, C., Hasboun, D., Clemenceau, S., Baulac, M., Dehaene, S., & Cohen, L. (2005). A direct intracranial record of emotions evoked by subliminal words. *Proceedings of the National Academy of Science, 102*, 7713–7717.

Ochsner, K. N., & Lieberman, M. D. (2001). The emergence of social cognitive neuroscience. *American Psychologist, 56*, 717–734.

Ochsner K. N., & Gross, J. J. (2005). The cognitive control of emotion. *Trends in Cognitive Sciences, 9*(5), 242–249.

Phelps, E. A. (2006). Emotion and cognition: Insights from Studies of the Human Amygdala. *Annual Review of Psychology, 57*, 27–53.

Rodin, J. (1986). Aging and health: effects of the sense of control. *Science, 233*, 1271–1276.

Sapolski, R.M. (2002). *A Primate's Memoir: A Neuroscientist's Unconventional Life Among the Baboons.* Scribner.

Schultz, W. (1999). The Reward Signal of Midbrain Dopamine Neurons. News in *Physiological Sciences, 14*(6), 249–255.

Scott, Dapretto, et al., under review (2008). *Social Cognitive and Affective Neuroscience Journal.*

Semler, R. (1993). *Maverick: The Success Story behind the World's Most Unusual Workplace.* Warner Books.

Seymour, B., Singer, T., & Dolan, R. (2007). The neurobiology of punishment. *Nature Reviews Neuroscience, 8*, 300–311.

Singer, T., Seymour, B., O'Doherty, J.P., Stephan, K.E., Dolan, R.J., Frith, C.D., (2006). Empathic neural responses are modulated by the perceived fairness of others. *Nature, 439*, 466–469.

Subramaniam, K., Kounios, J., Bowden, E.M., Parrish, T.B., & Jung-Beeman, M. (in press 2008). Positive mood and anxiety modulate anterior cingulate activity and cognitive preparation for insight. *Journal of Cognitive Neuroscience.*

Tabibnia, G., & Lieberman M. D. (2007). Fairness and Cooperation Are Rewarding: Evidence from Social Cognitive Neuroscience. *Annals of the New York Academy of Sciences, 1118*, 90–101.

Zak, P. J., Kurzban, R., Matzner, W. T. (2005). Oxytocin is associated with human trustworthiness, *Hormones and Behavior, 48*(5), 522–527.

Zink, C. F., Tong, Y., Chen, Q., Bassett, D. S., Stein, J. L., & Meyer-Lindenberg A. (2008). Know Your Place: Neural Processing of Social Hierarchy in Humans. *Neuron, 58*, 273–283.

Rock, D. (2008). SCARF: A brain-based model for collaborating with and influencing others. *NeuroLeadership Journal* 1(1), 44–52. Used by permission of the NeuroLeadership Institute.

Difficult Conversations:
How to Discuss What Matters Most

By Douglas Stone, Bruce Patton, and Sheila Heen

Points to Consider

1. What are the three difficult conversations in which individuals engage? How can an individual use the understanding of these conversations to more effectively deal with conflict?

2. In what ways can individuals utilize the Truth Assumption to navigate difficult conversations? To what extent is understanding the Truth Assumption and the ways it has an impact on difficult conversations important when working with small groups?

3. Why is keeping balance important for individuals, small groups and organizations?

4. What is a learning conversation? To what degree can learning conversations help individuals, small groups and organizations be more productive?

Difficult Conversations: How to Discuss What Matters Most

Introduction

Asking for a raise. Ending a relationship. Giving a critical performance review. Saying no to someone in need. Confronting disrespectful or harmful behavior. Disagreeing with the majority of the group. Apologizing.

At work, at home, and across the backyard fence, difficult conversations are attempted or avoided every day.

A Difficult Conversation Is Anything You Find It Hard to Talk About

Sexuality, race, gender, politics, and religion come quickly to mind as difficult topics to discuss, and for many of us they are. But discomfort and awkwardness are not limited to topics on the editorial page. Anytime we feel vulnerable or our self-esteem is implicated, when the issues at stake are important and the outcome uncertain, when we care deeply about what is being discussed or about the people with whom we are discussing it, there is potential for us to experience the conversation as difficult.

We all have conversations that we dread and find unpleasant, that we avoid or face up to like bad medicine:

> One of the senior engineers at your company, an old friend, has become a liability. Management has picked you to fire him.

> You overheard your mother-in-law telling a neighbor that your sons are spoiled and undisciplined. As you prepare to spend the holidays at her house, you're not sure the two of you can get through the week without a confrontation.

> The project you are working on took twice as long as you told the client it would. You can't afford not to bill for the extra time, but you dread informing the client.

UNIT
8

You want to tell your father how much you love him, but fear that the intimacy might make both of you feel awkward.

You recently learned that several black colleagues on the police force refer to you as an Uncle Tom. You are infuriated, but you aren't sure whether talking about it would accomplish anything.

And, of course, there's the stuff of everyday life, conversations that feel more ordinary but cause anxiety nonetheless: returning merchandise without a receipt, asking your secretary to do some photocopying, telling the painters not to smoke in the house. These are the interactions we put off when we can and stumble through when we must. The ones we practice over and over in our head, trying to figure out in advance what to say and wondering afterward what we should have said.

What makes these situations so hard to face? It's our fear of the consequences—whether we raise the issue or try to avoid it.

The Dilemma: Avoid or Confront, It Seems There Is No Good Path

We all know this dilemma. We go round and round on the same questions—Should I raise this? Or should I keep it to myself?

Perhaps the neighbors' dog keeps you up at night. "Should I talk to them?" you wonder. At first, you decide not to: "Maybe the barking will stop. Maybe I'll get used to it." But then the dog barks again, and you resolve that tomorrow you are going to talk to the neighbors once and for all.

Now you lie awake for a different reason. The thought of getting into a fight with the neighbors about their dog makes you nervous. You want the neighbors to like you; maybe you're overreacting. Eventually, you come back to thinking it's better to say nothing and this calms your nerves. But just as you drop off to sleep, that darn dog howls again, and your cycle of indecision starts anew.

There doesn't seem to be any choice that will allow you to sleep.

Why is it so difficult to decide whether to avoid or to confront? Because at some level we know the truth: If we try to avoid the problem, we'll feel taken advantage of, our feelings will fester, we'll wonder why we don't stick up for ourselves, and we'll rob the other person of the opportunity to improve things. But if we confront the problem, things might get even worse. We may be rejected or attacked; we might hurt the other person in ways we didn't intend; and the relationship might suffer.

There Is No Such Thing as a Diplomatic Hand Grenade

Desperate for a way out of the dilemma, we wonder if it is possible to be so tactful, so overwhelmingly pleasant that everything ends up fine.

Tact is good, but it's not the answer to difficult conversations. Tact won't make conversations with your father more intimate or take away your clients' anger over the increased bill. Nor is there a simple diplomatic way to fire your friend, to let your mother-in-law know that she drives you crazy, or to confront your colleagues' hurtful prejudices.

Delivering a difficult message is like throwing a hand grenade. Coated with sugar, thrown hard or soft, a hand grenade is still going to do damage. Try as you may, there's no way to throw a hand grenade with tact or to outrun the consequences. And keeping it to yourself is no better. Choosing not to deliver a difficult message is like hanging on to a hand grenade once you've pulled the pin.

So we feel stuck. We need advice that is more powerful than "Be diplomatic" or "Try to stay positive." The problems run deeper than that; so must the answers.

This Book Can Help

There is hope. Working at the Harvard Negotiation Project with thousands of people on all kinds of difficult conversations, we have found a way to make these conversations less stressful and more productive. A way to deal creatively with tough problems while treating people with decency and integrity. An approach that is helpful to *your* peace of mind, whether or not others join in.

We are going to help you get out of the hand grenade business altogether, by getting you out of the business of delivering (and receiving) messages. We will show you how to turn the damaging battle of warring messages into the more constructive approach we call a *learning conversation*.

UNIT
8

The Rewards Are Worth the Effort

Of course, changing how you deal with difficult conversations takes work. Like changing your golf swing, adapting to drive on the other side of the road, or learning a new language, the change can feel awkward at first. And it can feel threatening: breaking out of your comfort zone is rarely easy and is never risk-free. It requires you to look hard at yourself, and sometimes to change and grow. But better the ache of muscles growing from an unaccustomed workout than the sting of wounds from an unnecessary fight.

And the potential rewards are rich. If you follow the steps presented in this book, you will find difficult conversations becoming easier and causing less anxiety. You will be more effective and happier with the results. And as your anxiety goes down and your satisfaction goes up, you will find that you are choosing to engage more often in conversations that you should have been having all along.

In fact, the people we've worked with, who have learned new approaches to dealing with their most challenging conversations, report less anxiety and greater effectiveness in *all* of their conversations. They find they are less afraid of what others might say. They have a heightened sense of freedom of action in tough situations, more self-confidence, and a stronger sense of integrity and self-respect. They also learn that, more often than not, dealing constructively with tough topics and awkward situations strengthens a relationship. And that's an opportunity too good to pass up.

Skeptical? A Few Thoughts

If you're skeptical, that's understandable. You may have been struggling with these issues for weeks, months, or years. The problems are complex, and the people involved are not easy to deal with. How can reading a book make a difference?

There *are* limits to how much you can learn about human interaction from a book. We don't know the specifics of your situation, what is at stake for you, or where your particular weaknesses and strengths lie. But we have discovered that regardless of context, the things that make difficult conversations difficult, and the errors in thinking and acting that compound those difficulties, are the same. We all share the same fears and fall into the same few traps. No matter what you are facing, or whom, there is something in this book that can help.

It is true that some situations are unlikely to improve regardless of how skilled you become. The people involved may be so emotionally troubled, the stakes so high, or the conflict so intense that a book—or even a professional intervention—is unlikely to help. However, for every case that is truly hopeless, there are a thousand that appear hopeless but are not. People often come to us saying, "I want some advice, but I have to warn you, this situation is beyond fixing." And they are wrong. Together we are able to find some avenue of change that ends up having *significant* positive impact on the conversation.

Of course, you may not be ready or able to engage or reengage fully in a difficult situation or relationship. You may be grieving, licking your wounds, or just needing time away. You may be lost in anger or confused about what you want. But even if you are not yet ready to take on an actual conversation, this book can help you sort through your feelings and assist you as you find your way to a healthier place.

We Need to Look in New Places

What can we suggest that you haven't already thought of? Probably quite a bit. Because the question isn't whether you've been looking hard enough for the "answer" to difficult conversations, it's whether you've been looking in the right places. At heart, the problem isn't in your actions, it's in your thinking. So long as you focus only on what to do differently in difficult conversations you will fail to break new ground.

This book offers plenty of advice on how to conduct a difficult conversation. But first and more important, it will help you understand better what you're up against and why it makes sense to shift from a "message delivery stance" to a "learning stance." Only then will you be able to understand and implement the steps of a learning conversation.

Difficult Conversations Are a Normal Part of Life

No matter how good you get, difficult conversations will always challenge you. The authors know this from experiences in our own lives. We know what it feels like to be deeply afraid of hurting someone or of getting hurt. We know what it means to be consumed by guilt for how our actions have affected others, or for how we have let ourselves down. We know that even with the best of intentions, human relationships can corrode or become tangled, and, if we are honest, we also know that we don't always have the best of intentions. We know just how fragile are the heart and the soul.

So it is best to keep our goals realistic. Eliminating fear and anxiety is an unrealistic goal. *Reducing* fear and anxiety and learning how to manage that which remains are more obtainable. Achieving perfect results with no risk will not happen. Getting *better* results in the face of tolerable odds might.

And that, for most of us, is good enough. For if we are fragile, we are also remarkably resilient.

Sort Out the Three Conversations

Jack is about to have a difficult conversation.

He explains: "Late one afternoon I got a call from Michael, a good friend and occasional client. 'I'm in a tight spot,' he told me. 'I need a financial brochure laid out and printed by tomorrow afternoon.' He said his regular designer was out and that he was under a lot of pressure.

"'I was in the middle of another project, but Michael was a friend, so I dropped everything and worked late into the night on his brochure.

"Early the next morning, Michael reviewed the mock-up and gave the go-ahead to have it printed. I had the copies on his desk by noon. I was exhausted, but I was glad I'd been able to help him out.

"Then I got back to my office and discovered this voice-mail message from Michael:

> Well, you really screwed this one up! Look, Jack, I know you were under time pressure on this, but….[sigh]. The earnings chart isn't presented clearly enough, and it's slightly off. It's just a disaster. This is an important client. I assume you'll fix it right away. Give me a call as soon as you get in.

"Well, you can imagine how I felt about *that* message. The chart was off, but microscopically. I called Michael right away."

Their conversation went like this:

> Jack: Hi, Michael, I got your message—
>
> Michael: Yeah, look Jack, this thing has to be done over.
>
> Jack: Well, wait a second, I agree it's not perfect, but the chart is clearly labeled. Nobody's going to misunderstand—
>
> Michael: C'mon, Jack. You know as well as I do that we can't send this thing out like this.
>
> Jack: Well, I think that—
>
> Michael: There's really nothing to argue about here. Look, we all screw up. Just fix it and let's move on.
>
> Jack: Why didn't you say something about this when you looked at it this morning?
>
> Michael: I'm not the one who's supposed to be proofreading. Jack, I'm under tremendous pressure to get this done and to get it done right. Either you're on the team or you're not. I need a yes or a no. Are you going to redo it?
>
> Jack: [pause] Alright, alright. I'll do it.

This exchange has all the hallmarks of a difficult conversation going off the rails. Months later, Jack still feels lousy about this conversation and his relationship with Michael remains strained. He wonders what he could have done differently, and what he should do about it now.

But before we get to that, let's look at what Jack and Michael's conversation can teach us about how difficult conversations work.

Decoding the Structure of Difficult Conversations

Surprisingly, despite what appear to be infinite variations, all difficult conversations share a common structure. When you're caught up in the details and anxiety of a particular difficult conversation, this structure is hard to see. But understanding that structure is essential to improving how you handle your most challenging conversations.

There's More Here Than Meets the Ear

In the conversation between Jack and Michael recounted above, the words reveal only the surface of what is really going on. To make the structure of a difficult conversation visible, we need to understand not only what is said, but also what is *not* said. We need to understand what the people involved are thinking and feeling, but not saying to each other. In a difficult conversation this is usually where the real action is.

Look at what Jack is thinking and feeling, but not saying, as this conversation proceeds:

What Jack Thought and Felt But Didn't Say	What Jack and Michael Actually Said
How could he leave a message like that?! After I drop everything, break a dinner date with my wife, and stay up all night, that's the thanks I get?	
	Jack: Hi, Michael, I got your message—
	Michael: Yeah, look Jack, this thing has to be done over.
A total overreaction. Not even a CPA would be able to tell that graph is off. At the same time, I'm angry with myself for making such a stupid mistake.	
	Jack: Well, wait a second, I agree it's not perfect, but the chart is clearly labeled. Nobody's going to misunderstand—
	Michael: C'mon, Jack, you know as well as I do that we can't send this thing out like this.
Michael tries to intimidate colleagues into getting his way. But he shouldn't treat *me* that way. I am a friend! I want to stand up for myself, but I don't' want to get into a big fight about this. I can't afford to lose Michael as a client or as a friend. I feel stuck.	
	Jack: Well, I think that—
	Michael: There's really nothing to argue about here. Look, we all screw up. Just fix it and let's move on.
Screw up?! This isn't *my* fault. *You* approved it, remember?	**Jack:** Why didn't you say something about this when you looked at it this morning?
	Michael: I'm not the one who's supposed to be proofreading. I'm under tremendous pressure to get this done and to get it done *right*. Either you're on the team or you're not. I need a yes or a no. Are you going to redo it?
Is that how you see me? As a proofreader?	
I'm sick of this whole thing. I'm going to be bigger than whatever pettiness is driving him. The best way out is for me just to be generous and redo it.	
	Jack: [pause] Alright, alright. I'll do it.

Meanwhile, there's plenty that Michael is thinking and feeling but not saying. Michael is wondering whether he should have hired Jack in the first place. He hasn't been all that happy with Jack's work in the past, but he decided to go out on a limb with his partners to give his friend another chance. Michael is now frustrated with Jack and confused about whether hiring Jack was a good decision—personally or professionally.

The first insight, then, is a simple one: there's an awful lot going on between Jack and Michael that is not being spoken.

That's typical. In fact, the gap between what you're really thinking and what you're saying is part of what makes a conversation difficult. You're distracted by all that's going on inside. You're uncertain about what's okay to share, and what's better left unsaid. And you know that just saying what you're thinking would probably not make the conversation any easier.

Each Difficult Conversation Is Really Three Conversations

In studying hundreds of conversations of every kind we have discovered that there is an underlying structure to what's going on, and understanding this structure, in itself, is a powerful first step in improving how we deal with these conversations. It turns out that no matter what the subject, our thoughts and feelings fall into the same three categories, or "conversations." And in each of these conversations we make predictable errors that distort our thoughts and feelings, and get us into trouble.

UNIT 8

Everything problematic that Michael and Jack say, think, and feel falls into one of these three "conversations." And everything in your difficult conversations does too.

1. **The "What Happened?" Conversation**. Most difficult conversations involve disagreement about what has happened or what should happen. Who said what and who did what? Who's right, who meant what, or who's to blame? Jack and Michael tussle over these issues, both out loud and internally. *Does* the chart need to be redone? Is Michael trying to intimidate Jack? Who *should* have caught the error?

2. **The Feelings Conversation**. Every difficult conversation also asks and answers questions about feelings. Are my feelings valid? Appropriate? Should I acknowledge or deny them, put them on the table or check them at the door? What do I do about the other person's feelings? What if they are angry or hurt? Jack's and Michael's thoughts are littered with feelings. For example, "This is the thanks I get?!" signals hurt or anger, and "I'm under tremendous pressure" reveals anxiety. These feelings are not addressed directly in the conversation, but they leak in anyway.

3. **The Identity Conversation**. This is the conversation we each have with ourselves about what this situation means to us. We conduct an internal debate over whether this means we are competent or incompetent, a good person or bad, worthy of love or unlovable. What impact might it have on our self-image and self-esteem, our future and our well-being? Our answers to these questions determine in large part whether we feel "balanced" during the conversation, or whether we feel off-center and anxious. In the conversation between Jack and Michael, Jack is struggling with the sense that he has been incompetent, which makes him feel less balanced. And Michael is wondering whether he acted foolishly in hiring Jack.

Every difficult conversation involves grappling with these Three Conversations, so engaging successfully requires learning to operate effectively in each of these three realms. Managing all three simultaneously may seem hard, but it's easier than facing the consequences of engaging in difficult conversations blindly.

What We Can't Change, and What We Can

No matter how skilled we become, there are certain challenges in each of the Three Conversations that we can't change. We will still run into situations where untangling "what happened" is more complicated than we initially suspect. We will each have information the other person is unaware of, and raising each other's awareness is not easy. And we will still face emotionally charged situations that feel threatening because they put important aspects of our identity at risk.

What we *can* change is the way we respond to each of these challenges. Typically, instead of exploring what information the other person might have that we don't, we assume we know all we need to know to understand and explain things. Instead of working to manage our feelings constructively, we either try to hide them or let loose in ways that we later regret. Instead of exploring the identity issues that may be deeply at stake for us (or them), we proceed with the conversation as if it says nothing about us—and never come to grips with what is at the heart of our anxiety.

By understanding these errors and the havoc they wreak, we can begin to craft better approaches. Let's explore each conversation in more depth.

The "What Happened?" Conversation: What's the Story Here?

The "What Happened?" Conversation is where we spend much of our time in difficult conversations as we struggle with our different stories about who's right, who meant what, and who's to blame. On each of these three fronts—truth, intentions, and blame—we make a common but crippling assumption. Straightening out each of these assumptions is essential to improving our ability to handle difficult conversations well.

The Truth Assumption

As we argue vociferously for our view, we often fail to question one critical assumption upon which our whole stance in the conversation is built: I am right, you are wrong. This simple assumption causes endless grief.

What am I right about? I am right that you drive too fast. I am right that you are unable to mentor younger colleagues. I am right that your comments at Thanksgiving were inappropriate. I am right that the patient should have received more medication after such a painful operation. I am right that the contractor overcharged me. I am right that I deserve a raise. I am right that the brochure is fine as it is. The number of things I am right about would fill a book.

There's only one hitch: I am not right.

How could this be so? It seems impossible. Surely I must be right *sometimes*!

Well, no. The point is this: difficult conversations are almost never about getting the facts right. They are about conflicting perceptions, interpretations, and values. They are not about what a contract states, they are about what a contract *means*. They are not about which child-rearing book is most popular, they are about which child-rearing book should *we* follow.

They are not about what is true, they are about what is important.

Let's come back to Jack and Michael. There is no dispute about whether the graph is accurate or not. They both agree it is not. The dispute is over whether the error is worth worrying about and if so, how to handle it. These are not questions of right and wrong, but questions of interpretation and judgment. Interpretations and judgments are important to explore. In contrast, the quest to determine who is right and who is wrong is a dead end.

In the "What Happened?" Conversation, moving away from the truth assumption frees us to shift our purpose from proving we are right to understanding the perceptions, interpretations, and values of both sides. It allows us to move away from delivering messages and toward asking questions, exploring how each person is making sense of the world. And to offer our views as perceptions, interpretations, and values—not as "the truth."

The Intention Invention

The second argument in the "What Happened?" Conversation is over intentions—yours and mine. Did you yell at me to hurt my feelings or merely to emphasize your point? Did you throw my cigarettes out because you're trying to control my behavior or because you want to help me live up to my commitment to quit? What I think about your intentions will affect how I think about you and, ultimately, how our conversation goes.

The error we make in the realm of intentions is simple but profound: we assume we know the intentions of others when we don't. Worse still, when we are unsure about someone's intentions, we too often decide they are bad.

UNIT
8

The truth is, intentions are invisible. We assume them from other people's behavior. In other words, we make them up, we invent them. But our invented stories about other people's intentions are accurate much less often than we think. Why? Because people's intentions, like so much else in difficult conversations, are complex. Sometimes people act with mixed intentions. Sometimes they act with no intention or at least none related to us. And sometimes they act on good intentions that nonetheless hurt us.

Because our views of others' intentions (and their views of ours) are so important in difficult conversations, leaping to unfounded assumptions can be a disaster.

The Blame Frame

The third error we make in the "What Happened?" Conversation has to do with blame. Most difficult conversations focus significant attention on who's to blame for the mess we're in. When the company loses its biggest client, for example, we know that there will shortly ensue a ruthless game of blame roulette. We don't care where the ball lands, as long as it doesn't land on us. Personal relationships are no different. Your relationship with your stepmother is strained? She's to blame. She should stop bugging you about your messy room and the kids you hang out with.

In the conflict between Jack and Michael, Jack believes the problem is Michael's fault: the time to declare your hypersensitivity to formatting is before the brochure goes to print, not after. And, of course, Michael believes the problem is Jack's fault: Jack did the layout, mistakes are his responsibility.

But talking about fault is similar to talking about truth—it produces disagreement, denial, and little learning. It evokes fears of punishment and insists on an either/or answer. Nobody wants to be blamed, especially unfairly, so our energy goes into defending ourselves.

Parents of small children know this well. When the twins act up in the back seat of the car, we know that trying to affix blame will always yield to an outcry: "But she hit me first!" or "I hit her because she called me a baby." Each child denies blame not just to avoid losing her dessert, but also from a sense of justice. Neither feels like the problem is solely her fault, because it isn't.

From the front seat looking back, it is easy to see how each child has contributed to the fight. It's much more difficult to see how we've contributed to the problem in which we ourselves are involved. But in situations that give rise to difficult conversations, it is almost always true that what happened is the result of things *both* people did—or failed to do. And punishment is rarely relevant or appropriate. When competent, sensible people do something stupid, the smartest move is to try to figure out, first, what kept them from seeing it coming and, second, how to prevent the problem from happening again.

Talking about blame distracts us from exploring why things went wrong and how we might correct them going forward. Focusing instead on understanding the contribution system allows us to learn about the real causes of the problem, and to work on correcting them. The distinction between blame and contribution may seem subtle. But it is a distinction worth working to understand, because it will make a significant difference in your ability to handle difficult conversations.

The Feelings Conversation: What Should We Do with Our Emotions?

Difficult conversations are not just about what happened; they also involve emotion. The question is not whether strong feelings will arise, but how to handle them when they do. Should you tell your boss how you *really* feel about this management style, or about the colleague who stole your idea? Should you share with your sister how hurt you feel that she stayed friends with your ex? And what should you do with the anger you are likely to experience if you decide to talk with that vendor about his sexist remarks?

In the presence of strong feelings, many of us work hard to stay rational. Getting too deep into feelings is messy, clouds good judgment, and in some contexts—for example, at work—can seem just plain inappropriate. Bringing up feelings can also be scary or uncomfortable, and can make us feel vulnerable. After all, what if the other person dismisses our feelings or responds without real understanding? Or takes our feelings to heart in a way that wounds them or irrevocably damages the relationship? And once we've gotten our feelings off our chest, it's their turn. Are we up to hearing all about their anger and pain?

This line of reasoning suggests that we stay out of the Feelings Conversation altogether—that Jack is better off not sharing his feelings of anger and hurt, or Michael his sense of disappointment. Better to stick to questions about the brochure. Better to stick to "business."

Or is it?

An Opera Without Music

The problem with this reasoning is that it fails to take account of one simple fact: difficult conversations do not just *involve* feelings, they are at their very core *about* feelings. Feelings are not some noisy byproduct of engaging in difficult talk, they are an integral part of the conflict. Engaging in a difficult conversation without talking about feelings is like staging an opera without music. You'll get the plot but miss the point. In the conversation between Jack and Michael, for example, Jack never explicitly says that he feels mistreated or underappreciated, yet months later Jack can still summon his anger and resentment toward Michael.

Consider some of your own difficult conversations. What feelings are involved? Hurt or anger? Disappointment, shame, confusion? Do you feel treated unfairly or without respect? For some of us, even saying "I love you" or "I'm proud of you" can feel risky.

In the short term, engaging in a difficult conversation without talking about feelings may save you time and reduce your anxiety. It may also seem like a way to avoid certain serious risks—to you, to others, and to the relationship. But the question remains: if feelings are an issue, what have you accomplished if you don't address them?

Understanding feelings, talking about feelings, managing feelings—these are among the greatest challenges of being human. There is nothing that will make dealing with feelings easy and risk-free. Most of us, however, can do a better job in the Feelings Conversation than we are now. It may not seem like it, but talking about feelings is a skill that can be learned.

Of course, it doesn't always make sense to discuss feelings. As the saying goes, sometimes you should let sleeping dogs lie. Unfortunately, a lack of skill in discussing feelings may cause you to avoid not only sleeping dogs, but all dogs—even those that won't let *you* sleep.

The Identity Conversation: What Does This Say About Me?

Of the Three Conversations, the Identity Conversation may be the most subtle and the most challenging. But it offers us significant leverage in managing our anxiety and improving our skills in the other two conversations.

The Identity Conversation looks inward: it's all about who we are and how we see ourselves. How does what happened affect my self-esteem, my self-image, my sense of who I am in my world? What impact will it have on my future? What self-doubts do I harbor? In short: before, during, and after the difficult conversation, the Identity Conversation is about what I am saying to myself *about me.*

UNIT
8

You might think, "I'm just trying to ask my boss for a raise. Why does my sense of who I am in the world matter here?" Or Jack might be thinking, "This is about the brochure, not about me." In fact, anytime a conversation feels difficult, it is in part precisely because it is about You, with a capital Y. Something beyond the apparent substance of the conversation is at stake for you.

It may be something simple. What does it say about you when you talk to your neighbor about their dog? It may be that growing up in a small town gave you a strong sense of self-image as a friendly person and good neighbor, so you are uncomfortable with the possibility that your neighbors might see you as aggressive or as a trouble maker.

Asking for a raise? What if you get turned down? In fact, what if your boss gives you good reasons for turning you down? What will that do to your self-image as a competent and respected employee? Ostensibly the subject is money, but what's really making you sweat is your self-image is on the line.

Even when you are the one delivering the bad news, the Identity Conversation is in play. Imagine, for example, that you have to turn down an attractive new project proposal from Creative. The prospect of telling the people involved makes you anxious, even if you aren't responsible for the decision. In part, it's because you fear how the conversation will make you feel about yourself: "I'm not the kind of person who lets people down and crushes enthusiasm. I'm the person people respect for *finding* a way to do it, not for shutting the door." Your self-image as a person who helps others get things done butts up against the reality that you are going to be saying no. If you're no longer the hero, will people see you as the villain?

Keeping Your Balance

As you begin to sense the implications of the conversation for your self-image, you may begin to lose your balance. The eager young head of Creative who reminds you so much of yourself at that age looks disbelieving and betrayed. You suddenly feel confused; your anxiety skyrockets. You wonder whether it really makes sense to drop the idea so early in the process. Before you know it, you stammer out something about the possibility that the rejection will be reconsidered, even though you have absolutely no reason to believe that's likely.

In its mildest form, losing your balance may cause us to lose confidence in ourselves, to lose concentration, or to forget what we were going to say. In more extreme cases, it can feel earth-shattering. We may feel paralyzed, overcome by panic, stricken with an urge to flee, or even have trouble breathing.

Just knowing that the Identity Conversation is a component of difficult conversations can help. And, as in the other two conversations you can do much better than mere awareness. While losing your balance sometimes is inevitable, the Identity Conversation need not cause as much anxiety as it does. Like dealing with feelings, grappling with the Identity Conversation gets easier with the development of certain skills. Indeed, once you find your footing in the identity conversation, you can turn what is often a source of anxiety into a source of strength.

Moving Toward a Learning Conversation

Despite what we sometimes pretend, our initial purpose for having a difficult conversation is often to prove a point, to give them a piece of our mind, or to get them to do or be what we want. In other words, to deliver a message.

Once you understand the challenges inherent in the Three Conversations and the mistakes we make in each, you are likely to find that your purpose for having a particular conversation begins to shift. You come to appreciate the complexity of the perceptions and intentions involved the reality of joint contribution to the problem, the central role feelings have to play, and what the issues mean to each person's self-esteem and identity. And you find that a message delivery stance no longer makes sense. In fact, you may find that you no longer have a message to deliver, but rather some information to share and some questions to ask.

Instead of wanting to persuade and get your way, you want to understand what has happened from the other person's point of view, share and understand feelings, and work together to figure out a way to manage the problem going forward. In so doing, you make it more likely that the other person will be open to being persuaded, and that you will learn something that significantly changes the way you understand the problem.

Changing our stance means inviting the other person into the conversation with us, to help us figure things out. If we're going to achieve our purposes we have lots we need to learn from them and lots they need to learn from us. We need to have a learning conversation.

The differences between a typical battle of messages and a learning conversation are summarized in the chart on the following pages.

	A Battle of Messages	A Learning Conversation
The "What Happened?" Conversation Challenge: The situation is more complex than either person can see.	**Assumption:** I know all I need to know to understand what happened. **Goal:** Persuade them I'm right.	**Assumption:** Each of us is bringing different information and perceptions to the table; there are likely to be important things that each of us doesn't know. **Goal:** Explore each other's stories: how we understand the situation and why.
	Assumption: I know what they intended. **Goal:** Let them know what they did was wrong.	**Assumption:** I know what I intended, and the impact their actions had on me. I don't and can't know what's' in their head. **Goal:** Share the impact on me, and find out what they were thinking. Also find out what impact I'm having on them.
	Assumption: It's all their fault. (Or it's all my fault.) **Goal:** Get them to admit blame and take responsibility for making amends.	**Assumption:** We have probably *both* contributed to this mess. **Goal:** Understand the contribution system: how our actions interact to produce this result.
The Feelings Conversation Challenge: The situation is emotionally charged.	**Assumption:** Feelings are irrelevant and wouldn't be helpful to share. (Or, my feelings are their fault and they need to hear about them.) **Goal:** Avoid taking about feelings. (Or, let 'em have it!)	**Assumption:** Feelings are the heart of the situation. Feelings are usually complex. I may have to dig a bit to understand my feelings. **Goal:** Address feelings (mine and theirs) without judgments or attributions. Acknowledge feelings before problem-solving.
The Identity Conversation Challenge: The situation threatens our identity.	**Assumption:** I'm competent or incompetent, good or bad, loveable or unlovable. There is no in-between. **Goal:** Protect my all-or-nothing self-Image.	**Assumption:** There may be a lot at stake psychologically for both of us. Each of us is complex, neither of us is perfect. **Goal:** Understand the identity issues on the line for each of us. Build a more complex self-image to maintain by balance better.

UNIT

8

This book will help you turn difficult conversations into learning conversations by helping you handle each of the Three Conversations more productively and improving your ability to handle all three at once.

The next five chapters explore in depth the mistakes people commonly make in each of the Three Conversations. This will help you shift to a learning stance when it's your difficult conversation and you aren't feeling very open. Chapters 2, 3, and 4 investigate the three assumptions in the "What Happened?" Conversation. Chapter 5 shifts to the Feelings Conversation and Chapter 6 takes up the Identity Conversation. These chapters will help you sort out your thoughts and feelings. This preparation is essential before you step into any difficult conversation.

In the final six chapters we turn to the conversation itself, beginning with when to raise an issue and when to let go, and if you're going to raise it, what you can hope to achieve and what you can't—what purpose makes sense. Then we turn to the mechanics of how to talk productively about the issues that matter to you: finding the best ways to begin, inquiring and listening to learn, expressing yourself with power and clarity, and solving problems jointly, including how to get the conversation back on track when the going gets rough. Finally, we return to how Jack might have a follow up conversation with Michael to illustrate how this all might look in practice.

FILM STUDIES

All the President's Men (1976)

Based on the book by Bob Woodward and Carl Bernstein
Screenplay by William Goldman
Directed by Alan J. Pakula

UNIT
8

Character Guide

Bob Woodward.	Robert Redford
Carl Bernstein	Dustin Hoffman
Ben Bradlee	Jason Robards
Harry Rosenfeld	Jack Warden
Deep Throat	Hal Holbrooke
Howard Simons	Martin Balsam
Bookkeeper	Jane Alexander
Hugh Sloan Jr.	Stephen Collins
Mrs. Debbie Sloan	Meredith Baxter
D.A. Dardis	Ned Beatty
Sally Aiken	Penny Fuller
Foreign Editor	John McMartin
Donald Segretti.	Robert Walden
Dardis' Secretary	Polly Holliday

Introduction

All The President's Men is based on the true story of Richard M. Nixon, his political operatives and the Watergate Scandal during the 1972 presidential election that resulted in his unprecedented resignation from office on August 8, 1974. *Washington Post* reporters Bob Woodward and Carl Bernstein were individually working on stories about the break-in at the Democratic Party headquarters which was located in the Watergate complex. Initially, the story was deemed unimportant, so Woodward and Bernstein, both relatively new *Post* reporters, were told by their editor to work together on the story. The unimportant story became one of the most significant in late-twentieth-century United States political history. Conflicts between Woodward and Bernstein; the two reporters and their editors; Woodward and his anonymous source, "Deep Throat"; and White House officials and the *Washington Post* dramatize the persistence and resilience it took for Woodward and Bernstein to follow the money trail related to the Watergate break-in all the way to the Nixon White House.

Dialogue Questions

1. What factors caused conflict between Bob Woodward and Carl Bernstein? How were they able to successfully navigate through the conflict while maintaining their individual personalities and styles?

2. When the Watergate story became more important than *Post* editors initially thought and the editorial team wanted to give the assignment to a more experienced reporter, how did Woodward and Bernstein handle the difficult conversation? What was the result?

3. In what ways did the editorial team at the *Washington Post* successfully handle the conflict between Woodward and Bernstein and the *Post* and White House officials? How did the editorial team handle the conflict over the Watergate story between themselves?

4. How and why did Woodward and Bernstein ultimately overcome the various levels of conflict to break the Watergate story?

Freedom Writers (2007)

Based on the books by Erin Gruwell and the Freedom Writers
Screenplay by Richard LaGravenese
Directed by Richard LaGravenese

Character Guide

Erin Gruwell	Hillary Swank
Scott Casey	Patrick Dempsey
Steve Gruwell	Scott Glenn
Margaret Campbell	Imelda Staunton
Eva Benitez	April L. Hernandez
Andre Bryant	Mario
Gloria Munez	Kristin Herrera
Sindy	Jaclyn Ngan
Alejandro Santiago	Sergio Montalvo
Marcus	Jacob Finn
Jamal Hill	Deance Wyatt
Brandy Ross	Vanetta Smith
Tito	Gabriel Chavarria
Ben Daniels	Hunter Parrish
Miguel	Antonio Garcia
Victoria	Giovannie Samuels
Brian Gelford	John Benjamin Hickey
Dr. Carl Cohn	Robert Wisdom
Miep Gies	Pat Carroll
Paco	Will Morales
Eva's Father	Ricardo Molina
Eva's Mother	Angela Alvarado
Sindy's Boyfriend	Anh Tuan Nguyen
Sindy's Friend	Katie Soo
Brandy's Mother	Liisa Cohen
Brandy's Father	Brian Bennett
Horace Hall	Himself
Principal Banning	Tim Halligan

Introduction

Freedom Writers is based on the story of Erin Gruwell, a young English teacher, and her at-risk students at Woodrow Wilson Classical High School in Long Beach, California. Gruwell's students, known as the "unteachables," are wary of Gruwell. She is initially surprised to be teaching students who do not appear to be interested in learning. Determined to reach her students and overcome the conflicts in their lives and her own, Gruwell uses a racist drawing she intercepted from a student in one of her classes to teach them about the Holocaust. She invites Holocaust survivors as guest speakers to her classes. The following semester, the students read *The Diary of Anne Frank* and decide to raise the funds to bring Miep Gies, the woman who had sheltered Frank's family during the Holocaust, to Woodrow Wilson High School. Their discussion with Gies has a profound effect on the students' lives. Over the course of several years the students keep diaries about their thoughts and learning experiences. Writing and opening up to one another and the possibilities education has to offer helps them cope with conflicts amongst themselves and their friends, their families and the school system.

Dialogue Questions

1. Many of the characters show intense resentment and bitterness toward individuals and groups with whom they must interact every day. What creates these emotions? Conflicts easily and often result. What do you think might reduce the resentment and bitterness?

2. How and why was there conflict between Erin Gruwell and her department chair? How did they overcome their differences?

3. How and why did the "unteachables" become a team of "Freedom Writers" despite their earlier conflicts?

4. How did Gruwell and the school district for which she worked solve the conflict between them over her not being able to teach the "Freedom Writers" during their junior and senior years of high school?

EXERCISE

The Iliad:
Create an Explanatory Skit

Introduction

Your Instructor will divide the class into small groups. Each group should think about what other conflicts are similar to the type of conflict that existed between Achilles and Agamemnon. The examples you think of could be generic, everyday conflicts in families, businesses, or organizations; they could be historical, real conflicts; they could be fictional from literature or the movies.

Instructions

Using your imagination and creativity, your small group will develop a short dramatization of one of these examples. Your skit should demonstrate the root cause of the conflict and a possible solution to address the issues involved.

Plan on creating a skit of approximately ten minutes. Your instructor will indicate how much time your small group will have to develop the skit and the order in which the small groups will make their presentations.

UNIT

8

SUGGESTED READING

This selected bibliography is intended to supplement the excerpts and articles of authors included in this Unit. There is an emphasis on books that are pivotal and recent publications. Numerous journals regularly offer articles related to these topics, but are not included in this selected bibliography. For further research, you may wish to include searches of the following journals: (alphabetically) *Academy of Management Executive, Academy of Management Journal, Harvard Business Review, Journal of Leadership Studies, Leadership in Action, Leadership Quarterly,* and *Leader To Leader.*

This list is organized by author's last name using Modern Language Association-style citations.

Flaxington, Beverly. *Understanding Other People: The Five Secrets to Human Behavior.* Carlsbad, CA: Motivational Press, 2010.
Flaxington discusses the importance of understanding our own filters and the ways we connect with people. Listening to what people are really saying when they speak with you and learning strategies for dealing with difficult people in your life are keys to successfully leading individuals, teams and organizations through conflict.

Gerzon, Mark. *Leading Through Conflict: How Successful Leaders Transform Differences Into Opportunities.* Cambridge: Harvard Business Review Press, 2006.
Gerzon describes ways individuals, groups and organizations can turn conflict into opportunities for growth and success. An important factor in developing conflict-literate individuals through such strategies as teaching diversity, providing spaces for open dialogues and creating opportunities for civic engagement.

Goleman, Daniel. *Social Intelligence: The New Science of Human Relations.* New York: Bantam, 2007.
Goleman coined the phrase "Emotional Intelligence" or EQ in his 1995 book, *Emotional Intelligence.* He explains how brain science is showing we are wired to connect and communicate with others. Goleman contends the way we react to others and the ways they react to us have biological implications. Understanding more effectively how individuals are empathic, cooperative and altruistic helps people increase their social intelligence and, as a result, be better able to successfully navigate conflict.

Johnson, Clive, and Jackie Keddy. *Managing Conflict at Work: Understanding and Resolving Conflict for Productive Working Relationships.* London: Korgan Page, 2010.
Johnson and Keddy explore the nature of conflict in the workplace, the true cost of not managing conflict, and benefits of leading individuals and work groups through their conflicts.

Simmons, Steve, and John C. Simmons. *Measuring Emotional Intelligence: The Groundbreaking Guide to Applying the Principles of Emotional Intelligence.* Arlington: Summit Publishing, 1997.
This book describes all the facets of emotional intelligence, demonstrates how to measure them, and shows how to use this knowledge.

UNIT 9

REALIZING CHANGE

INTRODUCTION

Pressures for change often exist in an organization, and the leader must not fall into the trap of denying, resisting, or avoiding these pressures. One of the most important tasks of the leader is to encourage the ongoing rejuvenation of the organization he or she leads. This can be accomplished only if the leader understands the relationship between continuity and change. Leaders need to have a sense not only of their relationship with the organization's present and future, but with its past as well. This is particularly important in times of change.

Rosabeth Moss Kanter observes in *The Change Masters* that it is during times of change that people find stability and security in the culture and long-term direction of the organization. "It requires," she says, "that they feel integrated with the whole rather than identified with the particular territory of the moment, since that is changeable." Leaders can reduce the trauma of change by demonstrating that the change is not discontinuous, but rather that it is a natural outgrowth of the organization's inheritance from the past.

The point is that the traditions of an organization have great value. They are the storehouse of the organization's collective wisdom. These traditions grow out of the past and are adapted to the present without any break in continuity. A leader who does not recognize their importance can easily destroy, but not easily rebuild, them. Any effort to change an organization, therefore, should be implemented carefully so that the changes are in agreement with its history and its tradition.

Understanding an organization's history may be as important as understanding what its future will be. To add "part-historian" to the job description of a leader may seem overly demanding, but in times of rapid change, a sense of organizational continuity based on historical perspective may be as necessary as an awareness of where the organization is headed. Henry Ford told a *Chicago Tribune* reporter in 1916 that "history is more or less bunk." History is not bunk, as an older but wiser Henry Ford evidently discovered later in his career. He ordered that the following words be emblazoned over the entrance to the Ford Museum in Dearborn, Michigan: "The farther you look back, the farther you can see ahead." These are wise words for leaders in the midst of unprecedented change.

But making change in an organization, as this Unit reveals, requires more than merely an interest in the past. It requires a leader to become a "change agent," a person who leads or guides the process of change in an organization. To assume this role effectively means understanding the process of change and the reasons that change is difficult to initiate and implement.

Far too often, leaders discover that change—within themselves and within their organizations—is unplanned; reactive instead of proactive. An effective leader plans and manages change. This Unit includes readings that deal with the forces which create the need for change, the ability to recognize that the need for change has come, and ways to overcome resistance to change.

In the Classic Case "Allegory of the Cave," Plato explains the problems a leader faces when he or she tries to change the organization. Plato was a reformer. He sought to change Athens according to his standards of excellence and vision for the future just as any contemporary leader wants to change an organization. This is what makes Plato's most famous dialogue, *The Republic*, superb reading for leaders as well as philosophers. It is history's first consultant's report to the leaders of an organization!

Two women leaders are the focus of the Leadership Profile component of Unit Nine: Elizabeth Cady Stanton and Susan B. Anthony. Stanton and Anthony understood the difficulties in overcoming resistance to the change they sought, yet worked tirelessly until their deaths to overcome the resistance. Unfortunately, in their lifetimes they did not see the change they sought to implement—the nation-wide right to vote for American women—but their efforts made suffrage possible for millions of women.

The readings for this Unit include "Letter from Birmingham Jail," by Martin Luther King, Jr. Like Stanton and Anthony, King sought dramatic and significant change. In the Letter, he deals with his critics and detractors among the Southern Christian Leadership Conference. He writes about the need for change and how change can happen. He argues logically and forcefully that change should, and will, take place. He powerfully invokes tradition, the past, and shared values to convince critics and opponents that the time is right for change and that the change is the right change to make. Stanton, Anthony, and King all understood that the changes they advocated were consistent with the history of the United States and its philosophical foundations; they were eloquent and persistent in articulating their positions in order to break down resistance. A reading from Peter Senge on the practice of innovation underscores the importance of values, mission, and vision in advocating for change.

While leaders in national reform movements often seek wide-ranging change, Charles Darwin argued in *Origin of Species* that change, to be effective, need not always be dramatic or wide-ranging. According to Darwin, minor adjustments to adapt to the environment could make the difference between survival and extinction. An additional reading focuses on approaches individuals can take to initiate even small changes that can make a powerful difference. Jeff Brown, Mark Fenske, and Liz Neporent explore strategies using brain science that can help us realize change in our personal and professional lives.

Viewing *Inherit the Wind* and *Lincoln* provides an opportunity to consider the challenges and opportunities involved in leading change for others. Finally, the Exercise "Spacejam" will require you to significantly change your thinking in order to solve an increasingly difficult problem of dwindling "resources."

UNIT
9

Learning Objectives

- Recognize the importance of initiating and leading change as a leadership skill

- Identify positive and negative effects of change within an organization, group, community, or institution

- Describe the leader's role to realize change within his/her organization

- Evaluate personal readiness to respond to change, and/or adapt to change as a leader

- Discuss ways to overcome resistance to change

- Appreciate the contributions made by the Classic Case and Leadership Profile in this Unit toward understanding the challenge of initiating and realizing change in an organization, group, community, or institution

CLASSIC CASE

"The Allegory of the Cave"

By Plato (428–347 B.C.E.)
Greek Philosopher

Introduction and Historical Background

Plato, along with Socrates, his teacher, and Aristotle, his student, laid the philosophical foundations of Western culture. In fact, Alfred North Whitehead once described the history of philosophy as merely "a series of footnotes to Plato."

Plato wrote in dialogue form. Philosophical ideas were advanced, discussed, and criticized in the context of conversations or debates. By the time of his death in 347 B.C.E., Plato had completed thirty-five dialogues. Today, after 2400 years, these dialogues are still incomparable studies of the basic issues that confront human beings.

In addition to his writings, Plato, in 387 B.C.E., established the Academy in Athens as an institute for the systematic pursuit of philosophical and scientific research. It was a true educational innovation in that tedious lecturing was mercifully not allowed. Instead, students, encouraged by their teachers, discussed, argued, and analyzed problems.

The Republic, Plato's most noted dialogue, was a response to the catastrophic leadership failure that led to the defeat of Athens in the Peloponnesian War. American essayist Ralph Waldo Emerson, referring to *The Republic*, once declared, "Burn all the libraries, for their value is in this one book." It is superb reading for leaders as well as philosophers.

As Plato looked back on the history of Athens, reflecting on its greatness during the Golden Age under Pericles, he could not help but wonder how such a great organization could be brought to its knees. Plato was a reformer. He sought to change Athens, just as any contemporary leader wants to "change" an organization. Thus, in *The Republic*, Plato argues against the leadership style of Periclean Athens and offers his ideas for a new kind of leadership for his organization, a style of leadership that he believed would return Athens to her greatness. It is history's first consultant's report to the leaders of an organization that is being badly beaten by the competition!

You were introduced to Plato's *Republic* in Unit One where he addressed the important question of identifying and selecting capable leaders. The following excerpt from *The Republic* addresses the important issue of change within an organization. You will have an opportunity to discover just how relevant Plato's thoughts are to creating innovation and change in any organization, ancient or modern.

As you read this Classic Case and enter the "underground den," consider the difficulties you face in making change and, perhaps more important, think about the challenge of being a leader.

Points to Consider

1. To what extent, according to Plato, is it easy to change people? To what extent does he believe it is easier to change ideas?

2. Why does Plato consider it easier to maintain the status quo, rather than to implement change?

3. What role does insight play in defining and influencing change within an organization?

4. What does Plato consider to be the highest duty of the legislator or leader of the state?

"The Allegory of the Cave"

(Excerpt from *The Republic*, Book 7)
Translated by C.D.C. Reeve

Socrates' Narration Continues:

Socrates: Next, then, compare the effect of education and that of the lack of it on our nature to an experience like this. Imagine human beings living in an underground, cavelike dwelling, with an entrance a long way up that is open to the light and as wide as the cave itself. They have been there since childhood, with their necks and legs fettered, so that they are fixed in the same place, able to see only in front of them, because their fetter prevents them from turning their heads around. Light is provided by a fire burning far above and behind them. Between the prisoners and the fire, there is an elevated road stretching. Imagine that along this road a low wall has been built—like the screen in front of people that is provided by puppeteers, and above which they show their puppets.

Glaucon: I am imagining it.

Socrates: Also imagine, then, that there are people alongside the wall carrying multifarious artifacts that project above it—statues of people and other animals, made of stone, wood, and every material. And as you would expect, some of the carriers are talking and some are silent.

Glaucon: It is a strange image you are describing, and strange prisoners.

UNIT
9

Socrates: They are like us. I mean, in the first place, do you think these prisoners have ever seen anything of themselves and one another besides the shadows that the fire casts on the wall of the cave in front of them?

Glaucon: How could they, if they have to keep their heads motionless throughout life?

Socrates: What about the things carried along the wall? Isn't the same true where they are concerned?

Glaucon: Of course.

Socrates: And if they could engage in discussion with one another, don't you think they would assume that the words they used applied to the things they see passing in front of them?

Glaucon: They would have to.

Socrates: What if their prison also had an echo from the wall facing them? When one of the carriers passing along the wall spoke, do you think they would believe that anything other than the shadow passing in front of them was speaking?

Glaucon: I do not, by Zeus.

Socrates: All in all, then, what the prisoners would take for true reality is nothing other than the shadows of those artifacts.

Glaucon: That's entirely inevitable.

Socrates: Consider, then, what being released from their bonds and cured of their foolishness would naturally be like, if something like this should happen to them. When one was freed and suddenly compelled to stand up, turn his neck around, walk, and look up toward the light, he would be pained by doing all these things and be unable to see the things whose shadows he had seen before, because of the flashing lights. What do you think he would say if we told him that what he had seen before was silly nonsense, but that now—because he is a bit closer to what is, and is turned toward things that are more—he sees more correctly? And in particular, if we pointed to each of the things passing by and compelled him to answer what each of them is, don't you think he would be puzzled and believe that the things he saw earlier were more truly real than the ones he was being shown?

Glaucon: Much more so.

Socrates: And if he were compelled to look at the light itself, wouldn't his eyes be pained and wouldn't he turn around and flee toward the things he is able to see, and believe that they are really clearer than the ones he is being shown?

Glaucon: He would.

Socrates: And if someone dragged him by force away from there, along the rough, steep, upward path, and did not let him go until he had dragged him into the light of the sun, wouldn't he be pained and angry at being treated that way? And when he came into the light, wouldn't he have his eyes filled with sunlight and be unable to see a single one of the things now said to be truly real?

Glaucon: No, he would not be able to—at least not right away.

Socrates: He would need time to get adjusted, I suppose, if he is going to see the things in the world above. At first, he would see shadows most easily, then images of men and other things in water, then the things themselves. From these, it would be easier for him to go on to look at the things in the sky and the sky itself at night, gazing at the light of the stars and the moon, than during the day, gazing at the sun and the light of the sun.

Glaucon: Of course.

Socrates: Finally, I suppose, he would be able to see the sun—not reflections of it in water or some alien place, but the sun just by itself in its own place—and be able to look at it and see what it is like.

Glaucon: He would have to.

Socrates: After that, he would already be able to conclude about it that it provides the seasons and the years, governs everything in the visible world, and is in some way the cause of all the things that he and his fellows used to see.

Glaucon: That would clearly be his next step.

Socrates: What about when he reminds himself of his first dwelling place, what passed for wisdom there, and his fellow prisoners? Don't you think he would count himself happy for the change and pity the others?

Glaucon: Certainly.

Socrates: And if there had been honors, praises, or prizes among them for the one who was sharpest at identifying the shadows as they passed by; and was best able to remember which usually came earlier, which later, and which simultaneously; and who was thus best able to prophesize the future, do you think that our man would desire these rewards or envy those among the prisoners who were honored and held power? Or do you think he would feel with Homer that he would much prefer to "work the earth as a serf for another man, a man without possessions of his own," and go through any sufferings, rather than share their beliefs and live as they do?

Glaucon: Yes, I think he would rather suffer anything than live like that.

Socrates: Consider this too, then. If this man went back down into the cave and sat down in

his same seat, wouldn't his eyes be filled with darkness, coming suddenly out of the sun like that?

Glaucon: Certainly.

Socrates: Now, if he had to compete once again with the perpetual prisoners in recognizing the shadows, while his sight was still dim and before his eyes had recovered, and if the time required for readjustment was not short, wouldn't he provoke ridicule? Wouldn't it be said of him that he had returned from his upward journey with his eyes ruined, and that it is not worthwhile even to try and travel upward? And as for anyone who tried to free the prisoners and lead them upward, if they could somehow get their hands on him, wouldn't they kill him?

Glaucon: They certainly would.

Socrates: This image, my dear Glaucon, must be fitted together as a whole with what we said before. The realm revealed through sight should be likened to the prison dwelling, and the light of the fire inside it to the sun's power. And if you think of the upward journey and the seeing of things above as the upward journey of the soul to the intelligible realm, you won't mistake my intention—since it is what you wanted to hear about. Only the god knows whether it is true. But this is how these phenomena seem to me: in the knowable realm, the last thing to be seen is the form of the good, and it is seen only with toil and trouble. Once one has seen it, however, one must infer that it is the cause of all that is correct and beautiful in anything, that in the visible realm it produces both light and its source, and that in the intelligible realm it controls and provides truth and understanding; and that anyone who is to act sensibly in private or public must see it.

Glaucon: I agree, so far as I am able.

Socrates: Come on, then, and join me in this further thought: you should not be surprised that the ones who get to this point are not willing to occupy themselves with human affairs, but that, on the contrary, their souls are always eager to spend their time above. I mean, that

is surely what we would expect, if indeed the image I described before is also accurate here.

Glaucon: It is what we would expect.

Socrates: What about when someone, coming from looking at divine things, looks to the evils of human life? Do you think it is surprising that he behaves awkwardly and appears completely ridiculous, if—while his sight is still dim and he has not yet become accustomed to the darkness around him—he is compelled, either in the courts or elsewhere, to compete about the shadows of justice, or about the statues of which they are the shadows; and to dispute the way these things are understood by people who have never seen justice itself?

Glaucon: It is not surprising at all.

Socrates: On the contrary, anyone with any sense, at any rate, would remember that eyes may be confused in two ways and from two causes: when they change from the light into the darkness, or from the darkness into the light. If he kept in mind that the same applies to the soul, then when he saw a soul disturbed and unable to see something, he would not laugh absurdly. Instead, he would see whether it had come from a brighter life and was dimmed through not having yet become accustomed to the dark, or from greater ignorance into greater light and was dazzled by the increased brilliance. Then he would consider the first soul happy in its experience and life, and pity the latter. But even if he wanted to ridicule it, at least his ridiculing it would make him less ridiculous than ridiculing a soul that had come from the light above.

Glaucon: That's an entirely reasonable claim.

Socrates: Then here is how we must think about these matters, if that is true: education is not what some people boastfully declare it to be. They presumably say they can put knowledge into souls that lack it, as if they could put sight into blind eyes.

Glaucon: Yes, they do say that.

Socrates: But here is what our present account shows about this power to learn that is present in everyone's soul, and the instrument with which each of us learns: just as an eye cannot be turned around from darkness to light except by turning the whole body, so this instrument must be turned around from what-comes-to-be together with the whole soul, until it is able to bear to look at what is and at the brightest thing that is—the one we call the good. Isn't that right?

Glaucon: Yes.

Socrates: Of this very thing, then, there would be a craft—namely, of this turning around—concerned with how this instrument can be most easily and effectively turned around, not of putting sight into it. On the contrary, it takes for granted that sight is there, though not turned in the right way or looking where it should look, and contrives to redirect it appropriately.

Glaucon: That's probably right.

Socrates: Then the other so-called virtues of the soul do seem to be closely akin to those of the body: they really are not present in it initially, but are added later by habit and practice. The virtue of wisdom, on the other hand, belongs above all, so it seems, to something more divine, which never loses its power, but is either useful and beneficial or useless and harmful, depending on the way it is turned. Or haven't you ever noticed in people who are said to be bad, but clever, how keen the vision of their little soul is and how sharply it distinguishes the things it is turned toward? This shows that its sight is not inferior, but is forced to serve vice, so that the sharper it sees, the more evils it accomplishes.

Glaucon: I certainly have.

Socrates: However, if this element of this sort of nature had been hammered at right from childhood, and struck free of the leaden weights, as it were, of kinship with becoming, which have been fastened to it by eating and other such pleasure and indulgences, which pull its soul's vision downward—if, I say, I got rid of these and turned toward truly real things, then the same element of the same people would see them most sharply, just as it now does the things it is now turned toward.

Glaucon: That's probably right.

Socrates: Isn't it also probable, then—indeed, doesn't it follow necessarily from what was said before—that uneducated people who have no experience of true reality will never adequately govern a city, and neither will people who have been allowed to spend their whole lives in education. The former fail because they do not have a single goal in life at which all their actions, public and private, inevitably aim; the latter because they would refuse to act, thinking they had emigrated, while still alive, to the Isles of the Blessed.

Glaucon: True.

Socrates: It is our task as founders, then, to compel the best natures to learn what was said before to be the most important thing: namely, to see the good; to ascend that ascent. And when they have ascended and looked sufficiently, we must not allow them to do what they are allowed to do now.

Glaucon: What's that, then?

Socrates: To stay there and refuse to go down again to the prisoners in the cave and share their labors and honors, whether the inferior ones or the more excellent ones.

Glaucon: You mean we are to treat them unjustly, making them live a worse life when they could live a better one?

Socrates: You have forgotten again, my friend, that the law is not concerned with making any one class in the city do outstandingly well, but is contriving to produce this condition in the city as a whole, harmonizing the citizens together through persuasion or compulsion, and making them share with each other the benefit they can confer on the community. It produces such men in the city, not in order to allow them to turn in whatever direction each one wants, but to make use of them to bind the city together.

Glaucon: That's true. Yes, I had forgotten.

Socrates: Observe, then, Glaucon, that we won't be unjustly treating those who have become philosophers in our city, but that what we will say to them, when we compel them to take care of the others and guard them, will be just. We will say: "When people like you come to be in other cities, they are justified in not sharing in the others' labors. After all, they have grown there spontaneously, against the will of the constitution in each of them. And when something grows of its own accord and owed no debt for its upbringing, it has justice on its side when it is not keen to pay anyone for its upbringing. But both for your own sakes and for that of the rest of the city, we have bred you to be leaders and kings in the hive, so to speak. You are better and more completely educated than the others, and better able to share in both types of life. So each of you in turn must go down to live in the common dwelling place of the other citizens and grow accustomed to seeing in the dark. For when you are used to it, you will see infinitely better than the people there and know precisely what each image is, and also what it is an image of, because you have seen the truth about fine, just, and good things. So the city will be awake, governed by us and by you; not dreaming like the majority of cities nowadays, governed by men who fight against one another over shadows and form factions in order to rule—as if that were a great good. No, the truth of the matter is surely this: a city in which those who are going to rule are least eager to rule is necessarily best and freest from faction, whereas a city with the opposite kind of rulers is governed in the opposite way."

Glaucon: Yes, indeed.

Socrates: Then do you think the people we have nurtured will disobey us when they hear these things, and be unwilling to share the labors of the city, each in turn, and wish instead to live the greater part of their time with one another in the pure realm?

Glaucon: No, they couldn't possibly. After all, we will be giving just orders to just people. However, each of them will certainly go to rule as to something necessary, which is exactly the opposite of what is done by those who now rule in each city.

Socrates: That's right, comrade. If you can find a way of life that is better than ruling for those who are going to rule, your well-governed city will become a possibility. You see, in it alone the truly rich will rule—those who are rich not in gold, but in the wealth the happy must have: namely, a good and rational life. But if beggars—people hungry for private goods of their own—go into public life, thinking that the good is there for the seizing, then such a city is impossible. For when ruling is something fought over, such civil and domestic war destroys these men and the rest of the city as well.

Glaucon: That's absolutely true.

Socrates: Do you know of any other sort of life that looks down on political offices besides that of true philosophy?

Glaucon: No, by Zeus, I do not.

UNIT
9

LEADERSHIP PROFILES

Susan B. Anthony (1820–1906) and Elizabeth Cady Stanton (1815–1902)

Leaders in the United States Woman Suffrage Movement

Introduction and Historical Background

Elizabeth Cady Stanton and Susan B. Anthony shared a fruitful, fifty-year friendship that ultimately yielded greater rights for women, including the right to vote in the United States. Along the way, Stanton and Anthony endured barbs. They were called, among other epithets, ugly, unfeminine, promiscuous, and downright dangerous. Still, Stanton and Anthony articulated a vision of a world in which women enjoyed rights equal to those of men, and they managed their conflicts of both style and substance as they struggled to achieve their goals. Their friendship transcended their differences and, to the ends of their lives, Stanton and Anthony relied on one another for feedback and support. The story of their friendship offers students an opportunity to learn valuable leadership lessons. Stanton and Anthony spent their adult lives as activists for a cause that was at times extraordinarily unpopular. Still, they fervently believed that, in Stanton's words, "If one-half the effort had been expended to exalt the feminine element that has been

Library of Congress, Prints and Photographs Division, LC-USZ61-791

made to degrade it, we should have reached the natural equilibrium long ago. Either sex, in isolation, is robbed of one-half its power for the accomplishment of any given work." Stanton and Anthony were, to paraphrase the words one writer for *The New York Graphic* used to describe Anthony, "women who dared."

Stanton and Anthony were contemporaries who came from dissimilar backgrounds and had distinct personalities. Stanton was a charming and witty, if often uncompromising, revolutionary. She loved beautiful clothes, good food, great books, and afternoon naps. Her family was well-to-do. She had hoped to follow her father into a career in law but was abruptly told a law career was not a suitable profession for a woman. Sorely disappointed, Stanton still secured a fine education and as an adult became an activist in the abolitionist movement and the founder of the first wave of the women's rights movement in the United States. Though in many ways Stanton was radical, she took a traditional path in one way. Stanton married and had seven children. She found, however, that working in her home brought her little joy and she longed for a more publicly active life. She initially found that life in Boston's public salons, the Unitarian Church, and the abolitionist movement. Tired of theory and unhappy with a family move to New York State, Stanton found her calling in her work organizing the Seneca Falls Convention in 1848.

Anthony was plainspoken, disciplined, and single-minded. She was a canny tactician who willingly built consensus to achieve her goals. She grew up in a New York Quaker family, and,

though she had several opportunities, never married. The independent Anthony served as head-mistress of the female department of the Canajoharie Academy and, like Stanton, enjoyed fine clothes and intellectual challenges. She ultimately became the more popular and famous of the two friends, in large part because of her considerable skills as a consensus builder. By the time she met Stanton in 1851, Anthony was ready to build "…a happier and more glorious world."

Anthony tempered Stanton's fiery personality and remained Stanton's staunchest ally and cheer-leader. When Stanton died on October 26, 1902 at age eighty-five, Anthony continued their work. Before her own death on March 13, 1906 at age eighty-six, Anthony wrote one family member, "…remember that I want there should be no tears. Pass on, and go on with the work." And so women suffragists did just that. For nearly fourteen more years they continued the work begun at Seneca Falls in 1848. In 1920, women throughout the United States voted in their first national election.

Points to Consider

1. What lessons can you learn from Stanton and Anthony about how you articulate a vision involving controversial change and then work to build support for that change amongst people with different ideas about why and whether your vision should be implemented?

2. How did Stanton and Anthony connect with people to affect change?

3. How did Stanton and Anthony stay focused on achieving their goal for so long? Do you think they should have compromised somehow? Why or why not?

4. How and why do you think Stanton and Anthony motivated themselves to work for their vision even when the odds were against them and when they were not likely to personally benefit from those changes?

UNIT 9

"The 1873 Sentencing of Susan B. Anthony for the Crime of Voting"

(Excerpt from the Court Transcript)

The trial judge had taken the decision out of the hands of the jury, had pronounced Anthony guilty, and had further denied the motion for a new trial.

The Court: The prisoner will stand up. Has the prisoner anything to say why sentence shall not be pronounced?

Miss Anthony: Yes, your honor, I have many things to say; for in your ordered verdict of guilty, you have trampled underfoot every vital principle of our government. My natural rights, my civil rights, my political rights, are all alike ignored. Robbed of the fundamental privilege of citizenship, I am degraded from the status of a citizen to that of a subject; and not only myself individually, but all of my sex, are, by your honor's verdict, doomed to political subjection under this so-called Republican government.

Judge Hunt: The Court can not listen to a rehearsal of arguments the prisoner's counsel has already consumed three hours in presenting.

Miss Anthony: May it please your honor, I am not arguing the question, I am simply stating the reasons why sentence can not, in justice, be pronounced against me. Your denial of my citizen's right to vote is the denial of my right of consent as one of the governed, the denial of my right of representation as one of the taxed, the denial of my right to a trial by a jury of my peers as an offender against law, therefore, the denial of my sacred rights of life, liberty, property, and—

Judge Hunt: The Court can not allow the prisoner to go on.

Miss Anthony: But your honor will not deny me this one and only poor privilege of protest against this high-handed outrage upon my citizen's rights. May it please the Court to remember that since the day of my arrest last November, this is the first time that either myself or any person of my disfranchised class has been allowed a word of defense before judge or jury—

Judge Hunt: The prisoner must sit down; the Court can not allow it.

Miss Anthony: All my prosecutors, from the 8th Ward corner grocery politician, who entered the complaint, to the United States Marshal, Commissioner, District Attorney, District Judge, your honor on the bench, not one is my peer, but each and all are my political sovereigns; and had your honor submitted my case to the jury, as was clearly your duty, even then I should have had just cause of protest, for not one of those men was my peer; but, native or foreign, white or black, rich or poor, educated or ignorant, awake or asleep, sober or drunk, each and every man of them was my political superior; hence, in no sense, my peer. Even, under such circumstances, a commoner of England, tried before a jury of lords, would have far less cause to complain than should I, a woman, tried before a jury of men. Even my counsel, the Hon. Henry R. Selden, who has argued my cause so ably, so earnestly, so unanswerably before your honor, is my political sovereign. Precisely as no disfranchised person is entitled to sit upon a jury, and no woman is entitled to the franchise, so, none but a regularly admitted lawyer is allowed to practice in the courts, and no woman can gain admission to the bar—hence, jury, judge, counsel, must all be of the superior class.

Judge Hunt: The Court must insist—the prisoner has been tried according to the established forms of law.

Miss Anthony: Yes, your honor, but by forms of law all made by men, interpreted by men, administered by men, in favor of men, and against women; and hence, your honor's ordered verdict of guilty, against a United States citizen for the exercise of "that citizen's right to vote," simply because that citizen was a woman and not a man. But, yesterday, the same man-made forms of law declared it a crime punishable with $1,000 fine and six months' imprisonment, for you, or me, or any of us, to give a cup of cold water, a crust of bread, or a night's shelter to a panting fugitive as he was tracking his way to Canada. And every man or woman in whose veins coursed a drop of human sympathy violated that wicked law, reckless of consequences, and was justified in so doing. As then the slaves who got their freedom must take it over, or under, or through the unjust forms of law, precisely so now must women, to get their right to a voice in this Government, take it; and I have taken mine, and mean to take it at every possible opportunity.

Judge Hunt: The Court orders the prisoner to sit down. It will not allow another word.

Miss Anthony: When I was brought before your honor for trial, I hoped for a broad and liberal interpretation of the Constitution and its recent amendments, that should declare all United States citizens under its protecting ægis—that should declare equality of rights the national guarantee to all persons born or naturalized in the United States. But failing to get this justice—failing, even, to get a trial by a jury *not* of my peers—I ask not leniency at your hands—but rather the full rigors of the law.

Judge Hunt: The Court must insist—(Here the prisoner sat down.)

Judge Hunt: The prisoner will stand up. (Here Miss Anthony arose again.) The sentence of the Court is that you pay a fine of one hundred dollars and the costs of the prosecution.

Miss Anthony: May it please your honor, I shall never pay a dollar of your unjust penalty. All the stock in trade I possess is a $10,000 debt, incurred by publishing my paper—*The Revolution*—four years ago, the sole object of which was to educate all women to do precisely as I have done, rebel against your man-made, unjust, unconstitutional forms of law, that tax, fine, imprison, and hang women, while they deny them the right of representation in the Government; and I shall work on with might and main to pay every dollar of that honest debt, but not a penny shall go to this unjust claim. And I shall earnestly and persistently continue to urge all women to the practical recognition of the old revolutionary maxim, that "Resistance to tyranny is obedience to God."

Judge Hunt: Madam, the Court will not order you committed until the fine is paid.

"The Solitude of Self"

(Excerpt from a speech on January 17, 1892)
By Elizabeth Cady Stanton

UNIT 9

Elizabeth Cady Stanton, Susan B. Anthony, Lucy Stone, and Isabella Beecher Hooker appeared before the Judiciary Committee of the House of Representatives to plead their cause. According to the report of the Washington Star, *"The new members of the committee were apparently surprised at receiving such a talk from a woman and there was the most marked attention on the part of every one present. Their surprise was still greater when they found that Mrs. Stanton was not a phenomenal exception, but that every woman there could make an argument which would do credit to the best of public men."*

The point I wish plainly to bring before you on this occasion is the individuality of each human soul—our Protestant idea, the right of individual conscience and judgment—our republican idea, individual citizenship. In discussing the rights of woman, we are to consider, first, what belongs to her as an individual, in a world of her own, the arbiter of her own destiny, an imaginary Robinson Crusoe with her woman Friday on a solitary island. Her rights under such circumstances are to use all her faculties for her own safety and happiness.

Secondly, if we consider her as a citizen, as a member of a great nation, she must have the same rights as all other members, according to the fundamental principles of our Government.

Thirdly, viewed as a woman, an equal factor in civilization, her rights and duties are still the same—individual happiness and development.

Fourthly, it is only the incidental relations of life, such as mother, wife, sister, daughter, which may involve some special duties and training. In the usual discussion in regard to woman's sphere, such men as Herbert Spencer, Frederick Harrison and Grant Allen uniformly subordinate her rights and duties as an individual, as a citizen, as a woman, to the necessities of these incidental relations, some of which a large class of women never assume. In discussing the sphere of man we do not decide his rights as an individual, as a citizen, as a man, by his duties as a father, a husband, a brother or a son, some of which he may never undertake. Moreover he would be better fitted for these very relations, and whatever special work he might choose to do to earn his bread, by the complete development of all his faculties as an individual. Just so with woman. The education which will fit her to discharge the duties in the largest sphere of human usefulness, will best fit her for whatever special work she may be compelled to do.

The isolation of every human soul and the necessity of self-dependence must give each individual the right to choose his own surroundings. The strongest reason for giving woman all the opportunities for higher education, for the full development of her faculties, her forces of mind and body; for giving her the most enlarged freedom of thought and action; a complete emancipation from all forms of bondage, of custom, dependence, superstition; from all the crippling influences of fear—is the solitude and personal responsibility of her own individual life. The strongest reason why we ask for woman a voice in the government under which she lives; in the religion she is asked to believe; equality in social life, where she is the chief factor; a place in the trades and professions, where she may earn her bread, is because of her birthright to self-sovereignty; because, as an individual, she must rely on herself...

To throw obstacles in the way of a complete education is like putting out the eyes; to deny the rights of property is like cutting off the hands. To refuse political equality is to rob the ostracized of all self-respect, of credit in the market place, of recompense in the world of work, of a voice in choosing those who make and administer the law, a choice in the jury before whom they are tried, and in the judge who decides their punishment. Shakespeare's play of *Titus and Andronicus* contains a terrible satire on woman's position in the nineteenth century—"Rude men seized the king's daughter, cut out her tongue, cut off her hands, and then bade her go call for water and wash her hands." What a picture of woman's position! Robbed of her natural rights, handicapped by law and custom at every turn, yet compelled to fight her own battles, and in the emergencies of life to fall back on herself for protection...

How the little courtesies of life on the surface of society, deemed so important from man towards woman, fade into utter insignificance in view of the deeper tragedies in which she must play her part alone, where no human aid is possible!

Nothing strengthens the judgment and quickens the conscience like individual responsibility. Nothing adds such dignity to character as the recognition of one's self-sovereignty; the right to an equal place, everywhere conceded—a place earned by personal merit, not an artificial attainment by inheritance, wealth, family and position. Conceding then that the responsibilities of life rest equally on man and woman, that their destiny is the same, they need the same preparation for time and eternity. The talk of sheltering woman from the fierce storms of life is the sheerest mockery, for they beat on her from every point of the compass, just as they do on man, and with more fatal results, for he has been trained to protect himself, to resist, to conquer...

In music women speak again the language of Mendelssohn, Beethoven, Chopin, Schumann, and are worthy interpreters of their great thoughts. The poetry and novels of the century are theirs, and they have touched the keynote of reform in religion, politics and social life. They fill the editor's and professor's chair, plead at the bar of justice, walk the wards of the hospital, speak from the pulpit and the platform. Such is the type of womanhood that an enlightened public sentiment welcomes to-day, and such the triumph of the facts of life over the false theories of the past.

Is it, then, consistent to hold the developed woman of this day within the same narrow political limits as the dame with the spinning wheel and knitting needle occupied in the past? No, no! Machinery has taken the labors of woman as well as man on its tireless shoulders; the loom and the spinning wheel are but dreams of the past; the pen, the brush, the easel, the chisel, have taken their places, while the hopes and ambitions of women are essentially changed.

We see reason sufficient in the outer conditions of human beings for individual liberty and development, but when we consider the self-dependence of every human soul, we see the need of courage, judgment and the exercise of every faculty of mind and body, strengthened and developed by use, in woman as well as man...

Introduction and Historical Background by Susan Hult Edwards. Used by permission of Susan Hult Edwards.

Stanton, E. C., Anthony, S. B., & Gage, M. J. (1881). *History of Women's Suffrage, Volume II*. Fowler & Wells. Pp. 687–689

Stanton, E. C., Anthony, S. B., & Gage, M. J. (1881). *History of Women's Suffrage, Volume IV*. Fowler & Wells. Pp. 189–191

UNIT

9

476

"People don't resist change as much as the way they are changed."

—Winston Churchill (1874–1965), British Prime Minister

REFLECT & FOCUS

READINGS

"The Practice of Innovation"

By Peter M. Senge

Points to Consider

1. Senge writes that leaders' fundamental task is to help people do more together than they could individually. To what extent do you agree or disagree?

2. In what ways can Drucker's three ingredients of the discipline of innovation help small groups achieve their goals?

3. What does Senge mean by the statement "the process of innovation is a process of failure"? To what extent do you agree or disagree with Senge's assessment? To what degree is this true for organizations as well as individuals?

4. In what ways are Senge's clarifications of the words *mission*, *vision*, and *values* helpful?

UNIT

9

"The Practice of Innovation"

Peter Drucker has elegantly presented the three ingredients of the *discipline of innovation*: focus on mission, define significant results, and do rigorous assessment. But if it sounds so simple, why is it so difficult for institutions to innovate?

There are two possible explanations, representing dramatically different worldviews. These opposing outlooks were first clarified nearly 40 years ago by Douglas McGregor in his groundbreaking *Human Side of Enterprise*: Theory X (employees as unreliable and uncommitted, chasing a paycheck) versus Theory Y (employees as responsible adults wanting to contribute).

One possibility for difficulties innovating is that most people really don't care about innovation. After all, Theory X is still the prevailing philosophy in most large institutions—certainly in the American corporate world. Few people in positions of authority would admit to that view, but our practices belie our espoused values. If we look honestly at how organizations manage people, most appear to operate with the belief that people cannot work without careful supervision. As Arie de Geus has shown in his recent book *The Living Company*, we treat the business enterprise as a machine for making money rather than as a living community. Consequently, we view people as "human resources" waiting to be employed (or disemployed) to the organizations' needs. (The word *resource* literally means "standing in reserve, waiting to be used.")

From the Theory X perspective, institutions fail to innovate because most people lack the desire to innovate; forget Drucker's theory of innovation. The answer to that problem is simple: find more capable people. But that's a never-ending story. "We don't have the right people" is an excuse that suits all times and all circumstances; it is a refuge for scoundrels. Moreover, it obscures leaders' fundamental task of helping people do more together than they could individually.

If, on the other hand, we take the Theory Y perspective, that most people come to work (or at least came to work at one time) truly desiring to make a difference, to gain, as Peter Drucker puts it, a "return on their citizenship," then the failure to innovate becomes a bigger puzzle. It cannot be laid off on not having the right people. It must have more to do with why Peter Drucker's three core practices are more difficult than meets the eye. It requires that we try to understand how it is that good people, desiring to learn and innovate, can consistently fail to produce what they intend.

Know Your Purpose

We can start by inquiring into what we mean by *mission* anyway. It is very hard to focus on what you cannot define, and my experience is that there can be some very fuzzy thinking about mission, vision, and values.

Most organizations today have mission statements, purpose statements, official visions, and little cards with the organization's values. But precious few of us can say our organization's mission statement has transformed the enterprise. And there has grown an understandable cynicism around lofty ideals that don't match the realities of organizational life.

The first obstacle to understanding mission is a problem of language. Many leaders use *mission* and *vision* interchangeably, or think that the words—and the differences between them—matter little. But words do matter. Language is messy by nature, which is why we must be careful in how we use it. As leaders, after all, we have little else to work with. We typically don't use hammers and saws, heavy equipment, or even computers to do our real work. The essence of leadership—what we do with 98 percent of our time—is communication. To master any management practice, we must start by bringing discipline to the domain in which we spend most of our time, the domain of words.

The dictionary—which, unlike the computer, *is* an essential leadership tool—contains multiple definitions of the word *mission*; the most appropriate here is, "purpose, reason for being." *Vision*, by contrast, is "a picture or image of the future we seek to create," and *values* articulate how we intend to live as we pursue our mission. Paradoxically, if an organization's mission is truly motivating it is never really achieved. Mission provides an orientation, not a checklist of accomplishments. It defines a direction, not a destination. It tells the members of an organization why they are working together, how they intend to contribute to the world. Without a sense of mission, there is no foundation for establishing why some intended results are more important than others.

But, there is a big difference between having a mission statement and being truly mission-based. To be truly mission-based means that key decisions can be referred back to the mission—our reason for being. It means that people can and should object to management edicts that they do not see as connected to the mission. It means that thinking about and continually clarifying the mission is everybody's job because, as de Geus points out, it expresses the aspirations and fundamental identity of a human community. By contrast, most mission statements are nice ideas that might have some meaning for a few but communicate little to the community as a whole. In most organizations, no one would dream of challenging a management decision on the grounds that it does not serve the mission. In other words, most organizations serve those in power rather than a mission.

This also gives some clue as to why being mission-based is so difficult. It gets to the core of power and authority. It is profoundly radical. It says, in essence, those in positions of authority are not the source of authority. It says rather, that the source of legitimate power in the organization is its guiding ideas. Remember, "We hold these truths to be self evident…?" The cornerstone of a truly democratic system of governance is not voting or any other particular mechanism. It is the belief that power ultimately flows from ideas, not people. To be truly mission-based is to be democratic in this way, to make the mission more important than the boss, something that not too many corporations have yet demonstrated an ability to do.

While this might appeal to our ideals, living this way is extraordinarily challenging. We are all closet authoritarians. For most of us it is the only system of management we have ever known, starting in school. To be mission-based, and to be values-guided, is to hold up lofty standards against which every person's behavior can be judged. Moreover, mission is inherently fuzzy, abstract. It is so much easier to make decisions based on "the numbers," habit, and unexamined emotions. To be mission-based requires everyone to think continuously.

But it can be done, and when done it can work. The largest commercial enterprise in the world, in terms of market value, is not Microsoft, General Electric, or Mashushita. It is VISA International, whose annual volume exceeded $1.25 trillion in 1997. If its different member organizations' balance sheets of VISA products were combined and assessed according to common banking practices, it is estimated that its market value would exceed $333 billion. But VISA is not a typical corporation. It's a network of 20,000 owner-members, who are simultaneously one another's "customers, suppliers, and competitors," in the words of founding CEO Dee Hock. VISA's innovative governance system grew from an extraordinary effort to clarify purpose, which, after several years, emerged as: "to create the world's premier system for the exchange of value." "Truly clarifying purpose and the principles which elaborate our deepest beliefs can be the hardest work you will ever do," says Hock. "But without it, there is no way to create an enterprise that can truly self-organize, where you can balance broadly distributed decision-making function and control at the most local level with coherence and cohesion at any scale up to the global."

UNIT
9

Define Vision

The second requirement for innovation—define results—is easier in some ways. Managers by nature are pragmatic; ultimately they are concerned about results and must concentrate on how, not just why. The danger is that short-term goals can obscure larger purposes. Here again, language matters. After all, vision—an image of the future we seek to create—is synonymous with intended results. As such, vision is a practical tool, not an abstract concept. Visions can be long term or intermediate term. Multiple visions can coexist, capturing complementary facets of what people seek to create and encompassing different time frames. Leaders who lack vision fail to define what they hope to accomplish in terms that can ultimately be assessed. While mission is foundational, it is also insufficient because, by its nature, it is extraordinarily difficult to assess how we are doing by looking only at the mission. For this we need to stick our necks out and articulate "an image of the future we seek to create."

Results-oriented leaders, therefore, must have both a mission and a vision. Results mean little without purpose, for a very practical and powerful reason: a mission instills both the passion and the patience for the long journey. While vision inspires passion, many failed ventures are characterized by passion without patience.

Clarity about mission and vision is both an operational and a spiritual necessity. Mission provides a guiding star, a long-term purpose that allows you to balance the inevitable pressures between the short term and long term. Vision translates mission into truly meaningful intended results— and guides the allocation of time, energy, and resources. In my experience, it is only through a compelling vision that a deep sense of purpose comes alive. People's passions flow naturally into creating something that truly excites them. Taken together, mission and vision fill a deep need: All human beings have a purpose, a reason for being. Most of us believe that there is something more important than what you can buy, acquire, or market. The passion at the heart of every great undertaking comes from the deep longing of human beings to make a difference, to have an impact. It comes from what you contribute rather than what you get.

Now, these ideas might sound good, but if we take a deeper look we realize that they are radical statements in today's society. The return-on-investment orientation—the view that people go to work primarily for material gain—is the bedrock of our beliefs about people in contemporary industrial society. Thus, the real discipline of innovation not only threatens established power relations, it also runs counter to our cultural norms.

Consider, for example, the saying "People do what they're rewarded for." What management is about in many people's minds is creating the right set of incentives and rewards so people will do what the enterprise needs them to do. As W. Edwards Deming saw clearly, our system of management—in all organizations—is based almost totally on extrinsic motivation. It is pure Theory X thinking. It is why, in the last years of his life, Deming said that "our system of management has destroyed our people." This may not be our intent, but it is the consequence of our actions. If we didn't view the human being as an amoeba that does only what it's rewarded to do, then why would we spend so much time worrying about incentives?

Just ask people in the organization if they think the senior management really believes that people come to work every day, as Deming said, "seeking joy in work." That's intrinsic motivation, and it's assumed to be in scarce supply in today's management. Joy in work comes from being true to your purpose. It is the source of the passion, patience, and perseverance we need to thrive as individuals and as organizations. However, people cannot define results that relate to their deeper passions unless leaders cultivate an environment in which those passions can be safely articulated.

While there are some extraordinarily principled and value-driven organizations, the defining characteristic of far too many enterprises is cynicism. And cynicism comes from disappointment. As the saying goes, "Scratch the shell of any cynic and you'll find a frustrated idealist." Make speeches to your organization about upholding high ideals or contributing to a better world, and most people will roll their eyes (if they're in corporations they'll almost certainly roll their eyes). That reaction is the product of thwarted expectations, and it is the reason so many organizations fail to innovate. They are afraid to let the genie—passionate purpose—out of the bottle. With good cause. Passion is a powerful force, but, when frustrated, it is also dangerous.

Assess Results

The third dimension of innovation is assessment. We must continually gauge how we can best use our scarce resources. As managers we all know what assessing is about; it's one of the fundamental activities of all management.

Assessment has two components: measurement and interpretation. The problem is that the second and more difficult component of assessment—interpretation—requires understanding, participation, and physical presence. Statistical measures of an activity may be disappointing, but if you're actually involved, you may see that people are engaged and learning. They may be on the brink of a breakthrough. Incomplete or premature assessment destroys learning. As Bill O'Brien, retired CEO of Hanover Insurance, says, "managers are always pulling up the radishes to see how they're growing." Thus assessment is fundamentally about awareness and understanding without which any set of measures can mislead. Someone sitting on the outside judging, rather than fully understanding, can make effective assessment impossible.

But with awareness comes yet another problem, as Drucker has pointed out: after assessing results, we must be willing to abandon what doesn't work. Abandonment often precedes innovation. It clears the decks for trying something new. Again, this sounds so simple. Yet, how many of us have ever found that it is difficult for organizations to abandon what isn't working? To stop doing something that has been done for years? To remove a person from a position who really does not have credibility with his or her colleagues? "I worry about organizations that cannot fire one person but can fire a thousand," says O'Brien. There are good reasons why abandonment is a challenging organizational practice.

The first step in practicing abandonment is openness—creating an environment in which, at a critical moment, somebody with lots at stake can tell a boss, "This is not working." Building a culture in which people can express their views without fear of reprisal is a huge challenge for most organizations.

How often, for instance, have you noticed that when a group of people gets together informally the night before a staff meeting, their conversation bears almost no resemblance to the same group's discussion at the official meeting the next day? How many meetings have you attended where the real meeting takes place not in the conference room but in the hallway or the rest room afterward, when the very people who asked lots of intelligent questions in the meeting say, "What nonsense?" Furthermore, when people do feel safe enough to speak openly in a meeting, insiders, those with the most on the line, tend to discount what is said. When, for instance, a junior salesperson, a young woman (or an old one), tells the boss something is not working, you see how quickly an ostensibly open organization can reject unwelcome news.

I've never seen an institution that isn't deeply afflicted with these dynamics. Even the best managed corporations in the world fall short of their full potential, mostly because people know that the official meeting is not where the issues are really discussed or decided.

The litmus test for measuring openness is simple: How fast does bad news travel upward? In most organizations good news travels upward faster than the speed of light. But failure is denied before the word can be spoken: "Whose failure? What failure? That wasn't a failure, we just didn't have enough funding." Make no mistake, the process of innovation is a process of failure. By nature, innovation is a continual learning process. You must experience, assess, reflect on mission, identify results, experiment some more. Yet from an early age in school, and continuing in work, we have been trained to avoid failure, and thus real learning.

Chris Argyris, in his 1991 *Harvard Business Review* article "Teaching Smart People How to Learn," lays out a basic problem of learning in organizations. He notes that most people in organizations are quite smart, but that to succeed, they've learned to find correct answers and cover up incorrect ones. This undermines the inquiry skills essential to real innovation and leadership because these skills revolve around how to "uncover" what isn't working in ways that do not invoke defensiveness.

Consider this true story: A top management team of exceptionally bright, committed people is discussing key issues facing a major American corporation. In three hours, not a single genuine question is asked. Of course, trivial questions get asked, like "Didn't we go over this issue two years ago?" Or, "Don't our experienced salespeople disagree with that view?" Or "When's lunch?" Each implies that we are wasting our time with the subject, that we already have the answer.

Genuine inquiry starts when people ask questions to which they do not have an answer. That is rare in organizations. In most large corporations, people rise to the top because they're very good at a combination of two factors: merit and gamesmanship. In a good organization the mix may be 50/50; in a great one, 80/20. The problem is that even the best leaders—those who create a terrific impression and get results—actually know very little. In today's world how could they know much? Obviously, organizations want people at all levels who can produce results. But often the most important act of executive leadership is the ability to ask a question that hasn't been asked before, the ability to inquire, not just dictate or advocate. Unfortunately, most people in executive leadership positions are great at advocacy but poor at inquiry.

These are just a few of the issues revolving around effective assessment. This is an extraordinarily complex issue, with complex intellectual issues ("How do we know how long the radishes should take to grow?"), complex emotional issues (Who is not attached to ideas they believe in, many of which are wrong?), complex interpersonal issues ("I didn't want to tell him what I really think because it would hurt his feelings.") and complex political issues ("But it is the boss' pet program that is not working and the company has invested millions in it.") It is one thing for an organization with Peter Drucker advising it to "abandon practices that are not working." It is another for the rest of us who can only learn from peers.

For those reasons, assessment is a core research initiative within the new Society for Organizational Learning (SoL), leading companies, researchers, and consultants working together to advance the state of the art of how organizations learn. We are coming to believe that there is a big difference between "assessment for learning" and "assessment for evaluation." Because most of the assessment we have encountered in our lives was the latter, the very word tends to invoke defensiveness. But no learning can take place without continuous assessment. The key is that the assessment is done by the learners and the purpose is to learn, that is, to enhance capacity to produce intended outcomes, not to judge someone else.

From Habit to Discipline

Taken together, mission, vision, and assessment create an ecology, a set of fundamental relationships forming the bedrock of real leadership. These tools allow people, regardless of job title, to help shape their future. The failure of Industrial Age institutions to embrace the three components of innovation shows how far there is to go to meet the challenge of the next century. Moreover, Drucker is exactly right that innovation is a "discipline," a word having its root in the Latin *disciplina*, one of the oldest words for "to learn." Many have talent but real learning requires discipline, the process through which we draw out our potential through commitment, practice, passion, patience, and perseverance.

It is a difficult process, but there is reason for hope. The discipline of innovation is practiced successfully in many domains of human affairs, notably the arts and science. Interestingly, when it is practiced effectively it is invariably done so within communities, among diverse individuals who share a common purpose. Energized communities, for example, characterize most periods of innovation in the arts, such as the birth of impressionism, or modern dance, or jazz. Likewise, science at its best is an intensely collaborative undertaking; even when the "collaborators" are strong individuals competing with one another, their competition occurs within a larger mediating community. Likewise in business, real innovation is often much more collaborative than it first appears. For example, studies such as those by MIT's Eric von Hippel have shown that many of the best new product innovations come from customers. The problem is that most companies are not organized to tap this source of innovative thinking.

My guess is that mastering the discipline of innovation will require organizations working together, learning from one another's efforts. We must learn to do what artists have done for millennia, what scientists do when science works. To do something new, people invariably experience periods of profound discomfort. Confronting the threat and uncertainty such change brings is best done together, not in isolation.

Several years ago, at one of our early SoL community meetings (then called the MIT Organizational Learning Center), a manager approached me and said, "I see exactly what you're talking about, all these organizations learning from one another. This is Alcoholics Anonymous for Managers." I laughed, but I think he hit the nail on the head. We are all addicted to maintaining control, to avoiding failure, to doing things the way we always have. We can't help it. And we need one another to break the habit.

Senge, Peter M. "The Practice of Innovation." *Leader to Leader* 9 (1998), 16–22. Reprinted with permission of John Wiley and Sons, Inc.

"Letter from Birmingham Jail"

By Martin Luther King, Jr. (1929–1968)
American Clergyman, Civil Rights Leader, and Nobel Laureate

Introduction

In April 1963, Birmingham authorities arrested King for leading a campaign of civil disobedience. The civil rights activists were protesting the discriminatory policies of the City of Birmingham against blacks in both employment and the use of public facilities. They were also demonstrating for the rights of individuals to protest peacefully in public against policies with which they disagreed. The city government responded with force and jailed many of the demonstrators, including King. While King was in jail, eight of his fellow clergymen publicly criticized King's actions as "unwise and untimely."

The following excerpts are from a letter to the eight clergymen King wrote while jailed. He composed it under somewhat restricted circumstances; he started it on the margins of the newspaper in which the clergymen's statement appeared, and continued the letter on scraps of writing paper that a friendly trusty supplied, and concluded it on a pad his attorneys were eventually permitted to leave him. The letter is an eloquent response to the criticism and a cogent argument for the need for change in the treatment of blacks and other minorities.

UNIT 9

Points to Consider

1. Why do you think King encountered resistance to his tactics and goals from individuals within the Civil Rights movement?

2. When a group is working to realize change, how can an individual use King's advice to help reach consensus about the group's objectives?

3. What does King assert are four basic steps to take in a nonviolent campaign to change the status quo? To what extent do these work to help when organizations are hoping to realize change? Can you think of other steps you might add to the process of realizing change?

4. Why was King's philosophy of nonviolent direct action met with resistance and, often, violence?

"Letter from Birmingham Jail"

April 16, 1963

My Dear Fellow Clergymen:

While confined here in the Birmingham city jail, I came across your recent statement calling my present activities "unwise and untimely." Seldom do I pause to answer criticism of my work and ideas. If I sought to answer all the criticisms that cross my desk, my secretaries would have little time for anything other than such correspondence in the course of the day, and I would have no time for constructive work. But since I feel that you are men of genuine good will and that your criticisms are sincerely set forth, I want to try to answer your statement in what I hope will be patient and reasonable terms.

I think I should indicate why I am here in Birmingham, since you have been influenced by the view which argues against "outsiders coming in." I have the honor of serving as president of the Southern Christian Leadership Conference, an organization operating in every southern state, with headquarters in Atlanta, Georgia. We have some eighty-five affiliated organizations across the South, and one of them is the Alabama Christian Movement for Human Rights. Frequently we share staff, educational and financial resources with our affiliates. Several months ago the affiliate here in Birmingham asked us to be on call to engage in a nonviolent direct-action program if such were deemed necessary. We readily consented, and when the hour came we lived up to our promise. So I, along with several members of my staff, am here because I was invited here, I am here because I have organizational ties here.

But more basically, I am in Birmingham because injustice is here. Just as the prophets of the eight century B.C. left their villages and carried their "thus saith the Lord" far beyond the boundaries of their home towns, and just as the Apostle Paul left his village of Tarsus and carried the gospel of Jesus Christ to the far corners of the Greco-Roman world, so I am compelled to carry the gospel of freedom beyond my own home town. Like Paul, I must constantly respond to the Macedonian call for aid.

Moreover, I am cognizant of the interrelatedness of all communities and states. I cannot sit idly by in Atlanta and not be concerned about what happens in Birmingham.

Injustice anywhere is a threat to justice everywhere. We are caught in an inescapable network of mutuality, tied in a single garment of destiny. Whatever affects one directly, affects all indirectly. Never again can we afford to live with the narrow, provincial, "outside agitator" idea. Anyone who lives inside the United States can never be considered an outsider anywhere within its bounds.

You deplore the demonstrations taking place in Birmingham. But your statement, I am sorry to say, fails to express a similar concern for the conditions that brought the demonstrations. I am sure that none of you would want to rest content with the superficial kind of social analysis that deals merely with effects and does not grapple with underlying causes. It is unfortunate that demonstrations are taking place in Birmingham, but it is even more unfortunate that the city's white power structure left the Negro community with no alternative.

In any nonviolent campaign there are four basic steps: collection of the facts to determine whether injustices exist; negotiation; self-purification; and direct action. We have gone through all these steps in Birmingham. There can be no gainsaying the fact that racial injustice engulfs this community. Birmingham is probably the most thoroughly segregated city in the United States. Its ugly record of brutality is widely known. Negroes have experienced grossly unjust treatment in the courts. There have been more unsolved bombings of Negro homes and churches in Birmingham than in any other city in the nation. These are the hard, brutal facts of the case. On the basis of these conditions, Negro leaders sought to negotiate with the city fathers. But the latter consistently refused to engage in good-faith negotiation.

Then, last September, came the opportunity to talk with leaders of Birmingham's economic community. In the course of the negotiations, certain promises were made by the merchants—for example, to remove the stores' humiliating racial signs. On the basis of these promises, the Reverend Fred Shuttlesworth and the leaders of the Alabama Christian Movement for Human Rights agreed to a moratorium on all demonstrations. As the weeks and months went by, we realized that we were the victims of a broken promise. A few signs, briefly removed, returned; the others remained.

As in so many past experiences, our hopes had been blasted, and the shadow of deep disappointment settled upon us. We had no alternative except to prepare for direct action, whereby we would present our very bodies as a means of laying our case before the conscience of the local and the national community. Mindful of the difficulties involved, we decided to undertake a process of self-purification. We began a series of workshops on nonviolence, and we repeatedly asked ourselves: "Are you able to accept blows without retaliating?" "Are you able to endure the ordeal of jail?" We decided to schedule our direct-action program for the Easter season, realizing that except for Christmas, this is the main shopping period of the year. Knowing that a strong economic withdrawal would be the by-product of direct action, we felt that this would be the best time to bring pressure to bear on the merchants for the needed change.

Then it occurred to us that Birmingham's mayoralty election was coming up in March, and we speedily decided to postpone action until after election day. When we discovered that the Commissioner of Public Safety, Eugene "Bull" Connor, had piled up enough votes to be in the run-off we decided again to postpone action until the day after the run-off so that the demonstrations could not be used to cloud the issues. Like many others, we waited to see Mr. Connor defeated, and to this end we endured postponement after postponement. Having aided in this community need, we felt that our direct-action program could be delayed no longer.

You may well ask: "Why direct action? Why sit-ins, marches and so forth? Isn't negotiation a better path?" You are quite right in calling for negotiations. Indeed this is the very purpose of direct action. Nonviolent direct action seeks to create such a crisis and foster such a tension that a community which has constantly refused to negotiate is forced to confront the issue. It seeks so to dramatize the issue that it can no longer be ignored. My citing the creation of tension as part of the work of the nonviolent-resister may sound rather shocking. But I must confess that I am not afraid of the word "tension." I have earnestly opposed violent tension, but there is a type of constructive, nonviolent tension which is necessary for growth. Just as Socrates felt that it was necessary to create a tension in the mind so that individuals could rise from the bondage of myths and half-truths to the unfettered realm of creative analysis and objective appraisal, so must we see the need for nonviolent gadflies to create the kind of tension in society that will help men rise from the dark depths of prejudice and racism to the majestic heights of understanding and brotherhood.

The purpose of our direct-action program is to create a situation so crisis-packed that it will inevitably open the door to negotiation. I therefore concur with you in your call for negotiation. Too long has our beloved Southland been bogged down in a tragic effort to live in monologue rather than dialogue.

One of the basic points in your statement is that the action that I and my associates have taken in Birmingham is untimely. Some have asked: "Why didn't you give the new city administration time to act?" The only answer that I can give to this query is that the new Birmingham administration must be prodded about as much as the outgoing one, before it will act. We are sadly mistaken if we feel that the election of Albert Boutwell as mayor will bring the millennium to Birmingham. While Mr. Boutwell is a much more gentle person than Mr. Connor, they are both segregationists, dedicated to maintenance of the status quo. I have hope that Mr. Boutwell will be reasonable enough to see the futility of massive resistance to desegregation. But he will not see this without pressure from devotees of civil rights. My friends, I must say to you that we have not made a single gain in civil rights without determined legal and nonviolent pressure. Lamentably, it is an historical fact that privileged groups seldom give up their privileges voluntarily. Individuals may see the moral light and voluntarily give up their unjust posture; but, as Reinhold Niebuhr has reminded us, groups tend to be more immoral than individuals.

We know through painful experience that freedom is never voluntarily given by the oppressor; it must be demanded by the oppressed. Frankly, I have yet to engage in a direct-action campaign that was "well timed" in the view of those who have not suffered unduly from the disease of segregation. For years now I have heard the word "Wait!" It rings in the ear of every Negro with piercing familiarity. This "Wait" has almost always meant "Never." We must come to see, with one of our distinguished jurists, that "justice too long delayed is justice denied."

We have waited for many more than 340 years for our constitutional and God-given rights. The nations of Asia and Africa are moving with jetlike speed toward gaining political independence, but we still creep at horse-and-buggy pace toward gaining a cup of coffee at a lunch counter. Perhaps it is easy for those who have never felt the stinging darts of segregation to say "Wait." But when you have seen vicious mobs lynch your mothers and fathers at will and drown your sisters and brothers at whim; when you have seen hate-filled policemen curse, kick and even kill your black brothers and sisters; when you see the vast majority of your twenty million Negro brothers smothering in an airtight cage of poverty in the midst of an affluent society; when you suddenly find your tongue twisted and your speech stammering as you seek to explain to your six-year-old daughter why she can't go to the public amusement park that has just been advertised on television, and see tears welling up in her eyes when she is told that Funtown is closed to colored children, and see ominous clouds of inferiority beginning to form in her little mental sky, and see her beginning to distort her personality by developing an unconscious bitterness toward white people; when you have to concoct an answer for a five-year-old son who is asking: "Daddy, why do white people treat colored people so mean?"; when you take a cross-county drive and find it necessary to sleep night after night in the uncomfortable corners of your automobile because no motel will accept you; when you are humiliated day in and day out by nagging signs reading "white" and "colored"; when your first name becomes "nigger," your middle name becomes "boy" (however old you are) and your last name becomes "John," and your wife and mother are never given the respected title "Mrs."; when you are harried by day and haunted by night by the fact that you are a Negro, living constantly at tiptoe stance, never quite knowing what to expect next, and are plagued with inner fears and outer resentments; when you are forever fighting a degenerating sense of "nobodiness"—then you will understand why we find it difficult to wait. There comes a time when the cup of endurance runs over, and men are no longer willing to be plunged into the abyss of despair. I hope, sirs, you can understand our legitimate and unavoidable impatience.

You express a great deal of anxiety over our willingness to break laws. This is certainly a legitimate concern. Since we do diligently urge people to obey the Supreme Court's decision of 1954 outlawing segregation in public schools, at first glance it may seem rather paradoxical for us consciously to break laws. One may well ask: "How can you advocate breaking some laws and obeying others?" The answer lies in the fact that there are two types of laws: just and unjust. I would be the first to advocate obeying just laws. One has not only a legal but a moral responsibility to obey just laws. Conversely, one has a moral responsibility to disobey unjust laws. I would agree with St. Augustine that "an unjust law is no law at all".

Now, what is the difference between the two? How does one determine whether a law is just or unjust? A just law is a man-made code that squares with the moral law or the law of God. An unjust law is a code that is out of harmony with the moral law. To put it in the terms of St. Thomas Aquinas: An unjust law is a human law that is not rooted in eternal law and natural law. Any law that uplifts human personality is just. Any law that degrades human personality is unjust. All segregation statutes are unjust because segregation distorts the soul and damages the personality. It gives the segregator a false sense of superiority and the segregated a false sense of inferiority. Segregation, to use the terminology of the Jewish philosopher Martin Buber, substitutes an "I-it" relationship for an "I-thou" relationship and ends up relegating persons to the status of things. Hence segregation is not only politically, economically and sociologically unsound, it is morally wrong and sinful. Paul Tillich said that sin is separation. Is not segregation an existential expression of man's tragic separation, his awful estrangement, his terrible sinfulness? Thus it is that I can urge men to obey the 1954 decision of the Supreme Court, for it is morally right; and I can urge them to disobey segregation ordinances, for they are morally wrong.

Let us consider a more concrete example of just and unjust laws. An unjust law is a code that a numerical or power majority group compels a minority group to obey but does not make binding on itself. This is difference made legal. By the same token, a just law is a code that a majority compels a minority to follow and that it is willing to follow itself. This is sameness made legal.

Let me give another explanation. A law is unjust if it is inflicted on a minority that, as a result of being denied the right to vote, had no part in enacting or devising the law. Who can say that the legislature of Alabama which set up that state's segregation laws was democratically elected? Throughout Alabama all sorts of devious methods are used to prevent Negroes from becoming registered voters, and there are some counties in which, even though Negroes constitute a majority of the population, not a single Negro is registered. Can any law enacted under such circumstances be considered democratically structured?

Sometimes a law is just on its face and unjust in its application. For instance, I have been arrested on a charge of parading without a permit. Now, there is nothing wrong in having an ordinance which requires a permit for a parade. But such an ordinance becomes unjust when it is used to maintain segregation and to deny citizens the First Amendment privilege of peaceful assembly and protest.

I hope you are able to see the distinction I am trying to point out. In no sense do I advocate evading or defying the law, as would the rabid segregationist. That would lead to anarchy. One who breaks an unjust law must do so openly, lovingly, and with a willingness to accept the penalty. I submit that an individual who breaks a law that conscience tells him is unjust and who willingly accepts the penalty of imprisonment in order to arouse the conscience of the community over its injustice, is in reality expressing the highest respect for law.

Of course, there is nothing new about this kind of civil disobedience. It was evidenced sublimely in the refusal of Shadrach, Meshach and Abednego to obey the laws of Nebuchadnezzar, on the ground that a higher moral law was at stake. It was practiced superbly by the early Christians, who were willing to face hungry lions and the excruciating pain of chopping blocks rather than submit to certain unjust laws of the Roman Empire. To a degree, academic freedom is a reality today because Socrates practiced civil disobedience. In our own nation, the Boston Tea Party represented a massive act of civil disobedience.

We should never forget that everything Adolf Hitler did in Germany was "legal" and everything the Hungarian freedom fighters did in Hungary was "illegal." It was "illegal" to aid and comfort a Jew in Hitler's Germany. Even so, I am sure that, had I lived in Germany at the time, I would have aided and comforted my Jewish brothers. If today I lived in a Communist country where certain principles dear to the Christian faith are suppressed, I would openly advocate disobeying that country's antireligious laws.

I must make two honest confessions to you, my Christian and Jewish brothers. First, I must confess that over the past few years I have been gravely disappointed with the white moderate. I have almost reached the regrettable conclusion that the Negro's great stumbling block in his stride toward freedom is not the White Citizen's Counciler or the Ku Klux Klanner, but the white moderate, who is more devoted to "order" than to justice; who prefers a negative peace which is the absence of tension to a positive peace which is the presence of justice; who constantly says: "I agree with you in the goal you seek, but I cannot agree with your methods of direct action"; who paternalistically believes he can set the timetable for another man's freedom; who lives by a mythical concept of time and who constantly advises the Negro to wait for a "more convenient season." Shallow understanding from people of good will is more frustrating than absolute misunderstanding from people of ill will. Lukewarm acceptance is much more bewildering than outright rejection.

I had hoped that the white moderate would understand that law and order exist for the purpose of establishing justice and that when they fail in this purpose they become the dangerously structured dams that block the flow of social progress. I had hoped that the white moderate would understand that the present tension in the South is a necessary phase of the transition from an obnoxious negative peace, in which the Negro passively accepted his unjust plight, to a substantive and positive peace, in which all men will respect the dignity and worth of human personality. Actually, we who engage in nonviolent direct action are not the creators of tension. We merely bring to the surface the hidden tension that is already alive. We bring it out in the open, where it can be seen and dealt with. Like a boil that can never be cured so long as it is covered up but must be opened with all its ugliness to the natural medicines of air and light, injustice must be exposed, with all the tension its exposure creates, to the light of human conscience and the air of national opinion before it can be cured.

In your statement you assert that our actions, even though peaceful, must be condemned because they precipitate violence. But is this a logical assertion? Isn't this like condemning a robbed man because his possession of money precipitated the evil act of robbery? Isn't this like condemning Socrates because his unswerving commitment to truth and his philosophical inquiries precipitated the act by the misguided populace in which they made him drink hemlock? Isn't this like condemning Jesus because his unique God-consciousness and never-ceasing devotion to God's will precipitated the evil act of crucifixion? We must come to see that, as the federal courts have consistently affirmed, it is wrong to urge an individual to cease his efforts to gain his basic constitutional rights because the quest may precipitate violence. Society must protect the robbed and punish the robber.

I had also hoped that the white moderate would reject the myth concerning time in relation to the struggle for freedom. I have just received a letter from a white brother in Texas. He writes: "All Christians know that the colored people will receive equal rights eventually, but it is possible that you are in too great a religious hurry. It has taken Christianity almost two thousand years to accomplish what it has. The teachings of Christ take time to come to earth." Such an attitude stems from a tragic misconception of time, from the strangely rational notion that there is something in the very flow of time that will inevitably cure all ills. Actually, time itself is neutral; it can be used either destructively or constructively. More and more I feel that the people of ill will have used time much more effectively than have the people of good will. We will have to repent in this generation not merely for the hateful words and actions of the bad people but for the appalling silence of the good people. Human progress never rolls in on wheels of inevitability; it comes through the tireless efforts of men willing to be co-workers with God, and without this 'hard work,' time itself becomes an ally of the forces of social stagnation. We must use time creatively, in the knowledge that the time is always ripe to do right. Now is the time to make real the promise of democracy and transform our pending national elegy into a creative psalm of brotherhood. Now is the time to lift our national policy from the quicksand of racial injustice to the solid rock of human dignity.

You speak of our activity in Birmingham as extreme. At first I was rather disappointed that fellow clergymen would see my nonviolent efforts as those of an extremist. I began thinking about the fact that I stand in the middle of two opposing forces in the Negro community. One is a force of complacency, made up in part of Negroes who, as a result of long years of oppression, are so drained of self-respect and a sense of "somebodiness" that they have adjusted to segregation; and made up in part of a few middle class Negroes who, because of a degree of academic and economic security and because in some ways they profit by segregation, have become insensitive to the problems of the masses. The other force is one of bitterness and hatred, and it comes perilously close to advocating violence. It is expressed in the various black nationalist groups that are springing up across the nation, the largest and best-known being Elijah Muhammad's Muslim movement. Nourished by the Negro's frustration over the continued existence of racial discrimination, this movement is made up of people who have lost faith in America, who have absolutely repudiated Christianity, and who have concluded that the white man is an incorrigible "devil."

I have tried to stand between these two forces, saying that we need emulate neither the "do-nothingism" of the complacent nor the hatred and despair of the black nationalist. For there is the more excellent way of love and nonviolent protest. I am grateful to God that, through the influence of the Negro church, the way of nonviolence became an integral part of our struggle.

If this philosophy had not emerged, by now many streets of the South would, I am convinced, be flowing with blood. And I am further convinced that if our white brothers dismiss as "rabble-rousers" and "outside agitators" those of us who employ nonviolent direct action, and if they refuse to support our nonviolent efforts, millions of Negroes will, out of frustration and despair, seek solace and security in black-nationalist ideologies—a development that would inevitably lead to a frightening racial nightmare.

Oppressed people cannot remain oppressed forever. The yearning for freedom eventually manifests itself, and that is what has happened to the American Negro. Something within has reminded him of his birthright of freedom, and something without has reminded him that it can be gained. Consciously or unconsciously, he has been caught up by the Zeitgeist, and with his black brothers of Africa and his brown and yellow brothers of Asia, South America and the Caribbean, the United States Negro is moving with a sense of great urgency toward the promised land of racial justice. If one recognizes this vital urge that has engulfed the Negro community, one should readily understand why public demonstrations are taking place. The Negro has many pent-up resentments and latent frustrations, and he must release them. So let him march; let him make prayer pilgrimages to the city hall; let him go on freedom rides—and try to understand why he must do so. If his repressed emotions are not released in nonviolent ways, they will seek expression through violence; this is not a threat but a fact of history. So I have not said to my people: "Get rid of your discontent." Rather, I have tried to say that this normal and healthy discontent can be channeled into the creative outlet of nonviolent direct action. And now this approach is being termed extremist.

But though I was initially disappointed at being categorized as an extremist, as I continued to think about the matter I gradually gained a measure of satisfaction from the label. Was not Jesus an extremist for love: "Love your enemies, bless them that curse you, do good to them that hate you, and pray for them which despitefully use you, and persecute you." Was not Amos an extremist for justice: "Let justice roll down like waters and righteousness like an ever-flowing stream." Was not Paul an extremist for the Christian gospel: "I bear in my body the marks of the Lord Jesus." Was not Martin Luther an extremist: "Here I stand; I cannot do otherwise, so help me God." And John Bunyan: "I will stay in jail to the end of my days before I make a butchery of my conscience." And Abraham Lincoln: "This nation cannot survive half slave and half free." And Thomas Jefferson: "We hold these truths to be self-evident, that all men are created equal..." So the question is not whether we will be extremists, but what kind of extremist we will be. Will we be extremists for hate or for love? Will we be extremists for the preservation of injustice or for the extension of justice? In that dramatic scene on Calvary's hill three men were crucified. We must never forget that all three were crucified for the same crime—the crime of extremism. Two were extremists for immorality, and thus fell below their environment. The other, Jesus Christ, was an extremist for love, truth and goodness, and thereby rose above his environment. Perhaps the South, the nation and the world are in dire need of creative extremists.

UNIT

9

I had hoped that the white moderate would see this need. Perhaps I was too optimistic; perhaps I expected too much. I suppose I should have realized that few members of the oppressor race can understand the deep groans and passionate yearnings of the oppressed race, and still fewer have the vision to see that injustice must be rooted out by strong, persistent and determined action. I am thankful, however, that some of our white brothers in the South have grasped the meaning of this social revolution and committed themselves to it. They are still too few in quantity, but they are big in quality. Some—such as Ralph McGill, Lillian Smith, Harry Golden, James McBride Dabbs, Ann Braden and Sarah Patton Boyle—have written about our struggle in eloquent and prophetic terms. Others have marched with us down nameless streets of the South. They have languished in filthy, roach-infested jails, suffering the abuse and brutality of policemen who view them as "dirty nigger lovers." Unlike so many of their moderate brothers and sisters, they have recognized the urgency of the moment and sensed the need for powerful "action" antidotes to combat the disease of segregation.

Let me take note of my other major disappointment. I have been so greatly disappointed with the white church and its leadership. Of course, there are some notable exceptions. I am not unmindful of the fact that each of you has taken some significant stands on this issue. I commend you, Reverend Stallings, for your Christian stand on this past Sunday, in welcoming Negroes to your worship service on a non-segregated basis. I commend the Catholic leaders of this state for integrating Spring Hill College several years ago.

But despite these notable exceptions, I must honestly reiterate that I have been disappointed with the church. I do not say this as one of those negative critics who can always find something wrong with the church. I say this as a minister of the gospel, who loves the church; who was nurtured in its bosom; who has been sustained by its spiritual blessings and who will remain true to it as long as the cord of life shall lengthen.

When I was suddenly catapulted into the leadership of the bus protest in Montgomery, Alabama, a few years ago, I felt we would be supported by the white church. I felt that the white ministers, priests and rabbis of the South would be among our strongest allies. Instead, some have been outright opponents, refusing to understand the freedom movement and misrepresenting its leadership; and too many others have been more cautious than courageous and have remained silent behind the anesthetizing security of stained-glass windows.

In spite of my shattered dreams, I came to Birmingham with the hope that the white religious leadership of this community would see the justice of our cause and, with deep moral concern, would serve as the channel through which our just grievances could reach the power structure. I had hoped that each of you would understand. But again I have been disappointed.

I have heard numerous southern religious leaders admonish their worshipers to comply with a desegregation decision because it is the law, but I have longed to hear white ministers declare: "Follow this decree because integration is morally right and because the Negro is your brother." In the midst of blatant injustices inflicted upon the Negro, I have watched white churchmen stand on the sideline and mouth pious irrelevancies and sanctimonious trivialities. In the midst of a mighty struggle to rid our nation of racial and economic injustice, I have heard many ministers say: "Those are social issues, with which the gospel has no real concern." And I have watched many churches commit themselves to a completely other-worldly religion which makes a strange, un-Biblical distinction between body and soul, between the sacred and the secular.

I have traveled the length and breadth of Alabama, Mississippi and all the other southern states. On sweltering summer days and crisp autumn mornings I have looked at the South's beautiful churches with their lofty spires pointing heavenward. I have beheld the impressive outlines of her massive religious-education buildings. Over and over I have found myself asking: "What kind of people worship here? Who is their God? Where were their voices when the lips of Governor Barnett dripped with words of interposition and nullification? Where were they when Governor Wallace gave a clarion call for defiance and hatred? Where were their voices of support when bruised and weary Negro men and women decided to rise from the dark dungeons of complacency to the bright hills of creative protest?"

Yes, these questions are still in my mind. In deep disappointment I have wept over the laxity of the church. But be assured that my tears have been tears of love. There can be no deep disappointment where there is not deep love. Yes, I love the church. How could I do otherwise? I am in the rather unique position of being the son, the grandson and the great-grandson of preachers. Yes, I see the church as the body of Christ. But, oh! How we have blemished and scarred that body through social neglect and through fear of being nonconformists.

There was a time when the church was very powerful—in the time when the early Christians rejoiced at being deemed worthy to suffer for what they believed. In those days the church was not merely a thermometer that recorded the ideas and principles of popular opinion; it was a thermostat that transformed the mores of society. Whenever the early Christians entered a town, the people in power became disturbed and immediately sought to convict the Christians for being "disturbers of the peace" and "outside agitators." But the Christians pressed on, in the conviction that they were "a colony of heaven," called to obey God rather than man. Small in number, they were big in commitment. They were too God intoxicated to be "astronomically intimidated." By their effort and example they brought an end to such ancient evils as infanticide and gladiatorial contests.

Things are different now. So often the contemporary church is a weak, ineffectual voice with an uncertain sound. So often it is an archdefender of the status quo. Far from being disturbed by the presence of the church, the power structure of the average community is consoled by the church's silent—and often even vocal—sanction of things as they are.

But the judgment of God is upon the church as never before. If today's church does not recapture the sacrificial spirit of the early church, it will lose its authenticity, forfeit the loyalty of millions, and be dismissed as an irrelevant social club with no meaning for the twentieth century. Every day I meet young people whose disappointment with the church has turned into outright disgust.

Perhaps I have once again been too optimistic. Is organized religion too inextricably bound to the status quo to save our nation and the world? Perhaps I must turn my faith to the inner spiritual church, the church within the church, as the true ekklesia and the hope of the world. But again I am thankful to God that some noble souls from the ranks of organized religion have broken loose from the paralyzing chains of conformity and joined us as active partners in the struggle for freedom, They have left their secure congregations and walked the streets of Albany, Georgia, with us. They have gone down the highways of the South on tortuous rides for freedom. Yes, they have gone to jail with us. Some have been dismissed from their churches, have lost the support of their bishops and fellow ministers. But they have acted in the faith that right defeated is stronger than evil triumphant. Their witness has been the spiritual salt that has preserved the true meaning of the gospel in these troubled times. They have carved a tunnel of hope through the dark mountain of disappointment.

I hope the church as a whole will meet the challenge of this decisive hour. But even if the church does not come to the aid of justice, I have no despair about the future. I have no fear about the outcome of our struggle in Birmingham, even if our motives are at present misunderstood. We will reach the goal of freedom in Birmingham and all over the nation, because the goal of America is freedom. Abused and scorned though we may be, our destiny is tied up with America's destiny. Before the pilgrims landed at Plymouth, we were here. Before the pen of Jefferson etched the majestic words of the Declaration of Independence across the pages of history, we were here. For more than two centuries our forebears labored in this country without wages; they made cotton king; they built the homes of their masters while suffering gross injustice and shameful humiliation—and yet out of a bottomless vitality they continued to thrive and develop. If the inexpressible cruelties of slavery could not stop us, the opposition we now face will surely fail. We will win our freedom because the sacred heritage of our nation and the eternal will of God are embodied in our echoing demands.

Before closing I feel impelled to mention one other point in your statement that has troubled me profoundly. You warmly commended the Birmingham police force for keeping "order" and "preventing violence." I doubt that you would have so warmly commended the police force if you had seen its dogs sinking their teeth into unarmed, nonviolent Negroes. I doubt that you would so quickly commend the policemen if you were to observe their ugly and inhumane treatment of Negroes here in the city jail; if you were to watch them push and curse old Negro women and young Negro girls; if you were to see them slap and kick old Negro men and young boys; and if you were to observe them, as they did on two occasions, refuse to give us food because we want to sing our grace together. I cannot join you in your praise of the Birmingham police department.

It is true that the police have exercised a degree of discipline in handling the demonstrators. In this sense they have conducted themselves rather "nonviolently" in public. But for what purpose? To preserve the evil system of segregation. Over the past few years I have consistently preached that nonviolence demands that the means we use must be as pure as the ends we seek. I have tried to make clear that it is wrong to use immoral means to attain moral ends. But now I must affirm that it is just as wrong, or perhaps even more so, to use moral means to preserve immoral ends. Perhaps Mr. Connor and his policemen have been rather nonviolent in public, as was Chief Pritchett in Albany, Georgia but they have used the moral means of nonviolence to maintain the immoral end of racial injustice. As T. S. Eliot has said: "The last temptation is the greatest treason: To do the right deed for the wrong reason."

I wish you had commended the Negro sit-inners and demonstrators of Birmingham for their sublime courage, their willingness to suffer and their amazing discipline in the midst of great provocation. One day the South will recognize its real heroes. They will be the James Merediths, with the noble sense of purpose that enables them to face jeering and hostile mobs, and with agonizing loneliness that characterizes the life of the pioneer. They will be old, oppressed, battered Negro women, symbolized in a seventy-two-year-old woman in Montgomery, Alabama, who rose up with a sense of dignity and with her people decided not to ride segregated buses, and who responded with ungrammatical profundity to one who inquired about her weariness: "My feets is tired, but my soul is at rest." They will be the young high school and college students, the young ministers of the gospel and a host of their elders, courageously and nonviolently sitting at lunch counters and willingly going to jail for conscience' sake. One day the South will know that when these disinherited children of God sat down at lunch counters, they were in reality standing up for what is best in the American dream and for the most sacred values in our Judaeo-Christian heritage, thereby bringing our nation back to those great wells of democracy which were dug deep by the founding fathers in their formulation of the Constitution and the Declaration of Independence.

Never before have I written so long a letter. I'm afraid it is much too long to take your precious time. I can assure you that it would have been much shorter if I had been writing from a comfortable desk, but what else can one do when he is alone in a narrow jail cell, other than write long letters, think long thoughts and pray long prayers?

If I have said anything in this letter that overstates the truth and indicates an unreasonable impatience, I beg you to forgive me. If I have said anything that understates truth and indicates my having a patience that allows me to settle for anything less than brotherhood, I beg God to forgive me.

I hope this letter finds you strong in the faith... Let us all hope that the dark clouds of racial prejudice will soon pass away and the deep fog of misunderstanding will be lifted from our fear-drenched communities, and in some not too distant tomorrow the radiant stars of love and brotherhood will shine over our great nation with all their scintillating beauty.

Yours for the cause of Peace and Brotherhood,

Martin Luther King, Jr.

The Winner's Brain: 8 Strategies Great Minds Use to Achieve Success

By Jeff Brown, Mark Fenske, and Liz Neporent

Points to Consider

1. To what extent do you agree with the author's definition of individual success?

2. What strategies can you utilize to push beyond what you perceive are our limitations to realize change and achieve success, both individually and in group settings?

3. To what degree can you use the author's strategies to realize change in an organization?

4. At what point is an individual's success counterproductive to a group's success? At what point is an organization's success counterproductive to an individual's growth?

The Winner's Brain: 8 Strategies Great Minds Use to Achieve Success

Introduction

People who are successful in life have one thing in common: They all seem to be doing something different and special with their neurocircuitry to maximize their potential and achieve their goals. We believe that's what gives these people a Winner's Brain.

The average brain does a pretty good job of getting by day to day. After all, it has over one hundred billion brain cells serviced by a superhighway of blood vessels to help you think your thoughts, move your body, and experience the world around you, acting with a combination of speed and efficiency that even the most advanced computers can't rival. But presumably you are reading this book because of a desire to move beyond just getting by. You want to excel in life and achieve the goals that matter to you most.

re considering a career change or launching a new business, yet haven't had the where-
ke the leap. Maybe you feel stuck at work and are unclear how to get ahead. Perhaps
your job and are searching for a better situation. Wherever you are in life, whatever
you want to expand your limits and open up your possibilities.

Contrary to popular belief, high personal achievement has very little to do with your IQ, your life circumstances, your financial resources, knowing the right people, or even luck. Take, for example, the great French sculptor Auguste Rodin, who came from a poor family and was rejected from art school three times. Despite butting up against constant rejection, he bounced hack time and again, using each failure and disappointment as an opportunity to fuel his talents and his passions. As you shall see once you dive into the upcoming chapters, Resilience and Motivation are two of the critical abilities for which Winner's Brains are wired.

The Partnership of Brain and Behavior

Our combined expertise as a cognitive behavioral psychologist (Jeff) and a cognitive neuroscientist (Mark) places us in a unique position to explain how the cognitive mechanisms of the human brain are associated with success. We have seen from our respective work how the strategies shared in this book can influence thoughts and behavior and help individuals push past unpleasant life circumstances, allowing them to blossom and grow. Seeing people routinely rise above challenges—sometimes incredibly harsh ones—and consistently flourish is one of the primary reasons Jeff became so interested in the science of success. And we've also seen evidence that these same strategies can literally reshape the brain. Brains that perform successfully really do "light up" differently and work more efficiently, and Mark has investigated just how the structure and function of brains are altered as a result of how their owners use them.

Winner's Brains actually operate differently than the average brain. We know this, in part, because of technological advances that let us see individual differences in how neural areas light up on scans of brains as they spring into action. By measuring physiological changes related to neural activity, such as increases in blood flow within the brain, techniques such as fMRI (functional Magnetic Resonance Imaging) can help us see which areas of the brain are relatively more active and participating as a corresponding thought, emotion, or behavior is playing out. (If, for example, someone sneaks up behind you and yells "Boo!" that instant jolt of fear that surges through your body is associated with increased activity within the amygdala, an almond-shaped structure in the medial temporal lobe—the structure that's most closely associated with identifying threats and evaluating the possibility of harm.) We've found the following:

A Winner's Brain is very good at tuning out distractions and choosing the best way to focus on a task (there are different types of focus the brain is capable of) in order to get the best outcome. A study led by Daniel Weissman at the University of Michigan showed that participants were able to stop and reorient their brain's processing power to help them perform better despite interruptions. We call the deliberate form of this strategy focus reinvestment. With practice, this type of skill is something you can develop for yourself to reduce your own attention-related errors. Even if previous tries to change jobs, find a mate, or attain any other objective have failed in the past, an extra dose of focus may be just what you need to get you over the hump.

Winner's Brains seem to maintain a bottomless effort supply. A youngster who is forced to practice his piano lessons one hour every day, even if he doesn't want to and has no interest in playing, is unlikely to become an accomplished pianist. But a child who loves music, is interested in playing, and understands the potential of success will prioritize and complete her practice sessions—even at the end of her most tiring days. She is more likely to become a proficient, successful player because of her ability to sustain the effort.

Support for this idea comes from studies like one by Debra Gusnard and colleagues at Washington University School of Medicine, who measured people's brain activity while they viewed a random series of images that were either emotionally stimulating or dull. These people also filled out self-assessments regarding their day-to-day level of persistence in completing tasks. Subjects with high persistence scores showed, during periods of the experiment containing mostly dull images, increased activity in brain regions known to contribute to motivational drive. Subjects with low persistence scores showed decreased activity in these regions. Winner's Brains fire up Motivation to push through boredom, while brains of less tenacious individuals seem to run out of steam.

Winner's Brains adapt in exceptional ways over time, harnessing a process known as neuroplasticity. Every time you think a thought, feel an emotion, or execute a behavior, there is always some sort of corresponding change within your brain. In some instances we can detect these alterations in the brain's physical landscape. Later in this book, you'll read about London Black Cab drivers who have regions of the hippocampus—an area of the brain involved in memory and spatial navigation—that are considerably larger than that of the average person. Research by Eleanor Maguire and colleagues at University College London suggests that these cab drivers likely started out with fairly ordinary brains. But when motivated to commit routes to memory, they quite literally built a better brain, neuron by neuron. This is something virtually anyone should be able to do—including you—if you quite literally put your mind to it.

Many people view the brain as a mysterious, abstract structure—almost like a set of master controls that run on autopilot behind a locked door to which one has no real access. This simply isn't the case. You have the ability to unlock the door and consciously, deliberately, and successfully control much of your brain's switchboard in order to better position yourself to achieve your goals and dreams. The brain is active and subject to change no matter what you do—this is one of the key discoveries of modern neuroscience. What sets the owner of a Winner's Brain apart is the desire and the know-how to take charge of the process.

Our definition of Winners encompasses the usual conception: people who meet with extraordinary success in the particular aspects of life they value the most. Winners achieve what they set out to accomplish, whether they wish to master a golf swing, raise a confident child, or climb the corporate ladder. But we would add more: The kind of Winners we are talking about revel in the journey toward their goals almost as much as the destination itself, and they strive for the type of success that helps make the world a better place. And whether they realize it or not, virtually all Winners rely on the specific brain strategies we lay out in this book to come out on top.

Throughout this book, dozens of our Winners tell their stories, which illuminate the science and theories. They come from all walks of life: artists and inventors, musicians and business people, a high-altitude window washer, an Olympic champion. Many are well known, like blues great B. B. King, Olympic gold medalist Kerri Strug, actress Laura Linney, and motivational speaker Trisha Meili, the Central Park jogger. They all meet the definition of success in their own unique way. Our interviews reveal surprising, often touching, and enlightening information aimed at showing how anyone can change their thinking to improve their life.

To be clear, not everyone with a Winner's Brain walks around with a gold medal, an Oscar, or a million-dollar paycheck. Some of the people you'll meet consider their greatest accomplishment being a college graduate, a superb cab driver, or a working artist. They are every bit as amazing as the celebrities you will meet in this book because they have accomplished the things in life that are most important to them personally, often in the face of extreme adversity.

UNIT
9

What It *Doesn't* Take

We'd also like to dispel the myth that achievers are all born hardwired for success, that you are either born with a high-functioning brain or you aren't. We know that the brain changes based on what its owner chooses to do with it. And yes, you do have a certain amount of control over the process. Many of the studies we present in this book demonstrate this cause and effect convincingly. What has emerged from this research and our representative interviews is that Winners are often forced to do some extensive rewiring so they can leap over life's obstacles and stay on the path to success. In addition, many didn't start with the vast financial resources or the important personal connections you might expect. And very few fit the definition of lucky. All of them demonstrate a strategic and proactive use of brain power—they take charge of their brain's Adaptability rather than leaving it to chance or waiting for the perfect set of circumstances to present themselves.

In the case of how your brain operates, nature does not always trump nurture: They work together. One of the central themes of this book is that there are many ways to shape your brain to more fully express its genetic potential. As you'll learn in the chapter on Adaptability, your brain's structure and functioning will continue to change over time even if you don't do anything strategic with it—just not necessarily the way you wish. So why not take the reins and nurture the nature you have? Even into old age, we all can adapt our brain. Indeed, one of the well-established laws of neuroscience is that the brain retains a capacity for change until the day you die. You are not enslaved by a brain that can only respond in one way. There are endless opportunities for improvement; and when you actively take charge of how your brain works, you have a better chance of influencing your fortunes.

…

BrainPower Tools: Five Essential Elements of Success

Winner's Brains have specific traits in common that we call BrainPower Tools. Some brains may possess some or all of these BrainPower Tools naturally—and if so, that's great—but we believe that almost anyone can enhance them by using the techniques in this book.

The Winner's Profile Quiz

Before you read this chapter, take this quick quiz to see if you currently have what it takes to set yourself up for success. This quiz isn't brain science per se, but it is derived from our experience and research associated with the psychological traits that appear to help people achieve and succeed. You were not born with these tools fully developed, but we believe it is possible to use your brain to strengthen them. As you will learn in this book, you can adapt the way your brain operates by consciously driving your thoughts, emotions, and behaviors in a specific direction.

To take the quiz, indicate how strongly you believe the statements or ideas below. Total your score by totaling up the numbers from all of your answers, then see how you measure up on the Winner's Brain continuum right now. After you've read through the chapters on the Win Factor strategies and given yourself at least a month to apply what you've learned, take the quiz again to see how your score changes. You may be surprised how your scores in your weaker areas have improved. You may find yourself responding in a more resilient way, staying more focused on the things you consider important or be better able to identify which talents are going to move you ahead in life.

Don't agree at all (1)   Somewhat agree (2)   Completely agree (3)

Goal Laser

1. Nothing ever distracts me from my goals.   _____
2. I strive for my goals until I reach them—no matter what.   _____
3. I always see a project through to the end.   _____

Optimal Risk Gauge

4. I easily tolerate being outside of my comfort zone.   _____
5. My decisions never lead to regret.   _____
6. If something's too good to be true, then it usually is.   _____

Talent Meter

7. If I'm not good at something, I find out how to improve.   _____
8. I can accurately identify potential in others and myself.   _____
9. It's easy for me to recognize what I don't know.   _____

Opportunity Radar

10. I'm good at finding solutions when none seem to exist.   _____
11. When something goes wrong, I try to see not the failure,
    but the opportunity in the setback.   _____
12. When I try something and it doesn't work out the way I want it to,
    I reboot and find a new way to come at the problem.   _____

Effort Accelerator

13. I can motivate myself easily.   _____
14. I rarely procrastinate.   _____
15. Even if I'm in last place, I find the strength to finish the race. _____

Score

45–40: You've got a head start; this book will help you put it all together. Your BrainPower Tools are well developed—now polish them to make them even stronger and more useful to you.

39–30: You're getting there but still have room for growth. You'll be a quick study. Some of your BrainPower Tools are operating smoothly, but others could use a bit of fine tuning. The strategies in this book are going to help you get to the next level.

29–20: You're just starting out, but you can get there. You have an awareness of your own potential. By taking on the brain-enhancing strategies we outline in this book, you will learn to direct your abilities to take you in the direction you want to go.

20 and below: Perhaps you thought you could never achieve success. You can. Like almost everyone, you have the raw materials it takes to get what you want from life, you just need some help developing the strategies and skills to get there.

As we began to write this book, it became remarkably clear how Winner's Brains tend to do many of the same things and operate in similar ways regardless of the direction their owners choose to take them. When we put our heads together to decide exactly what makes a Winner's Brain tick—Jeff in his capacity as a cognitive behavioral psychologist and Mark as a cognitive neuroscientist—the result was a profile consisting of eight Win Factors (more on those in a bit)

UNIT
9

that contribute to five different areas that we call BrainPower Tools: your Opportunity Radar, Optimal Risk Gauge, Goal Laser, Effort Accelerator, and Talent Meter.

How did we pinpoint these? First, we spent a lot of time reviewing how extraordinary brains operate differently in the moment and how they reshape themselves over time in response to the way they are used. From that emerged a picture of how Winners tend to use their brains to achieve success. Next, we discussed both our findings and our conclusions with some of the world's most respected experts in the various branches of neuroscience and psychology to confirm and refine our interpretation of the research. Speaking to top minds in the field helped us confidently reach conclusions that the research can actually support.

Finally, we wanted to illustrate how what is true in the lab can also be translated into real-life success. That's where the interviews come in with dozens of people we consider to be Winners. Every Winner in this book not only had to be successful in the area of their choosing, they had to clearly demonstrate the use of the BrainPower Tools and the Win Factor strategies we outline. In addition, no one featured here is to the manor born or has been handed anything without having to work hard and smart to get it. It was both gratifying and amazing to see how well the neuroscience and psychology match up to what actually helps people get what they want out of life.

We also concluded that some people quickly emerge with each BrainPower Tool firing on all cylinders. They may not always realize they are using their brains in this way, but research indicates they are. Some of the studies we detail in this book start out by identifying people who already have the ability to do something well, then go on to examine how others might learn the particular strategy or trait. Other studies teach the success strategy and then look to neuroscience and psychology to explain how it works. Both types of studies are useful because they emphasize the average person's ability to move his or her brain in the direction of Winner.

So let's start by looking at each of the five BrainPower Tools and how they align with a Winner's Brain. In the process, you'll meet some of the Winners you'll learn more about later on and you'll get a taste of the science of success.

Tool #1: Opportunity Radar

No one can mistake Phyllis Diller's deep, staccato laugh for anyone's but hers. Hearing that signature cackle, you might think it's all been fun and games, but remember, she started out in the 1950s, an era that didn't exactly embrace female comics with open arms (unless you were Lucille Ball). Yet even with all of the challenges she faced as a young comedian, she would often pass up higher-paying gigs for ones that paid zilch as long as she thought it would allow her to do the act she wanted to do and be seen by the people she wanted to be seen by. That's a pretty gutsy move for someone who was barely making ends meet.

Like many of the Winners you'll meet throughout this book, Diller has the head (plus the hair!) for putting herself in the right place at the right time. We call this almost magical ability to spot a hot prospect Opportunity Radar.

Winners are continually scanning for blips on life's radar screen, and when a blip looks interesting, they investigate. Another great example is George de Mestral, the Swiss engineer who invented Velcro after examining the mountain thistle burrs he removed from his dog's fur. How many millions of people before de Mestral treated those burrs as nothing but a nuisance? People with exceptional Opportunity Radar recognize that opportunities don't always come gift-wrapped; more often than not, they come wrapped in a problem or an idea that everyone else has simply missed. This is a skill that serves everyone well. If a project you are working on bombs, you may not be thrilled, but if you can seize upon the things you learned along the way, perhaps there is one aspect you can develop into something great.

Recent research shows that people like Diller and de Mestral rely on what some have called the brain's promotion system, the aspects of the brain that are primed to search for and recognize a good Opportunity. A team of researchers led by William Cunningham, for example, measured activity in emotion-related brain regions on an fMRI scanner, such as the amygdala and anterior cingulate, as individuals experienced emotionally positive and negative words. They found that the emotion-related regions were more sensitive to positive information in individuals who tend to seek advancement and accomplishment and were more reactive to negative information in those who tend to be more concerned with safety and responsibility. In addition to their ability to hone in on what may be potentially good, Winners may often depend on what most of us describe as intuition; however, digging a little deeper, we see that intuition is another aspect of Opportunity Radar that is stoked by an openness to view things with a fresh eye. This is why Diller was always able to spark new life into topics as well-worn as mothers-in-law and lazy husbands.

Was every career choice Diller made a good one? There's that famous laugh again as she admits to her share of face plants. You see, even the most winning of Winners will occasionally misread the blips on the Opportunity Radar screen. But having a keen radar helps stack the odds in your favor by helping you anticipate which opportunities may lead to success and which won't. You learn to avoid mistakes by slowing down and taking the time to assess the pros and cons of each opportunity. And when you stumble, your skin grows thicker with the confidence to carry on until the next good option comes along.

Tool #2: Optimal Risk Gauge

When Stephen Harris flashes that killer smile, right away most women think: Rock Star. Harris was a boy from a small working-class Welsh town who made it big in the 1980s playing bass for bands such as The Cult and Guns N' Roses—until he walked away from the scene to pursue other interests like painting and rock climbing. In September 2001, Harris had a life-changing epiphany after witnessing firsthand the pain and suffering following the terrorist attacks on the World Trade Center in New York City. Although he was never an enthusiastic student, he decided to go back to school and become a doctor. So at the age of 36, Harris took the risk and walked away from a comfortable existence to travel down a road where he won't officially pick up a stethoscope until he's 45. In the end, he says, taking the leap was an easy decision. He shrugs his shoulders when he points out that he would eventually be 45 in any case, so the greater risk would be looking back and realizing he hadn't pursued his dream. How many times have you wanted to take a leap but weren't sure how to evaluate the consequences?

People like Harris dovetail their Opportunity Radars with the BrainPower Tool we call *Optimal Risk Gauge*. The sorts of risk taking they consider important don't involve betting your life savings on a horse race or highly speculative investments, nor are they casual risks like buying a lottery ticket or playing penny poker with the gang. For your Risk Gauge to be effective, you must be good at recognizing what the risks are, determine how much risk you can tolerate and whether or not you are willing and able to pay the consequences if you fail. You don't want to crash and burn from taking the plunge too often, but you do want to aim for a high enough payoff to make it worth your while.

Winners also try to better their situation (and sometimes the world) by taking risks that are substantial enough that they have a personal stake in the outcome, yet more gratifying than if they sat on the sidelines playing it safe. This is because lightweight goals aren't rewarding and insurmountable ones are a waste of time.

UNIT

9

Evidence for this came in 2007 when Sabrina Tom and colleagues at the University of California, Los Angeles conducted a neuroeconomics experiment to see how the brain evaluates risk. Brain scans of 16 people who had a 50/50 chance of winning a bet for a small amount of cash showed that a broad set of regions associated with reward lit up as the potential gains increased—but those same areas dimmed as potential losses increased. Individuals with more pronounced levels of this neural "loss aversion" in regions such as the prefrontal cortex and ventral striatum (part of the basal ganglia) also tended to be those whose behavior showed greater sensitivity to potential losses. Winners like Harris are particularly good at calibrating this type of risk threshold to decide whether or not there is a chance worth taking. They know when to dive in headfirst and when to walk away.

Tool #3: Goal Laser

Iranian-born Ramin Karimloo first saw Andrew Lloyd Webber's musical *The Phantom of the Opera* at age 12, and he was hooked. Now, as he hurries into makeup before a night's performance in London's West End production of *Phantom*, you can tell he is just as excited and enthusiastic as that first moment he decided that playing the Phantom is what he wanted to do with his life.

Talk about follow-through! Karimloo has an impressive *Goal Laser*, the Brainpower Tool that helps you take aim at what you want out of life without allowing the static of distractions and stressors to interfere. It gives you the patience to delay gratification, often for years, without getting sidetracked along the way. Karimloo, for example, started by honing his skills singing in rock bands, then took parts in regional theater, eventually graduating to national touring companies. By his early twenties he was getting understudy roles on the London stage in hits such as *Les Misérables* and *Miss Saigon*. Finally, two weeks before his 25th birthday, he was awarded the lead role as the Phantom at London's Her Majesty's Theatre, where he continued until he left to prepare for his role as the main character in the premiere of *Love Never Dies*, the much-anticipated sequel to *Phantom*. (He was hand-picked for the role by Andrew Lloyd Webber himself.)

As studies show, people who have highly focused Goal Lasers like Karimloo tend to outperform their less self-directed peers because they intentionally and deliberately take steps to accomplish the things that are important to them. For example, a 2007 study of 22.3 salespeople by University of Texas at Arlington's Fernando Jaramillo and his colleagues found that the go-getters—those who showed the greatest amount of initiative—had an easier time translating their goals into actions compared to peers who had trouble taking initiative. So Goal Laser is about more than just having hopes and dreams: it's about locking on to them for as long as it takes to achieve them.

Tool #4: Effort Accelerator

Olympic gold medalist Kerri Strug is living proof of how valuable it is to have a strong *Effort Accelerator*, as we call the BrainPower Tool that supplies the push needed to keep on rolling over obstacles and sidestepping distractions as you march steadily toward achievement. As anyone who has ever tried to get in shape before knows, going to the gym day after day, year after year, and enduring hours of practice and physical punishment, as Strug did leading up to her heroic vault in the 1996 Summer Olympics, takes an incredible work ethic that goes well beyond simple motivation. There were certainly days where Strug wasn't particularly pumped up about what she had to do. But she did it. And she did it steadily, reliably, consistently. When she shares her lifelong motto "Never put off until tomorrow what you can do today," you can almost hear her revving up her Effort Accelerator.

The truth is, there are plenty of people who enjoy success when they aren't particularly motivated, but they seem to have the sort of self-directed energy inherent to the Effort Accelerator that keeps them chugging along. We see this in studies, such as that led by Debra Gusnard, where subjects who score high on the persistence scale (and show a lot of activity in the brain regions associated with motivational drive) are able to perform well even when tasks are boring and *unmotivating*. Comparatively, low-persistence individuals show decreased activity in those same regions when faced with such tasks.

This provides insight into Winners like Strug who use Motivation as the fuel in the tank and Effort Accelerator as the foot that presses down firmly on the gas pedal. Research has shown that the neurotransmitter dopamine plays a key role in providing this corresponding "urge to do something" through a key neural pathway joining structures in the midbrain and the ventral striatum. These regions kick into gear to move you from intention into action. In a recent fMRI study, Kari Eddington and colleagues at Duke University found that these brain areas are highly active when someone feels very motivated and action-oriented about a specific goal.

Tool #5: Talent Meter

Neuroimaging studies demonstrate how important a highly developed prefrontal cortex is for helping high achievers in a variety of fields gauge their own competence. Among other things, the medial aspect of this brain region contributes strongly to their *Talent Meter*, the BrainPower Tool that gives you a sense of what you're good at and what you're not.

One top LPGA golfer's Talent Meter kicked into high gear at a young age. Golfing didn't immediately emerge as her top gift—it was soccer then—but even as a preteen she had enough insight about herself to realize her destiny was on the links. Actually she excelled at a lot of things, both physically and academically, but her Talent Meter did a good job of divining the most successful path for her to take. It continues to guide her as she transitions from professional golf to other pursuits. Neuroimaging studies, such as a 2007 investigation led in Belgium by Arnaud D'Argembeau, suggest that a forward-most region of the medial prefrontal cortex is particularly important in helping a person reflect on their traits and abilities versus those of others. Such self-awareness is critical for maintaining a properly calibrated Talent Meter.

Indeed, having a well-calibrated Talent Meter is probably as important as possessing the actual talent itself. You might have the potential of becoming a great public speaker, an amazing parent, or an incredible teacher, but if you don't recognize those abilities within yourself you won't take the time to develop those natural talents. And all the hard work in the world won't turn you into a master chef if that sort of endeavor doesn't play to your strengths.

A finely tuned Talent Meter means being aware of weaknesses, too. The golf champion says she is brutally honest with herself: whether she is learning a new shot or now dipping a toe into the clothing business, she assesses what she knows and doesn't know. When she identifies a weakness, she is knowingly fanatical about learning as much as she can to minimize it. In this way she usually avoids the sand trap, so to speak, that many other people fall into when they judge themselves good at things, at which they in fact aren't.

This is what scientists have dubbed "the double whammy of incompetence"—and it can get you into trouble if you're not careful. Work by researchers such as Justin Kruger and David Dunning of Cornell University suggests that if you don't even realize you have gaps in your abilities, it may never occur to you to try and make improvements. Like everyone else, even great talents have opportunities for improvement.

UNIT
9

All five BrainPower Tools are interrelated. We found this to be true over and over in both the studies we reviewed and on the stage of real life where Winners strut their stuff. And, while we believe it is possible to meet with some success with only a partial list of BrainPower Tools in your belt, we think you are more apt to achieve the things you want to in life when all of your bases are covered. Since everyone seems to be blessed with the capacity to strengthen every single tool to at least some degree—and often to a large degree—we don't see any reason why you shouldn't try. In doing so you are likely to meet with even more success.

The good news is there are strategies you can use to strengthen your BrainPower Tools, and they fall into one of eight general categories we call Win Factors. Each group of Win Factors addresses particular networks of brain regions to help make them operate more effectively. When you actively develop these on a consistent basis, your BrainPower Tools will take hold and become the overriding traits your brain displays in your everyday life. As a result, you are more likely to engage in activities that lead to success. You'll learn about these eight Winner's Brain strategies in detail in the next section of this book, but in short, they are:

Win Factor #1: Self-Awareness

A well-developed sense of Self-Awareness makes you more effective in your relationships, your job, and every other aspect of your life. When you take it to the level of a Winner's Brain, you are not only aware of how you relate to the rest of the world but also how the rest of the world relates to you. For some people, the fact that Self-Awareness is a skill to develop is surprising, but a number of recent studies show how it is possible and how much of a difference it makes when you do. Get ready to know yourself better.

Win Factor #2: Motivation

Though it may seem like Motivation is something that hits you like a bolt of lightning, research suggests that it flows through you like the phases of an electrical current. In a Winner's Brain, Motivation allows the individual to glide right over obstacles that often stop less determined people cold. It helps them push through challenges even when there is little external impetus to spur it on. Motivation primes the brain to see rewards even when they are a long way off and, indeed, even when there are no guarantees those rewards will ever come.

Win Factor #3: Focus

Emails! Phone calls! Instant messages! The brain is faced with a zoo of distractions that compete for our attention on a nearly constant basis. Winner's Brains have the ability to focus on tasks and activities in the moment, especially when the moment is also full of stressors and distractions. They deliberately calibrate their level of Focus under a wide variety of circumstances and can call on the best type of Focus for the task at hand.

Win Factor #4: Emotional Balance

The word "emotions" carries a negative connotation for some people, as if they're something to be avoided or they represent weakness. In fact, emotional responses are an important source of information that can have powerful effects on our decisions and behavior. When emotions are in balance, you can make them work in your favor and put feelings to good use rather than being driven blindly by them. As the research suggests, getting a handle on the aspects of the brain that control emotion will help you be more mindful of your feelings and allow you to channel them in productive ways—and we'll teach you how.

Win Factor #5: Memory

Winners don't just rely on Memory to help recollect Sunday dinners from long ago. It is most productive and useful when it's called upon to help anticipate the future and make predictions about the best way to respond to a novel situation. Individuals with a Winner's Brain excel at rapidly scanning their minds for old information that can help them anticipate and better understand novel circumstances. Winners can also recognize what they don't know and have mechanisms in place for uncovering that information quickly and accurately so they can integrate it and perform better.

Win Factor #6: Resilience

A common misconception is that past failures are an accurate representation of the future. Winners understand and embrace the importance of failing and, simply put, they get up at least one more time than anyone else. It's this act of "'getting up"—be it mental or physical—that equals bounce, our term for Resilience. The resilient brain is about the big comeback and about not backing down.

Win Factor #7: Adaptability

The brain is surprisingly plastic and pliable. Winners embrace this fact. They take advantage of the fact that the brain keeps on changing no matter what and that the shape it takes will be directly molded by how they use it. This Adaptability is not confined to one region of the brain; it applies to areas throughout the brain. Any change to a thought, behavior, or emotion causes the brain to adapt even if the difference can't be immediately seen in brain scans. More substantial physical changes to the brain may come as the result of hard, conscious work, but even making small adjustments can alter how your brain responds. This is the foundation of every single Winner's Brain strategy and tip we offer.

Win Factor #8: Brain Care

Just because you can't see it stretching or flexing its muscles doesn't mean your brain doesn't do these things—at least metaphorically. Winners take good care of their brains. They feed it the right foods, give it plenty of sleep, and exercise it, just as they would their abs or their pecs. Like every other part of your body, how you treat your brain is how it will operate. And when you handle your brain with care, you are on your way to having a Winner's Brain.

UNIT

9

FILM STUDIES

Inherit the Wind (1960)

Based on a novel by Jerome Lawrence and Robert Edwin Lee
Screenplay by Robert Edwin Lee, Harold Jacob Smith, Nedrick Young and Jerome Lawrence
Directed by Stanley Kramer

Character Guide

Henry Drummond . . . . Spencer Tracy

Matthew Harrison Brady . . . . . Frederic March

E.K. Hornbeck . . . . Gene Kelly

Bertram T. Cates . . . . Dick York

Rachel Brown . . . . Donna Anderson

Judge Mel Coffey . . . . Harry Morgan

Reverend Jeremiah Brown . . . . . Claude Akins

Prosecutor Tom Davenport . . . . Elliott Reid

Introduction

Academy Award-nominated *Inherit the Wind* is a fictionalized version of the real-life "Scopes Monkey Trial" (1925) which took place in Dayton, Tennessee and featured debates about evolution versus creation between Clarence Darrow and William Jennings Bryan. In the film, science teacher B.T. Cates is prosecuted for teaching Charles Darwin's theory of evolution when it was expressly forbidden by Tennessee law and is defended by renowned attorney Henry Drummond. The prosecution's key witness is national politician Matthew Harrison Brady who was well-known for his fundamentalist beliefs. The film highlights the struggle between people who hope to realize change and those who seek to protect tradition.

Dialogue Questions

1. How does the film illustrate that one person's actions can begin the process of change?

2. In what ways did Henry Drummond and Matthew Harrison Brady react to change in *Inherit the Wind*? In what ways do they represent groups of people who share their views?

3. What are the similarities and differences between Drummond and Brady?

4. What factors make societal change difficult for people?

Lincoln (2012)

Based on *Team of Rivals: The Political Genius of Abraham Lincoln* by Doris Kearns Goodwin
Screenplay by Tony Kushner
Directed by Steven Spielberg

Character Guide

Abraham Lincoln. . . . . Daniel Day-Lewis

Thaddeus Stevens. . . . . Tommy Lee Jones

Mary Todd Lincoln . . . . Sally Field

Robert Todd Lincoln . . . . Joseph Gordon-Levitt

W.N. Bilbo . . . . James Spader

William H. Seward . . . . David Strathairn

UNIT
9

Introduction

The Academy Award-winning film *Lincoln* explores the final months of Abraham Lincoln's presidency. Lincoln sought an end to the Civil War that had divided the nation and restoration of the Union while working with a Cabinet derived of a team of brilliant rivals who had differing views about the best way to realize change in the United States beyond the war. The questions of how to unite a divided nation and how to abolish slavery were two of the significant issues facing Lincoln and his Cabinet. The President uses his considerable people skills, intelligence, passion and humor to focus his team of talented and equally passionate rivals on finding solutions to the nation's greatest problems.

Dialogue Questions

1. What characteristics does the film show Lincoln possessed that help him navigate tumult and realize change?

2. In what ways did Lincoln utilize the considerable talents of each member of his Cabinet to reach viable solutions to problems and to realize change?

3. How can the strategies used by Lincoln and his Cabinet to unite a divided nation be adapted by organizations in the midst of change?

4. When seeking to realize change, to what extent must opposing voices be taken into consideration?

EXERCISE

Spacejam

Introduction

This exercise is meant to convince a group that it has the capacity to innovate and change, to press the edge of the envelope with regard to the challenge it is facing. For participants, doing Spacejam feels a lot like doing Musical Chairs. What differentiates the two is that Spacejam promotes creative change through collaboration rather than competition, inclusion rather than exclusion, thoughtful shepherding of resources rather than forced expropriation of limited resources. Making this change on purpose—from the purpose of Musical Chairs to the purpose of Spacejam—will not be easy! Pay attention to the group dynamics as ideas for change or innovation are introduced.

Instructions

Your Instructor will provide further directions.

Kaagan. S. (1999). Spacejam. In *Leadership Games: Experiential Learning for Organizational Development*. Sage. Pp. 31–33. Used by permission of SAGE.

SUGGESTED READING

This selected bibliography is intended to supplement the excerpts and articles of authors included in this Unit. There is an emphasis on books that are pivotal and recent publications. Numerous journals regularly offer articles related to these topics, but are not included in this selected bibliography. For further research, you may wish to include searches of the following journals: (alphabetically) *Academy of Management Executive, Academy of Management Journal, Harvard Business Review, Journal of Leadership Studies, Leadership in Action, Leadership Quarterly,* and *Leader To Leader.*

This list is organized by author's last name using Modern Language Association-style citations.

Duncan, Rodger D., and Stephen Covey. *Change-Friendly Leadership: How to Transform Good Intentions Into Great Performance*. New York: Maxwell Stone Publishing, 2012.
The authors investigate the power of character-driven change, the process of taking action to address problems, the ways to better understand resistance and ways to nurture networks of people who can help an individual or organization realize change. The book includes a self-assessment at the end of each chapter.

Ginzberg, Lori D. *Elizabeth Cady Stanton: An American Life*. New York: Hill and Wang, 2010.
Ginzberg explores Stanton's life and the influences, including Susan B. Anthony, that guided her interest in and passion for realizing change for women in the United States.

Heath, Chip, and Dan Heath. *Switch: How to Change Things When Change is Hard*. New York: Crown Business, 2010.
Heath and Heath contend each individual has a rational mind and an emotional mind that complete for control. They explore brain science and psychology to uncover ways to embrace the rational brain to realize change.

Kegan, Robert and Lisa L. Lahey. *Immunity to Change: How to Overcome It and Unlock the Potential in Yourself and Your Organization*. Cambridge: Harvard Business Review Press, 2009.
Kegan and Lahey explore how our individual and collective beliefs create immunity to change. They offer strategies to determine what holds individuals and organizations back and approaches that allow them to move forward and realize change.

Kotter, John P. *Leading Change, With a New Preface from the Author*. New York: Harvard Business Review Press, 2012.
Kotter explores the ways management, which often deals with the status quo, and leadership are different. He offers an eight-step process for leading change.

Phillips, Donald T. *Lincoln on Leadership: Executive Strategies for Tough Times*. New York: Warner, 1993.
Phillips uses history lessons to illustrate leadership principles in times of change.

Senge, Peter. *The Dance of Change: The Challenges of Sustaining Momentum in Learning Organizations*. New York: Doubleday/Currency, 1999.
This book details the four challenges in organizational change: getting started, initiating change, sustaining transformation, and redesigning and rethinking. It also discusses how to overcome common problems with change. The book includes solo and team exercises.

UNIT

9

Senge, Peter. *The Fifth Discipline: The Art and Practice of the Learning Organization.* **New York: Doubleday/Currency, 2006.**
Senge introduced key principles of learning organizations with the first edition of this book in 1990. He explains organizational "learning disabilities" that threaten productivity and creativity and the shifts in thinking necessary to overcome them. Systems thinking is an important topic of the book.

UNIT 10

EMPOWERING OTHERS

INTRODUCTION

Empowerment is a key concept to understand for leaders to be the most effective they can be. In a nutshell, leaders can actually gain more power by giving power away to others. Unit Ten explores this paradox.

Empowerment is more than delegation. Delegation is the assignment of formal authority and the accountability for carrying out specific tasks. It involves explaining to the delegate the "what and why" of the assignment while leaving the "how" to the delegate. It is transactional in nature. A leader engaging in the empowerment process provides direction via strong ideals, vision, and purpose. Instead of assigning specific tasks, the leader encourages followers to be creative rather than reactive. The empowering leader commits people to action, inspires followers to accept and work toward a common goal, and converts followers into leaders and agents of change. Empowering is transformational in nature. The distinction between transactional and transformational leadership is further explained in the reading by Bernard M. Bass, "From Transactional to Transformational Leadership: Learning to Share the Vision."

Neither of these concepts, delegation nor empowerment, is a renouncement of responsibility on the part of the leader. Nor are they avoidance techniques which enable the leader to abdicate responsibility for making decisions or the consequences of making decisions. They both produce results, however, that are critical to effective leadership, even when the leader may not hold a leadership position or authority to lead. The Classic Case, *The Night Is Darkest Before the Dawn*, by Abi Morgan, is just such a situation; the women of the play have no structural or formal power to bring about change, yet they strive to give power and meaning to the lives of others. This modern play, set in Afghanistan, offers a unique look at the concept of empowerment. The Leadership Profile of Nelson Mandela examines a different scenario, one in which a leader is removed from the arena—actually imprisoned—and yet remains an effective leader, continuing to grow and evolve the movement he led before his imprisonment.

In addition to the Reading, Classic Case, and Leadership Profile mentioned above, this Unit includes two additional readings, underscoring the importance of empowerment to effective leaders. Daniel Goleman and Richard Boyatzis discuss the "emotional and social intelligence" of leaders that is so important to creating an empowering environment. Stephen Covey explains three key roles of effective, empowering leaders in a rapidly and constantly changing environment.

The Film Studies for the Unit are *Norma Rae* (1979) and *Invictus* (2009). *Norma Rae* portrays the transformation of a textile worker whose life is changed by the arrival of a union organizer. Norma Rae in turn empowers others in the textile mill to accomplish goals and a vision that she cannot produce on her own. *Invictus* tells the story of the South African rugby team that won the 1995 World Cup and how Nelson Mandela contributed to their empowerment, indirectly—as before while imprisoned, but now as President of South Africa. The team in turn contributed to the unification of the nation following decades of racial division and violence during apartheid.

The Exercise "Shaping the Future" provides an opportunity for your group to learn from each other how to accomplish a task that at first may seem the group is powerless or incapable of completing. Everyone will need to practice empowering behaviors to succeed.

Learning Objectives

- Distinguish between transactional and transformational leadership

- Understand the relationship between power, delegation, and empowerment

- Define the principles of empowerment necessary for the effective exercise of leadership

- Recognize the benefits of effective empowerment

- Understand "emotional intelligence" and "social intelligence" and the correlation with empowering others

- Appreciate the contributions made by the Classic Case and Leadership Profile in this Unit toward understanding empowerment

UNIT

10

CLASSIC CASE

The Night Is Darkest Before the Dawn

By Abi Morgan (b. 1968)

Introduction and Historical Background

This short play set in Afghanistan in the early 2000s is part of a British series of 12 plays that together recount 150 years of Afghan history. The collection of plays, *The Great Game: Afghanistan*, takes its name from the geopolitical struggle for control of central Asia, including Afghanistan, since the early 19th century. Acclaimed British Director Nicholas Kent commissioned the plays when he noticed that the place and history and wars of Afghanistan received little attention from writers.

The 12 plays of *The Great Game* are divided into a trilogy: Part I, "Invasions and Independence" begins in 1842, when Britain invaded to pre-empt Russian control of Afghanistan, through the 1920s; Part II is "Communism, the Mujahideen and the Taliban," and covers 1966 to 1979; and Part III, "Enduring Freedom," covers from before September 11, 2001 to the present. *The Great Game: Afghanistan* premiered in London in 2009, and returned there in 2010 before a U.S. tour in New York, Washington, D.C., Minneapolis, and Berkeley. When *The Great Game: Afghanistan* returned to Washington, D.C. in 2011, special, free encore performances for U.S. soldiers and military and government officials involved in Afghanistan were scheduled due to significant interest shown by the Pentagon in the production for its value as an educational experience.

Playwright Abi Morgan has been recognized for bringing powerful stories to stage and screen. She won an Emmy Award in 2013 for the British mini-series, *The Hour. The Night Is Darkest Before the Dawn* is layered with several poignant messages through the story of an Afghan widow who seeks to re-open the school for girls at which her husband taught. The theme of empowerment through education for girls and women of the geographic region that includes Afghanistan and neighboring nations remains relevant as time passes. Shot on her school bus in Pakistan in 2012, Malala Yousafzai is a strong voice advocating for girls' education, and exemplifies the struggle for empowerment through education that continues.

Points to Consider

1. Who is exercising leadership that empowers others? In what ways? Who is empowered? In what ways?

2. What are the obstacles to empowerment for different characters?

3. In what ways is collaboration contributing to empowerment?

4. How can organizations effectively empower others?

The Night Is Darkest Before the Dawn

Editors' Note: The play is reprinted faithfully to the original manuscript.

Character Guide
Minoo (early 50s Afghan)

Huma (late 20–30s Afghan)

Alex (late 30s/early 40s American)

Omaid (early 30s Afghan)

Behrukh (mid-teens Afghan)

Commandhan Elmar (late 40s Afghan)

3 Tribesmen

Setting: The play is set in a rural smallholding, south of Kandahar. It is April 2002.

Dusk—

A bombed out building—

Minoo (early 50s) sits making bread by a fire. She is dressed in the familiar blue burkah of the Taliban era.

Huma (late 20s/early 30s) stands waiting, in modern dress, her hair covered, a soft briefcase in her hand.

Alex (late 30s/early 40s) sits, in shirt and slacks, drinking a small glass of tea. He is wearing a flak jacket.

Beyond endless chalky fields specked with poppies.

Huma: It's good.

Alex: Oh yeah its fine as long you tuck that sugar cube—

Huma: Under the tongue.

Alex: Right.

Huma: Yes.

Alex: …right under the tongue.

Minoo nods, reaching for a kettle of tea going to pour Alex more.

No. I'm good.

Huma: He's had enough thank you.

Minoo ignores Huma, pouring more tea, resuming making bread.

Alex: Oh, OK … OK …

Alex shrugs, drinks.

Thanks…Great…

Alex drinks.

I don't know how much more of this stuff I can drink. Couldn't we just go out there to talk to them?

Huma: They'll be back soon. They're coming back?

Minoo shrugs—

Alex: What did she say?

Huma: It is nearly sunset.

Alex nods, looking out.

Alex: We've been here two hours.

Huma: Ten more minutes OK?

Alex: You said that yesterday.

Alex shrugs, silently looking about him. Minoo reaches for the kettle, goes to pour more tea.

No. Thank you.

Minoo hesitates, shrugs, and hangs the teapot back on the fire.

Tashakkur.

Huma: I am surprised she even gave you tea.

Alex hesitates mid-sip, raising his glass to Minoo, clearly embarrassed.

I guess it's because you're American.

Distant rumble of a truck—

Let me talk.

Alex instinctively stands, Huma gently moving in front of him.

Alex: Won't it be better—

Huma: No…I know the family.

Alex: You need to make it clear.

Huma: Yes.

Alex: Only nine. Nine is not…It's not a class yet.

Huma: I know what to say.

Omaid (late 30s) a tall dark man, swathed in robes and headdress enters surrounded by his tribesmen. Many have guns slung across backs, and rifles in hand. Behrukh (15 years) a few yards behind follows, carrying a hoe.

Aasalaamu Aleikum.

Omaid hesitates, considering, his tribesman close by.

Omaid: Who's the American?

Omaid joins his tribesmen washing by a tap, the ritual before pray, washing hands, feet, nose, ears, mouth.

Alex: Alex Braiton.

Alex holds out his hand, ready to greet Omaid.

Al-Salaam.

Omaid does not look up from washing.

Omaid: I don't talk to journalists.

Huma: He's not a journalist.

Alex: Can you tell him—?

Huma: He works for an international charity.

Omaid: You run with the Americans now?

Silence.

Huma: They want to put funding into our school.

Alex: We've been waiting over two hours. Two hours.

Omaid looks at Alex blankly, enjoying not understanding.

Yeah, you keep smiling at me.

Alex shakes his head wearily.

Really, there's no place I'd rather be. We have been here two hours waiting for you.

Huma: Please.

Alex shrugs, concedes.

Behrukh, is that you?

Behrukh hesitates, hands back, tentative.

You've grown.

Huma wants to touch Behrukh, raising her hands to touch her, hesitating on seeing Behrukh's resistance.

We miss you. We've all missed you.

A tribesman tuts, Behrukh hurries to fetch a towel for the tribesmen, than falls into line, laying out plates, preparing food with Minoo.

We have opened the school again.

Silence.

I have nine girls already who have agreed to return.

Omaid hesitates, smiles, amused.

Omaid: Nine? *(Beat.)* You do not have a school. You have a university.

Omaid considers Alex, washing his face and hands; snorting water through his nostrils, hitting the dust on the ground.

Alex: Are we OK? Is everything OK?

Alex looks nervously at a passing tribesman, a gun still slung across his back.

Huma?

Huma: We're fine.

Alex: What's he saying?

Huma: I'm telling him about the school.

Alex: Charity? We are giving money. You have daughters?

Huma: Please.

Alex: Sir? Are you hearing me?

Omaid looks to Alex, unwavering.

Forgive me if my temper is a little frayed, Sir, but it is the fourth time we have been here this week. Every time you say you will meet us and every time… It takes us over an hour each way…And my ass right now is kindasore. Those craters in the road, it doesn't make for a pleasant ride. So the least you can do now, Sir, now we are here—

Omaid smiles.

There's that smile again.

Alex shakes his head, laughs, exasperated, reaching for a small pair of binoculars in his bag.

Omaid: So brave today, sister, with your American.

Huma: He's not my American.

Alex looks up, from his binoculars, considering.

Alex: Are those poppies in that field?

Huma hesitates, nods.

Omaid: I heard they killed your husband.

Huma holds his look unwavering.

I go to watch the football.

Huma: All the way to Kabul? I didn't know you liked it so much.

Omaid shrugs, moving on, avoiding Huma's gaze.

I want Behrukh.

Huma holds the forms and pens out to Omaid, to look at.

I have brought the forms for her to register. I can fill them in with you now. *(Silence.)* I am not leaving unless you give her to me.

Omaid stands, looking at her. He starts to laugh.

Huma searches in her bag, taking out a pencil sharpener.

Huma: Behrukh?

She places it on the ground in front of her.

UNIT
10

Behrukh, do you know what this is?

Behrukh hesitates, looks to Omaid, almost fearful.

You remember?

Behrukh hesitates, nods.

Can you still write your name?

Minoo tuts, holding a bucket to Behrukh. Behrukh looks to Omaid, he nods. Behrukh makes to tend to distant livestock, rattling the bucket of meal.

His organization is interested in funding the school. They are willing to supply all the writing materials, books, stationery. Fifteen scholarships.

Omaid: No.

Huma: Give her to me for one year.

Omaid's gaze follows Alex, taking in the distant poppy field.

Omaid: You bring an American here?

Huma: Brother—

Omaid: After everything, you return and you bring him.

Huma: He is here to help us, Omaid.

Omaid: Us?

Omaid laughs.

Alex: What does he say?

Alex looks to Huma for understanding.

Omaid: That is very nice. That is very funny. You are very funny Huma.

Huma packs up her papers, pencils and sharpener into her bag.

Alex: Are we going?

Alex looks to Omaid, weary.

That's a pity. I'm sorry. Can you tell him...I am sorry.

Alex peers out across the fields, squinting his eyes, the sun casting its fading light, revealing the sway of green poppy plants.

I thought it was just wheat. That they'd assigned wheat to these fields.

Huma: He's asking why you are not growing wheat.

Omaid looks to Alex, attempting to be understood.

Omaid: 5000 dollars...one field.

Omaid smiles, close to Alex now.

Opium. *(Beat.)* For the non-believers.

Behrukh returns, tipping up her bucket, draining the last of the meal on the ground for the chickens, slapping the bottom of the bucket.

Where is the mullah to tell me not?

Alex: They'll come and destroy them. The military will destroy all of it. Huma?

Huma: He wants to know if you realize the military will destroy your fields.

Omaid: Tell him build me a dam and maybe I will grow something other than poppies.

Omaid pushes an elderly tribesman toward Alex.

Tell him take one of these other idiots if he wants to waste his money educating us.

Alex looks to Huma, searching for understanding.

Tell him they may have rid us of the Taliban but they must offer us more than their bombs and packets of onion seeds.

Huma: He's angry. We're wasting our time here.

Omaid: We don't have flak jackets—

Omaid points to Alex's chest. Alex looks down, half understanding.

...to protect us.

Alex: This?...I promised my wife. My wife? She said she'd shoot me if I didn't wear it.

Alex hesitates, sees Omaid is unamused.

Omaid makes to go, tutting Behrukh to follow.

Huma: 'He who has a slave girl and teaches her good manners and improves her education will be rewarded twice.'

Omaid: And when the Taliban return? What good will your education do then? They will not be so merciful a second time Huma. Your husband learnt that.

Huma: And you?

Omaid laughs, joining his tribesmen as they kneel to pray, in line, facing the setting sun.

Alex: What the…? What…am I doing here? Really I should have…Gone to Mali…built toilets for elementary in Zambia…I mean we come to these places…we drink tea…we offer them free education and they just laugh at us.

Huma: (*Beat.*) You see the man on the right.

Huma nods to a tribesman kneeling to pray next to Omaid.

That is his chief tribesman. On left is a cousin of his brother. They work for him but if he not grow opium they will cut his throat. They closed the markets so they sell it across the border. They cross through the mountains if they can. On mules or trucks—

The steady ritual of praying, the men bow back and forth.

The short one? He carries it. He has sister married to border guard. He was in my husband's class. A good boy. The fat one? He is father-in-law of Kandahar Chief of Police. Worse happens? Americans come and destroy the fields. Poppy always comes back, even if there is no water. Bombs ripping the earth…Poppy always comes back. Our blessing and our curse. What thrives here, also kills us.

Alex: You know Omaid well?

Huma nods.

Huma: I married his brother. He was killed by the Taliban.

Alex: Oh…OK…Right…

Huma: (*Beat.*) They didn't tell you that in the office?

Alex shakes his head.

Now I know you are being polite.

Behrukh passes, sorting through a pile of old sacking.

Behrukh?

Silence.

So quiet? You were always chatter chatter chatter. When you were five you did not sit still before your mouth would run away.

Silence.

We have classrooms. And a computer. Maybe one day you could be a teacher too.

Behrukh finishes up sorting bags, going to wash. Huma, hesitates, joins her. Together they wash.

Hidi. And Muna. Gzifa was the first to come. Her mother brought her to the school herself.

Omaid: (*Calling over.*) Behrukh.

Behrukh reaches for a towel, dries her face, hands, moving on.

Behrukh: Our mother is dead.

Huma: Yes.

Behrukh can barely look at Alex, standing across the yard.

But we are free—

Behrukh: I still carry water every day.

Minoo and Behrukh join the others, kneeling to pray. Huma looking on. Huma looks back, a row of guns resting up against the wall. Huma makes to go. Alex stops her.

Alex: You have nine girls. You need fifteen.

UNIT
10

Huma: He won't.

Alex: Six more girls, Huma. Let him pray and after—

Huma: After?

Alex: Let's hope we eat.

Alex resumes watching through his binoculars. Huma considers waiting—

Prayers over, Omaid and his Tribesmen return, ready to eat. Omaid considers Alex standing close by, shrugging to him to join us.

Omaid: You? *(Pointing to Alex.)* New York?

Minoo, Behrukh, hurry to get things ready, hovering close by, passing food. Alex and Huma join them making to eat.

Huma: He's asking where you're from?

Alex: Amherst, just north-east of Buffalo. It is officially America's safest town. Some days we don't even lock our front doors.

Omaid smiles, quietly ridiculing Alex.

There's that smile again.

Omaid: New York.

Omaid mimes a plane with his hand, absently.

Boom. Boom.

Omaid laughs, shoveling more food into his mouth.

Alex: Motherfucker.

Alex puts down his plate.

Look I know your wife and two sons were killed by American bombs. Huma?

Alex looks to Huma to translate. Huma hesitates.

Huma: He's saying—

Alex pushes on.

Alex: I know they were driving back from Kandahar market. Kandahar. I know your wife

was pregnant with your fifth child. I am sincerely sorry for your loss.

Huma: He's saying—

Alex: Many many innocent lives have been and will be lost in this war but I truly believe that it should not stop you from sending your daughters to school. We need six more girls to qualify for our charity's funding. It would be one classroom. All girls. You sent them six years ago.

Huma: I have the old papers that Ara used to register. But it is important that if you want them to re-register—

Huma searches the papers, pulling a thick file out of her briefcase, handing it to Omaid.

Omaid: It was Ara who signed them…Ara wanted her to go to school.

Huma: Yes.

Omaid: Because you and Farrin talked to her.

Huma: It was of her own free will Omaid.

Omaid: Was it? 'She must go to school,' she said. I saw other men beat their wives. But she is strong…was strong…'Take them then,' I said. 'While you can.' '94 the Taliban arrived. Ara cried that night. I said 'Why are you crying? Now she can stay home and cook. Now she can learn from you. At least our boys can still go to school.' So OK…they go to the Madrassa. They pray. They grow beards. We all look like old men. But still at least my boys had an education.

But Farrin says 'So what happens to Behrukh?' I say 'Brother don't make trouble for yourself.' He promised me.

Huma: Your brother wanted to see his niece educated.

Omaid stands as if to strike Huma. Huma screams. Alex goes to protect her. Omaid steps back.

Omaid: My brother is dead.

Distant rumble of trucks—

You just arrive. Suddenly you are back with your American. You say 'Come on, learn again.' *(Beat.)* We have learnt enough for one lifetime.

Huma: You used to listen to your brother. She is a bright girl. I taught her how to sharpen a pencil. I taught her to write her name. Can she write her name still?

Omaid: My sons are gone. Now Behrukh must stay and help with the land.

Omaid makes to go. Huma desperately searches in her bag.

Huma: Behrukh—

Huma places a pencil, sharpener and piece of paper down in front of Behrukh.

Show me. Show me if you can still write your name.

Behrukh hesitates, takes the pencil. Omaid makes to go.

This girl was a storyteller.

Behrukh struggles to write, but slowly writes her name until—

I used to ask her to stand in front of the class and read to everyone what she had written. Now she cannot even write her name. It is not enough. Not for one lifetime. Omaid please—

Behrukh shakes her head, clearly already forgotten. Huma holds up the half written name.

Omaid: You think the Taliban has gone far? They are only a few kilometers away. Hiding across a border or in the mountains. They do not go away.

Omaid, close to Huma now, almost gentle.

I saw what they did to my brother. You did not, Sister. Farrin was a big man, a strong man. His body was built for the land but always he was head in a book. If he had stayed here, stayed on the land. *(Beat.)* They tied his arms to one truck, his legs to another. They disemboweled

him. They made the people watch and then the footballers come on. Kicking the ball, his guts still on the ground. The Taliban with the guns, shouting at them 'Play on…Play on' And 'Keep your head up…Keep watching. Don't look down…Watch the game.' *(Tapping the side of his head.)* I will be watching that game all my life.

Distant laughter—

She is all I have left.

Huma: Then teach her. Educate her as you did your sons. Or are you too scared?

Omaid: I was not the one who was too scared, Huma. You were.

Huma hesitates, shaken. Omaid shakes his head, moves away.

Alex: What did he say?

Omaid walks across the yard, to greet an arriving truck.

Huma: It doesn't matter.

The rise of smoke, a cluster of Tribesmen still lost in their card game, an opium pipe passed amongst them.

Alex: Who are they?

Omaid in conversation with arriving mujahideen, with weapons sunk on the back of distant truck. Elmar (40s) sits in a truck, a gun slung across his back, clearly the head of the group.

Huma: (Shrugs.) Commandhan. Everyone knows him. He works with the military. They are needed to keep the Taliban at bay.

Minoo, sunk against the wall, plucks a chicken, the blood smearing her blue burkah as Elmar passes, a gun slung across his back, head swathed in the turban of the mujahideen.

Elmar: It is our teacher.

Huma instinctively straightens, facing Elmar, quietly imposing yet Huma maintains her stance.

Good day, Sir.

UNIT
10

Omaid nods to Behrukh to make tea.

Alex: Aasalaamu Aleikum.

Elmar: Wa-AleikumAassalaam.

Huma nods, avoiding Elmar's gaze.

The road is up. *(To Alex.)* One of your mines.

Elmar smiles at Alex.

No cars will be getting out tonight.

Huma: This is—

Huma goes to introduce Alex to Elmar.

Alex: Alex Braiton. I'm from—

Elmar smiles.

Elmar: I know who he is.

Huma: He's giving funding to our school. *(To Alex.)* I'm telling him you why you come.

Elmar: I hear of this.

Huma: I have nine girls. I came to ask if Behrukh would like to join our class.

Elmar: So you have come to educate us?

Huma goes to translate. Elmar waves him away.

No need. No need. I speak your English very well. So you have come—

Alex: … to facilitate the re-establishment of the schools.

Elmar: She is a good teacher?

Elmar points to Huma, laughs to himself.

Alex: That's what I hear.

Elmar: You have a lot of woman teachers?

Alex: A handful. We'd like to see more.

Omaid hovers.

Elmar: You OK?

Omaid: Yes. All fine.

Elmar: You have worms in your ass?

The tribesmen smile.

Omaid: You wish to eat, Commandhan.

Elmar: No.

Elmar looks to Alex.

American. I like your films.

Elmar smiles, gaze lingering on Huma.

Gladiator?

Alex: You know *Gladiator*? Yeah. Yeah. Russell Crowe. That's a great movie.

Elmar: And *Titanic*. You know *Titanic*?

Alex: Uh huh.

Elmar: It is very very moving. I like this film.

Alex: You and the rest of the world…Me not so much but…It's a favorite of my wife's.

Elmar: They teach you much about life.

Alex: I guess.

Elmar takes a cup of tea, considering Huma.

Elmar: You have got fat.

Huma: A little.

Elmar: Who is going to run this school?

Huma: I will.

Elmar: Farrin was a very good teacher.

Alex: Teacher? Right. Farrin? Do we have him on our books?

Huma: No. Not anymore.

Elmar: He married a local girl. We were not sure about her but he insisted he wanted an intelligent wife. You understand?

Omaid: Commandhan, do you wish to look around the farm now?

Elmar tuts, silencing Omaid.

Elmar: Farrin says 'I am going to build school.' Build?

Alex: Right. Yeah…I think I understand.

Elmar: Good school. Everyone come and he teach them how to read and right. With Huma. *(Pointing at Huma.)* Wife?

Alex nods, turning to look at Huma, slowly understanding.

Then Taliban come. Taliban close down. We say 'Farrin, please…' But Farrin has intelligent wife. 'Ssh,' she says. 'You shall teach at night.'

Omaid: Commandhan please.

Elmar: 'No one will know.' Farrin loved his wife. Why not? She is a beautiful woman. Is she not a beautiful woman?

Alex hesitates, nods.

Alex: Beautiful? Yes. Yes she is.

Elmar: Like Kate Winslet.

Alex: Kate Winslet. Right. Back on course, films again.

Elmar: And love…He loved her.

Huma looks down, tears pricking her face.

For a bright man he was very stupid. Taliban come. They take him to Kabul. But not his wife.

Elmar looks to Huma.

Why did he die and you survive? Because you are beautiful? Now I think you grow a little fat. Huma, you know what they say? They say you survived because you were not stupid.

Alex: Huma?

Omaid: She just came to ask about the school.

Elmar: And you will not disappoint her.

Omaid: I need Behrukh to work the land.

Behrukh passes, Elmar reaches out, pats her head.

Elmar: We must look to our daughters now, Omaid. They are the intelligent ones.

Elmar puts an arm around Alex, gently leading him towards the Tribesmen, joining them as the opium pipe is passed around.

Education is important now. We must all be intelligent to survive.

Alex: OK…Huma are you OK?

Huma nods, unable to look at him.

Elmar: There has been too much dying, too much blood in these hills. We have been fighting for too long. First the Russians, then the Taliban. So many martyrs, so many mujahideen fallen in this land. We must make their sacrifice worth it. We should talk. I would like to give money to this school.

Omaid looks on. Huma, head hung, visibly shaken. Omaid makes to follow. Huma looks up.

Huma: Is it true? Do they say that? Brother…

Omaid hesitates.

Omaid: They say the night they came for Farrin, you hid and would not open the door. They say you were the one that taught at night but every day you got more scared. They say the girls would come to you and find Farrin teaching them. They say you were too sick with fear. They say you looked to him to take your class. *(Beat.)* A man alone with ten little girls, what were you thinking of?

They say in court you said 'I did not know. He would not tell me. My husband was a mystery to me.' But they say it was you that found paper. You smuggled pencils and sharpeners under your dress. Is that true? Is that true?

Huma hesitates, nods her head.

Behrukh: Abba, no. No.

Omaid pushes Huma away, broken.

Omaid: You break my heart, Sister.

Huma suddenly sinks to the ground, weeping bitterly.

Behrukh: Don't cry. Don't cry Aunty.

Omaid looks on, before moving away.

Huma: I am sorry I could not fight for you. I am sorry I did not come and find you. I am sorry I did not bring my books here and teach you in the dark of night so you could spell your name. I was not as brave…I was not as brave—

Behrukh runs and gets water, a cloth, coming back, helping Huma to bed. Dabbing her face with a cloth Behrukh washes her, gently dries her face and hands.

Huma: You are a good girl. You were always such a good kind clever girl.

Far off, distant laughter. Alex sits with Elmar and others, smoking from the opium pipe. Behrukh lays out a bed roll encouraging Huma to sleep.

You will be brighter and quicker and cleverer than any of us. *(Beat.)* And maybe braver.

Omaid looks back, now sat with Alex and Elmar. He waves the opium pipe away. He looks back. Huma sleeps, Behrukh close by.

Alex: Holy mother of God.

Alex clutches his head, the opium smoke hitting him.

Omaid: You like?

Alex: Huh?

Omaid laughs to himself, licking a Rizla paper, lighting his cigarette. Alex looks at him, clearly not understanding.

Omaid: I do not like but my men…they like…Every day is party now.

Alex stands, steadies himself, walking over to the tap to drink. He gulps, stands, wipes his mouth, looks up.

My wife is buried beyond that tree. *(Points.)* My eldest son Dehgan. It means farmer… *(Points.)* My youngest. Atash. Fire. He would shout at the tanks, running after them throwing rocks.

All the little kids. 'No, no, I'd say. They have come to set us free.'

Omaid gestures, to the Elmar, sitting with the tribesmen smoking.

Commandhan?

Omaid shrugs gives up. Alex, resigned, smiles, washing his face, half listening yet not understanding Omaid as he talks to himself.

He is better than some. He takes what he makes from the land and puts back into this community. Maybe he will even give you money for your school. But what happens after?

Omaid attempts to try and speak again, in broken English to Alex.

They will come back.

Alex: I'm sorry I don't understand.

Omaid shakes his head, heading off to take a piss.

I'm not built for this country.

Alex reels a little as he tries to stand. Elmar laughs.

Elmar: But we are built for you. You like the pipe?

Alex: Wow…yeah…It's…quite something…

Elmar: That's what they all say. We are built for America. Why else do you come to help us?

Alex: Excuse me.

Elmar: Taliban go. America come. Why else are you here?

Alex: No, I don't think…no really.

Elmar: Poppy is our future. Poppy survives, even if we don't. Stronger than we are. You have to learn from it. Bend, grow, war, peace. You have to be like the poppy.

Alex: I don't think so.

Elmar laughs. Alex gestures towards the fields.

They'll rip all your fields up you know.

Elmar laughs, waving him away.

Not me…But someone will…So…*(Almost to self.)* gather your poppies while you can.

Around them the tribesmen sleep. Minoo nudges a fire into life as Behrukh picks firewood.

Elmar: You father?

Alex: Huh? Oh right…Father? Yes.

Alex nods, holding up three fingers.

Boy. Two girls. Three…Three…I haven't seen them in…five months…

Elmar: I'm a father. Five girls.

Alex: That's a lot of wedding cake.

Elmar: You teach my girls. You make them clever. When Taliban comes back, if Taliban comes back, they know something at least. I give you money for school. Money from poppies.

Elmar smiles, sinking down to rest.

Alex: What am I doing here?

Alex touches his chest, realizes he's not wearing his flak jacket. He looks around, searching, stopping on seeing Minoo wearing it. He hesitates, shrugs, resigned. Alex looks to the bombed out building. Omaid passes, half listening.

I take my kids to school every day. I don't even think about it. My eldest. She wants to be famous. I'm ashamed of that. I say 'You can be anything you want to be. A doctor? A lawyer?' 'I just want to be on the TV dad.' She'll change her mind. I'll change her mind. I say 'Don't you know how lucky you are? You have the world. You are waking up every day and you have the world.' She laughs.

Omaid looks at him bemused, clearly not understanding a word.

That's why I'm here.

Omaid shakes his head, smiles.

Omaid: I don't know what you're saying.

Huma wakes with a start, disoriented. Alex reaches for his cellphone.

Alex: Do you ever get a signal here?

Alex moving away, trying to find a signal with his phone.

Elmar: Can't sleep teacher?

Huma hesitates, nods to Elmar, sitting with Omaid.

I am going to send my girls. And you will do the same. You can have one of my own men. He will help you in the fields.

'Proclaim! And your Lord is the Most Bountiful Who taught the pen. Who taught man that which he knew not…'

It will not bring our sons back but…

You have a class, teacher. So teach them.

Elmar scoops up the rough sacks of raw opium, nodding to his tribesmen to help, heading back towards his truck. Omaid goes to help him, clocking Behrukh sitting by herself with a pencil and paper.

Omaid: So she says you are a storyteller?

Omaid considers, waiting for Behrukh's response; Behrukh stands, hesitant yet unwavering.

Behrukh: Yes Abba.

Omaid: As a little girl, you use to sit with your brothers whispering. They would sit listening, what were you telling them?

Behrukh: Just stories I heard at school.

Omaid considers, lifting up the sacks.

Omaid: We sleep—

Behrukh: And after I use tell them story of the farmer and the silver. *(Beat.)* Once there was a poor farmer who worked all his life very hard and lived carefully. But every year he would have no money. After a lifetime he said to himself, if I am to have anything in this world, I will have to trust in the most merciful Allah,

UNIT
10

Peace be unto him, that it will appear to me. So he prayed and he prayed but nothing. Then one day he was returning home when a thorn tore his robes. He was very angry so he dug up the bramble at the roots and destroyed it when underneath he saw an earthenware jar. He opened it and inside was more silver than he had ever seen in his life. But he said 'No, I wished for riches upon my own hearth, instead I have found this here. This is not what I asked for.' And he buried the jar of silver where he found it and went home to his wife. His wife was very angry and told a neighbor 'Go back and find that jar and I will share the silver with you.' So the neighbor returned and found the jar. But when he opened it it was filled with poisonous snakes. Thinking that the man and his wife had played a trick on him, he grew very angry. So he took the jar and climbed onto the roof of the man's house and threw it down the chimney while they were asleep. But when the man woke, it was not snakes he found, but a thousand silver coins scattered in his hearth. 'Finally' the man said, 'I can accept these riches.'

Omaid hesitates, looking to Huma.

She came to our house, Abba. After everything, she came back. Please, Abba—

Omaid: One week. You go for one week and then…We will see.

Behrukh smiles her thanks, falling into unrolling her bedroll. Behrukh looks on, Huma close by.

At night, Ara comes to me, she is calling and I am running but I can never get to her in time.

(Beat.) I always wondered why you were never blessed with children. He punishes us in different ways.

Omaid makes to go, picking up the sacks, taking them over to Elmar waiting.

Huma: Did he for ask for me when they—?

Omaid: No.

Huma nods. Omaid moves away to load the last of the sacks on the truck.

Huma: Tomorrow you will write that story down, yes?

Behrukh nods, Huma bends down and picks up the pencil and the sharpener, holding it out to Behrukh.

Push it in.

Behrukh hesitantly takes the sharpener, pushing the pencil inside.

Now turn. A little more pressure.

A long thread of pencil sharpening falling from the sharpener.

Steady. Steady.

Alex on his cellphone, hesitates, watching Behrukh and Huma.

The hum of cicadas—

The night hangs heavy—

The End

Morgan, Abi. "The Night is Darkest Before the Dawn." *The Great Game: Afghanistan*. Oberon Modern Plays. London: Oberon, 2010. Print.

LEADERSHIP PROFILE

Nelson Mandela (1918–2013)

South African Leader against Apartheid,
President of the Republic of South Africa, 1994–1999
Long Walk to Freedom, by Nelson Mandela

Introduction and Historical Background

Photo by LSE Library

Nelson Rolihlahla Mandela was born into a royal clan of the Thembu, part of the Xhosa nation, in a rural area of the Eastern Cape, South Africa, in 1918. He was raised for the chieftainship, but while pursuing law studies at Fort Hare University he joined with Oliver Tambo and later Walter Sisulo, organizing the African National Congress Youth League that within five years seized control of the African National Congress (ANC). In 1961, when the police of the South African apartheid government killed 69 peaceful demonstrators in Sharpeville, Mandela led the ANC toward the path of armed rebellion, serving as the commander in chief of Spear of the Nation, the new guerrilla army.

Before he was arrested, he became a popular hero—called the "Black Pimpernel" (a reference to the "Scarlett Pimpernel," a French aristocrat who took daring risks to rescue revolutionaries from the guillotine during the French Revolution)—and at the trial his performance as lead defendant enhanced his popularity and leadership qualities. The defendants accepted responsibility for their actions, admitted the charges of the state, and used the trial as a platform for political action. His closing words at the trial stand as a testament to his creed: "I have fought against white domination, and I have fought against black domination. I have cherished the ideal of a democratic and free society in which all persons live together in harmony and equal opportunities. It is an ideal which I hope to live for and to achieve. But if need be, it is an ideal for which I am prepared to die."

Mandela and his fellow defendants were sentenced in 1964 to life for plotting sabotage. He spent most of his prison years on Robben Island, six miles off the coast of Cape Town, where he wrote major portions of his autobiography. In 1990, he was freed from prison after 27 years. The country's first national, nonracial, one-person-one-vote election was held on April 27, 1994, and the resulting constituent assembly elected Mandela President of the Republic of South Africa, a position he held until 1999. Charlene Smith, Mandela's authorized biographer who wrote *Mandela: In Celebration of a Great Life*, sums up his legacy: social justice, careful listening, the integrity to risk popularity, and the humility to apologize when wrong.

UNIT
10

Points to Consider

1. In Mandela's account of his imprisonment, he consciously makes decisions that he frames as the exercise of leadership. What is the basis of his ability to exercise leadership while in prison?

2. How does Mandela empower others inside and outside of the prison?

3. How do you think Mandela sustains his own personal empowerment and ability to exercise leadership within a nation of apartheid, the laws and practices that restrict personal power and rights? What are the knowledge, skills, attitudes, and strategies that contribute to his personal empowerment in such an environment?

4. How does Mandela balance his ideals of African democracy, unity, and peace with the policy of violence adopted by the African National Congress (ANC)? Is his justification acceptable to you? Why or why not?

Long Walk to Freedom

(Excerpts)
By Nelson Mandela

Part Nine—Robben Island: Beginning to Hope

Chapter 79

In 1976, I received an extraordinary visit: Jimmy Kruger, the minister of prisons, a prominent member of the prime minister's cabinet, came to see me. Kruger was not only influential about prisons policy but he was critical of the government's handling of the liberation struggle.

I had an inkling as to why he had come. The government was then engaged in a massive effort to make a success of its separate development policy, and "quasi-independent" homelands. The showpiece of separate development was the Transkei, led by my nephew and one-time benefactor, K.D. Matanzima, who had successfully repressed almost all legitimate opposition to his rule. I recalled that the commanding officer had recently said to me in a bantering way, "Mandela, you ought to retire to the Transkei and take a good long rest."

As it turned out, that was precisely what Jimmy Kruger was proposing as well. He was a stout, blunt man, not nearly as polished as I would have expected from a cabinet minister. I approached the meeting as another opportunity to present our grievances, and at first he seemed content to listen. I began by reminding him of the letter we had sent him in 1969, which had gone unanswered. He merely shrugged. I then detailed the poor conditions on the island, reiterating once more that we were political prisoners, not criminals, and expected to be treated as such. But Kruger scoffed at this, saying, "Nah, you are all violent Communists!"

I then began to tell him a bit about the history of our organization and why we had turned to violence. It was clear that he knew almost nothing about the ANC, and what he did know was gleaned from the propaganda of the right-wing press. When I told him the organization was far older than the National Party, he was dumb-founded. I said that if he considered us Communists he should reread the Freedom Charter. He looked at me blankly. He had never heard of the Freedom Charter. I found it extraordinary that a cabinet minister should be so uninformed. Yet I should not have been surprised; Nationalist politicians routinely condemned what they didn't understand.

I raised the question of our release and reminded him of the case of the 1914 Afrikaaner rebels, who had resorted to violence though they were represented in Parliament, could hold meetings, and could even vote. Even though General de Wet and General Kemp had led a force of twelve thousand and occupied towns and caused many deaths, they were both released soon after their convictions for high treason. I mentioned the case of Robey Leibbrandt, who set up an underground organization during the Second World War to oppose South Africa's support for the Allies; he was sentenced to life imprisonment but soon pardoned. Kruger seemed as ignorant of these episodes in the history of his own people as he was of the Freedom Charter. It is difficult to negotiate with those who do not share the same frame of reference.

Kruger waved all of this aside. "That is ancient history," he said. He came armed with a specific offer. Despite his reputation for brusqueness, he made his proposal in a deferential manner. He stated the matter simply: if I recognized the legitimacy of the Transkei government and was willing to move there, my sentence would be dramatically reduced.

I listened respectfully until he finished. First, I said, I wholly rejected the Bantustan [Separatist] policy, and would do nothing to support it, and second, I was from Johannesburg, and it was to Johannesburg that I would return. Kruger remonstrated with me, but to no avail. A month later he returned with the same proposal, and again I turned him down. It was an offer only a turncoat could accept.

Chapter 80

As diligent as we were in gathering news and information, our knowledge of current events was always sketchy. Happenings in the outside world were muffled by the fact that we heard of them first through rumor; only later might they be confirmed by a newspaper account or an outside visitor.

In June of 1976, we began to hear vague reports of a great uprising in the country. The whispers were fanciful and improbable: the youth of Soweto had overthrown the military and the soldiers had dropped their guns and fled. It was only when the first young prisoners who had been involved in the June 16 uprising began to arrive on Robben Island in August that we learned what truly happened.

UNIT 10

On June 16, 1976, fifteen thousand schoolchildren gathered in Soweto to protest the government's ruling that half of all classes in secondary schools must be taught in Afrikaans. Students did not want to learn and teachers did not want to teach in the language of the oppressor. Pleadings and petitions by parents and teachers had fallen on deaf ears. A detachment of police confronted this army of earnest schoolchildren and without warning opened fire, killing thirteen-year-old Hector Pieterson and many others. The children fought with sticks and stones, and mass chaos ensued, with hundreds of children wounded, and two white men stoned to death.

The events of that day reverberated in every town and township of South Africa. The uprising triggered riots and violence across the country. Mass funerals for the victims of state violence became national rallying points. Suddenly the young people of South Africa were fired with the spirit of protest and rebellion. Students boycotted schools all across the country. ANC organizers joined with students to actively support the protest. Bantu Education had come back to haunt its creators, for these angry and audacious young people were its progeny.

In September, the isolation section was filled with young men who had been arrested in the aftermath of the uprising. Through whispered conversations in an adjacent hallway we learned firsthand what had taken place. My comrades and I were enormously cheered; the spirit of mass protest that had seemed dormant through the 1960s was erupting in the 1970s. Many of these young people had left the country to join our own military movement, and then smuggled themselves back home. Thousands of them were trained in our camps in Tanzania, Angola, and Mozambique. There is nothing so encouraging in prison as learning that the people outside are supporting the cause for which you are inside.

These young men were a different breed of prisoner than we had ever seen before. They were brave, hostile, and aggressive; they would not take orders, and shouted "Amandla!" at every opportunity. Their instinct was to confront rather than cooperate. The authorities did not know how to handle them, and they turned the island upside down. During the Rivonia Trial, I remarked to a security policeman that if the government did not reform itself, the freedom fighters who would take our place would someday make the authorities yearn for us. That day had indeed come on Robben Island.

In these young men we saw the angry revolutionary spirit of the times. I had had some warning. At a visit with Winnie a few months before, she had managed to tell me through our coded conversation that there was a rising class of discontented youth who were militant and Africanist in orientation. She said they were changing the nature of the struggle and that I should be aware of them.

The new prisoners were appalled by what they considered the barbaric conditions of the island, and said they could not understand how we could live in such a way. We told them that they should have seen the island in 1964. But they were almost as skeptical of us as they were of the authorities. They chose to ignore our calls for discipline and thought our advice feeble and unassertive.

It was obvious that they regarded us, the Rivonia Trialists, as moderates. After so many years of being branded a radical revolutionary, to be perceived as a moderate was a novel and not altogether pleasant feeling. I knew that I could react in one of two ways: I could scold them for their impertinence or I could listen to what they were saying. I chose the latter.

When some of these men, such as Strini Moodley of the South African Students' Organization and Saths Cooper of the Black People's Convention, came into our section, I had them give us papers on their movement and philosophy. I wanted to know what had brought them to the struggle, what motivated them, what their ideas were for the future.

Shortly after their arrival on the island, the commanding officer came to me and asked me as a favor to address the young men. He wanted me to tell them to restrain themselves, to recognize the fact that they were in prison and to accept the discipline of prison life. I told him that I was not prepared to do that. Under the circumstances, they would have regarded me as a collaborator of the oppressor.

These fellows refused to conform to even basic prison regulations. One day I was at the Head Office conferring with the commanding officer. As I was walking out with the major, we came upon a young prisoner being interviewed by a prison official. The young man who was no more than eighteen years old, was wearing his prison cap in the presence of senior officers, a violation of regulations. Nor did he stand up when the major entered the room, another violation.

The major looked at him and said, "Please, take off your cap." The prisoner ignored him. Then in an irritated tone, the major said, "Take off your cap." The prisoner turned and looked at the major, and said, "What for?"

I could hardly believe what I had just heard. It was a revolutionary question: What for? The major also seemed taken aback, but managed a reply. "It is against regulations," he said. The younger

prisoner responded, "Why do you have this regulation? What is the purpose of it?" This questioning on the part of the prisoner was too much for the major, and he stomped out of the room, saying, "Mandela, you talk to him." But I would not intervene on his behalf, and simply bowed in the direction of the prisoner to let him know that I was on his side.

This was our first exposure to the Black Consciousness Movement. With the banning of the ANC, PAC, and Communist Party, the Black Consciousness Movement helped fill a vacuum among young people. Black Consciousness was less a movement than a philosophy and grew out of the idea that blacks must first liberate themselves from the sense of psychological inferiority bred by three centuries of white rule. Only then could the people rise up in confidence and truly liberate themselves from repression. While the Black Consciousness Movement advocated a nonracial society, they excluded whites from playing a role in achieving that society.

These concepts were not unfamiliar to me: they closely mirrored ideas I myself held at the time of the founding of the ANC Youth League a quarter-century before. We, too, were Africanists; we, too, stressed ethnic pride and racial self-confidence; we, too, rejected white assistance in the struggle. In many ways, Black Consciousness represented the same response to the same problem that had never gone away.

But just as we had outgrown our Youth League outlook, I was confident that these young men would transcend some of the strictures of Black Consciousness. While I was encouraged by their militancy, I thought that their philosophy, in its concentration on blackness, was exclusionary, and represented an intermediate view that was not fully mature. I saw my role as an elder statesman who might help them move on to the more inclusive ideas of the Congress Movement. I knew also that these young men would eventually become frustrated because Black Consciousness offered no program of action, no outlet for their protest.

Although we viewed the ranks of the BCM as a fertile ground for the ANC, we did not attempt to recruit these men. We knew that this would alienate both them and the other parties on the island. Our policy was to be friendly, to take an interest, to compliment them on their achievements, but not to proselytize. If they came to us and asked questions—"What is the ANC policy on the Bantustans?" "What does the Freedom Charter say about nationalization?" we would answer them—and a great many of them did come to us with questions.

I myself contacted some of these men through smuggled notes. I spoke with some who were from the Transkei and asked questions about my old home. Some of the men who arrived were already well known in the struggle. I had heard reports of the bravery of Patrick "Terror" Lekota, a leader of the South African Students' Organization, and sent him a note of welcome to Robben Island.

Terror's nickname comes from his prowess on the soccer field, but he was just as formidable in a debate. He disagreed with some of his colleagues on the issue of racial exclusiveness and inched closer to the ideas of the ANC. Once on the island, Terror decided that he wanted to join us, but we discouraged him—not because we did not want him but because we thought such a maneuver would create tensions in the general section.

But Terror would not take no for an answer and publicly switched his allegiance to the ANC. One day, not long afterward, he was assaulted with a garden fork by disgruntled BC members. After he was treated, the authorities charged the attackers and planned to put them on trial. But in the interest of harmony, we advised Terror not to lodge a complaint. He agreed, and refused to testify against those who had hurt him. The case was dropped. Such a trial, I felt, would only play into the hands of the authorities. I wanted these young men to see that the ANC was a great tent that could accommodate many different views and affiliations.

After that incident, the floodgates seemed to open and dozens of BC men decided to join the ANC, including some of those who had planned the attack on Terror. Terror rose to the top of the ANC hierarchy in the general section, and was soon teaching ANC policies to other prisoners. The courage and vision of men like Lekota [Terror] confirmed to us that our views remained potent, and still represented the best hope for unifying the liberation struggle as a whole.

Political feuding continued in [sections] F and G. We learned of a clash among the ANC, the PAC, and the BCM in the general section. A number of ANC people had been beaten. A large number of ANC members were charged by the authorities, and a trial was set for the island's administrative court. The ANC men brought in an outside lawyer to handle the case. Although I had not witnessed the fight, I was asked to be a character witness. This was a troubling prospect. While I was more than willing to give testimonials for my comrades, I did not want to take any action that would heighten the bitterness between the ANC, the PAC, and the BCM.

I regarded my role in prison not just as the leader of the ANC, but as a promoter of unity, an honest broker, a peacemaker, and I was reluctant to take a side in this dispute, even if it was the side of my own organization. If I testified on behalf of the ANC, I would jeopardize my chances of bringing about reconciliation among the different groups. If I preached unity, I must act like a unifier, even at the risk of perhaps alienating some of my own colleagues.

I decided not to testify. This disappointed some of my colleagues, but I thought the issue was serious enough to risk their displeasure. It was more important to show the young Black Consciousness men that the struggle was indivisible and that we all had the same enemy.

Chapter 81

In their anxiousness to deal with these young lions, the authorities more or less let us fend for ourselves. We were in the second year of a go-slow strike at the quarry, demanding a complete end to all manual labor. Our requirement was for the right to do something useful with our days, like studying or learning a trade. We no longer even went through the motions of working at the quarry; we simply talked among ourselves. In early 1977, the authorities announced the end of manual labor. Instead, we could spend our days in our section. They arranged some type of work for us to do in the courtyard, but it was merely a fig leaf to hide their capitulation.

This victory was the combined result of our own unceasing protests and simple logistics. The authorities normally preferred to have a ratio of one warder for every three prisoners. Even before the arrival of the post-Soweto prisoners, there was a shortage of warders, and the rebellious young men required even greater supervision. They were so bold that each man seemed to require his own warder. If we remained in our section, we required less supervision.

The end of manual labor was liberating. I could now spend the day reading, writing letters, discussing issues with my comrades, or formulating legal briefs. The free time allowed me to pursue what became two of my favorite hobbies on Robben Island: gardening and tennis.

To survive in prison, one must develop ways to take satisfaction in one's daily life. One can feel fulfilled by washing one's clothes so that they are particularly clean, by sweeping a hallway so that it is empty of dust, by organizing one's cell to conserve as much space as possible. The same pride one takes in more consequential tasks outside of prison one can find in doing small things inside prison.

Almost from the beginning of my sentence on Robben Island, I asked the authorities for permission to start a garden in the courtyard. For years, they refused without offering a reason. But eventually they relented, and we were able to cut out a small garden on a narrow patch of earth against the far wall.

The soil in the courtyard was dry and rocky. The courtyard had been constructed over a landfill, and in order to start my garden, I had to excavate a great many rocks to allow the plants room to grow. At the time, some of my comrades jested that I was a miner at heart, for I spent my days at the quarry and my free time digging in the courtyard.

The authorities supplied me with seeds. I initially planted tomatoes, chilies, and onions—hardy plants that did not require rich earth or constant care. The early harvests were poor, but they soon improved. The authorities did not regret giving permission, for once the garden began to flourish, I often provided the warders with some of my best tomatoes and onions.

While I have always enjoyed gardening, it was not until I was behind bars that I was able to tend my own garden. My first experience in the garden was at Fort Hare where, as part of the university's manual labor requirement, I worked in one of my professors' gardens and enjoyed the contact with the soil as an antidote to my intellectual labors. Once I was in Johannesburg studying and then working, I had neither the time nor the space to cultivate a garden.

I began to order books on gardening and horticulture. I studied different gardening techniques and types of fertilizer. I did not have many of the materials that the books discussed, but I learned through trial and error. For a time, I attempted to grow peanuts, and used different soils and fertilizers, but finally I gave up. It was one of my only failures.

A garden was one of the few things in prison that one could control. To plant a seed, watch it grow, to tend it and then harvest it, offered a simple but enduring satisfaction. The sense of being the custodian of this small patch of earth offered a small taste of freedom.

In some ways, I saw the garden as a metaphor for certain aspects of my life. A leader must also tend his garden; he, too, plants seeds, and then watches, cultivates, and harvests the result. Like the gardener, a leader must take responsibility for what he cultivates; he must mind his work, try to repel enemies, preserve what can be preserved, and eliminate what cannot succeed.

I wrote Winnie two letters about a particularly beautiful tomato plant, how I coaxed it from a tender seedling to a robust plant that produced deep red fruit. But, then, either through some mistake or lack of care, the plant began to wither and decline, and nothing I did would bring it back to health. When it finally died, I removed the roots from the soil, washed them, and buried them in a corner of the garden.

I narrated this small story at great length. I do not know what she read into that letter, but when I wrote it I had a mixture of feelings: I did not want our relationship to go the way of that plant, and yet I felt I had been unable to nourish many of the most important relationships in my life. Sometimes there is nothing one can do to save something that must die.

One unanticipated result of ending labor was that I began to gain weight. Though we were doing barely enough labor at the quarry to work up a sweat, the walk there and back was enough to keep me trim.

I have always believed that exercise is not only a key to physical health but to peace of mind. Many times in the old days I unleashed my anger and frustration on a punching bag rather than taking it out on a comrade or even a policeman. Exercise dissipates tension, and tension is the enemy of serenity. I found that I worked better and thought more clearly when I was in good physical condition, and so training became one of the inflexible disciplines of my life. In prison, having an outlet for one's frustrations was absolutely essential.

Even on the island, I attempted to follow my old boxing routine of doing roadwork and muscle-building from Monday through Thursday and then resting for the next three days. On Monday through Thursday, I would do stationary running in my cell in the morning for up to forty-five minutes. I would also perform one hundred fingertip push-ups, two hundred sit-ups, fifty deep knee-bends, and various other calisthenics.

In my letters to my children, I regularly urged them to exercise, to play some fast-moving sport like basketball, soccer, or tennis to take their mind off whatever might be bothering them. While I was not always successful with my children, I did manage to influence some of my more sedentary colleagues. Exercise was unusual for African men of my age and generation. After a while, even Walter began to take a few turns around the courtyard in the morning. I know that some of my younger comrades looked at me and said to themselves, "If that old man can do it, why can't I?" They too began to exercise.

From the very first meetings I had with outside visitors and the International Red Cross, I stressed the importance of having the time and facilities for proper exercise. Only in the mid-1970's, under the auspices of the International Red Cross, did we begin to receive things like volleyball equipment and a Ping-Pong table.

At roughly the same time we finished working at the quarry, one of the warders had the idea of converting our courtyard into a tennis court. Its dimensions were perfect. Prisoners from the general section painted the cement surface green and then fashioned the traditional configuration of white lines. A few days later a net was put up and suddenly we had our own Wimbledon in our front yard.

I had played a bit of tennis when I was at Fort Hare, but I was by no means an expert. My forehand was relatively strong, my backhand regrettably weak. But I pursued the sport for exercise, not style; it was the best and only replacement for the walks to and from the quarry. I was one of the first in our section to play regularly. I was a back-court player, only rushing the net when I had a clean slam.

Once manual labor ended, I had much more time for reading, but the books I had been using were now out-of-bounds. When my studies were canceled, I was still in the midst of pursuing my L.L.B. [Bachelor of Laws] at the University of London. I had started studying for the L.L.B. during the Rivonia Trial and the suspension of study privileges for four years would undoubtedly assure me of the university record for the most number of years pursuing that degree.

But the suspension of study privileges had an unintended benefit, and that was that I began to read books that I would not otherwise have read. Instead of poring over tomes about contract law, I was now absorbed by novels.

I did not have an unlimited library to choose from on Robben Island. We had access to many unremembered mysteries and detective novels and all the works of Daphne du Maurier, but little more. Political books were off-limits. Any book about socialism or communism was definitely out. A request for a book with the word *red* in the title, even if it was *Little Red Riding Hood*, would be rejected by the censors. *War of the Worlds* by H. G. Wells, though it is a work of science fiction, would be turned down because the word *war* appeared in its title.

From the first, I tried to read books about South Africa or by South African writers. I read all the unbanned novels of Nadine Gordimer and learned a great deal about the white liberal sensibility. I read many American novels, and recall especially John Steinbeck's *The Grapes of Wrath*, in which I found many similarities between the plight of the migrant workers in that novel and our own laborers and farmworkers.

One book that I returned to many times was Tolstoy's great work, *War and Peace*. (Although the word *war* was in the title, this book was permitted.) I was particularly taken with the portrait of General Kutuzov, whom everyone at the Russian court underestimated. Kutuzov defeated Napoleon precisely because he was not swayed by the ephemeral and superficial values of the court, and made his decisions on a visceral understanding of his men and his people. It reminded me once again that to truly lead one's people one must also truly know them.

Part 10—Talking with the Enemy

Chapter 88

...

The government had sent "feelers" to me over the years, beginning with Minister Kruger's efforts to persuade me to move to the Transkei. These were not efforts to negotiate, but attempts to isolate me from my organization. On several other occasions, Kruger said to me: "Mandela, we can work with you, but not your colleagues. Be reasonable." Although I did not respond to these overtures, the mere fact that they were talking rather than attacking could be seen as a prelude to genuine negotiations.

The government was testing the waters. In late 1984 and early 1985, I had visits from two prominent Western statesmen, Lord Nicholas Bethell, a member of the British House of Lords and the European Parliament, and Samuel Dash, a professor of law at Georgetown University and a former counsel to the U.S. Senate Watergate Committee. Both visits were authorized by the new minister of justice, Kobie Coetsee, who appeared to be a new sort of Afrikaner leader.

I met Lord Bethell in the prison commander's office, which was dominated by a large photograph of a glowering President Botha. Bethell was a jovial, rotund man and when I first met him, I teased him about his stoutness. "You look like you are related to Winston Churchill," I said as we shook hands, and he laughed.

Lord Bethell wanted to know about our conditions at Pollsmoor and I told him. We discussed the armed struggle and I explained to him it was not up to us to renounce violence, but the government. I reaffirmed that we aimed for hard military targets, not people. "I would not want our men to assassinate, for instance, the major here," I said, pointing to Major Fritz van Sittert, who was monitoring the talks. Van Sittert was a good-natured fellow who did not say much, but he started at my remark.

In my visit with Professor Dash, which quickly followed that of Lord Bethell, I laid out what I saw as the minimum for a future nonracial South Africa: a unitary state without homelands; nonracial elections for the central Parliament; and one-person-one-vote. Professor Dash asked me whether I took any encouragement from the government's stated intention of repealing the mixed-marriage laws and certain other apartheid statutes. "This is a pinprick," I said. "It is not my ambition to marry a white woman or swim in a white pool. It is political equality that we want." I told Dash quite candidly that at the moment we could not defeat the government on the battlefield, but could make governing difficult for them.

UNIT
10

I had one not-so-pleasant visit from two Americans, editors of the conservative newspaper the *Washington Times*. They seemed less intent on finding out my views than on proving that I was a Communist and a terrorist. All of their questions were slanted in that direction, and when I reiterated that I was neither a Communist nor a terrorist, they attempted to show that I was not a Christian either by asserting that the Reverend Martin Luther King never resorted to violence. I told them that the conditions in which Martin Luther King struggled were totally different from my own: the United States was a democracy with constitutional guarantees of equal rights that protected nonviolent protest (though there was still prejudice against blacks); South Africa was a police state with a constitution that enshrined inequality and an army that responded to nonviolence with force. I told them that I was a Christian and had always been a Christian. Even Christ, I said, when he was left with no alternative, used force to expel the moneylenders from the temple. He was not a man of violence, but had no choice but to use force against evil. I do not think I persuaded them.

Faced with trouble at home and pressure from abroad, P.W. Botha offered a tepid, halfway measure. On January 31, 1985, in a debate in Parliament, the state president publicly offered me my freedom if I "unconditionally rejected violence as a political instrument." This offer was extended to all political prisoners. Then, as if he were staking me to a public challenge, he added, "It is therefore not the South African government which now stands in the way of Mr. Mandela's freedom. It is he himself."

I had been warned by the authorities that the government was going to make a proposal involving my freedom, but I had not been prepared for the fact that it would be made in Parliament by the state president. By my reckoning, it was the sixth conditional offer the government had made for my release in the past ten years. After I listened to the speech on radio, I made a request to the commander of the prison for an urgent visit by my wife and my lawyer, Ismail Ayob, so that I could dictate my response to the state president's offer.

Winnie and Ismail were not given permission to visit for a week, and in the meantime I wrote a letter to the foreign minister, Pik Botha, rejecting the conditions for my release, while also preparing a public response, because [P.W.] Botha's offer was an attempt to drive a wedge between me and my colleagues by tempting me to accept a policy the ANC rejected. I wanted to reassure the ANC in general and Oliver in particular that my loyalty to the organization was beyond question. I also wished to send a message to the government that while I rejected its offer because of the conditions attached to it, I nevertheless thought negotiation, not war, was the path to a solution.

Botha wanted the onus of violence to rest on my shoulders and I wanted to reaffirm to the world that we were only responding to the violence done to us. I intended to make it clear that if I emerged from prison into the same circumstances in which I was arrested, I would be forced to resume the same activities for which I was arrested.

I met with Winnie and Ismail on a Friday; on Sunday, a UDF [political party opposing the Nationalist party of apartheid] rally was to be held in Soweto's Jabulani Stadium, where my response would be made public. Some guards with whom I was not familiar supervised the visit, and as we began discussing my response to the state president, one of the warders, a relatively young fellow, interrupted to say that only family matters were permitted to be discussed. I ignored him, and he returned minutes later with a senior warder whom I barely knew. This warder said that I must cease discussing politics, and I told him that I was dealing with a matter of national importance involving an offer from the state president. I warned him that if he wanted to halt the discussion he must get direct orders from the state president himself. "If you are not willing to telephone the state president to get those orders," I said coldly, "then kindly do not interrupt us again." He did not.

I gave Ismail and Winnie the speech I had prepared. In addition to responding to the government, I wanted to thank publicly the UDF for its fine work and to congratulate Bishop Tutu on his prize, adding that his award belonged to all the people. On Sunday, February 10, 1985, my daughter Zindzi read my response to a cheering crowd of people who had not been able to hear my words legally anywhere in South Africa for more than twenty years.

Zindzi was a dynamic speaker like her mother, and said that her father should be at the stadium to speak the words himself. I was proud to know that it was she who spoke my words.

I am a member of the African National Congress. I have always been a member of the African National Congress and I will remain a member of the African National Congress until the day I die. Oliver Tambo is more than a brother to me. He is my greatest friend and comrade for nearly fifty years. If there is any one amongst you who cherishes my freedom, Oliver Tambo cherishes it more, and I know that he would give his life to see me free...

I am surprised at the conditions that the government wants to impose on me. I am not a violent man.... It was only then, when all other forms of resistance were no longer open to us, that we turned to armed struggle. Let Botha show that he is different to Malan, Strijdom and Verwoerd. Let him renounce violence. Let him say that he will dismantle apartheid. Let him unban the people's organization, the African National Congress. Let him free all who have been imprisoned, banished or exiled for their opposition to apartheid. Let him guarantee free political activity so that people may decide who will govern them.

I cherish my own freedom dearly, but I care even more for your freedom. Too many have died since I went to prison. Too many have suffered for the love of freedom. I owe it to their widows, to their orphans, to their mothers, and to their fathers who have grieved and wept for them. Not only I have suffered during these long, lonely, wasted years. I am not less life-loving than you are. But I cannot sell my birthright, nor am I prepared to sell the birthright of the people to be free...

What freedom am I being offered when I may be arrested on a pass offense? What freedom am I being offered to live my life as a family with my dear wife who remains in banishment in Brandfort? What freedom am I being offered when I must ask for permission to live in an urban area?...What freedom am I being offered when my very South African citizenship is not respected?

UNIT
10

Only free men can negotiate. Prisoners cannot enter into contracts...I cannot and will not give any undertaking at a time when I and you, the people, are not free. Your freedom and mine cannot be separated. I will return.

Excerpts from *Long Walk to Freedom* by Nelson Mandela. Pages 481–492, 519–523. Copyright © 1994 by Nelson Rolihlahla Mandela. Used by permission of Little, Brown and Company, Inc.

"…You lead by empowering your people, by developing them, by educating them to be leaders. The leader is a teacher, and you lead not only by creating systems and assigning work but also by developing people. Effective empowerment is based on a simple formula, the product of autonomy, direction, and support: $E = A \times D \times S$."

—Peter Koestenbaum, Philosophy Professor and Leadership Consultant
Quoted from *Leadership: The Inner Side of Greatness*
(San Francisco: Jossey-Bass, 1991)

REFLECT & FOCUS

READINGS

"From Transactional to Transformational Leadership: Learning to Share the Vision"

By Bernard M. Bass

Points to Consider

1. What is the distinction between transformational behavior and personal style?

2. Why does Bass characterize transformational leadership as an "art and science" rather than a skill?

3. Why do you think teams can be stronger with transformational leadership?

4. What would be different in the exercise of transformational leadership when it is an organization or a community that is in need of change or growth?

"From Transactional to Transformational Leadership: Learning to Share the Vision"

Sir Edmund Hillary of Mount Everest fame liked to tell a story about one of Captain Robert Falcon Scott's earlier attempts, from 1901 to 1904, to reach the South Pole. Scott led an expedition made up of men from the Royal Navy and the merchant marine, as well as a group of scientists. Scott had considerable trouble dealing with the merchant marine personnel, who were unaccustomed to the rigid discipline of Scott's Royal Navy. Scott wanted to send one seaman home because he would not take orders, but the seaman refused, arguing that he had signed a contract and knew his rights. Since the seaman was not subject to Royal Navy disciplinary action, Scott did not know what to do. Then Ernest Shackleton, a merchant navy officer in Scott's party, calmly informed the seaman that he, the seaman, was returning to Britain. Again the seaman refused—and Shackleton knocked him to the ship's deck. After another refusal, followed by a second flooring, the seaman decided he would return home. Scott later became one of the victims of his own inadequacies as a leader in his 1911 race to the South Pole. Shackleton went on to lead many memorable expeditions; once, seeking help for the rest of his party, who were stranded on the Antarctic Coast, he journeyed with a small crew in a small open boat from the edge of Antarctica to South Georgia Island.

Leadership Today

Most relationships between supervisors and their employees are quite different today. Few managers depend mainly on their legitimate power, as Scott did, or on their coercive power, as Shackleton did, to persuade people to do as they're told. Rather, managers engage in a transaction with their employees: they explain what is required of them and what compensation they will receive if they fulfill these requirements.

A shift in management style at Xerox's Reprographic Business Group (RBG) provides a good example. In the first step toward establishing management in which managers take the initiative and show consideration for others, 44 specific, effective management behaviors were identified.

Two factors that characterize modern leadership were found in many of these behaviors. One factor—initiating and organizing work—concentrates on accomplishing the tasks at hand. The second factor—showing consideration for employees—focuses on satisfying the self-interest of those who do good work. The leader gets things done by making, and fulfilling, promises of recognition, pay increases, and advancement for employees who perform well. By contrast, employees who do not do good work are penalized. This transaction or exchange—this promise and reward for good performance, or threat and discipline for poor performance—characterizes effective leadership. These kinds of transactions took place in most of the effective 44 leadership behaviors identified at Xerox's RBG. This kind of leadership, which is based on transactions between manager and employees, is called "transactional leadership."

In many instances, however, such transactional leadership is a prescription for mediocrity. This is particularly true if the leader relies heavily on passive management-by-exception, intervening with his or her group only when procedures and standards for accomplishing tasks are not being met. My colleagues and I have arrived at this surprising but consistent finding in a number of research analyses. Such a manager espouses the popular adage, "If it ain't broke, don't fix it." He or she stands in back of the caboose of a moving freight train and says, "Now I know where we are going." This kind of manager may use disciplinary threats to bring a group's performance up to standards—a technique that is ineffective and, in the long run, likely to be counterproductive.

Moreover, whether the promise of rewards or the avoidance of penalties motivates the employees depends on whether the leader has control of the rewards or penalties. In many organizations, pay increases depend mainly on seniority, and promotions depend on qualifications and policies about which the leader has little to say. The breaking of regulations may be the main cause of penalties. Many an executive has found his or her hands tied by contract provisions, organizational politics, and inadequate resources.

Transformational Leadership

Superior leadership performance—transformational leadership—occurs when leaders broaden and elevate the interests of their employees, when they generate awareness and acceptance of the purposes and mission of the group, and when they stir their employees to look beyond their own self-interest for the good of the group. Transformational leaders achieve these results in one or more ways: they may be charismatic to their followers and thus inspire them; they may meet the emotional needs of each employee; and/or they may intellectually stimulate employees. Exhibit 1 lists the characteristics of transformational and transactional leadership; these listings are based on the findings of a series of surveys and on clinical and case evidence.

Attaining charisma in the eyes of one's employees is central to succeeding as a transformational leader. Charismatic leaders have great power and influence. Employees want to identify with them, and they have a high degree of trust and confidence in them. Charismatic leaders inspire and excite their employees with the idea that they may be able to accomplish great things with great effort. Further, transformational leaders are individually considerate, that is, they pay close attention to differences among their employees; they act as mentors to those who need to grow and develop. Intellectual stimulation of employees is a third factor in transformational leadership. Intellectually stimulating leaders are willing and able to show their employees new ways of looking at old problems, to teach them to see difficulties as problems to be solved, and to emphasize rational solutions. Such a leader was Lorenz Iverson, a former president of the Mesta Machine Company, who said to his employees, "We got this job because you're the best mechanics in the world!" He practiced management-by-walking-around and stimulated the development of many of Mesta's patented inventions. He is remembered for instilling pride and commitment in his employees.

Exhibit 1

Characteristics [possible for] Transformational and Transactional Leaders:

Transformational Leader

Charisma: Provides vision and sense of mission, instills pride, gains respect and trust.

Inspiration: Communicates high expectations, uses symbols to focus efforts, expresses important purposes in simple ways.

Intellectual stimulation: Promotes intelligence, rationality, and careful problem solving.

Individualized consideration: Gives personal attention, treats each employee individually, coaches, advises.

Transactional Leader

Contingent reward: Contracts exchange of rewards for effort, promises reward for good performance, recognizes accomplishments.

Management by exception (active): Watches and searches for deviations from rules and standards, takes corrective action.

Management by exception (passive): Intervenes only if standards are not met.

Laissez-faire: Abdicates responsibilities, avoids making decisions.

UNIT
10

The Big Payoff

Managers who behave like transformational leaders are more likely to be seen by their colleagues and employees as satisfying and effective leaders than are those who behave like transactional leaders, according to their colleagues', supervisors', and employees' responses on the Multifactor Leadership Questionnaire (MLQ). Similar results have been found in various organizational settings. Leaders studied have come from an extremely broad variety of organizations: chief executive officers and senior and middle level managers in business and industrial firms in the United States, Canada, and British Army field grade officers; United States Navy senior officers and junior surface fleet officers; Annapolis midshipmen; educational administrators; and religious leaders.

Moreover, various types of evaluations—including performance rating by both supervisors and direct reports, as well as standard financial measures—have produced a similar correlation between transformational behavior and high ratings. Managers tagged as high performers by their supervisors were also rated, in a separate evaluation by their followers, as more transformational than transactional. Their organizations do better financially. The same pattern emerged between followers' descriptions of shipboard Naval officers and those officers' supervisors' performance appraisals and recommendations for early promotion. And among Methodist ministers, transformational—not transactional—leadership behavior was positively related to high church attendance among congregants and growth in church membership.

Results were the same for evaluation of team performance in complex business simulations. Considerable credit for Boeing's turnaround since its 1969 crisis can be given to its chief executive, T.A. Wilson, who has emphasized technological progress, aggressive marketing, and a willingness to take calculated business risks. The confidence that Boeing employees have in Wilson, and their respect for him as a brilliant engineer and an outstanding leader, have instilled in them great pride in the company and its products.

Extra Effort from Below

Transformational leaders have better relationships with their supervisors and make more of a contribution to the organization than do those who are only transactional. Moreover, employees say they themselves exert a lot of extra effort on behalf of managers who are transformational leaders. Organizations whose leaders are transactional are less effective than those whose leaders are transformational—particularly if much of the transactional leadership is passive management-by-exception (intervening only when standards are not being met). Employees say they exert little effort for such leaders. Nevertheless, leader-follower transactions dependent on contingent reward may also work reasonably well if the leaders can provide rewards that are valued by the followers.

Exhibit 2 illustrates the effect that transformational, as compared with transactional, leadership has on employee effort. The data were collected from 228 employees of 58 managers in a large engineering firm. The managers were ranked according to their leadership factor scores, which were based on descriptions of leaders by their employees and colleagues on the Multifactor Leadership Questionnaire. "Four-star" leaders were those who ranked in the top 25% on a leadership factor score; "one-star" leaders were among the bottom 25% of managers on the leadership factor score. From 75% to 82% of the "four-star" transformational managers had employees who indicated they frequently exerted extra effort on their jobs. Of the "one-star" transformational managers, only 22% to 24% had employees who said they frequently exerted extra effort.

It is interesting to note that, as Exhibit 2 illustrates, being rated as "four-star" rather than "one-star" in *transactional* leadership did not have the same impact on employees' extra effort as a high rating had for the transformational leaders. Similar findings have emerged from studies of leaders and their immediate employees at a diverse range of organizations, including Digital Equipment Corporation and Federal Express.

Exhibit 2

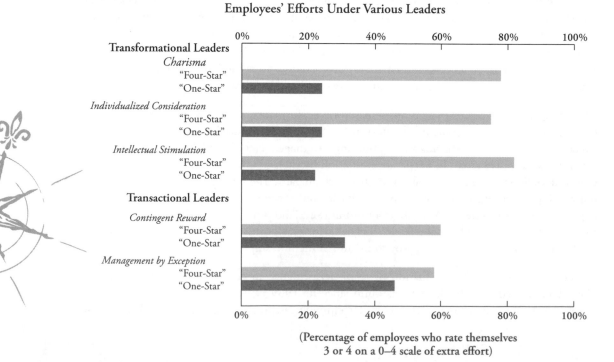

Employees' Efforts Under Various Leaders

(Percentage of employees who rate themselves
3 or 4 on a 0–4 scale of extra effort)

Different Styles of Transformational Leadership

As noted earlier, certain types of behavior characterize the transformational leader. Yet transformational leaders vary widely in their personal styles. H. Ross Perot is self-effacing: "I don't look impressive," he says. "To a lot of guys I don't look like I could afford a car." But Perot created the $2.5 billion EDS organization from his vision, initiative, emphasis on hard work, and a special organizational culture with strict codes of morality and dress and quasi-military management. His personal involvement in the rescue of two of his employees trapped as hostages in Iran in 1979 is an extreme example of individualized consideration, a transformational factor. Leslie Wexner of The Limited, Inc. enjoys a more flamboyant lifestyle. But like Perot, Wexner converted his vision of a nationwide chain of women's sportswear stores into a reality through his own hard work. He stimulates employee participation in discussions and decisions and encourages them to share his vision of the company's future.

Many on *Fortune*'s list of the ten toughest bosses would not live up to modern behavioral science's prescriptions for the good leader: one who initiates the structure for interaction among his colleagues, and who does so with consideration for their welfare. Nevertheless, these tough bosses are highly successful as a consequence of the transformational qualities they display; Boeing's Wilson is a case in point. Although they do initiate structure and may be considerate of their employees, these leaders succeed through such transformational factors as charisma and the ability and willingness to treat different subordinates differently, as well as by providing intellectual stimulation for the employees. They frequently raise standards, take calculated risks, and get others to join them in their vision of the future. Rather than work with the organizational culture, they challenge and change that culture, as Roger Smith of General Motors Corporation did. Self-determination and self-confidence are characteristic of them. They succeed because of these transformational elements—even if they, like Wilson, have authoritarian tendencies.

Transformational Leaders Make the Difference between Success and Failure

Fighting with fewer men and tanks than his enemy had, against superior equipment, Ernst Rommel, the Desert Fox, won a series of victories in 1941 and 1942 against the British in North Africa, until he was overwhelmed at El Alamein. Because he was up front at the scene of the action, he could make more rapid assessments and decisions than could his British counterparts, who stayed 20 miles back in headquarters. This, and his willingness to accept calculated risks, contributed to his legendary speed, surprise, and boldness, as well as the continuing high morale of his troops.

Napoleon declared that an army of rabbits commanded by a lion could do better than an army of lions commanded by a rabbit. He was not far from the truth. With all due respect to social, economic, political, and market forces, and to human resources policies that affect an organization's health, having a lion—or, in Rommel's case, a fox—in command rather than a rabbit frequently means success for the organization. Lee Iacocca of Chrysler Corporation and Jack Welch of General Electric, who have become folk heroes (or folk devils, to some), are contemporary examples of the importance of transformational leaders to their organizations.

Leadership makes its presence felt throughout the organization and its activities. We found that employees not only do a better job when they believe their supervisors are transformational leaders, but they also are much more satisfied with the company's performance appraisal system. Likewise, mass communications directed toward individual employees are much more likely to have an impact if the messages are reinforced face-to-face by their supervisors at all organizational levels.

Transformational leadership should be encouraged, for it can make a big difference in the firm's performance at all levels. Managers need to do more than focus on the exchange of material, social, and personal benefits for services satisfactorily rendered. The charismatic leader, like the flamboyant Ted Turner of Turner Broadcasting System, Inc., can instill a sense of mission; the individually considerate leader, like the shy and self-effacing Roberto Goizueta of the Coca Cola Corporation, can lead employees to take an interest in higher-level concerns; the intellectually stimulating leader, like the innovative Roger Smith at General Motors Corporation, can articulate a shared vision of jointly acceptable possibilities. This is not to say that transformational leaders are always prosocial in their efforts, for some fulfill grandiose dreams at the expense of their followers.

Despite the many successes with management development programs and the leadership development programs in our military academies, many executives still feel that leadership is like the water—something to talk about, but about which not much can be done. Others say leadership ability is mystical—one needs to be born with it.

In fact, much can be done to improve leadership in an organization and to change the presiding style from transactional to transformational. The overall amount of transformational leadership in an organization can be increased substantially by suitable organizational and human resources policies. The new model of transformational leadership presents opportunities from enhancing a corporation's image and for improving its success in recruitment, selection, and promotion. This model also has implications for the organization's training and development activities and for the design of its jobs and organizational structure.

Implications for Corporate Image

It is no accident that many of the firms identified in Tom Peters and Robert Waterman's *In Search of Excellence* (Warner Books, 1982) as excellently managed have large numbers of transformational leaders. Conversely, the poorly managed "dinosaurs" among the firms they describe need to implement a lot more transformational leadership. A firm that is permeated with transformational leadership from top to bottom conveys to its own personnel as well as to customers, suppliers, financial backers, and the community at large that it has its eyes on the future; is confident; has personnel who are pulling together for the common good; and places a premium on its intellectual resources and flexibility and on the development of its people.

Implications for Recruiting

Increasing transformational leadership within the organization may help in recruitment. Candidates are likely to be attracted to an organization whose CEO is charismatic and enjoys a public image as a confident, successful, optimistic, dynamic leader. In addition, prospects are likely to be attracted by interview experiences with other members of management who exhibit individualized consideration. More intelligent prospects will be particularly impressed with intellectually stimulating contacts they make during the recruiting and hiring process.

Implications for Selection, Promotion, and Transfer

Since we can identify and measure the factors associated with transformational leadership, these factors should be incorporated into managerial assessment, selection, placement, and guidance programs—along with related assessments of relevant personal dimensions and individual differences. Somewhat more transformational leadership is generally expected and found as managers move to successively higher levels in the organization, but it is reasonable to expect that an individual's performance at one level will be similar to his or her performance at the next. Direct reports, and/or supervisors can be asked to describe the manager's current leadership with the Multifactor Leadership Questionnaire; their responses should be considered when decisions are made regarding a manager's promotion or transfer into a position of greater supervisory responsibility. Feedback from these results can also be used for counseling, coaching, and mentoring.

Further, the organization can tap the personal characteristics and strengths that underlie the manager's transformational behavior. Charismatic leaders are characterized by energy, self-confidence, determination, intellect, verbal skills, and strong ego ideals. Each of these traits can be assessed in individual managers. Similarly, we can assess some of the traits underlying individualized consideration, such as coaching skills; preference for two-way, face-to-face communication; and willingness to delegate. Again, in the area of intellectual stimulation, candidates for promotion could be assessed with an eye toward the type of intellectual stimulation—general, creative, or mathematical—that would be most effective at the higher level of management. Appropriate intelligence tests may be used to select intellectually stimulating candidates.

Research findings indicate that when employees rate their managers on the MLQ, they describe new business leaders as significantly more transformational than established business leaders. Thus MLQ scores can be used profitably to identify executives to head new ventures.

Implications for Development

A management trainee's first supervisor can make a big difference in his or her subsequent career success. For example, six years after they joined Exxon, many managers who were highly rated by their supervisors reported that they had been given challenging assignments by their initial supervisor (i.e., they had received individualized consideration). Many had been assigned to supervisors with good reputations in the firm. It is important to note that managers tend to model their own leadership style after that of their immediate supervisors. Thus if more higher-ups are transformational, more lower-level employees will emulate transformational behavior—and will be likely to act as transformational leaders as they rise in the organization.

Organizational policy needs to support an understanding and appreciation of the maverick who is willing to take unpopular positions, who knows when to reject the conventional wisdom, and who takes reasonable risks. For example, when R. Gordon McGovern took over as president of Campbell Soup, he introduced the "right to fail" policy, which shook up the stodgy organization. On the other hand, the fine line between self-confidence and obstinacy needs to be drawn. The determined Winston Churchill who contributed so much to the survival of Britain in 1940 was the same Churchill whose obstinacy contributed to the mistakes in 1941 of failing to prepare Singapore adequately and of committing British troops to unnecessary disaster in Crete and Greece.

Intellectual stimulation also needs to be nurtured and cultivated as a way of life in the organization. The "best and the brightest" people should be hired, nourished, and encouraged. Innovation and creativity should be fostered at all levels in the firm.

UNIT
10

Implications for Training

Despite conventional wisdom to the contrary, transformational leadership is a widespread phenomenon. True, more of it occurs at the top than at the bottom of an organization; but it has also been observed by many employees in their first-level supervisors. Transformational leadership can be learned, and it can—and should—be the subject of management training and development. Research has shown that leaders at all levels can be trained to be charismatic in both verbal and nonverbal performance. Successful programs have been conducted for first-level project leaders in hi-tech computer firms as well as for senior executives of insurance firms.

That transformational leadership can be increased through training was verified in an experiment when Multifactor Leadership Questionnaire scores were obtained on shop supervisors from their trainees, who were inmates in minimum, medium, and maximum security prisons. The supervisors worked directly with the inmates in industrial shops to produce various products for sale within and outside the prison system. The experiment compared four groups of supervisors on their pre- and post-training effectiveness in various industrial and vocational shops in the prison. One group was trained in transformational leadership, one group was trained in transactional leadership, one was untrained but measured "before and after," and one was untrained and measured only "after." The performances of both trained groups improved, but in comparison to the three other groups of supervisors, those who were trained in transformational leadership did as well or better at improving productivity, absenteeism, and "citizenship" behavior among the inmates; they also won more respect from the inmates.

Training Managers

Practical training that teaches people how to be transformational is similar to that used in the Xerox RPG strategy to modify management style. A counselor, mediator, or supervisor gives a manager a detailed, standardized description of his or her transformational and transactional leadership performance as rated by the manager's employees and/or colleagues. The Multifactor Leadership Questionnaire is used for this purpose. The manager also sees a chart showing the effects of his or her leadership on employee satisfaction, motivation, and perception of organizational effectiveness. Anonymity is maintained, although the manager sees the individual differences among the responses.

Participating managers complete a parallel questionnaire about their own leadership. The discrepancies between how they rate themselves and how their employees rate them may be examined scale-by-scale and item-by-item. The counselor may pose such questions as: "Why do you think you gave yourself a much higher score than your employees gave you in individualized consideration?" and "Why did your employees disagree with you on how rapidly you get to the heart of complex problems or the extent to which they trust you to overcome any obstacles?" It is important for managers to be aware of and accept their employees' view of their performance. A study of United States Naval officers found that those who agreed with their direct reports about their transformational leadership behavior were also likely to earn higher fitness ratings and recommendations for early promotion from their supervisors.

The manager and the counselor discuss in detail why certain results may have appeared and what can be done to improve ratings. For example, a manager may be asked: "What specific behavior on your part makes your employees say they are proud to work with you?" or "What have you done that results in your colleagues' saying you foster a sense of mission?" The collected responses to these questions can create a useful picture of what the manager can do to raise his or her performance on particular items.

In addition to working individually with a counselor, the manager also may participate in a workshop with other managers who are working toward becoming more transformational leaders. Workshop participants who received high ratings from their employees on a particular item are asked what they, the participants, specifically did to achieve these ratings. Questions might include: "Why did all of your employees say that you frequently enabled them to think about old problems in new ways?" or "Why did they all say that you increased their optimism for the future?"

Conversely, questions may focus on why a participant's employees varied widely in their ratings. If the data printout shows a wide divergence of opinion about whether a manager made the employees enthusiastic about assignments, he or she might be asked to suggest possible reasons for such differences of opinion among the employees.

Other Approaches to Training

Several other approaches to teaching transformational leadership make use of the specific data gathered in the workshop. For instance, participants are asked to think of an effective leader they have known and the behavior the leader displayed. Many examples of charisma, individual consideration, and intellectual stimulation are usually noted. The effective leaders who are mentioned typically come from many levels inside and outside the organization; the workshop leader may point out that transformational leadership is neither particularly uncommon nor limited only to world class leaders. Moreover, these leaders' specific behaviors can be described, observed, and adopted. After viewing videotapes of charismatic, individually considerate, and intellectually stimulating managers in action, workshop participants may be asked to create their own scenarios and videotapes, in which they emulate the transformational leaders they have observed. The other participants may then offer critiques and suggest improvements.

The workshop also aims to increase other aspects of transformational leadership. The transformational leader develops and changes the organizational culture, and to show participants that they have such capabilities, the workshop leader asks them to imagine what the organization might be like in two to five years if it were fully aligned with their own ideas and interests. Then, in small teams based on their actual functions at work, they proceed to redesign the organization.

Similarly, training in mentoring can be used to promote the transformational factor of individualized consideration. For example, one participant can counsel another while a third acts as an observer and a source of feedback about the performance. And many creativity exercises show a manager how he or she can be more intellectually stimulating. Action plans emerge from workshop sessions. Examples include the following:

- I am going to sit down with all my employees and review this data with them.

- I am going to ask for another "reading" in a year; in the meantime I will try to reduce the discrepancies between where I am and where I should be.

- I'm going to talk with my mentor about these results and ask him what he thinks I should do about them.

UNIT
10

Implications for Leadership Education

Military academies have traditionally emphasized leadership education, and today we are seeing a surge of interest in leadership courses in liberal arts colleges as well. At least 600 such courses were being offered, according to a recently completed survey of colleges. The Center for Creative Leadership holds conferences on leadership courses in undergraduate education, most recently in the summer of 1986. The subject of transformational leadership also has been added to leadership courses at the U.S. Air Force Academy at Colorado Springs. In one such course, both faculty and students examined how Air Force officers who are transformational leaders serve as role models for cadets. Scales from the Multifactor Leadership Questionnaire were used to show that the transformational leaders among the instructors and staff provided role models for their students. The faculty and students discussed the questionnaire results and their implications.

Clearly, training cannot turn a purely transactional leader into a transformational leader. Moreover, some managers, while striving to be transformational leaders, misuse their training; their pseudo-transformational efforts only further the manager's self-interest and values. Under the influence of such a manager, employees can be misdirected away from their own best interests and those of the organization as a whole. In one such case, Donald Burr of People's Express Airlines displayed many transformational qualities that rapidly built and then rapidly ruined the firm.

For too long, leadership development has been seen as mainly a matter of skill development. But leadership—particularly transformational leadership—should be regarded as an art and a science. It is encouraging to see that the Council for Liberal Learning of the Association of American Colleges now sponsors week-long conferences on leadership for scholars, prominent citizens, and national leaders.

Implications for Job Design and Job Assignment

As we have noted earlier, the results of a study of Exxon managers showed that highly-rated managers had had challenging tasks delegated to them by their supervisors when they first joined the company. Jobs can—and should—be designed to provide greater challenges. Delegation with guidance and follow-up can become an individualizing and developmental way of life in a firm.

Transformational leaders show individualized consideration by paying attention to the particular development needs of each of their employees. Employees' jobs are designed with those needs in mind, as well as the needs of the organization. One employee needs experience leading a project team. Another needs an opportunity to reinforce what she has learned in an advanced computer programming class. Their transformational leader assigns them tasks accordingly.

Leaders can be intellectually stimulating to their employees if their own jobs allow them to explore new opportunities, to diagnose organizational problems, and to generate solutions. Leaders whose jobs force them to focus on solving small, immediate problems are likely to be less intellectually stimulating than those who have time to think ahead and in larger terms.

Implications for Organizational Structure

Transformational leadership is not a panacea. In many situations, it is inappropriate and transactional processes are indicated. In general, firms that are functioning in stable markets can afford to depend on their "one-minute" managers to provide the necessary, day-to-day leadership. If the technology, workforce, and environment are stable as well, then things are likely to move along quite well with managers who simply promise and deliver rewards to employees for carrying out assignments. And in stable organizations, even management-by-exception can be quite effective if the manager monitors employee performance and takes corrective action as needed. Rules and regulations for getting things done, when clearly understood and accepted by the employees, can eliminate the need for leadership under some circumstances.

But when the firm is faced with a turbulent marketplace; when its products are born, live, and die within the span of a few years; and/or when its current technology can become obsolete before it is fully depreciated; then transformational leadership needs to be fostered at all levels in the firm. In order to succeed, the firm needs to have the flexibility to forecast and meet new demands and changes as they occur—and only transformational leadership can enable the firm to do so.

Problems, rapid changes, and uncertainties call for a flexible organization with determined leaders who can inspire employees to participate enthusiastically in team efforts and share in organizational goals. In short, charisma, attention to individualized development, and the ability and willingness to provide intellectual stimulation are critical in leaders whose firms are faced with demands for renewal and change. At these organizations, fostering transformational leadership through policies of recruitment, selection, promotion, training, and development is likely to pay off in the health, well-being, and effective performance of the organization.

From Transactional to Transformational Leadership: Learning to Share the Vision by Bernard M. Bass from Organizational Dynamics, January 1990, Vol. 18, Issue 3, p. 19. Used by permission.

"Social Intelligence and the Biology of Leadership"

By Daniel Goleman and Richard Boyatzis

Points to Consider

1. What personal examples can you think of when your social behavior reinforced positive feelings for yourself and others?

2. What are some specific socially intelligent behaviors that positively affect a group or organizational climate?

3. What are some ways to deliver a tough message in a positive way, and thus minimize negative feelings for others?

"Social Intelligence and the Biology of Leadership"

New studies of the brain show that leaders can improve group performance by understanding the biology of empathy.

In 1998, one of us, Daniel Goleman, published in these pages his first article on emotional intelligence and leadership. The response to "What Makes a Leader?" was enthusiastic. People throughout and beyond the business community started talking about the vital role that empathy and self-knowledge play in effective leadership. The concept of emotional intelligence continues to occupy a prominent space in the leadership literature and in everyday coaching practices. But in the past five years, research in the emerging field of social neuroscience—the study of what happens in the brain while people interact—is beginning to reveal subtle new truths about what makes a good leader.

The salient discovery is that certain things leaders do—specifically, exhibit empathy and become attuned to others' moods—literally affect both their own brain chemistry and that of their followers. Indeed, researchers have found that the leader-follower dynamic is not a case of two (or more) independent brains reacting consciously or unconsciously to each other. Rather, the individual minds become, in a sense, fused into a single system. We believe that great leaders are those whose behavior powerfully leverages the system of brain interconnectedness. We place them on the opposite end of the neural continuum from people with serious social disorders, such as autism or Asperger's syndrome, that are characterized by underdevelopment in the areas of the brain associated with social interactions. If we are correct, it follows that a potent way of becoming a better leader is to find authentic contexts in which to learn the kinds of social behavior that reinforce the brain's social circuitry. Leading effectively is, in other words, less about mastering situations—or even mastering social skill sets—than about developing a genuine interest in and talent for fostering positive feelings in the people whose cooperation and support you need.

The notion that effective leadership is about having powerful social circuits in the brain has prompted us to extend our concept of emotional intelligence, which we had grounded in theories of individual psychology. A more relationship-based construct for assessing leadership is social intelligence, which we define as a set of interpersonal competencies built on specific neural circuits (and related endocrine systems) that inspire others to be effective.

The idea that leaders need social skills is not new, of course. In 1920, Columbia University psychologist Edward Thorndike pointed out that "the best mechanic in a factory may fail as a foreman for lack of social intelligence." More recently, our colleague Claudio Fernández-Aráoz found in an analysis of new C-level executives that those who had been hired for their self-discipline, drive, and intellect were sometimes later fired for lacking basic social skills. In other words, the people Fernández-Aráoz studied had smarts in spades, but their inability to get along socially on the job was professionally self-defeating.

What's new about our definition of social intelligence is its biological underpinning, which we will explore in the following pages. Drawing on the work of neuroscientists, our own research and consulting endeavors, and the findings of researchers affiliated with the Consortium for Research on Emotional Intelligence in Organizations, we will show you how to translate newly acquired knowledge about mirror neurons, spindle cells, and oscillators into practical, socially intelligent behaviors that can reinforce the neural links between you and your followers.

Followers Mirror Their Leaders—Literally

Perhaps the most stunning recent discovery in behavioral neuroscience is the identification of mirror neurons in widely dispersed areas of the brain. Italian neuroscientists found them by accident while monitoring a particular cell in a monkey's brain that fired only when the monkey raised its arm. One day a lab assistant lifted an ice cream cone to his own mouth and triggered a reaction in the monkey's cell. It was the first evidence that the brain is peppered with neurons that mimic, or mirror, what another being does. This previously unknown class of brain cells operates as neural Wi-Fi, allowing us to navigate our social world. When we consciously or unconsciously detect someone else's emotions through their actions, our mirror neurons reproduce those emotions. Collectively, these neurons create an instant sense of shared experience.

Mirror neurons have particular importance in organizations, because leaders' emotions and actions prompt followers to mirror those feelings and deeds. The effects of activating neural circuitry in followers' brains can be very powerful. In a recent study, our colleague Marie Dasborough observed two groups: One received negative performance feedback accompanied by positive emotional signals—namely, nods and smiles; the other was given positive feedback that was delivered critically, with frowns and narrowed eyes. In subsequent interviews conducted to compare the emotional states of the two groups, the people who had received positive feedback accompanied by negative emotional signals reported feeling worse about their performance than did the participants who had received good-natured negative feedback. In effect, the delivery was more important than the message itself. And everybody knows that when people feel better, they perform better. So, if leaders hope to get the best out of their people, they should continue to be demanding but in ways that foster a positive mood in their teams. The old carrot-and-stick approach alone doesn't make neural sense; traditional incentive systems are simply not enough to get the best performance from followers.

Here's an example of what does work. It turns out that there's a subset of mirror neurons whose only job is to detect other people's smiles and laughter, prompting smiles and laughter in return. A boss who is self-controlled and humorless will rarely engage those neurons in his team members, but a boss who laughs and sets an easygoing tone puts those neurons to work, triggering spontaneous laughter and knitting his team together in the process. A bonded group is one that performs well, as our colleague Fabio Sala has shown in his research. He found that top-performing leaders elicited laughter from their subordinates three times as often, on average, as did mid-performing leaders. Being in a good mood, other research finds, helps people take in information effectively and respond nimbly and creatively. In other words, laughter is serious business.

It certainly made a difference at one university-based hospital in Boston. Two doctors we'll call Dr. Burke and Dr. Humboldt were in contention for the post of CEO of the corporation that ran this hospital and others. Both of them headed up departments, were superb physicians, and had published many widely cited research articles in prestigious medical journals. But the two had very different personalities. Burke was intense, task focused, and impersonal. He was a relentless perfectionist with a combative tone that kept his staff continually on edge. Humboldt was no less demanding, but he was very approachable, even playful, in relating to staff, colleagues, and patients. Observers noted that people smiled and teased one another—and even spoke their minds—more in Humboldt's department than in Burke's. Prized talent often ended up leaving Burke's department; in contrast, outstanding folks gravitated to Humboldt's warmer working climate. Recognizing Humboldt's socially intelligent leadership style, the hospital corporation's board picked him as the new CEO.

The "Finely Attuned" Leader

Great executives often talk about leading from the gut. Indeed, having good instincts is widely recognized as an advantage for a leader in any context, whether in reading the mood of one's organization or in conducting a delicate negotiation with the competition. Leadership scholars characterize this talent as an ability to recognize patterns, usually born of extensive experience. Their advice: Trust your gut, but get lots of input as you make decisions. That's sound practice, of course, but managers don't always have the time to consult dozens of people.

Findings in neuroscience suggest that this approach is probably too cautious. Intuition, too, is in the brain, produced in part by a class of neurons called spindle cells because of their shape. They have a body size about four times that of other brain cells, with an extra-long branch to make attaching to other cells easier and transmitting thoughts and feelings to them quicker. This ultrarapid connection of emotions, beliefs, and judgments creates what behavioral scientists call our social guidance system. Spindle cells trigger neural networks that come into play whenever we have to choose the best response among many—even for a task as routine as prioritizing a to-do list. These cells also help us gauge whether someone is trustworthy and right (or wrong) for a job. Within one-twentieth of a second, our spindle cells fire with information about how we feel about that person; such "thin-slice" judgments can be very accurate, as follow-up metrics reveal. Therefore, leaders should not fear to act on those judgments, provided that they are also attuned to others' moods.

Such attunement is literally physical. Followers of an effective leader experience rapport with her—or what we and our colleague Annie McKee call "resonance." Much of this feeling arises unconsciously, thanks to mirror neurons and spindle-cell circuitry. But another class of neurons is also involved: Oscillators coordinate people physically by regulating how and when their bodies move together. You can see oscillators in action when you watch people about to kiss; their movements look like a dance, one body responding to the other seamlessly. The same dynamic occurs when two cellists play together. Not only do they hit their notes in unison, but thanks to oscillators, the two musicians' right brain hemispheres are more closely coordinated than are the left and right sides of their individual brains.

UNIT
10

Do Women Have Stronger Social Circuits?

People often ask whether gender differences factor into the social intelligence skills needed for outstanding leadership. The answer is yes and no. It's true that women tend, on average, to be better than men at immediately sensing other people's emotions, whereas men tend to have more social confidence, at least in work settings. However, gender differences in social intelligence that are dramatic in the general population are all but absent among the most successful leaders.

When the University of Toledo's Margaret Hopkins studied several hundred executives from a major bank, she found gender differences in social intelligence in the overall group but not between the most effective men and the most effective women. Ruth Malloy of the Hay Group uncovered a similar pattern in her study of CEOs of international companies. Gender, clearly, is not neural destiny.

Firing Up Your Social Neurons

The firing of social neurons is evident all around us. We once analyzed a video of Herb Kelleher, a cofounder and former CEO of Southwest Airlines, strolling down the corridors of Love Field in Dallas, the airline's hub. We could practically see him activate the mirror neurons, oscillators, and other social circuitry in each person he encountered. He offered beaming smiles, shook hands with customers as he told them how much he appreciated their business, hugged employees as he thanked them for their good work. And he got back exactly what he gave. Typical was the flight attendant whose face lit up when she unexpectedly encountered her boss. "Oh, my honey!" she blurted, brimming with warmth, and gave him a big hug. She later explained, "Everyone just feels like family with him."

Unfortunately, it's not easy to turn yourself into a Herb Kelleher or a Dr. Humboldt if you're not one already. We know of no clear-cut methods to strengthen mirror neurons, spindle cells, and oscillators; they activate by the thousands per second during any encounter, and their precise firing patterns remain elusive. What's more, self-conscious attempts to display social intelligence can often backfire. When you make an intentional effort to coordinate movements with another person, it is not only oscillators that fire. In such situations the brain uses other, less adept circuitry to initiate and guide movements; as a result, the interaction feels forced.

The only way to develop your social circuitry effectively is to undertake the hard work of changing your behavior (see "Primal Leadership: The Hidden Driver of Great Performance," our December 2001 HBR article with Annie McKee). Companies interested in leadership development need to begin by assessing the willingness of individuals to enter a change program. Eager candidates should first develop a personal vision for change and then undergo a thorough diagnostic assessment, akin to a medical workup, to identify areas of social weakness and strength. Armed with the feedback, the aspiring leader can be trained in specific areas where developing better social skills will have the greatest payoff. The training can range from rehearsing better

> *The way to develop your social circuitry is to undertake the hard work of changing your behavior.*

ways of interacting and trying them out at every opportunity, to being shadowed by a coach and then debriefed about what he observes, to learning directly from a role model. The options are many, but the road to success is always tough.

How to Become Socially Smarter

To see what social intelligence training involves, consider the case of a top executive we'll call Janice. She had been hired as a marketing manager by a Fortune 500 company because of her business expertise, outstanding track record as a strategic thinker and planner, reputation as a straight talker, and ability to anticipate business issues that were crucial for meeting goals. Within her first six months on the job, however, Janice was floundering; other executives saw her as aggressive and opinionated, lacking in political astuteness, and careless about what she said and to whom, especially higher-ups.

To save this promising leader, Janice's boss called in Kathleen Cavallo, an organizational psychologist and senior consultant with the Hay Group, who immediately put Janice through a 360-degree evaluation. Her direct reports, peers, and managers gave Janice low ratings on empathy, service orientation, adaptability, and managing conflicts. Cavallo learned more by having confidential conversations with the people who worked most closely with Janice. Their complaints focused on her failure to establish rapport with people or even notice their reactions. The bottom line: Janice was adept neither at reading the social norms of a group nor at recognizing people's emotional cues when she violated those norms. Even more dangerous, Janice did not realize she was being too blunt in managing upward. When she had a strong difference of opinion with a manager, she did not sense when to back off. Her "let's get it all on the table and mix it up" approach was threatening her job; top management was getting fed up.

When Cavallo presented this performance feedback as a wake-up call to Janice, she was of course shaken to discover that her job might be in danger. What upset her more, though, was the realization that she was not having her desired impact on other people. Cavallo initiated coaching sessions in which Janice would describe notable successes and failures from her day. The more time Janice spent reviewing these incidents, the better she became at recognizing the difference between expressing an idea with conviction and acting like a pit bull. She began to anticipate how people might react to her in a meeting or during a negative performance review; she rehearsed more-astute ways to present her opinions; and she developed a personal vision for change. Such mental preparation activates the social circuitry of the brain, strengthening the neural connections you need to act effectively; that's why Olympic athletes put hundreds of hours into mental review of their moves.

At one point, Cavallo asked Janice to name a leader in her organization who had excellent social intelligence skills. Janice identified a veteran senior manager who was masterly both in the art of the critique and at expressing disagreement in meetings without damaging relationships. She asked him to help coach her, and she switched to a job where she could work with him—a post she held for two years. Janice was lucky to find a mentor who believed that part of a leader's job is to develop human capital. Many bosses would rather manage around a problem employee than help her get better. Janice's new boss took her on because he recognized her other strengths as invaluable, and his gut told him that Janice could improve with guidance.

Before meetings, Janice's mentor coached her on how to express her viewpoint about contentious issues and how to talk to higher-ups, and he modeled for her the art of performance feedback. By observing him day in and day out, Janice learned to affirm people even as she challenged their positions or critiqued their performance. Spending time with a living, breathing model of effective behavior provides the perfect stimulation for our mirror neurons, which allow us to directly experience, internalize, and ultimately emulate what we observe.

Janice's transformation was genuine and comprehensive. In a sense, she went in one person and came out another. If you think about it, that's an important lesson from neuroscience: Because our behavior creates and develops neural networks, we are not necessarily prisoners of our genes and our early childhood experiences. Leaders can change if, like Janice, they are ready to put in the effort. As she progressed in her training, the social behaviors she was learning became more like second nature to her. In scientific terms, Janice was strengthening her social circuits through practice. And as others responded to her, their brains connected with hers more profoundly and effectively, thereby reinforcing Janice's circuits in a virtuous circle. The upshot: Janice went from being on the verge of dismissal to getting promoted to a position two levels up.

A few years later, some members of Janice's staff left the company because they were not happy—so she asked Cavallo to come back. Cavallo discovered that although Janice had mastered the ability to communicate and connect with management and peers, she still sometimes missed cues from her direct reports when they tried to signal their frustration. With more help from Cavallo, Janice was able to turn the situation around by refocusing her attention on her staff's emotional needs and fine-tuning her communication style. Opinion surveys conducted with Janice's staff before and after Cavallo's second round of coaching documented dramatic increases in their emotional commitment and intention to stay in the organization. Janice and the staff also delivered a 6% increase in annual sales, and after another successful year she was made president of a multibillion-dollar unit. Companies can clearly benefit a lot from putting people through the kind of program Janice completed.

Hard Metrics of Social Intelligence

Our research over the past decade has confirmed that there is a large performance gap between socially intelligent and socially unintelligent leaders. At a major national bank, for example, we found that levels of an executive's social intelligence competencies predicted yearly performance appraisals more powerfully than did the emotional intelligence competencies of self-awareness and self-management. (For a brief explanation of our assessment tool, which focuses on seven dimensions, see the exhibit "Are You a Socially Intelligent Leader?")

Are You a Socially Intelligent Leader?

To measure an executive's social intelligence and help him or her develop a plan for improving it, we have a specialist administer our behavioral assessment tool, the Emotional and Social Competency Inventory. It is a 360-degree evaluation instrument by which bosses, peers, direct reports, clients, and sometimes even family members assess a leader according to seven social intelligence qualities.

We came up with these seven by integrating our existing emotional intelligence framework with data assembled by our colleagues at the Hay Group, who used hard metrics to capture the behavior of top-performing leaders at hundreds of corporations over two decades. Listed here are each of the qualities, followed by some of the questions we use to assess them.

Empathy

☐ Do you understand what motivates other people, even those from different backgrounds?

☒ Are you sensitive to others' needs?

Attunement

☒ Do you listen attentively and think about how others feel?

☒ Are you attuned to others' moods?

Organizational Awareness

☒ Do you appreciate the culture and values of the group or organization?

☐ Do you understand social networks and know their unspoken norms?

Influence

☒ Do you persuade others by engaging them in discussion and appealing to their self-interests?

☐ Do you get support from key people?

Developing Others

☒ Do you coach and mentor others with compassion and personally invest time and energy in mentoring?

☐ Do you provide feedback that people find helpful for their professional development?

Inspiration

☐ Do you articulate a compelling vision, build group pride, and foster a positive emotional tone?

☐ Do you lead by bringing out the best in people?

Teamwork

☐ Do you solicit input from everyone on the team?

☐ Do you support all team members and encourage cooperation?

UNIT

10

The Chemistry of Stress

When people are under stress, surges in the stress hormones adrenaline and cortisol strongly affect their reasoning and cognition. At low levels, cortisol facilitates thinking and other mental functions, so well-timed pressure to perform and targeted critiques of subordinates certainly have their place. When a leader's demands become too great for a subordinate to handle, however, soaring cortisol levels and an added hard kick of adrenaline can paralyze the mind's critical abilities. Attention fixates on the threat from the boss rather than the work at hand; memory, planning, and creativity go out the window. People fall back on old habits, no matter how unsuitable those are for addressing new challenges.

Poorly delivered criticism and displays of anger by leaders are common triggers of hormonal surges. In fact, when laboratory scientists want to study the highest levels of stress hormones, they simulate a job interview in which an applicant receives intense face-to-face criticism—an analogue of a boss's tearing apart a subordinate's performance. Researchers likewise find that when someone who is very important to a person expresses contempt or disgust toward him, his stress circuitry triggers an explosion of stress hormones and a spike in heart rate by 30 to 40 beats per minute. Then, because of the interpersonal dynamic of mirror neurons and oscillators, the tension spreads to other people. Before you know it, the destructive emotions have infected an entire group and inhibited its performance.

Leaders are themselves not immune to the contagion of stress. All the more reason they should take the time to understand the biology of their emotions.

Social intelligence turns out to be especially important in crisis situations. Consider the experience of workers at a large Canadian provincial health care system that had gone through drastic cutbacks and a reorganization. Internal surveys revealed that the frontline workers had become frustrated that they were no longer able to give their patients a high level of care. Notably, workers whose leaders scored low in social intelligence reported unmet patient-care needs at three times the rate—and emotional exhaustion at four times the rate—of their colleagues who had supportive leaders. At the same time, nurses with socially intelligent bosses reported good emotional health and an enhanced ability to care for their patients, even during the stress of layoffs (see the sidebar "The Chemistry of Stress"). These results should be compulsory reading for the boards of companies in crisis. Such boards typically favor expertise over social intelligence when selecting someone to guide the institution through tough times. A crisis manager needs both.

As we explore the discoveries of neuroscience, we are struck by how closely the best psychological theories of development map to the newly charted hardwiring of the brain. Back in the 1950s, for example, British pediatrician and psychoanalyst D.W. Winnicott was advocating for play as a way to accelerate children's learning. Similarly, British physician and psychoanalyst John Bowlby emphasized the importance of providing a secure base from which people can strive toward goals, take risks without unwarranted fear, and freely explore new possibilities. Hard-bitten executives may consider it absurdly indulgent and financially untenable to concern themselves with such theories in a world where bottom-line performance is the yardstick of success. But as new ways of scientifically measuring human development start to bear out these theories and link them directly with performance, the so-called soft side of business begins to look not so soft after all.

Goleman, Daniel and Boyatzis, Richard (2008). Social intelligence and the biology of leadership. *Harvard Business Review*, September, 75–81.

"Three Roles of the Leader in the New Paradigm"

By Stephen R. Covey

Points to Consider

1. What values would you add or subtract from Covey's list of "inviolable principles—natural laws in the human dimension": fairness, service, equity, justice, integrity, honesty, and trust?

2. Covey employs several analogies in the article: "a white-water world," a compass, a family. To what degree are they useful or helpful to you to understand the new paradigm and the exercise of leadership in groups?

3. What are the challenges of aligning people with mission and vision in a large organization or in a community? What does Covey suggest are the ways to meet these challenges?

"Three Roles of the Leader in the New Paradigm"

The leader of the future, of the next millennium, will be one who creates a culture or a value system centered upon principles. Creating such a culture in a business, government, school, hospital, nonprofit organization, family, or other organization will be a tremendous and exciting challenge in this new era and will only be achieved by leaders, be they emerging or seasoned, who have the vision, courage, and humility to constantly learn and grow. Those people and organizations who have a passion for learning—learning through listening, seeing emerging trends, sensing and anticipating needs in the marketplace, evaluating past successes and mistakes, and absorbing the lessons that conscience and principles teach us, to mention just a few ways—will have enduring influence. Such learning leaders will not resist change; they will embrace it.

A White-Water World

The world has changed in a very profound way. This change continues to happen all around us, all the time. It is a white-water world. The consumer revolution has accelerated enormously. People are so much more enlightened and aware. So many more dynamic, competitive forces are operating. Quality standards have risen, particularly in the global marketplace, to the point where there is simply no way to fake it. It may be possible to survive in a local marketplace without meeting these standards, perhaps even in a regional marketplace, but certainly not in a global marketplace.

In all sectors—business, government, health care, social, or nonprofit—the marketplace is demanding that organizations transform themselves. They must be able to produce services and goods and deliver them in a fast, friendly, and flexible way and on a consistent basis that serves the needs of both internal and external customers. This requires a work force that is not only allowed to give of its full creativity and talent, but enabled, encouraged, and rewarded for doing so. Even though tens of thousands of organizations are deeply involved in quality initiatives designed to produce those very results, transformation is not being achieved. The fundamental reason most quality initiatives do not work is because of a lack of trust in the culture—in the relationships between people. Just as you cannot fake world-class quality, so also is it impossible to fake high trust. It has to come out of trustworthiness.

UNIT
10

I put more faith in what the global economy is doing to drive quality than in any other factor. It is teaching us that principles such as empowerment, trust, and trustworthiness ultimately control the effective results we seek. The most effective leaders are, first, *models* of what I call principle-centered leadership. They have come to realize that we're all subject to natural laws or governing principles, which operate regardless of our awareness of them or our obedience to them. Our effectiveness is predicated upon alignment with these inviolable principles—natural laws in the human dimension that are just as real, just as unchanging, as laws such as gravity are in the physical dimension. These principles are woven into the fabric of every civilized society and constitute the roots of every organization that has endured.

To the degree that we recognize and live in harmony with such basic principles as fairness, service, equity, justice, integrity, honesty, and trust, we move toward either survival and stability on the one hand or disintegration and destruction on the other. Principles are self-evident, self-validating natural laws. In fact, the best way to realize that a principle is self-evident is by trying to imagine a world or, for that matter, *any* effective, enduring society, organization, or family based upon its opposite.

Correct principles are like compasses: they are always pointing the way. They don't change or shift, and if we know how to read them, we won't get lost, confused, or fooled by conflicting voices and values. They provide the true north direction to our lives as we navigate the "streams" of our environments. Thus we see that a changeless, principle-centered core is the key to having the confidence, security, power, guidance, and wisdom to change the way we address the changing needs and opportunities around us.

So the first role of the leader is to be a model of principle-centered leadership. Whenever a person or organization is principle-centered, that person or organization becomes a model—an example—to other people and organizations. It is that kind of modeling, that kind of character, competence, and action, that produces trust among people, causing them to identify with this modeling and be influenced by it. Modeling, then, is a combination of character (who you are as a person) and competence (what you can do). These two qualities represent your potential. But when you actually *do* it—when you put action together with character—you've got modeling.

Three Roles of a Leader

What is it, then, that the principle-centered leader models? I suggest that you can break leadership into three basic functions or activities: pathfinding, aligning, and empowering. Let's explore each one in turn.

Pathfinding

The essence and power of *pathfinding* are found in a compelling vision and mission. Pathfinding deals with the larger sense of the future. It gets the culture imbued with and excited about a tremendous, transcendent purpose. But in relation to what? To meeting the needs of your customers and other stakeholders. Pathfinding, then, ties together your value system and vision with the needs of customers and other stakeholders through a strategic plan. I call this the strategic pathway.

Aligning

The second activity of a leader is *aligning*. It consists of ensuring that your organizational structure, systems, and operational processes all contribute to achieving your mission and vision of meeting the needs of customers and other stakeholders. They don't interfere with it, they don't compete with it, and they don't dominate it. They're only there for one purpose—to contribute

to it. Far and away the greatest leverage of the principle of alignment comes when your people are in alignment with your mission, vision, and strategy. When people are filled with true understanding of the needs, when they share a powerful commitment to accomplishing the vision, when they are invited to create and continually improve the structures and systems that will meet the needs, then you have alignment. Without these human conditions, you cannot have world-class quality; all you have is brittle programs. Ultimately, we must learn that programs and systems are vital, but that *people* are the programmers.

Empowering

The third activity of a leader is *empowering*. What does that mean? People have enormous talent, ingenuity, intelligence, and creativity. Most of it lies dormant. When you have true alignment toward a common vision, a common mission, you begin to co-mission with those people. Individual purpose and mission are commingled with the mission of the organization. When these purposes overlap, great synergy is created. A fire is ignited within people that unleashes their latent talent, ingenuity, and creativity to do whatever is necessary and consistent with the principles agreed upon to accomplish their common values, vision, and mission in serving customers and other stakeholders. This is what we mean by empowerment.

But then you have to study what happens. What are the results? Are we really meeting the needs of the customers and the other stakeholders? Data and information that indicate whether these needs are truly being met must be fed back to the empowered people and teams inside the culture so that they can use it to make the necessary course corrections and improvements and continue to do whatever it takes to fulfill the mission and to serve the needs.

A New Paradigm of Leadership

These roles of modeling principle-centered leadership—pathfinding, aligning, and empowering—represent a paradigm that is different in kind from traditional management thinking. There is a very significant difference between management and leadership. Both are vital functions, and because they are, it's critical to understand how they are different so one isn't mistaken for the other.

UNIT
10

Leadership focuses on doing the right things; management focuses on doing things right. Leadership makes sure the ladders we are climbing are leaning against the right wall; management makes sure we are climbing the ladders in the most efficient way possible. Most managers and executives operate within existing paradigms or ways of thinking, but leaders have the courage to bring those paradigms to the surface, identify the underlying assumptions and motivations, and challenge them by asking, "Does this still hold water?" For example:

- In health care, new leaders might challenge the assumption that medicine should focus upon the diagnosis and treatment of disease. Some medical schools today don't even teach nutrition, even though one-third of all cancers are nutrition-related and two-thirds of all diseases are tied to lifestyle. Still, the medical community heads down the path of diagnosis and treatment of disease. They claim that they deal with the whole package—the health and welfare of people—but they have a treatment paradigm. Fortunately, new leaders are creating more preventive-medicine alternatives.

- In law, new leaders might challenge the assumption that law is best practiced in courtrooms using confrontational, win-lose litigation. They might move toward the use of synergy and win-win thinking to prevent and settle disputes. Alternative dispute resolution usually results in compromise. New leaders will seek "win-win or no deal" options that lead to synergy. Synergy is more than cooperation; it's creating better solutions. It requires empathic listening and courage in expressing one's views and opinions in ways that show respect for the other person's views. Out of genuine interaction come synergistic insights.

- In business, new leaders will challenge the assumption that "total customer satisfaction" represents the ultimate service ethic. They will move toward the total stakeholder satisfaction, caring for everyone who has a stake in the success of the operation and making decisions that benefit all stakeholders. To bring about this new mind-set, leaders must develop a new skill-set of synergy. Synergy comes naturally from the quality of the relationship—the friendship, trust, and love that unites people.

- If you can put the new skill-set of synergy together with the new mind-set of interdependence, you have the perfect one-two punch for achieving competitive advantage. When you have the mind-set and the skill-set, you create effective structures, systems, and processes that are aligned with your vision and mission. Every organization is perfectly designed and aligned to get the results it gets. If you want different results, you need a new mind-set and a new skill-set to create synergistic solutions. It's only enlightened self-interest to keep all stakeholders in mind when making decisions, because we are so interdependent.

Who Is the Leader of the Future?

In many cases, the leader of the future will be the same as the leader of the present. There will be no change in personnel, but rather an internal change: the person becomes the leader of the future by an inside-out transformation. What drives leaders to change, to become more centered on principles?

I think the main source of *personnel* change is pain; this pain may come from disappointment, failure, death, troubled or broken relationships with family or friends, violated trust, personal weakness, discouragement, poor health, the consequences of poor decisions, loneliness, mediocrity, fear, financial stress, job insecurity, or life imbalance. If you aren't feeling pain, people tend to be too deeply invested in themselves and their world to rise above their own interests or the politics of running things, both at work and at home. When people are experiencing personal pain, they tend to be more open to a new model of living in which the common elements of humility and personal sacrifice lead to inside-out, principle-centered change.

The primary driving force of *organizational* change is the global economy. The standard of quality is now so high that unless you have an empowered work force and a spirit of partnership with all stakeholders, you can't compete, whether you work in the private sector, public sector, or social sector. When you're facing competitors who think more ecologically and interdependently, eventually the force of circumstances drives you to be humble. That's what is driving the quest for quality, learning, process reengineering, and other initiatives. But many of these initiatives don't go far enough. The mind shift is not great enough. The interests of all stakeholders must be dealt with in an orchestrated way.

We either are forced by circumstances to be humble or can choose to be humble out of a recognition that principles ultimately govern. To be humble is good, regardless of the reason. But it's better to be humbled by conscience rather than by circumstances.

The Leader of the Future—A Family Within

The leader of the future has the humility to accept principles and the courage to align with them, which takes a great personal sacrifice. Out of this humility, courage, and sacrifice comes the person of integrity. In fact, I like to think of this kind of leader as having an entire family within him or her: humility and courage the parents, and integrity the child.

Humility and Courage the Parents

Humility says, "I am not in control; principles ultimately govern and control." It understands that the key to long-term success is learning to align with "true north" principles. That takes humility because the traditional mind-set is "I am in control; my destiny lies in my hands." This mind-set leads to arrogance—the sort of pride that comes before the fall.

Leaders of the future will have the courage to align with principles and go against the grain of old assumptions or paradigms. It takes tremendous courage and stamina to say, "I'm going to align my personal value system, my lifestyle, my direction and my habits with timeless principles." Courage is the quality of every principle at its highest testing point. Every virtue is ultimately tested at the highest level. That's where courage comes into play. When you confront an old approach directly, you experience the fear of ripping out an old habit and replacing it with something new.

Integrity the Child

Out of the marriage of humility and courage is born the child of integrity. We all want to be known and remembered as men and women of integrity. Having integrity means integrating ourselves with principles. The leaders of the future must be men and women of integrity who internalize these principles. They grow in wisdom and cultivate an abundance mind-set—a sense that there are opportunities for all. If you have integrity, you are not caught up in a constant state of comparison with others. Nor do you feel the need to play political games, because your security comes from within. As soon as you change the source of your security, everything else flows from it. Your security, power, wisdom, and guidance increase, because you can constantly draw upon the strength of these principles as you apply them.

UNIT

10

A Final Note

We are becoming increasingly and painfully aware of the perilous weakening of our social structure. Drugs, gangs, illiteracy, poverty, crime, violence, breakdown of the family—these all continue in a downward spiral. Leaders of the present are beginning to recognize that such social problems put at risk every aspect of society. The leaders of the future realize that the solutions to these problems are far beyond the ability of the sectors that have traditionally been expected to deal with them—namely, the government and social sectors. My intent is not to criticize these sectors. In fact, I believe that they would be the first to admit that they are bound to fail without a broader network of helping hands.

The problem is that, on the whole, there has been a marked weakening of the responsibility that neighborhoods, communities, churches, families, and individuals feel toward volunteering. It has become too easy to absolve ourselves from this responsibility to our communities. I believe that it is a family responsibility and that everyone should have a sense of stewardship about the community—every man, every woman, and every child. There should be some real sense of stewardship around service on the part of the young people, particularly those who are at the most idealistic age, the late teens and early twenties.

The leader of the future will be a leader in every area of life, especially family life. The enormous needs and opportunities in society call for a great responsibility toward service. There is no place where this spirit of service can be cultivated like the home. The spirit of the home, and also of the school, is that they prepare young people to go forth and serve. People are supposed to serve. Life is a mission, not a career. The whole spirit of this philosophy should pervade our society. I also think that it is a source of happiness, because you don't get happiness directly. It only comes as a by-product of service. You can get pleasure directly, but it is fleeting.

How, then, do we influence our children toward the spirit of service and meaningful contribution? First, we must look inward and ask: Am I a *model* of this principle of service myself? Does my family see me dedicating my time and abilities to serving them and the community? Second, have I taken time to immerse myself and my family in the needs of others in the community in order to create a sense of vision about how our family and each of us as individuals can make unique and meaningful contributions to meet those needs (*pathfinding*)? Third, have I, as a leader in my home, *aligned* the priorities and structures of our life so that this desire to serve is supported, not undermined? Finally, have I created conditions and opportunities in the home that will empower my children to serve? Do I encourage and support the development of their minds and talents? Do I organize service opportunities for the entire family and do all I can to create a fun environment around those activities? Even if the answer to every one of those questions is no, we all still have the capacity to decide what our lives will be about from today on.

This inherent capacity to choose, to develop a new vision for ourselves, to rescript our life, to begin a new habit or let go of an old one, to forgive someone, to apologize, to make a promise and then keep it, in any area of life, is, always has been, and always will be a moment of truth for every true leader.

Appears in Hesselbein, Frances, Marshall Goldsmith, and Richard Beckhard, eds. *The Leader of the Future*. San Francisco: Jossey-Bass, 1996. Pp. 149–159. Used by permission of Franklin Covey Company.

FILM STUDIES

Norma Rae (1979)

Screenplay by Irving Ravetch and Harriet Frank, Jr.
Directed by Martin Ritt

Character Guide

Norma Rae . . . . .Sally Field

Reuben Warshinski . .Ron Leibman

Introduction

This film showcases the leadership skills of two different characters: a New York labor organizer and a southern textile factory worker. Both exhibit leadership qualities, particularly the ability to empower others to accomplish the overall goal of organizing a group of powerless textile factory workers.

Norma Rae is a woman "trapped" who yearns for knowledge and a better life. She is employed as a factory worker in the 1970s. Reuben Warshinski, a labor union organizer, appears at her home. As an outsider, Reuben is shunned by the townspeople who fear "loss of their jobs" when talk of a union surfaces. Norma befriends Reuben and the leadership skills of both begin to emerge.

As you view the film, consider the Dialogue Questions and be prepared to share your responses.

UNIT

10

Dialogue Questions

1. What is the leadership style of the factory management team?

2. What effect did the style have on the factory workers?

3. What leadership qualities are exhibited by Reuben Warshinski?

4. What leadership qualities are exhibited by Norma Rae?

5. How does Reuben empower Norma?

6. How does Norma empower her co-workers?

7. What happens when the exercise of leadership effectively empowers others?

Invictus (2009)

Screenplay by Anthony Peckham based on the book by John Carlin
Directed by Clint Eastwood

Character Guide

Nelson Mandela . . . . Morgan Freeman

Francois Pienaar . . . . Matt Damon

Jason Tshabalala . . . . Tony Kgoroge

Etienne Feyder . . . . Julian Lewis Jones

Chester Williams . . . . McNeil Hendricks

Brenda Mozibuko . . . . Adjoa Andoh

Introduction

Invictus is set in South Africa in the 1990s, when Nelson Mandela was released from prison after nearly 26 years as a political prisoner, and during his subsequent presidency of the nation. Mandela's release marked the end of apartheid in South Africa, but not the tensions between the white and black South Africans. The South African rugby team, the Springboks, is a symbol of South Africa under apartheid. There is only one black member of the Springboks, and fewer black fans of the team. The new black South African sports governing body seeks to disband the Springboks, but Mandela believes that the team can be an avenue to reconciliation.

Dialogue Questions

1. How complex are the challenges facing Mandela as president of South Africa? What is his vision?

2. Why is empowering others important to Mandela?

3. When Mandela invites the Sprinkboks' captain/coach, Pienaar, to tea, he brings up leadership and motivation. What does their conversation illuminate about the leadership style and values of each?

4. Pienaar leaves the meeting believing that Mandela has suggested the importance of winning the World Cup, yet Mandela never mentioned it specifically. How did Mandela accomplish this? In what ways is it significant that Pienaar himself realizes that this is an important goal?

5. At a later time during the rugby season, Pienaar takes the Springboks on a tour of Robben Island where Mandela had been imprisoned. Why does he do this?

6. How does Pienaar exercise leadership beyond the team? In what ways does it empower the team?

7. How are inspiration and empowerment distinct? How are they connected?

UNIT

10

EXERCISE

Shaping the Future

Introduction

Whenever people embark on a new assignment together, they are unsighted in important respects. They do not know what the future will bring. The demands imposed by their task are unknown to them. If they have not worked together as a group, they do not know what their interactions will be like.

"Shaping the Future" offers you the opportunity to work together at a task without the benefit of sight. It invites you to achieve a greater common understanding of a task and to determine responsibilities for evaluating progress in accomplishing it—in short, it invites you to empower each other. Because the exercise presents problems of both goal definition and mutual accountability for evaluation, it is also an excellent team-building experience.

Instructions

Your Instructor will provide the directions and instructions for you to complete this exercise.

Kaagan. S. (1999). Shaping the future. In *Leadership Games: Experiential Learning for Organizational Development*. Sage. Pp. 91–95. Used by permission of SAGE.

SUGGESTED READING

This selected bibliography is intended to supplement the excerpts and articles of authors included in this Unit. There is an emphasis on books that are pivotal and recent publications. Numerous journals regularly offer articles related to these topics, but are not included in this selected bibliography. For further research, you may wish to include searches of the following journals: (alphabetically) *Academy of Management Executive, Academy of Management Journal, Harvard Business Review, Journal of Leadership Studies, Leadership in Action, Leadership Quarterly*, and *Leader To Leader*.

This list is organized by author's last name using Modern Language Association-style citations.

Heifetz, Ronald A. *Leadership Without Easy Answers.* Cambridge: Harvard University Press, 1998.
Pioneering study on "adaptive leadership" based on Heifetz's ten years of experience as the Executive Director of the Leadership Education Project at Harvard University's Kennedy School of Government. The study offers a visionary model of leadership which defines leadership as a process that empowers others rather than merely aggrandizes the authority of the leader.

Juckes, Tim J. *Opposition in South Africa: The Leadership of Z. K. Matthews, Nelson Mandela, and Stephen Biko.* Westport: Praeger, 1995.
This is a retrospective of 20th-century political activities in South Africa. It focuses on three key individuals who led an apartheid-opposition movement that restructured a society.

Kouzes, James M., and Barry Z. Posner. *Encouraging the Heart: A Leader's Guide to Rewarding and Recognizing Others.* San Francisco: Jossey-Bass, 2003.
The authors identify "Seven Essentials of Encouraging" that leaders can use to energize and recognize people.

Riggio, Ronald and Sherylle J. Tan, (Eds.). *Leader Interpersonal and Influence Skills: The Soft Skills of Leadership.* New York: Routledge, 2013.
Characterized as providing "hard data on soft skills" this volume has an evidence-based approach to making the case for soft skills, and a practical approach to building them.

Senge, Peter M. *The Fifth Discipline: The Art and Practice of the Learning Organization.* New York: Doubleday Currency, 2006.
Senge teaches the theory and techniques of team learning. Each individual on the team learns and grows beyond his or her ability to do so alone.

Tichy, Noel M., and Eli Cohen. *The Leadership Engine: How Winning Companies Build Leaders at Every Level.* New York: Harper Business, 2007.
Using examples from real companies, Tichy identifies four areas in which good leaders help others to develop: generating positive energy, making tough decisions, developing good business ideas, and instilling values that will help support those ideas.

UNIT

10

UNIT11

EXPLORING THE HISTORY OF LEADERSHIP STUDIES

INTRODUCTION

This Unit of *Phi Theta Kappa Leadership Development Studies: A Humanities Approach* explores how the observation and study of leadership differs depending upon the time and place in which such study took place. As mentioned in the introduction to this text, this course overall has an emphasis on transformational leadership and on the exercise of leadership as the driver of progress for individuals, a group, a community, or society; this Unit seeks to answer the questions "When did this view of leadership emerge?" and "How has this view of leadership changed over time?" As the readings will illustrate, this transformational focus and a focus on servant leadership to benefit others, groups, communities, societies, and the world appears in very early writing on leadership, despite the common contention among contemporary leadership scholars who point to James MacGregor Burns' writing on transformational leadership in his book *Leadership* (1975) and Robert Greenleaf's work *Servant Leadership* (1977) for the origins of this leadership model. In fact, the concept of servant leadership has evolved alongside more authoritarian models of leadership for centuries and this Unit begins with two ancient sources to illustrate this juxtaposition: Aristotle's "The Sole Proper Claim to Political Power" from *The Politics*, which he probably wrote sometime during the last twelve years of his life (335–323 B.C.E.) and which explains the reasoning prevalent in the Western tradition that particular "Great Men" were natural, authoritarian leaders; and Lao Tzu's *Tao Te Ching*, written in 526 B.C.E., which elaborates on the view that *"Man at his best, like water, serves as he goes along."*

References to the concept of servant leadership can be found in many other early cultures and persist through history even as powerful rulers conquered many of them. One of the most-recognized examples is the Christian view articulated by Jesus Christ and his followers. In the Bible, Mark quotes Jesus:

> *"You know that among the Gentiles those whom they recognize as their rulers lord it over them, but it is not so with you; whoever wishes to become great among you must be your servant…"* (Mark 10: 35–45)

Another example comes from the western plains of what is now the United States, before the arrival of the Europeans, in the words of Black Elk of the Oglala Sioux:

> *"(One day) the head man picked out the best hunters and said: 'Good young warriors, what you do is always good and today you shall feed the helpless. Perhaps there are some who are old and feeble or who have little, whatever you kill shall be theirs.' This was a great honor for the young men."*

By the middle of the 19th century this general philosophy was spreading widely. Alfred Nobel, who invented dynamite in 1866, gave his fortune to the Swedish Academy with a stipulation that a Peace Prize be granted to "the person who conferred the greatest benefit to mankind and performed the best work for the abolition of standing armies." More varied examples, some included in other units of this textbook, include Harriet Tubman, Florence Nightingale, Mohandas Gandhi, Martin Luther King Jr., Ceśar Chávez, and Mother Teresa. History is replete with countless servant leaders, but historians have often buried their contributions beneath the violent contributions of authoritarian leaders and governments who changed the history of the world through war, conquest, domination, or oppression.

The more visible and familiar authoritarian form of leadership grew out of fear and the need for protection, or desire for power and resources. Competition to acquire more security, more power, and more resources precipitated conflict and wars between peoples in ages past and explains the conflicts of the present, too. Competitive, "zero sum" thinking became accepted as the norm,

UNIT
11

and in this paradigm successful leaders are those who amass victories and riches, recounting their conquests through grand oral histories and endless documents. However, as empires came and went, to some they represented futility. Percy Bysshe Shelley expressed a longing for a better way in 1817 in his poem "Ozymandias," the Greek name for King Ramses II of Egypt:

> *I met a traveler from an antique land,*
> *Who said — "Two vast and trunkless legs of stone*
> *Stand in the desert…Near them on the sand,*
> *Half sunk a shattered visage lies…*
> *And on the pedestal, these words appear:*
> *My name is Ozymandias, King of Kings,*
> *Look on my Works, ye mighty and despair!*
> *Nothing remains, Round the decay*
> *Of that colossal Wreck, boundless and bare*
> *The lone and level sands stretch far away.*

Shelley's poem represents an undercurrent of doubt that authoritarian forms of leadership created true progress or were more effective than servant leadership. Both forms of leadership had existed side by side for centuries, but the more egocentric form had always seemed to dominate the collective consciousness. Perhaps the majority of attention went to authoritarian leaders because from pre-history on, great men and women and the common people took pleasure in hearing and reading about the accounts of battles, conquests, and victories. In medieval Europe, as in other areas of the world, bards and storytellers told stories of the heroic deeds of historic and mythical figures, symbolic of all that was good within a particular culture defeating external or evil forces.

In this Unit, the reader will explore several perspectives on leadership from both ends of this dichotomy—authoritarian leadership and servant leadership—and some in between. The oldest readings of the Unit, from Aristotle and Lao Tzu, both contain notions of what is important in leadership and contain the seeds of ideas or theories which now have modern names—Great Man/Woman Theory and Servant Leadership Theory—but these ancient writers didn't keep them separate, seeking to name and describe a "theory of leadership" as modern leadership theorists do. Their ideas come from a "big picture" perspective on what is important to know about effective leadership, and they emphasize both the characteristics a great leader must possess and service to humankind.

After the readings representing the importance of the ancient European sources and ancient Asian sources, additional readings in this Unit show that these same ideas emerge again and again through history up to the present, but with modifications according to the time and place. Authors T. H. White, Upton Sinclair, Abraham Maslow, and Aung San Suu Kyi will show how the ideas become separated, distilled in new ways, or evolve through time and allow us to look more closely at several additional leadership theories important in the historiography of leadership. We will read an excerpt from *The Once and Future King* as an example of the thinking in Great Man/Woman Theory which long dominated Western thinking on leadership. An excerpt from *The Jungle* provides us with an opportunity to study the emergence of the Scientific Management Era. An additional reading from Abraham Maslow highlights his profound influence on management and leadership theory and helps us to understand the Human Relations Movement, and finally, the writing of Aung San Suu Kyi helps illustrate a modern Systems approach to thinking about leadership. She synthesizes anew the ideas that the integrity of the leader and the circumstances in which they lead both shape the direction and success of the leader, and that service to people must also be important.

This journey through time and place shows us that a body of collective wisdom beginning long ago continues to influence our thinking on leadership. The Film Studies for this Unit are *Elizabeth* and *42*, about Queen Elizabeth I and Jackie Robinson—again spanning time and geography to examine changes in thinking and theorizing about leadership. The experiential Exercise prompts students to develop a "Unified Theory of Leadership" which they believe encompasses what is most important to them about leadership and that explains what is necessary for excellent leadership to occur.

The Readings, Film, and Exercise will provide historical perspective regarding leadership theory and prepare students to think analytically and critically about leadership theory before embarking on future, more detailed explorations of the work of recent leadership theorists.

Learning Objectives

- Distinguish among the main schools of leadership studies or theory
- Explain how theories of leadership and leadership studies changed through history
- Recognize how literature reflects the dominant leadership theory of the time
- Appreciate the contributions made by the humanities selections of the Unit toward understanding the history of leadership studies

CLASSIC CASE

"The Sole Proper Claim to Political Power"

By Aristotle (384–322 B.C.E.)
Greek Philosopher

Introduction and Historical Background

Aristotle's thoughts on leadership represent for this Unit the extensive influence of the ancient Greeks on leadership studies. Some ideas in this excerpt remain important in our collective wisdom and thinking about leadership.

Psychologist Carl Jung calls the body of shared wisdom the "collective unconscious." In his book, *Man and His Symbols*, he suggests that there are many shared symbols that arise in different cultures and become recognizable to a broad range of people. These common symbols are what Jung calls "archetypes." Archetypes are "the expression of universal themes that transcend differences of time and place because they are fundamentally symbolic," says Jung. These common archetypes often appear in either the oral or written accounts of a group's history or myths. Some of the most common myths describe the hero who possesses super-human strength or a unique power or quality. The hero rises to power from common origins, although he/she may have been originally born to royalty (think of Moses or King Arthur). The hero triumphs over forces of evil in a gigantic struggle but his/her fallibility (often the sin of pride or "hubris") leads to a tragic fall or inevitable failure. These elements of the myth of the leader appear in almost every culture and even invaded modern pop culture through films such as the *Star Wars* series.

The ancient Greeks had enormous influence on leadership studies through the archetypes represented in Greek mythology and through the explorations of leadership of great Greek philosophers and authors. Plato along with Socrates, his teacher, and Aristotle, his student, laid the philosophical foundations of Western culture and much of early leadership theory. In "The Philosopher King," an excerpt from Plato's *The Republic*, some of the earliest discussion of leadership and the traits of leaders can be found (Unit One). Plato believed that only a few people in an organization or society are capable of leadership. These people were older members of the group who had learned through their experiences and also possessed critical traits of leadership such as integrity, honesty, and a strong concern for the welfare of the group. These character traits that Plato identifies as being integral to leadership are similarly viewed in many other cultures and are thus archetypal elements of leadership theory.

"The Allegory of the Cave," another excerpt from *The Republic*, discusses the difficulty individuals have in making changes in their lives and how this affects organizations (Unit Nine). The other contribution that "The Allegory of the Cave" makes to leadership theory is the introduction of the concept that the leader has responsibility for the welfare of the group. This concept of leaders as shepherds and protectors would also dominate leadership theory for centuries.

Another significant contributor to the understanding of universal principles of leadership is the Greek dramatist

Sophocles. Many contemporary scholars consider him to be one of the greatest Greek tragedians along with Aeschylus and Euripides. In his play *Antigone*, Sophocles looks at ethical decision making, respect for higher powers, and the tragic consequences of leaders' flawed decision making. The Greeks and especially Sophocles gave leadership a particularly ominous tone by suggesting that the leader, in failing to recognize inherent weaknesses in his personality, could make serious mistakes leading to tragic consequences for him and the group. This potential for dramatic failures of judgment in the era of the Great Man/Woman leaders, where leadership authority was centered in one individual, made leadership a very dangerous endeavor for those born to it. This view of leadership as a "divine right of kings and queens" and as a drama centered on the leader's personal story, dominated much of the worldview for many centuries and influenced numerous authors who portrayed the great leaders of their time, including William Shakespeare.

Homer, also an ancient Greek author, reinforces the concept of the leader as archetypal hero. In *The Iliad*, Homer illustrates several egocentric leaders (Unit Eight). In *The Odyssey*, Homer continues to build images creating a symbolic, heroic, and trait-driven representation of leadership. Ulysses' journey home and his triumph over monsters and demons is a foundational, classical rendering of the leader as a hero who triumphs over evil.

Clearly, the ancient Greeks perhaps more than any other group defined the Great Man/Woman Theory of leadership and the archetypes symbolizing it. From pre-history to the modern era, royalty—aided by mystic or religious figures who reinforced the divine right to rule—dominated much of leadership thinking and practice. The Enlightenment period and the American Revolution began the process of introducing more democratic forms of leadership, but the cult of personality was still the most revered form of leadership for many years after the Greeks first described the concept.

This Unit excerpts *The Politics*, among the most famous of Aristotle's prolific writing. *The Politics* has had great influence on the field of philosophy, and continues to hold a prominent place among the philosophical works studied and debated today. Aristotle's Lyceum school was a research institution as well as a teaching/learning institution and by the time that Aristotle was recording his teachings on politics, the Lyceum had amassed 158 constitutions for student members to describe and study. Aristotle thus had taken a turn away from Plato's idealistic explorations on the leadership of a state toward practical research of real states, laws, rulers, and definitions of citizens. From such research Aristotle drew conclusions and grand statements such as the following "The Sole Proper Claim to Political Power." Interestingly, Aristotle did not lose all Platonic idealism and while he admits that various claims to real political power may compete (wealth, birth, and superior strength) and have a certain partial or relative "justice," he goes on to deny that any of these claims to political power are "just" in an absolute sense; the only claim that is absolutely just is that of "virtue," concluding that moral and intellectual abilities are always needed in a citizen leader, and when a man ascends to a superlative level in virtue he should reign with supreme power above the law—the ultimate version of Plato's "Philosopher King."

Points to Consider

1. Do you agree that education and virtue should have the highest claim for justifying political power? Why or why not?

2. Aristotle seems to assume that everyone in a state would be very happy to have a truly superior, virtuous individual take over the existing government and that it would happen because "nature takes its course." What does this tell you about Aristotle's view of humanity?

3. What examples can you think of, in the present or the past, of highly intellectual and benevolent individuals who exercised leadership with absolute power?

4. Aristotle says the question of how to treat a person or people who consider themselves superior to the rulers is one which bad as well as good forms of government have always dealt with—tyrants quite naturally eliminate someone who is a threat to their rule, and he expects that a democratic state would "ostracize" or marginalize anyone who disagrees with the majority—but he believes there could be a person who truly is superior in virtue, "a god among men," who should be allowed to govern and would do so better than any government could. How do you suppose Aristotle would expect this ultimate ruler to deal with the question of how to treat someone who speaks out against his rule?

"The Sole Proper Claim to Political Power"

(Excerpt from *The Politics*)
Translated by T. A. Sinclair, revised and
re-presented by T. J. Saunders

Book III, Chapter xiii

Some or all of these things [wealth, birth or nobility, superior strength, greater numbers in a mass of people] would seem to have a proper claim to be contributions to a state's existence; but I repeat that, in order to secure the good life, education and virtue would have the most just claim of all. But since those who are equal in one particular ought not to enjoy equality in all things, nor those who are unequal in one respect have inequality in all, it follows that all constitutions in which such a state of affairs prevails must be deviations.

It has already been stated that while all men have some kind of justice in their claims, not all of them have a claim that is just in an absolute sense. (a) The *rich* argue that they have a greater share in the land, and the land is of social interest; and further, that they are more to be relied upon to fulfill their contracts. (b) The claims of the *free* and *well-born* are closely related: the more nobly born are more fully citizens than the non-noble, good birth being held in esteem in every country; and the offspring of the better sort are likely to be better men, for good birth is excellence of stock. (c) Next we shall mention the equally just claims of *virtue*, for we always speak of justice as a social virtue, and one which is sure to bring all the other virtues along with it. (d) And surely the *majority* have a better claim than the minority, as being stronger, richer and better,

if we balance the larger numbers against the smaller.

Now suppose all these to be present in a single city—that is to say, the good, the rich and the well-born, and beside them a mass of citizens—will there or will there not be dispute as to which should rule? Now in the three types of constitution of which we spoke earlier the decision provokes no dispute, because they differ from each other in just this respect, sovereignty being exercised in oligarchy by the rich, in aristocracy by the sound, and so on. But we have to ask ourselves how to reach a conclusion when these elements are present at one and the same time. Suppose for example that those who have virtue are exceedingly few in number—how is the matter to be settled? Are we to regard their fewness in the light of the work to be done, asking whether they are strong enough to run the state? Or are we to ask whether their numbers are sufficient to make a state?

The problem arises in regard to all claimants to honours in the state. Those who base their claim to rule on wealth would seem to have no just claim at all, nor those who base themselves on birth; for if one man is very much richer than the rest, then clearly by the same principle of justice, he will have to be sole ruler over them all, and similarly one who is superior in good birth will have to rule over all whose claim is based on free status. This same thing could well happen where the constitution is an aristocracy, based on virtue; for if one man is better than all the sound men in the citizen-body, then on the same principle of justice he ought to be sovereign over them. Again, suppose that the multitude ought to be sovereign because they are stronger than the few, and suppose one man, or more than one but still fewer than the many, to be stronger than the rest—then these would have to be sovereign rather than the multitude.

All these considerations seem to show that none of these criteria is right by which one set of men claim that they themselves should rule and all the rest be subject to them. For surely, whether their claim to sovereignty over the citizen-body rests on wealth or on virtue, it remains true that against their arguments the multitude will have some justice on their side; for it is quite possible on occasion for the multitude to be better than the few, and richer too, when considered not singly but together.

So it is possible in this fashion to meet also a difficulty which some people pose and debate, namely whether a lawgiver, who seeks to lay down the laws that are most right, ought, given the circumstance mentioned, to legislate for the benefit of the majority or for the benefit of the better sort. By "right" we ought to mean "equally" right, i.e. right with respect to the benefit of the whole state and the common interest of the citizens. (A citizen is in general one who has a share in ruling and in being ruled; but he will not be identical in every kind of constitution. So far as the best constitution is concerned, he is a man who is able and who chooses to rule and to be ruled with a view to a life that is in accordance with virtue.)

But if there is one man (or several, but not enough to make up the whole complement of a state) of such superlative virtue that the capacity for statecraft and the virtue of all the rest are simply not to be compared with his (or theirs), such men we must take not to be part of the state. To judge them worthy of mere equality with the rest would be to do

them an injustice, so far unequal to them are they in virtue and in the capacity for statecraft. We may reasonably regard such a one as a god among men—which shows, clearly, that legislation too must apply only to equals in birth and capacity. But there is no law that embraces men of that caliber: they are themselves law, and anyone who tried to legislate for them would be snubbed for his pains. They might well say what the lions in Antisthenes' fable said to the hares who asserted their claim to equality with them.

It is for this kind of reason that democratically organized states establish also the practice of ostracism. They appear to attach such immense importance to the principle of equality above all else that they ostracized and removed out of the state for fixed periods anyone whose power was deemed to be excessive, whether this power was due to wealth or popularity or any other influence in the state. (Here is an example from mythology: the Argonauts left Heracles behind for some such reason—because the Argo would not have on Board one so vastly bigger than the rest of the crew.) This is why critics of tyranny who disapprove of the advice given by Periander are not to be considered fully justified. It is said that to Thrasybulus' messenger, who had come for advice, Periander returned no answer; but while walking in a field, reduced all the ears of corn to one level by lopping off the tallest. The messenger did not understand the motive for this action, but reported the action to Thrasybulus, who perceived that he ought to remove the outstanding men. The method is useful not only to tyrants, and tyrants are not alone in practicing it: oligarchies and democracies are in just the same position, for ostracism has very much the same effect as lopping off and exiling the leading men. And it is the regular practice of the holders of sovereign power, in their dealings with other states and with foreign nations. For example, the Athenians, as soon as their empire was strong enough, reduced Lesbos, Chios, and Samos to submission, contrary to the terms of the agreement; and the Persian king often trimmed the Medes, Babylonians, and others who prided themselves on their earlier supremacy. Indeed this whole question

UNIT
11

concerns all constitutions, not merely the divergent ones, which resort to such methods for their own advantage, but also right forms of constitution, which aim at the common good.

This same point may be observed also in the other skills and fields of knowledge. A painter would not allow his representation to have one foot disproportionately large, however magnificent the foot might be. A shipbuilder would not let the stern, or any other part of the ship, be out of proportion. A chorus-master will not allow among the members a performer whose voice is finer and more powerful than all the others. On this showing there is no reason at all why monarchs should not remain on good terms with their states, provided that in taking this action their own rule is beneficial to those states. Therefore the theory behind ostracism has some measure of political justice, in cases of admitted disproportion. Of course if the lawgiver can so construct the constitution from the start that there will never be any need of this kind of medicine, so much the better. Otherwise the best we can do, if occasion arises, is to put matters right by some such method. (In fact this is not the way it worked out in the states, because instead of seeking the advantage of their own constitution, men used ostracism as a weapon in factional strife.)

So in the deviation forms of constitution ostracism is obviously exercised for some personal benefit, and is just; though it is perhaps equally obvious that it is just in a limited sense only. But when it comes to the best type of constitution, there is a real difficulty, not in the cases of superiority of the other goods, such as strength or riches or popularity, but where a man is pre-eminent in virtue. What are we to do then? Men will not say that such a person ought to be banished or deported; nor yet that they ought to rule over him, for that would be like claiming to rule over Zeus, by dividing up the offices. It only remains therefore to let nature take its course; he will govern and we will all gladly obey him. Thus such men will be permanent kings in their states.

Aristotle. *The Politics*. Translated by T. A. Sinclair, revised and re-presented by Trevor J. Saunders. (Penguin Classics 1962, Revised edition 1981). The 1962 translation Copyright © Trevor J. Saunders, 1981. Reproduced by permission of Penguin Books Ltd.

LEADERSHIP PROFILE

Lao Tzu (570–490 B.C.E.)

Chinese Chou Dynasty Archivist and Teacher
Excerpts from *Tao Te Ching*

Introduction and Historical Background

More than Plato and Aristotle, who both suggested that a great leader served society, Lao Tzu and his contemporary, Confucius (Unit Three), show us the deep, ancient roots for Servant Leadership theory. Lao Tzu's thoughts on leadership here provide evidence of the extensive influence of ancient Asian cultures on leadership studies.

Biographical information about Lao Tzu states simply that he was "the keeper of the imperial archives at Loyang, an ancient capital of the Chinese province of Honan," in the sixth century B.C.E. But throughout his life Lao Tzu was also developing ways of being and doing what he later related in his book translated as "The Way of Life." A careful reading of this text of eighty-one sayings or verses reveals that this may be one of the oldest texts to describe more specifically the way of life of a leader and what constitutes good leadership.

Fotolio

Historians of China describe China in the sixth and fifth century B.C.E. as a culture in transition. The complex systems that had evolved to govern and bring order to such a large country had begun to deteriorate into corruption and bureaucracy. Societal norms that may have served the people well initially were now surrendering to dishonesty, hypocrisy and empty displays. Despite this decline in societal norms, Lao Tzu was hesitant to record a set of rules that would guide human behavior in this difficult time because he believed a true sense of the "way of life" evolved from an inward contemplation of a natural way of behavior that was instinctive rather than learned. Witter Bynner's account suggests that in his later years, saddened by the "perversity of society" and its failure to accept his teachings, Lao Tzu decided to ride into exile. At the boundary of his country, the border guard, Yin Hsi, who had dreamed of his coming, recognized him. Yin Hsi persuaded Lao Tzu to record his teachings rather than simply disappear in frustration. *Tao Te Ching*, a text of 5,000 words divided into eighty-one sayings or verses, was the result.

The sparse poetry of the verses advocating the *Tao* or Way is vague enough to be timeless and open to application and interpretation even 2,500 years later. Scholars agree that the verses are intended to be both mystical, universal or absolute truths and a practical, political handbook of sorts about ruling and surviving in chaotic times. More recent leadership philosophies and writings ranging from Gandhi's "Satyagraha" (Unit Three) to Hermann Hesse's *Journey to the East* and Robert Greenleaf's *The Leader as Servant* (both excerpted in Unit Two) or Margaret Wheatley's *Leadership and the New Science* likewise merge mysticism and pragmatic advice and emphasize serving others. Eleven verses have been selected that reveal Lao Tzu's view of leadership as selflessness and acts of outward giving. There are themes of assisting and encouraging growth among followers, setting the example of the highest character, humility, and guiding, but not directing, all of which are recurrent themes in Eastern philosophy and which resonate in much modern leadership theory.

Points to Consider

1. In your own words, how did Lao Tzu view the role of the leader?

2. What was the leader's relationship with the group according to Lao Tzu?

3. To Lao Tzu, is the leader's role with the organization a passive or active one?

4. How does Lao Tzu's *Tao* lay the groundwork for the concept of servant leadership? (See Unit Two, particularly "The Servant as Leader" by Robert Greenleaf.)

Tao Te Ching

(Excerpts)
By Lao Tzu
Translated by Witter Bynner

8

Man at his best, like water,
Serves as he goes along:
Like water he seeks his own level,
The common level of life,
Loves living close to the earth,
Living clear down in his heart,
Loves kinship with his neighbors,
The pick of words that tell the truth,
The even tenor of a well-run state,
The fair profit of able dealing,
The right timing of useful deeds,
And for blocking no one's way
No one blames him.

17

A leader is best
When people barely know that he exists,
Not so good when people obey and acclaim him,
Worst when they despise him.
'Fail to honor people,
They fail to honor you;'
But of a good leader, who talks little,
When his work is done, his aim fulfilled,
They will all say, 'We did this ourselves.'

18

When people lost sight of the way to live
Came codes of love and honesty,
Learning came, charity came,
Hypocrisy took charge;
When differences weakened family ties
Came benevolent fathers and dutiful sons;
And when lands were disrupted and misgoverned
Came ministers commended as loyal.

29

Those who would take over the earth
And shape it to their will
Never, I notice, succeed.
The earth is like a vessel so sacred
That at the mere approach of the profane
It is marred
And when they reach out their fingers it is gone.
For a time in the world some force themselves ahead
And some are left behind,
For a time in the world some make a great noise
And some are held silent,
For a time in the world some are puffed fat
And some are kept hungry,
For a time in the world some push aboard
And some are tipped out:
At no time in the world will a man who is sane
Over-reach himself,
Over-spend himself,
Over-rate himself.

30

One who would guide a leader of men in the uses of life
Will warn him against the uses of arms for conquest.
Weapons often turn upon the wielder,
An army's harvest is a waste of thorns,
Conscription of a multitude of men
Drains the next year dry.
A good general, daring to march, dares also to halt,
Will never press his triumph beyond need.
What he must do he does but not for glory,
What he must do he does but not for show,
What he must do he does but not for self;
He has done it because it had to be done,
Not from a hot head.

Let life ripen and then fall,
Force is not the way at all:
Deny the way of life and you are dead.

37

The way to use life is to do nothing through acting,
The way to use life is to do everything through being.
When a leader knows this,
His land naturally goes straight.
And the world's passion to stray from straightness
Is checked at the core
By the simple unnamable cleanness
Through which men cease from coveting,
And to a land where men cease from coveting
Peace comes of course.

46

In a land where the way of life is understood
Race-horses are led back to serve the field;
In a land where the way of life is not understood
War-horses are bred on the autumn yield.
Owning is the entanglement,
Wanting is the bewilderment,
Taking is the presentiment:
Only he who contains content
Remains content.

56

Those who know do not tell,
Those who tell do not know.
Not to set the tongue loose
But to curb it,
Not to have edges that catch
But to remain untangled,
Unblinded,
Unconfused,
Is to find balance,
And he who holds the balance beyond sway of love or hate,
Beyond reach of profit or loss,
Beyond care of praise or blame,
Has attained the highest post in the world.

57

A realm is governed by ordinary acts,
A battle is governed by extraordinary acts;
The world is governed by no acts at all.
And how do I know?
This is how I know.
Act after act prohibits
Everything but poverty,
Weapon after weapon conquers
Everything but chaos,
Business after business provides
A craze of waste,
Law after law breeds
A multitude of thieves.
Therefore a sensible man says:
If I keep from meddling with people, they take care of themselves,
If I keep from commanding people, they behave themselves,
If I keep from preaching at people, they improve themselves,
If I keep from imposing on people, they become themselves.

58

The less a leader does and says
The happier his people,
The more a leader struts and brags
The sorrier his people.
Often what appears to be unhappiness is happiness
And what appears to be happiness is unhappiness.
Who can see what leads to what
When happiness appears and yet is not,
When what should be is nothing but a mask
Disguising what should not be? Who can but ask
An end to such a stupid plot!
Therefore a sound man shall so square the circle
And circle the square as not to injure, not to impede:
The glow of his life shall not daze,
It shall lead.

UNIT
11

81

Real words are not in vain,
Vain words are not real;
And since those who argue prove nothing
A sensible man does not argue.
A sensible man is wiser than he knows,
While a fool knows more than is wise.
Therefore a sensible man does not devise resources:
The greater his use to others
The greater their use to him,
The more he yields to others
The more they yield to him.
The way of life cleaves without cutting:
Which, without need to say,
Should be man's way.

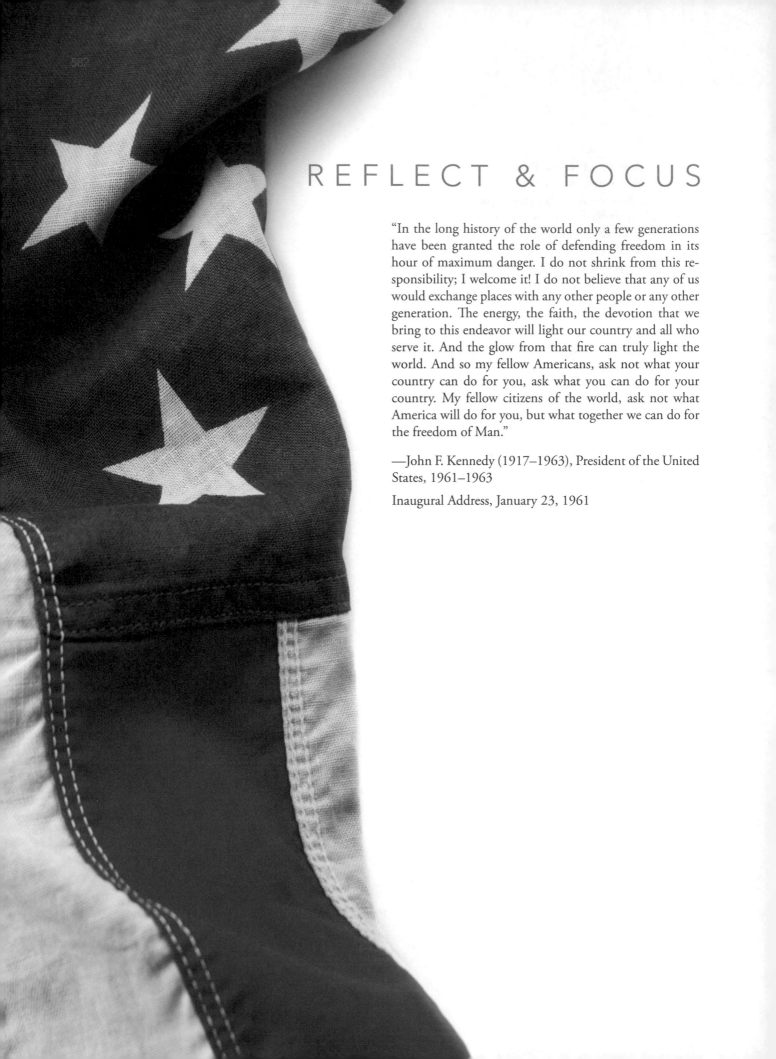

REFLECT & FOCUS

"In the long history of the world only a few generations have been granted the role of defending freedom in its hour of maximum danger. I do not shrink from this responsibility; I welcome it! I do not believe that any of us would exchange places with any other people or any other generation. The energy, the faith, the devotion that we bring to this endeavor will light our country and all who serve it. And the glow from that fire can truly light the world. And so my fellow Americans, ask not what your country can do for you, ask what you can do for your country. My fellow citizens of the world, ask not what America will do for you, but what together we can do for the freedom of Man."

—John F. Kennedy (1917–1963), President of the United States, 1961–1963

Inaugural Address, January 23, 1961

READINGS

The Once and Future King

By T. H. White (1906–1964)
English Writer

Introduction and Historical Background

One of the earliest and longest periods in the development of leadership theory is characterized by emphasis on great men and great women and the traits and characteristics that contributed to their success as leaders. This era that stretches from pre-history into the twentieth century has dominated much of the beliefs people have about leadership and reinforces the symbols and archetypes that so many people associate with leadership. In this theory, the leader is seen as almost a superhuman figure who embodies the positive characteristics that everyone desires. Juliette Wood of the Folklore Society of England describes this phenomenon: "All countries have figures who represent the sum of all that is thought to be good." In this paradigm, or belief system, it is conventional wisdom and assumed that leaders are born, not made. This theory of leadership was perhaps most prevalent and strongly adhered to in the age of Absolutism in which leaders possess the "divine right" to lead because of their birth into a royal family, although assessment instruments for emerging leaders to identify their strongest leadership traits exist today and research seeking to identify the most important traits for a leader to possess continues to the present! Thus born, these individuals must naturally, divinely possess the traits of successful leaders admired and codified first by the Greeks. These traits, such as honesty, integrity and a respect for the truth, increase the admiration of followers. Developing and perfecting these traits prepare the leaders for their roles as battle leaders, protectors of the faith, and keepers of the countries' traditions and values.

This view of leadership nearly always includes a set of responsibilities for the natural-born leader to fulfill. Foremost of these responsibilities is the protection of his/her people. People of many cultures viewed the divine leader who is a successful protector of the people as the highest example of leadership. We have already read examples of this view from ancient European civilization in the selections by Plato and Aristotle, and this view prevailed among people of Medieval Europe as well, which we examine more closely in this reading, and also among Asian people. In Japan, the rise of a warrior class—the "Samurai"—is directly related to the belief among nobles that they had a responsibility to care for and protect the peasants living on their lands.

It is this same concept of a noble warrior class protecting the people that reached a peak in twelfth-century Europe and spawned the myths surrounding Charlemagne (Charles the Great of France) and King Arthur of England. Though the existence of an actual figure called King Arthur and his knights, Sir Lancelot, Sir Gawain, and Sir Galahad, can be disputed, the myth promulgated by Chretien de Troyes of France in the twelfth century and Sir Thomas Malory's *Morte D'Arthur* in the late fifteenth century served to reinforce the concept of the Great Man and revered protector for the kings of those times. King Arthur and his Knights of the Round Table engage in heroic feats to protect the populace. To inspire confidence among the people they must protect, the great mythic leaders of the Middle Ages also complete "heroic epic journeys" of some sort, in which they prove their bravery and courage and will to defeat forces of evil.

The other prevalent aspect of Great Man/Great Woman theories of leadership is the frequent inclusion of the qualities of spirituality, mysticism, and the influence of religion. We see this in the tales of great leaders in the history of many cultures, ranging from the Pharaohs of ancient Egypt to the European Kings and Queens, to the czars of Russia and the sheiks of the Middle East or emperors of China or Japan, but it is present in modern great man/great woman theorizing on leadership, too, evidenced by such recent book titles as *Leadership: The Inner Side of Greatness* (Peter Koestenbaum, 1991), or *The Inner Work of Leaders* (Barbara Mackoff and Gary Wenet, 2001).

The following excerpt from T. H. White's *The Once and Future King* clearly illustrates the key elements of the Great Man/Great Woman Theory of leadership. White was born in India, where his parents lived while his father served in the Civil Service, and he was educated in England. He devoted his life to writing after spending several years teaching English. His subjects were wide-ranging, but he seems to have been most fascinated with social history and Arthurian legends; his most famous works are the four novels of Arthur that are his brilliant adaptation of Sir Thomas Malory's *Morte d'Arthur* and which together form *The Once and Future King*, published in 1958.

Points to Consider

1. What traits and characteristics does Arthur possess that are important for the exercise of leadership?

2. Merlin seems to know that Arthur possesses a trait that he is not using and seeks to change this situation. What is it? Are there traits or talents you possess and could nurture and use more than you do?

3. Arthur is at risk of failing at the exercise of leadership. How and why?

The Once and Future King

(Excerpt)

Chapter II

On the battlements of their castle at Camelot, during an interval of peace between the two Gaelic Wars, the young king of England was standing with his tutor, looking across the purple wastes of evening. A soft light flooded the land below them, and the slow river wound between venerable abbey and stately castle, while the flaming water of sunset reflected spires and turrets and pennoncells hanging motionless in the calm air.

The world was laid out before the two watchers like a toy, for they were on a high keep which dominated the town. At their feet they could see the grass of the outer bailey—it was horrible looking down on it—and a small foreshortened man, with two buckets on a yoke, making his way across to the menagerie. They could see, further off at the gatehouse, which was not so horrible to look at because it was not vertically below, the night guard taking over from the sergeant. They were clicking their heels and saluting and presenting pikes and exchanging passwords as merrily as a marriage bell—but it was done in silence for the two, because it was so far below. They looked like lead soldiers, the little gallow-glasses, and their footsteps could not sound upon the luscious sheep-nibbled green. Then, outside the curtain wall, there was the distant noise of old wives bargaining, and brats bawling, and corporals quaffing, and a few goats mixed with it, and two or three lepers in white hoods ringing bells as they walked, and the swishing robes of nuns who were kindly visiting the poor, two by two, and a fight going on between some gentlemen who were interested in horses. On the other side of the river, which ran directly beneath the castle wall, there was a man ploughing in the fields, with his plough tied to the horse's tail. The

UNIT
11

wooden plough squeaked. There was a silent person near him, fishing for salmon with worms—the rivers were not polluted in those days—and further off, there was a donkey giving his musical concert to the coming night. All these noises came up to the two on the tower smally, as though they were listening through the wrong end of a megaphone.

Arthur was a young man, just on the threshold of life. He had fair hair and a stupid face, or at any rate there was a lack of cunning in it. It was an open face, with kind eyes and a reliable or faithful expression, as though he were a good learner who enjoyed being alive and did not believe in original sin. He had never been unjustly treated, for one thing, so he was kind to other people.

The King was dressed in a robe of velvet which had belonged to Uther the Conqueror, his father, trimmed with the beards of fourteen kings who had been vanquished in the olden days. Unfortunately some of these kings had had red hair, some black, some pepper-and-salt, while their growth of beard had been uneven. The trimming looked like a feather boa. The moustaches were stuck on round the buttons.

Merlyn had a white beard which reached to his middle, horn-rimmed spectacles, and a conical hat. He wore it in compliment to the Saxon serfs of the country, whose national headgear was either a kind of diving-cap, or the Phrygian cap, or else this cone of straw.

The two of them were speaking sometimes, as the words came to them, between spells of listening to the evening.

"Well," said Arthur, "I must say it is nice to be a king. It was a splendid battle."

"Do you think so?"

"Of course it was splendid. Look at the way Lot of Orkney ran, after I had begun to use Excalibur."

"He got you down first."

"That was nothing. It was because I was not using Excalibur. As soon as I drew my trusty sword they ran like rabbits."

"They will come again," said the magician, "all six. The Kings of Orkney, Garloth, Gore, Scotland, The Tower, and the Hundred Knights have started already—in fact, the Gaelic Confederation. You must remember that your claim to the throne is hardly a conventional one."

"Let them come," replied the King. "I don't mind. I will beat them properly this time, and then we will see who is master."

The old man crammed his beard in his mouth and began to chew it, as he generally did when he was put about. He bit through one of the hairs, which stuck between two teeth. He tried to lick it off, then took it out with his fingers. Finally he began curling it into two points.

"I suppose you will learn some day," he said, "but God knows it is heartbreaking, uphill work."

"Oh?"

"Yes," cried Merlyn passionately. "Oh? oh? oh? That is all you can say. Oh? oh? oh? Like a schoolboy."

"I shall cut off your head if you are not careful."

"Cut it off. It would be a good thing if you did. I should not have to keep on tutoring, at any rate."

Arthur shifted his elbow on the battlement and looked at his ancient friend.

"What is the matter, Merlyn?" he asked. "Have I been doing something wrong? I am sorry if I have."

The magician uncurled his beard and blew his nose.

"It is not so much what you are doing" he said. "It is how you are thinking. If there is one thing I can't stand, it is stupidity. I always say that stupidity is the Sin against the Holy Ghost."

"I know you do."

"Now you are being sarcastic."

The King took him by the shoulder and turned him round. "Look," he said, "what is wrong?" Are you in a bad temper? If I have done something stupid, tell me. Don't be in a bad temper."

It had the effect of making the aged nigromant angrier than before.

"Tell you!" he exclaimed. "And what is going to happen when there is nobody to tell you? Are you never going to think for yourself? What is going to happen when I am locked up in this wretched tumulus of mine, I should like to know?"

"I didn't know there was a tumulus in it."

"Oh, hang the tumulus! What tumulus? What am I supposed to be talking about?"

"Stupidity," said Arthur. "It was stupidity when we started."

"Exactly."

"Well, it's no good saying Exactly. You were going to say something about it."

"I don't know what I was going to say about it. You put one in such a passion with all your this and that, that I am sure nobody would know what they were talking about for two minutes together. How did it begin?"

"It began about the battle."

"Now I remember," said Merlyn. "That is exactly where it did begin."

"I said it was a good battle."

"So I recollect."

"Well, it was a good battle," he repeated defensively. "It was a jolly battle, and I won it myself, and it was fun."

The magician's eyes veiled themselves like a vulture's, as he vanished inside his mind. There was a silence on the battlements for several minutes, while a pair of peregrines that were being hacked in a nearby field flew over their heads in a playful chase, crying out Kik-kik-kik, their bells ringing. Merlyn looked out of his eyes once more.

"It was clever of you," he said slowly, "to win the battle."

Arthur had been taught that he ought to be modest, and he was too simple to notice that the vulture was going to pounce.

"Oh well. It was luck."

"Very clever," repeated Merlyn. "How many of your kerns were killed?"

"I don't remember."

"No."

"Kay said —"

The King stopped in the middle of the sentence, and looked at him.

"Well," he said. "It was not fun then. I had not thought."

"The tally was more than seven hundred. They were all kerns, of course. None of the knights were injured, except the one who broke his leg falling off the horse."

When he saw that Arthur was not going to answer, the old fellow went on in a bitter voice.

"I was forgetting," he added, "that you had some really nasty bruises."

Arthur glared at his finger-nails.

"I hate when you are a prig."

Merlyn was charmed.

"That's the spirit," he said, putting his arm through the King's and smiling cheerfully. "That's more like it. Stand up for yourself, that's the ticket. Asking advice is the fatal thing. Besides, I won't be here to advise you fairly soon."

"What is this you keep talking about, about not being here, and the tumulus and so on?"

"It is nothing. I am due to fall in love with a girl called Nimue in a short time, and then she learns my spells and locks me up in a cave for several centuries. It is one of those things which are going to happen."

"But, Merlyn, how horrible! To be stuck in a cave for centuries like a toad in a hole! We must do something about it."

"Nonsense," said the magician. "What was I talking about?"

"About this maiden…."

"I was talking about advice, and how you must never take it. Well, I am going to give you some now. I advise you to think about battles, and about your realm of Gramarye, and about the sort of things a king has to do. Will you do that?"

"I will. Of course I will. But about this girl who learns your spells…"

"You see, it is a question of the people, as well as of the kings. When you said about the battle being a lovely one, you were thinking like your father. I want you to think like yourself, so that you will be a credit to all this education I have been giving you—afterwards, when I am only an old man locked up in a hole."

"Merlyn!"

"There, there! I was playing for sympathy. Never mind. I said it for effect. As a matter of fact, it will be charming to have a rest for a few hundred years, and, as for Nimue, I am looking backward to her a good deal. No, no, the important thing is this thinking-for-yourself business and the matter of battles. Have you ever thought seriously about the state of your country, for instance, or are you going to go on all your life being like Uther Pendragon? After all, you are the King of the place."

"I have not thought very much."

"No. Then let me do some thinking with you. Suppose we think about your Gaelic friend, Sir Bruce Sans Pitié."

"That fellow!"

"Exactly. And why do you say it like that?"

"He is a swine. He goes murdering maidens—and, as soon as a real knight turns up to rescue them, he gallops off for all he is worth. He breeds special fast horses so that nobody can catch him, and he stabs people in the back. He's a marauder. I would kill him at once if I could catch him."

"Well," said Merlyn, "I don't think he is very different from the others. What is all this chivalry, anyway? It simply means being rich enough to have a castle and a suit of armour, and then, when you have them, you make the Saxon people do what you like. The only risk you run is getting a few bruises if you happen to come across another knight. Look at that tilt you saw between Pellinore and Grummore, when you were small. It is this armour that does it. All the barons can slice the poor people about as much as they want, and it is a day's work to hurt each other, and the result is that the country is devastated. Might is Right, that's the motto. Bruce Sans Pitié is only an example of the general situation. Look at Lot and Nentres and Uriens and all that Gaelic crew, fighting against you for the Kingdom. Pulling swords out of stones is not a legal proof of paternity, I admit, but the kings of the Old Ones are not fighting you about that. They have rebelled, although you are their feudal sovereign, simply because the throne is insecure. England's difficulty, we used to say, is Ireland's opportunity. This is their chance to pay off racial scores, and to have some blood-letting as sport, and to make a bit of money in ransoms. Their turbulence does not cost them anything themselves because they are dressed in armour—and you seem to enjoy it too. But look at the country. Look at the barns burnt, and dead men's legs sticking out of ponds, and horses with swelled bellies by the roadside, and mills falling down, and money buried, and nobody daring to walk abroad with gold or ornaments on their clothes. That is chivalry nowadays. That is the Uther Pendragon touch. And then you talk about a battle being fun!"

"I was thinking of myself."

"I know."

"I ought to have thought of the people who had no armour."

"Quite."

"Might isn't Right, is it, Merlyn?"

"Aha!" replied the magician, beaming. "Aha! You are a cunning lad, Arthur, but you won't catch your old tutor like that. You are trying to put me in a passion by making me do the thinking. But I am not to be caught. I am too old a fox for that. You will have to think the rest yourself. Is might right—and if not, why not, give reasons and draw a plan. Besides, what are you going to do about it?"

"What…" began the King, but he saw the gathering frown.

"Very well," he said. "I will think about it."

And he began thinking, stroking his upper lip, where the moustache was going to be.

There was a small incident before they left the keep. The man who had been carrying the two buckets to the menagerie came back with his buckets empty. He passed directly under them, looking small, on his way to the kitchen door. Arthur, who had been playing with a loose stone which he had dislodged from one of the machicolations, got tired of thinking and leaned over with the stone in his hand.

"How small Curselaine looks."

"He is tiny."

"I wonder what would happen if I dropped this stone on his head?"

Merlyn measured the distance.

"At thirty-two feet per second," he said, "I think it would kill him dead. Four hundred g is enough to shatter the skull."

"I have never killed anybody like that," said the boy, in an inquisitive tone.

Merlyn was watching.

"You are the King," he said.

Then he added, "Nobody can say anything to you if you try."

Arthur stayed motionless, leaning out with the stone in his hand. Then, without his body moving, his eyes slid sideways to meet his tutor's.

The stone knocked Merlyn's hat off clean as a whistle, and the old gentleman chased him featly down the stairs, waving his wand of lignum vitae.

Arthur was happy. Like the man in Eden before the fall, he was enjoying his innocence and fortune. Instead of being a poor squire, he was a king. Instead of being an orphan, he was loved by nearly everybody except the Gaels, and he loved everybody in return.

So far as he was concerned, as yet, there might never have been such a thing as a simple particle of sorrow on the gay, sweet surface of the dew-glittering world.

Chapter III

Sir Kay had heard stories about the Queen of Orkney, and he was inquisitive about her.

"Who is Queen Morgause?" he asked one day. "I was told that she is beautiful. What did these Old Ones want to fight us about? And what is her husband like, King Lot? What is his proper name? I heard somebody calling him the King of the Out Isles, and then there are others who call him the King of Lothian and Orkney. Where is Lothian? Is it near Hy Brazil? I can't understand what the revolt was about. Everybody knows that the King of England is their feudal overlord. I heard that she has four sons. Is it true that she doesn't get on with her husband?"

They were riding back from a day on the mountain, where they had been hunting grouse with peregrines, and Merlyn had gone with them for the sake of the ride. He had become a vegetarian lately—an opponent of blood-sports on principle—although he had gone through most of them during his thoughtless youth—and even now he secretly adored to watch the falcons for themselves. Their masterly circles, as they waited on—mere specks in the sky—and the bur-r-r with which they scythed on the grouse, and the way in which the wretched quarry, killed instantaneously, went end-over tip into the heather—these were a temptation to which he yielded in the uncomfortable knowledge that it was sin. He consoled himself by saying that the grouse were for the pot. But it was a shallow excuse, for he did not believe in eating meat either.

Arthur, who was riding watchfully like a sensible young monarch, withdrew his eye from a clump of whins which might have held an ambush in those early days of anarchy, and cocked one eyebrow at his tutor. He was wondering with half his mind which of Kay's questions the magician would choose to answer, but the other half was still upon the martial possibilities of the landscape. He knew how far the falconers were behind them—the cadger carrying the hooded hawks on a square framework slung from his shoulders, with a man-at-arms on either side—and how far in front was the next likely place for a William Rufus arrow.

Merlyn chose the second question.

"Wars are never fought for one reason," he said. "They are fought for dozens of reasons, in a muddle. It is the same with revolts."

"But there must have been a main reason," said Kay.

"Not necessarily."

Arthur observed: "We might have to trot now. It is clear going for two miles since those whins, and we can have a canter back again, to keep with the men. It would breath the horses."

Merlyn's hat blew off. They had to stop and pick it up. Afterwards they walked their horses sedately in a row.

"One reason," said the magician, "is the immortal feud of Gael and Gall. The Gaelic Confederation are representatives of an ancient race which has been harried out of England by several races which are represented by you. Naturally they want to be as nasty as possible to you when they can."

"Racial history is beyond me," said Kay. "Nobody knows which race is which. They are all serfs, in any case."

The old man looked at him with something like amusement.

"One of the startling things about the Norman," he said, "is that he really does not know a single thing about anybody except himself. And you, Kay, as a Norman gentleman, carry the peculiarity to its limit. I wonder if you even know what a Gael is? Some people call them Celts."

"A celt is a kind of battle-axe," said Arthur, surprising the magician with this piece of information more than he had been surprised for several generations. For it was true, in one of the meanings of the word, although Arthur ought not to have known it.

"Not that kind of celt. I am talking about the people. Let's stick to calling them Gaels. I mean the Old Ones who live in Brittany and Cornwall and Wales and Ireland and Scotland. Picts and that."

"Picts?" asked Kay. "I think I have heard about Picts. Pictures. They were painted blue."

"And I am supposed to have managed your education!"

The King said thoughtfully: "Would you mind telling me about the races, Merlyn? I supposed I ought to understand the situation, if there has to be a second war."

This time it was Kay who looked surprised.

"Is there to be a war?" he asked. "This is the first I've heard of it. I thought the revolt was crushed last year?"

"They have made a new confederation since they went home, with five new kings, which makes them eleven altogether. The new ones belong to the old blood too. They are Clariance of North Humberland, Idres of Cornwall, Cradelmas of North Wales, Brandegoris of Stranggore and Anguish of Ireland. It will be a proper war, I'm afraid."

"And all about races," said his foster-brother in disgust. "Still, it may be fun."

The King ignored him.

"Go on," he said to Merlyn. "I want you to explain."

"Only," he added quickly, as the magician opened his mouth, "not too many details."

Merlyn opened his mouth and shut it twice, before he was able to comply with this restriction.

"About three thousand years ago," he said, "the country you are riding through belonged to a Gaelic race who fought with copper hatchets. Two thousand years ago they were hunted west by another Gaelic race with bronze swords. A thousand years ago there was a Teuton invasion by people who had iron weapons, but it didn't reach the whole of the Pictish Isles because the Romans arrived in the middle and got mixed up with it. The Romans went away about eight hundred years ago, and then another Teuton invasion—of people mainly called Saxons—drove the whole rag-bag west as usual. The Saxons were just beginning to settle down when your father the Conqueror arrived with his pack of Normans, and that is where we are today. Robin Wood was a Saxon partizan."

"I thought we were called the British Isles."

"So we are. People have got the B's and P's muddled up. Nothing like the Teuton race for confusing its consonants. In Ireland they are still chattering away about some people called Fomorians, who were really Pomeranians, while…"

Arthur interrupted him at the critical moment.

"So it comes to this," he said, "that we Normans have the Saxons for serfs, while the Saxons once had a sort of under-surfs, who were called the Gaels—the Old Ones. In that case I don't see why the Gaelic Confederation should want to fight against me—as a Norman king—when it was really the Saxons who hunted them, and when it was hundreds of years ago in any case."

"You are under-rating the Gaelic memory, dear boy. They don't distinguish between you. The Normans are a Teuton race, like the Saxons whom your father conquered. So far as the ancient Gaels are concerned, they just regard both your races as branches of the same alien people, who have driven them north and west."

Kay said definitely: "I can't stand any more history. After all, we are supposed to be grown up. If we go on, we shall be doing dictation."

Arthur grinned and began in the well-remembered sing-song voice: Barbara Celarent Darii Ferioque Prioris, while Kay sang the next four lines with him antiphonically.

Merlyn said: "You asked for it."

"And now we have it."

"The main thing is that the war is going to happen because the Teutons or the Galls or whatever you call them upset the Gaels long ago."

"Certainly not," exclaimed the magician. "I never said anything of the sort."

They gaped.

"I said the war will happen for dozens of reasons, not for one. Another of the reasons for this particular war is because Queen Morgause wears the trousers. Perhaps I ought to say the trews."

Arthur asked painstakingly: "Let me get this clear. First I was given to understand that Lot and the rest had rebelled because they were Gaels and we were Galls, but now I am told that it deals with the Queen of Orkney's trousers. Could you be more definite?"

"There is the feud of Gael and Gall which we have been talking about, but there are other feuds too. Surely you have not forgotten that your father killed the Earl of Cornwall before you were born? Queen Morgause was one of the daughters of that Earl."

"The Lovely Cornwall Sisters," observed Kay.

"Exactly. You met one of them yourselves—Queen Morgan le Fay. That was when you were friends with Robin Wood, and you found her on a bed of lard. The third sister was Elaine. All three of them are witches of one sort or another, though Morgan is the only one who takes it seriously."

"If my father," said the King, "killed the Queen of Orkney's father, then I think she had a good reason for wanting her husband to rebel against me."

"It is only a personal reason. Personal reasons are no excuse for war."

"And furthermore," the King continued, "if my race has driven out the Gaelic race, then I think the Queen of Orkney's subjects have a good reason too."

Merlyn scratched his chin in the middle of the beard, with the hand which held the reins, and pondered.

"Uther," he said at length, "your lamented father, was an aggressor. So were his predecessors the Saxons, who drove the Old Ones away. But if we go on living backward like that, we shall never come to the end of it. The Old Ones themselves were aggressors, against the earlier race of the copper hatchets, and even the hatchet fellows were aggressors, against some earlier crew of ex-quimaux who lived on shells. You simply go on and on, until you get to Cain and Abel. But the point is that the Saxon Conquest did succeed, and so did the Norman Conquest of the Saxons. Your father settled the unfortunate Saxons long ago, however brutally he did it, and when a great many years have passed one ought to be ready to accept a *status quo*. Also I would like to point out that the Norman Conquest was a process of welding small units into bigger ones—while the

UNIT
11

present revolt of the Gaelic Confederation is a process of disintegration. They want to smash up what we may call their United Kingdom into a lot of piffling little kingdoms of their own. That is why their reason is not what you might call a good one."

He scratched his chin again, and became wrathful.

"I never could stomach these nationalists," he exclaimed. "The destiny of Man is to unite, not to divide. If you keep on dividing you end up as a collection of monkeys throwing nuts at each other out of separate trees."

"All the same," said the King, "there seems to have been a good deal of provocation. Perhaps I ought not to fight?"

"And give in?" asked Kay, more in amusement than dismay.

"I could abdicate."

They looked at Merlyn, who refused to meet their eyes. He rode on, staring straight in front of him, munching his beard.

"Ought I to give in?"

"You are the King," said the old man stubbornly. "Nobody can say anything if you do."

Later on, he began to speak in a gentler tone.

"Did you know," he asked rather wistfully, "that I was one of the Old Ones myself? My father was a demon, they say, but my mother was a Gael. The only human blood I have comes from the Old Ones. Yet here I am denouncing their ideas of nationalism, being what their politicians would call a traitor—because, by calling names, they can score the cheap debating points. And do you know another thing, Arthur? Life is too bitter already, without territories and wars and noble feuds."

The Jungle

By Upton Sinclair (1878–1968)
American Writer

Introduction and Historical Background

Political and social revolutions that forged the modern nation-states of America and France during the eighteenth century were major influences in a change in focus from viewing leaders as strictly divinely selected and perfect (or "perfectable") individuals to the idea that people should have a say in who leads them. To understand how threatening this concept was to the world's governments of the time, it takes only a reminder that American and French revolutionaries alike were referred to first as rebels and traitors or even terrorists and only later as patriots. However, even modern democracies and republics without kings or queens by divine right still emphasized traits and characteristics in examining leaders or potential leaders. It was not political ideology that produced real change in thinking about leadership, but the invention of machines and industrialization that first ushered in a new era of leadership theorizing referred to as Scientific Management.

Scientific Management Theory took the tools, inventions, and processes of the Industrial Revolution to redefine the traditional view of leadership. In Scientific Management Theory, the leader is not a person born to leadership with a set of positive and inspirational traits and characteristics, but a person who can control the means of production, including other people. F.W. Taylor is known as the "Father of Scientific Management" and earned the nickname "Speedy" for his reputation as an efficiency expert. Improving the efficiency of workers, increasing the production of goods through technical advances, and lowering costs to make consumer products available to larger groups of people were the hallmarks and responsibilities of leaders. In order to codify these principles within the complex industrial environments being created, rules and standards emerged. These rules and standards for leaders to learn and implement included such things as the Scalar Principle (separation between administration and workers), and Unity of Command (having no more than one supervisor and span of control, including usually no more than 3–6 subordinates). As the twentieth century progressed, some of the leadership theories sought to be increasingly scientific with charts and grids and measurements and the language of science and a belief that training better leaders was as possible as training a scientist. Scientific Management, through strictly organizing the workplace, created new efficiencies and new levels of productivity, but it also dehumanized the relationships between leaders and followers and spawned abuses. The movement toward worker control was not accompanied by worker protections. Without workmen's compensation, workplace safety standards, and child labor laws, the workplace in many cases became an extraordinarily dangerous place for workers while managers and owners prospered through effective, scientific management. In Upton Sinclair's novel *The Jungle*, the shortcomings—even abuses—of Scientific Management Theory of leadership are clearly illustrated.

Sinclair is one of the most prolific American writers with over 80 fiction and nonfiction books to his credit. He was profoundly concerned with social and political problems, and his best-known work, *The Jungle*, exposes the serious dangers to employees and health risks to consumers created in the meat packing industry of the early 20th century. Look for examples of Sinclair's use of mechanical language or the language of business and productivity when talking about people. The novel was a great influence in the passage of The Pure Food and Drug Act (1906).

Points to Consider

1. How does the experience of the workers in *The Jungle* contrast with contemporary thinking about "human resources"?

2. The story is about the workers, not the business owners, managers, or leaders, but from the few places they are mentioned and from the experiences of the workers in the passage, what do you learn about the leadership in the packing house?

3. What are the costs and risks of focusing on *efficiency* in an organization? To what extent should leadership be concerned with efficiency?

The Jungle

(Excerpt)

Now, the dreadful winter was come upon them. In the forests, all summer long, the branches of the trees do battle for light, and some of them lose and die; and then come the raging blasts, and the storms of snow and hail, and strew the ground with these weaker branches. Just so it was in Packingtown; the whole district braced itself for the struggle that was an agony, and those whose time was come died off in hordes. All the year round they had been serving as cogs in the great packing machine, and now was the time for the renovating of it, and the replacing of damaged parts. There came pneumonia and grippe, stalking among them, seeking for weakened constitutions; there was the annual harvest of those whom tuberculosis had been dragging down. There came cruel, cold, and biting winds, and blizzards of snow, all testing relentlessly for failing muscles and impoverished blood. Sooner or later came the day when the unfit one did not report for work; and then, with no time lost in waiting, and no inquiries or regrets, there was a chance for a new hand.

The new hands were here by the thousands. All day long the gates of the packing houses were besieged by starving and penniless men; they came, literally, by the thousands every single morning, fighting with each other for a chance for life. Blizzards and cold made no difference to them, they were always on hand; they were on hand two hours before the sun rose, an hour before the work began. Sometimes their faces froze, sometimes their feet and their hands; sometimes they froze all together—but still they came, for they had no other place to go. One day Durham advertised in the paper for two hundred men to cut ice; and all that day the homeless and starving of the city came trudging through the snow from all over its two hundred square miles. That night forty score of them crowded into the station house of the stockyards district—they filled the rooms, sleeping in each other's laps, toboggan-fashion, and they piled on top of each other in the outside. On the morrow, before daybreak, there were three thousand at Durham's, and the police reserves had to be sent for to quell the riot. Then Durham's bosses picked out twenty of the biggest; the "two hundred" proved to have been a printer's error.

Four or five miles to the eastward lay the lake, and over this the bitter winds came raging. Sometimes the thermometer would fall to ten or twenty degrees below zero at night, and in the morning the street would be piled with snowdrifts up to the first-floor windows. The streets through which our friends had to go to their work were all unpaved and full of deep holes and gullies; in summer, when it rained hard, a man might have to wade to his waist to get to his house, and now in winter it was no joke getting through these places, before light in the morning and after dark at night. They would wrap up in all they owned, but they could not wrap up against exhaustion, and many a man gave out in these battles with the snowdrifts, and lay down and fell asleep.

And if it was bad for the men, one may imagine how the women and children fared. Some would ride in the cars, if the cars were running, but when you are making only five cents an hour, as was little Stanislovas, you do not like to spend that much to ride two miles. The children would come to the yards with great shawls about their ears, and so tied up that you could hardly find them— and still there would be accidents. One bitter morning in February the little boy who worked at the lard machine with Stanislovas came about an hour late, and screaming with pain. They unwrapped him, and a man began vigorously rubbing his ears, and as they were frozen stiff, it took only two or three rubs to break them short off. As a result of this, little Stanislovas conceived a terror of the cold that was almost mania. Every morning, when it came time to start for the yards, he would begin to cry and protest. Nobody knew quite how to manage him, for threats did no good—it seemed to be something that he could not control, and they feared sometimes that he would go into convulsions. In the end it had to be arranged that he always went with Jurgis, and came home with him again, and often, when the snow was deep, the man would carry him the whole way on his shoulders. Sometimes Jurgis would be working until late at night, and then it was pitiful, for there was no place for the little fellow to wait, save in the doorways or in a corner of the killing beds, and he would all but fall asleep there, and freeze to death.

There was no heat upon the killing beds; the men might exactly as well have worked out of doors all winter. For that matter, there was very little heat anywhere in the building, except in the cooking rooms and such places—and it was the men who worked in these who ran the most risk of all, because whenever they had to pass to another room they had to go through ice-cold corridors, and sometimes with nothing on above the waist except a sleeveless undershirt. On the killing beds you were apt to be covered with blood, and it would freeze solid; if you leaned against a pillar, you would freeze to that, and if you put your hand upon the blade of your knife, you would run the chance of leaving your skin on it. The men would tie up their feet in newspapers and old sacks, and these would be soaked in blood and frozen, and then soaked again, and so on, until by nighttime a man would be walking on great lumps the size of the feet of an elephant. Now and then, when the bosses were not looking, you would see them plunging their feet and ankles into the steaming hot carcass of the steer, or darting across the room to the hot-water jets. The cruelest thing of all was that nearly all of them—all of those who used knives—were unable to wear gloves, and their arms would be white with frost and their hands would grow numb, and then of course there would be accidents. Also the air would be full of steam, from the hot water and the hot blood, so that you could not see five feet before you; and then, with men rushing about at the speed they kept up on the killing beds, and all with butcher knives, like razors, in their hands— well, it was to be counted as a wonder that there were not more men slaughtered than cattle.

And yet all this inconvenience they might have put up with, if only it had not been for one thing—if only there had been some place where they might eat. Jurgis had either to eat his dinner amid the stench in which he had worked, or else to rush, as did all his companions, to any one of the hundreds of liquor stores which stretched out their arms to him. To the west of the yards ran Ashland Avenue, and here was an unbroken line of saloons—"Whiskey Row," they called it; to the north was Forty-seventh Street, where there were half a dozen to the block, and at the angle of the two was "Whiskey Point," a space of fifteen or twenty acres, and containing one glue factory and about two hundred saloons.

One might walk among these and take his choice: "Hot pea soup and boiled cabbage today." "Sauerkraut and hot frankfurters. Walk in." "Bean soup and stewed lamb. Welcome." All of these things were printed in many languages, as were also the names of the resorts, which were infinite in their variety and appeal. There was the "Home Circle" and the "Cosey Corner"; there were "Firesides" and "Hearthstones" and "Pleasure Places" and "Wonderlands" and "Dream Castles" and "Love's Delights." Whatever else they were called, they were sure to be called "Union Headquarters," and to hold out a welcome to workingmen; and there was always a warm stove, and a chair near it, and some friends to laugh and talk with. There was only one condition attached,—you must drink. If you went in not intending to drink, you would be put out in no time, and if you were slow about going, like as not you would get your head split open with a beer bottle in the bargain. But all of the men understood the convention and drank; they believed that by it they were getting something for nothing—for they did not need to take more than one drink, and upon the strength of it they might fill themselves up with a good hot dinner. This did not always work out in practice, however, for there was pretty sure to be a friend who would treat

UNIT
11

you, and then you would have to treat him. Then some one else would come in—and, anyhow, a few drinks were good for a man who worked hard. As he went back he did not shiver so, he had more courage for his task; the deadly brutalizing monotony of it did not afflict him so—he had ideas while he worked, and took a more cheerful view of his circumstances. On the way home, however, the shivering was apt to come on him again; and so he would have to stop once or twice to warm up against the cruel cold. As there were hot things to eat in this saloon too, he might get home late to his supper, or he might not get home at all. And then his wife might set out to look for him, and she too would feel the cold; and perhaps she would have some of the children with her—and so a whole family would drift into drinking, as the current of a river drifts downstream. As if to complete the chain, the packers all paid their men in checks, refusing all requests to pay in coin; and where in Packingtown could a man go to have his check cashed but to a saloon, where he could pay for the favor by spending a part of the money?

From all of these things Jurgis was saved because of Ona. He never would take but the one drink at noontime; and so he got the reputation of being a surly fellow, and was not quite welcome at the saloons, and had to drift about from one to another. Then at night he would go straight home, helping Ona and Stanislovas, or often putting the former on a car. And when he got home perhaps he would have to trudge several blocks, and come staggering back through the snow-drifts with a bag of coal upon his shoulder. Home was not a very attractive place—at least not this winter. They had only been able to buy one stove, and this was a small one, and proved not to be big enough to warm even the kitchen in the bitterest weather. This made it hard for Teta Elzbieta all day, and for the children when they could not get to school. At night they would sit huddled around this stove, while they ate their supper off their laps; and then Jurgis and Jonas would smoke a pipe, after which they would all crawl into their beds to get warm, after putting out the fire to save the coal. Then they would have some frightful experiences with the cold. They would sleep with all their clothes on, including their overcoats, and put over them all the bedding and spare clothing they owned; the children would sleep all crowded into one bed, and yet even so they could not keep warm. The outside ones would be shivering and sobbing, crawling over the others and trying to get down into the center, and causing a fight. This old house with the leaky weather boards was a very different thing from their cabins at home, with great thick walls plastered inside and outside with mud; and the cold which came upon them was a living thing, a demon-presence in the room. They would waken in the midnight hours, when everything was black; perhaps they would hear it yelling outside, or perhaps there would be deathlike stillness—and that would be worse yet. They could feel the cold as it crept in through the cracks, reaching out for them with its icy, death-dealing fingers, and they would crouch and cower, and try to hide from it, all in vain. It would come, and it would come; a grisly thing, a specter born in the black caverns of terror; a power primeval, cosmic, shadowing the tortures of the lost souls flung out to chaos and destruction. It was cruel, iron-hard; and hour after hour they would cringe in its grasp, alone, alone. There would be no one to hear them if they cried out; there would be no help, no mercy. And so on until morning—when they would go out to another day of toil, a little weaker, a little nearer to the time when it would be their turn to be shaken from the tree.

Sinclair, U. (1905). *The Jungle*. Signet. Pp. 81–86

Motivation and Personality

By Abraham Maslow (1908–1970)
American Psychologist

Introduction and Historical Background

In Scientific Management Theory it was assumed that each job could be reduced to a series of discrete steps and workers could be plugged into these steps like cogs in a machine. Industrial scientists developed time and motion studies to determine the most efficient way to perform a certain task and then workers were trained to perform the job in exactly that manner. At the time, little thought was given to the idea of motivating workers to better perform their tasks. It was assumed that wages and the threat of losing their jobs would be enough to ensure high productivity and efficiency.

The economic growth in the years following the Industrial Revolution and the Scientific Management era hid the fact that many workers and their families were suffering under tremendous financial and personal hardships. Mary Parker Follett (1868–1933), a Boston social worker, had viewed some of the abuses the Industrial Revolution had brought upon the working class and determined that different, fundamental factors could drive people in the workplace. Through her writings she became a bridge between the industrial psychologists who designed workplace studies and leaders who adhered to the scientific management theories. Follet was instrumental in demonstrating the need for studies on how human factors affected production and efficiency, and pioneered the Human Relations Movement.

Into this environment and new thinking about how people are motivated in the workplace came Elton Mayo (1880–1949). Mayo was a Harvard professor trained in psychopathology who was commissioned by the National Research Council and the Western Electric plant near Chicago to study the effects of illumination on worker productivity. The study seemed straightforward to the researchers but the results were not. Mayo and his associates thought by reducing the illumination in one part of the factory they could determine how lighting affected efficiency and productivity. It was thought that at some point, reduced illumination would result in lowered productivity and efficiency but this was not the case. The workers in the study actually increased productivity as the illumination decreased. The control group whose lighting was not decreased also increased their productivity. This brought Mayo and others to the conclusion that many more emotional factors must be at work in determining workers' productivity than had been previously thought. For example, perhaps the workers enjoyed the attention they received from being in the "experiment" and therefore worked harder. Mayo suggested that the reason workers are motivated by such studies and research is that individuals have a deep psychological need to believe that the organization cares about them. This realization that there were strong emotional components relating to employee productivity launched a period of major change in a variety of fields such as psychology and management. New ideas such as "employee-centered management" were truly revolutionary.

It was not long before a brilliant psychologist, Abraham Maslow, began writing on human motivation and brought about a major shift in the field of psychology which in turn influenced a number of leadership and management theorists, including Chris Argyris and his Immaturity-Maturity Theory, Fred Herzberg and his Motivation-Hygiene Theory, Ikie Victor Vroom and his Expectancy Theory, and Douglas McGregor and his Theory X/Theory Y Management Theory.

Abraham Maslow was born in Brooklyn, New York to Russian immigrant parents. Biographies describe him as an "extraordinarily shy, neurotic young man, depressed, terribly unhappy, lonely, and self-rejecting." He wrote that he "grew up in libraries and among books, without friends." He was a brilliant student, and briefly tried law school to please his father, but left to "study everything," settling eventually on a major in psychology. He learned to love psychology among the great scholars of behaviorism, but it did not fulfill his desire to understand the complete human. He felt that psychology could provide a "philosophy of life, a conception of human nature…a guide to living, to values, to choices."

Today, students in varied disciplines, including psychology, education, business, and leadership studies, continue to learn the name Abraham Maslow and study his defining work, *the hierarchy of needs*. The hierarchy of needs applies to such a number of disciplines because it so simply and accurately describes the human experience in almost any context. Maslow was a Humanist—he viewed human potential as a vastly underestimated and an unexplained territory. Diagrams such as the one on the following page to illustrate the hierarchy of needs and even build upon it have become almost ubiquitous (Self-Actualization topped Maslow's original hierarchy, but he did state that he felt his work was a transitional step in the process toward the development of a "transhuman" psychology, so the addition of Transcendence to the traditional hierarchy of needs likely would not upset Maslow).

Maslow contended that as long as lower-level needs went unsatisfied, or even if there was fear that they might be unsatisfied, higher-level potential in areas such as learning, creativity, innovation, or self-esteem would never be reached. If the lower-level needs become reasonably and confidently satisfied, successively higher needs become more influential in motivating human behavior. Note that this is not to say that when lower-level needs are satisfied, they are no longer an issue. On the contrary, Maslow noted that people seem to easily become dissatisfied with what he referred to as "environmental factors."

Motivation and Personality, first published in 1954, is a humanistic critique of the theories of motivation existing at the time, known as behaviorist theories. Maslow lays out for the first time the foundations for a truly human theory of motivation. One of his greatest strengths was his courage and ability to ask significant questions and then explore them with an unprejudiced sense of wonder. He brought questions that are important to all of us to the attention of the field of psychology—questions like, "What is it to be a good human being? Of what are human beings capable? What makes a happy, creative, fulfilled human being? How do we know when a human being has reached his or her full potential?" Maslow dedicated his life to studying people whom he considered psychologically healthy and many he considered "self-actualized"—"those who have come to a high level of maturation, health, and self-fulfillment."

Maslow's Hierarchy of Needs (1990s Eight-Stage Model)

Transcendence
helping others
to self-actualize

Self-actualization
personal growth, self-fulfillment

Cognitive Needs
knowledge, meaning, self-awareness

Esteem Needs
achievement, status, responsibility, reputation

Belongingness and Love Needs
family, affection, relationships, work group, etc.

Safety Needs
protection, security, order, law, limits, stability, etc.

Biological and Physiological Needs
basic life needs—air, food, drink, shelter, warmth, sleep, etc.

Maslow's extensive studies of human nature produced these central ideas:

1. Human beings have an innate tendency to move toward higher levels of health, creativity, and self-fulfillment.

2. Neurosis may be regarded as a blockage of the tendency toward self-actualization.

3. The evolution of a synergistic society is a natural and essential process. This is a society in which all individuals may reach a high level of self-development, without restricting each others' freedom.

4. Business efficiency and personal growth are not incompatible. In fact, the process of self-actualization leads each individual to the highest levels of efficiency. [Frager, Robert. "Foreword" in *Motivation and Personality*, 3rd edition. New York: Addison-Wesley Longman, 1987.]

Motivation and Personality had profound influence in creating a positive and holistic view of human nature and human potential. It began a trend toward a growing emphasis on the power of choice, values, and human potential for good in many fields, including Leadership Studies. Maslow himself wrote in 1968: "I must confess that I have come to think of this humanist trend in psychology as a revolution in the truest, oldest sense of the word, the sense in which Galileo, Darwin, Einstein, Freud, and Marx made revolutions, i.e. new ways of perceiving and thinking, new images of man and of society, new conceptions of ethics and of values, new directions in which to move."

UNIT
11

Points to Consider

1. Which of the various leaders portrayed in the text seem to have the most of Maslow's characteristics of self-actualization?

2. What are some specific examples of both "growth motivation" and "deprivation motivation"?

3. How does Maslow's description of life being like a jungle for some people fit with Upton Sinclair's description of life in his novel *The Jungle*?

4. Why do you think there are a number of similarities between psychologically healthy children and self-actualized adults?

Motivation and Personality

(Excerpt)

Chapter 11—Self-actualizing People: A Study of Psychological Health

[Editors' Note: Footnotes and the details regarding the subjects and methodology of the study have been omitted]

The study to be reported in this chapter is unusual in various ways. It was not planned as an ordinary research; it was not a social venture but a private one, motivated by my own curiosity and pointed toward the solution of various personal, moral, ethical, and scientific problems. I sought only to convince and to teach myself rather than to prove or to demonstrate to others. [Editor's note: Maslow's study of self-actualizing people was an informal personal inquiry that he continued throughout his life.]

Quite unexpectedly, however, these studies have proved to be so enlightening to me, and so laden with exciting implications, that it seems fair that some sort of report should be made to others in spite of its methodological shortcomings.

…

The Observations

Holistic analysis of the total impressions yields the following characteristics of self-actualizing people for further clinical and experimental study: perception of reality, acceptance, spontaneity, problem centering, solitude, autonomy, fresh appreciation, peak experiences, human kinship, humility and respect, interpersonal relationships, ethics, means and ends, humor, creativity, resistance to enculturation, imperfections, values, and resolutions of dichotomies.

Perception of Reality

The first form in which this capacity was noticed was as an unusual ability to detect the spurious, the fake, and the dishonest in personality, and in general to judge people correctly and efficiently. In an informal experiment with a group of college students, a clear tendency was discerned for the more secure (the more healthy) to judge their professors more accurately than did the less secure students, that is, high scorers in the S-I test (Maslow, 1952).

As the study progressed, it slowly became apparent that this efficiency extended to many other areas of life—indeed *all* areas that were observed. In art and music, in things of the intellect, in scientific matters, in politics and public affairs, they seemed as a group to be able to see concealed or confused realities more swiftly and more correctly than others. Thus an informal survey indicated that their predictions of the future from whatever facts were in hand at the time seemed to be more often correct, because less based upon wish, desire, anxiety, fear, or upon generalized, character-determined optimism or pessimism.

At first this was phrased as good taste or good judgment, the implication being relative and not absolute. But for many reasons (some to be detailed below), it has become progressively more clear that this had better be called perception (not taste) of something that was absolutely there (reality, not a set of opinions). It is hoped that this conclusion—or hypothesis—can one day be put to the experimental test.

If this is so, it would be impossible to overstress its importance. Money-Kyrle (1944), an English psychoanalyst, has indicated that he believes it possible to call neurotic people not only *relatively* but *absolutely* inefficient, simply because they do not perceive the real world so accurately or so efficiently as do healthy persons. Neurotics are not emotionally sick—they are cognitively *wrong*! If health and neurosis are, respectively, correct and incorrect perceptions of reality, propositions of value merge in this area, and, in principle, value propositions should then be empirically demonstrable rather than merely matters of taste or exhortation. For those who have wrestled with this problem it will be clear that we may have here a partial basis for a true science of values, and consequently of ethics, social relations, politics, religion, and so forth.

It is definitely possible that maladjustment or even extreme neurosis would disturb perception enough to affect acuity of perception of light or touch or odor. But it is *probable* that this effect can be demonstrated in spheres of perception removed from the merely physiological. It should also follow that the effects of wish, desire, or prejudice upon perception as in many recent experiments should be very much less in healthy people than in sick. [*A priori*] considerations encourage the hypothesis that this superiority in the perception of reality eventuates in a superior ability to reason, to perceive the truth, to come to conclusions, to be logical, and to be cognitively efficient, in general.

One particularly impressive and instructive aspect of this superior relationship with reality will be discussed at length in Chapter 13. It was found that self-actualizing people distinguished far more easily than most the fresh, concrete, and idiographic from the generic, abstract, and categorized. The consequence is that they live more in the real world of nature than in the human-made mass of concepts, abstractions, expectations, beliefs, and stereotypes that most people confuse with the world. They are therefore far more apt to perceive what is there rather than their own wishes, hopes, fears, anxieties, their own theories and beliefs, or those of their cultural group. "The innocent eye," Herbert Read has very effectively called it.

The relationship with the unknown seems to be of exceptional promise as another bridge between academic and clinical psychology. Our healthy subjects are generally unthreatened and unfrightened by the unknown, being therein quite different from average people. They accept it, are comfortable with it, and, often are even *more* attracted by it than by the known. They not only tolerate the ambiguous and unstructured (Frenkel-Brunswik, 1949); they like it. Quite characteristic is Einstein's statement, "The most beautiful thing we can experience is the mysterious. It is the source of all art and science."

These people, it is true, are the intellectuals, the researchers, and the scientists, so that perhaps the major determinant here is intellectual power. And yet we all know how many scientists with high IQ, through timidity, conventionality, anxiety, or other character defects, occupy themselves exclusively with what is known, with polishing it, arranging and rearranging it, classifying it, and otherwise puttering with it instead of discovering, as they are supposed to do.

UNIT
11

Since for healthy people the unknown is not frightening, they do not have to spend any time laying the ghost, whistling past the cemetery, or otherwise protecting themselves against imagined dangers. They do not neglect the unknown, or deny it, or run away from it, or try to make believe it is really known, nor do they organize, dichotomize, or categorize it prematurely. They do not cling to the familiar, nor is their quest for the truth a catastrophic need for certainty, safety, definiteness, and order, such as we see in an exaggerated form from Goldstein's brain-injured patients (1939) or in the compulsive-obsessive neurotic. They can be, when the total objective situation calls for it, comfortably disorderly, sloppy, anarchic, chaotic, vague, doubtful, uncertain, indefinite, approximate, inexact, or inaccurate (all, at certain moments in science, art, or life in general, quite desirable).

Thus it comes about that doubt, tentativeness, uncertainty, with the consequent necessity for abeyance of decision, which is for most a torture, can be for some a pleasantly stimulating challenge, a high spot in life rather than a low.

Acceptance

A good many personal qualities that can be perceived on the surface and that seem at first to be various and unconnected may be understood as manifestations or derivatives of a more fundamental single attitude, namely, of a relative lack of overriding guilt, of crippling shame, and of extreme or severe anxiety. This is in direct contrast with the neurotic person who in every instance may be described as crippled by guilt and/or shame and/or anxiety. Even the normal member of our culture feels unnecessarily guilty or ashamed about too many things and has anxiety in too many unnecessary situations. Our healthy individuals find it possible to accept themselves and their own nature without chagrin or complaint or, for that matter, even without thinking about the matter very much.

They can accept their own human nature in the stoic style, with all its shortcomings, with all its discrepancies from the ideal image without feeling real concern. It would convey the wrong impression to say that they are self-satisfied. What we must say rather is that they can take the frailties and sins, weaknesses, and evils of human nature in the same unquestioning spirit with which one accepts the characteristics of nature. One does not complain about water because it is wet, or about rocks because they are hard, or about trees because they are green. As children look out upon the world with wide, uncritical, undemanding, innocent eyes, simply noting and observing what is the case, without either arguing the matter or demanding that it be otherwise, so do self-actualizing people tend to look upon human nature in themselves and in others. This is of course not the same as resignation, but resignation too can be observed in our subjects, especially in the face of illness and death.

Be it observed that this amounts to saying in another form what we have already described; namely, that the self-actualized person sees reality more clearly: our subjects see human nature as it *is* and not as they would prefer it to be. Their eyes see what is before them without being strained through spectacles of various sorts to distort or shape or color the reality (Bergson, 1944).

The first and most obvious level of acceptance is at the so-called animal level. Those self-actualizing people tend to be good animals, hearty in their appetites and enjoying themselves without regret or shame or apology. They seem to have a uniformly good appetite for food; they seem to sleep well; they seem to enjoy their sexual lives without unnecessary inhibition and so on for all the relatively physiological impulses. They are able to accept themselves not only on these low levels, but at all levels as well; for example, love, safety, belongingness, honor, self-respect. All of these are accepted without question as worth while, simply because these people are inclining to accept the work of nature rather than to argue with it for not having constructed things to a different pattern. This shows itself in a relative lack of the disgusts and aversions seen in average people and especially in neurotics, such as food annoyances, disgust with body products, body odors, and body functions.

Closely related to self-acceptance and to acceptance of others is (1) their lack of defensiveness, protective coloration, or pose, and (2) their distaste for such artificialities in others. Cant, guile, hypocrisy, front, face, playing a game, trying to impress in conventional ways: these are all absent in themselves to an unusual degree. Since they can live comfortably even with their own short-comings, these finally come to be perceived, especially in later life, as not shortcomings at all, but simply as neutral personal characteristics.

This is not an absolute lack of guilt, shame, sadness, anxiety, or defensiveness; it is a lack of un-necessary or neurotic (because unrealistic) guilt, and the like. The animal processes (e.g., sex, uri-nation, pregnancy, menstruation, growing old, etc.) are part of reality and so must be accepted.

What healthy people *do* feel guilty about (or ashamed, anxious, sad, or regretful) are (1) improv-able shortcomings (e.g., laziness, thoughtlessness, loss of temper, hurting others); (2) stubborn remnants of psychological ill health (e.g., prejudice, jealousy, envy); (3) habits, which, though relatively independent of character structure may yet be very strong, or (4) shortcomings of the species or of the culture or of the group with which they have identified. The general formula seems to be that healthy people will feel bad about discrepancies between what is and what might very well be or ought to be (Adler, 1939; Fromm, 1947; Horney, 1950).

Spontaneity

Self-actualizing people can all be described as relatively spontaneous in behavior and far more spontaneous than that in their inner life, thoughts, impulses, and so on. Their behavior is marked by simplicity and naturalness, and by lack of artificiality or straining for effect. This does not necessarily mean consistently unconventional behavior. If we were to take an actual count of the number of times that self-actualizing people behaved in an unconventional manner the tally would not be high. Their unconventionality is not superficial but essential or internal. It is their impulses, thought, and consciousness that are so unusually unconventional, spontaneous, and natural. Apparently recognizing that the world of people in which they live could not understand or accept this, and since they have no wish to hurt them or to fight with them over every trivial-ity, they will go through the ceremonies and rituals of convention with a good-humored shrug and with the best possible grace. Thus I have seen a man accept an honor he laughed at and even despised in private, rather than make an issue of it and hurt the people who thought they were pleasing him.

That this conventionality is a cloak that rests very lightly upon their shoulders and is easily cast aside can be seen from the fact that self-actualizing people infrequently allow convention to ham-per them or inhibit them from doing anything that they consider very important or basic. It is at such moments that their essential lack of conventionality appears, and not as with the average Bohemian or authority-rebel, who makes great issues of trivial things and who will fight against some unimportant regulation as if it were a world issue.

This same inner attitude can also be seen in those moments when such persons become keenly absorbed in something that is close to one of their main interests. They can then be seen quite casually to drop off all sorts of rules of behavior to which at other times they conform; it is as if they have to make a conscious effort to be conventional; as if they were conventional voluntarily and by design.

UNIT
11

Finally, this external habit of behavior can be voluntarily dropped when in the company of people who do not demand or expect routine behavior. That this relative control of behavior is felt as something of a burden is seen by our subjects' preference for such company as allows them to be more free, natural, and spontaneous, and that relieves them of what they find sometimes to be effortful conduct.

One consequence or correlate of this characteristic is that these people have codes of ethics that are relatively autonomous and individual rather than conventional. The unthinking observer might sometimes believe them to be unethical, since they can break down not only conventions but laws when the situation seems to demand it. But the very opposite is the case. They are the most ethical of people even though their ethics are not necessarily the same as those of the people around them. It is this kind of observation that leads us to understand very assuredly that the ordinary ethical behavior of the average person is largely conventional behavior rather than truly ethical behavior (e.g., behavior based on fundamentally accepted principles, which are perceived to be true).

Because of this alienation from ordinary conventions and from the ordinarily accepted hypocrisies, lies, and inconsistencies of social life, they sometimes feel like spies or aliens in a foreign land and sometimes behave so.

I should not give the impression that they try to hide what they are like. Sometimes they let themselves go deliberately, out of momentary irritation with customary rigidity or with conventional blindness. They may, for instance, be trying to teach someone or they may be trying to protect someone from hurt or injustice or they may sometimes find emotions bubbling up from within them that are so pleasant or even ecstatic that it seems almost sacrilegious to suppress them. In such instances I have observed that they are not anxious or guilty or ashamed of the impression that they make on the onlooker. It is their claim that they usually behave in a conventional fashion simply because no great issues are involved or because they know people will be hurt or embarrassed by any other kind of behavior.

Their ease of penetration to reality, their closer approach to an animallike or childlike acceptance and spontaneity imply a superior awareness of their own impulses, desires, opinion, and subjective reactions in general (Fromm, 1947; Ran, 1943; Reik, 1948). Clinical study of this capacity confirms beyond a doubt the opinion of, for example, Fromm (1941) that average, normal, well-adjusted people often have not the slightest idea of what they are, of what they want, of what their own opinions are.

It was such findings as these that led ultimately to the discovery of a most profound difference between self-actualizing people and others; namely, that the motivational life of self-actualizing people is not only quantitatively different but also qualitatively different from that of ordinary people. It seems probable that we must construct a profoundly different psychology of motivation for self-actualizing people, such as metamotivation or growth motivation, rather than deficiency motivation. Perhaps it will be useful to make a distinction between living and preparing to live. Perhaps the ordinary concept of motivation should apply *only* to nonself-actualizers. Our subjects no longer strive in the ordinary sense, but rather develop. They attempt to grow to perfection and to develop more and more fully in their own style. The motivation of ordinary people is a striving for the basic need gratifications that they lack. But self-actualizing people in fact lack none of these gratifications; and yet they have impulses. They work, they try, and they are ambitious, even though in an unusual sense. For them motivation is just character growth, character expression, maturation, and development; in a word self-actualization. Could these self-actualizing people be more human, more revealing of the original nature of the species, closer to the species type in the taxonomical sense? Ought a biological species to be judged by its crippled, warped, only partially developed specimens, or by examples that have been overdomesticated, caged, and trained?

Problem Centering

Our subjects are in general strongly focused on problems outside themselves. In current terminology they are problem centered rather than ego centered. They generally are not problems for themselves and are not generally much concerned about themselves (e.g., as contrasted with the ordinary introspectiveness that one finds in insecure people). These individuals customarily have some mission in life, some task to fulfill, some problem outside themselves which enlists much of their energies (Bühler & Massarik, 1968; Frankl, 1969).

This is not necessarily a task that they would prefer or choose for themselves; it may be a task that they feel is their responsibility, duty, or obligation. This is why we use the phrase "a task that they must do" rather than the phrase "a task that they want to do." In general these tasks are nonpersonal or unselfish, concerned rather with the good of humanity in general, or of a nation in general, or of a few individuals in the subject's family.

With few exceptions we can say that our objects are ordinarily concerned with basic issues and eternal questions of the type that we have learned to call philosophical or ethical. Such people live customarily in the widest possible frame of reference. They seem never to get so close to the trees that they fail to see the forest. They work within a framework of values that are broad and not petty, universal and not local, and in terms of a century rather than the moment. In a word, these people are all in one sense or another philosophers, however homely.

Of course, such an attitude carries with it dozens of implications for every area of daily living. For instance, one of the main presenting symptoms originally worked with (bigness, lack of smallness, triviality, or pettiness) can be subsumed under this more general heading. This impression of being above small things, of having a larger horizon, a wider breadth of vision, of living in the widest frame of reference, *sub specie aeternitatis*, is of the utmost social and interpersonal importance; it seems to impart a certain serenity and lack of worry over immediate concerns that make life easier not only for themselves but for all who are associated with them.

Solitude

For all my subjects it is true that they can be solitary without harm to themselves and without discomfort. Furthermore, it is true for almost all that they positively *like* solitude and privacy to a definitely greater degree than the average person.

It is often possible for them to remain above the battle, to remain unruffled, undisturbed by that which produces turmoil in others. They find it easy to be aloof, reserved, and also calm and serene; thus it becomes possible for them to take personal misfortunes without reacting violently as the ordinary person does. They seem to be able to retain their dignity even in undignified surroundings and situations. Perhaps this comes in part from their tendency to stick by their own interpretation of a situation rather than to rely upon what other people feel or think about the matter. This reserve may shade over into austerity and remoteness.

This quality of detachment may have some connection with certain other qualities as well. For one thing it is possible to call my subjects more objective (in *all* senses of the word) than average people. We have seen that they are more problem centered than ego centered. This is true even when the problem concerns themselves, their own wishes, motives, hopes, or aspirations. Consequently, they have the ability to concentrate to a degree not usual for ordinary people. Intense concentration produces as a by-product such phenomena as absent-mindedness, the ability to forget and to be oblivious of outer surroundings. Examples are the ability to sleep soundly, to have undisturbed appetite, and to be able to smile and laugh through a period of problems, worry, and responsibility.

UNIT
11

In social relations with most people, detachment creates certain troubles and problems. It is easily interpreted by "normal" people as coldness, snobbishness, lack of affection, unfriendliness, or even hostility. By contrast, the ordinary friendship relationship is more clinging, more demanding, more desirous of reassurance, compliment, support, warmth, and exclusiveness. It is true that self-actualizing people do not need others in the ordinary sense. But since this being needed or being missed is the usual earnest of friendship, it is evident that detachment will not easily be accepted by average people.

Another meaning of autonomy is self-decision, self-government, being an active, responsible, self-disciplined, deciding agent rather than a pawn, or helplessly "determined" by others, being strong rather than weak. My subjects make up their own minds, come to their own decisions, are self-starters, and are responsible for themselves and their own destinies. It is a subtle quality, difficult to describe in words, and yet profoundly important. They taught me to see as profoundly sick, abnormal, or weak what I had always taken for granted as humanly normal; namely, that too many people do not make up their own minds, but have their minds made up for them by salesmen, advertisers, parents, propagandists, TV, newspapers, and so on. They are pawns to be moved by others rather than self-moving, self-determined individuals. Therefore they are apt to feel helpless, weak, and totally determined; they are prey for predators, flabby whiners rather than self-determining, responsible persons. What this nonresponsibility means for self-choice politics and economics is of course obvious; it is catastrophic. Democratic self-choice society must have self-movers, self-deciders, self-choosers who make up their own minds, free agents, free-willers.

The extensive experiments by Asch (1956) and by McClelland (McClelland, 1961, 1964; McClelland & Winter, 1969) permit us to guess that self-deteminers come to perhaps 5 percent to 30 percent of our population depending on the particular circumstances. Of my self-actualizing subjects, 100 percent are self-movers.

Finally I must make a statement, even though it will certainly be disturbing to many theologians, philosophers, and scientists: self-actualizing individuals have more "free will" and are less "determined" than average people are. However the words *free will* and *determinism* may come to be operationally defined, in this investigation they are empirical realities. Furthermore, they are degree concepts, varying in amount; they are not all-or-none packages.

Autonomy

One of the characteristics of self-actualizing people, which to a certain extent crosscuts much of what we have already described, is their relative independence of the physical and social environment. Since they are propelled by growth motivation rather than by deficiency motivation, self-actualizing people are not dependent for their main satisfactions on the real world, or other people or culture or means to ends or, in general, on extrinsic satisfactions. Rather they are dependent for their own development and continued growth on their own potentialities and latent resources. Just as the tree needs sunshine and water and food, so do most people need love, safety, and other basic need gratifications that can come only from without. But once these external satisfiers are obtained, once these inner deficiencies are satiated by outside satisfiers, the true problem of individual human development begins, namely self-actualization.

This independence of environment means a relative stability in the face of hard knocks, blows, deprivations, frustrations, and the like. These people can maintain a relative serenity in the midst of circumstances that would drive other people to suicide; they have also been described as "self-contained."

Deficiency-motivated people *must* have other people available, since most of their main need gratifications (love, safety, respect, prestige, belongingness) can come only from other human beings. But growth-motivated people may actually be *hampered* by others. The determinants of satisfaction and of the good life are for them now inner-individual and *not* social. They have become strong enough to be independent of the good opinion of other people, or even of their affection. The honors, the status, the rewards, the popularity, the prestige, and the love they can bestow must have become less important than self-development and inner growth (Huxley, 1944; Northrop, 1947; Rand, 1943; Rogers, 1961). We must remember that the best technique we know, even though not the only one, for getting to this point of relative independence from love and respect is to have been given plenty of this very same love and respect in the past.

Fresh Appreciation

Self-actualizing people have the wonderful capacity to appreciate again and again, freshly and naively, the basic goods of life, with awe, pleasure, wonder, and even ecstasy, however stale these experiences may have become to others—what C. Wilson has called "newness" (1969). Thus, for such a person, any sunset may be as beautiful as the first one, any flower may be of breath-taking loveliness, even after a million flowers have been seen. The thousandth baby seen is just as miraculous a product as the first. A man remains as convinced of his luck in marriage 30 years after his marriage and is as surprised by his wife's beauty when she is 60 as he was 40 years before. For such people, even the casual workaday, moment-to-moment business of living can be thrilling, exciting, and ecstatic. These intense feelings do not come all the time; they come occasionally rather than usually, but at the most unexpected moments. The person may cross the river on the ferry ten times and at the eleventh crossing have a strong recurrence of the same feelings, reaction of beauty, and excitement as when riding the ferry for the first time (Eastman, 1928).

There are some differences in choice of beautiful objects. Some subjects go primarily to nature. For others it is primarily children, and for a few subjects it has been primarily great music; but it may certainly be said that they derive ecstasy, inspiration, and strength from the basic experiences of life. No one of them, for instance, will get this same sort of reaction from going to a night club or getting a lot of money or having a good time at a party…

It is probable that this acute richness of subjective experience is an aspect of closeness of relationship to the concrete and fresh, per se reality discussed above. Perhaps what we call staleness in experience is a consequence of categorizing or ticketing off a rich perception into one or another category or rubric as it proves to be no longer advantageous, or useful, or threatening, or otherwise ego involved (Bergson, 1944).

I have also become convinced that getting used to our blessings is one of the most important nonevil generators of human evil, tragedy, and suffering. What we take for granted we undervalue, and we are therefore too apt to sell a valuable birthright for a mess of pottage, leaving behind regret, remorse, and a lowering of self-esteem. Wives, husbands, children, friends are unfortunately more apt to be loved and appreciated after they have died than while they are still available. Something similar is true for physical health, for political freedoms, for economic well-being; we learn their true value after we have lost them.

Herzberg's studies of "hygiene" factors in industry (1966), Wilson's observations about the St. Neot's margin (1967, 1969), and my study of "low grumbles high grumbles and metagrumbles" (1965b) all show that life could be vastly improved if we could count our blessings as self-actualizing people can and do and if we could retain their constant sense of good fortune and gratitude for it.

UNIT
11

Peak Experiences

Those subjective expressions that have been called the mystic experience and described so well by William James (1958) are a fairly common experience for our subjects, though not for all. The strong emotions described in the previous section sometimes get strong, chaotic, and widespread enough to be called mystical experiences…. There were the same feelings of limitless horizons, opening up to the vision, the feeling of being simultaneously more powerful and also more helpless than one ever was before, the feeling of great ecstasy and wonder and awe, the loss of placing in time and space with, finally, the conviction that something extremely important and valuable had happened, so that the subject is to some extent transformed and strengthened even in daily life by such experiences.

It is quite important to dissociate this experience from any theological or supernatural reference, even though for thousands of years they have been linked. Because this experience is a natural experience, well within the jurisdiction of science, I call it the peak experience.

We may also learn from our subjects that such experiences can occur in a lesser degree of intensity. The theological literature has generally assumed an absolute, qualitative difference between the mystic experience and all others. As soon as it is divorced from supernatural reference and studied as a natural phenomenon, it becomes possible to place the mystic experience on a quantitative continuum from intense to mild. We discover then that the *mild* mystic experience occurs in many, perhaps even most, individuals, and that in the favored individual it occurs often, perhaps even daily.

Apparently the acute mystic or peak experience is a tremendous intensification of *any* of the experiences in which there is loss of self or transcendence of it, such as problem centering, intense concentration, intense sensuous experience, or self-forgetful and intense enjoyment of music or art.

I have learned through the years since this study was first begun in 1935 to lay far greater stress than I had at first on the differences between "peakers" and "nonpeakers." Most likely this is a difference of degree or amount, but it is a very important difference. Some of its consequences are set forth in considerable detail in Maslow, 1969b. If I had to sum it up very briefly, I would say that the nonpeaking self-actualizers seem so far to tend to be practical, effective people, mesomorphs living in the world and doing very well in it. Peakers seem *also* to live in the realm of Being; of poetry, aesthetics; symbols; transcendence; "religion" of the mystical, personal, noninstitutional sort; and of end experiences. My prediction is that this will turn out to be one of the crucial characterological "class differences," crucial especially for social life because it looks as though the "merely healthy" nonpeaking self-actualizers seem likely to be the social world improvers, the politicians, the workers in society, the reformers, the crusaders, whereas the transcending peakers are more apt to write the poetry, the music, the philosophies, and the religions.

Human Kinship

Self-actualizing people have a deep feeling of identification, sympathy, and affection for human beings in general. They feel kinship and connection, as if all people were members of a single family. One's feelings toward siblings would be on the whole affectionate, even if they were foolish, weak, or even if they were sometimes nasty. They would still be more easily forgiven than strangers. Because of this, self-actualizing people have a genuine desire to help the human race.

If one's view is not general enough and if it is not spread over a long period of time, then one may not see this feeling of identification with mankind. Self-actualizing people are after all very different from other people in thought, impulse, behavior, and emotion. When it comes down to it, in certain basic ways they are like aliens in a strange land. Very few really understand them, however much they may like them. They are often saddened, exasperated, and even enraged by the shortcomings of the average person, and while these are ordinarily no more than a nuisance, they sometimes become bitter tragedy. However far apart they are at times, they nevertheless feel a basic underlying kinship with these creatures whom they must regard with, if not condescension, at least the knowledge that they themselves can do many things better than others can, that they can see things that others cannot see, and that the truth that is so clear to them is for most people veiled and hidden.

Humility and Respect

All my subjects without exception may be said to be democratic people in the deepest possible sense. I say this on the basis of a previous analysis of authoritarian (Maslow, 1943) and democratic character structures that is too elaborate to present here; it is possible only to describe some aspects of this behavior in short space. These people have all the obvious or superficial democratic characteristics. They can be and are friendly with anyone of suitable character regardless of class, education, political belief, race, or color. As a matter of fact it often seems as if they are not even aware of these differences, which are for the average person so obvious and so important.

They have not only this most obvious quality but their democratic feeling goes deeper as well. For instance they find it possible to learn from anybody who has something to teach them—no matter what other characteristics he or she may have. In such a learning relationship they do not try to maintain any outward dignity or to maintain status or age prestige and the like. It should even be said that my subjects share a quality that could be called humility of a certain type. They are all quite well aware of how little they know in comparison with what *could* be known and what *is* known by others. Because of this it is possible for them without pose to be honestly respectful and even humble before people who can teach them something that they do not know or who have a skill they do not possess. They give this honest respect to a carpenter who is a good carpenter, or for that matter to anybody who is a master of his own tools or his own craft.

The careful distinction must be made between this democratic feeling and a lack of discrimination in taste, of an undiscriminating equalizing of any one human being with any other. These individuals, themselves elite, select for their friends elite, but this is an elite of character, capacity, and talent, rather than of birth, race, blood, name, family, age, youth, fame, or power.

Most profound, but also most vague is the hard-to-get-at tendency to give a certain quantum of respect to *any* human being just because he or she is a human individual; our subjects seem not to wish to go beyond a certain minimum point, even with scoundrels, of demeaning, of derogating, or robbing of dignity. And yet this goes along with their strong sense of right and wrong, of good and evil. They are more likely rather than less likely to counterattack against evil people and evil behavior. They are far less ambivalent, confused, or weak-willed about their own anger than average people are.

Interpersonal Relationships

Self-actualizing people have deeper and more profound interpersonal relations than any other adults (although not necessarily deeper than those of children). They are capable of more fusion, greater love, more perfect identification, more obliteration of the ego boundaries than other people would consider possible. There are, however, certain special characteristics of these relationships. In the first place, it is my observation that the other members of these relationships are likely to be healthier and closer to self-actualization than the average, often *much* closer. There is high selectiveness here, considering the small proportion of such people in the general population.

One consequence of this phenomenon and of certain others as well is that self-actualizing people have these especially deep ties with rather few individuals. Their circle of friends is rather small. The ones that they love profoundly are few in number. Partly this is for the reason that being very close to someone in this self-actualizing style seems to require a good deal of time. Devotion is not a matter of a moment. One subject expressed it like this: "I haven't got time for many friends. Nobody has, that is, if they are to be *real* friends." This exclusiveness of devotion can and does exist side by side with a widespreading human warmth, benevolence, affection, and friendliness (as qualified above). These people *tend* to be kind or at least patient to almost everyone. They have an especially tender love for children and are easily touched by them. In a very real even though special sense, they love or rather have compassion for all humanity.

This love does not imply lack of discrimination. The fact is that they can and do speak realistically and harshly of those who deserve it, and especially of the hypocritical, the pretentious, the pompous, or the self-inflated. But the face-to-face relationships even with these people do not always show signs of realistically low evaluations. One explanatory statement was about as follows: "Most people, after all, do not amount to much but they *could* have. They make all sorts of foolish mistakes and wind up being miserable and not knowing how they got that way when their intentions were good. Those who are not nice are usually paying for it in deep unhappiness. They should be pitied rather than attacked."

Perhaps the briefest possible description is to say that their hostile reactions to others are (1) deserved, and (2) for the good of the person attacked or for someone else's good. This is to say, with Fromm, that their hostility is not character based, but is reactive or situational.

All the subjects for whom I have data show in common another characteristic that is appropriate to mention here, namely, that they attract at least some admirers, friends, or even disciples or worshippers. The relation between the individual and his or her train of admirers is apt to be rather one-sided. The admirers are apt to demand more than our individual is willing to give. And, furthermore, these devotions can be rather embarrassing, distressing, and even distasteful to the self-actualizing person, since they often go beyond ordinary bounds. The usual picture is of our subject being kind and pleasant when forced into these relationships, but ordinarily trying to avoid them as gracefully as possible.

Ethics

I have found none of my subjects to be chronically unsure about the difference between right and wrong in their actual living. Whether or not they could verbalize the matter, they rarely showed in their day-to-day living the chaos, the confusion, the inconsistency, or the conflict that are so common in the average person's ethical dealings. This may be phrased also in the following terms: these individuals are strongly ethical, they have definite moral standards, they do right and do not do wrong. Needless to say, their notions of right and wrong and of good and evil are often not the conventional ones.

One way of expressing the quality I am trying to describe was suggested by Dr. David Levy, who pointed out that a few centuries ago these would all have been described as men who walk in the path of God or as godly men. A few say that they believe in a God, but describe this God more as a metaphysical concept than as a personal figure. If religion is defined only in social-behavioral terms, then these are all religious people, the atheists included. But if more conservatively we use the term *religion* to stress the supernatural element and institutional orthodoxy (certainly the more common usage) then our answer must be quite different, for then very few of them are religious.

Means and Ends

Self-actualizing people most of the time behave as though, for them, means and ends are clearly distinguishable. In general, they are fixed on ends rather than on means, and means are quite definitely subordinated to these ends. This, however, is an overly simple statement. Our subjects make the situation more complex by often regarding as ends in themselves many experiences and activities that are, for other people, only means. Our subjects are somewhat more likely to appreciate for its own sake, and in an absolute way, the doing itself; they can often enjoy for its own sake the getting to some place as well as the arriving. It is occasionally possible for them to make out of the most trivial and routine activity an intrinsically enjoyable game or dance or play. Wertheimer pointed out that most children are so creative that they can transform hackneyed routine, mechanical, and rote experiences (e.g., as in one of his experiments, transporting books from one set of shelves to another) into a structured and amusing game of a sort by doing this according to a certain system or with a certain rhythm.

Humor

One very early finding that was quite easy to make, because it was common to all my subjects, was that their sense of humor is not of the ordinary type. They do not consider funny what the average person considers to be funny. Thus they do not laugh at hostile humor (making people laugh by hurting someone) or superiority humor (laughing at someone else's inferiority) or authority-rebellion humor (the unfunny, Oedipal, or smutty joke). Characteristically what they consider humor is more closely allied to philosophy than to anything else. It may also be called the humor of the real because it consists in large part in poking fun at human beings in general when they are foolish, or forget their place in the universe, or try to be big when they are actually small. This can take the form of poking fun at themselves, but this is not done in any masochistic or clownlike way. Lincoln's humor can serve as a suitable example. Probably Lincoln never made a joke that hurt anybody else; it is also likely that many or even most of his jokes had something to say, had a function beyond just producing a laugh. They often seemed to be education in a more palatable form, akin to parables or fables.

On a simple quantitative basis, our subjects may be said to be humorous less often than the average of the population. Punning, joking, witty remarks, gay repartee, persiflage of the ordinary sort is much less often seen than the rather thoughtful, philosophical humor that elicits a smile more usually than a laugh, that is intrinsic to the situation rather than added to it, that is spontaneous rather than planned, and that very often can never be repeated. It should not be surprising that average people, accustomed as they are to joke books and belly laughs, consider our subjects to be rather on the sober and serious side.

Such humor can be very pervasive; the human situation, human pride, seriousness, busy-ness, bustle, ambition, striving and planning can all be seen as amusing, humorous, even funny. I once understood this attitude, I thought, in a room full of "kinetic art," which seemed to me to be a humorous parody of human life, with the noise, movement, turmoil, hurry and bustle, all of it going no place. This attitude also rubs off on professional work itself, which in a certain sense is also play, and which, though taken seriously, is somehow also taken lightly.

Creativity

This is a universal characteristic of all the people studied or observed (see Chapter 13, "Creativity in Self-actualizing People"). There is no exception. Each one shows in one way or another a special kind of creativeness or originality or inventiveness that has certain peculiar characteristics. These special characteristics can be understood more fully in the light of discussion later in this chapter. For one thing, it is different from the special-talent creativeness of the Mozart type. We may as well face the fact that the so-called geniuses display ability that we do not understand. All we can say of them is that they seem to be specially endowed with a drive and a capacity that may have rather little relationship to the rest of the personality and with which, from all evidence, the individuals seem to be born. Such talent we have no concern with here since it does not rest upon psychic health or basic satisfaction. The creativeness of the self-actualized person seems rather to be kin to the naïve and universal creativeness of unspoiled children. It seems to be more a fundamental characteristic of common human nature—a potentiality given to all human beings at birth. Most human beings lose this as they become enculturated, but some few individuals seem either to retain this fresh and naïve, direct way of looking at life, or if they have lost it, as most people do, they later in life recover it. Santayana called this the "second naiveté," a very good name for it.

This creativeness appears in some of our subjects not in the usual forms of writing books, composing music, or producing artistic objects, but rather may be much more humble. It is as if this special type of creativeness, being an expression of healthy personality, is projected out upon the world or touches whatever activity the person is engaged in. In this sense there can be creative shoemakers or carpenters or clerks. Whatever one does can be done with a certain attitude, a certain spirit that arises out of the nature of the character of the person performing the act. One can even *see* creatively as the child does.

This quality is differentiated out here for the sake of discussion, as if it were something separate from the characteristics that precede it and follow it, but this is not actually the case. Perhaps when we speak of creativeness here we are simply describing from another point of view, namely, from the point of view of consequences, what we have described above as a greater freshness, penetration, and efficiency of perception. These people seem to see the true and the real more easily. It is because of this that they seem to other more limited men creative.

Furthermore, as we have seen, these individuals are less inhibited, less constricted, less bound, in a word, less enculturated. In more positive terms, they are more spontaneous, more natural, more human. This too would have as one of its consequences what would seem to other people to be creativeness. If we assume, as we may from our study of children, that all people were once spontaneous, and perhaps in their deepest roots still are, but that these people have in addition to the deep spontaneity a superficial but powerful set of inhibitions, then this spontaneity must be checked so as not to appear very often. If there were no choking-off forces, we might expect that every human being would show this special type of creativeness (Anderson, 1959; Maslow, 1958).

Resistance to Enculturation

Self-actualizing people are not well adjusted (in the naïve sense of approval of and identification with the culture). They get along with the culture in various ways, but of all of them it may be said that in a certain profound and meaningful sense they resist enculturation and maintain a certain inner detachment from the culture in which they are immersed. Since in the culture-and-personality literature very little has been said about resistance to molding by the culture, and since, as Riesman (1950) has clearly pointed out, the saving remnant is especially important for American society, even our meager data are of some importance.

On the whole the relationship of these healthy people with their much less healthy culture is a complex one; from it can be teased out at least the following components.

1. All these people fall well within the limits of apparent conventionality in choice of clothes, of language, of food, of ways of doing things in our culture. And yet they are not *really* conventional, certainly not fashionable or smart or chic. The expressed inner attitude is usually that

it is ordinarily of no great consequence which folkways are used, that one set of traffic rules is as good as any other set, that while they make life smoother they do not really matter enough to make a fuss about. Here again we see the general tendency of these people to accept most states of affairs that they consider unimportant or unchangeable or not of primary concern to them as individuals. Since choice of shoes, or style of haircut or politeness, or manner of behaving at a party are not of primary concern to any of the individuals studied, they are apt to elicit as a reaction only a shrug of the shoulders. These are not moral issues. But since this tolerant acceptance of harmless folkways is not warm approval with identification, their yielding to convention is apt to be rather casual and perfunctory, with cutting of corners in favor of directness, honesty, saving of energy, and so on. In the pinch, when yielding to conventions is too annoying or too expensive, the apparent conventionality reveals itself for the superficial thing that it is, and is tossed off as easily as a cloak.

2.   Hardly any of these people can be called authority rebels in the adolescent or hot sense. They show no active impatience or moment-to-moment, chronic, long-time discontent with the culture or preoccupation with changing it quickly, although they often enough show bursts of indignation with injustice. One of these subjects, who was a hot rebel in his younger days, a union organizer in the days when this was a highly dangerous occupation, has given up in disgust and hopelessness. As he became resigned to the slowness of social change (in this culture and in this era) he turned finally to education of the young. All the others show what might be called a calm, long-time concern with culture improvement that seems to me to imply an acceptance of slowness of change along with the unquestioned desirability and necessity of such change. This is by no means a lack of fight. When quick change is possible or when resolution and courage are needed, it is available in these people. Although they are not a a radical group of people in the ordinary sense, I think they easily *could* be. First of all, this is primarily an intellectual group (it must be remembered who selected them), most of whom already have a mission and feel that they are doing something really important to improve the world. Second, they are a realistic group and seem to be unwilling to make great but useless sacrifices. In a more drastic situation it seems very likely that they would be willing to drop their work in favor of radical social action (e.g., the anti-Nazi underground in Germany or in France). My impression is that they are not against fighting but only against ineffective fighting. Another point that came up very commonly in discussion was the desirability of enjoying life and having a good time. This seems to all but one to be incompatible with hot and full-time rebelliousness. Furthermore, it seems to them that this is too great a sacrifice to make for the small returns expected. Most of them have had their episodes of fighting, impatience, and eagerness in youth, and in most cases have learned that their optimism about quick change was unwarranted. What they settled down to as a group was an accepting, calm, good-humored everyday effort to improve the culture, usually from within, rather than to reject it wholly and fight it from without.

3.   An inner feeling of detachment from the culture is not necessarily conscious but is displayed by almost all, particularly in discussions of the American culture as a whole, in various comparisons with other cultures, and in the fact that they very frequently seem to be able to stand off from it as if they did not quite belong to it. The mixture of varying proportions of affection or approval and hostility or criticism indicated that they select from American culture what is good in it by their lights and reject what they think bad in it. In a word they weigh it, assay it, taste it, and then make their own decisions. This is certainly very different from the ordinary sort of passive yielding to cultural shaping displayed for instance by the ethnocentric subjects of the many studies of authoritarian personalities. It is also different from the total rejection of what after all is a relatively good culture, that is, when compared

with other cultures that actually *exist*, rather than fantasied heavens of perfection (or as one lapel button put it, Nirvana *Now!*). Detachment from the culture is probably also reflected in our self-actualizing subjects' detachment from people and their liking for privacy, which has been described above, as also in their less than average need for the familiar and customary.

4. For these and other reasons they may be called autonomous, that is, ruled by the laws of their own character rather than by the rules of society. It is in this sense that they are not only or merely Americans, but also, to a greater degree than others, members at large of the human species. To say that they are above or beyond the American culture would be misleading if interpreted strictly, for after all they speak American, act American, have American characters, and so forth. And yet if we compare them with the oversocialized, the robotized, or the ethnocentric, we are irresistibly tempted to hypothesize that this group is not simply another subcultural group, but rather less enculturated, less flattened out, less molded. This implies degree, and placing on a continuum that ranges from relative acceptance of the cuture to relative detachment from it. If this turns out to be a tenable hypothesis, at least one other hypotheses can be deduced from it: that those individuals in different cultures who are more detached from their own culture should not only have less national character but also should be more like each other in certain respects than they are like the less developed members of their own societies.

In summary the perennial question "Is it possible to be a good or healthy man in an imperfect culture?" has been answered by the observation that it is possible for relatively healthy people to develop in the American culture. They manage to get along by a complex combination of inner autonomy and outer acceptance that of course will be possible only so long as the culture remains tolerant of this kind of detached withholding from complete cultural identification.

Of course this is not ideal health. Our imperfect society clearly forces inhibitions and restraints upon our subjects. To the extent that they have to maintain their little secrecies, to that extent is their spontaneity lessened and to that extent are some of their potentialities not actualized. And since only few people can attain health in our culture (or perhaps in any culture), those who do attain it are lonely for their own kind and are therefore less spontaneous and less actualized.

Imperfections

The ordinary mistake that is made by novelists, poets, and essayists about good human beings is to make them so good that they are caricatures, so that nobody would like to be like them. The individual's own wishes for perfection and guilt and shame about shortcomings are projected upon various kinds of people from whom average people demand much more than they themselves give. Thus teachers and ministers are sometimes conceived to be rather joyless people who have no mundane desires and who have no weaknesses. It is my belief that most of the novelists who have attempted to portray good (healthy) people did this sort of thing, making them into stuffed shirts or marionettes or unreal projections of unreal ideals, rather than into the robust, hearty, lusty individuals they really are. Our subjects show many of the lesser human failings. They too are equipped with silly, wasteful, or thoughtless habits. They can be boring, stubborn, irritating. They are by no means free from a rather superficial vanity, pride, partiality to their own productions, family, friends, and children. Temper outbursts are not rare.

Our subjects are occasionally capable of an extraordinary and unexpected ruthlessness. It must be remembered that they are very strong people. This makes it possible for them to display a surgical coldness when this is called for, beyond the power of average people. The man who found that a long-trusted acquaintance was dishonest cut himself off from this friendship sharply and abruptly and without any observable pangs whatsoever. A woman who was married to someone she did not love, when she decided on divorce, did it with such decisiveness that looked almost like ruthlessness. Some of them recover so quickly from the death of people close to them as to seem heartless.

We may mention one more example that arises primarily from the absorption of our subjects in an impersonal world. In their concentration, in the fascinated interest, in their intense concentration on some phenomenon or question, they may become absent-minded or humorless and forget their ordinary social politeness. In such circumstances, they are apt to show themselves more clearly as essentially not interested in chatting, gay conversation, party-going, or the like; they may use language or behavior that may be very distressing, shocking, insulting, or hurtful to others. Other undesirable (at least from the point of view of others) consequences of detachment have been listed above.

Even their kindness can lead them into mistakes, such as marrying out of pity, getting too closely involved with neurotics, bores, or unhappy people and then being sorry for it, allowing scoundrels to impose on them for a while, or giving more than they should so that occasionally they encourage parasites and psychopaths.

Finally, it has already been pointed out that these people are *not* free of guilt, anxiety, sadness, self-castigation, internal strife, and conflict. The fact that these arise out of nonneurotic sources is of little consequence to most people today (even to most psychologists) who are therefore apt to think them *un*healthy for this reason.

What this has taught me I think all of us had better learn. *There are no perfect human beings!* Persons can be found who are good, very good indeed, in fact, great. There do in fact exist creators, seers, sages, saints, shakers, and movers. This can certainly give us hope for the future of the species even if they can at times be boring, irritating, petulant, selfish, angry, or depressed. To avoid disillusionment with human nature, we must first give up our illusions about it.

Values

A firm foundation for a value system is automatically furnished to self-actualizers by their philosophic acceptance of the nature of self, of human nature, of much of social life, and of nature and physical reality. These acceptance values account for a high percentage of the total of their individual value judgments from day to day. What they approve of, disapprove of, are loyal to, oppose or propose, what pleases them or displeases them can often be understood as surface derivations of the source trait of acceptance.

Not only is this foundation automatically (and universally) supplied to *all* self-actualizers by their intrinsic dynamics (so that in at least this respect fully developed human nature may be universal and cross-cultural); other determiners are supplied as well by these same dynamics. Among these are (1) their peculiarly comfortable relationships with reality, (2) their feeling of human kinship, (3) their basically satisfied condition from which flow, as epiphenomena, various consequences of surplus, of wealth, overflowing abundance, (4) their characteristically discriminating relations to means and ends, and so on (see above).

One most important consequence of this attitude toward the world—as well as a validation of it—is the fact that conflict and struggle, ambivalence and uncertainty over choice lessen or disappear in many areas of life. Apparently much so-called morality is largely an epiphenomenon of nonacceptance or dissatisfaction. Many problems are seen to be gratuitous and fade out of existence in the atmosphere of pagan acceptance. It is not so much that the problem is solved as that it becomes clearly seen that it never was an intrinsic problem in the first place, but only a sick-person-created one, such as card playing, dancing, wearing short dresses, exposing the head (in some churches) or *not* exposing the head (in others), drinking wine, or eating some meats and not others, or eating them on some days but not on others. Not only are such trivialities deflated; the process also goes on at a more important level, such as in the relations between the sexes, attitudes toward the structure of the body and toward its functioning, and toward death itself.

The pursuit of this finding to more profound levels has suggested to the writer that much else of what passes for morals, ethics, and values may be simple by-products of the pervasive psychopathology of the average. Many conflicts, frustrations, and threats (which force the kind of choice in which value is expressed) evaporate or resolve for self-actualizing people in the same way as do, let us say, conflicts over dancing. For them the seemingly irreconcilable battle of the sexes becomes no conflict at all but rather a delightful collaboration. The antagonistic interests of adults and children turn out to be not so antagonistic after all. Just as with sex and age differences, so also is it with natural differences, class and caste differences, political differences, role differences, religious differences, and the like. As we know, these are each fertile breeding grounds for anxiety, fear, hostility, aggression, defensiveness, and jealousy. But it begins to appear that they *need not be*, for our subjects' reaction to differences is much less often of this undesirable type. They are more apt to enjoy differences than to fear them.

To take the teacher-student relationship as a specific paradigm, our teacher subjects behaved in a very unneurotic way simply by interpreting the whole situation differently, for example, as a pleasant collaboration rather than as a clash of wills, of authority, of dignity, and so on; the replacement of artificial dignity—which is easily and inevitably threatened—with the natural simplicity, which is *not* easily threatened; the giving up of the attempt to be omniscient and omnipotent; the absence of student-threatening authoritarianism; the refusal to regard the students as competing with each other or with the teacher; the refusal to assume the professor stereotype and the insistence on remaining as realistically human as say, a plumber or a carpenter; all of these create a classroom atmosphere in which suspicion, wariness, defensiveness, hostility, and anxiety tend to disappear. So also do similar threat responses tend to disappear in marriages, in families, and in other interpersonal situations when threat itself is reduced.

The principles and the values of the desperate person and of the psychologically healthy person must be different in at least some ways. They have profoundly different perceptions (interpretations) of the physical world, the social world, and the private psychological world, whose organization and economy is in part the responsibility of the person's value system. For basically deprived people the world is a dangerous place, a jungle, an enemy territory populated by (1) those whom they can dominate and (2) those who can dominate them. Their value systems are of necessity, like those of any jungle denizen, dominated and organized by the lower needs, especially the creature needs and the safety needs. Basically satisfied people are a different case. They can afford out of their abundance to take these needs and their satisfaction for granted and can devote themselves to higher gratifications. This is to say that their value systems are different, in fact *must* be different.

The topmost portion of the value system of the self-actualized person is entirely unique and idiosyncratic-character-structure-expressive. This must be true by definition, for self-actualization is actualization of a self, and no two selves are altogether alike. There is only one Renoir, one Brahms, one Spinoza. Our subjects had very much in common, as we have seen, and yet at the same time were more completely individualized, more unmistakably themselves, less easily confounded with others than any average control group could possibly be. That is to say, they are simultaneously very much alike and very much unlike each other. They are more completely individual than any group that has ever been described, and yet are also more completely socialized, more identified with humanity than any other group yet described. They are closer to *both* their specieshood and to their unique individuality.

Resolution of Dichotomies

At this point we may finally allow ourselves to generalize and underscore a very important theoretical conclusion derivable from the study of self-actualizing people. At several points in this chapter—and in other chapters as well—it was concluded that what had been considered in the past to be polarities or opposites or dichotomies were so *only in less healthy people*. In healthy people, these dichotomies were resolved, the polarities disappeared, and many oppositions thought to be intrinsic merged and coalesced with each other to form unities. See also Chenault (1969).

For example the age-old opposition between heart and head, reason and instinct, or cognition and conation was seen to disappear in healthy people where they become synergic rather than antagonists, and where conflict between them disappears because they say the same thing and point to the same conclusion. In a word in these people, desires are in excellent accord with reason. St. Augustine's "Love God and do as you will" can easily be translated "Be healthy and then you may trust your impulses."

The dichotomy between selfishness and unselfishness disappears altogether in healthy people because in principle every act is *both* selfish and unselfish. Our subjects are simultaneously very spiritual and very pagan and sensual even to the point where sexuality becomes a *path* to the spiritual and "religious." Duty cannot be contrasted with pleasure nor work with play when duty is pleasure, when work is play, and people doing their duty and being virtuous are simultaneously seeking their pleasure and being happy. If the most socially identified people are themselves also the most individualistic people, of what use is it to retain the polarity? If the most mature are also childlike? And if the most ethical and moral people are also the lustiest and most animal?

Similar findings have been reached for kindness-ruthlessness, concreteness-abstractness, acceptance-rebellion, self-society, adjustment-maladjustment, detachment from others-identification with others, serious-humorous, Dionysian-Apollonian, introverted-extraverted, intense-casual, serious-frivolous, conventional-unconventional, mystic-realistic, active-passive, masculine-feminine, lust-love, and Eros-Agape. In these people, the id, the ego, and the superego are collaborative and synergic; they do not war with each other nor are their interests in basic disagreement as they are in neurotic people. So also do the cognitive, the impulsive, and the emotional coalesce into an organismic unity and into a non-Aristotelian interpenetration. The higher and the lower are not in opposition but in agreement, and a thousand serious philosophical dilemmas are discovered to have more than two horns or, paradoxically, no horns at all. If the war between the sexes turns out to be no war at all in matured people, but only a sign of crippling and stunting of growth, who then would wish to choose sides? Who would deliberately and knowingly choose psychopathology? Is it necessary to choose between the good woman and the bad, as if they were mutually exclusive, when we have found that the really healthy woman is both at the same time?

In this, as in other ways, healthy people are so different from average ones, not only in degree but in kind as well, that they generate two very different kinds of psychology. It becomes more and more clear that the study of crippled, stunted, immature, and unhealthy specimens can yield only a cripple psychology and cripple philosophy. The study of self-actualizing people must be the basis for a more universal science of psychology.

"Freedom from Fear"

By Aung San Suu Kyi (1945–)
Burmese Pro-Democracy Activist and Political Leader

Introduction and Historical Background

The increasing complexity of organizations by the 1950s demanded new definitions and observations of how systems work. In his book, *General System Theory*, Ludwig von Bertalanffy made a breakthrough in organizational thinking. Bertalanffy was a biologist who was used to observing living organisms. His observations led him to conclude that organizations were like life forms. Not only were they both made up of hundreds of elements interacting with each other, but they also responded to input from outside. These observations led to the development of what is called Systems Theory.

Systems Theory suggests that all complex systems, such as organizations, are made up of subsystems. Further, because systems react to outside input, there are multiple and numerous possible causes for an event. This concept of multiple-causation is at the heart of Systems thinking. Leaders in the era of Systems Theory began to realize that they must pay attention to multiple influences: the nature of the work or task or mission, the relationships among people, and the environment. Each individual may be affected differently by these things, so Systems Theory assumes a high level of sophistication on the part of the leader, particularly in understanding human behavior. Within each contact the leader must decide the right course of action and approach to the follower. The leader is constantly asking the question: Do I focus on the task and give direction or do I focus on my relationship with the employee and give support? From Systems Theory thinking come leadership theories like Contingency Theory from Fred Fiedler and Situational Leadership from Paul Hersey and Kenneth Blanchard. In the broad category of Systems Theory, environments are assumed to be multi-dimensional and possess identifiable characteristics like climate and culture. These climates are invisible and are formed over time by the physical dimensions of the environment and the interaction of the people within it. These patterns eventually become accepted by the group although never officially identified or acknowledged.

In Systems Theory, conflict is seen as inevitable and the leader's ability to mediate conflict is highly prized. Communication in this theory is both informal and participatory, resulting in group decision making. In Systems Theory the leader must also be skilled at motivating the members of the group or organization. Answering the question correctly and providing the appropriate response to employee needs is critical in Systems Theory.

Aung San Suu Kyi is a contemporary leader seeking to establish democracy in her country Burma, known as Myanmar under the military rule that has existed there since 1962. Her writing provides an example of Systems Theory thinking in action: she shows an awareness of the complexity of her country's situation and multiple strong influences including its history and international sanctions; she emphasizes the political, social, and economic environment; she understands the importance of communications to keep people engaged and informed of these circumstances and the direction she advocates. She combines historical context and her desires for democracy and better conditions for the Burmese people effectively, paradoxically acknowledging both her unique leadership and insisting on loyalty to ideas and to the people rather than relying on a single leader for the opposition movement. Adding further complexity, not to mention significant hardship, the military government has detained her or kept her under house arrest for most of the past 15 years.

Aung San Suu Kyi was born in 1945, daughter of national hero General Aung San who led the Burma Independence Movement and was assassinated in 1947 (Burma was under British rule from 1885 until 1948). Aung San Suu Kyi first left Burma in 1960 with her mother, whom the government had appointed Ambassador to India. She later earned a degree from Oxford and eventually married an English academic, Michael Aris, in 1972. She remained devoted to her family and country, however, and her husband related that she constantly reminded him that one day she would have to return to Burma. She did not return to Burma until 1988 when she received news of her mother's illness. In the same month, the military dictator announced his resignation after 26 years of rule, sparking pro-democracy demonstrations. By August, there were mass uprisings against the military government, and the government cracked down, killing thousands. Aung San Suu Kyi delivered a speech before hundreds of thousands of people in Rangoon following the crackdown and emerged as the leader of the democracy movement. In September, Aung San Suu Kyi became head of the new National League for Democracy (NLD). The NLD and Aung San Suu Kyi campaigned furiously during the coming months under constant threat from the military. In July 1989, she was detained and kept under house arrest without charges, a hearing, or trial. Despite her continuing detention, the NLD won a huge majority in the general elections in April of 1990, securing 82 percent of the seats in the legislature, but the military junta refused to recognize the results of the election. The military retroactively changed the law under which they held her, stating that they would enforce the detention for up to five years, but would allow her to leave Burma to be with her husband and sons "on humanitarian grounds." Understanding that she would be exiled and not allowed to return, Aung San Suu Kyi chose to remain in Burma. Between 1989 and 2010, she spent a total of 15 years under house arrest, often to prevent her participation in events the military organized for public participation to appear more democratic. In 1991, she was awarded the Nobel Peace Prize, in absentia.

In 2006, the military rulers convened a constitutional convention and prevented Aung San Suu Kyi's participation. A revised constitution was published in 2008 to begin transition to a democratic state, but the referendum to adopt it and national elections in 2010 were criticized for widespread alleged fraud on the part of the ruling military party. In 2010, after winning a majority in parliament, the military released Aung San Suu Kyi from house arrest. She ran for a parliamentary seat and won in the 2012 elections.

Points to Consider

1. Aung San Suu Kyi focuses on both inner attributes of those seeking democracy in Burma and the conditions imposed by the military government. What are some of these inner attributes of people she admires and encourages? What are the conditions she describes in the country? Is it realistic for these attributes to overcome and change the conditions in Burma? Why or why not?

2. Vaclav Havel has written that "Aung San Suu Kyi cannot be silenced because she speaks the truth and because her words reflect basic Burmese and universal concepts." What concepts does she present in this reading that you agree are universal?

"Freedom from Fear"

(Excerpt)

The following was first released for publication by the editor to commemorate the European Parliament's award to Aung San Suu Kyi of the 1990 Sakharov Prize for Freedom of Thought. The award ceremony took place in her absence at Strasbourg on 10 July 1991. In the same week the essay appeared in full or in part in The Times Literary Supplement, The New York Times, The Far Eastern Economic Review, The Bangkok Post, the Times of India *and in the German, Norwegian and Icelandic press. [This reading is one chapter in a collection of Aung San Suu Kyi's writing and speeches edited by her husband, Michael Aris, who died in 1997.]*

It is not power that corrupts but fear. Fear of losing power corrupts those who wield it and fear of the scourge of power corrupts those who are subject to it. Most Burmese are familiar with the four *a-gati*, the four kinds of corruption. *Chanda-gati*, corruption induced by desire, is deviation from the right path in pursuit of bribes or for the sake of those one loves. *Dosa-gati* is taking the wrong path to spite those against whom one bears ill will, and *moha-gati* is aberration due to ignorance. But perhaps the worst of the four is *bhaya-gati*, for not only does *bhaya*, fear, stifle and slowly destroy all sense of right and wrong, it so often lies at the root of the other three kinds of corruption.

Just as *chanda-gati*, when not the result of sheer avarice, can be caused by fear of want or fear of losing the goodwill of those one loves, so fear of being surpassed, humiliated or injured in some way can provide the impetus for ill will. And it would be difficult to dispel ignorance unless there is freedom to pursue the truth unfettered by fear. With so close a relationship between fear and corruption it is little wonder that in any society where fear is rife corruption in all forms becomes deeply entrenched.

Public dissatisfaction with economic hardships has been seen as the chief cause of the movement for democracy in Burma, sparked off by the student demonstrations of 1988. It is true that years of incoherent policies, inept official measures, burgeoning inflation and falling real income had turned the country into an economic shambles. But it was more than the difficulties of eking out a barely acceptable standard of living that had eroded the patience of a traditionally good-natured, quiescent people—it was also the humiliation of a way of life disfigured by corruption and fear. The students were protesting not just against the death of their comrades but against the denial of their right to life by a totalitarian regime which deprived the present of meaning-fulness and held out no hope for the future. And because the students' protests articulated the frustrations of the people at large, the demonstrations quickly grew into a nationwide movement. Some of its keenest supporters were businessmen who had developed the skills and the contacts necessary not only to survive but to prosper within the system. But their affluence offered them no genuine sense of security or fulfillment, and they could not but see that if they and their fellow citizens, regardless of economic status, were to achieve a worthwhile existence, an accountable administration was at least a necessary if not a sufficient condition. The people of Burma had wearied of a precarious state of passive apprehension where they were "as water in the cupped hands" of the powers that be.

> Emerald cool we may be
> As water in cupped hands
> But oh that we might be
> As splinters of glass
> In cupped hands.

Glass splinters, the smallest with its sharp, glinting power to defend itself against hands that try to crush, could be seen as a vivid symbol of the spark of courage that is an essential attribute of those who would free themselves from the grip of oppression. Bogyoke Aung San regarded himself as a revolutionary and searched tirelessly for answers to the problems that beset Burma during her times of trial. He exhorted the people to develop courage: "Don't just depend on the courage and intrepidity of others. Each and every one of you must make sacrifices to become a hero possessed of courage and intrepidity. Then only shall we all be able to enjoy true freedom."

The effort necessary to remain uncorrupted in an environment where fear is an integral part of everyday existence is not immediately apparent to those fortunate enough to live in states governed by the rule of law. Just laws do not merely prevent corruption by meting out impartial punishment to offenders. They also help to create a society in which people can fulfil [sic] the basic requirements necessary for the preservation of human dignity without recourse to corrupt practices. Where there are no such laws, the burden of upholding the principles of justice and common decency falls on the ordinary people. It is the cumulative effect of their sustained effort and steady endurance which will change a nation where reason and conscience are warped by fear into one where legal rules exist to promote man's desire for harmony and justice while restraining the less desirable destructive traits in his nature.

In an age when immense technological advances have created lethal weapons which could be, and are, used by the powerful and the unprincipled to dominate the weak and the helpless, there is a compelling need for a closer relationship between politics and ethics at both the national and international levels. The Universal Declaration of Human Rights of the United Nations proclaims that "every individual and every organ of society" should strive to promote the basic rights and freedoms to which all human beings regardless of race, nationality or religion are entitled. But as long as there are governments whose authority is founded on coercion rather than on the mandate of the people, and interest groups which place short-term profits above long-term peace and prosperity, concerted international action to protect and promote human rights will remain at best a partially realized ideal. There will continue to be arenas of struggle where victims of oppression have to draw on their own inner resources to defend their inalienable rights as members of the human family.

The quintessential revolution is that of the spirit, born of an intellectual conviction of the need for change in those mental attitudes and values which shape the course of a nation's development. A revolution which aims merely at changing official policies and institutions with a view to an improvement in material conditions has little chance of genuine success. Without a revolution of the spirit, the forces which produced the iniquities of the old order would continue to be operative, posing a constant threat to the process of reform and regeneration. It is not enough merely to call for freedom, democracy and human rights. There has to be a united determination to persevere in the struggle, to make sacrifices in the name of enduring truths, to resist the corrupting influences of desire, ill will, ignorance and fear.

Saints, it has been said, are the sinners who go on trying. So free men are the oppressed who go on trying and who in the process make themselves fit to bear the responsibilities and to uphold the disciplines which will maintain a free society. Among the basic freedoms to which men aspire that their lives might be full and uncramped, freedom from fear stands out as both a means and an end. A people who would build a nation in which strong, democratic institutions are firmly established as a guarantee against state-induced power must first learn to liberate their own minds from apathy and fear.

Always one to practice what he preached, Aung San himself constantly demonstrated courage—not just the physical sort but the kind that enabled him to speak the truth, to stand by his word, to accept criticism, to admit his faults, to correct his mistakes, to respect the opposition, to parley with the enemy and to let people be the judge of his worthiness as a leader. It is for such moral courage that he will always be loved and respected in Burma—not merely as a warrior hero but as the inspiration and conscience of the nation. The words used by Jawaharlal Nehru to describe Mahatma Gandhi could well be applied to Aung San: "The essence of his teaching was fearlessness and truth, and action allied to those, always keeping the welfare of the masses in view."

Gandhi, that great apostle of non-violence, and Aung San, the founder of a national army, were very different personalities, but as there is an inevitable sameness about the challenges of authoritarian rule anywhere at any time, so there is a similarity in the intrinsic qualities of those who rise up to meet the challenge. Nehru, who considered the instillation of courage in the people of India one of Gandhi's greatest achievements, was a political modernist, but as he assessed the needs for a twentieth-century movement for independence, he found himself looking back to the philosophy of ancient India: "The greatest gift for an individual or a nation…was *abhaya*, fearlessness, not merely bodily courage but absence of fear from the mind."

Fearlessness may be a gift but perhaps more precious is the courage acquired through endeavour, courage that comes from cultivating the habit of refusing to let fear dictate one's actions, courage that could be described as "grace under pressure"—grace which is renewed repeatedly in the face of harsh, unremitting pressure.

Within a system which denies the existence of basic human rights, fear tends to be the order of the day. Fear of imprisonment, fear of torture, fear of death, fear of losing friends, family, property or means of livelihood, fear of poverty, fear of isolation, fear of failure. A most insidious form of fear is that which masquerades as common sense or even wisdom, condemning as foolish, reckless, insignificant or futile the small, daily acts of courage which help to preserve man's self-respect and inherent human dignity. It is not easy for a people conditioned by the iron rule of the principle that might is right to free themselves from the enervating miasma of fear. Yet even under the most crushing state machinery courage rises up again and again, for fear is not the natural state of civilized man.

The wellspring of courage and endurance in the face of unbridled power is generally a firm belief in the sanctity of ethical principles combined with a historical sense that despite all setbacks the condition of man is set on an ultimate course for both spiritual and material advancement. It is his capacity for self-improvement and self-redemption which most distinguishes man from the mere brute. At the root of human responsibility is the concept of perfection, the urge to achieve it, the intelligence to find a path towards it, and the will to follow that path if not to the end at least the distance needed to rise above individual limitations and environmental impediments. It is man's vision of a world fit for rational, civilized humanity which leads him to dare and to suffer to build societies free from want and fear. Concepts such as truth, justice and compassion cannot be dismissed as trite when these are often the only bulwarks which stand against ruthless power.

FILM STUDIES

Elizabeth (1998)

Screenplay by Michael Hirst
Directed by Shekhar Kapur

Character Guide

Queen Elizabeth I . . . . Cate Blanchett

Sir William Cecil . . . . Richard Attenborough

Earl of Leicester . . . . Joseph Fiennes

Sir Francis Walsingham . . . . . . Geoffrey Rush

Duke of Norfolk . . . . Christopher Eccleston

Archbishop of Canterbury . . . . . John Gielgud

Introduction

In 1554 Elizabeth Tudor was thrust into the role of Queen of England upon the death of her father, Henry VIII, and subsequent death of her half-sister Mary Tudor. Never expecting to be queen she was not only unprepared for her new position but inherited the throne of a country fraught with political and religious conflict and threats from overseas neighbors. In order to bring about stability, Elizabeth had to call upon all her skills as an emerging leader. Elizabeth I represents not only one of the greatest and most powerful monarchs of all time but also a leader who exemplifies multiple styles and approaches to leadership.

Dialogue Questions

1. Identify some of the conflicts causing turmoil inside England as Elizabeth takes the throne.

2. What factions must Elizabeth unite in order to bring order and stability to her country?

3. In what ways does Elizabeth use an authoritarian style and in what ways is her approach like servant leadership? What allows her to blend both of the approaches?

4. Does Elizabeth take an inward focus to leadership or does she focus on her followers?

5. What does Elizabeth sacrifice in order to be successful as a leader?

6. In what ways does Elizabeth adapt and/or increase her leadership abilities?

42 (2012)

Screenplay by Brian Helgeland
Directed by Brian Helgeland

UNIT
11

Character Guide

Jackie Robinson . . . . Chadwick Boseman

Branch Rickey . . . . Harrison Ford

Rachel Robinson . . . . Nicole Behanie

Leo Durocher . . . . Christopher Meloni

Dixie Walker . . . . Ryan Merriman

Pee Wee Reese . . . . Lucas Black

Introduction

42 is a biographical film of the early baseball career of Jackie Robinson, the first black player in the major leagues. We first see Robinson's rather rebellious spirit in his play in the Negro league, then Branch Rickey recruits him to play, possibly, for the majors, if he can overcome his natural rebellious tendencies. Robinson is put to the test by discrimination, both subtle and vehemently outward, on many fronts, but manages to build a reputation as a great player *and* a "gentleman."

Dialogue Questions

1. What do you think motivates Branch Rickey to step out of his expected role and make the controversial and eventually successful decision to recruit Robinson?

2. How does Rickey go about convincing Robinson to attempt the difficult task of changing his behavior? Is it purely the reward—playing for a major league—or does Rickey appeal to other aspects of human behavior and character?

3. It takes a long time, with some people, for Robinson to find his place on his new team of white players. What enables the kind of patience required, waiting for people to change? Can patience be taught? Learned?

4. What do you think is important in Branch Rickey's philosophy of leadership? Jackie Robinson's?

5. How does the "little picture" in which one acts daily relate to the "big picture" of change in society, hopefully for the better? How can one find inspiration in glimpses of the big picture for continuing with the difficult task of acting in the little?

EXERCISE

Developing a Theory of Leadership

Introduction

According to Dr. Mark McCabe, Dean of Students at Colorado Mountain College and National Facilitator for The Phi Theta Kappa Leadership Development Program, there are over one thousand definitions of leadership. With so many definitions it would appear that practitioners are selecting definitions to fit particular situations or events. One other way to view the proliferation of leadership definitions is to assume that each person is developing a somewhat different leadership style, philosophy, and personality and that each definition reflects this. It seems that it would be difficult to study and even create academic departments devoted to researching a field for which there is no single accepted definition of what researchers and students are studying!

Nevertheless, Leadership Studies as a field has flourished in the late 20th and early 21st centuries, and researchers seek to find commonalities despite the thousands of definitions of leadership. They have developed many ideas—theories—about what makes a good and successful leader. In this Unit and indeed throughout this text, some of these theories have surfaced: Servant Leadership, Transformational Leadership, Trait Theory or Great Man/Great Woman Theory, Situational Theory, Contingency Theory. But is the good leader of the past still effective today? What about in the future? This exercise challenges you to develop a personal theoretical statement or conceptualization of leadership that would assist and guide someone desiring to take on a leadership role and lead well and that you could even perhaps research one day.

What Is Your Leadership Theory?

Instructions

Take a moment to consider the different theories and approaches to leadership mentioned in this Unit and other Units of the text (for example, Transformational Leadership Theory is explored in Bernard Bass' article in Unit Ten). Which of them seems to resonate most strongly in you? Which of them seems to make the most sense to you based upon your experiences leading or observing other leaders? What is "right on" about the theory, and what raises questions or doubts for you? What is missing? What would you "tweak" about it? Write down a draft theoretical statement.

Share your theoretical statement with three or four other people in your group. See if there are similarities between your theories. Collaborate on a group theoretical statement to present to the class. Use the following Points to Consider to guide your group's dialogue.

Points to Consider

1. After reviewing the different influences contributing to our understanding of leadership, what do you consider the most important aspects?

2. How important are personality traits for the effective exercise of leadership?

3. Should someone called to exercise leadership be focused inwardly to develop traits and abilities, or focused outwardly on the traits and abilities of others? Explain your response in detail.

4. There are over one thousand definitions of leadership, indicating that no one definition fits every situation, and/or that it is an extremely complex phenomenon. Nevertheless, researchers develop and propose their ideas to explain what makes leadership effective. What do *you* think makes an important, positive difference in the exercise of leadership?

5. How can you state this as a theory?

6. What are the key elements of this theory?

SUGGESTED READING

This selected bibliography is intended to supplement the excerpts and articles of authors included in this Unit. There is an emphasis on books that are pivotal and recent publications. Numerous journals regularly offer articles related to these topics, but are not included in this selected bibliography. For further research, you may wish to include searches of the following journals: (alphabetically) *Academy of Management Executive, Academy of Management Journal, Harvard Business Review, Journal of Leadership Studies, Leadership in Action, Leadership Quarterly,* and *Leader To Leader.*

This list is organized by author's last name using Modern Language Association-style citations.

Bass, Bernard. M., and Ruth Bass. *The Bass Handbook of Leadership: Theory, Research, and Managerial Application.* **4th ed. New York: Free Press, 2008.**
Intended for students of leadership, this handbook covers a broad range of leadership definitions, concepts, and theories. Also included are chapters on personal traits, charisma, intellect and political tactics.

Burns, James MacGregor. *Leadership.* **New York: Harper Torch Books, 1975.**
This book was winner of the Pulitzer Prize and the National Book Award. Many scholars believe that James MacGregor Burns was the first person to differentiate between management and leadership and define leadership as a separate discipline. Burns' introduction of the concept of "transformational" leadership also set the tone for a shift toward an outward focus on followers rather than the inward focus on the traits and style of the leader. Burns includes a great deal of history on leadership theory.

Carlyle, Thomas. *On Heroes, Hero-Worship, and the Heroic in History.* **Boston: Houghton Mifflin, 1907.**
Originally a lecture Carlyle delivered in 1841, this is the classic position that "men make history," and not the other way around. Carlyle also suggests that for society to survive, we must continue to revere great men and recognize and appreciate the heroes among us.

Grint, Keith, ed. *Leadership: Classical, Contemporary, and Critical Approaches.* **Oxford: Oxford University Press, 1997.**
A collection of writings by different authors from five different perspectives to answer the question "What is leadership?" The perspectives are: Classical, with writers including Plato and Machiavelli; Traditional, with chapters by Chester Barnard and R. M. Stogdill; Modern, including readings on democratic leadership and the glass ceiling; Mythical, with a chapter by Manfred Kets de Vries; and Alternative, addressed by Martin Luther King, Jr. as well as feminist and postmodernist writers.

Heider, John. *The Tao of Leadership: Lao Tzu's* Tao Te Ching *Adapted for a New Age.* **Atlanta: Humanics New Age, 1985.**
Heider has written down his versions of Lao Tzu's classic book of lessons on how things happen, how to live in conscious harmony with natural law, and how to govern or educate others in accordance with natural law.

Hesselbein, Frances, Marshall Goldsmith, and Richard Beckhard, Eds. *The Leader of the Future 2: New Vision, Strategies and Practices for the Next Era.* **San Francisco: Jossey-Bass, 2006.**
This collection of essays from some of the best-known names in leadership provides views on important trends in current leadership thought.

Northouse, Peter G. *Leadership Theory and Practice*. Thousand Oaks, CA: Sage Publications, 2012.

Northouse includes thorough overviews of the primary leadership theories and includes case studies and assessment exercises.

Nye, Joseph S. *The Powers to Lead*. New York: Oxford University Press, 2008.

Nye gives leadership a sweeping treatment—historical, political, psychological—and explains the big changes unfolding in our present understanding of effective leadership.

Pierce, Jon L., and John W. Newstrom. *The Manager's Bookshelf: A Mosaic of Contemporary Views*. 7th edition. Upper Saddle River, NJ: Prentice Hall, 2005.

This collection of leadership essays from the best-selling leadership texts is an excellent start to any leadership library. Though the cost seems high, the purchase of all the texts included would be tenfold. Numerous leadership issues are covered, including diversity, change, conflict, and decision making. This is a must read for an aspiring leader who chooses to become better informed on current leadership thoughts and practices.

Popham, Peter. *The Lady and the Peacock: The Life of Aung San Suu Kyi*. New York: The Experiment Publishing, 2012.

One of the most recent accounts of this famous dissident's life that includes details about the confrontations with the ruling junta.

Rost, Joseph C. *Leadership for the Twenty-first Century*. New York: Praeger, 1991.

A critique of 150 writings on leadership since 1930, this book explores old definitions of leadership and proposes a new one. Fundamental concepts of great man theories, psychological traits, behavior, and situation are criticized for oversimplifying a complex set of relationships.

von Bertalanffy, Ludwig. *General System Theory: Foundations, Development, Applications*. New York: George Braziller, 1976.

Biologist von Bertalanffy first proposed System Theory in the 1940s. This work is his definitive exploration of it as it applies to other things beyond living organisms, including organizations.

EPILOGUE

Each of the preceding eleven units presented ideas and issues on leadership and nine of these emphasized a particular leadership skill required for the effective exercise of leadership. As you seek to exercise leadership, you may feel overwhelmed at the prospect of attempting to apply all of these skills in just the right way at just the right time. Some of you may be experienced leaders seeking to bring your skills to a new level and likewise have many, many things to think about and apply. It is important to remember that leaders do not develop or change or improve overnight!

Development takes place gradually and progressively as you take on increasingly responsible leadership roles. Each new leadership experience presents a different set of challenges and provides new opportunities or contexts in which to apply ideas and skills—whether skills you have already mastered or newly acquired ones. Your philosophy of leadership will continue to evolve, as it likely has during this course. You will continue to learn more about yourself and others. These things influence your interactions with others and shape your exercise of leadership.

Development occurs like a spiral that might begin as follows. When you articulate a vision and set some goals to achieve the vision, there will be successes and failures. Reflection on these successes and failures provides you with opportunities to strengthen your character by clarifying your sense of right and wrong, illuminating what is important to you, and developing relationships that are truly meaningful and helpful with those who are on the journey with you—your awareness of ethics, values, and serving increases. This heightened awareness assists with new decisions you must make. As you develop your decision-making skills, your confidence grows. A new level of confidence frees you to concentrate on additional areas of human relations that will accelerate the process of achieving a vision, like dealing with conflicts and creating a cohesive team. When conflicts do not destroy and teams stick together, trust and respect emerge. An atmosphere of trust and respect makes empowerment possible. When you more effectively empower others, new changes and growth for an organization or community involve more people and have greater possibilities of success, and you can refine and re-articulate your vision and begin again. The cycle renews, but at a higher level. With increased trust and respect, others begin to follow you up the spiral—assisting them to begin exercising leadership themselves is the essence of servant leadership.

Leading is not a static condition. Conditions and situations demand adjustments and innovations based on inquiry and reflection. Existing challenges and newly emerging ones need dynamic and transformational leaders if we are to overcome them. True and great leaders seek progress for humankind and constantly develop their own abilities and those of others in service to a worthy mission. The process is never finished.

INDEX

M

ABOUT THE EDITORS

Monika Byrd serves as Dean of Leadership and Service Learning for Phi Theta Kappa Honor Society. She has facilitated leadership development and leadership studies for college, professional, and community audiences, and was the editor of the 3rd and 4th editions of *Leadership Development Studies: A Humanities Approach*. She currently serves on the Board of Directors and the curriculum development team of the International Public Safety Leadership and Ethics Institute and as a National Facilitator for both Phi Theta Kappa's Leadership Development Program's Certification Seminars and training programs for the International Public Safety Leadership and Ethics Institute.

Susan Edwards serves as Dean of Academic Affairs and Honors Programs for Phi Theta Kappa Honor Society and teaches history and the humanities for Lone Star College–CyFair. She is a graduate of Leadership Houston, Leadership Texas, and Leadership America and a former President of the Texas Community College Teachers Association. She currently serves on the Board for the National Council for Student Development and the Two-Year College Directorate for the American College Personnel Association. She is a National Facilitator for Phi Theta Kappa's Leadership Development Program's Certification Seminars and chairs the Society's Honors Program Council.